THE QUR'AN AND LATE ANTIQUITY

OXFORD STUDIES IN LATE ANTIQUITY

Series Editor
Ralph Mathisen

Late Antiquity has unified what in the past were disparate disciplinary, chronological, and geographical areas of study. Welcoming a wide array of methodological approaches, this book series provides a venue for the finest new scholarship on the period, ranging from the later Roman Empire to the Byzantine, Sasanid, early Islamic, and early Carolingian worlds.

Explaining the Cosmos
Creation and Cultural Interaction in Late-Antique Gaza
Michael W. Champion

Contested Monarchy
Integrating the Roman Empire in the Fourth Century AD
Edited by Johannes Wienand

Universal Salvation in Late Antiquity
Porphyry of Tyre and the Pagan-Christian Debate in Late Antiquity
Michael Bland Simmons

The Poetics of Late Antique Literature
Edited by Jás Elsner and Jesús Hernández-Lobato

Rome's Holy Mountain
The Capitoline Hill in Late Antiquity
Jason Moralee

Columbanus and the Peoples of Post-Roman Europe
Edited by Alexander O'Hara

Jonas of Bobbio and the Legacy of Columbanus
Sanctity and Community in the Seventh Century
Alexander O'Hara

Sacred Stimulus
Jerusalem in the Visual Christianization of Rome
Galit Noga-Banai

The Qur'an and Late Antiquity
A Shared Heritage
Angelika Neuwirth

The Qur'an and Late Antiquity

A Shared Heritage

Angelika Neuwirth
Translated by Samuel Wilder

OXFORD
UNIVERSITY PRESS

OXFORD
UNIVERSITY PRESS

Oxford University Press is a department of the University of Oxford. It furthers the University's objective of excellence in research, scholarship, and education by publishing worldwide. Oxford is a registered trade mark of Oxford University Press in the UK and certain other countries.

Published in the United States of America by Oxford University Press
198 Madison Avenue, New York, NY 10016, United States of America.

Library of Congress Cataloging-in-Publication Data
Names: Neuwirth, Angelika, author. | Wilder, Samuel (Translator).
Title: The Qur'an and late antiquity / Angelika Neuwirth ; translated
by Samuel Wilder.
Other titles: Koran als Text der Spätantike. English
Description: New York, NY : Oxford Univerity Press, [2019] | Series: Oxford
studies in late antiquity | Includes bibliographical references and index.
Identifiers: LCCN 2018015795 (print) | LCCN 2018016947 (ebook) |
ISBN 9780199928965 (updf) | ISBN 9780190921316 (oso) |
ISBN 9780190921309 (epub) | ISBN 9780199928958 (hardcover)
Subjects: LCSH: Qur'an—History. | Qur'an as literature. | Qur'an—Criticism,
Textual. | Qur'an—Evidences, authority, etc. | Qur'an—Manuscripts. |
Qur'an—Relation to the Bible.
Classification: LCC BP131 (ebook) | LCC BP131 .N48913 2019 (print) |
DDC 297.1/2209—dc23
LC record available at https://lccn.loc.gov/2018015795

1 3 5 7 9 8 6 4 2

Printed by Sheridan Books, Inc., United States of America

Publication was made possible by the generous support of VolkswagenStiftung

Contents

Preface

This book could not have been written were it not for my long-term cohabitation with the three monotheistic religions in the place of their birth, or at least of their spiritual origin. It is rooted ultimately in insights that reach back far in time, to my time as a student in Jerusalem, living in the Old City, in immediate proximity to the Haram al-Sharif and the eastern churches and synagogues. What elsewhere would have to be collected in the imagination—the sound of Qur'an recitation as a clearly audible voice in a concert of various liturgical chants and the presence of Qur'anic script, its calligraphy, as a strikingly abstract-geometrical representation amidst the omnipresent images exhibited in the other religions—belonged there to everyday experience. Accordingly, the Qur'an could scarcely be perceived other than as part of an ensemble of related holy scriptures, all of them sensually present side by side. It is this experience above all that is reflected in the volume presented here.

At the same time, however, one cannot ignore that the Qur'an is the core testimony of Arabic verbal creativity. I was fortunate to enjoy the unique possibility to experience this language in its daily performance and as an object of zealous scholarly discussions about its subtlest nuances, not only as an observer but as a participant as well, during a six-year guest professorship at the University of Jordan, in Amman. The explanations that are set forth in the present volume have been nourished hermeneutically by the numerous and diverse suggestions offered to me by Arabic-speaking students and colleagues in Jordan, with whom I had the opportunity to read texts of classical Arabic literature over the course of several years. These early experiences were re-actualized often, above all during periods of teaching in Egypt, during my work as the director of the Orient Institute in Beirut and Istanbul and, not least, during my still ongoing annual teaching activities at the Dormitio Abbey in Jerusalem.

But teaching experience in Germany has also played into this book. My work at diverse German universities made me painfully aware that important preconditions for a synopsis of the widely divergent perceptions of the Qur'an and of the Arabic language in the East and the West are still missing. Arabic-Islamic studies are pursued in the universities of Europe and the Islamic world in almost complete isolation from one another. The two academic traditions remain bound to their respective hermeneutic principles, so that the interpretation of the foundational writings of Islam, especially the Qur'an, often leads to incompatible, even contrary results. These often idiosyncratic views on the Qur'an have research fanned out in Western research into vastly differing models of reading the Qur'an. To track one's way through the thicket of these competing theses and hypotheses, a comprehensive presentation of the results of research achieved up to now is required. It is hoped that such an overview is accomplished here; a mere retracing of the differences will not suffice.

Western research on the Qur'an is not only almost unmanageably subdivided and ramified but is also highly controversial. Though more recently, in research into the Qur'an's "milieu" or tradition, linguistic and theological data from the neighboring religions are being systematically taken into account, their reflection in the Qur'an is most often assessed in the framework of "reception history," as data testifying to the survival and vitality of Jewish and Christian traditions beyond their narrow religious realms. To avoid such a "Eurocentric" reading, it is therefore essential to re-pose the question of the historical anchoring of the Qur'an in time and place. A radical turning of perspective is required, away from the focus on reception history and toward the history of the text's emergence as a scripture in its own right. This entails a new reflection on the Qur'an in relation to Late Antiquity research, a field that has only in recent times been extended to encompass the Arabian Peninsula.

Although the initial intention for this volume was to lay the ground for a concise commentary on the Qur'an, to be published in several subsequent volumes, it can also be read as a general introduction to the Qur'an, setting it systematically for the first time into the context of its milieu of emergence, the Near Eastern culture of Late Antiquity. This requires that the Qur'an no longer be treated *hagiographically*, as part of the vita of the prophet, the *Sīra*, as has so frequently been the case in introductions up to now, that is, as part of Islamic tradition, but rather *historically*, as a document of "community formation" within a "sectarian milieu," a landscape of debate, of arguments fought out between diverse groups, Christians, Jews, and pagans alike. This implies a 180-degree turn of perspective, from the Islamic Qur'an to the Late Antique Qur'an, a turn that bears culture-critical implications that are highly relevant for the current moment. To claim that the Qur'an emerged from Late Antique culture makes this scripture, which has so far been treated only as an Islamic document—to put it acutely—recognizable as a European legacy as well, a voice in the concert of traditions of an age that is now being recognized as a formative epoch for later European culture. The Qur'an thus becomes a text that should be significant for Europeans, a text that binds together Muslims and non-Muslims alike.

In order to reach scholarly oriented readers as well as those interested more generally in religions, certain compromises have been necessary in the presentation of the text. Individual sub-chapters of this volume, which have grown from lectures on subjects already quite well known, may appear more easily accessible than others that set forth new theses and seek to challenge the reader to undertake a critical examination of the existing research literature. But wherever it was deemed necessary, particular problems, in the interest of fostering a broader comprehension, have been explained with reference to their wider context. Occasional repetitions that were produced thereby have been allowed to stand, in order to make the individual chapters comprehensible if read individually. Through the explanation of technical terms and the systematic translation of all quotations, effort has been made to ease access to the text also for nonspecialists. The use of scientific transliteration, even of long original Arabic citations, may seem irritating at first view; it was unavoidable, however, as the linguistic guise of Qur'anic discourse is an essential part of the message itself, and textual discussions must therefore make reference to the exact linguistic form. Citations cannot be replaced by mere references to the printed original text, since the printed text merges Qur'anic verses into unstructured text blocks obscuring their original poetic character. Readers who are not familiar with Arabic and have no interest in the sound-image of the Qur'an can easily skip over the transliterations, which are set into italic type.

Postscript

The original German text of this volume, *Der Koran als Text der Spätantike: Ein europäischer Zugang*, which appeared in 2010, was the outcome of long-term scholarly exchange with colleagues, co-workers, and students in various parts of the world, who are gratefully remembered. Meanwhile, I am indebted to still another supporter of my cause, my patient and enduring translator, Sam Wilder, who has coped successfully with the often complicated issues of my German style. I equally owe thanks to the VolkswagenStiftung, whose generous funding made the translation possible. Seven years have passed since the publication of the original—a time span in which our thesis that the Qur'an is part and parcel of the Late Antique culture of the Eastern Mediterranean has found approval in wide parts of the scholarly world. During these years, further evidence could be provided in a number of new publications: It is now possible to consult the historical literary "concise" commentary on nearly half of the Meccan sura corpus (Angelika Neuwirth, *Der Koran Band I: Frühmekkanische Suren*, Berlin, 2011, and *Der Koran Band 2/1: Frühmittelmekkanische Suren*, Berlin, 2017). In addition, a collective volume of articles on both literary and theological aspects of the Qur'an has been published (*Scripture, Poetry, and the Making of a Community: Reading the Qur'an as a Literary Text*, London, 2014), as well as more recently an extended essay on the development of the Qur'anic proclamation viewed as a dialectical process of an enchantment and a subsequent disenchantment of the world (*Die koranische Verzauberung der Welt und ihre Entzauberung in der Geschichte*). Many of the ideas expounded in the present programmatic volume have been developed further in these later publications.

The translator wishes to thank Michael Ladner, Charly Wilder, and Harlene Hipsh, for their help in the completion of this work.

Beirut, December 2017

Abbreviations

AIEO	*Annales d l'Institut d'Études Orientales de l'Université d'Alger*
BO	*Bibliotheca Orientalis*
BSOAS	*Bulletin of the School of Oriental and African Studies*
EI²	*Encyclopaedia of Islam*, 2nd ed., 11 vols., Leiden, 1975–2002
EJ²	*Encyclopaedia Judaica*, 2nd ed., 22 vols., Jerusalem and New York, 2007
EQ	*Encyclopedia of the Qurʾān*, ed. Jane Dammen McAuliffe, 5 vols., Leiden, 2001–2006
GdQ	Theodor Nöldeke, *Geschichte des Qorans*, Göttingen, 1860
GdQ2	Friedrich Schwally, *Geschichte des Qorans von Theodor Nöldeke. Völlig umgearbeitet von F. S.*; part 1: *Über den Ursprung des Qorans*, Leipzig, 1909; part 2: *Die Sammlung des Qorans, mit einem literaturhistorischen Anhang über die muhammedanischen Quellen und die neuere christliche Forschung*, Leipzig 1919; Gotthelf Bergsträsser, *Geschichte des Qorans; part 3: Die Geschichte des Qorantexts*, Leipzig, 1938
JAOS	*Journal of the American Oriental Society*
JQR	*Jewish Quarterly Review*
JQS	*Journal of Qurʾanic Studies*
JRAS	*Journal of the Royal Asiatic Society*
JSAI	*Jerusalem Studies of Arabic and Islam*
MIDEO	*Mélanges de l'Institut Dominicain d'Études Orinetales du Caire*
OLZ	*Orientalistische Literaturzeitung*
ThWAT	*Theologisches Wörterbuch zum AltenTestament*
ZDMG	*Zeitschrift der Deutschen Morgenländischen Gesellschaft*
ZRGG	*Zeitschrift für Religions- und Geistesgeschichte*
ZS	*Zeitschrift für Semitistik und verwandte Gebiete*

THE QUR'AN AND LATE ANTIQUITY

Introduction

I.1 The Qur'an as the Document of the Emergence of a Religion

The objective of this volume, to discern the emergence of a new religion through the gradually unfolding textual form of its foundational document, may seem overly ambitious. But in the case of Islam, there is no serious alternative. Later historical evidence, such as the biographies of the Prophet, reflect the final victory of Islam as it was ultimately achieved, to which they in turn give literary form. Only the Qur'an is the genuine testimony of the development of the cultically marked movement from which the earliest community emerged, already during the lifetime of the Prophet. Today, such a focus on the "emergent Qur'an text" appears as unfamiliar as ever. Such a focus must not only compete hermeneutically with the challenges of very divergent approaches and projects but has to proceed from a conception of the Qur'an that is not identical with that of research up to now. This is because it is not in the transmitted "anthological" form of the text, with its 114 suras organized by text length, that the new religion inscribed itself first, but rather in the pre-form of this text: the oral proclamation that preceded the text's codification.

The distinction between these two manifestations of the Qur'an is no trivial matter for textual history; rather, a focus on the oral "proclamation" implies a significant hermeneutic revision, one that resets the Qur'an into an epoch to which it has not yet been closely connected. In its pre-canonic oral manifestation, the Qur'an text can no longer be considered as exclusively "Islamic," but instead forms an integral part of the debate culture of Late Antiquity, an epoch that has only in recent times gained the attention it deserves in Near Eastern studies.[1] To uncover this oral proclamation, which remains, as it were, hidden beneath the final canonized text of scripture and to retrieve the interaction between the speaker and his hearers engaged in the discussion of prior traditions is a central aim of this book. Despite its experimental character, and despite the numerous hypotheses that must be entertained in course, the radical alteration of research perspective that is attempted here—a turn from the final canonical text to the communication process of Qur'anic proclamation that must first be

1. See the discussion in Hoyland, *Seeing Islam*, 12–17.

reconstructed—appears to be the only viable route to the restoration of an important semantic dimension of the Qur'an that tradition has submerged. Only when the text is read as a "transcript" that accompanied an oral proclamation can the Qur'an be reconceptualized as a novel and rhetorically plausible response to central questions of its time, a response that proved persuasive to its hearers and united them into that new community that only a short time later would transform the cultural map of the wider region.

I.2 A "European Reading"

The project that is developed here pursues several goals. On the one hand, it is primarily an attempt to contribute to the inner-European or "Western" state of research. A critical discussion of modern contributions to research should bring some order to a body of Western scholarship that is heterogeneous in method and divided among a number of divergent schools, and simultaneously draw attention to the political dimension of the knowledge production involved in Qur'an research that is all too often neglected. This should be a contribution to bridging the prevailing hermeneutic polarity between Muslim and Western research projects. At the current moment, when Islam has long been a part of the European lifeworld, Western and Muslim Qur'an researchers remain separated more than ever by hermeneutic barriers. Western researchers accuse Muslims of being beholden to theological dogmas, while Muslim researchers perceive their Western colleagues as polemical and triumphalist, devoid of the most elementary empathy for Islam. Although the period between the two world wars saw European researchers of Islam being appointed to positions at Arab universities, and visiting professorships by German scholars of the Qur'an were welcomed in Jordan and Egypt as late as the 1970s and 1980s, such mutual curiosity and openness have now become things of the past. Between then and now lie decisive political events and developments, which have led to the ubiquitous present-day phenomenon of a *ṣaḥwa islāmīya*, an "Islamic awakening." In the scholarly arena, there have also been conflicts, "text wars," which have led to a notable breakdown in the East-West academic relationship, a breach of mutual trust. In this situation, itself scandalous, where two great research traditions stand opposite each other without entering into creative exchange, Qur'an research as such must be newly rethought. The present book offers a contribution toward the fulfillment of the desideratum of (self-)critique within Western research, in order to prepare the way for an open conversation engaging inner-Islamic research on the Qur'an.

But this project is not only European in that it problematizes various Western discourses; more crucially, it is also European in its historical perspective. This volume, and the commentary volumes that will appear subsequently, aim to make the Qur'an recognizable again to Western readers for what it was at the time of its emergence in the early community: a literarily extraordinary and intellectually engaging text. Because the Qur'an emerged out of an engagement with Late Antique discourses and inscribed itself in those already extant Christian and Jewish traditions commonly held to be a European heritage, it too is itself a part of the historical legacy of Late Antiquity to Europe. To read the Qur'an anew can and should open European readers who are grounded in the Western-Christian tradition to a new view of their own theological and spiritual history and empower them to grasp the Qur'an as a vital part of the reception history of their own familiar texts. It is hoped that this book will make Western readers aware of the Qur'an's close connection to an epoch that has been reclaimed for European identity.

This does not entail, however, that this book has nothing to say to Muslim readers. Certainly, the historical-critical and literary method followed here is the outcome of a long hermeneutic tradition honed on Western texts, and its systematic application to the Qur'an may therefore appear new and perhaps even foreign—despite the various projects aimed at historicization that took root within the traditional inner-Islamic literature, such as the scholarship on the "circumstances of revelation," *asbāb al-nuzūl*,[2] the "disputes over abrogation," *al-nāsikh wa-l-mansūkh*, the discussions of Medinan additions,[3] and the modern "literary exegesis," or *tafsīr adabī*.[4] The ambivalent impression often imparted to Muslim readers by historical Qur'an research, especially by older scholarly works not always devoid of prejudice,[5] has been reinforced in recent times by research on early Islam that is heavily colored by polemic. It is for just this reason that this book does not seek, despite its orientation toward the historical methods of Europe, to remain in conversation only with readers acculturated within the West, but rather seeks at the same time to offer a contribution to the long-overdue convergence of Western and inner-Islamic research.

Indeed, this work starts from the recognition that the first step toward understanding must consist in placing the Qur'an on the same eye level in Western perception as the scriptures of the two older religions, Judaism and Christianity.[6] The disentanglement of the Qur'an from the context of something that is essentially "other" and therefore admits of arbitrary interpretation is the necessary

2. See also Rippin, "The Exegetical Genre '*asbāb al-nuzūl*,'" and Rippin, "The Function of '*Asbāb al-nuzūl*.'"

3. See Nagel, *Medinensische Einschübe*.

4. See Wielandt, *Offenbarung und Geschichte*, and Wieland, "Exegesis, modern"; cf. also "History of Research" in chap. 1.

5. See William Muir's biography of Muhammad, *The Life of Mohammad*, and Khalidi, *Image*, 249–251, on earlier Western-Eastern scholarship.

6. This objective is in keeping with Mohamed Arkoun's *Lectures du Coran*, which takes Western scholarship's historical-critical approach to task for the contemporary malaise. Without a historical rehabilitation of the Koran, the comparison Arkoun is trying to make between the Koran and other texts cannot be accomplished in a hermeneutically adequate way. The present writer offers an Arabic summary of the earlier work on the Late Antique Koran, "*An yuʿallam al-Qurʾān fī Urūba ka-naṣṣ ʾurūbī*," (Teaching the Koran in Europe—as a European text).

precondition for all further steps of reliable Qur'an research. Put into practice, this entails a methodological insistence on treating the Qur'an in the same manner as the two other scriptures, as will be presented here through examples. Our project therefore aims at an "inner-European revision": the critique of individual, historically problematic premises maintained in Western research, to which an opposing model will be offered by the re-embedding of the Qur'an in an epoch shared by both Near Eastern and Western history.

With this goal in mind, our reading offers a "cultural translation," rather than an attempt at a comprehensive interpretation of the Qur'an text. Let there be no illusion about this: a truly adequate *interpretation* of the Qur'an as the scripture of the Muslims must include the great hermeneutic tradition of Islamic scholarship, that is, the living Islamic tradition that embeds the Qur'an into the lifeworld of Islam. This necessary second step, the integration of the Islamic tradition, can only occur through intensive collaboration with Muslim scholars, a practice toward which we hope this work will do something to prepare the way.

But what emerges positively from the investigations set forth here is that just as the Qur'an belongs to the Islamic tradition, so too does it belong to the European tradition; the proclamation recorded in the Qur'an is part of a discourse that crosses the boundaries of religions. It is a new and consistently perceptible voice in the concert of theological-philosophical discussions of its time, which were fundamental not only for the emergence of the Islamic religion but also, to put the emphasis elsewhere, for the formation of Europe. The Qur'an is an integral part of this process of development, which began in the close interaction between religious cultures. In that we read the Qur'an both as an innovative answer to Christian and Jewish questions of Late Antiquity and as a challenge raised in opposition to them, our reading is of significance not only for the historically informed European reader. Rather, these very discussions into which the Qur'an enters also gain new historical relevance for Muslim readers, who can reclaim the entire debate culture of Late Antiquity, in which the Qur'an participates, as a part of their own spiritual history.

I.3 The Qur'an as Proclamation

The Qur'an, although available since the death of the Prophet as a collection of text units, or "suras" (Arabic *sūra*, pl. *suwar*), is nevertheless *not* a book composed in writing. All too clearly, the form and content of the suras make evident their function as oral proclamation. Accordingly, the text is not—as one might conclude from its frequent self-designation *al-kitāb*, "the writing"—a "book" conceived by an author that unfolds according to a preconceived plan; rather, as is clear from its equally frequent self-designation *qurʾān*, "lecture, reading," it is a proclamation. Given that this proclamation took place over a span of some two decades, it is no wonder that differing styles of language supersede and follow each other and that after a long period of poetic speech, a more prosaic and instructive discourse becomes the rule. But there is a rich set of characteristics shared between these two differing discourse forms, which allows us to speak of a formal and thematic continuity, evidence of one and the same language-forming genius. Even if we rarely find explicit personal references or specifications of time and place in the Qur'an, nevertheless the transmitted text of the Qur'an can plausibly fit into the frame given by Islamic tradition. According to this tradition, the Qur'anic texts were communicated by their proclaimer, who entered history as the Prophet Muhammad, in the years between 610 and 632, to a growing number of hearers and followers. Though we will proceed heuristically from this rough framework in what follows (if not from all its traditional details and specific interpretations of events), the legitimacy even of this framework can only be proven through the results of a literary description of the Qur'an.

Because the proclaimer cannot be separated from the proclamation, at least a summary reconstruction of the outer circumstances of the appearance of Muhammad as a prophet cannot be dispensed with. This epitome can only be partly brought out through the Qur'an itself but must also be derived in part from the contemporary milieu of the Qur'an's emergence—here, the results of critical research into the biographies of the Prophet (*sīra*) cannot be excluded entirely.[7] Perhaps the most important characteristic of his appearance is the proclaimer's increasingly forceful claim to communicate divine inspirations, followed by his claim to play the role of a prophet in his society.[8] This manifests itself in the Qur'an on the one hand in mantic discourse forms in direct "you" address, maintained throughout the entire text, and on the other in the strongly pronounced and continuous biblical intertextuality of the Qur'an. If one follows the references in the Qur'an itself, during his ministry in Mecca (610–622), the audience consisted, alongside pagan followers of the local cult,[9] mainly of monotheistically oriented though not confessionally bound hearers, whose religious knowledge would have been part of the formation of the local elites. On the other hand, after their compelled migration (*hijra*) in the year 622 to the oasis settlement Medina, the proclaimer and his community also encountered learned Christians and, above all, Jews knowledgeable in tradition, with whom they entered into controversial disputes and orally conducted discussions, as is shown by a great number of negotiations of Jewish traditions in the Qur'an.

7. See also Motzki, *Biography of Muhammad*, and Schoeler, *Charakter und Authentie*, and now also Goerke and Schoeler, *Korpus 'Urwa b. az-Zubair*, and, in contrast, Berg, *Development of Exegesis*.

8. Andrae, *Ursprung*, Bobzin, *Muhammad*, and recently Schöller, *Muhammad*, offer an overview of the life and works of the proclaimer. On the problems with the Prophet's biography, see Rubin, *Biography*, and Chabbi, "Histoire et tradition sacrée."

9. See Ammann, *Geburt des Islam*, and Krone, *Al-Lāt*.

The turn that occurred at this time, when the proclaimer and his community entered into an increasingly significant political role and a political entity emerged,[10] is set up by the Islamic calendar as the beginning of a new era. Although the *hijra* itself is not mentioned explicitly in the Qur'an nor granted any of its later aura as the primal scene of political self-determination for the Islamic religious community, or *umma*,[11] the migration to Medina marks a new factual beginning. In terms of textual development, this fissure can hardly be overestimated, since political engagement in Medina brought about sustainable religious-political consequences that are reflected in the text. What had been the freely available stock of monotheistic traditions that circulated in Mecca became the object of controversy in Medina, so that biblical and post-biblical traditions were now represented by concrete interpretive communities and reclaimed as monopoly by learned Jews and Christians, so that the new community was obliged to make claims against them—an interaction that still needs to be reconstructed critically in detail.[12]

Alongside and in parallel to the process of proclamation, we see already in Mecca the formation of a belief community possessing a distinctive cult, a process—as can be gleaned from the Qur'an itself—that is supported ideologically and documented textually by the proclamation. This occurs in a kind of zigzag movement: after a time in which the cult was shared with the pagan Meccans,[13] we see a clear turning point toward monotheistic liturgical models already familiar to many pious people of the region, then later in Medina the local ancient Arab cult forms and orientations are again granted an important rank. Islamic cult practices, which at the end of the development consist of several daily prayers, fasting, and pilgrimage, reflect these several changes in orientation.

I.3.1 Two Simultaneously Acquired Achievements: A Scripture and a Community

The proclamation process thus at once generates a new scripture *and* a new community—a unique simultaneous "twin birth" of two historically crucial achievements, which does not occur in the emergence of either the Hebrew Bible or the New Testament.[14] This double development is no longer recognizable in the traditional reading of the Qur'an accompanied by commentary, as a text already fixed in writing. In that reading, historical developments that were only later implemented are read teleologically back into the narrative of the emergence of the Qur'an, thus ideas still being the object of negotiation in the Qur'an,

10. Noth, "Früher Islam."

11. See the critical examination of the early Islamic concept of *hijra* in Crone, "Concept of Hijra."

12. For the topics debated here, see Busse's account, *Theologische Beziehungen*, 8–29.

13. Our knowledge of this phase is largely due to Uri Rubin's studies; above all see Rubin, "Morning and Evening Prayers."

14. On the development of the Hebrew Bible from scribal culture, see Van der Toorn, *Scribal Culture*.

because they loom large in later Islam, are no longer palpable in the earlier effective power they wielded in the Qur'an. This double emergence of a text and a community is also elided from the synchronic reading that is predominant in current Western research, which takes the entire text into view as a fait accompli. It only becomes evident from a chronologically oriented reading of the text, which traces the process of development of the various fundamental ideas treated by proclaimer and community and seeks to explain their sequence in time plausibly. This progressive treatment has until now remained beyond the horizon of Muslim researchers, even of such scholars as Fazlur Rahman[15] and the (post-)modern Turkish exegetes,[16] despite the fact that they postulate the necessity of a historical reading, that is, a reading oriented toward the transmitted "circumstances of revelation," the *asbāb al-nuzūl.*

The form in which the proclamation was dressed is the sura. It is attested in the manuscript tradition from the very beginning; thus its validity not only literally but also in terms of the history of the tradition must stand beyond question. It is a textual unit unknown in liturgy up to that time, polythematic and consisting of various elements such as address, prayer, hymn, and narrative. It undergoes substantial alterations during the proclamation process. The Qur'an in its final form, which appeared already in the seventh century, includes 114 such suras, arranged into a text corpus by order of decreasing length. The first (incomplete) manuscript evidence dates to around forty to sixty years after the death of the Prophet in 632;[17] the oldest Qur'anic inscriptions are explicitly dated to the year 691. Since manuscripts and inscriptions are extant from a time shortly after the proclamation, if not from the time of the Prophet himself, the surviving state of the text handed down to us can be referred back with high probability almost to the time of its genesis. Although the existence of early manuscripts indicates that the redaction of the Qur'an occurred already during the seventh century, without, however, confirming the positive emergence of the text in precisely the time presupposed by tradition, still no serious reason compels us to doubt the genesis of the text from the proclamation of the Prophet at the point in time asserted by tradition. The final redaction and authoritative publication of a *textus ne varietur*, a text claimed to be binding and based on preceding written and intensive oral tradition, is to be placed at the latest in the time of the Umayyad caliph ʿAbd al-Malik (ruled 65–86 / 685–705), it thus followed the emergence of the text much more quickly than in the cases of the Old and New Testaments. Alongside the Qur'an, Islamic tradition also developed a grand narrative of the birth of Islam, clad in the form of the Life of the Prophet (*sīra*; in what follows

15. Rahman, *Major Themes in the Qur'an.*

16. See Körner, *Koranhermeutik in der Türkei.*

17. See now Déroche, *La transmission écrite du Coran*; Marcus Fraser (unpublished lecture) has drawn attention to even earlier manuscripts.

"Sira") compiled by Ibn Isḥāq (d. 150/768) and revised by Ibn Hishām (d. 214/829 or 219/834),[18] which, however, clearly reflects the perspective of a later stage in the history of mentalities.

The presentation in this volume will build essentially not on this Prophet vita, which is frequently relied on for Qur'anic history, but rather on the Qur'an itself and the evidence of its spatial and temporal environment, even if certain basic data are adopted from the Prophet vita, such as the scenario "proclaimer Muhammad—Meccan and Medinan hearers" and the skeletal outline of the most important political events.

The text of the Qur'an is available in numerous printed editions, among which the textual tradition of Ḥafṣ (d. 180/796) according to ʿĀṣim (d. 128/745), the Ḥafs ʿan ʿĀṣim text, has become particularly widespread due to the impact of the first inner-Islamic Qur'an printing prompted by the Azhar school (Cairo 1925).[19] This edition, and all other printed editions in circulation today, is based on the so-called Uthmanic consonantal text, which Islamic tradition dates to the 750s. European translations of the Qur'an are widely available. Among those in German, that of Rudi Paret[20] still enjoys the highest prominence in scholarly usage. The Qur'an quotations in this volume are based on an original translation, which attempts to display the character of the text as proclamation; it should be read alongside the sequence of critical Qur'an commentaries that will follow this volume.

I.3.2 Autonomy of the Qur'an as "Oral Scripture"

It is not accidental that from the beginning, the Qur'an declares itself to be an oral text through its Arabic name *al-qurʾān*, "recitation"—this is a marked difference from the case of the Bible, whose name goes back to Latin *biblia* "the book (as such)" or Greek *ta biblia*, "the (canonical) books." The accent on orality in the name *al-qurʾān* touches upon an essential point in several respects: the Qur'an is not only a text composed orally but one that was also transmitted orally throughout history and is today represented primarily in this way. Nevertheless, as Western readers we have become accustomed to perceive it as a book like the Bible, or even as something that is irritatingly close to it, a book that therefore bears the onerous reputation of epigonality, precisely because of this closeness. This is no light verdict, since the Bible not only possesses status as "the book of books" from a religious perspective but also makes further universal claims

18. Rotter offers a partial German translation of the Life of the Prophet in *Das Leben des Propheten*; a complete English translation is available in Guillaume, *Life of Mohammad*.

19. *Al-Qurʾān al-karīm*, Cairo, 1925. Other text traditions, some in print but primarily circulating in the form of lithographs, do not offer an essentially different version of the text but, rather, deviations in spelling and orthography; see chap. 4, 161–163. On the principles of the Cairo edition, see Bergsträsser, "Koranlesung in Kairo."

20. Paret, *Koran*. Newer German translations exist: Khoury, *Koran*, Zirker, *Koran*, und Karimi, *Koran*; a literarily sophisticated translation by Bobzin was published in early 2010.

of a unique kind. It is not by accident that it has cleared away all other monuments of ancient Near Eastern literature from the field,[21] so that it is the only continuously read and taught work from its various eras of emergence. Offering prophetic discourse, narrative, wisdom, and poetry that claim to be worthy of permanent memory, it has set standards in literature that are virtually unattainable, becoming the "canonical text" as such. Because the Qur'an for its community of believers came to substitute for the Bible, the Qur'an's status within Islam seems to give substance to the Western accusation of epigonality, an accusation that developed quite early: a book similar to the Bible but coming *after* the Bible could only be a pale imitation. Perhaps it is this tense closeness to the Bible that is chiefly responsible for the widespread denigrating judgments of the form and contents of the Qur'an that have long been prominent in Western perception.[22]

In order to free the Qur'an from this verdict of epigonality, we have taken a number of routes. There is a current trend in American research to read the Qur'an simply as an updating of the Bible, one that makes the biblical memory meaningful for its new recipients by bridging the ontological gap between the biblical past and the Qur'anic present" through particular literary exegeses.[23] The problematic nature of the often cryptic Qur'anic narratives is solved through interpreting them as attempts to decenter the linearity of the biblical textual environment, to undermine Jewish and Christian scripture and thus eliminate the idea of a clearly restorable message.[24] The Qur'an is thus treated as a biblical apocryphon, the outcome of a preconceived textual intention. Such an exegetical concept would only be comprehensible for a text compiled by an author, which is here assumed as a matter of course for the Qur'an. This presently prevalent research trend, which reads the Qur'an purely synchronically and exclusively in terms of text-referentiality, steers clear of the problematic of the Qur'an's emergence, which is—as has to be admitted—loaded with hypotheses. By renouncing the text's temporal and spatial coordinates, this approach, however, takes the question of historical emergence too lightly. Insofar as this reading does not treat the relative chronology of each of the discussed texts, its reconstructions of Qur'anic developments must fall apart as arbitrary and often untenable.[25]

In this introductory volume, as against that, the difficult attempt will be made to place the Qur'anic proclamation into its historical sequence, because only in this way does the processuality of its textual genesis *and* its communal formation become recognizable. It is here that the most significant analogy that binds the emergence of the Qur'an to that of the two other monotheistic traditions emerges, since the central texts of each of these traditions also reflect a communal

21. Cf., for instance, Pritchard, *Ancient Near Eastern Texts.*
22. See also Wild, "Schauerliche Öde."
23. Hughes, "The Stranger at the Sea."
24. See Brown, *The Apocalypse of Islam*, 87.
25. See also, in general, Sinai, "Qur'an as Process."

process of dealing with tradition. The Qur'an represents a religious genesis that corresponds to these other two major processes of religious genesis; it is not a post-biblical text with no commitment whose conditions of emergence are of no interest. Precisely because the Qur'an is a scripture that is so disputed between East and West, to reckon with it seriously is to do much more than simply interpret a text. What must be reconstructed is the development of the Qur'an as a communal document, that is, as the genuine evidence of the emergence of a religion in Late Antiquity, analogous to the emergences of the two other traditions. The opposite approach to the Qur'an as a written fait accompli either implicitly denies or willfully ignores its worthiness of this rank. The exclusively synchronic approach cannot be justified through the argument that it was only the later readings of the community that first laid the foundations for the inner-Islamic understanding of the Qur'an today, and these therefore must form the ideal basis for a dialogue with Islam. The Qur'an can only be perceived appropriately in terms of the history of knowledge, that is, in terms of its engagement with the two other traditions, when it is considered as evidence of the "drama of argumentation" that played out between the community and the contemporary representatives of the contemporaneous traditions. The logic and hermeneutics of the Qur'an only become clear when viewed as a recourse to the great questions of its time, an antithesis to the premises current in its particular space, and not as the context-free discourse of an isolated speaker or, worse, an author. This requires an arsenal of methods, including the philological approach offered here, which perhaps today enjoys the weakest reputation. Although the Qur'an appears to many researchers as a textual challenge to be taken up primarily by literary scholarship, it is of primary importance that Qur'an research first engages the tasks of philology and the history of theology, in order to lay a solid foundation for literary-critical undertakings.

I.3.3 "Multi-mediality"

With respect to its media of representation, the Qur'an holds a very special status in religious history. In a much more vital way than in the case of the other scriptures, the Qur'an was and is still present audibly in daily life, where it is recited in various forms of cantilene. Its unique *Sitz im Leben* has always been liturgy: each of the five daily prayers of Islam includes several Qur'an recitations, chosen independently by the worshipper and recited by heart in melodic recitation. The Qur'an is thus tied inextricably with performance intended for aesthetic affect, whose emotional potential becomes unrecognizable in the mute reading of the text that so often forms the basis of critical research.[26] This additional acoustic-aesthetic dimension, which for the scriptures of the other religions is confined

26. An approach to this aesthetic dimension is introduced by Kermani, *Gott its schön*.

to the social context of collective worship, is the ubiquitous form of presence of the Qur'an, which maintains its affective power outside of collective worship as well.[27] Since claims for aesthetic quality were already involved in its emergence and earliest diffusion, it is no surprise that the Qur'an soon took on a further aesthetic manifestation beyond the acoustic as it was set into writing in Arabic letters: the Qur'an is also omnipresent visually, in calligraphic reproductions of individual suras and verses that are present in public and private space. As the reference text par excellence for calligraphic art, it has exercised an effect on Islamic aesthetics throughout history that cannot be overstated.[28]

That this formal plurality of appearances, this "multi-mediality," is a unique quality of the Qur'an, and that a special attraction adheres to its visual and auditory manifestation, has often been noted in research, but serious conclusions have rarely been drawn from this. The Qur'an's three forms of appearance have never been studied together in Western research, the visual appearance of the Qur'an being the subject of art history, while the acoustic one remains a special area of ethnomusicology. On the other hand, the textual appearance of the Qur'an, as a post-biblical prophetic writing, is excluded from the only discipline that might be entitled to comprehend it, theology. Instead, the Qur'an has been considered exclusively through the lens of Arabic philology, which, concerned with the study of the entire stock of Islamic writing, took the Qur'an to be one among the various bodies of evidence of Arabic literature, ignoring its special status as the founding document of a world religion. Accordingly, the Qur'an has been submitted mainly to grammatical and stylistic analyses. Though many of these foundational works—produced by outstanding scholars—are still of great value, they have rarely been able to bring the Qur'an closer to the Western reader aesthetically or hermeneutically—a failure that is due not least to the application of inappropriate standards. The criteria for judgments about the linguistic correctness, level of style, and literary rank of the Qur'an have been derived from the same sources by which one measured Arabic literature as a whole, being derived from the grammatical and lexicological writings on the "classical" Arabic language, the *ʿarabīya*,[29] which were all composed some centuries after the Qur'an. Although this body of rules and regulations is invaluable for any approach to the development of secular post-Qur'anic classical Arabic, its strict application to the Qur'an is an anachronism, since the Qur'an emerged well before the fixing of "classical" grammar. Taking into account the further important aspect that the Qur'an cannot be isolated stylistically from biblical tradition, it becomes clear that the paradigms developed in later Arabic literature that are applied to the Qur'an in Western research offer only arbitrary standards. It is no surprise, then,

27. Nelson, *Art of Reciting*.
28. Blair, *Calligraphy*.
29. Spitaler, "Arabisch."

that philological analyses have sometimes amounted to "catalogues of vices" rather than elaborations of a poetics of the Qur'an.[30] Indeed, it would be no exaggeration to claim that until the end of the last century,[31] with the single exception of the German poet and "imitative stylist" of Near Eastern literature Friedrich Rückert (1788–1866),[32] no researcher in the German-speaking world has taken a noteworthy interest in the Qur'anic speech style—a judgment that probably can be extended to the rest of the European research tradition, where it was only translators, including George Sale (1697–1736)[33] and his later countryman Arthur Arberry (1905–1969),[34] who alone showed any evidence of a sensibility for Qur'anic literary form.[35] In the German-speaking world, we can, however, expect a feedback of the Qur'an into German literature in the near future; two literary translations, by Hartmut Bobzin and Stefan Weidner, are presently in preparation, or have already appeared.[36]

I.4 Two Misreflections of the Qur'an: Teleology and the Syndrome of Epigonality

The list of false perceptions of the Qur'an can be continued. Above all, two continuously encountered research perspectives stand in the way of an objective and open-ended textual investigation: teleology and, often in conjunction with it, the assumption of epigonality. We constantly encounter an unquestioned conception of the Qur'an as a "finished book," whether in the sense of a great authorial venture by the Prophet that still during his lifetime would alter world history or in the sense of a successful later compilation that grounded this success retroactively in salvation history. This reduction of the genesis of the Qur'an to a "parthenogenesis," to the production of a consummate book intended as such, is accompanied by a second reductive conception, which claims that the text is a mere surrogate of the Bible, or at most an epigonal attempt to recreate it in Arabic. With few exceptions, modern Qur'an researchers shy away from granting the Qur'an its own creative process of emergence and avoid granting the final sacral-coded text any dimension of meaning that exceeds its verbal pronouncements; above all, they avoid recognizing it as a document of communal history.

Qur'an research, and research in early Islam in general, is thus beholden to the teleological conception of the appearance of the Qur'an as a "primal scene"—this is so regardless of whether the Qur'an is seen as Muhammad's "book" in

30. Nöldecke, "Zur Sprache des Koran" ("register of sins").
31. That is, up to the publication of Kermani, *Gott its schön*, in 1999.
32. Rückert, *Koran* (completed 1844, first edition 1888).
33. Sale, *Koran*, London, 1734.
34. Arberry, *Koran*, Oxford, 1964.
35. Some short suras were analyzed for their tonality in the exceptional study of Michael Sells, "Sound, Spirit, and Gender"; this is an approach he adopts also in his synoptic work *Approaching the Qur'an*.
36. Bobzin, *Der Koran*.

its traditional temporal and spatial coordinates, as in traditional research, or whether it is construed by skeptical researchers as a "book" produced by anonymous redactors. The "book" is conceived as an authorial text or, put briefly, a finished theological design, a fait accompli that marks a new historical beginning or, in the eyes of the skeptics assuming a later, politically conditioned compilation, asserts in retrospect a new beginning for an already established Islamic society. In the cases of the individual phases of development of the Qur'an's genesis, however, such as the migration of the Prophet from Mecca to Medina in the year 622, the construction of a primal scene has recently been sharply critiqued and debunked as untenable. Thus a recent study shows that the event of the *hijra*, which occurs during the Qur'an genesis itself, was not initially a foundational act that set the standards for a new epoch in Islamic history, but only became such retrospectively, through a hindsight that underlays it with teleological necessity.[37] The most crucial such event, the emergence of a "book," the gradual "hypostasizing" of the proclamation into the word of God manifest in codex form, should be subject to just such an interpretive archaeology. It is evident that the "closure of the text," which is a necessary precondition for this hypostasizing, did not occur during the period of the Qur'an's genesis. Within the Qur'an itself, one can detect traces of an adaptation of a Late Antique logos theology, which raised the audibly recited Qur'an, *al-qur'ān in statu nascendi*, to the rank of a "hypostasis," a manifestation of the word of God perceivable to the senses. The Qur'an's elevation to a transcendent status as a materialized "book" is a later phenomenon, one that is often carried forward in modern apologetics. Islamic reform thinkers such as Muhammad Shahrur begin their critique here;[38] likewise, structuralist researchers such as Mohammed Arkoun have long called for the deconstruction of the sacralized "book," or what Arkoun called the "*livre-livre*"; but this critique has not been pursued in connection to historical analysis.[39] Even in "skeptical" research, the task of historically criticizing the construction of Islamic primal scenes and their mythical ramifications has only barely been perceived, and often short-circuited through the "transportation" of the Qur'an text out of its "primary milieu," the Hijaz of the seventh century, into a later, "demythologized historical period" or a more "historically transparent" geographical region such as Syria. It is on this crucial point of Qur'an research that the volume here presented adopts a fundamentally new position: the Qur'an should be perceived as a text that grew historically, prior to its later achievement of a unique religious aura. It must be loosed from both the historically later discourse of Islamic tradition and the speculative horizon of Western projections and placed back into the Late Antique milieu of its emergence—as a unique and new voice in the theological

37. Crone, "Concept of Hijra."
38. Eickelman, "Muslim Politics."
39. Arkoun, *Lectures du Coran*; Arkoun, *Rethinking Islam*.

debates of its time. In this project, it will not always be possible to proceed beyond hypotheses.

This project of freeing the Qur'an from its teleological cocoon has a culture-critical dimension that goes beyond academic concerns and that touches upon not only the very position of Western research but also the position of research in the Near East, which does not appear much better off than that of Western research. According to the dominant Islamic view, relevant Arab history begins with the Qur'anic revelation, and "only a chaotic image remains from the previous time, condensed in the concept of *jāhilīya*, which is understood as the 'Time of Ignorance.' "[40] As the Lebanese historian Samir Kassir emphasizes, this origin myth, which refers everything back to the "role of Muhammad," reduces prehistory to an epoch characterized almost exclusively by nomadic forms of life. The *jāhilīya*, construed as pre-Islamic "barbarism" and "ignorance," thus serves as a pure binary contrast to the new civilization brought about by Islam. But *jāhilīya* understood in this sense,

> of which Arabic historiography preserves only poetic evidence and genealogical myth, would in the best case cover the immediate hundred years preceding the Prophet only. The chaotic image cannot be maintained if one reviews the results of research into Hellenistic and Roman history documented by archaeology, epigraphy, and numismatics. Indeed, the Arab cities in the northern Hijāz were fully Romanized, even to the point that they gave rise to Roman emperors. Warlike nomadism, a notion nourished in the later Arabic conceptual world, should then be thoroughly relativized, so that one can imagine what sort of Copernican revolution would be initiated by the recognition of a golden age that preceded the actual golden ages.[41]

Kassir pleads for the freeing of the Arabic-Islamic vision from the teleological compulsion of the assumption of religious predetermination, the assumption that all Arab history stems originally from the revelation proclaimed by Muhammad—a mythologizing of history that, mutatis mutandis, also underlies the alternative nationalistic vision that attributes a "golden age" to the Arabic expansion movement under the first caliphs. Kassir's plea is valuable for its recontextualization of Arabic-Islamic history alongside Jewish-Christian, syncretistic, and pagan Late Antiquity, and for its opening of Islamic history to a pre-Islamic pluricultural past that releases the Qur'an and early Islam from their respective isolation.

The burning question of the evaluation of the *jāhilīya* current in Islamic discussions has its counterpart in discussions around the European construction of

40. Kassir, *Das arabische Unglück*, 38ff., cf. below 22ff.
41. Ibid., 39.

Late Antiquity. *Jāhilīya* and Late Antiquity are two sides of the same coin. But they are difficult to bring together, as each in turn is based on a principle of exclusion. Though the Islamic *jāhilīya* construction, with its ostracizing of the pre-Islamic mentality, is geared above all to the pagan way of life, it consigns however—with the denigration of an entire epoch as an obsolete "pre-time"—those processes and actors not in conformity with later Islam to historical oblivion. Late Antique Arabia has become an "empty Hijaz,"[42] as James E. Montgomery has pointedly expressed it, a region emptied of its cultural setting. The traditional conception of a "culturally remote" Hijaz has not only caused skeptical researchers to search for the milieu of the Qur'an's emergence in another region; it also seems co-responsible for the exclusivist Western construction of Late Antiquity, which has long excluded Islam. Islam was received as signaling a cultural break, inducing the "decline" of the plural older cultures of the Near East that had survived into Late Antiquity—a construction that has only begun in recent times to be weakened by a more inclusive view.[43] But the Qur'an itself has not yet been given a place in the world of Late Antiquity.

I.4.1 Epigonality

The second distorting mirror, the projection of the Qur'an as an epigonal reprise of the Bible, has effects that are no less disfiguring. If nearly all available introductory presentations show traces of a pejorative assessment of Qur'anic religious discourse[44] and draw a strikingly dismissive picture of the development of the Qur'an's textual form, this is largely due to a conception of the Qur'an as a weaker replica of the Bible, with nothing essentially new to offer. These reservations about the text have even deeper roots: if we read the Qur'an as a mere replica of the Bible, the text seems to put forth trains of thought and images in a way that has long become obsolete in the secular West. Qur'anic practices and positions, such as ritualized piety and the awareness of standing within primordially concluded covenantal bonds, would thus appear too outdated and obsolete to deserve a systematic review of their gradual development as results of a long and constant religious conversation.[45]

The Qur'an, as a post-biblical scripture, is also caught between the meshes of a new secularized reading of the "Bible as literature."[46] As a paraenetic text, a communication with admonishing-instructing intentions, the Qur'an does not meet the classical standards of biblical narrative, where strict narrative logic and artistic composition of theological elements take precedent. It is even

42. Montgomery, "The Empty Ḥijāz"; see also his rehabilitation of the *'ayyām al-'Arab* literature, which had up that point been completely ignored in literature on the Koran: Montgomery, *Vagaries*, 10–51.

43. Bowersock, *Hellenism*; Hoyland, *Arabia*; Brown, "Late Antiquity and Islam."

44. Wild's compilation, "Schauerliche Öde," could easily be expanded to new cases.

45. See also Wild's observations in "Why Self-Referentiality?," 1–14.

46. See Schmidt and Weidner, *Bibel als Literatur*.

further from fulfilling the expectation imposed on the text today, that it should be "rooted in reality" and "animate." The Bible itself has only recently been widely rediscovered as "literature," a discovery whose representatives boldly discredit previous exegetical readings oriented to allegory and typology as hindrances to the recognition of the full "humanistic dimension" of biblical discourse. Here too a judgment emerges that is drawn exclusively from Western secular ideals. This verdict hits the Qur'an all the harder, since this scripture as such already reflects an exegetical reading of biblical narratives, and thus is not highly amenable to readings rooted in reality or concentrating only on narrative techniques.

The teleological conception of the Qur'an as a pregiven book and the refusal to include a reading of its sacral coding (the "religious ballast" long disregarded in the Western tradition) have operated as distorting mirrors and ultimately eliminated the Qur'an's epistemic dimension, the process of dealing with diverse older traditions. That which is revolutionarily new, what the reading of the Qur'an makes most attractive intellectually, thus remains unrecognized. In this volume, special significance and constant attention will be given to the contextualizing of the Qur'an not only with the Bible but also with rabbinic, patristic, and liturgical literature. Of course, "parallels" and "models" for Qur'anic texts have long been recognized, but they have generally been treated as mere evidence for comparative studies. Here, by contrast, their re-functioning in the context of communal formation will become the central point of focus.

We will also oppose the widespread notion that the Qur'an can be understood in isolation from ancient Arabic poetry. It is not enough to concede that the Qur'an inverted the heroic ethos of *murūʾa*, "heroism," or integrated it where possible into new Islamic categories. The confrontation of the Qur'anic community with this local "great tradition" brought forth a complex new discourse, which, no less dramatically than the biblical-Qur'anic discourse, radically overturned central conventions of thought. Perhaps the most significant rewriting is to be seen in the rigorous new formation of the ancient Arabic construction of space, which is given form in the *nasīb*, the opening section of the qasida (*qaṣīda*) that includes the convention of the poet's lamenting at the abandoned campsite. The space of the ruins, emptied of sense, in which the ancient Arab speaker locates himself, is not only reversed in its qualities but raised in its reformulation to the rank of a linchpin for the new eschatologically marked worldview: it returns in the form of a garden full of sensory fulfillment, which awaits the pious in the hereafter.[47]

47. Neuwirth, "Zeit und Ewigkeit in den Psalmen und im Koran."

I.5 The "Qur'anic Community"

A third new aspect of our approach lies in the focus on the Qur'anic community. We do not assume an "author" behind the Qur'an, but rather—apart from the very first suras, which reflect an individual conversation between God and man—a protracted communal discussion that lasts over the whole period of the Prophet's ministry. The expectation of the hearers that is fulfilled in the Qur'an is conditioned by their previous knowledge: successful communication is conditioned on a body of knowledge that existed already in ongoing discussions. This is not to discard the assumption, firmly held also in our hypotheses, that it was the proclaimer himself who ultimately gave the text its verbal and literary form. But in terms of content, the pronouncements also belong simultaneously to the early community, which is constantly present in the text. In what follows, particular attention will be given to the hearers—here termed the "Qur'anic community"—as co-formers of the discourse and intended hearers of the text, though the central actor in the interaction scenario remains, just as before, the proclaimer himself. While older works speak in general of "Muhammad" and newer ones of "the Qur'an," here we speak generally of the "proclaimer," with respect to the communication process that overrides all of this; this term can be understood as the common denominator of his frequent self-designations as "warner," *nadhīr*; later "apostle," *rasūl*; and then yet later "prophet," *nabī*. The name Muhammad appears first in Medinan texts, perhaps as an honorific, at a time when the proclaimer already occupies a ruling and ceremonial function evoking theocratic models. Account should be given to the Qur'anic language usage as it developed through a number of stages; to avoid anachronisms, referring to the "proclaimer" therefore appears to be most rewarding.[48]

I.6 Qur'an Research as Historical and Literary-Critical Project

It is hard to deny that the Qur'an remains a text that is difficult to approach for the Western reader. In its transmitted form, it does not invite a continuous reading. But its unapproachability is not based primarily on its historical age, on the fact that it is a Late Antique text dating to the seventh century and thus stands at a distance from the modern thought world; nor is it based on the fact that it is an Arabic text, the particular cultural references of which are not familiar to the European reader. Rather, the text's unique obstacle lies in its particular formal traits, as a document of proclamation in a mantic discourse form that has not yet been analyzed through literary-critical methods. In common perception, the Qur'an stands as an erratic block within its own literary landscape, disconnected

48. On scholarly uncertainty, see Crone, "What Do We Actually Know about Mohammed?"

from the Arabic literature that preceded it and isolated in its textual position from the neighboring, more familiar Jewish and Christian literatures. "Uprooted" in this way from its semantic and aesthetic context, the text appears full of forced metaphors, occasionally labored mysteriousness, and trains of thought that are ambiguous to the untrained eye; above all, it is the order of suras, which evinces no chronological or narrative logic, that makes the Qur'an appear to be a text that undercuts any continuous reading. Added to this is the centuries-old perception of the text's foreignness in the Western world, of simultaneous nearness to and distance from the Bible, a trait that has been willfully overplayed again in recent scholarly literature. The contemporary call for a re-reading of classical Greek poetry that would concentrate on aesthetics and not overemphasize cultural specificity and foreignness is relevant also, mutatis mutandis, for the Qur'an—even if, in our case, the historical reconstruction of the milieu of emergence is still far from achieved. An additional hindrance to this project is the teleological ballast of a traditional Western reading, which is based on the preconceived notion that the Qur'an is a kind of "reduced form" of the Bible and thus a literary fossil. This ballast must be discarded, if one wants to make comprehensible the actual and irrefutable aesthetic affective power of the Qur'an, which has been so powerful throughout the centuries and remains so.

Indeed, we find that all of the text-specific obstacles to understanding listed above can be explained and dispelled historically. Each must be worked through, if the new reading is not to remain speculative. And the conditions for this are more amenable than ever: not only has our knowledge of the environment of the Qur'an and its historical, religious-historical, and social-political conditions of emergence progressed significantly in recent times, so that one speaks now of regionally different "Late Antiquities" in the broader region in which the Qur'an emerges;[49] additionally, promising new methodological approaches are being developed for the study of the formal particularities of the Qur'an. It is therefore not too ambitious to suggest a new reading, through the laying out of the conditions of emergence as well as the functions and forms of Qur'anic discourse, and through a detailed commentary: a new reading will invite the reader of the Qur'an to discover the historical complexity of the text and to recognize its complex rhetorical structure as an integral part of the religious message itself.

This optimism may be surprising given the current state of Qur'an research, where the most diverse projects and methodologies are employed side by side but hardly ever checked against each other. Certainly, the project of an introduction to the Qur'an that brings together all relevant aspects will remain illusory, in view of the diverse innovative individual research projects that now stand only in their beginning phases. Yet just such an introduction is long overdue, if only as a

49. On this, see Neuwirth, Sinai, and Marx, *Qur'ān in Context*. Robin has presented important new insights on the historical context of Late Antiquity in Southern Arabia; see especially his "Himyar et Israël."

practical attempt to break through the hermeneutical barriers erected in Qur'an research between the different methodologies. This confidence is based in the conviction that through the linking of literary-critical and historical approaches, a firm basis for new Qur'an research can be laid. This means that we must develop a linking model that also allows the knowledge attained within disciplines that have until now been kept distinct from philological or historical studies, such as cultural anthropology[50] or art theory,[51] to be bundled and made fruitful for a more complex understanding of the Qur'an. The present volume, which situates itself in the tradition of philological-literary studies, assumes that serious academic Qur'an research cannot proceed without an interest in the historical dimensions of the Qur'an, and that even an inexperienced, less ambitious reader applying an ahistorical reading would make it only halfway through the Qur'an. At least heuristically, the text must be placed within a cultural milieu.

I.6.1 The Indispensability of Chronology

A crucial precondition of this project is the reconstruction of the chronology that is no longer immediately evident in the transmitted textual form, despite the fact that such a reconstruction has often been discredited in modern studies as an obsolete research goal.[52] It is chronology that constitutes the scaffolding for the understanding of the pre-redactional text, that is, the successive *proclamation* of the Qur'anic message that should be the centerpiece of historical comprehension of the Qur'an, whereas chronology for the understanding of the post-redactional text interpreted by the exegetes is not as urgently required.

Still, questions surrounding the chronology of individual texts have played no insignificant role in the Islamic tradition from the beginning. They were the object of theology and legal science, where the interpretation of Qur'anic citations often requires one to confront the question of when and under what circumstances the texts under scrutiny were proclaimed. Assigning a historic sequence to the individual Qur'an texts, the traditional Islamic sciences distinguish between Meccan and Medinan suras.[53] This differentiation does not, however, affect the interpretation in general, but rather remains limited to verses already problematized theologically or in terms of legal specifics. Initiatives toward a chronological ordering of texts have also been developed in the discipline of the determination of the "circumstances of the revelation," *asbāb al-nuzūl*; but since this discipline involves the Sira and therefore merges with hagiographic literature, its results cannot be evaluated as historical in strict sense.

50. See, e.g., Toelle, *Coran revisité*; Chabbi, *Seigneur*; and Martin, *Cultural Perspective*; Toelle, *Local Contexts*.

51. See, e.g., Fowden, *Hellenism, Christianity and the Umayyads*.

52. This seems to be characteristic of British and American work on the Koran; cf. for example the works of Hawting, Rippin, and Martin.

53. A compilation of statements within the traditional literature is offered by Nagel, *Medinensische Einschübe*.

On the other hand, specialized European research—above all Gustav Weil (1808–1889),[54] followed significantly by Theodor Nöldeke (1836–1930), whose *Geschichte des Qorans (The History of the Qur'an)* appeared in 1860—refined the division into two periods of emergence established in Islamic tradition. Primarily on the basis of formal observations, Nöldeke distinguished between three Meccan periods and one Medinan period. For several generations, European research relied on this chronology as the backbone of its understanding of the Qur'an, taking interest above all in a reconstruction of the development of the proclaimer and his message. Though Nöldeke's work remained beholden to several prejudices, and although he treated the Qur'an as above all an authorial work rather than the reflection of an interaction between speaker and community, nonetheless his *The History of the Qur'ān* laid the basis for all later work on the formation and development of the Qur'anic message. In the time since, it has been possible to refine the chronology he laid out in essential ways.[55] For the development of the pre-redactional text, that is, the proclamation itself, chronology, though it remains ultimately hypothetical, must serve as an indispensable guideline if the succession of discourses and theological positions is to be comprehended.

I.6.2 The Problem of Historicity

The Qur'an is not only a difficult text but also a contested one in the contemporary moment, one whose historical location is controversial in Islamic and Western research. Certainly, in view of the disproportionately short time that Islamic tradition assigns to Muhammad's lifework, it is to be expected that doubts may arise about the unprecedentedly grand career of a man from a remote corner of the contemporary oecumene. If we follow the historical reports, he was born around 570, first appeared publicly in Mecca in 610, and was forced into exile to Medina in 622, where, after the successful spread of his teaching across a wide range of the Arabian Peninsula, he died ten years later in 632.[56] Much of this presentation seems to differ from what is familiar from religious history: the Qur'an, a message to the pagans of the Arabian Peninsula, led within only twenty-two years to the founding of a new religion? A holy scripture becomes fixed and canonized a short time after the death of the founder, and then transmitted authentically down to the present? It is thus hardly surprising that hypotheses drawing on the course of developments in Judaism and Christianity have been continually formulated, not only in recent times, seeking to rewrite early Islamic history and place the emergence of the Qur'an in another region, another time,[57] occasionally

54. Weil, *Historisch-kritische Einleitung.*

55. See Sinai, "Qur'an as Process."

56. An overview of the proclaimer's life and work is offered by Bobzin, *Muhammad*, and recently by Schöller, *Mohammed.*

57. Wansbrough, *Quranic Studies*; Wansbrough, *Sectarian Milieu*; Crone and Cook, *Hagarism.*

even without the participation of Muhammad.[58] But these new reconstructions cannot be brought into agreement, nor do they yield a plausible new picture of events, raising instead innumerable new questions. It has not been possible so far to construct an alternative history of the emergence of Islam. The risk assumed by the skeptical elimination of the inner-Islamic historical tradition has so far yielded no historically viable result.

But the inner-Islamic positioning of the Qur'an in history is also not without its problems, as the critique of the historian Samir Kassir has already made clear.[59] There is a tendency here to construct a pure historical origin in the Qur'an and to denigrate the preceding times as an "age of ignorance." The fact that Samir Kassir, in his call for the reconnection of Arabian history to Late Antique culture, has in mind primarily the social and ideological links with non-Arabian actors[60] and does not problematize inner-Arab verbal and literary relationships is not due to his personal specialization as a historian alone. Arabic research looks back to a long tradition of linguistic and literary work on the Qur'an and ancient Arabic poetry stretching back over many centuries, so that the urgency of venturing new readings in this realm may not be immediately felt. But critical Qur'an research must take up, as a second axis of the undertaking, so to speak, a new cultural-critical *and* literary study of the evidence of poetry and epic of the sixth and seventh centuries.

Indeed, ancient Arabic poetry, whose reincorporation into Late Antiquity is now being advocated by ever more voices,[61] has not been adequately studied with a view to its rich intertextuality reaching across languages and cultures. This poetry has long been explained in conformity with indigenous Arabic language scholarship, as originating entirely from a nomadic, or in exceptional cases provincial and courtly, culture; it has thus appeared as essentially particular and wholly limited to Arab culture. But, as James E. Montgomery has shown, what we are dealing with here is rather a consciously Bedouinizing elitist poetry, that fits into the Hellenistically imprinted culture of its wider environment. Particular characteristics, such as the wistful call to that which has passed on, the *ubi sunt qui ante nos in mundo fuere*[62] motif that is so characteristic of the Hellenistic period and which is repeated in ancient Arabic poetry, come immediately to mind. As these ideas also undergo a new interpretation in the Qur'an, this poetry is to be considered one of the formative foundations for the Qur'an community, comparable in rank to the monotheistic religions. That the Qur'an employs and

58. Luxenberg, *Syro-aramäische Lesart*.

59. Kassir, *Das arabische Unglück*. Chabbi argues similarly in *Le Coran décrypté*. Chabbi, however, is primarily interested in eliminating mythical excesses from the history of Islam.

60. See, e.g., Ali, *Al-Mufassal*, Ajina, *Mausūʿat*, and al-Saʿfi, *al-Qurbān*. Crucial advances have been made in the study of epigraphy and papyrus; for more recent Arabic scholarship, see Hussein, *Nashʾat al-Dawla*.

61. Montgomery, "Dichotomy"; Zwettler, *Oral Tradition*; cf. also Bauer, "The Relevance of Early Arabic Poetry"; Dmitriev, *Das poetische Werk*; Toral-Niehoff, *Stammesfürsten*.

62. Becker, "Ubi sunt qui ante nos in mundo fuere."

further develops the poetic language has long been recognized. But this research path has rarely been pursued in any detail since the work of Alfred Bloch.[63] It is obvious that a treatment of the Qur'an that neglects its literary form and its reference to poetry—a deficit that is reflected still in the Western Qur'an commentaries presently in use[64]—cannot adequately capture the dimensions of the text's significance.

I.6.3 Plurality of Methods

Only thirty years ago, one could make the claim, with an apologetic but also optimistic tone, that "Qur'an research still stands in children's shoes." In the time since, it has grown up into a complex discipline, in which a diversity of methodological projects are being tested anew. Yet these complex approaches to the Qur'an do not tend to build on each other, but rather give rise to a kind of chaos, in which the actual object of research, the Qur'an itself, no longer comes into focus. However welcome this diversity of research methods may be, it remains ineffectual so long as the individual projects and their results are not brought together and the respective underlying hypothetical premises are not explicitly expounded.

At present, the Qur'an's textual history and exegesis are more controversial than ever.[65] Above all, we are further away than ever from the important goal of setting the third monotheistic scripture on the same level with the two others, of setting the Qur'an into relief as a reference text equal to the Bible, a text to which no less promising historical, literary, and theological questions can be set than to the biblical writings themselves. This justifies the urgency of a serious analysis of the structures of the text that is to be informed by biblical studies, a treatment that handles it not in an "essentialist" way, as an exotic text, but rather with an "egalitarian" method, that is, with the same methodical apparatus and corresponding strategies as employed for the biblical writings. According to the guiding principle of biblical studies, which calls for the primacy of "lower criticism," the Qur'an must first be submitted heuristically, in its current state of transmission, to a microstructural reading, which will test the coherence of its unities, the suras, before it can be made the object of such textual experiments as have become frequent in recent studies, seeking to prove hypothetical pre-Islamic precedents or the contrary, a text produced later within Islam.

It is thus no longer possible to base oneself on a single, particular method. The present study is principally dedicated to the historical-critical approach, an approach that is being questioned, however, from various perspectives in recent times.[66] Alongside the numerous alternative synchronic Bible readings, which

63. Bloch, *Vers und Sprache*; see as well Spitaler's review.
64. This also applies to Paret, *Koran: Kommentar*; Bell, *Commentary*; and Khoury, *Koran*.
65. Motzki, "Alternative Accounts of the Qur'an's Formation."
66. See also Barton, *Cambridge Companion to Biblical Interpretation*.

are not applicable to the pre-canonic Qur'an, an approach oriented toward reception history,[67] poses new challenges to Qur'an research. Thus, certain Jewish[68] and Christian[69] exegetes plead that the Bible should no longer be understood from outside the context of its beginnings, but should rather be re-embedded into its living liturgical and theological tradition, which has been maintained down to today. In this, they point to the decisive break with tradition that began with the secularization of biblical studies in the eighteenth/nineteenth century, when the traditional hermeneutic rules were displaced through the rigorous application of historical-critical methods, and, to put this briefly, the study of the prehistory of the Bible came to replace the study of the Bible itself.

But Qur'an research, unlike this new direction of biblical studies, is not faced with the task of reconnecting the Qur'an to its traditional exegetical context. In contrast to the Bible (at least in its mainstream interpretations), the Qur'an stands within a virtually unbroken tradition of dogmatically bound exegesis. But Qur'an research, even as it adopts principles from the historical-critical method, should learn from these new reflections in biblical studies. What is still required for the Qur'an is focus on it as a text that *already reflects* the traditional Jewish and Christian traditions of exegesis that are now being rediscovered in biblical studies. What is called for now is not, as in new Jewish and Christian Bible research, the reconstruction of the Qur'an's own traditional exegesis; rather, because the Qur'an itself is a part of the history of post-biblical exegesis and presents reworkings of allegorical and typological interpretations of earlier writings; what is demanded is the laying open of these particular post-biblical intertextualities *in* the Qur'an itself. From this perspective, the inclusion of post-biblical exegetical traditions newly reclaimed in biblical studies and historical-critical analysis can be meaningfully brought together. Apart from this, the fact that a reading of the Qur'an embedded in its exegetical tradition still presents a challenging field of research in itself is shown fully by exemplary new studies on the commentary literature.[70]

What must be brought up to speed in Qur'an research, however, are attempts to anchor the text historically in Late Antiquity, a task wherein the historical-critical method must be combined with newer approaches: the investigation presented here will in no way end in literary-critical "deconstruction," since the primary object of study on which it seeks to shed light consists of the individual suras in their complete and final form. The single suras are not to be treated in isolation, however, but rather should be regarded as parts of the sequence of suras that must be reconstructed, that is, as phases of the proclamation. In this, the

67. Reiser, *Bibelkritik und Auslegung.*

68. Kugel, "Early Interpretation"; Kugel, *The Bible as It Was.*

69. Wilken, "In Defense of Allegory."

70. Most recently see Saleh, *Qur'an Commentary of al-Tha'labi*; Saleh, *In Defense of the Bible*; Lane, *Kashshaf of Jar Allah al-Zamakhshari*; and Sinai, *Studien zur frühen Koraninterpretation.*

posing of questions about the history of redaction connects to the interests of the so-called canonical reading (canonical approach), which has been propagated since the 1970s in American biblical studies.[71] The *canonical approach* understands the genesis of a canon as a process of growth. Canon in this context no longer means simply the binding, codified final form of a scripture but rather "a consciousness deeply rooted in this very writing of obligation, which is established through processes of updating and intertextuality that are reflected in the text."[72]—"Even if this genesis, conceived as a canonic process, comes to an end with the end of the growth of the text, the final form of the writing offers neither a form without tension nor one that levels out the traces of the gradually grown text. With the final form, the site of interpretation is displaced. Up to that point it has occurred in the text as productive updating or redaction, and from that point on it occurs through commentary and interpretation alongside, or on, the text."[73]

Differently than in, for example, the case of the Psalms, with the Qur'an we are not attempting to stitch together a meaningfully ordered total corpus of proclamations—for in the case of the Qur'an, these proclamations never constituted a meaningfully ordered written ensemble, but rather consisted at most of a virtual corpus made up of the suras assigned to their historical sequence. The most important goal of the reconstruction of a Qur'an chronology is, rather, an understanding of the suras themselves that meets the demands of literary critical scholarship. That the suras are rich in intertextual references has already been highlighted by John Wansbrough;[74] but Qur'anic intertextuality does not make reference exclusively to extra-Qur'anic texts that arise out of the biblical tradition. Rather, the Qur'an—as has been highlighted by Navid Kermani,[75] who most recently has made the case for the poeticity of the Qur'an—predisposes its addressees "through announcements, open and hidden signals, familiar characteristics or implicit references, to a very particular kind of reception. . . . In the case of the Qur'an it must be added that the Qur'an is to a high degree a self-referential text, a text which reflects on itself in many places, which comments on itself, which makes a theme of its own linguistic awareness, more than any other scripture in the history of world religions."[76]

Literary research into the Qur'an thus stands before a double task: it must on the one hand take into its horizon the insights of the hermeneutics developed within Islam, that is, integrate classical Arabic linguistic stylistics and modern literary exegesis, *tafsīr adabī*. This important task is yet to be attempted. Its other

71. See especially Childs, *Biblical Theology*; Childs, *Old Testament as Scripture*; Childs, *New Testament as Canon*; and Childs, *Theologie der einen Bibel*.

72. Dohmen and Oeming, *Biblischer Kanon*, 25.

73. Ibid.

74. Wansbrough, *Quranic Studies*.

75. Kermani, *Gott ist schön*.

76. Ibid., 97.

task is a "poetological analysis" in the Western tradition, and here important precedents already exist in Psalm research; "the approaches of structural literary studies, aesthetic stylistics and rhetoric, speech-act theory, but also research in motifs and symbols, allow one to treat the differing images and communication structures, and especially the ornamental and structural form . . . , in the most precise way possible. This endeavor is combined with the program of *close reading* of the so-called final-text exegesis, which, in contrast to the frequent privileging of the "first form" of a text, demands that the 'end form' of a text be taken seriously."[77] In the Psalms as well as the Qur'an, the dialogue between individual texts plays a decisive role. In the first instance, the recognition of the inner-Qur'anic intertexts, as they emerge on the basis of chronological analysis, allows a full understanding of an individual sura. The reconstruction of a chronology is thus above all a desideratum for further literary studies, even while it itself is carried out in turn through the initial investigatory steps of literary studies.

That all of these projected steps in our limited frame cannot be dealt with in more than a programmatic way at best, is self-evident. The knowledge required for this, belonging as it does to various disciplines, does not converge in the minds of individual researchers, but can only be generated through the cooperation of research teams. The project Corpus Coranicum, which has been underway since 2007 in the Berlin-Brandenburg Academy of Sciences, has envisaged this new kind of work on the Qur'an text reaching across disciplinary boundaries, bringing together literary scholars, historians, Arabists, Semiticists, scholars of Judaism, and researchers on the Christian Orient.[78] The present is meant to lay the basis for a concise commentary on the Qur'an that will appear in successive volumes, and which in turn is conceived as a kind of pilot project for the publication of a major commentary work, to be made available online, edited by the Berlin-Brandenburg Academy of Sciences.

I.7 The Qur'an as Panorama—Illuminated in Thirteen Chapters

The present volume consists of three parts. The first part consists of three introductory chapters (chaps. 1–3), the first of which is an overview of research. This overview consciously does not limit itself to a recital of the approaches and results of earlier research,[79] but attempts to summarize them critically, to draw attention to the problematics and occasional prejudices of Western research. But the current self-imposed isolation of research into the Qur'an and early Islam, highlighted by Samir Kassir, is only partially due to the indigenous Islamic tradition

77. Hossfeld, *Die Psalmen*, 1:20.
78. Marx, "Programmatik des Akademienvorhabens *Corpus Coranicum*."
79. This is the aim of the article by Motzki, "Alternative Accounts."

itself. It is also a reaction to Western approaches, in particular those of the so-called skeptics, whose research has until now not been successfully explained to Muslim readers "constructively," as products of a given critique-provoking research tradition, nor has the Western approach of connecting the Qur'an to its biblical intertexts.

It immediately stands out that alongside the "traditional" Western research interests in the Qur'an, as a text read through the lens of the Prophet's biography and thus already "Muslim," there was and still is a parallel interest in generating an "archaeology" of the Qur'an, following the tradition of historical-critical Bible exegesis. This search to find the foundational "source texts" of the Qur'an rarely contented itself with illuminating the Qur'an historically, but rather corroborated the image of the Qur'an's substantial dependence on biblical and post-biblical traditions, its epigonality.

The results of this "source research" are apt to bring to light the biblical or Late Antique intertexts that served as premises for Qur'anic argumentation. Such intertexts should be considered part of the image store of Late Antiquity, a collective stock of knowledge familiar to the proclaimer and his first hearers from oral tradition, that needed to be negotiated and tested for their compatibility with the new worldview taking shape. The historical overview presented here follows discussions of the Qur'an back into the nineteenth century (chap. 1, "Sketch of Research").

In research up to now, the already canonized text has almost without exception consistently occupied the foreground. While individual verses have been recognized as results of the appropriation of older traditions, this did not result in the perception of the Qur'anic communication process as a continuous negotiation of traditions. These two projects—the assessment of the already completed Qur'an and the appraisal of the preceding processes of its communication addressing a not yet Islamic, pluricultural listenership—have not been presented adequately in their dialectical tension in the research up to now, but have regularly been simply conflated. In place of the "Islamic revelation" or the Qur'an already fixed literarily, the "Qur'anic proclamation" must therefore be brought to the fore, and the dialectic tension between both manifestations of the Qur'an should be described. A glance on Qur'anic self-referentiality is helpful here, since it shows how the Qur'an itself reflects on the process of the mediation of its message, and thus reflects on its own emergence. What is at stake is the gradual taking shape of the Qur'anic end form and its sacral coding, which has triggered irritation in Western discussions, even giving rise to the formulation of a "theory of inlibration" in analogy to the incarnation of the divine word in Christianity (chap. 2, "Qur'an and Scripture").

The relationship between the Qur'an and history is an area of particular controversy. The question of the status of history in the Qur'anic worldview has up to now been addressed only cursorily,[80] and has been answered generally in an entirely negative way. The Qur'anic conception of history itself is considered to be cyclical, a judgment that disregards the complex ideological developments in the course of the Qur'an's genesis, being derived almost entirely from the early suras. This view cannot be maintained if one takes into account all the evidence concerning history in the Qur'an. Above all, it has gone unnoticed up to now that the Qur'an takes serious positions on contemporary "history discourses": on the one hand it offers a new view of the biblical valuation of history as a history of providence, and on the other it takes up historically specific questions current in ancient Arabia and employs them as groundwork for new conceptions. Moreover, the later texts of the Qur'an exhibit a successive expansion of the inherited salvation history, finally involving the development of the Qur'anic community itself. Viewed within the project of understanding the Qur'an as a text of Late Antiquity, the Qur'an's view of history seems in a sense to "run backwards," taking into account disputes with Late Antique hearers and their expectations. In that this project connects Qur'anic content and form with the debates of Late Antiquity, it necessarily builds on foundations that are both historical and literary (chap. 3, "Qur'an and History").

This general introductory section is followed in the second part (chaps. 4–9) by sketches of individual domains of scholarship within Qur'an research, beginning with the history of the text and its redaction. The prehistory of the later fixed codex, despite its extraordinarily rich documentation, is not an object of widespread scholarly consensus; mutually exclusive heuristic scenarios still compete against each other in research. As a matter of fact, the history of Qur'anic discourse itself reaches back in time before this redactional history. It is through the persuasiveness of the arguments brought forward in the reconstruction of the sequence of Qur'anic discourses on the one hand and through an accurate history of the transmission of the codex on the other that the historicity of the Qur'an, which has been questioned by some researchers, has to be tested. (chap. 4, "History of the Text and Its Redaction").

Equally of fundamental significance is the reconstruction of the chronology of the Qur'an. In which way—continuing, modifying, or revoking—do individual suras build on each other? Although an abundance of material has already been brought together for the assessment of extra-Qur'anic intertextuality,[81] the inner-Qur'anic references between suras have hardly been noted or studied at all. The basis for the reconstruction of the chronology is the textual unit of the sura, the semantic and formal-structural elements of which can be traced across the course of the Qur'anic development. It is surprising to find that Western research

80. Paret, "Das Geschichtsbild Mohammeds."

81. Speyer, *Die biblischen Erzählungen im Qoran*, and many others; cf. as well Hartwig, "Die 'Wissenschaft des Judentums.'"

has only rarely chosen to investigate the unit of the sura, the (re)discovery of the sura being a relatively recent phenomenon. Nevertheless, a structural analysis of the sura is indispensible, since only if chronological ascriptions are based on a multiplicity of formal and semantic evidence can the reconstruction of a Qur'anic chronology be safeguarded against circular reasoning. As a third category of chronological evidence, alongside form and semantics, the strategies for the authorization of the Qur'anic message reflected in the texts must be taken into account (chap. 5, "Sura Structure and Chronology").

The fait accompli of the "book" Qur'aneasily allows one to forget that the text represents, so to speak, a twin of the Qur'anic community, which enters into history simultaneously alongside it, and which first constitutes itself as a community of worshippers. In view of the fact that the Qur'anic proclamation documents the emergence of the community, while also acting as a liturgical text to influence the formation of this community, the two should be treated in close connection. This duplicity is supported by the distinction made in the early Islamic tradition itself between two manifestations of the Qur'an: *qurʾān*, "recitation, reading," and *muṣḥaf*, "codex." In the mostly synchronic readings of the Qur'an in recent Western research, only the fixed text is considered, without attention paid to the dynamic development of its thought and its continuous engagement with a pre-Islamic milieu. Parallel to the development of the text, a development of cult takes place, which has gone largely ignored, and which reaches a turning point in the middle Meccan and again in the Medinan period. Two mutually opposing processes are manifest here: the emergence of complex sura structures and, later on, their dissolution, both achieved within the Qur'anic development. It is the investigation of the text as to the traces of its performance, set within particular coordinates of place and time, that can set the Qur'an into relief as a liturgical text and allow it to be comprehended as a dynamic confrontation with pre-Islamic traditions (chap. 6, "The Liturgical Qur'an").

Once one does not set up the person Muhammad as author but rather recognizes a steadily growing and changing group of actors standing in discussions with the proclaimer, it becomes legitimate to search for particular "discourses," following onto each other that should have occupied the minds of the proclaimer and the community successively. We must elicit key questions for the individual periods, the sequence of which can lead to insight about the ideological development undergone by the community. In this process, a number of thematic complexes can be recognized, ranging from consolation, affirmation of providential care, Prophetic warning, and an elementary theology of signs in the early Meccan phase, to the self-construction of the community as a new people of God and a new self-presentation in cult in the middle Meccan period, to the production of, and reflection on, the textual genre of the parable or "likeness," which in the late Meccan phase provides not only a new forum for the critique of tradition but also a strategy of self-authorization. In Medina, we note a new reflection on the covenant with God, reflections on violence in the context of military activities, legislation, and, above all, the integration of the ancient Arabic cult into the new ritual. Finally, the new religious-political situation proves challenging, since the new community is confronted by learned representatives of Jewish and occasionally Christian exegesis, not only raising claims for the interpretive monopoly over the biblical tradition but also putting forward significant and novel statements of belief developed within their own exegesis. A comprehensive "theologizing," a sharpening of insight into the ideological significance of tradition, becomes manifest, often in the form of polemic, leading in the Medinan period to a profound re-reading of individual suras that were already proclaimed in Mecca. This sequence of discourses, resulting frequently in later revisions of earlier texts, is only plausible against the background of a continuous oral proclamation (chaps. 7–9, "Stations of Community Formation").

A third part (chaps. 10–13) is dedicated to the literary, kerygmatic, and theological dimensions of the Qur'an. It first explores the relation between Qur'an and Bible. Eliciting the similarities and differences between the two corpora in their entirety allows us to refine the hermeneutical and theological questions that can be adapted from Jewish and Christian scholarship on the Bible and applied to the Qur'an, above all the question of the either allegorical or literal reading of textual passages. While we find only occasional and reticent employment of allegorical discourse, and biblical and post-biblical allegories are occasionally even resolved veritatively in the Qur'an, the hermeneutical tool of typology proves crucial in the Qur'an. The new positioning of the Qur'an in Late Antiquity invites investigations in the exegetical strategies developed post-biblically and then employed in the Qur'an as means of connecting to the biblical paradigm of a scriptural religion. A comparison of biblical and Qur'anic prophetic speech as appellatory, and a treatment of the narrative forms in both text corpora, allows us to set the Qur'an's autonomy more sharply into relief (chap. 10, "Qur'an and Bible").

The characterization of the Qur'an's particular narrative technique is still heavily contested in Qur'an research. Here, the question of authorship presents a difficult problem, in that we cannot assume for the proclaimer a continuously maintained and intentional mode of presentation. Narrative in the Qur'an seems to convey a different intention than that of biblical narrative: as in Jewish and Christian traditional literature, rather than in the Bible itself, the Qur'an privileges references to authoritative texts and their norms, over an interest in the imitation of lived reality. Moreover, the appellatory gesture of speech entailed in the communication of "prophecy," by which a divine plan "behind the things" is made present, persistently colors the narrative presentation. Reading the Qur'anic narratives not as communications about biblical protagonists but rather as evocations of authority-inspiring models, and above all as the reflection of a sharpening consciousness of the significance of these figures for the gradually forming communal vision of history, one should attend less to the deviations from putative biblical models and more to Late Antique strategies of persuasion, interpretation, and typology (chap. 11, "Biblical-Qur'anic Figures").

Bound up with the sequence of discourses is the question of the distinct "Arab character" of the Qur'an, and thus its relationship to the literary corpus of ancient Arabic poetry that already laid claim to paramount collective significance before the Qur'an's appearance. In the biblical tradition, not only are prophecy and poetry closely interweaved, but the relationship between these two modes is even an object of controversy within the Bible, as it is in the Qur'anic context. Yet a contextualization of the Qur'an alongside ancient Arabic poetry is almost entirely lacking in contemporary research. The existing comparative studies that seek to connect the ethical orientations of Qur'an and poetry present the Qur'an as testimony of a worldview sketched in opposition to poetry, where particular values upheld in poetry are inverted.[82] This approach, since it is pursued synchronically, does not pay due attention to the dynamic quality of the debates between the traditions that were in contest with each other at the time of the genesis of the Qur'an. The Qur'an texts still await to be studied more systematically in relation to the broader spectrum of intellectual-historical questions raised in the poetry (chap. 12, "Qur'an and Poetry").

Not least, the Qur'an is also a document of a community and a society that was familiar with highly developed rhetorical and intellectual poetry, for whom language itself stood out as an object of artistic experiment and reflection. As a Late Antique text, standing within a culture of debate, the Qur'an is not always spontaneous prophetic speech but is also, and to a large degree, exegesis, reflective engagement with predecessor traditions both sacred and profane; it is therefore, to a much higher degree than the Bible, a text founded in rhetoric. The rhetorical dimension of the Qur'an is inextricable from its liturgical function; the primacy of the mode of realization of formal recitation is manifest clearly in the textual form. The aural form of presentation, whose affective power can hardly be overstated, carries forth a tradition of performance of scriptural texts refined and backed by cantilena that was ubiquitous in the religious cultures of the Near East. Acoustically, and above all as a clearly rhetorically marked theological text, the Qur'an shows itself to be a document of Late Antiquity (chap 13, "The Rhetorical Qur'an").

I.7.1 The Two Faces of the Qur'an

Like a number of other research initiatives on the Near East currently being undertaken, the description of the Qur'an offered here is meant as a contribution to the project of integrating early Islam into Late Antiquity. Through the strict observance of chronology, and the combination of historical and literary-critical

82. Izutsu, *God and Man in the Koran*.

approaches, this volume aims to contribute to the setting of the Qur'an on the same level with the biblical scriptures, and thus to contribute something new alongside the two companion volumes to the Qur'an[83].

This new element consists in the discovery of the "not yet Islamic," Late Antique dimension, which complements the Qur'an's significance as the founding document of the Islamic religion. The Qur'an has two faces, and they are difficult to hold in view at once. One needs to resort to a maneuver familiar from visual representation: one can treat the Qur'an as a puzzle-picture, revealing two quite different faces, depending on the perspective of the beholder. From one perspective, we see the founding text of Islam; from the other, we see a "Near Eastern–European" text that participates in the formation of later Europe. This latter face, which has been so little noticed, should become more visible and nuanced in what follows. By inscribing itself in the complex cultural palimpsest of Late Antiquity as the last world-historically significant scripture, the Qur'an became interwoven forever into the texts that preceded it. By virtue of its historical effects as scripture, the Qur'an can still be viewed as the exclusive inheritance of the Muslims; but at the same time it makes its entry into the Western textual canon and offers a significant legacy of Late Antiquity to Europe.[84]

83. McAuliffe, *Cambridge Companion*; Rippin, *Blackwell Companion*.

84. Maria Teodorova, "Europa als Palimpsest," differentiates between "legacy as continuity" or "inheritance" and "legacy through perception." While the former pertains to the safeguarded relationship Muslims have with the Koran, the latter is more of a latent connection that should be claimed for the relationship of Europeans to the Koran, even if they have not yet become aware of their relationship to the Koran.

1

How the Qur'an Has Been Read So Far

A SKETCH OF RESEARCH

1.1 Projects of Biblical Scholarship

The historical-critical reading of the Qur'an that forms the basis of this study is indebted to models from biblical scholarship.[1] In that field, for more than two hundred years, historical-critical reading has constituted the backbone of research and laid the foundations not only for a historically conscious micro-structural reading of the text but also for the variety of new, no longer diachronically oriented approaches that now fill out our image of the text. Although since the 1970s, a paradigm shift has taken place—one now reads the Bible in modes that are poststructuralist,[2] psychoanalytical,[3] ideological,[4] feminist,[5] and not least narratological and poetological—it remains the historical reading, that which seeks to understand the text as a document of its cultural environment and the ideological currents of its time, that provides the necessary pre-condition for any recognition of what is decisively new in the text.[6] It is the step of historical-critical research, the freeing of the scriptures from their theological context, that makes possible all later, secularly oriented approaches. But there are problems within this historical-critical reading project that must not be overlooked. Recent Jewish and Christian exegetes have drawn attention to the fact that the onset of the historical-critical method around the middle of the eighteenth century signaled a severe break in the history of biblical interpretation, a rupture that, according to Marius Reiser, "was more decisive than all earlier breaks. . . . With the emergence of the historical disciplines in the eighteenth century, Bible scholarship became its own world,"[7] adopting as its object a new context, far removed from religion. It is well known that no comparable change of orientation has

1. Individual parts of this chapter are based on an overview of scholarship published in 2007, "Ein Versuch der historischen und forschungsgeschichtlichen Verortung des Koran," and on the essay "Die Korangenese zwischen Mythos und Geschichte." For a brief introduction, see Andrew Rippin, "Western Scholarship and the Qur'an," and Fred Donner, "The Qur'an in Recent Scholarship." Critical assessments are offered in contributions by Harald Motzki, "Alternative Accounts," and Marco Schöller, "Post-enlightenment Academic Study."

2. Carroll, "Poststructuralist approaches."

3. Ricœur, *Hermeneutik und Psychoanalyse.*

4. Sternberg, *Poetics of Biblical Narrative.*

5. Loades, "Feminist Interpretation."

6. For an introduction and defense, see Barton, "Introduction," and Barton, "Historical-Critical Approaches."

7. Reiser, *Bibelkritik und Auslegung.*

occurred in the inner-Islamic reception of the Qur'an. It is true that a number of Islamic exegetes heralded the arrival of a historicizing approach to the Qur'an as early as the nineteenth century.[8] Their readings of the Qur'an in isolation from its centuries-old tradition however appeared too theologically explosive to be hermeneutically acceptable to the majority of traditional Muslim scholars. But it would be an exaggeration to speak of any systematic inner-Islamic historical-critical research program centered on the Qur'an. Furthermore, even if such a project were applied to the transmitted text as it stands, this would not lead to a break with tradition comparable to that in the Jewish-Christian tradition, since the most serious result of such a project, the breaking down of the scripture into individual texts of various origin and authorship, is not feasible for the Qur'an in view of the text's original emergence over a period of scarcely more than twenty years. Thus, Richard Bell (1876–1952)—in his attempted "documentary analysis" of the Qur'an[9] was compelled to attribute all the individual traditions that he declared as "doublets" to a single, original author, the Prophet himself. His deconstruction of the text into numerous short units shows itself to be a methodological dead end. John Wansbrough (1928–2001),[10] in his related attempt to elicit varying individual transmissions by means of form criticism, had to extend the traditionally accepted period of the Qur'an's emergence by more than a hundred years in order to allow for the participation in the Qur'an's genesis all the plural authors and traditions that he posited. Wansbrough's deconstruction of the Qur'an by means of form criticism led to results that have since been refuted on the basis of the external facts of textual history. What, then, if we turn to the second fundamental pillar of historical-critical research, that is, the probing of a new context of scripture, the replacement of "exegetical tradition" by "historical environment"? To what extent does a historical reading distinguish itself from a traditional one? If one considers that between the emergence of the text and its canonical reception no breaks occurred comparable with the Jewish-Christian situation, then one must assume a smoother transition from the collective of hearers to the later religious community. For unlike in the case of the Hebrew language, which had ceased to be spoken in its biblical form, no such extraordinary linguistic development took place in Arabic in this intervening phase; nor did a centralized religious authority appear, as in the case of the New Testament, to enforce the dogmatic obligation of new interpretations often quite far from the literal sense. What changed fundamentally between the collective of hearers and

8. On the modern Muslim exegetes of the Qur'an, see primarily Rotraud Wielandt, *Offenbarung und Geschichte*, and Wielandt, "Exegesis, Modern." On Arkoun, see Rippin, "God"; on the contemporary aspects of Muslim intellectuals' dealing with the Qur'an in general, see Stefan Wild, *Mensch, Prophet*; on the Turkish exegetes, see Felix Körner, *Koranhermeneutik in der Türkei heute*, and Körner, *Revisionist Koran Hermeneutics*. Apart from the exegetes introduced here, who are trained in methods of Western scholarship, there are also the traditional, encyclopedic Qur'an commentators; see Johanna Pink, "Sunnitische Korankommentare."

9. Bell, *Qur'an*.

10. Wansbrough, *Quranic Studies*.

the later religious community is less the semantic understanding of individual pronouncements than, as will be shown, the hermeneutic approach to the text as a whole. The post-canonical Qur'an, that is, the text read through commentary, loses its dialectical tension once it is uprooted from the debate landscape of Late Antiquity. By its loosing from the communication situation and its exclusive binding to a transcendent source, the text is "immobilized," so to speak, it changes from a polyphonic, aural text, a document of processes of exchange, into a monologic text, a transcendent discourse. A fundamental break in the perception of the Qur'an is thus achieved, whose long-term effects cannot be ignored. The full dimensions of this break can only be grasped through diachronic studies.

New methodological approaches are now available for the redressing of this break. In biblical scholarship, a number of researchers are working toward a reassessment of the text's hermeneutical development, considering the possibilities of a renewed linking of the biblical text back to the exegetical tradition.[11] At the same time the rigorous analytical orientation of the historical-critical is being relaxed. The initial search for a putative "original text" and "original meaning" has long since given way to an interest in the process of the text's development as a site of interaction between writers and recipients, between proclaimers and their hearers. One speaks now of a "canonic process"[12] leading through many intervening phases to the end form of the text. But while in the case of the Bible, this continual writing and rewriting of a growing nucleus of texts reached across centuries,[13] in the case of the orally communicated Qur'an the canonic process stretches over slightly more than twenty years, a period in which the Qur'an existed as an open-ended communal engagement with earlier texts, in which we can trace the successive canonization of text units through the acceptance of the hearers.[14] If one wants to treat the Qur'an not as post-canonical fait accompli, a published text for reading, but rather as the pre-canonical manifestation of a proclamation, one must engage with both historical-critical analysis and with the complementary "canonical approach" to reading.

But since this proclamation occurred in poetic language, it also requires a literary analysis. Here, certain new approaches in current Bible scholarship, oriented more toward rhetoric than the narratively focused approaches mentioned above, seem to provide the most promising avenues for progress.[15] Indeed, the Qur'an is not a narrative but rather a discursive text, one that is marked, to put it briefly, by engagement with other, mostly equally discursive texts. This "origin of the Qur'an from textual engagements" is reflected in the text's literary from,

11. Wilken, "In Defense of Allegory," and Kugel, *The Bible as It Was*.

12. Childs, *Biblical Theology*; Sanders, *Canon and Community*. This approach has been probed for the Qur'an in Neuwirth, "Referentiality and Textuality."

13. On this, see primarily Kugel, *The Bible as It Was*.

14. Cf. Sinai, "The Qur'ān as Process."

15. See Ricœur, *Biblical Interpretation*, and Brueggemann, *Theology of the Old Testament*.

which discourages and impedes cursory reading and immediate understanding. For this reason, research began from early on to attempt the reconstruction of the historical context of the Qur'an, but it has greatly oversimplified this task, relying on the Sira tradition, that is the biography of the Prophet that arose a century and a half after the emergence of the Qur'an. This often uncritical recourse to a myth of origin[16] not only has led to the drawing of an image of the emergence of the Qur'an that remains anachronistic but also, even more seriously, has introduced an element of teleology to the history of the Qur'an, so that both the Qur'an as it is available to us today and the early triumph of the Islamic community appear to be the necessary results of divine revelation and right guidance given to Muhammad, his inspired speech and charismatic action. What a historical reading requires, then, is both releasing the Qur'anic genesis and the formation of the community epistemically from the later framing within Islam and relocating the text and listenership within the epoch from which Islam emerged. The Qur'an must be recognized as a Late Antique text that arose alongside a community of hearers that gradually took shape, who were acculturated to Late Antiquity. In our view, such a contextual reading stands in agreement with the readings of individual Islamic scholars, such as Amin al-Khuli, Fazlur Rahman, Nasr Hamid Abu Zaid, Mehmet Paçacı, and Ömer Özsoy.[17] Thus, Abu Zaid distinguishes between the universal Qur'anic message and the contingent "code" in which it was dressed.[18] But we must go yet a step further and decline to treat the text as a fait accompli, focusing instead on the engagement of the community with the pluricultural traditions of the period, an approach which carries with it theological consequences.

It would be an oversimplification, however, to treat the Qur'an according to the modern Protestant conception of the Bible and to describe it, for example, as "a universal message in a contingent code." As is evident from the strong reservations of wide circles of observant Muslims to any approach to the Qur'an that suppresses its transcendent claim that this text does not merely correspond to a scripture, understood as "subjected to the conditions of understanding of any other literature"[19] but constitutes the hypostasized word of God, capable of being experienced sensibly in recitation, a conception that comes close to that of the incarnate word of God.[20] An accurate reading of the Qur'an as a Late Antique text must include in its horizon the complexly differentiated concepts of God's word that developed in this epoch and which had already prevailed in the two

16. The model of the Qur'an's genesis in Wansbrough, *Quranic Studies*, only appears as an exception, since he also contextualizes the Qur'an with the Sira, judging both of them to be contemporaneous later historical constructions.

17. On Rahman, see Saeed, "Fazlur Rahman"; on Paçacı and Özsoy, see Körner, *Revisionist Koran Hermeneutics*.

18. Abu Zaid, *Mafhūm al-Naṣṣ*; see Kermani, *Offenbarung als Kommunikation*.

19. See Bultmann, *Glauben und Verstehen*, 2:231.

20. See Wild, *Mensch, Prophet*, 6ff., cf. chap. 2, 89–95.

older religions by the time of the Qur'an's genesis. What is revolutionarily new in the Qur'anic proclamation can only be extracted from a study of the synergism between speaker, community, and the representatives of traditions present in this environment.

The reading suggested here is primarily an engagement with historically oriented Western research, but it also attempts to give an account of the complexity of the Qur'anic forms of appearance by paying attention to particular forms of inner-Qur'anic intertextuality. The Western tradition of research demands an initial approach oriented to biblical scholarship, if only to warrant an equal treatment for the Qur'an and to "synchronize" the three scriptures, to set their respective perceptions on the same level. The following presentation will sketch the path of Western research up to now, so that, viewed through a critical lens occasional excesses of historical analysis can be discerned. Apparently what is lacking here is the hermeneutic corrective of knowledge accumulated in the inner-Arabic linguistic-stylistic tradition. At present, historical Western research is only breathing with one lung, so to speak. The second lung, the Arabicity and poeticity[21] of the Qur'an, has not yet been utilized. Engagement with the aesthetic dimension of the Qur'an still remains the exclusive domain of inner-Islamic exegesis. It has hardly been treated in Western research and, consequently, is only discussed marginally in this volume (see chapters 12 and 13). But the aesthetic knowledge that awaits discovery, and which could ultimately permit the Qur'an to be set into relief as an "Arabic scripture" in an Arabic literary context, is necessary for any future comprehensive interpretation of the Qur'an.

1.2 A Great Research Tradition and its Violent Interruption

1.2.1 *The Science of Judaism (Wissenschaft des Judentums) as Founding Discipline of Critical Qur'an Research*

The challenge to read the Qur'an more as a Late Antique text than an Islamic one, that is, to assign it back into its pre-Islamic pluricultural milieu, become an urgency only in recent times.[22] It is however not at all new: it is a direction of research that bore fruit for over a century, originating within the Science of Judaism.[23] Already from the 1830s onward, scholars within this field began to read the Qur'an historically against the background of the plural cultures of Late Antiquity. Abraham Geiger (1810–1874), in his groundbreaking work *Was hat*

21. Here, the works by Kermani, *Gott ist schön*, and Graham, "Recitation and Aesthetic Reception," deserve attention as rare exceptions. Cf. also Sells, "A Literary Approach to the Hymnic Surahs"; Sells, "Sounds, Spirit and Gender in Sūrat al-Qadr"; Sells, "Sound and Meaning in Sūrat al-Qāri'a."

22. The discussion was initiated by Wansbrough, *Quranic Studies*; see also his *Sectarian Milieu*, and cf. Rippin, "The Qur'an as literature"; Rippin, "Quranic Studies, Part IV," 39–46; and Rippin, *The Qur'an: Style and Content.*

23. On this, see now Neuwirth, "Im vollen Licht der Geschichte"; Hartwig, "Die 'Wissenschaft des Judentums.'"

Mohammed aus dem Judenthume aufgenommen (*What did Muhammad adopt from Judaism*) (1833), was the first to attempt to identify the biblical and post-biblical traditions reflected in the Qur'an. The critical Qur'an research introduced by Geiger,[24] which built on the historical-critical research of the Bible, was carried forward by other researchers with Jewish training (after Geiger, above all Hartwig Hirschfeld [1854–1934] and Ignaz Goldziher [1850–1921]), in conjunction with scholars trained in classical Arabic literature or biblical texts (such as Theodor Nöldeke [1836–1930] or Julius Wellhausen [1844–1918]). Later researchers from the tradition of the Science of Judaism, above all Josef Horovitz (1874–1931) and his school, especially Heinrich Speyer [1897–1935]), further refined this approach in the first half of the twentieth century and employed it fruitfully in important studies on personal names,[25] narrative forms,[26] eschatology,[27] polemics,[28] and prayer.[29] In recognizing the receptions of biblical and, above all, post-biblical Jewish literature in the Qur'an, they made a decisive contribution toward the transfer of the Qur'an from its traditional frame of reference in relation to a stereotyped and "wholly other" paganism, *jāhilīya*, connecting the Islamic revelation to the wider context of formative Near Eastern traditions. The contextualization of the Qur'an text alongside rabbinic literature,[30] introduced by Abraham Geiger, was to characterize Qur'an research decisively and until the violent abruption of this research tradition with the seizure of power by National Socialism produced a number of standard works that remain indispensable down to today. The last significant work of this school, Henrich Speyer's *Die biblischen Erzählungen im Qoran*,[31] makes conveniently available the Jewish traditions reflected in the Qur'an, as far as they were known up to that time, without laying claim to these traditions as direct templates for the Qur'an.

But we must not neglect the fact that the perspective adopted in Qur'an research within the Science of Judaism, according to which Muhammad was viewed as slavishly dependent on the earlier traditions the Qur'anic texts being presented as reproductions or often distortions of older texts, constitutes a serious weak point in this research, marring its results especially in the beginning. Here traces are recognizable of the old established Christian polemical tradition against Islam, which asserted Muhammad's responsibility as author of the Qur'an only in order to indict him as a willful falsifier of divine truth.[32] Even if, after the

24. For the preliminary, prescientific interpretation of the Qur'an, see Bobzin, *Koran im Zeitalter der Reformation*.

25. Horovitz, *Jewish Proper Names*.

26. Horovitz, *Koranische Untersuchungen*.

27. Horovitz, "Das koranische Paradies."

28. Ettinghausen, *Antiheidnische Polemik*.

29. Goitein, *Gebet im Koran*.

30. Lassner, "Abraham Geiger."

31. Speyer, *Die biblischen Erzählungen im Qoran*. The work had to be backdated to the year 1931, in order for it to be published in Nazi Germany in 1935; see Rosenthal, "Speyer."

32. Bobzin, "Pre-1800 Preoccupations of Qur'anic Studies."

Enlightenment, the person of the Prophet was rehabilitated as a sincere seeker of God without false intentions,[33] nevertheless the Qur'an itself was reduced, despite this new evaluation, to the lesser dimensions of an epigonal text produced by an author of only moderate theological understanding.

This perception was supported not least by the historical-critical approach itself, one of whose primary objectives is the search for the "original" text, the urtext. In relation to the Bible, this search had brought to the fore a great number of ancient Near Eastern traditions apt to illuminate the historical context of the biblical texts and thus facilitated their earliest meaning. But while these early traditions were scarcely ever seen to seriously compete with the Bible in their literary form and theological significance, in the case of the Qur'an the opposite was true: what came to light in the form of predecessor texts was not mere documents of "cultural precursors" but rather the most prestigious text of all, the Hebrew Bible itself. Its authority was to overshadow the Qur'an from the very beginning. What was bear on the image of the Qur'an most heavily was the exclusivity of the historical analysis, which did not allow for alternatives: unlike the Bible, which was familiar to every educated person even beyond the context of historical-critical research, the Qur'an, at least at the time when it was submitted to Geiger's rigorous source criticism by Geiger, was a widely unknown text even in scholarly circles. Thus, what in Western biblical scholarship represented a critical turning point and renewal was taken in Western Qur'an research not as a re-thinking but as an absolute and unprepared beginning. The variety of methods prevalent in Bible scholarship were not accessible to Qur'anic scholarship, which was historical-critical without alternatives. Since its critical deconstruction was not preceded by overarching studies of the Qur'an as a whole, there was no image of the Qur'an as a scripture in its own right,. fit to balance or to cancel the hasty verdict of epigonality.

In the wake of the Science of Judaism, the measuring stick for the evaluation of the Qur'an was provided almost exclusively by biblical texts—which being more ancient counted as more "authentic." The early representatives of the Science of Judaism, who oriented their evaluation of the Qur'an exclusively toward more ancient texts, were not unique in underestimating the Qur'an: others arrived to a pejorative evaluation of the Qur'an by measuring it against the standards of earlier secular literature. The founder father of Qur'anic philology, Theodor Nöldeke, whose *Geschichte des Qorans* (*History of the Qur'an*) (1860) offers a still unsurpassed chronology of the suras and who assumed Muhammad's role as author to be self-evident granted him an essentially lower artistic status than the ancient Arabic poets, on grounds of linguistic and stylistic deviations from the poetic language.[34]

33. Sinai, "Orientalism."

34. Nöldeke, "Zur Sprache des Korans."

All these initiatives were pursued in a space wholly aloof from contemporary Muslim scholarship. It is astonishing to discover that the critical Qur'an scholars of the nineteenth and early twentieth century almost never took notice of contemporary Muslim research activities, although some outstanding researchers, such as Alois Sprenger (1813–1893) and later Ignaz Goldziher (1850–1921) and Josef Horovitz (1874–1931), did cooperate closely for some time with Muslim scholars. In fact, in the nineteenth century and especially the early twentieth, new approaches developed in India and above all in Egypt were opening the Qur'an for new modern questions independently of the premodern commentary literature that had served as the exegetical basis up to that point. This inner-Islamic work on the Qur'an not only remained wholly absent from contemporaneous Western Qur'an research (apart from Gotthelf Bergsträsser's [1886–1933] text-historical researches which he carried out in cooperation with Arab scholarly circles)[35] but also has never been adequately integrated into the Western horizon of research in the time since. Rather, this period of inner-Islamic research has been "objectified" in retrospect, made an *object of* rather than a *contribution to* research. Western Qur'an research thus begins with a double asynchrony: on the one hand in relation to biblical scholarship, to which it ultimately connects only superficially, and on the other hand in relation to Muslim research, which it excludes from its scope from the start.

1.3 Retreat to Islam-Historical Positions

1.3.1 The "Life of Muhammad Research"

The innumerable "intertexts" of the Qur'an, that is, those biblical and post-biblical traditions reflected in the text that were identified by representatives of the Science of Judaism, are currently being amassed and studied in the framework of the Berlin project Corpus Coranicum. But these intertexts will only be fruitful for Qur'an research if they are evaluated in relation to Qur'anic the discourse, that is, if the decisive questions around their reworking and refunctioning in the frame of the Qur'anic communication process between proclaimer and community are addressed. Nonetheless, the early research, in its uncovering of the polyphony of the Qur'an, has the unquestioned merit of having reopened the possibility of recognizing texts as what they were in the phase of their emergence, prior to the canonization of the Qur'an as the founding document of a new religion, namely: answers to burning questions of the time, confrontations with theological positions of the neighboring religions—partly to be accepted, partly negotiated, altered, refuted, or replaced by new ones. It is this process that above

35. See Marx, "The Koran According to Agfa."

all illuminates the success of the proclamation manifest in the emergence of a community that lasted beyond the death of the proclaimer.

The loss that set in with the politically compelled deletion of this tradition of research and the expulsion of Jewish scholars from German universities cannot be overstated. The researchers of the Science of Judaism had viewed the Qur'an as a *text* still untouched by exegesis, and thus focused on its transitional state during the phase in which the new pious were still on their way toward their later self-understanding as a religious community. The disappearance of this direction of research within German scholarship brought about a serious downturn in Qur'an research, the salient contributions of the Science of Judaism not only remaining without further progress but also soon downplayed in their significance. Although in the 1920s, researchers such as Tor Andrae[36] (1885–1948), Richard Bell,[37] Wilhelm Rudolph (1891–1987),[38] and Karl Ahrens[39] uncovered traces of Christian traditions in the Qur'an in analogy to the reception research of the Science of Judaism, by the 1930s a new tendency was setting in. Most prominently, the Arabicist Johann Fück[40] (1894–1974) laid the stress on the "originality of the Arabian prophet" and viewed the "examination of questions of dependency" as a dead end that entailed the "dismantling [of] the being of the Prophet into a sum of a thousand particulars." The "Muhammad research" that became prominent at this point took up the task of showing "how the Prophet, drawing from the spiritual stimulations of his environment, succeeded in uniting a number of elements of the most various kinds into a synthesis that was original and viable in its consummation."[41] Additionally, they looked to the Qur'an as a document of the psychological development of the Prophet, an impulse that led positively to the composition of several biographies of the Prophet.[42] But an unmistakable narrowing of the previous horizon of considerations was evident: in its view toward the genesis of the Qur'an itself, scholarship became oriented, anachronistically, to the Islamic biographies of the Prophet that were fixed in writing from about a century after his lifetime.

There is a notable exception in the approach followed by Richard Bell in his translation of the Qur'an, where he turns back to the text itself to test a "documentary hypothesis."[43] His two-volume 1953 translation[44] is still valuable

36. Andrae, *Ursprung*; Andrae, *Mohammad, sein Leben und sein Glaube.*

37. Bell, *Origin of Islam.*

38. Rudolph, *Abhängigkeit des Qorans.*

39. Ahrens, "Christliches im Qoran."

40. Fück, "Die Originalität des arabischen Propheten."

41. Ibid., 510. For a more recent evaluation of this "life of Muhammed scholarship," see the overview by Peters, "The Quest of the Historical Muhammad."

42. Andrae, *Mohammed*; Buhl, *Leben Muhammeds.*

43. Bell, *Qur'an*; cf. Nagel, "Vom 'Qur'an' zur Schrift."

44. Bell, *Qur'ān*; Bell, *Introduction*, revised by Watt, *Bell's Introduction*. Cf. Rippin, "Reading the Qur'an with Richard Bell."

today and is one of the most dependable Qur'an renderings. But in his reordering of the text, Bell pursues the no longer tenable thesis that the striking phenomenon of the multiple formulations of individual stories and themes in the Qur'an is to be explained mechanically by the external circumstance of the limited availability of writing materials. Recurring text elements, considered as doublets, would then be explained as new versions written on the reverse sides of older ones, thus leading to multiple versions being included in the final text collection. Bell, who drew here on biblical source criticism, disassembled the text into a variety of individual revelations, which he assigned to various contexts of emergence, thus fragmenting the text into unrecognizability.

In the Qur'an research of the postwar period, which was largely marked by W. Montgomery Watt (1909–2006),[45] Regis Blachère (1900–1973),[46] and Rudi Paret (1901–1983),[47] but for which the standards had already been set by August Fischer (1865–1949) and Johann Fück, the person of the Prophet generally stood as the central point of interest—an emphasis that can best be explained in relation to the model of the critical "life of Jesus" research that was pursued vigorously in Germany in the nineteenth and early twentieth centuries. Disenchanted by the philological treatments of the Qur'an because of the lack of literary-critical criteria,[48] and unable to appreciate its dialectical relation to the religious predecessor texts due to a lack of the necessary knowledge of Jewish traditions, they turned to the psychological development of the putative "author" of the Qur'an, that is, the Prophet. Earlier approaches had attempted to illuminate the textual form, if not in terms of literary-artistic criteria, then at least in terms of formal ones. Thus, Karl Vollers (1857–1909)[49] investigated the language of the Qur'an for its dialect interferences, and Alphonse Mingana (1878–1937)[50] attempted to determine its Syriac interferences. Around the same time, Anton Baumstark (1872–1948)[51] contributed fundamentally to a new appreciation of the Qur'an as a liturgical text by pointing out the Jewish and Christian liturgical formulas echoed in the Qur'an. The only contribution that was literary-critical in a strict sense, after David Heinrich Müller's (1846–1912) early and still rough attempt to detect biblical-prophetic speech forms in the Qur'an,[52] was Gustav Richter's (1906–1934) *Der Sprachstil des Koran* (The rhetorical style of the Qur'an), which remained incomplete.[53]

45. Watt, *Muhammad at Mecca*; Watt, *Muhammad at Medina*.
46. Blachère, *Coran*, Blachère, *Introduction*, Blachère, *Littérature arabe*.
47. Paret, *Mohammed und der Koran*; Paret, "Der Koran als Geschichtsquelle."
48. On the current literary evaluation of the Qur'an, see Wild, " 'Schauerliche Öde.' "
49. Vollers, *Volkssprache und Schriftsprache*.
50. Mingana, "Syriac Influences on the Style of the Kur'an."
51. Baumstark, "Jüdischer und christlicher Gebetstypus im Koran."
52. D. H. Müller, *Grundgesetze der ursemitischen Poesie*.
53. Richter, *Sprachstil des Koran*.

Approaches within literary studies remained largely invisible in the postwar period; only text-critical work continued to be pursued.[54] In retrospect, we can see in this option a significant step backwards, in that the attempt to deal with the reception of earlier materials in the text is given up, and even the most fundamental groundwork of historical Qur'an research itself was relinquished, namely, the chronology of the suras worked out by Theodor Nöldeke. In Rudi Paret's commentary, which has been treated as standard since its appearance,[55] the chronology of the suras is given hardly any significance. The commentary treats the texts in the order of their occurrence in the text corpus and gives hardly any notice to the chronological sequence and accompanying functional relationships between the suras. However useful as Paret's work remains, including as it does what is widely considered the most reliable translation[56] into German alongside his reissuing of a collection of earlier research into the Qur'an,[57] his strongly simplifying perception of the Qur'anic text expounded in his summary presentation *Muhammad und der Koran,* where he attempts to explain the Qur'an entirely in terms of the personal disposition of the Prophet, is utterly disappointing. This perspective, which remains aloof from the text, had already impaired his commentary. Since it does not allow to recognize the Qur'an's complex intertextuality and substantially new approach to predecessor texts, this discursive level falls short of that of earlier authors such as Josef Horovitz and Tor Andrae, whose work he himself reissued.

In the time since, we can document a true boom of presentations of Muhammad—occasionally in fulfillment of demands for concise new summaries—but most notably two extensive monographs by Tilman Nagel,[58] which, however, do not mark any revolutionary step forward. Although Nagel's extensive studies explicate the life of the Prophet in detail, the mode of presentation remains selective and ultimately arbitrary, drawing on hadith traditions without employing the requisite methodological step of *isnād*-cum-*matn* analysis, and thus mixing late material with early.[59] A wholly new approach is ventured by Tarif Khalidi, who, in his detailed history of the inner-Islamic reception of Muhammad, takes account also of the biographies of Muhammad that have emerged in the

54. See the works of Bergsträsser and Pretzl, and also Beck, "Der uthmanische Kodex in der Koranlesung des zweiten Jahrhunderts," and Beck, "Studien zur Geschichte der kufischen Koranlesung." The most recent monograph on textual history and textual criticism including oral tradition is Kellermann, *Koranlesung im Maghreb* (still unpublished dissertation from 1994).

55. Paret, *Koran: Kommentar und Konkordanz.*

56. Paret, *Koran: Übersetzung.*

57. Paret, *Der Koran.*

58. See Bobzin, *Muhammad*; Bobzin, *Der Koran*; Cook, *Muhammad*; Schöller, *Mohammed*; Nagel, *Muhammad*; and Nagel, *Allahs Liebling.*

59. On this, see Schoeler (lecture, Frankfurt, November 2009). Engagement with the international research on early Islam that has emerged in recent years is missing in Nagel's work.

Arab world since the 1920s, which are elsewhere often disregarded in Western research.[60]

The Qur'an research that has occurred in the postwar period and later seems, if treated summarily, to be characterized by a narrowing of perspective. This "Muhammad research" has not been able to avoid the tendency to assume Muhammad to be the lone decisive actor in communal formation and the authorial composer of the Qur'an. It also harbors a simplified conception of the emergence of the Qur'an and of Islam, failing to interrogate critically the traditional Islamic image of the miraculous nature and transhistoricity of the Qur'anic event, but only, in the best case, reversing it: in place of the miracle of "a holy book virtually falling out of the sky," the new image—no less miraculous—of the refashioning of older traditions by Muhammad himself, raising the figure of the proclaimer to the rank of the sole actor responsible for the theological development reflected in the Qur'an and the formation of the nascent Islamic community. With this understanding, Muhammad's individual "correct" or "false" understanding of previous textual traditions would alone be decisive for the emergence and shaping of the new belief as it takes shape, ignoring the continuous interaction between proclaimer and community and allowing no shared creative treatment of previous traditions. The Qur'anic question of authorship is not to be solved simply by substituting the person of Muhammad for God, nor can the history of the Qur'an's genesis be written merely on the basis of the Sira.

1.3.2 Problematic Bird's-Eye Views

Flashing out the open question of the development of the Qur'anic message, Gustav von Grunebaum attempted in 1960,[61] and then again in 1965,[62] to explain the success of the Qur'anic message by means of a particularly suggestive theological sketch of the Prophet. Von Grunebaum's (1909–1972) impressive presentation is still worthy of attention as an understanding of the reform work brought about through the Qur'an.[63] But it is heavily impaired by a lack of criticism of tradition and, more so, by the author's teleological projection of later cultural polarizations back into the period of the Qur'an's genesis. Von Grunebaum finds that "from an Arabic standpoint, the teaching of Muhammad [signifies]unmistakable progress toward greater religious and intellectual maturity."[64] But he stipulates teleologically that "the Arabs" were the intended "receivers of the teaching of Muhammad," thus removing them by essentialist logic from the wider circles of listeners educated in Late Antique lore and establishing a firm polarity between the Jews and Christians (who appear only later as theological opponents) on the

60. Khalidi, *Images of Muhammad.*
61. Von Grunebaum, "Ausbreitungs- und Anpassungsfähigkeit."
62. Von Grunebaum, "Experience of the Holy and Concept of Man."
63. Additionally see Noth, "Früher Islam."
64. Von Grunebaum, "Ausbreitungs- und Anpassungsfähigkeit," 14.

one hand and the putative pure "Arabs" on the other. Although he highlights central characteristics of the Qur'anic message, these characteristics do not seem to have constituted any doctrinal program during the period of Muhammad's ministry. Von Grunebaum does, however, convey the impression that there is an effective economy in the treatment of theological themes in the Qur'an:

> It must be maintained that the Qur'anic revelation limits itself to relatively few themes, all of extraordinary significance for the peoples of the Middle East in the seventh century, both within and outside the Arabian Peninsula. This begins with the revelation through the elected speaker, and the securing of inviolable authority in the life of the community, and the assurance of direct divine guidance; this is followed by monotheism and the book. The recognition of these concepts opened a level of religious thought to the Arabs that had arrived to their future subjects some centuries earlier, and without which the conqueror would not have been capable of dialogue or intellectual respectability. (One should be clear that the reliance on revelation and a book contributes to the development of identical criteria of what is cognitively acceptable and the recognition of similar theological and epistemological problems—a further factor in the creation of an atmosphere in which shared basic beliefs ensure the success of a new teaching.) In any case, for quite a long period the belief in a Final Judgment that would hurl sinners into eternal fire and the pious into paradise, alongside the conviction in a pre-existing end of the world, created a cluster of themes of extraordinary emotional power.[65]

As apt as this characterization of the Qur'anic message may be from the birds-eye view of theology, it grants no rightful place to the characteristics of the Qur'an that consist not simply in the assumption or discarding of earlier *theologumena* but in such novelties as the crucial interpretation of the world as a "sign system" of God[66] and the granting of the faculty of understanding, logos, which is bound up in creation. Von Grunebaum conceives of the genesis of the Qur'anic teaching as a kind of pre-meditated project with the goal of simplifying the available theologies thus offering a promise of salvation that is more easily won:

> The discarding of an overly complicated Trinitarianism, that recourse to *Docetism* that among Christian sects fulfilled the function of a certain primitive rationalism; the rejection of original sin and of the burden of unavoidable original guilt that also represents the personal responsibility of the believer; an optimistic view of human nature as more in need of guidance than salvation, and thus the elimination of the more extreme

65. Ibid., 14–15.
66. See chap. 7, 264–277.

> forms of askesis . . . ; in short, Islam's more realistic but also more crude alignment with this world provided the average believer with a system of beliefs that satisfied his essential religious needs and freed him from the Christian paradox of being *in* but not *of* the world, and which further freed him from participation in the debates over doctrinal subtleties the acceptance or rejection of which all too often bore actual consequences. With this different view of man and his contractual relation (*ḥukm*) to the majesty of God, all lived significance fell away from the mysteries of salvation through the suffering of God-man, who was God's son but not a second divinity, mysteries the formulation of which had so often led into error—indeed, the Islamic God is above all *will*, which can be felt by man in the experience of his majesty; obedience becomes the door to salvation, a door that is not difficult to open.[67]

In von Grunebaum's work, the Qur'an is presented as a teaching that reflects, and was developed by, the proclaimer, for which he presupposes uncritically the scenario sketched in the Sira, where Muhammad is confronted predominantly by "the Arabs," and not a heterodox or syncretistic group of people with pluricultural formation within a peripheral space of Late Antiquity. The birds-eye view adopted here not only arrives at a de-historicization of the Qur'an but also leads at the same time to an affirmation of its otherness, its origin from a putative purely Arab context, and its exclusive designation for "the Arabs." With the demotion of the theological points recognized in the Qur'an to the status of mere conveniences or maneuvers required tactically to achieve politically advantageous facilities in debate, this perspective relinquishes the possibility of perceiving the Qur'anic teachings as the result of behaviors and adaptations of the theological traditions of the Late Antique environment and, above all, fails to understand them as communicative contributions to debates that reach across religious borders. Von Grunebaum's perspective is closed to the perception of the Qur'an as a new voice in the polyphonic concert of Late Antique post-biblical traditions that has today come to be seen as the spiritual underpinning of Europe's later development, a heritage from which the Qur'an has been excluded due to such perspectives. Von Grunebaum's influential presentations have strongly impacted later research, without the methodological flaw of the teleological projection of later developments back into the Qur'anic beginnings having been objected. Wherever a theological-historical contextualization of the Qur'an has been undertaken in recent research, it has been in a summary form, as if the codification of the Qur'an text was not preceded by successive negotiations of the positions of belief that were current in that space and time. Most notably, the

67. Von Grunebaum, "Ausbreitungs- und Anpassungsfähigkeit," 15.

essentialist scenario of interaction involving an "Arab proclaimer" and "Arabs as hearers" has widely been maintained.

1.4 The Qur'an Without the Memory of the Community? New Voices in the "Authenticity Debate"

1.4.1 Wansbrough, Crone, and Cook

In part as a response to such tendencies to "flatten" the text, we should consider the revolutionary work of John Wansbrough, who categorically questioned the notion of the Prophet's authorship that had been accepted up to that point, sketching a new scenario. It is hardly an exaggeration to claim that Wansbrough's *Quranic Studies*[68] introduced a decisive turn in research on early Islam.[69] Through his work, the entire historical paradigm developed by the Islamic tradition, held as foundational up to that point, was called into question: in view of its striking echoes of biblical and post-biblical traditions, the Qur'an appears, according to Wansbrough's thesis, to be the product of inter-religious debates that can best be conceived as having occurred in Mesopotamia during the eighth/ninth centuries, among scholars of a syncretistic community containing Jewish and Christian adversaries. The Qur'an would thus appear to be a later compilation, and the scenario of the Arabian Peninsula and the depiction of the Prophet would appear to be retrojections supplied as necessary proofs of the Arabian "rootedness" of the origins of the new religion. Wansbrough's *Quranic Studies* was followed in the same year, 1977, by a similarly rigorous attempt at deconstruction by Patricia Crone and Michael Cook, who in *Hagarism* introduced an alternative origin scenario in the form of a messianic movement connected to Palestine. In this presentation, distilled wholly from non-Islamic sources, Muhammad acted politically as a messianic proclaimer, not, however, as the proclaimer of the transmitted Qur'an. While his original teaching within the messianic movement that he led focused on the genealogical derivation of the Arabs from Abraham and Hagar (thus "Hagarenes" and "hagarism"), this teaching later, following the Umayyad caliph ʿAbd al-Malik's break with the Jews, had to be universalized, thus leading to the stylization of the person of Muhammad as a prophet on the model of Moses in the Qur'an as it was now being compiled.[70]

These works, with their classification of the Qur'an as a compilation achieved later with political considerations in mind, introduced a turn, primarily in Anglosaxon research on early Islam (Andrew Rippin, Patricia Crone, Michael

68. See the reviews by Graham, Ullendorff, Nemoy, and Neuwirth.

69. For a detailed, tradition-critical discussion of Wansbrough's thesis, see Radtke, *Offenbarung*, and see now Sinai, *Studien zur frühen Koraninterpretation*, 23–31.

70. An extensive presentation, with criticisms of sources and methods, is offered by Robinson, *Discovering the Qur'an*, 47–59. See now also Sinai, *Studien zur frühen Koraninterpretation*, 35–38.

Cook, Gerald Hawting).[71] Only few researchers, such as Neal Robinson[72] and David Marshall,[73] resisted this change in orientation and saw through the problematics of its complete suppression of the memory of the community. According to the revisionist researchers of the Wansbrough school, it is not Muhammad who "took over" the traditions of other religions; rather, a circle of redactors, who cannot be further defined, members of a sectarian milieu in Syria or southern Iraq, introduced questionable doctrines into the text. Alongside this, they embedded the "logia" of a mythical Prophet in diverse text sorts, chiefly simulations of disputes, thus compiling a "Meccan-Muhammadan" gospel, with the goal of rooting the later-developed founding myth of Islam's origin in the original homeland of the Arabs. Any notification of Islamic tradition would thus be groundless, since historical reality had been so fundamentally deformed by ideological compulsions that nothing precise could be yielded regarding the prehistory of the Islamic scripture. The form-historical approach introduced into Qur'an research by Wansbrough, that once had been developed in biblical scholarship to deal with secondarily compiled texts of various authors, was applied in isolation from the rest of philological methods, such as the preconditional step of lower criticism; it equally led far away from the drama-theoretical approach required for the analysis of the communication process. Even within his ambitious project, Wansbrough is not consistent: he omits lower criticism, as a means of testing the unity or secondary compilation of the individual Qur'anic texts, the first step required in the sequence of methods of biblical scholarship. The suras, which are clearly delineated already in early manuscripts, and which are clearly intended units whose formal design suggests a genetic coherence, go unnoticed by him. Wansbrough's form-critical attempt at atomization of a text that, if treated with a consistent method, is clearly recognizable as coherent, is a theoretical dead end. His thesis of a late dating, developed in analogy to the redaction of the Mishna and the New Testament Gospels, stands as a whole-cloth judgment rather than the result of concrete comparative analysis. But *Quranic Studies*, by breaking down hardened positions and raising a wide spectrum of new questions, represented an epistemological breakthrough. Although his important assertion of the processuality of the emergence of the Qur'an "threw out the baby with the bathwater" by leaping to a late dating and foreign ascriptions, nevertheless the idea that the Qur'an is the result of a dynamic, complex communication process is a step forward from which Qur'an research can no more

71. On Rippin's position, see his introduction in Rippin, *Approaches*. Furthermore, see Cook, *The Koran*; Hawting, *The Idea of Idolatry and the Emergence of Islam*. This thesis is repeated in Hawting, "Introduction." Hawting's continued adherence to a later emergence of the Qur'an outside of the Hijaz is difficult to comprehend in view of clear evidence for an early complete text of the Qur'an.

72. See Robinson, *Discovering the Qur'an*, who adopts the Qur'an analysis of Neuwirth, *Komposition der mekkanischen Suren*, which appeared contemporaneously with the works of Wansbrough and Crone/Cook.

73. See Marshall, *God, Muhammad and the Unbelievers*.

retreat. It is however not enough to accept this claim alone, but the further step of reconstructing this process, a step that has not been attempted by the revisionist researchers is still due. Indeed, because codicological research now indicates a much earlier final Qur'an redaction,[74] much of the revisionist approach to reconstruction has become obsolete.[75]

It should not go unmentioned that almost twenty years later, in an article published in 1994,[76] Patricia Crone suggested a softening of the late dating put forward earlier, but still assuming the drafting of the final text to have occurred later, in the Umayyad period. This is based above all on "a whole sequence of anomalies in early Islamic Qur'anic usage, which indicate a striking discontinuity between the Qur'an on one side and *tafsīr* and *fiqh* on the other, . . . which are not to be explained against the background of the conventional scenario of the Qur'an's emergence."[77] Nicolai Sinai has examined all of the individual arguments critically and found convincing explanations for the phenomena that Crone claims make a late dating necessary. But the basic error, the *proton pseudos*, lies rather in the approach itself. What probably would require no special pleading in the case of any other premodern text must always be stressed again in the case of the Qur'an: as long as one renounces a microstructural reading of the text on the basis of philological research previously conducted and does not consider the text's Late Antique references, no adequate judgment can be rendered about the text's drafting. External testimonies gleaned from the reception of the text that argue *against* a composition of the text in the time of Muhammad must be taken seriously and checked, but they cannot be taken to outweigh the internal indices that argue *for* such a drafting. The revisionist research in de-embedding the Qur'an from its coordinates of place and time and brusquely assigning the genesis of a Meccan-Medinan original community to the realm of legend turns away high-handedly from these traces of the contemporaneous development of text and community.

Revisionist scholarship induced a paradigm shift. The removal of temporal-spatial definition from the Qur'an genesis and the shift of the historical event that occurred with this genesis to another time and place was, after initial recognition, brought into doubt and rejected by later research, yet it did introduce a sustained reinterpretation of the Qur'an: the Qur'an became an "open" text, that is, a text that was ultimately not to be defined safely in terms of time, space, and authorship. What was to remain effective was a rigorous de-historicizing of

74. Cf. chap. 4, 158–161.

75. It should be noted that certain hermeneutically insensitive formulations of the revolutionary hypotheses of the Wansbrough school, whose publications were rapidly disseminated in the Middle East due to the English language and the authors' prominence, contributed to a palpable decline in the relationships between Muslim scholars of early Islam and their Western colleagues; see Neuwirth, "De-mythifying Islam."

76. Crone, "Two legal problems."

77. Sinai, *Studien zur frühen Koraninterpretation*, 35.

the Qur'an; the new perspectives on the Qur'an as a historically undefinable text seemed for some time to have removed the foundations from the philological approach that had been pursued up to that point. Thus, for example the *Studien zur Kompositin der mekkanischen Suren* (*Inverstigations into the Composition of the Meccan Suras)* that appeared by the present author in 1981, offering the first form- and genre-critical analysis of the individual Meccan suras, was long disregarded, overshadowed by the revisionist theses. Likewise, an opposing model that was contemporary with Wansbrough's negation of the Qur'an's genesis, and which conformed to tradition, developed in another British university by John Burton,[78] was scarcely taken into consideration. Supported by observations drawn from legal history and hadith criticism, Burton argued for a text collection already completed by the Prophet himself.

Is Wansbrough's work a long overdue introduction of methods of biblical scholarship into Qur'an research? It appears rather to be an ambitious attempt in this direction that runs up against a fundamental objection. It targets his procedure to derive entire models of thought, concepts of genre, and historical conceptions from biblical scholarship and to impose them on the Qur'an or early Islam. Wansbrough attempts to generate a kind of "form history" on the model of biblical studies, that is, to explain forms through their history, which however first needs to be reconstructed. But this had already been recognized within biblical studies as producing a vicious cycle.[79] In Qur'an research, it is a rash step. What is first required is a form analysis that closely reads the particularities of the various suras and sura sections, a close description of this formal texture.[80]

1.4.2 *The Qur'an—An Originally Christian Writing?*

Two other attempts at a revision of the traditional image of the Qur'an genesis, developed in German research, show themselves to be essentially simpler and more positivist, claiming that the Islamic Qur'an should be considered merely a corruption of a Christian predecessor. Already in 1972, Günther Lülling[81] had started a controversy, claiming that the Qur'an text transmitted to us was not authentic, but that behind it, as an ur-Qur'an, lay a collection of Christian strophic songs in Arabic dialect that was then reworked into a new text by Muhammad, who, as the "author" of the text, exploited the ambiguity of the old Arabic script that was not yet vocalized. In the form in which we have it, the Qur'an text would then be due to yet a later redaction, which, as Nicolai Sinai summarizes, "inverted Muhammad's original message, which had been a radical critique of monotheist

78. Burton, *The Collection of the Qur'an*. See also Neuwirth's review of Burton.
79. Bultmann, *Geschichte der synoptischen Tradition*, 5.
80. Cf. Richter, *Exegese als Literaturwissenschaft*, 72–79.
81. Lüling, *Ur-Qur'an*.

high religion from the standpoint of ancient Arabian polytheism, into its very opposite, due to political opportunism."[82]

Lülling, who resumes Karl Vollers's (1906)[83] hypothesis of an originally dialectical form of the Qur'an, presupposes a background for his "ur-Qur'an" that is heretical Christian, or at least positioned against the imperial church. The Arabian Peninsula of Late Antiquity would then be "the refuge of an anti-Trinitarian Jewish Christianity, not yet contaminated by the speculations on the Trinity in Greek theology. Byzantine orthodoxy, armed with the imperial means of compulsion, would have pushed this authentic ur-Christianity back ever more on the defensive, ultimately into Arabia, and Muhammad responded to this through a sharpening of the Jewish-Christian critique of Hellenized theology, with the intention of restoring a pagan fertility cult," which Lülling also sees as a driving force of ur-Christianity. Jesus and Muhammad thus share the same fate: both revolted against a type of militant orthodoxy for which they were appropriated posthumously. . . . Lülling's undertaking is motivated by a fundamental impulse that is radically civilization-critical, whereby human history appears as a history of human self-forgetting and self-deception, a chronicle of the fall from good origins.[84]

Critics found his theory to be conspiratorial and selective, and, above all, beholden to a circular logic[85]—but what seems even more grave is the basic attitude of the author, whose own reconstructions of the "ur-Qur'an" text, in contrast to the transmitted Qur'an, sound conventional and without tension: Lülling's "authenticity parameter," the maximal closeness of the texts of the "ur-Qur'an" to Christian hymns, is ultimately based on a prejudice, which affords to Christianity alone a genuine religious self-expression and sees Muhammad or his community as nothing more than manipulators of Christian poetry. The correct observation, that certain Qur'anic forms developed according to earlier Christian ones, all too quickly turns into a claim of one-sided dependency, into epigonality.

In more recent times, Christoph Luxenberg has offered a further attempt at reconstruction in his book *Die syro-aramäische Lesart des Koran* (*The Syro-Aramaic Reading of the Koran*),[86] which appeared in 2000. He argues within the discourse of linguistic history. The work postulates a lectionary as the basis of the Qur'an, consisting of a translation from Syriac into a form of Arabic that did not have any literary precedent. In view of its strong proliferation of Syriac elements, this language would represent a Syriac-Arabic admixture, which would

82. Sinai, "Lülings apokalyptische Koranphilologie."

83. Vollers's thesis, which holds that the Qur'an was recorded in a Hijaz vernacular, was based on the assessment of dialectal variants in the non-canonical readings. This thesis was refuted in a review by Geyer and Nöldeke, "Zur Sprache des Korans."

84. Sinai, "Lülings apokalyptische Koranphilologie."

85. See Hawting's review of Lüling.

86. See Marx, "Ein neuer Impuls"; Marx, "Was ist eigentlich der Koran?"

have been immediately comprehensible to the addressees of the Qur'an but not to the later Arab elite that was removed in place and time from this place of origin, who reinterpreted the hybrid text as purely Arabic. For Luxenberg, a non-Arabic Christian original text lies behind the Qur'an, which was rewritten into an Arabic-Islamic text in a way that he himself cannot explain. Once again we find the accusation of epigonality.

Luxenberg demonstrates his method of reconstruction of the "original" wording, which often presupposes several steps of transformation, through a number of examples.[87] What is central is the elimination of two Qur'anic *theologumena*, which he holds to be irreconcilable with a post-biblical text: the communication of the proclamation through divine inspiration (*waḥy*), and the existence of maidens of paradise (*hurun ʿīn*). According to Luxenberg, both owe their presence in the Qur'an to errant conclusions drawn from misunderstood Syriac predecessor texts. The Qur'anic self-designation *wahy*, "inspiration," must signify, if clarified by means of Syriac etymology, nothing other than "translation." The Qur'an thus reveals itself as the translation of an earlier text. The conception of the maidens of paradise in the Qur'an also appears to be the result of misreading—in its place we should see reference to white grapes, an interpretation that ignores the fact that already in Syriac literature, such as in the Hymns of Ephrem, grapes within a paradisiacal context are not to be taken in the literal sense but rather stand allegorically for sensory pleasures, above all the erotic. Even the putative Syriac predecessors are, however, reproduced by Luxenberg in a curtailed form. In order to demonstrate his sensational thesis, a number of "misreadings" in the context of the passages involving the maidens, have to be "corrected" as well, again through recourse to Syriac etymologies, producing connections to grapes. It is a linguistic tour de force, whose positive provocation for research lies in the fact that it contests the exclusive interpretive monopoly of Arabic studies over the Qur'an; but along with this legitimate critique, which ably demonstrates that one cannot approach the historical situation of emergence without profound knowledge of the non-Arabic religious writing of Late Antiquity, Luxenberg himself attempts to lay claim to just such an interpretive monopoly. If one thinks Luxenberg's thesis through to its end, Arab readers would have no access to the "true Qur'an," which would be the exclusive domain of experts and specialists in the Syriac-Aramaic church language.

But perhaps the most convincing demonstration of the "reductionism" of the Luxenberg approach is provided by a contrast of his high-handed constructions of dependencies with examples of methodologically well-founded

87. Luxenberg's methods of linguistic derivation encountered intense criticism within Semitic studies; see De Blois, "Islam in Its Arabian Context"; see also his review of Luxenberg, and the review by Hopkins. See also Wild, "Lost in Philology?," and Saleh, "The Etymological Fallacy." In contrast, Luxenberg's theses were widely received as a welcome provocation by a number of scholars without linguistic access to the Qur'an, and by those unwilling to recognize the Qur'an as a literary artifact; see the reviews of Baasten and Jansen.

contextualizations of Qur'anic texts with their predecessor traditions in Syriac: here, above all, the works of Joseph Witztum are encouraging.[88] The Syriac predecessor traditions do not figure in his work as "urtexts," but rather constitute an exegetical "middle stage" in the palimpsest of traditions based on the Bible and its initial Jewish exegesis, then overlaid by Christian interpretation, into which the Qur'an ultimately enters. Witztum's investigations also open new insights into the Qur'an's particular approach to Christologically laden traditions and their earlier foundations; his work thus promises to yield important findings for the history of theology.

Such curiosity stands outside discussion in Luxenberg's tendentious approach. This is all the more deplorable since his thesis of the Christian origin of Islam has provoked far-reaching speculations on the part of researchers who are not specialists in the study of the Near East. The volume edited by the theologian Karl-Heinz Ohlig with Gert Rüdiger Puin, *Die dunklen Anfänge: Neue Forschungen zur Entstehung und frühen Geschichte des Islam* (*Dark beginnings: New research on the emergence and early history of Islam*) (2005),[89] and Ohlig's book, edited with Markus Groß, *Schlaglichter: Die beiden ersten islamischen Jahrhunderte* (Highlights: the first two Islamic centuries)(2008), attempt to rewrite the early history of Islam into one that is entirely Christian. Both initiatives gamble away a number of highly relevant individual results through an openly exhibited apologetic stance, which ridicules the requirements of unbiased research.

The construction of a supposed Christian history that extends for more than a century into the Islamic period is bound up with a new explanation of the name Muhammad, literally: "the praised," which is asserted, through the use of philological acrobatics, to designate Christ rather than the Arab Prophet. This interpretation permits the person of Muhammad to be eliminated from history. But even this foundational element of the argumentation has been called into doubt. The suggestive reinterpretation of the name cannot be maintained in view of the parallel cases documented in South Arabian research of the adoption of divine or theophoric titles of honor reclaimed by privileged persons from the circle of worshipers. The name Muhammad, "the praised," which first occurs in the Qur'an in the Medinan suras (Q 3:144, 33:40, 47:2, and 48:29), appears plausibly in this light as a title of honor given to the Prophet as one sent by God.[90]

88. See Witztum, "The Foundations of the House (Q 2:127)"; a more extensive study on the revision of Syrian treatments of Biblical stories (Joseph and Adam) in the Qur'an is now in preparation.

89. See Sinai's review, as well as the objection from the research group Corpus Coranicum to Ohlig's invective against Islamic scholarship, published in the feuilleton of the *Frankfurter Allgemeine Zeitung* on November 21, 2006: "Die Koranforschung tritt in die kritische Phase ein."

90. Comparable to the case of his rival Prophet, Musaylimah, called "Raḥmān al-Yamāma" after the name of his God, al-Raḥmān. Robin cites an earlier example from the third century: the designation of the Roman emperor Marcus Aurelius Antoninus as Elagabalus or Heliogabalus, the name of the god of Emesa, whose cult was introduced to Rome by the emperor. Following this analogy, Muhammad could have been named after his god; on this see Robin, "Himyar et Israel," 876.

In any case, the burdening of a single lexical element with serious real historical conclusions points to a reductive approach. Such equivalencies as the claim of a correspondence of Muhammad to "Benedictus," thus indicating Christ, or Luxenberg's equation of *qur'ān* and "lectionary," thus indicating a factual Syriac predecessor scripture to the Qur'an, could certainly arise within a Late Antique sectarian milieu, but this derivation of history from the explanations of single lexemes belongs rather to polemically motivated speculation than to serious scholarship. The immensely complex background of individual and collective naming is shown by the studies of Carsten Colpe,[91] who probes a Jewish-Christian characterization of the earliest community.

Despite the ideological coloring of the investigations presented in the Ohlig circle, its results must be checked in detail. The conference volume edited by Neuwirth, Sinai, and Marx, *The Qur'an in Context: Historical and Literary Investigations into the Qur'an*, confronts critically some of the ideas set out in the volumes compiled in the service of the hypothesis of Christian origin.[92] Above all, the studies by Norbert Nebes,[93] Barbara Finster,[94] Stefan Heidemann, Peter Stein,[95] and Mikhail Bukharin[96] demonstrate the significance of archaeology, architecture, numismatics, and epigraphy for the reconstruction of the original milieu of the Qur'an. A first general overview was offered in 2001 by Robert Hoyland.[97]

In the meantime, recent research on South Arabia has shaken the legitimacy of the long-unquestioned focus on the northern Hijaz and Syria as the primary cultural catchment area of the ministry of Muhammad, challenging also the derivation of early Islam from Christianity. Christian Robin,[98] whose research concentrates above all on pre-Islamic South Arabia, has opened a new scope on important religious phenomena that were previously derived summarily from the Syriac-Christian region. Meanwhile, Jewish mediations of concepts from South Arabia have been found to be central in the formation of ritual and liturgical elements that were previously set wholly in a Christian context, such as *zakāt*, "almsgiving," or *ṣalāt*, "prayer." It is nothing new that important ancient Arabian festivals that entered Islam not only coincide with Jewish festivals in their annual locations and earliest etiology but in part also have names identical to Jewish festivals. A connection to South Arabia, which was marked by Judaism for over two centuries, could plausibly clarify these correspondences that have

91. Colpe, *Das Siegel der Propheten*.

92. Heidemann, "Das Problem der frühislamischen Numismatik," responds to Popp's account, "Die frühe Islamgeschichte."

93. Nebes, "The Martyrs of Najrān and the End of Himyar."

94. Finster, "Arabia in Late Antiquity."

95. Stein, "Mecca on the Caravan Routes in Pre-Islamic antiquity."

96. Bukharin, "Literacy in Pre-Islamic Arabia."

97. Hoyland, *Arabia*; Hoyland, *Seeing Islam*.

98. Robin, "Himyar et Israel"; Robin, "Les Filles de Dieu"; Robin, "Des inscriptions aux traditions."

remained unexplained for so long. While the pre-Islamic and Qur'anic *ḥajj* is synonymous with the *ḥag ha-sukkot*, the Festival of Tabernacles, the pre-Islamic *ʿumra* corresponds to the Jewish spring festival, Pesach. [99] The fast that is not named explicitly in the Qur'an but identified unambiguously in the tradition, the "Ashura" fast[100] observed by the community before the institutionalizing of the Ramadan fast, carries a name in the tradition (but not in the Qur'an) that is derived from the Aramaic name (*ʿasora*) for the fast day known in Hebrew as Yom Kippur. The religious pluralism that we see here appears to have been formative for ancient Arabian culture, as we see with clarity in the anthologies edited by Gerald Hawting, *The Development of Islamic Ritual*, and Francis E. Peters, *Arabs and Ancient Arabia on the Eve of Islam*. This plurality is ill served by a distortion of history that limits it only to Christianity.

1.5 The Arabic Side of the Qur'an: Mirror of the Arabian Environment

Thomas Bauer has rightly denounced a further one-sidedness found in Qur'an research up to now, the fact that the Qur'an is systematically contextualized with its Christian and Jewish neighboring traditions, while its relation to its own Arabian environment remains thoroughly neglected. Although since Julius Wellhausen[101] early Arabic religious conditions have been studied and recognized as important reference points for Qur'an readings,[102] such attention has not been paid to the ideological coordinates, in a broader sense, that are reflected in the ancient profane texts. Rather, as Aaron Hughes points out,[103] a "hermeneutically sealed border" has been constructed between Islam and pre-Islam in the research, in a manner that follows the Islamic tradition.[104] Ludwig Ammann has rightly pointed out that between religion and poetry there exists a "division of labor, which assigns to religion the task of dealing with occasional conflicts and crises, and leaves to poetry the reflection on enduring malaise and aporia." Poetry must therefore be brought into view alongside ancient Arabic religion, if one wants to mark out the spiritual horizon of ancient Arabia. An important new approach is sketched by Bauer in his programmatic article "The Relevance of Early Arabic Poetry for Qur'anic Studies," which demonstrates a powerful "negative intertextuality" in Qur'anic citations of poetry.[105] Beyond this, the Qur'an reflects a

99. See Neuwirth, "Gewalttexte und Versöhnungsliturgien."

100. Hawting, "The Tawwābūn"; Hawting *Islamic Ritual*, 173–188.

101. Wellhausen, *Reste altarabischen Heidentums.*

102. Fahd, *Panthéon*; Krone, *Al-Lāt*; Chabbi, *Seigneur*; Peters, *Arabs and Arabia.*

103. See Hughes, "The Stranger at the Sea."

104. This construction doesn't allow for the Qur'anic reflections of older Arabian myths to be seen as reasonable adoptions. They are viewed merely as theologically polished retellings, for example, in J. Stetkevych, *Golden Bough*; cf. Hughes, "The Stranger at the Sea," 262.

105. One example is discussed in chap. 12, 436–441.

decisive reinterpretation of ancient Arabic concepts of time and fate, wherein the cyclical conception of time of ancient Arabic poetry is replaced by a linear one. This important change of orientation in the Qur'an has not yet been systematically studied,[106] and is less derived from explicit Qur'anic pronouncements than it is indirectly deduced from the positions taken on history and the future: the Qur'anic proclamation accomplishes this change of orientation through the fact that it throws into question the norms of behavior bound up in pre-Islamic poetry to the perception of cyclical time; above all, the Bedouin ethos founded on a cyclical perception of time is transmuted into an ethics oriented to the uniqueness of God and a linear construction of history.[107]

In the comparative analysis of poetry and Qur'an, special significance should be attached to the diverse literary genres and topoi that figure in both literary corpora. Deserving special attention here is the text type of the *mathal*,[108] the parable speech built up into a short narrative, which is already familiar from poetry,[109] but in the Qur'an also reflects New Testament and Jewish precedents.[110] Which tradition does the Qur'anic parable follow? Does it stand in the service of an "empirical explanation," as the poetry would suggest, or rather in the service of a theological interpretation of its object, as in religious tradition?[111] A further example can be found in "praise," *fakhr*, which recurs in the Qur'an as hymn, and "invective," *hijāʾ*, which is also known to the Qur'an.[112] Here too, systematic comparisons are still lacking. Finally, there are topoi, such as the unanswered question expressing an existential aporia, which belong to a repertoire of discourse forms employed in poetry and Qur'an alike.[113] Poetic topoi can also be transferred into an entirely new context, such as the "immortality discourse," *khulūd*, which is predominant in poetry, and which is transmuted from a hero's striving through physical endurance toward inner-worldly praise into an assurance of the timelessly preserved blessedness of the righteous. Certain pre-Islamic virtues recur in the Qur'an, such as *jūd* "generosity," which is transmuted from the hero's ultimately self-interested bravado expressed in self-expenditure on behalf of the Bedouin collective into the responsibility required of the individual toward the body politic of an urban society, or *ḥamāsa*, "bravery," which is repurposed into *ṣabr* "patience," a concept of heightened intensity and permanence. All of these terms are divested of their ancient Arabic excessiveness. The Qur'an is thus just as much a new reading of the poetry as it is a new reading of biblical traditions.

106. Tamer, *Zeit und Gott*, concentrates on poetry. For the Qur'an, he limits himself to an investigation of concepts of time, without however interrogating the text in its entirety in terms of statements about time.

107. Cf. chap. 12, 434–441.

108. Lohmann, "Die Gleichnisse im Koran"; Sister, "Metaphern und Vergleiche im Koran."

109. Cf. the introduction to Bauer, *Altarabische Dichtkunst*.

110. Ben-Shammai, "The Status of Parable and Simile."

111. Cf. chap. 8, 300–308.

112. See Fischer, *Wert der vorhandenen Koran-Übersetzungen*.

113. Ammann, *Die Geburt des Islam*.

This approach to the Arabic heritage has not yet been pursued, although important beginnings have been made, which we see in the studies of Omar Farukh[114] and M. M. Bravmann,[115] and, in more recent times, Jaroslav Stetkevych[116] and Suzanne P. Stetkevych,[117] Agnes Imhof,[118] and Salam al-Kindy.[119]

1.6 The New Center: Not Book or Prophet, But Community

1.6.1 In Western Research

In the wake of the critical rejection of the hypotheses of Lülling and Luxenberg, who posited a pre-Qur'anic Christian form of the Qur'an, and the failure of Wansbrough's reduction of the Qur'an to a kind of "Islamic Mishna," we must confront a new challenge: to make the Qur'an recognizable as a rhetorically marked text and a mirror of collective formation. This means that we must set the two great developments that were formative for the genesis of Islam into meaningful relation: the emergence of the community and the collection of texts with canonical authority that are united in the Qur'an. This task is evaded by the skeptical researchers, who obstruct their own access to this problematics and too quickly ignore the Qur'an itself, which must be the textual basis for this investigation, degrading it to a salvation-historical construct tailored to later collective requirements, or even to an ideologically motivated "rewriting" of ancient "original texts."

The accusation that is implied in this, which Andrew Rippin has made explicit,[120] that the Qur'an shows no stylistic continuity and therefore could scarcely be the creation of "one and the same forming hand," remains a mere prejudice, as Nicolai Sinai stresses, so long as composition and the gradually developing formation of the successive discourses and leitmotifs are not submitted to systematic study. "If one emphasizes, on the other hand, the emergence of the text not from a preexisting overall plan, but rather from the complex interaction between a charismatic leader, an increasingly heterogeneous set of followers, and a group of opponents setting his authority into question polemically, then the literary heterogeneity of the Qur'an appears to be thoroughly comprehensible."[121] The skeptical position, represented most often by historians, stands opposed to the positive view held by literary scholars, who recognize no substantial breaks in

114. Farrukh, *Das Bild des Frühislam*; see also Müller, "Die Barmherzigkeit Gottes."
115. Bravmann, *Spiritual Background of Early Islam*; Goldziher, "Muruwwa und Din."
116. J. Stetkevych, *Golden Bough*.
117. S. Stetkevych, *The Mute Immortals Speak*.
118. Imhof, *Religiöser Wandel*.
119. Al-Kindy, *Voyageur sans Orient*.
120. Rippin, review of Neuwirth, *Komposition der mekkanischen Suren*.
121. Sinai, *Studien zur frühen Koraninterpretation*, 35.

the stylistic development.[122] That the assumption of several forming hands would open up new historical questions, which remain unanswered by the proponents of these theories, makes this hypothesis even more problematic.

But after the shifting of positions once thought to be secure that was triggered by Wansbrough, one can no longer simply assert the person of the Prophet as the sole "originator" of the Qur'an but should rather assign more weight to the contribution of the hearers and transmitters. The very preservation of the proclamation, in oral tradition, was a task that lay on many shoulders, and its codification after the death of the proclaimer required further transmitters. Like the Bible, the Qur'an is not "author literature" but rather a piece of "tradition literature." What Ernst Axel Knauf stresses for the Bible is true, mutatis mutandis, for the Qur'an: "The biblical absence of the 'author' corresponds to the absence of the book as artifact, as product, as a good in the biblical world. Certainly there were books, i.e., scrolls, in the archives. . . . But literature remained the spiritual possession of each group that possessed it and had access to it. . . . The expectation of a particular author figure for a text referred by tradition back to divine inspiration ultimately stems from the Enlightenment and Romantic period, which did away with divine inspiration to make room for the 'genius of the original author.' "[123] In the Qur'an too, the concept of "tradition literature" should be rethought, as a designation for a text emerging from the interaction of a group "formed by tradition," even if this text may have received its final form through a single forming hand.

Here, Islamic tradition, if viewed critically, is of inestimable value. As the source-critical studies of Gregor Schoeler,[124] Harald Motzki,[125] Marco Schöller,[126] and Andreas Goerke[127] show, tradition supplies relevant historical contexts for the changing situations of the proclamation. It is doubtful, however, if a coherent image of the proclaimer will ever emerge such as was provided, for example, for Jesus by David Flusser (1917–2000),[128] who was able to check the words of the Gospels against the Hebrew and Aramaic traditions current at the time of Jesus for possible ideological reworkings. While Flusser proceeds with carefully sorting out later additions and reinterpretations of the Gospels to bring forth a clear image of Jesus, the procedure of the biographer of Muhammad, Tilman Nagel,[129] is marked by a contrary bias: to give voice to the bulk of traditional

122. See Neuwirth, "Form and Structure."

123. Knauf, "Pentateuch-Redaktion."

124. Schoeler, *Charakter und Authentie.*

125. Motzki, *Anfänge der islamischen Jurisprudenz.*

126. Schöller, *Exegetisches Denken.*

127. Goerke and Schoeler, *Korpus Urwa b. az-Zubair.*

128. Flusser, *Jesus* (1998). This work, building on an earlier presentation (1970), stands out among the numerous attempts put forward since 1970 to represent the historical, Jewish Jesus through a sensitive exploration of Jesus's exceptional, messianic self-image; on this scholarship, see Vermes, *Changing Faces of Jesus*, 267.

129. Nagel, *Mohammed.*

material that emerged in the century after Muhammad, failing however to convey Muhammad's personal aura and the factual impact of his ministry. The immense mass of material should not obscure the fact that it reflects a later perception; it stems from a phase in which the community no longer stood in dispute with others, but was already established as a religious community of its own. What positively can be brought to light about the proclaimer is essentially his convictions that resound in his proclamation. Since these proclamations—unlike in the case of Jesus—are not elaborations of firmly identifiable biblical traditions but rather answers to current questions and challenges that are today difficult to grasp, a biography of the proclaimer in the present state of research can in no way rely on secure foundations.

What is much more amenable to research is the Meccan and Medinan milieu.[130] Exemplary investigations of this are available in the works of the "Jerusalem school" around M. Y. Kister (1914–2010), who, building on Ignaz Goldziher's approach to the critical evaluation of hadith, succeeded in historically illuminating important stages in Muhammad's ministry.[131] His work has been continued by Michael Lecker.[132] Uri Rubin—a pioneer in the history of the early community's cult—in a number of groundbreaking studies has demonstrated how the intricate cultic practices of ancient Arabian Mecca and Medina that shed light on the religious personality of the Prophet can be reconstructed even from contradictory reports[133]—an approach that follows on the works of Shlomo Dov Goitein (1900–1985),[134] Julius Wellhausen (1844–1918),[135] and—despite his tendentiousness—Henri Lammens (1862–1937).[136] The new store of knowledge that Rubin gleans from hadith and historical texts is meanwhile being supported by the findings of epigraphical and archaeological studies, of which Robert Hoyland[137] has provided a first synoptic overview. An important further document, the work on pre-Islamic history preserved on papyrus by Wahb ibn Munabbih (110/728 or 114/732),[138] who drew extensively on non-Muslim sources, promises further insights into the historical picture of the environment of the Prophet.

While future Qur'anic research will not be able to do without either archaeological or epigraphical evidence, nor without the critical evaluation of Islamic tradition, it is not this archive of knowledge that should form the starting point for Qur'an research but rather the text itself, read as the mirror of a communication. The communication structure of the Qur'an, which has received little

130. See Noth, "Früher Islam."
131. Kister, "Labbayka."
132. Lecker, "On the Markets of Medina."
133. Rubin, "Ilaf"; Rubin, "Meccan Trade"; Rubin, "The Shrouded Messenger"; Rubin, "Hanifiyya and Kaʿba."
134. Goitein, *Islamic History and Institutions.*
135. Wellhausen, *Reste altarabischen Heidentums.*
136. Lammens, *L'Arabie occidentale.*
137. Hoyland, *Arabia and the Arabs.*
138. Khoury, *Wahb ibn Munabbih.*

attention up to now, finally has to be focused in its relation to the interaction between the proclaimer and his hearers. In Nicolai Sinai's words, the Qur'anic texts document a process that can be characterized as trial and error as a gradual mutual approach of text and hearers' expectations: the role of Muhammad must accordingly be thought of anew. It consists on the one hand of his speaking to the hearers, perceived by Muhammad himself more and more clearly as inspired speech, and on the other hand of his triggering of debates that were to engage the hearership. His import would thus rather consist in his role as a catalyst and ultimate form giver than in that of an author in the conventional sense.

What is required, then, is not to describe the Qur'an in retrospect as an already homogenized founding document or divinely designed unit—this has already been done in numerous presentations of the canonical Qur'an; rather—we must trace the text *in statu nascendi*, in its genesis through the interplay of multiple actors and traditions. The cultural and social environment of the Hijaz, which lay on the periphery of two great empires, is still widely unresearched, though the negative assessment of this region as being devoid of culture, barren, and monotonous has by now become obsolete.[139] It has also been contested energetically by Jacqueline Chabbi,[140] whose monograph *Le Seigneur des Tribus* is based on the conviction that it is above all local Bedouin traditions that mark the characteristics of the Qur'an. Though this requires a further discussion of details, it confirms the notion that the Hijaz poses no serious problems as a milieu for the emergence of the Qur'an.[141] The Hijaz is the homeland not only of ancient Arabic poetry but also of an epic-narrative tribal tradition that still awaits evaluation as historical evidence. At present, epigraphical and material evidence already attest amply to the liveliness of cultural activity intensive enough to render the search for another milieu of emergence for the Qur'an superfluous. One of the most careful and insightful experts in the history of this region, Robert Hoyland, summarizes: "This makes it difficult to see how historical scenarios that require for their acceptance a total discontinuity in the historical memory of the Muslim community—such as that Muḥammad did not exist, the Quran was not written in Arabic, Mecca was originally in a different place etc.—can really be justified. Many of these scenarios rely on absence of evidence, but it seems a shame to make such a recourse when there are so many very vocal forms of material evidence still waiting to be studied."[142] Recent studies show that neither the (non-Arabic) written sources from the period nor the received epigraphical and numismatic

139. Montgomery, "The Empty Ḥijāzī."

140. Chabbi, *Seigneur*, and recently Chabbi, *Le Coran décrypté*. The monotheistic intertexts do not however receive their deserved attention here. The attempt at a reconstruction of the "réalité vécue" is carried out as in self-delimitation against tradition, labeled "le phantasme et l'illusion" (*Le Coran décrypté*, 23). In doing so, the Judeo-Christian traditions already echoing in the Qur'an are suspected as reflections of later Islamic thought.

141. See also Finster, "Arabia in Late Antiquity"; Stein, "Literacy in Pre-Islamic Arabia"; and Bukharin, "Mecca on the Caravan Routes."

142. Hoyland, "New Documentary Texts and the Early Islamic State"; Hoyland, *Arabia and the Arabs*.

evidence call into question the localizing of the Qur'an in its traditional milieu of emergence. Religious diversity, held together by a shared Hellenism-imprinted culture, should be assumed for the Near East in general so also for the milieu and period of the ministry of the Prophet. What is required is not speculation but rather the comparative accounting of the diverse religious and profane traditions that were involved in this, so as to illuminate the cultural "space of resonance" in which the emergence and reception of the Qur'anic texts played out.[143]

1.6.2 In Arabic-Language Inner-Islamic Research

That being said, it is hard to overlook the fact that the text-centered, literary approach proposed here has a major correlate, baffling in certain important points, within inner-Islamic research, in the school of *tafsīr adabī*, "literary exegesis," as it was named by its founder, Amin al-Khuli (d. 1966).[144] The new Qur'an reading that was developed by al-Khuli, Bint al-Shati (A'isha Abd al-Rahman, d. 1998)[145] and Muhammad Ahmad Khalafallah (d. 1998)[146] stands in the tradition of the reform of religious thought that was introduced in the nineteenth century by Muhammad Abduh (d. 1905)[147] and Rashid Rida (d. 1935)[148] and the new critical philology endorsed by Taha Husayn (d. 1973).[149] With some daring, one could speak of this exegetical direction, which has not yet been made fruitful for Western scholarly dealings with the Qur'an, as an analogue to the somewhat earlier emergence of Western critical Qur'an research introduced by Abraham Geiger in 1833; indeed, both new directions are clearly historically directed. They move beyond the traditional Islamic commentary focusing on the text itself. The fact that in these two cases, the historicizing of the Qur'an was to proceed on two distinctly different paths—Western historical-critical research concentrating on *intertexts* versus inner-Islamic exegesis focused on the *form* of the Qur'an—renders the task to "synchronize" the two strains as phenomena of a period of rupture, in Europe the nineteenth century and in the Near East of the early twentieth century, no less urgent.

The "Egyptian school" of new Qur'an exegesis, in contrast to the beginnings of critical Qur'an research in the West, is still widely unresearched. The éclat caused by the censorship measures with which the local religious establishment reacted to the new approaches was internationally noted: bans on publication

143. A new, exemplary study of the genesis of the Qur'an that provides a long overdue, stringent model of reflection, is offered by Sinai, *Studien zur frühen Koraninterpretation*.

144. Al-Khuli, *Manāhij al-ṭaqālīd*.

145. Abd al-Rahman (Bint al-Shati'), *al-ʿIjāz al-Bayānī*. On her, see Boullata, "Modern Qur'an Exegesis"; on the *tafsīr adabī* in general, see Wild, "Die andere Seite."

146. Khalafallah, *al-Fann al-Qaṣaṣī*; Khalafallah, *al-Qurʾān wa-mushkilāt Ḥayātinā*.

147. Abduh and Rida, *Tafsīr al-Manār*. On Abduh, see Hasselblatt, *Herkunft und Auswirkungen*.

148. Ziyadeh, "Rachid Rida."

149. Husain, *Fī al-Shiʿr al-Jāhilī*. On him, see Cachia, *Taha Husayn*.

such as that imposed on Taha Husayn in the 1930s, and even firings, as experienced by Muhammad Khalafallah and, in more recent times, Nasr Hamid Abu Zaid;[150] Sayyid Qutb (executed 1966),[151] who in the early years of his work also belonged to this movement, fell victim to state power for more far-reaching religious reasons. The Arabic scholar Islam Dayeh, who works on the history of modern Arabic philology, notes: "All of these scholars pleaded for the necessity of treating the Qur'an as a literary and aesthetic work, alongside other prose or dramatic literature, visual art or music. The text appears to them as a verbal artefact, ruled by an inherent and coherent logic, stylistics, and grammar."[152] In *tafsir adabi*, the Qur'an is released from the confines of the centuries-old, dogmatically binding commentary tradition to be investigated as to its language, its literary topoi, and its imagery. Rotraud Wielandt, who has provided the most detailed analysis of the "literary exegesis" conducted by Khalafallah, cites the justification put forward by the author himself: "It is clear that the Qur'an is human in its means of expression, human in style, and that it appeared in agreement with what was customary among the Arabs in linguistic art and eloquence—in view of all this, how can one claim that one should not understand the Qur'an according to these rules and stylistic characteristics?"[153] Khalafallah goes one step further in his historical contextualization, claiming that "a new religion . . . will meet with belief only if it connects to what is long known," which for him entails not only the linguistic but also the earlier ideological positions and usages, which were "corrected" through the proclamation of Muhammad. The studies of Khalafallah and his circle, which have precursors in the often less rigorous work[154] of earlier scholars such as Muhammad Abduh, Rashid Rida, and al-Shatibi,[155] are interesting not least as engagements with the European thought models of the time.[156] But up to now, they have been taken into account only by means of a kind of "objectification," that is, as the object of research on modern exegesis, and not dialogically, as scholarly contributions as such toward an inclusive Western-Eastern Qur'an exegesis. The studies that emerged from the so-called Egyptian school, even if they often present themselves apologetically as demonstrations of the inimitability of the Qur'an, should be synchronized with the contemporaneous Western Qur'an research as important contributions to a critical Qur'an exegesis.

150. On this, see Wild, *Mensch, Prophet,* whose observations demonstrate that it was in particular the insistence on the nonhistoric paraenetic quality of the Qur'anic Prophet legends that led to the drastic measures taken by the religious authorities against modern exegetes in individual instances; this pattern has indeed been continued. On Sadek Jalal al-Azm (1934–2017), see ibid., 40ff.

151. Qutb, *Fī Ẓilāl al-Qur'ān.*

152. Dayeh, "Plain Sense and the Allegorical—Lessons from the Egyptian School."

153. Wielandt, *Offenbarung und Geschichte,* 147. She quotes Khalafallah, *Al-Fann al-Qasasī,* 137ff. See also Wielandt, "Exegesis, Modern."

154. Al-Shatibi, *Al-Muwāfiqāt.*

155. See above all Wielandt, *Offenbarung und Geschichte,* and Jomier, *Commentaire coranique du Manar;* Jomier, "Quelques positions actuelles"; and Caspar and Jomier, "L'exégèse scientifique."

156. See Haddad, *Contemporary Islam.*

Already through their focus on the text and its addressees, in place of the earlier concentration on the transcendent speaker, they deserve recognition as new contributions to literary Qur'an reading. In this, they go a decisive step further than those exegetes from the Indian subcontinent, Ashraf Ali Thanavi (d. 1943), Hamid al-Din al-Farahi (d. 1930), and Amin Ahsan Islahi (d. 1997), whose work has been brought to attention by Mustansir Mir.[157] Their pronounced interest in the Qur'an's composition, its *nazm*, is documented not least in the fact that they treat the individual sura as a unit of interpretation, which they attempt to understand through defined recurring ideas. Yet they do not go so far as to accept a reading of the Qur'an as a literary artifact like other texts.

What is true for the *tafsīr adabī*, which can be accounted not as a majoritarian exegesis but as a relatively well-known and thoroughly challenging reading, is true also for the approach of Nasr Hamid Abu Zaid,[158] who submits the Qur'an to text-linguistic analysis. "In his model, we find the following scheme: a code of the message, Arabic; a message, the Qur'an; the receivers of the message, the Prophet Muhammad and his contemporaries; and the sender of the message, God."[159] Abu Zaid introduces a concept of scholarship that—excluding from its purview of research the "inspiration," namely, the stage preceding the communication of the Qur'an to the hearers—makes the view clear toward the communication process: "What the researcher can provide is an understanding of the Qur'anic text as the contemporaries of the Prophet understood it. Language usage, cultural background, and the horizon of understanding of the contemporaries of the Prophet become the inherent factors in the understanding of the text."[160]

Though it is true that within Islamic scholarship the Qur'anic use of language—in the context of the proclamation's social setting—has already come to occupy the central place of a new interpretation, this is still not yet the case for the other languages involved in the history of the Qur'anic emergence. The cultural background, the landscape of debate of Late Antiquity, which can only be tapped through historical and theological-historical investigations that reach far into the non-Arabic language tradition, still remains a domain of Western scholarship. It is here that the dialogue must begin between Islamic and more recent Western Qur'an research, which is occupied with collecting and evaluating these plurilinguistic Syriac, Hebrew, and Greek intertexts. We must approach the Qur'an text from both perspectives—from the inner-Arabic aesthetic, linguistic, and hermeneutical perspective and from the historical-critical perspective—to rid ourselves of the currently prevailing one-sidedness and to achieve a theoretically well-founded modern Qur'an exegesis. Western and Eastern research

157. Mir, "The Sura as a Unity."
158. Abu Zaid, *Mafhūm al-Naṣṣ*. Cf. Kermani, *Offenbarung als Kommunikation*.
159. Wild, *Mensch, Prophet*, 49ff.
160. Ibid.

strains are already converging to a higher degree than it may seem. Even if Abu Zaid's Qur'an exegesis, whose ultimate interest is in the implementation of the "inner meaning" of the Qur'an, its *maghzā*, in social life, seems to be less a contribution to the historical or literary exploration of the text than a normative new reading of the Qur'an, its reform intention is nevertheless based on a reading of the Qur'an that remains very close to the text. This reformist direction, which already distinguished the modern interpretations of the "Egyptian School," may ultimately provide the most promising interface between the interpretations currently operating in East and West. Indeed, reflective Western research—when it is aware of its inescapable political role as cultural critique—is ultimately also an act of reform, if not of Islamic culture itself, then of the European perception of this culture. We must decisively reset our perspective on the Qur'an, recognizing it as a genuine and historically documentable testimony of the emergence of a new religion, if the third scripture of monotheism is finally to be set on the same plane as the others.

2

The Qur'an and Scripture

2.1 "Sending Down," *Tanzīl*, and "Inspiration," *Waḥy*

We are accustomed to designating the Qur'an immediately as the "revealed scripture" of the Muslims. In doing so, we carry out the transference onto Islam of a Jewish-Christian concept[1] whose appropriateness still requires systematic testing—even if this designation, frequent in Western media, has long been used also by Muslim researchers themselves. With this designation we direct our attention primarily to the transcendent dimension of the Qur'an, its being a revelation, which—deemed exclusively a matter of belief of Muslims[2]—frees us from the necessity of reflecting on the position of the Qur'an beyond the limits of its Islamic reception history, within our own theological history. In what follows, a change of perspective will be suggested: in place of the "Islamic revelation," the "Qur'anic proclamation" should come to the fore, entailing a reading of the Qur'an not as the exclusively Muslim founding document of a religion but rather "inclusively," as a document of Late Antique theological debates. At the same time, a view should be given to the process reflected in the Qur'an of the communication of its message, and thus its genesis. The Qur'an does indeed yield information self-referentially about the process of its emergence, information that is given already in the early suras through the depiction of various scenes of emergence. The designation "revelation,"[3] which is so commonly used today, in fact stands for several Qur'anic concepts at once: for *waḥy*, "inspiration,"[4] and for *tanzīl*, "sending down."[5] In what follows, we will seek to illuminate the central Qur'anic texts on *waḥy* and *tanzīl* and then present the Qur'anic conception of an orally recited scripture, alongside Late Antique reflections over heavenly and earthly writing. After a detour through debates conducted in Western research about the concept of "inlibration," an attempt will be made to sketch an overall image of the medialities of the Qur'an, which in reality are more complex than they might seem.

Yet, skepticism is warranted not only in relation to the Jewish-Christian designation "revelation": the two inner-Qur'anic designations *waḥy* and *tanzīl*,

1. On the biblical background of the concept, see Van der Toorn, *Scribal Culture*, 205–232.
2. Cf. Arkoun, *Lectures du Coran*; Arkoun, "The notion of revelation."
3. See Wiedenhöfer, "Offenbarung."
4. Abu Zaid, *Mafhūm al-Naṣṣ*; cf. Kermani, *Offenbarung als Kommunikation*.
5. See Wild, "We have sent down to thee the book."

which in Islamic exegesis are used without distinction for the whole Qur'an, also should not be accepted immediately as a Qur'anic-sanctioned fait accompli. For more than twenty years, the Qur'an was a communication process, before it became fixed as a text and was later canonized. It is precisely its self-referentiality, brought to expression in the images of "sending down" and "inspiration," that must be investigated and "historicized," that is, viewed in connection with the otherwise detectable traces of the process of text genesis, alongside an engagement with extra-Qur'anic predecessors.

Islamic tradition itself also clearly marks a distinction between two manifestations of the Qur'an, as fixed written text and oral communication, in that it distinguishes between the concepts *muṣḥaf*, "codex," and *qurʾān*, "reading/recitation."[6] It would be difficult to overstate the importance of this distinction. Only after the oral communication process, *qurʾān*, came to a standstill with the death of the proclaimer were the texts gathered systematically and perceived, through a process of textualization, as canonical scripture (*muṣḥaf*),[7] to be read both ahistorically as a divine monologue and historically as a document initiating a new epoch and marking the victory of Islam over the rivaling traditions. Once this latter manifestation of the Qur'an came to play a predominant role in the identity construction of the religious community, those traits of the Qur'an's genesis that are significant for the researcher of Late Antique religious history, the traces of the Qur'anic community's engagement with the older traditions, became virtually irrelevant for Islam. Accordingly, they were marginalized in inner-Islamic exegesis, and it is on this one-sided exegesis that Western Qur'an translations and overview presentations down to today are still strongly dependent,[8] so that both scholarly traditions draw the image of a largely homogenous Arab scenario of the Qur'an's emergence. Indeed, Islamic tradition allows for the participation in the Qur'anic communication scenario of individual Christians and Jews who were knowledgeable about, or even quite learned in, religious traditions, but these always remain minor characters. It is historically warranted, however, to assume that there was a lively exchange between members of the different traditions that went well beyond such a circle of people, since the Qur'an reflects a multiplicity of negotiations, modified appropriations, rewritings, and even decided rejections of earlier traditions.

2.1.1 *Tanzīl*

The image evoked by *tanzīl*, "sending down," the vertical communication of the divine message, is by no means present in the Qur'an from the very beginning.

6. Cf. chap. 3, 109–114.

7. The process of canonization should be seen as gradual. On its implications, see Al-Azmeh, "The Muslim Canon," and Al-Azmeh, "Chronophagous Discourse," and see now also Sinai, *Studien zur frühen Koranauslegung*, 1–22.

8. So in Fück, "Die Originalität des arabischen Propheten"; see also Watt, *Muhammad at Mecca*; Watt, *Muhammad at Medina*; Paret, *Mohammed und der Koran*; Paret, "Der Koran als Geschichtsquelle."

The idea of the sending down of the Qur'an through the divine sender, which occurs for the first time in early Meccan suras (Q 97:1, 69:43, and 56:80), seems on first view rather to cohere with the older Arabian conception of the vertically conceived communication of supernatural wisdom associated with poetic inspiration.[9] "God's sending down" could then be understood as a corrective of the common pre-Islamic imagination of supernatural verbal conveyances through inspiring spirits, jinns[10] or satans, which "bring down" their wisdom, gleaned through eavesdropping on the higher spheres, to the individuals to be inspired, that is, to poets or soothsayers. The associating of the proclaimer to these communicators is rejected implicitly in the middle Meccan sura Q 26:221–222.:

> *hal unabbiʾukum ʿalā man tanazzalū l-shayāṭīn*
> *tanazzalu ʿalā kulli affākin athīm*
>
> Shall I let you know upon whom the satans descend?
> They descend upon every sinning liar [i.e., poets]

Other early texts, such as Q 69:41–43, even turn explicitly against this insinuation of the proclaimer's inspiration on the model of the poets, whose "muses" in the ancient Arabian context are the inspiring demons. Their *qawl*, that is, their "speech," which is not guaranteed transcendently, is contrasted to the word of God:

> *wa-mā huwa bi-qawli shāʿirin qalīlan mā tuʾminūn*
> *wa-lā bi-qawli kāhinin qalīlan mā tadhakkarūn*
> *tanzīlun min rabbi l-ʿālamīn*
>
> It is not the speech of a poet—how little you believe!
> Nor that of a seer—how little indeed you recall!
> It is rather a sending down from the Lord of the worlds.[11]

So the sending down, set into this "pagan" context, should be understood at first in the sense of a "correction," that is, an apologetically motivated replacement of an existing mythic configuration, not the result of theological reflection. It is notable, however, that *tanzīl* in later Qur'anic texts is also the mode of communication of the other scriptures, which are viewed collectively as *munazzal*, "sent down," and represented as "excerpts" from a preexisting heavenly writing. In the later period, then, *tanzīl* is not a trait specific to the Qur'an.

But was *tanzīl* ever a trait specific to the Qur'an, a mode of reception that only occurred in the Qur'an? The earliest *tanzīl* verses suggest the possibility that the image of sending down connects to older monotheistic conceptions rather than

9. See Wild, "We have sent down to thee the book."
10. Cf. Chabbi, "Jinn"; on reflections of jinn in the Qur'an, see Hawting, "Eavesdropping."
11. On these texts, see chap. 12, 427–429.

pagan ones. In Q 97:1, we read *innā anzalnāhu fī laylati l-qadr*, "Truly, we sent it down in the night of destiny," a verse which, interpreting "it" in the sense of a determined text, would give rise to an interpretive aporia. The referent of—*hu*, "it," cannot be identical to that which has just been recited; Q 97:1 refers to a new usage. It stands rather for an authoritative manifestation of the word of God, an analogue to the "embodiment" of the word of God in the neighboring traditions.[12] In the Nicene Creed it is said of Christ, "He descended from the heavens" (Greek *katelthonta ek tōn ouranōn*, Arabic *nazala mina l-samā*ʾ). The image of the sending down should then be considered in the early Meccan period to be a manifestation of the word of God that goes beyond the verbal-semantic proclamation and thus stands as a "vocal embodiment" *alongside* the teaching and guidance given with scripture. Although the Qur'an becomes manifest not through incarnation but rather as the verbally delineated word of God, it nonetheless shows distinct structural analogies to the word of God becoming man, to the incarnate logos (see p. 90–92). It has recently even led to discussions of the Qur'an in terms of " 'inlibration," "the becoming book of God's word." This designation reflects a problematic understanding of the Qur'an, as will be shown below, and reveals how far apart we still are from a proper understanding of *al-qur*ʾ*ān* and *al-tanzīl* in relation to "writing," or in relation to a manifestation of God's word that transcends writing.

2.1.2 *Waḥy*

The mode whereby the message arrived to the proclaimer is presented in two distinct scenarios in the early texts. The first is a vision. Here, the message itself is designated as *waḥy*, "inspiration,"[13] and its authority is corroborated through the evocation of a divine communication, Q 53:4–12:[14]

in huwa illā waḥyun yūḥā
ʿallamahu shadīdu l-quwā
dhū mirratin fa-stawā
wa-huwa bi-l-ufuqi l-aʿlā
thumma danā fa-tadallā
fa-kāna qāba qawsayni aw adnā
fa-awḥā ilā ʿabdihi mā awḥā
mā kadhdhaba l-fuʾādu mā raʾā
a-fa-tumārūnahu ʿalā mā yarā

12. On the hypostatization of the word of God in the Jewish tradition of Late Antiquity, cf. Boyarin, "The Gospel of the Memra," and Van der Toorn, *Scribal Culture*, 221–227; cf. below, 91–94.

13. See Izutsu, "Revelation as a Linguistic Concept," and Izutsu, *God and Man in the Quran*, although he does not take account of biblical and non-biblical traditions. Cf. also Chabbi, *Le Coran décrypté*, 81–92, which connects the delivery of the message to an inspiration of jinns.

14. Cf. on the vision and its relationship to the narrative of calling.

> It [the reading] is but an inspiration inspired,
> taught to him by one immense in power
> of great prestige. Erected high he sat enthroned
> on the upper horizon,
> then he drew near and hung suspended
> and was two bows' distance away or nearer
> and inspired in his servant what he inspired.
> The mind did not question what it saw.
> Do you dispute with him what he saw?

This scenario reflects in some details Isaiah's vision in Isaiah 6:1–11:[15]

> In the year that King Uzziah died, I saw the Lord, high and exalted, seated on a throne; and the train of his robe filled the temple. Above him were seraphim, each with six wings: With two wings they covered their faces, with two they covered their feet, and with two they were flying. And they were calling to one another: "Holy, holy, holy is the Lord Almighty; The whole earth is full of his glory." . . . Then I heard the voice of the Lord saying, "Whom shall I send? And who will go for us?" And I said, "Here am I. Send me!" He said, "Go and tell this people . . ."

The historically embedded, dynastically dated first-person report of Isaiah's calling as a Prophet contrasts with the Qur'anic report of the communication of divine teachings to the proclaimer, which is told in the third person and not set into historical time. The proclaimer's vision is not reported for its own sake, but is embedded within an argument that sets out to authenticate the transcendent origin of the proclamation as such. But still, the two visions are related: in both scenes, the envisioned sits upright on the throne. The verb *istawā*, "to stand/sit upright," is to be understood as an abbreviation for *ʿalā l-ʿarshi stawā*, "he sits upright on the throne" (Q 20:5, 13:2, 10:3, passim); *dhū l-ʿarshi*, "he of the throne," "the enthroned," (Q 81:20), a frequent image in ancient Near Eastern and biblical tradition,[16] may reflect the image of the enthroned *pantokrator*,[17] which is frequent in Late Antique iconography and is present verbally in both Jewish and Christian liturgy.[18] In both vision scenes, something is proclaimed: in the biblical text the praise of God articulated by the seraphim, in the Qur'anic text an inspiration to the proclaimer. But the two throne visions differ in some crucial

15. On the scene with Isaiah, see Irsigler, "Gott als König."

16. Cf. Hooke, *Myth and Kingship*; Brettler, *God Is King*; Schmidt, *Königtum Gottes*.

17. Rippin, "God," bases the kingly image of God on the Qur'anic predications of God, without naming concrete biblical intertexts.

18. The Kedushah, an exclamation evoking the divine holiness within Jewish prayer, contains the encomium of the seraphim from Isaiah 6:3, "Holy, Holy, Holy, The Lord of Hosts, The entire world is filled with His Glory." The Christian liturgy recapitulates this calling in an anaphoric prayer during mass ("with Your Glory").

characteristics: in contrast to Isaiah, the divine appearance in the Qur'an is not static, but seems rather to move toward the onlooker.[19] The two prophet visions also part ways in further details: unlike the speech of God in Isaiah, the "inspiration," *waḥy*, in the Qur'an does not form part of a prophetic calling, even if the inspired speech is identical semantically with the proclamation whose transcendent source the report of the vision is meant to confirm. Above all, the biblical image of God undergoes decisive changes in the Qur'an that does not allow for anthropomorphic traits.

This is in tune with the report in the earlier sura Q 81:19–23 of the vision of a phenomenon that also appears on the horizon (*bi-l-ufuqi l-mubīn*), a report in which the proclamation is identified not as God's immediate speech but rather as the "word" (*qawl*) of a "noble messenger with power before the enthroned" (*rasūlin karīm / dhī qūwatin ʿinda dhī l-ʿarshi makīn*). Here too the entire proclamation is authorized through the vision of a supernatural phenomenon, but now of an angel, similar to the seraphim in Isaiah, one who is "closely related to the enthroned."

The two vision scenes that evoke Isaiah's vision (Q 81:19–23 and 53:4–12) are complemented by a third, immediately following Q 53:4–12, in which no divine communication is given to the proclaimer. Here, the experience of divine closeness is confined to the visual, the divine person manifesting himself only emblematically through a natural phenomenon, a bush changed in its appearance (Q 53:13–18)—an evident reference to the shrub figuring in the calling of Moses. All the three Qur'anic vision reports are clearly not immediate imitations of reality, but rather are "overdetermined," charges with biblical textual evocations. At the same time, the biblical models are also "corrected": in sura 81, an angel is interposed as speaker, so that God himself does not need to speak. In Q 53:4–12 a divine communication follows, but manifests itself, unlike in the biblical report, as *non*verbal speech. Again unlike the message of the angel, which appears as "(understandable) speech," *qawl*, God's address is introduced as *waḥy*, "(nonverbal) inspiration." The striking fact that God speaks directly in none of the visions is no accident: the Qur'anic presentation here undertakes a "correction," quite in concert with the theological tendencies of its time, of the anthropomorphism that dominated the biblical reports to various degrees. With *waḥy*, unlike in the case of angelic speech, no clear communication is intended—but what exactly then is meant by *waḥy*?

The word, already common in pre-Islamic poetry, indicates not an articulated message but rather one signaled through suggestive signs, as might exist

19. This is not a Qur'anic innovation, but rather reflects a biblical notion developed after Isaiah: James Kugel, *How to Read the Bible*, 600–606 (as suggested in a personal communication from Dirk Hartwig) points out that the throne was already understood to be in motion in Ezekiel's time; God left Jerusalem and was ascending to heaven in a transportable chariot throne, having left his temple during the first wave of exile to Babylon.

for example in the chirping of birds or in an unreadable writing on a rock.[20] The Egyptian thinker Nasr Hamid Abu Zaid[21] recontextualizes the Qur'anic *waḥy*, which is reclaimed in the Islamic tradition to mean divine speech, with its ancient Arabic usage, and determines that it refers to a communication that is not yet verbalized, a "suggestion" or "inspiration" that can only become comprehensible through a "translation" achieved by the recipient. Everything that precedes this process of resetting into human speech remains inaccessible to the outsider, and thus to the researcher as well (this is the important point for the reformist thinker Abu Zaid), who must properly limit himself to the already verbalized speech of the Prophet, that is, to his "horizontal" communication with his hearers,[22] dispensing with treating the transcendent side of the text. This "horizontal" manifestation of *waḥy* can be understood—to proceed beyond Abu Zaid's ideas—as part of a drama[23] that plays out between the proclaimer, the community as it forms, and which is reflected in the Qur'anic texts that have been "translated" by the proclaimer into verbal language. The Qur'an, it is true, is formally almost continuously the speech of a divine "I" or "we" to a Prophetic "you," through which one can, however, "hear" the social situation that is involved in the address. In light of its dramatic communication to the hearers, the text is polyphonic, in that some hearers and hearer groups enter the text alongside the proclaimer who is present as the addressee, or at least are spoken about in their absence.

Only in the post-Qur'anic period, after the death of the proclaimer, is *waḥy* generalized to become a designation of the Qur'anic message as a whole. With the proliferation of the dogma of the non-createdness of the Qur'an in the ninth/tenth century, the concept of *waḥy* grew massively in authority. But only in recent times has this authority come to operate so restrictively within conservative circles as to withdraw the Qur'an entirely from the access of analytic approach. Precanonically, that is, understood with Abu Zaid in the context of ancient Arabic, extra-Qur'anic evidence, *waḥy* means a preverbal inspiration that is far remote from its understanding in the later developed dogma of verbal inspiration.

2.1.3 *Vigils as Frames of "Inspiration"*

The visions, of which there are three recorded in the Qur'an, are rare exceptions as a frame for the communication of messages.[24] There is a second scenario that

20. Cf. the function of *waḥy* in early Arabic poetry, see chap. 12, 444–447.

21. Abu Zaid, *Mafhūm al-Naṣṣ*; see also Kermani, *Offenbarung als Kommunikation*.

22. This occurred in conjunction with the Muʿtazila theology, which, in the eighth/ninth century, assumes a distinction between the uncreated, intrinsic, knowledge of God and his created word, and asserts the existence of a necessarily not-eternal substrate for the retention of this word; see the evidence in Maalouf, *La place du verbe*. The fact that this position was replaced a century later with the dogma of the uncreatedness of the Qur'an is related to anti-Christian polemic.

23. See Neuwirth, "Structure and the Emergence of Community."

24. The Qur'an gives accounts of two visions in three places: Q 53:4–12; 53:13–18 and one, Q 81:23f., that is arguably identical with the first vision mentioned in sura 53.

presents the receipt of God's word less dramatically, namely, as the result of askesis, as new texts growing out of the nightly recitation of texts that were already in circulation. Here, the receipt of texts presents itself as resulting from the recitations performed by the proclaimer in his vigils, which must have been conducted with highly intense concentration. The most evident case is Q 73:1–9:

> *yā ayyuhā l-muzzammil*
> *qumi l-layla illā qalīlā*
> *niṣfahu awi nquṣ minhu qalīlā*
> *aw zid ʿalayhi wa-rattili l-qurʾāna tartīlā*
> *innā sa-nulqi ʿalayka qawlan thaqīlā*
> *inna nāshiʾata l-layli hiya ashaddu waṭʾan*
> *wa-aqwamu qīlā*
> *inna laka fī l-nahāri sabḥan ṭawīlā*
> *wa-dhkuri sma rabbika wa-tabattal ilayhi tabtīlā*
> *rabbu l-mashriqi wa-l-maghribi*
> *lā ilāha illā huwa fa-ttakhidhhu wakilā*

> You who are enwrapped in your garment,
> Stand the night, the large part of it,
> Half of it, or take away some of it,
> Or add something to it,
> And chant the reading in clear chant.
> We will charge you with a weighty speech.
> In the beginning of the night impression are strongest and words are the most collected.
> You have in the day long-lasting activity.
> So remember the name of your Lord
> and give yourself entirely to him.
> He is the lord of the sunrise and the sunset.
> There is no God but him! So take Him as a protector![25]

Although here we also find language related to divine visitation—God himself gives the proclaimer admonitions for the right disposition toward the reception of the messages and "gives to him heavy speech"—the new texts emerge not least through human effort, namely, through the recitation in vigils of texts already known. These vigils may have consisted of recitations of Psalm-like liturgical texts such as constituted by the early suras. The text itself reflects this close relation to the Psalms: verse 2, *qumi l-layla*, "stand the night," recalls "at midnight I stand up, to praise you" (Psalms 119:62); verse 8, *wa-dhkur sma rabbika*, "recall

25. On the relationship between text genesis and cult development, cf. chap. 6, 205–208.

the name of your Lord," recalls "praise the name of the Lord" (Psalms 113:1), and verse 9, *rabbu l-mashriqi wa-l-maghribi*, "Lord of the sunnrise and sunset," recalls "from rise to setting of the sun" (Psalms 50:1).

The early Qur'an consists to a large extent of paraphrases of psalms; it forms part of Late Antique psalmic piety which for the first time finds its place in the Arabic language, there being no Arabic translation of the Psalms extant before the ninth century.[26] At this early stage, the text is still very little interested in self-definition; the word *qurʾān* itself at the beginning refers to the process of recitation rather than to the text itself. Only with the growth of the community and the emergent necessity of self-assertion does the urgency of self-authorization arise, which, as we should expect, occurs on the one hand through self-distinction of the proclaimer against ancient Arabic predecessors, in particular the poets,[27] and on the other hand through contrast between the text and the preceding scriptures of the two older religions,[28] which are known in the form of scrolls or codices.

2.2 Al-Qurʾān: Communication of Texts from the Heavenly Scripture

In contrast to these scriptures, the Qur'an presents itself at first as a new formation in altered verbal dress, as a new message that follows, and confirms, the earlier scriptures. But above all, already in the earliest community, the conception took shape that the oral Qur'an stemmed from the "preserved tablet" that is with God, *al-lawḥ al-maḥfūẓ*, an original and heavenly writing;[29] cf. Q 85:21–22.: *bal innahu qurʾānun majīd / fī lawḥin maḥfūẓ*, "Truly, it is a glorious reading [*qurʾān*] / on a preserved tablet." The Qur'an thus has its origins and roots in a transcendent original writing, from which excerpts are "sent down," so to speak, as divine messages for recitation (Q 56:77–78: *innahu la-qurʾānun karīm / fī kitābin maknūn*, "Indeed, it is a generous reading [*qurʾān*] / preserved in a hidden writing").

Narratives in the later Meccan suras are often explicitly presented as elements of "the writing," *al-kitāb*. This writing is viewed as unchanging and extensive, perhaps a Qur'anic adaptation of the idea of the book of the heavenly register, which is found in the book of Jubilees, a Jewish apocryphon of the second century BCE, but which was a widely prevalent notion already in the ancient Near East.[30] The Qur'anic references to the writing, *al-kitāb*, presuppose a kind of archive, a store of narratives that exist already fixed in writing to be communicated

26. On the Arabic tradition of the psalms, see Schippers, "Psalms."

27. See Farrukh, *Das Bild des Frühislam*, and now also Bauer, "The Relevance of Early Arabic Poetry."

28. There have only been a few studies on this, primarily Speyer, *Die biblischen Erzählungen im Qoran*; Busse, *Die Theologischen Beziehungen*; and, on Qur'anic engagement with the Psalms, Neuwirth, "Psalmen."

29. See Jeffery, *The Qur'an as Scripture*; Madigan, *The Qur'an's Self-Image*.

30. On the role of writing in the book of Jubilees, see Najman, "Interpretation as Primordial Writing," and Kugel, *The Bible as It Was*. On the history of this idea, see Van Doorn, *Scribal Culture*, 214–227.

to the proclaimer by the sender in the form of clearly defined pericopes, resembling the textual units read out in the services of Jews and Christians. In the Qur'anic proclamation, these pericopes are framed by introductory and closing parts and are set into a Qur'anic unit of recitation, a sura, which includes various sorts of texts.

Narrative communications from the heavenly scripture are at first clearly distinguished from less universal elements, such as debates over ephemeral issues of the community. The particular rank and ceremonial function of the narratives transmitted from biblical tradition but ultimately originating from the heavenly scripture is underlined by introductory formulas such as *wa-dhkur fī l-kitāb*, "recall in [the communication of] the scripture" (Q 19:16). It is only in a later phase, in Medina, that the entire message communicated to the community is considered to constitute "scripture," that is, that communal issues discussed in Qur'anic speech are themselves recognized as a part of salvation history, so that entire suras are counted as manifestations of *al-kitāb*.[31]

But even at this stage of development, the distinction between the message and its transcendent sources is maintained. The claim raised so energetically today in fundamentalist circles of a transcendent rank also for the *materially* present text, a rank that withdraws it from scholarly analysis, is not founded in the Qur'an. It can rather be connected to the dogma of the uncreatedness of the Qur'an that became widespread in the ninth/tenth century,[32] according to which the Arabic language of the Qur'an does not stem from social convention but rather from divine imposition, so that exegesis of the Qur'an falls within strict theoretical limits of veritative, "literal" explanation. That the insistence on the transcendent character of the Qur'an as an exclusive feature of Islam is in no way an inherited tradition but rather something new, and that it represents a withdrawal into essentializing self-isolation that is obviously politically conditioned, is shown by the tradition of the Qur'an interpretation through the past 1,300 years. Throughout history, the Qur'an was in fact always of two natures: a scripture of transcendent origin and the inner-worldly focal point for a form of life, and thus the object of wide-ranging theological reflection.

Above all, to give a monopoly to the transcendent origin of the Qur'an contradicts the text itself, which insists on the shared origin of all three monotheistic scriptures and invites Jews and Christians, as older "possessors of scriptures," *ahl al-kitāb*, to acknowledge the shared genealogy of the three monotheistic religions, which according to the later evidence of the Qur'an all stem from one and the same transcendent archetype. The Qur'an here occupies a pioneering position, since, as William Graham emphasizes,[33] the concept of holy writings beyond

31. Cf. Neuwirth, "Structure and the Emergence of Community."
32. See Wild, *Mensch, Prophet*, 7.
33. Graham, "Scripture and the Qur'ān."

one's own religion, which has become widely familiar only since the nineteenth century, is already self-evident in the Qur'an: countless verses speak not only of the heavenly writing, *kitāb*, but also of its forms of appearance already established in this world, the "writings," *kutub*, of other religions, the Jews and Christians.

The later Qur'an sketches a "scriptural community," a concept that is then thwarted by the process of canonization after the closure of the proclamation. But while the Qur'anic text itself stresses at great length its consubstantiality with the other scriptures, it nonetheless features unambiguously in later Islamic theology as the final manifestation of divine speech that perfects all other scriptures. Between the statements of the proclaimed Qur'an text and its later interpretation lies the break of canonization,[34] which grants a new predominance to the transcendent dimension. The historic-dialogic character of the Qur'an at the time of the proclaimer, a polyphonic religious conversation with and about others, becomes a univocal text after the death of the proclaimer, a divine monologue. In the context of the reading of the Qur'an as a Late Antique text, we therefore have to go back behind canonization.

Canonicity, which involves the social recognition of the already victorious community, imposes a substantially new reading. It no longer reflects the historical drama of engagement with others characterized by trial and error, but rather sees the scripture as a triumphant symbol of victory, even granting it the authority to unseat chronometrical time. If we follow the historian and cultural critic Aziz al-Azmeh, the canonical text not only raises the claim of eternal validity but is also structured a-historically.[35] Canonization is a reconfiguration, so to speak, from a sequence of speeches conditioned by time into an array of timeless individual texts. In place of the historically developing genesis of the text as it unfolds under the eyes of the analytical-historicizing reader, the reader of the canon beholds an original myth, which henceforth covers the text like an opaque screen: namely, the myth of the event, transcending history, of the granting of the scripture to the Prophet. Each individual or collective Qur'an recitation is thus a restaging of the event of revelation, in that it repeats mimetically the act of the physical-acoustic recording of the heavenly writing by the Prophet Muhammad. Thus the universalist character of the Qur'an is drowned out by the emphasis laid on its "Islamic character," its particularistic belonging to one single religious community exclusively, which is conveyed by the daily prayer ritual. Yet this cultic role of the Qur'an over the course of Islamic history was only one of several manifestations of the text, which was simultaneously present as a literary text, as a rhetorical model, and as a kind of score for artistically sophisticated recitations.[36]

34. Sinai, *Studien zur frühen Koraninterpretation*, 1–22.
35. Al-Azmeh, "Chronophagous Discourse," 163–164.
36. On this image, cf. Kermani, *Gott ist schön*, 197–205.

2.3 Orality as Theologumenon

Like the other scriptures, the Qur'an emerged out of an extensive corpus of heterogeneous traditions, from which excerpts eventually crystallized into a coherent writing, a process which occurred through the proclamation to the emerging community. What distinguishes the Qur'anic situation is its specific milieu, in which scripture had already materialized into written codices and become a familiar phenomenon. As Nicolai Sinai has convincingly demonstrated,[37] the emerging Qur'an had to assert itself vis-a-vis Jewish-Christian conceptions of scripture, in order to set out its own claims to authority. It is surprising that in this process it was not the conception of a written manifestation of scripture that was followed, but a new concept, that of an "oral writing was developed. Daniel Madigan first propounded the thesis that "nothing about the Qur'ān suggests that it conceives of itself as identical with the *kitāb* [i.e., the heavenly book],"[38] that is, in no phase of its development did the Qur'an pursue the objective of a closed written corpus. This claim of "an ontological difference between the recitation and its transcendent sources" is linked to certain conditions, as Sinai shows.[39] The first requirement was the consciousness of an essentially oral character as the goal of the Qur'an in its process of formation, independent of the occasional use of writing as a mnemotechnic aid. Secondly, convincing arguments were required to explain the absence of the conventional ceremonial frameworks that surrounded the revealed word of God in the neighboring cultures.

The community's consciousness of the special feature of Qur'anic mediality took shape gradually. It is striking that in the earliest suras, there is not yet explicit language about the divine source of the recitation. Clearly, some time was required before the revelation claim implicit in the Prophetic second-person address was perceived reflexively enough that the problem of the relation of the Qur'an to written models could arise. This development, which was at first gradual, is easily comprehensible in view of the Qur'anic beginnings. The earliest suras stand in an already pre-founded tradition, that of the Psalms; they thus existed in a genre of oral liturgical speech and required no explicit authorization.

The important step toward Qur'anic self-legitimation, toward the introduction of an explicit reference to authority in the texts, was required only later, toward the end of the early Meccan period, and in reaction to a challenge from outside. This can be deduced from verses such as Q 69:40–42:[40]

37. Sinai, "Qur'anic Self-Referentiality."
38. Madigan, *The Qur'ān's Self-Image*, 177.
39. Sinai, "Qur'anic Self-Referentiality," 110.
40. Ibid, 111.

innahu la-qawlu rasūlin karīm
wa-mā huwa bi-qawli shāʿirin qalīlan mā tuʾminūn
wa-lā bi-qawli kāhinin qalīlan mā tadhdhakkarūn

It is the speech of a noble messenger
not the speech of a poet—how little you believe!
Nor the speech of a seer—how little you recall!

An antagonistic "misreading" of the literary genre of the recitation, with implications about its particular type of inspiration, is "corrected," through reference to its divine origin, verse 43: *tanzīlun min rabbi l-ʿālamīn*, "A sending down from the lord of the worlds."

This specific Qur'anic self-referentiality, which legitimizes speech through reference to its transcendent origin, "must thus be understood as having grown up successively out of the process of confrontation with the audience, whose expectations and views had to be convincingly addressed."[41]

2.3.1 Strategies of Justification for the Orality of Scripture

The Qur'an itself confronts the problem of its non-written form and the lack of the paraphernalia of writing. Sinai points to the problematic already raised by Madigan: according to Madigan, the central problem in every attempt to interpret the concept of *kitāb* lies in the fact that the Qur'an understands itself on the one hand as "of a piece with carefully guarded, lavishly appointed, and scrupulously copied sacred codices and scrolls, while itself remaining open-ended, unwritten, and at the mercy of frail human memory."[42] According to Sinai, this tension can best be explained via "a need to balance the obvious situatedness of Muḥammad's recitations with a strategic interest in imparting to them the glow of scripturality that was felt, by his audience, to be an indispensible concomitant of genuine revelations."[43]

The familiar complaint brought against the proclaimer by his opponents is brought to a point in the question in Q 25:32: *law lā nuzzila ʿalayhi l-qurʾānu jumlatan wāḥidatan*, "Why is the reading not sent down to him in one go, as a complete communication?" The incompleteness and situation-boundedness of the message were clearly perceived as defects by the hearers, which set these recitations apart from the conventional manifestations of God's word, and which therefore had to be compensated for through additional forms of authentication, so that they might better correspond to the familiar models. These had to do with writing, since revelation in the Jewish and Christian context was tied to the concept of a written corpus.

41. Ibid.
42. Madigan, *Self-Image*, 45, cited in Sinai, "Qur'anic Self-Referentiality," 113–114.
43. Sinai, "Qur'anic Self-Referentiality," 114.

Sinai sees this compensation realized in a group of early suras, which assert a connection to the heavenly book as a form of authorization. Thus, in Q 80:11–16, the Qur'anic communications are presented as a kind of excerpt from the heavenly original text:

kallā innahu tadhkirah
fa-man shāʾa dhakarah
fī ṣuḥufin mukarrama
marfūʿatin muṭahharah
bi-aydi safarah
kirāmin bararah[44]

No indeed, it is a reminder
—Who so desires may remember it—
inscribed in hallowed scrolls
sublime immaculate
by the hands of scribes
noble, virtuous.

The expectations of the hearers could only be fulfilled in this way because the "heavenly writing" as an emblem of authority was a firm component of the differentiated spiritual conceptions in Late Antiquity. Karel van der Toorn, who has retraced the long process of the Bible's formation as a corpus characterized by scribal culture, points to the conception, common since the books of Enoch (third century BCE) and Daniel (ca. 160 BCE), of the heavenly source of writing, which is accessible to individual Prophets through visions.[45] Such efficacious older traditions concerning heavenly writings as the sources of revelation should also—the real, physical, manifestations of writings in the neighboring traditions notwithstanding—have played a role in the Qur'anic authorization of the message through heavenly writing. The heavenly source of the Qur'anic message is elsewhere designated as a "tablet" (Q 85:22) and somewhat later, in the middle Meccan period, even as "the mother of the script," *umm al-kitāb* (Q 43:4), conceptions which may ultimately go back to the book of Jubilees. This apocryphal work,[46] which posits a heavenly tablet written by divine instruction on which all wisdom and the events of salvation history are recorded, had an intense reception in Late Antiquity and brings to a point the complex conceptions of writing that are reflected in various late books of the Bible.

44. See Q 85:21–22: *bal huwa qurʾānun majīd / fī lawḥin maḥfūẓ*, and 56:77–80.
45. Van der Toorn, *Scribal Culture*, 227–231.
46. Najman, "Interpretation as Primordial Writing"; Grintz, "Jubilees."

2.3.2 *Qurʾān versus Kitāb*

What is the relationship between the performed *qurʾān* and the heavenly *kitāb*? After the two had long been kept neatly separate from each other, the dichotomy between the Qur'anic recollections from the *kitāb* (i.e., biblical recollections) and other types of Qur'anic proclamation increasingly softens in the late Meccan suras: *al-kitāb* becomes the designation of a heavenly "mode of storage," as Sinai formulates it, while *al-qurʾān* comes to refer to earthly realization. But the two are never treated as wholly identical, since the proclaimer does not receive excerpts from the *kitāb* in an unchanged form, but rather these excerpts are adapted to the particular needs of the recipients in the course of their transmission. Sinai stresses this difference, which the Qur'an itself reclaims as a particular hermeneutic coding, even designating it with a particular technical term: *tafṣīl*. The locus classicus for this perception is Q 41:2–3:

tanzīlun mina l-raḥmāni l-raḥīm
kitābun fuṣṣilat āyātuhu qurʾānan ʿarabīyan
li-qawmin yaʿlamūn

A sending down from the Merciful, the Compassionate,
a scripture, whose verses are made distinct
an Arabic reading, for a people who have knowledge.

According to Sinai, *tafṣīl* thus implies a kind of paraphrase of the *kitāb*, by which the texts are adapted to the horizon of the hearers.[47] This observation also throws light on the fact, often perceived with irritation, that individual stories are recalled in more than one place and in differing versions in the Qur'an. In light of the *tafṣīl* hermeneutic, these differing narratives can be seen as successive repetitions of a single *kitāb* pericope, which are formulated anew multiple times and adapted to changing communal situations. Sinai then states: "From the qurʾānic perspective, then, the celestial scripture cannot be given to man in any other shape than *mufaṣṣalan* (Q 6:114). The kitāb is partially accessible, but never available: it can be tapped via divine revelation, but due to the need to tailor such revelations to a specific target audience, the kitāb as such is at no one's disposal, not even in the form of excerpts."[48] Thus, in late Meccan time, the orality of the holy script assumed the rank of a Qur'anic article of belief, a theologumenon—a phenomenon that is unknown in the case of any other scripture.

This being said, the basic conception of the possibility of adapting scripture to the changing situations of the recipients is not specifically Qur'anic, but is already a biblical stereotype. The textual growth of the Bible also incorporates the

47. A similar conception is advocated by Kadi and Mir, "Literature and the Qur'ān.
48. Sinai, "Qur'anic Self-Referentiality," 126.

advent of new expectations in the addressees. Multiple biblical books appeared that retold things already known but provided new aspects to the subject. James Kugel even sees this possibility of "self-actualization" as one of the principles of the Bible's development. The Qur'an, with its retelling of biblical stories, sets itself in this tradition, which was already established in the development of the Bible.[49] Indeed, it puts this praxis into the service of its own oral mediality. Orally communicated versions of the biblical stories are more flexible than written texts; they allow for back-references and even, on the occasion of the renewed performance of an already preached text, of clarifying expansions, a kind of oral glossing.

Only in Medina are there critical reflections on the medium of sacred scripture in human hands.[50] The members of the two older religions are now perceived as competitors vying with the Qur'anic community for the inheritance of the monotheistic tradition, which until that point was available to all, and was not assigned to particular confessions. It is in this function that the members of the older religions in the late Meccan period are designated as "possessors of scripture, *ahl al-kitab*, in their function as "rivals in a contest of inheritance," making claims on the basis of their writings as a kind of "title deed." Their first mention in Q 29:46 already stands in the context of a virtual conflict, which can only be pursued through "fair dispute": *wa-lā tujādilū ahla l-kitābi illā bi-llatī hiya aḥsanu*, "Do not dispute with the people of the scripture, except in a way that is seemly!" This first designation of the members of other religions as *ahl al-kitāb* should be surprising, since it seems to evoke a characteristic also shared by the Qur'anic community. Since there is no disparaging connotation in this quotation, the expression may reproduce a self-designation of the Jews and/or Christians, which perhaps was linked to their most important distinction: Jewish-Christian scripturality against the Qur'anic orality of God's word. In contrast to the scripture that was claimed by these others and reified *materialiter*, the Qur'an remained a "virtual sacred script" at the time of the Prophet, an orally preserved message.

2.4 Late Meccan Reflections on Heavenly and Earthly Scriptures

2.4.1 Announcements and Confirmations of Revelation

The late Meccan suras attest to a greater degree of attention paid to the function and significance of writing. Exegesis now comes to the foreground. The idea of

49. Kugel, *The Bible as It Was*. Furthermore, one could refer to the Targumim, which convey Bible texts not only in a new language but in one that would be appropriate to the expectations of later listeners and readers. Cf. also Shinan, "Midrash on Scripture."

50. On the differentiation made at this time between various kinds of written verses, unambiguous and ambiguous, see Neuwirth, "Mary and Jesus," and cf. chap. 9, 324–327.

God's people, which was already developed in the middle Meccan period, and which implied the idea that election is expressed through the communication of scripture, becomes the key point of a new discourse: the reflection about one's own role in the "scripture," that is, the status and function of the continuously unfolding or already unfolded communications of the heavenly "writing." In view of the expanding circle of hearers, which seem to also have included members of the neighboring religions, these communications had to be reflected on anew. This reflection is mirrored in the late Meccan period not only in later "corrections," that is, additions to older suras, but also in a critique of the handling of writing of the earlier possessors of scripture, whose idealized role comes into doubt in this phase.

The Qur'anic sign theology, according to which God manifests his presence in creation and intext,[51] is refined, so that the successive oral communication of transcendently written pericopes adapted to the respective situations of the hearers comes to be understood as a specifically Qur'anic privilege—this is quite different from the scriptures of the Jews and Christians, which are presented as having been revealed all at once.

In the late Meccan period, the sura structures become stereotyped to such a degree that a particular typus develops for the sura's beginning: the "announcement of revelation,"[52] a form that occurs only twice in the middle Meccan suras (suras 26 and 27).[53] As a rule, it correlates with a later mention of scripture, a "confirmation of revelation," that regularly introduces the sura's closing part. With only six exceptions, all late Meccan suras begin—either implicitly or explicitly deictically[54]—with an introduction that is related to scripture. This incipit sets the tone, so to speak, for the further course of the text, and is referred to again at the close of the sura.

One should perhaps imagine the frequently deictic announcement to have been underscored by gestures. In any case, a ceremonial significance comes to attach itself to this stereotyped beginning, which first becomes frequent in the late Meccan suras. Their introduction authorizes what follows as a speech of transcendent origin, and this is as a rule underlined again by the closing confirmation of revelation. That the recited text is thus itself understood as "signs" or a "sign system" seems to be confirmed by the initiatory naming of letters or letter combinations in the form of minimal textual units.[55] The majority of all late Meccan

51. See chap. 7, 244–277.

52. When labeling both kinds of texts, the term "revelation" is used for the Qur'an despite the preliminary problems with the term, since it most clearly relays the transcendental origin. Cf. chap. 5, passim.

53. Mentions of the Qur'an were also common before, but they rather assumed the form of an oath, see Neuwirth, *Studien zur Komposition*, 264–289.

54. That is, fifteen of twenty-one suras. For the exceptions, meaning those with a different introduction, such as with a hymn in suras 6, 34, 35, or suras without a distinctive introduction, such as Q 16, 29, 30, reference should be made to Neuwirth, *Studien zur Komposition*, 276–313.

55. Cf. chap. 4, 144–146.

suras that are introduced by references to writing also begin with detached letter names, such as for example *ṣād, alif lām rā*, etc. Although there is no consensus in the tradition or in Western research about the function of these letters, their interpretation as representing the smallest elements of the acoustic performance of the word of God seems to be the most convincing. More explicitly, this understanding of the text as signs, which sets before the listener/ reader the epistemic task of decoding, is evinced by its frequent designation as the "signs of scripture," *ayāt al-kitāb*. As in Q 12:1–2:[56]

alif lām rāʾ tilka āyātu l-kitābi l-mubīn
innā anzalnāhu qurʾānan ʿarabīyan laʿallakum taʿqulūn

Alif lam ra. Those are the signs of the clear scripture.
We send it down to be an Arabic reading,
so that you may understand.

The notion of signs of writing is supplemented by the further sign dimension of the hearers' native tongue,[57] through which knowledge (*ʿaql*) will be enacted. The frequency of the description of the *qurʾān* as "Arabic" seems to allow further conclusions: here clearly a transformation is attested, of a universal *kitāb* into a sensorily, aurally perceptible manifestation that serves to communicate the message but exceeds the semantics of the proclamation as something new and unique. In these verses, the Qur'an assumes a new dimension as a transcendent communication, which approaches a hypostasis, an "embodiment," in this case sonic, of the word of God. Nasr Hamid Abu Zaid has spoken in this connection of a "trans-formation" of God's word into the form of the Arabic language.[58]

At the conclusion of the sura, in Q 12:111, the intention standing behind the narration of biblical stories is named:

la-qad kāna fī qaṣaṣihim ʿibratun li-ūlī l-albābi mā kāna ḥadīthan yuftarā wa-lākin taṣdīqan li-lladhī bayna yadayhi wa-tafṣīla kulli shayʾin wa-hudan wa-raḥmatan li-qawmin yuʾminūn

In the telling of them is a lesson to those possessed of minds. It is no story that has been invented, but rather a confirmation of what came before it, a clear explication of all things and a guidance and mercy for a people who believe.

56. Also in suras 10, 11, 13, 28, 31, and 41.
57. On this particular self-referentiality, see Wild, "An Arabic Recitation."
58. See Abu Zaid, *Islam und Politik*, 63; cf. on "inlibration" 92–95.

The written signs confirm the message of the earlier revelations (*taṣdīq*); they set out their message as adapted for the respective proclamation situations (*tafṣīl*)[59] and teach those with understanding (*ūlū l-albāb*).

The introductory announcement of revelation and closing confirmation of revelation correlate also in sura 14, which in its opening verses (1–2) raises the high claim of leading the community out of the condition of ignorance into that of insight:

> *alif lām rā᾽ kitābun anzalnāhu ilayka li-tukhrija l-nāsa mina l-ẓulumāti ilā l-nūri*
>
> Alif lam ra. A scripture, which we have sent down upon you, so that you may lead men from darkness to light.

The initial pronouncement gains further pathos through the following hymnic recollection: *allāhu lladhī lahu mā fī l-samawāti wa-mā fī l-arḍi*, "It is God, to whom what is in heaven and earth belong" (verse 2). This entails an expressive statement about the transcendent dimension of the two works of creation: transcendent writing and cosmos. Yet, despite this sublime origin, scripture should serve the pragmatic goal of the teaching of men. The closing confirmation (verse 52) thus declines to offer an affirmation of the transcendent character, underlining instead the appellatory character of the message for those with understanding (*ūlū l-albāb*).

> *hādha balāghun li-l-nāsi wa-li-yundharū bihi wa-li-ya῾lamū annamā huwa ilāhun wāḥidun wa-li yadhdhakkarū ūlū l-albāb*
>
> This is a proclamation to the people. Let them be warned thereby, and recognize that He is but one God, so that those possessed of minds remember.

In sura 28, the announcement and confirmation of revelation are motivated apologetically (verses 1–3):

> *ṭa sīn mīm*
> *tilka āyātu l-kitābi l-mubīn*
> *natlū ῾alayka min naba᾽i Mūsā wa-Fir῾awna bi-l-ḥaqqi*
> *li-qawmin yu᾽minūn*
>
> Ta sin mim.
> Those are the signs of the clear scripture.
> We recite to you the reports about Moses and Pharaoh in truth,
> to the people who believe.

59. Sinai, "Qur'anic Self-Referentiality."

In this sura opening, the intermediary role of the proclaimer is confirmed alongside the authenticity of the scripture, whereas at the sura's end he is exonerated of the accusation of authorial interference; the sura's conclusion begins thus (verses 85–88):

inna lladhī faraḍa ʿalaya l-qurʾāna la-rādduka ilā maʿādin
qul rabbi aʿlamu man jāʾa bi-l-huda wa-man huwa fī ḍalālin mubīn
wa-mā kunta tarjū an yulqā ilayka l-kitābu illā raḥmatan min rabbika
fa-lā takūnanna ẓahīran li-l-kāfirīn
wa-lā yuṣuddunnaka ʿan āyāti llāhi baʿda idh unzilat ilayka

He who ordained the Qur'an upon you will bring you back to a home place. Say: my Lord knows better, who brings right guidance and who is in clear error.
You had not expected that scripture would come down to you,
it happens only through mercy of your lord.
So do not be a supporter to the unbelievers
And do not turn yourself away from the signs of God, after they have been sent down to you.[60]

This reflection over the status of scripture as a text world that opens itself to the receivers not through their own witnessing (Q 3:44), or through their appropriation of wisdom (Q 18:26–27), but only through inspiration is also thematized elsewhere; cf. Q 29:48.

That the proclaimer himself perceives signs of creation and of scripture as inextricably linked is shown in Q 45:1–6:

ḥā mīm
tanzīlu l-kitābi mina lladhī l-ʿazīzi l-ḥakīm
inna fī l-samawāti wa-l-arḍi la-āyātin li-l-muʾminīn
wa-fī khalqikum . . .
tilka āyātu llāhi natlūhā ʿalayka

Ha mim.
A sending down of scripture from God, the powerful and wise.
In the heaven and the earth are signs for the believers,
And in your creation . . .
Those are signs of God that we recite for you.

The neglect of the signs, which are not specified, is set into a description of hell as a reason for punishment, which is followed by a doxology that closes the sura; Q 45:35:

60. For an example of the resistance to similar misrepresentations, cf. Q29:48–49.

dhālikum bi-annakumu ttakhadhtum āyāti llāhi huquwan wa-gharratkumu l-ḥayātu l-dunyā

That, because you have taken God's signs lightly and this lowly world has beguiled you.[61]

The sign value of scripture is strengthened several times by the sign character of creation. Thus, there is the complaint in the closing part of sura 29, which begins exceptionally without *kitāb*-introduction, that the unbelievers require "[wonder] signs," even while the recitation itself consists of clear signs that can be understood by knowledgeable hearers; Q 29:50–51:

wa-qālū law lā unzila ʿalayhi āyātun min rabbihi qul innamā l-āyātu ʿinda llāhi wa-innamā anā nadhīrun mubīn
a-wa-lam yakfihim annā anzalnā ʿalayka l-kitāba yutlā ʿalayhim

They say: if only a sign came down to him from his Lord!
Say: the signs are with God; I am only a clear warner.
Is it not enough for them that we have sent down the scripture upon you, so that it can be read out to them?

Miracle signs and written signs are indicated through a homonym in Arabic, as in Syriac,[62] which is a shibboleth for the unbelievers, and at the same time a hermeneutic challenge for the pious. In the same sura, and for the first time in the Qur'an, we find mention of the existence of present hearers who are also in possession of scripture, with whom a disputation is clearly underway; Q 29:46:

wa-lā tujādilū ahla l-kitābi illā bi-llati hiya aḥsanu
illā lladhīna ẓalamū minhum
wa-qūlū amannā bi-lladhī unzila ilaynā wa-unzila ilaykum
wa-ilāhunā wa-ilāhukum wāḥidun
wa-naḥnu lahu muslimūn

Do not dispute with the people of the scripture except in a seemly way— save those who do wrong—
and say: we believe in what has been sent down to us and to you,
your God and our God are one, and to Him we submit.

Although the exhortation does not allow us to draw precise conclusions about the concrete content of the exegetical controversy, it transpires that the previous imagination of being able to deal with biblical tradition autonomously has begun to totter.

61. Furthermore cf. Q42:1–2, taken up again in Q42:48–49.
62. On the Qur'anic theology of signs in more detail, chap. 7, 264–277.

2.4.2 *Decryption of Signs as a Touchstone among the Receivers of Scripture*

While the signs (*āyāt*) still serve in these texts as pointers toward insights into the truthfulness and divine origin of one's own scripture,[63] they elsewhere become the object of struggle between religious parties. Sura 11 begins:

alif lām rāʾ kitābun uḥkimat āyātuhu
thumma fuṣṣilat min ladun ḥakīmin khabīr

Alif lam ra. A writing, of which the signs are set right,
and then made distinct from on high by one wise and knowing.

The hymnic statement is relativized at the beginning of the sura's close, which is not a confirmation of revelation of the Qur'anic message but rather confirms the revelation character of earlier messages, namely, the scripture of Moses. The message to Moses has triggered dissent, Q 11:110:

wa-la-qad ataynā Mūsā l-kitāba fa-khtulifa fīhi
wa-law lā kalimatun sabaqat min rabbika la-quḍiya baynahum
wa-innahum la-fī shakkin minhu murīb

We gave Moses the scripture, and disputes arose concerning it.
Were it not for a prior word from your Lord
judgment would have been passed upon them.
They are in perplexing doubts concerning it.[64]

Sura 10 begins similarly with an announcement of scripture signs; Q 10:1:

alif lām rāʾ tilka āyātu l-kitābi l-ḥakīm

Alif lam ra. Those are signs of the wise scripture.

Here too, the closing part of Q 10:93 makes reference not to the Qur'anic message but to the benefactions granted to the Israelites, and the same disunity is stated:

la-qad bawwaʾnā banī Isrāʾīla mubawwaʾa ṣidqin
wa-razaqnāhum mina l-ṭayyibāti
fa-mā khtalafū ḥattā jāʾahumu l-ʿilmu
inna rabbaka yaqḍī baynahum yawma l-qiyāmati
fī-ma kānū fīhi yakhtalifūn

63. Further suras, which argue apologetically in the opening section and/or closing section based on the signs of scripture and creation, are sura 46 (verse 1 and 29ff.), 40 (verse 1 and 77ff.), 39 (verse 1 and 41ff.), and 31 (verse 1 and 20ff.).

64. Also the case in sura 32, which in the closing section (verses 22–25) depicts the collapse of consensus; accordingly also Q41:1 and 41ff.

We have given to the Israelites an abode befitting the just
and supplied them with good things.
They quarreled not until knowledge came to them.
Your Lord will judge between them on the day of resurrection,
about that over which they quarreled.

The dissent is not named explicitly, but in terms of religious history it is probably best to think here of the Jewish-Christian schism, which also resonates in the polemical commentary on the story of Jesus in sura 43.[65] What is important is that the historical fact of the splitting of the earlier communities on account of disagreement over the meaning of given signs compromises them as predecessors of the community. The new community must rely on itself to cope with its problems. They now confront the hermeneutic problem that persists until the end of the Meccan period, that of communicating the signs probatively to those who do not yet believe: sura 30, which begins without a *kitāb* introduction, contains the passage Q 30:52–53:

fa-innaka lā tusmiʿu l-mawtā wa-lā tusmiʿu l-ṣumma l-duʿāʾa
idhā wallaw mudbirīn
wa-mā anta bi-hādi l-ʿumyi ʿan ḍalālatihim
in tusmiʿu illā man yuʾminu bi-āyātinā fa-hum muslimūn

You will not make the dead hear, nor make the deaf hear the call,
if they turn and walk away.
Nor can you guide the blind away from their error.
You will only make hear those who believe in our signs
and submit themselves.

The passage closes with a controversy over the much disputed Late Antique textual type of the parable (*mathal*), in which the Qur'anic speaker recognizes a particular medium for authorization of the message, but which is a weak point of his rhetoric in the eyes of the opponents. Q 30:58–60 states:[66]

wa-la-qad ḍarabnā li-l-nāsi fī hādhā l-qurʾāni min kulli mathalin,
wa-laʾin jiʾtahum bi-āyatin, la- yaqūlanna lladhīna kafarū,
in antum illā mubṭilūn
ka-dhālika yaṭbaʿu llāhu ʿalā qalbi lladhīna lā yaʿlamūn
fa-ṣbir inna waʿda llāhi ḥaqqun
wa-lā yastakhiffanka lladhīna lā yūqinūn

65. See chap. 8, 300–301.
66. See chap. 8., 305–310.

We have struck for people in this reading all kinds of parables. But when you bring them a sign/verse, those who disbelieve speak:
you only put forward what is preposterous.
So does God stamp the hearts of those who do not understand.
Have patience, the promise of God is true.
And be not disheartened by those who are not convinced.

Resignation is expressed even more drastically in sura 13, although the beginning confirms both the character of scripture as revelation and the election of the proclaimer, Q 13:1:

alif lām rāʾ tilka āyātu l-kitābi
wa-lladhī unzila ilayka min rabbika l-ḥaqqu

Alif lam ra. Those are the signs of the scripture.
What was sent down by your Lord to you is the truth.

The close of the sura, which again confirms the sending of the proclaimer, also complains of the stubborn unbelief of the opponents, who are not impressed even by the long history of punishment sentences. Even exceedingly clear signs such as miracles remain unnoticed, as Q 13:30–31 states:

ka-dhālika arsalnāka fī ummatin qad khalat min qablihā umamun
li-tatluwa ʿalayhimu lladhī awḥaynā ilayka
wa-hum yakfurūna bi-l-raḥmāni . . .
wa-law anna qurʾānan suyyirat bihi l-jibālu
aw quṭiʿat bihi l-arḍu aw kullima bihi l-mawtā
bal li-llāhi l-amru jamīʿan[67]

We have sent you to a nation, before whom many nations have passed away,
so that you may recite to them what has been inspired in you,
while they do not believe in the Merciful . . .
Even if it were a reading wherewith mountains are moved from their place,
or the earth is cut into pieces, or the dead are spoken to. Indeed, this entire matter is God's.

The signs themselves are not thrown into question by the failed handling of scripture by the earlier peoples, nor by the doubt of those without understanding. Nor are they shaken in their truth value by the "possessors of scripture," who appear on the stage later in Medina, and whose polemic brings to light the existence of divergences between the old and new scriptures.[68] Already in Mecca, one sees a

67. Sura 7 commences similarly, and it also remains apologetic in the closing mention of the proclamation.

68. In the dispute with these new adversaries, there was an increase in the frequency of the introduction of arguments that had already been tried and tested in the long tradition of biblical scriptural apologetics. See Lazarus-Yafeh, *Intertwined Worlds*, 19–28.

softening of the erstwhile firm conviction in the persuasive power of the scripture, as the sura dispenses in its final part with the positive confirmation of revelation and replaces it with the mention of the scripture of Moses with its schismatic consequences, thus sending out a negative signal. Though this reorientation does not affect the announcement of revelation at the start of the suras, which remains stable due to its ceremonial function, the previously prevailing ring composition of the late Meccan suras is broken. This maceration of the composition, alongside the replacement of the narrative section by a discursive middle part, which also occurs in the late Meccan period, is a further step toward a freer, or at least less predictable, sura structure.

But faith in scripture as such remains unshaken. The scriptural signs of God are presented as beyond measure. Q 31:27 takes up an idea also familiar from the Bible:

wa-law annamā fī l-arḍi min shajaratin aqlāmun
wa-l-baḥru yamudduhu min baʿdihi sabʿatu abḥurin
mā nafadat kalimātu llāhi inna llāha ʿazīzun ḥakīm

If all the trees of the earth were writing pens
and the sea [full of ink] extended so that beyond it were seven more seas, still the words of God would not be exhausted; God is powerful and wise.

2.5 Inlibration or Qur'anic Logos Theology?

The designation reserved for the members of the older religions, *ahl al-kitāb*, literally "people of scripture," which already occurs once in a neutral sense in a late Meccan sura (Q 29:50), becomes in Medina an expression of a decidedly critical perception of the Jewish and Christian treatment of scripture, to which is now ascribed an exclusivist and particularist bias that eliminates the new believers.

The very concept *ahl al-kitāb* has long been treated as an ideal starting point for interreligious dialogue.[69] The essential commonality between the three religions seemed to lie in their shared access to scriptures with a monotheistic message. According to this paradigm, Muhammad becomes a figure corresponding to Christ, in that both brought a message that would become a scripture.[70] But the fact that this analogy does not hold has long been recognized. What should instead be seen as analogous, as Stefan Wild and Daniel Madigan have stressed, are

69. Madigan, "Gottes Botschaft an die Welt."

70. This parallelization is the main content of the inscriptions in the Dome of the Rock from the year 691, which include almost exclusively Qur'anic verses; see Neuwirth, "The Spiritual Meaning of Jerusalem."

Christ and the Qur'an.[71] Madigan, who follows the traces of this insight through early Islamic theological history investigating the concept *kitāb*, "writing," arrives to the image of the Qur'an as a hypostasis of God's word.

But what we still lack is an investigation of the Qur'anic proclamation itself as to development of the understanding of the received word of God. The question arises to what extent the reception of the message was understood already by the community itself through the categories of Jewish or Christian logos-theology. The Qur'an was constituted in Late Antiquity, a period in which scripture-discourse had become highly differentiated. Alongside scripture, other forms of the appearance of God's word had manifested themselves by this time, such as wisdom, Sophia, or the "word," *memra* (Aramaic for logos), that functions to communicate divine knowledge to men. The perception of the divine logos, *memra,* at work in the world, which was upheld in early synagogue Judaism, but which—as a "second power in heaven,"[72]—was to draw heavy polemics from the rabbis, in Christian tradition is interpreted Christologically, most emphatically in the prologue of John.[73] The word of God, embodied in the logos or even incarnate in Christ, thus takes its place alongside the divine self-communication through scripture. This increase in complexity in the understanding of the word of God is reflected not only in the later treatment of the Qur'an, whose formal recitation in the Friday communal worship stands in the position of the Eucharist of the Christian service,[74] but also already in the genesis of the Qur'an itself. It has left behind clear traces, above all in the much-recited prologue to sura 55.[75]

2.5.1 *Preexistence of the Qurʾān?*

2.5.1.1 *Traces of a Logos Theology in the Qur'an*

This prologue (Q 55:1–4) presents a praise of the Qur'an as the preexistent word of God, in a solemn-pathetic tone that is unexampled elsewhere in the entire text corpus. With its linguistic style and its theological claim, it raises the expectation that an authoritative pronouncement from the older traditions is being answered.

al-Raḥmān
ʿallama l-qurʾān
khalaqa l-insān
ʿallamahu l-bayān

71. Wild, *Mensch, Prophet*, 6. Recognition of this problem was primarily advanced by Madigan, "Gottes Botschaft an die Welt." Madigan refers to Nathan Söderblom (1866–1931) as the first advocate of the analogy Christ-Qur'an.

72. Segal, *Two Powers*.

73. See Boyarin, *Borderlines*, 89–127; Boyarin, "The Gospel of the Memra."

74. On the dispute between early theologians, for whom the proximity of the Qur'an to the incarnate word of God itself became a problem, see van Ess, *Theologie und Gesellschaft*, 4:615, 6:411; Thomas, *Early Muslim Polemic against Christianity*, 37–59. On the Islamic dogma of the "inimitability of the Qur'an," cf. chap. 13, 458–462.

75. Cf. chap. 3, 125–127.

The compassionate,
He taught the reading,
He created man
And taught him understanding / clear speech.

The word *qurʾān* in verse 2 raises problems. It cannot mean the later-achieved text corpus, nor can it mean the praxis of recitation. That something else is intended here, something that transcends history and reality, comes out already from the naming of *qurʾān* before the naming of the act of creation. The power of divine-human communication that is at work here shows clear similarity to logos conceptions, which present this power as an intermediary between the divine and human spheres.

The particularly solemn form of the sura prologue is striking. It may have originated in a competitive situation, through the necessity of offering an equivalent to an already available and similarly outstanding text. Such a theological key text within the Christian tradition, dedicated to the same phenomenon of the word of God, is the prologue to the Gospel of John (Jo 1:1–5). As Daniel Boyarin has shown,[76] this text reflects a wisdom literature midrash on the creation report preserved in the Targumim, which tells of the *memra* that descends into the world in order to strengthen the bond between God and man, but which fails in this and. In the Christian version of the prologue it is only able to accomplish its work through incarnation.

In the beginning was the word,
And the word was by God, and God was the word.
The same was in the beginning by God
All things are created through it, without it nothing is created.
In it was life, and life was the light of men.
Light shines in the darkness, but the darkness has not taken it. . . .
He was in the world, the world arose through him, but they rejected him.

A short comparison of the texts yields no truly consistent parallels: both prologues present the word of God as preexistent—in the sura this is named simply as *qurʾān*, and is therefore not terminologically distinct from the Qur'an text itself. But the *qurʾān* possesses no power of creation, which belongs only to God. Rather, God manifests himself in the communication of wisdom insofar as it is "taught" (verse 2); the Qur'anic logos thus appears, not unlike the Torah in earlier Jewish tradition, in the form of the revelation. Its fate among men is not disclosed, but there is no indication either of its failure. The failure of the logos attested by the older traditions is avoided in the Qur'anic view through divine intervention. For the addressees are prepared for its reception, as shown by verse

76. Boyarin, "The Gospel of the Memra."

4, which displays yet another trace of the logos: *'allamahu l-bayān*, "he taught him understanding." This capability of understanding, which is granted to man, enables him to receive the logos. At the same time, it lends plausibility to the Qur'anic conception of the world as a sign system that man must read—a vision that recalls Philo's conception of the *kosmos noetos*, the archetypal world of ideas, which has its origin in logos and is made amenable to understanding through logos.[77] Thus on the one hand logos is hypostasized as *qur'ān*, as authoritative power that manufactures human-divine communication, and on the other hand logos is represented through the capability of understanding given to men by God, his *bayān*, through which the world becomes intelligible. A very particular significance thus comes to adhere to language, which again recalls Philo's logos teaching. "Philo idealizes language more than man. For him, the ideal language does not at all belong to the realm of createdness. It rather seems to have preexisted with God Himself."[78] In the Qur'an, this dimension of the logos is represented through *bayān*, which oscillates in meaning, and which can mean "clear speech," as well as "faculty of understanding."

Certainly, the thrust of the sura prologue is different from that of the Gospel's prologue. It does not aim to raise the logos up to a "second power in the heaven," as rabbinic polemic found objectionable in the early Jewish logos-teaching. Rather, the Qur'anic logos manifests itself in divine teaching and in the epistemic proliferation of creation. The Late Antique and Qur'anic conceptions of the working of the logos on the world are thus different. Yet it should not be overlooked that sura 55 engages with logos conceptions and reinterprets them in the light of the new manifestation of God's word. As the text treats the working of the logos from a new perspective, not as failure but rather as divinely prepared success, it inverts the negative prehistory of the Johannite incarnation. Since the logos is not dismissed but rather adopted, the theological necessity of incarnation is invalid. Although the logos given by the *qur'ān* does not possess far-reaching powers in comparison to the Jewish-Christian equivalent, it is still the logos that successfully penetrates the world and works in it. This initial investigation of a single text makes the exploration of the Qur'an's self-referentiality for further logos references appear a promising avenue of research.[79]

2.5.2 *Inlibration?*

What could be set in parallel, then, both in terms of theological history and in terms of the Qur'anic pronouncements themselves, is the becoming-human of

77. On the forces involved in Logos and Sophia, see Schäfer, *Weibliche Gottesbilder im Judentum*, 64–68.

78. Niehoff, "What Is in a Name?" 224, cited in Boyarin, "The Gospel of the Memra," 115.

79. The power to produce order is, however, granted to the Qur'an through the force of liturgical texts. An extensive litany commemorating the Laylat al-Qadr names a number of beneficial interventions in creation, which are solicited "through the Qur'an," *bi l-qur'ān*. (The age of these texts, which is taken for granted in contemporary usage, is difficult to determine.)

God's word in Christ, and the "becoming Qur'an" of God's word. The historian of philosophy Harry A. Wolfson attempted to bring the relationship between these two to a point with the neologism "inlibration," which he coined for this purpose.[80] The Qur'an would then be the embodiment in book form of God's word, just as Christ is the word's embodiment in the flesh. For the historian of philosophy, this abbreviation will possess particular suggestive power. At least on first view, it seems that later reflections over the eternality or createdness of the Qur'an cannot be imagined in isolation from the Christological challenge. Already soon after the death of the Prophet, the recording of the Qur'an on the "preserved tablet" appeared to some traditionists to have been accomplished *before* the creation of the world;[81] but it was only later, after the objections voiced by the rational theologians of the Mu'tazila, who felt the closeness to Christology to be a threat and who were partisans of the createdness of the Qur'an, that the preexistence of the Qur'an as a divine attribute became a precondition for correct belief in Sunni theology.[82] And it was only later still that its eternality became dogma.[83]

But even outside of theological speculation, the parallels between the becoming-human and "becoming Qur'an" of God's word go even further: the philosopher of religion Seyyed Nasr writes that "the medium of the divine message in Christianity is the Virgin Mary, while in Islam it is the soul of the Prophet,"[84] thus making a parallel between the virginity of Mary and the traditionally maintained illiteracy of the Prophet: just as Mary bore a child although she "knew no man" and God's work was thus accomplished, so according to Islamic tradition Muhammad is presented as wholly untouched by previously acquired knowledge of scripture. *Al-nabī al-ummī* (Q 7:157–158) is thus understood as "illiterate prophet,"[85] so that the Qur'an can be recognized as a purely divine work.

Despite these incontestable parallels, which were already recognized in early Islamic history, some skepticism regarding the designation "inlibration" is required, as Madigan has already pointed out. The designation not only reads Islamic phenomena through a Christian lens, transferring onto Islam the myth-imprinted Christian thought figure of the divine assumption of corporeality, despite the fact that Islam is broadly amythical and myth-critical. Even more misleading is the fact that the suggestion of an entelechy "book" or "writing" leads wrongly to the assumption that "while the Christians believe in a living, active and personal word of God, the Muslims have only a closed canon, dead

80. Wolfson, *The Philosophy of the Kalam*, 244–245.

81. See Madigan, "Preserved Tablet"; Maalouf, *La place du verbe*.

82. Madigan, "Gottes Botschaft an die Welt."

83. See van Ess, *Theologie und Gesellschaft*, 4:628.

84. Seyyed Nasr, *Ideals and Realities of Islam*, 43ff.

85. See Günther, "The Illiterate Prophet." This interpretation is not tenable in historical-critical scholarship. In the Qur'an, the designation of the proclaimer as *al-nabī al-ummī* designates rather his affiliation with the "faithful among the (non-Jewish) peoples"; see chap. 11, 402–405.

letters."[86] This sounds something like the Pauline polemic against the "dead letters" of the law, which are contrasted to the "heart writing" of the Christian Bible. But it is just such a writing of the heart that is reclaimed for Islam by the Muslim religious philosopher Seyyed Nasr, in arguing for the analogy Christ-Qur'an, when he claims that the medium of the divine message in Christianity is the Virgin Mary, while in Islam it is the soul of the Prophet.[87] We cannot deny in substance the analogy Christ-Qur'an that already struck some early Islamic theologians, whose verdict *makhlūq*, "created," can be recognized as a negative echo to the Nicene *genēthenta ou poiēthenta*, Arabic *mawlūd ghayr makhlūq*, "born, not created."[88] But the term "Qur'an" must be filled out differently. Thus, Seyyed Nasr does not speak explicitly of the Qur'an's manifestation as a book as analogue to Christ. This would scarcely be conceivable for a Muslim, because the written character of the Qur'an is only one, and by no means the central, manifestation of the divine message. The central manifestation is instead the recitation, performed by heart. What must be maintained then is the analogy of logos embodiment: the incarnated word of God in Christianity and the acoustically present word of God in Islam.

One cannot capture the dimension of significance of logos in the Qur'an if one reduces the Qur'an to its message. Hartmut Stegemann notes: "Bible and Qur'an are not merely 'holy scriptures'; beyond that, in both religions, they are the 'word of God,' but in quite different senses."[89] These differing "self-understandings in Islam and Christianity" that are illuminated by Stegemann cannot be reduced to contrasting statements: "For Islam, the Qur'an is the *direct word of God*, formulated by Allah himself and communicated only to the Prophet Muhammad. The Qur'an is a gift from God, which guides men rightly and enables them to lead their lives according to the directives of God. For Christians on the other hand, their Bible is only indirectly the word of God. It becomes the word of God in the sermon. . . . Apart from that, the Bible is at the same time the word of humans. . . . The Bible is testimony . . . on a scale that is personal."[90] Here, the evidence of the Qur'an itself is ignored, which never speaks of a pre-formulation by God (according to Stegemann, "Allah"). The Qur'an not only is "writing" and "word of God in the sense of right guidance," but also claims for itself, already during the course of the proclamation, the status of a unique, sensorily perceptible *self-manifestation* of God's word—its own reception of logos theology.

Nasr Hamid Abu Zaid has offered a challenging contribution to the clarification of the Christian-Islamic analogy, which, as Andreas Meier emphasizes,

86. Madigan, "Gottes Botschaft an die Welt."

87. Cf. note 84 above.

88. Thus, we can see here an attempt within the proclamation of the Qur'an to avoid proximity to a Trinitarian idea of God; see Nader, *Le systeme philosophique*, 101, and Maalouf, *La place du verbe*, 85–107.

89. Stegemann, "Gedanken zum Johannesprolog," 178.

90. Ibid.

draws for illustration on the concept of transformation (*taḥawwul*), which is related to traditional Christian dogma: "The Arabic language represents the medium of the Islamic revelation, into which and through which the transformation becomes real, just as flesh and blood, namely, Mary, represent in Christianity the medium into which and through which the transformation is made real." Meier's interpretation, that the "paradoxical reality of incarnation must be taken seriously in a view toward the Qur'an and humanity," is certainly applicable.[91] Abu Zaid's observation, which gives terminological priority to an early Islamic position,[92] gains even more weight if one considers the Qur'anic-Christian analogy not simply as a fait accompli, nor, as has been done up to now, merely as an object of early Islamic theological discussion, but rather takes into view the epistemic relationship with the Late Antique and incarnate logos that developed over the course of the revelation of the Qur'an. The observation then shows itself to be an important corrective to the inlibration theory, which is so widely taken at face value.

It is then not that a book stands in place of the incarnation as the embodiment of God's word, but rather, as Madigan also stresses, that a sensorily perceptible acoustic-linguistic manifestation takes on this status, which does not first come to the fore in the tradition studied by Madigan but is inherent in the Qur'an itself. A religious conversation with Islam that does not aim to remain arbitrarily selective therefore would gain substantially from a diachronic reading of the Qur'an. For the determination of the Qur'anic relation to Christian traditions, the negotiations of logos theology, that is, the dialectic of the Qur'anic self-localization in relation to the surrounding logos conceptions, must be taken into account—a task that can only be accomplished through a diachronic treatment of the Qur'an.

2.6 Medialities of the Qur'an

2.6.1 *The Restaging of the Sending Down in Recitation*

Writing is just one of the medialities of the Qur'an. With the conclusion of the canonization of the Qur'an, at the very latest, a third, new foundational experience is thus set beside the Old Testament and Christian myth of origin. Not the inscription of the tablets of the law for Moses as the document of God's covenant with the elected people nor the notion of "love as fulfilment of the law" guaranteed by Christ's self-sacrifice (Romans 13:10), but rather the divine teaching, continuously over many years, of God's verbal addresses to Muhammad and his

91. Meier, "Gottes Wort in Knechtsgestalt," 71–73, cited in Elsas, "Religionswissenschaftliche Vermittlung," 185–186.

92. Here we can think of someone like Ibn Kullāb, a contemporary of Ibn Ḥanbal, according to whom the message communicated by Gabriel to the Prophet is only a rendition, not the direct word of God; see van Ess, *Theologie und Gesellschaft*, vol. 4, 614–615.

community, stands as the central event in Islamic self-understanding. In comparison to this event, what is narrated in the Qur'an about other Prophets is downsized to the status of typological precedents. Since the speech of God is recalled as a decisive event of listening, the Qur'an remains, even later, chiefly an acoustic experience. From the very beginning, there is a particular "language" of the Qur'an that adheres to its acoustic realization.

According to Islamic tradition, the Qur'anic message begins with the challenge to announce the divine word: "Read, *iqra'*, in the name of your lord, who created" (Q 96:1). This verse is traditionally interpreted as the first divine address to the Prophet. Although what stands behind this exhortation maybe a current liturgical exhortation familiar from the Jewish and Christian tradition, the verse remains emblematic of the early Meccan suras, in which the occurrence of the proclamation, *qur'an*, is a central theme. Navid Kermani has justly spoken of the Qur'an as a score, which requires a musical resetting for its realization.[93] Indeed, the speech of God is cultic speech, which can only be adequately reflected through the backing of the text by a cantilena. This sacral performance of the text is not a new discovery of the Qur'anic community but rather an answer to the forms of worship of the plural cultures in the milieu of the Qur'an's emergence, which however assumes a central significance for Islam.

Already for the earliest Qur'anic community, the recited Qur'an had its own setting in life, its *Sitz im Leben* in ritual prayer, which in its form, fixed at the latest in the second Islamic century but probably already during Muhammad's ministry, and valid down to today, consists of a sequence of short formulas accompanied by gestures and, as its most crucial component, several instances of Qur'an recitation. Through this ceremony, the worshipper exits the profane frame of time and space and enters a sacral state that includes him in an imaginary simultaneity with all the other worshipers and places him in a spatial proximity to the central sanctuary. This sacral frame opens a space for different degrees of spiritual fulfillment, which were described by the medieval theologian Muḥammad al-Ghazālī (1058–1111): "If I recite, I hear the Qur'an immediately just as if a reciter performed it for me, then with greater profundity, as if the Prophet recited it for me, and then finally I hear it as if it were spoken out by God himself."[94] It is not by chance that the Qur'an's physical-spiritual reception, accomplished through recitation, has been compared with the taking-into-self of the Eucharist in Christian ritual.[95] Not the book, then, but the recitation is the manifestation of God's word approachable by humans.[96]

93. Cf. the discussion of the sura in chap. 7, 248–252.
94. Al-Ghazālī, *Iḥyā'*, 1:402.
95. Cf. Wild, *Mensch, Prophet.*
96. Cf. Lacocque, *Apocalyptic Symbolism.*

The anthropologist Kristina Nelson has referred to the Qur'an as a text that is oral in its very being.[97] In fact, one can easily extract the Qur'anic determination for recitation out of the text structure itself. Not only does the Qur'an consist of verses, first of short, rhythmically catchy poetic verses and later of long and syntactically complex speech units that manifests themselves as verses through their rhyming end colons.[98] It is also structured rhetorically so that units of sense and breath coincide—differently, for example, from the case in the speech units of the Hebrew Bible, the Gospels, or the letters of Paul. Namely, in its early parts the Qur'an comes very near to the Psalms or the speeches of the biblical prophets. But even in its later suras, where one must speak of artistic prose rather than poetry, the Qur'an is rhetorical to a very high degree. Here, in place of the tonally marked rhymes, closing clausulas are now formed, which allow the text to be scanned not only rhythmically but also semantically, or theologically, so to speak, again and again introducing references to transcendence into the text. Thus, many of the long narrative Qur'an verses end with a closing clausula such as *inna llāha l-samīʿu l-baṣīr*, "God is the hearing, the seeing" (Q 17:1), or *inna llāha yuḥibbu l-muqṣiṭīn*, "God loves those who act justly" (Q 60:8). These commentary formulas sprinkle divine evaluations of justly repaid human deeds or references to God's ubiquitous presence and almighty power throughout the text. The commenting clausulas are not monotone interruptions that halt the flow of speech, as is often claimed in the critical literature; rather, through their linking back of all events to the will of God, they form the backbone of Qur'anic discourse.[99] It is no wonder, then, that in the praxis of recitation they undergo a particular melodic design, similarly to the concluding half verses in Gregorian choral. The sacral recitation of the Qur'an is thus designed to strengthen the significance of the transcendent origin of the Qur'an, which has come to be regarded as so central in recent times. This particular speech praxis also re-enacts the emergence of the Qur'an, which is said in the origin myth to have come from a process of divine oral inspiration.

But independently of the linkage to prayer, Qur'an reading, as Andreas Kellermann stresses, is "in itself already ritual."[100] It creates a unity of reader and hearer that would never exist in a solitary reception of a written text. The performance as a "ceremonial making present of the social stock of sense"[101] repeats the proclaimed truth not with the goal of the communication of information but rather as "practiced wisdom," in order for "institutionalized forms of coming together" to come into existence.[102] A striking example of this is the widespread praxis in the countries of the Maghreb, especially Morocco and Algeria, of group

97. Nelson, *Art of Reciting*.
98. See chap. 5, 321–324.
99. See Neuwirth, "Yūsuf-Sure"; cf. chap. 13, 472–477.
100. Kellermann, " 'Die Mündlichkeit' des Koran."
101. Assmann, "Nachwort," 270.
102. Ibid., 274.

reading (*qirāʾa jamāʿīya*), in which those who have learned the Qur'an by heart or are currently learning it meet daily in order to recite together a thirtieth part of the Qur'an, *juz*, at a very fast tempo. This group reading is also practiced on festive occasions.[103] The performance, described in detail by Kellermann, is concerned above all with the rules of pronunciation, "orthoepy" (*tajwīd*), and the melodic shaping of the reading.[104] While the orthoepy of *tajwīd* within the canon of knowledge is no more than a propadeutic for the science of reading,[105] the *tajwīd* rules remain practically indispensable for the Qur'an reader.

> They come to be considered as a component of the text itself, so that their omission counts as a distortion of the text and thus a sin: *man lam yujawwidi l-qurʾāna athīm*, "He who does not recite the Qur'an with *tajwīd* is sinful."[106] We see here a clear position that emerged in the course of the tradition, taking the Qur'an to be the word of God even on the level of its expression; *tajwīd* preserves the text's archaic language condition, which guarantees the distinction of the divine speech from colloquial language and intensifies the effect of secondary complexity generated through poetic means, as it controls the text's intonation.[107]

Regarding the melodic forming of the reading, two styles are distinguished: *murattal* and *mujawwad*. The former is a relatively unadorned style used in teaching and liturgy, "characterized by a stereotyped melodic course. The emphasis lies in the exact realization of *tajwīd* rules. The latter, on the other hand, is formed as art music, characterized by frequent repetitions of single passages, strong contrasts of registers, and an interaction with the listeners that is articulated through cheers."[108] Kellermann concludes his presentation of the conditions of the Qur'anic performance thus: "A classification of the Qur'an into the category of purely written literature must . . . appear inadequate. The designation of the Prophet as author of the Qur'an, which was often adopted automatically by earlier Orientalists, is rooted in this kind of treatment, whereby the text is uprooted from its social situation and, in Goody's words, 'decontextualized,' thus having to rely on a 'name that supports it.' "[109] In contrast to this, the Qur'an always requires performance in a ritual context. Here, the individual metaphysical experience of the Prophet as the addressee of the revelation and sender of the message in its reenactment becomes a sonic experience that always manifests itself again as new and different, in which the personal religiosity of the reader finds its medium

103. Kellermann, *Koranlesung im Maghreb*, describes this in detail.
104. Kellermann also dwells on the particular of the text used (*qirāʾāt*); cf. chap. 4, 149–155.
105. Bergsträsser and Pretzl, *Geschichte des Korantexts*, 232.
106. Thus Ibn al-Jazarī in his didactic *tajwīd* poem, the so-called *Jazarīya*, 13.
107. Kellermann, "Die 'Mündlichkeit' des Koran," 18.
108. Ibid., 22.
109. Assmann and Assmann, "Nachwort," 276.

of expression, so that he has the possibility to encode his "I" for the purpose of "knowledge and determination of his own wisdom."[110] The ritual of Qur'an reading consists in the personal reliving of the act of revelation, so that not only an "initial speech act" but also the positioning of the receiver and of the contemporary oral transmitters are comprehended as a means toward the public glorification of God—and that is much more than can be represented with writing."[111]

It is notable that the aural performance of the Qur'an in no way remains limited to the private and collective cultic sphere, but also exists in more recent times as a means of the proliferation of the Qur'an alongside the printed volume. Since the 1960s, alongside the printed *muṣḥaf*, the "codex," there also exists a *muṣḥaf murattal*, a "recited codex." In 1961, Egyptian radio broadcast the first complete recording of the Qur'an, recited by the highest authority in Qur'an recitation at the time in al-Azhar University, Mahmud al-Husari.[112] Since then, innumerable recordings by various readers have become available, which are distributed on all the newest audio devices. Although already in the 1930s audio records of Qur'an readings were being produced and individual Qur'an recordings were broadcast on radio,[113] the regular radio broadcast of the *muṣḥaf murattal* represents something new. With the *muṣḥaf murattal*, according to Andreas Kellermann, "we find an intention that goes well beyond mere conservation, and throws light on the Muslim understanding of the Qur'an: namely, the usage of modern mass media for the maintenance of the tradition of performance of the Qur'an vis-à-vis the progressive textualization of Islamic culture. . . . For even today, with the unlimited written reproducibility and availability of the Qur'an, the conception has not been abandoned that the text must be made into sound in performance'[114]

2.6.2 *Writing as Coding*

The Qur'an not only is ubiquitous in discourse through its text, and in sound through its recitation, but also proliferates as calligraphy in Islamic art, so that one can speak of the visual as a further "language" of the Qur'an. The Arabic alphabet itself, although fully developed only through the praxis of Qur'an writing, is already a theme in the Qur'an itself: twenty-nine suras begin with the naming of one or several letter names, such as *ṣād, alif lām mīm*, etc.[115] The heavenly writing paraphernalia, the reed pen and above all the writing tablet, also play a striking role in the Qur'an and can be seen at the intersection of important developments, in a phase of the community's new orientation toward a writing-supported

110. Lotman, *Die Struktur literarischer Texte*, 101.

111. Kellermann, "Die 'Mündlichkeit' des Koran," 22.

112. Cf. Al-Sa'id, *al-Jam' al-Ṣawtī*; on its reception, see "Die 'Mündlichkeit' des Koran," 1–3.

113. On the reception, which was initially met with skepticism among religious scholars, see Jomier, "La place du Coran."

114. Kellermann, "Die 'Mündlichkeit' des Koran," 2.

115. On these letters groups, misleadingly denoted in scholarship as "ciphers," see chap. 4, 144–145.

biblically inspired self-understanding. Indeed, we can see an analogy between what occurred for Arabic culture in the genesis of the Qur'an and what has been described for various ancient cultures by Jan Assmann as a transition from "ritual" to "textual coherence" that occurs with the onset of writing.[116] After an early phase, in which the new proclamation still stood in the frame and context of the Kaaba rites, a profound process of change can be observed in the early Meccan community, namely, from an ancient Arab self-positioning to a biblically imprinted one. The biblical stories that had up to that point been evoked in short allusions now come to the foreground, and the protagonists of the early historical narratives, ancient figures of the Arabian Peninsula, give way to biblical figures, while the Holy Land itself—though less as a geographical space than a spatial oscillation between heaven and earth—enters as a backdrop in place of ancient Arabia. The biblical sacred-historical past, set in place of the inherited historical memory, crystalizes into a text world that competes with the now-problematic Meccan realities. This "other world" is referred to in gestures, enacted in prayer: through the new direction of prayer toward Jerusalem, the central biblical sanctuary. The act of writing plays an important role in this—it is in this phase that the proclamation is recorded for the first time (admittedly for purely mnemotechnic aims) in writing;[117] written scripture was the emblem of the older religions, the Jews and Christians who are later designated as "possessors of scripture." In the Qur'anic view, their revelations owe their authority to their relation to writing; like the emerging Qur'an, they are excerpts from the heavenly original writing, given visual form as the "preserved tablet," *al-lawḥ al-maḥfūẓ*. A poet of the early twentieth century, the Egyptian Ahmad Shawqi, presented the process of the communication of this "writing" to men as a kind of liquefaction of letters into drops of speech:[118]

wa-l-waḥyu yaqṭuru salsalan min salsalin
wa-l-lawḥu wa-l-qalamu l-badīʿu rawwāʿū
ismu l-jalālati fī bahāʾi ḥurūfihī
alifun hunālika wa-smu Ṭāhā l-bāʾū

Inspiration pours down in drops of pearls,
While the tablet and the astounding pen are shining
The name of Majesty in the glory of its letters
The A is there, and the name of the Prophet follows like B.

116. Assmann, "Kanon und Zensur"; on an application of the model to the Qur'an, see Neuwirth, "Vom Rezitationstext"; cf. also chap. 6, 205–208.

117. This newly introduced textualization is referred to in the introduction of the suras by the invocation formulation *bi-smi llāhi l-raḥmāni l-raḥīm* "In the name of God, the compassionate the merciful," the so-called Basmala—analogous to the Christian practice of preluding textual elements with the formulation, "In the name of the Father, the Son and the Holy Ghost."

118. Shawqi, *al-Aʿmāl al-Shiʿrīya al-Kāmila*, 34.

From this perspective, writing transcends its functionality as a sign system: a transcendent universe out of letter signs, which obtain their significance through their supernatural beauty, their "glory," corresponds to the writing that is perceptible in the world, which consists of semantically functional signs, granting to it and elsewhere unknown aura.

Although supported by the same object of the tablet, the Qur'anic process of becoming scripture is thus substantially different from the episode of the granting of the tablets in the Hebrew Bible, and even more so from its later Christian interpretation. The theologian Friedrich Wilhelm Graf has clearly outlined the significance of the description of the tablet for religious history, which is foundational above all from the Protestant perspective: "At Sinai, the transcendent God sealed a covenant with his people, of which the conditions are literally the moral laws. This sealing of the covenant at Sinai, seen from the perspective of religious history, signifies an entirely new conception of the relation between God and man, characterized by radical transcendence of God, an unconditioned claim to exclusive worship by his people, and a moralistic and legal order."[119]

It is true, already in rabbinic Judaism, a more comprehensive perception of the communication of God's word, the *tora mi-Sinai*, the teaching communicated on Sinai, had been superimposed onto the event of the handing down of the tablets, so that the post-Mosaic *tora she be-ʿal pe*, that is, the oral teaching, had come to outweigh the written. For the Qur'an, the Mosaic event is submerged into an episode that, reported in an entirely de-dramatized text in sura 7, has completely lost its history-generating dimension.[120] The Ten Commandments, which are listed three times in the Qur'an, are never linked to this event. Seen from the Qur'anic perspective, divine writing is withdrawn from human access, God sends only oral excerpts from the heavenly tablet to his Prophets—a transformation that negates the uniqueness of the biblical event without, however, devaluing it. What occurs in medieval Christian reception, where at the entrance to Gothic cathedrals we find the figure of the *synagoga*, a feminine figure blindfolded and with broken staff, symbolizing the "fall of the tablets," which literally slip down from the figure—an allegory of Judaism deemed obsolete in pre-modern Christian tradition —is not imaginable in an Islamic context.

The Islamic equivalent of the tablets, the heavenly writing, is a source of cultic rather than moral authority. It not only manifests God's transcendence but also remains transcendent itself. For that reason, not only is there no image of the handing down of the tablets in Islam, but there is also no historic precedent for such a representation in written form of the divine word such as is so common

119. Graf, *Moses Vermächtnis*.
120. See Neuwirth, "Meccan Texts, Medinan Additions?"

in Western reception[121]—an even stronger challenge to the imagination of the believers to take possession of this ultimately heavenly writing through art.

For according to the Qur'an, not only letters or the Qur'an verses but indeed all created things are "signs," *āyāt*, of God. Creation is understood as a sign system in analogy to writing, which man is constantly called upon to "read" in the Qur'an.[122] These signs of creation, such as the cosmic order, the blessings of nature, and the historical fortunes of the community, are unfolded narratively in the Qur'an, and thus take on a verbal form through the prophetic proclamation. But since they had already existed in written form in the original Qur'an, the "mother of the writing," *umm al-kitāb*, they are at the same time coded in writing. Without this coding, things could be represented figuratively without problem—as they are in other cultures. Instead, in view of their anchoring in the heavenly writing, it is the form of writing that suggests itself as their visual, inner-worldly presentation; in place of the image, we thus have the "script image." Language and writing unite in this image, which, as in Ahmad Shawqi's poem, glorifies the majestic name of God.

2.6.3 *Text, Sound, and Body*

In looking for commonalities between the three monotheistic religions, it is problematic to rely on external shared traits, which can be represented in suggestive coinages such as "Abrahamic religions,"[123] "possessors of scripture,"[124] or "revealed religions." More interesting are the differences, expressed for instance in the diverse medialities of the respective proclamations. We could observe here that what we are accustomed to designating as "Qur'anic revelation" was connected by its receivers with other, completely different experiences. Alongside the communication that was experienced quasi-vertically, the "sending down" (*tanzīl*) and the "inspiration" (*waḥy*), which both also describe the experience of earlier prophets, there was the completely amythical emergence of performance texts, generated during the intensive ascetic practice of the proclaimer during his vigils. Here, it was an aural experience, also called *waḥy*, that came about in the course of the recitation of already received texts. An important feature is the still preverbal quality of the "inspiration" *waḥy*, discussed by Nasr Hamid Abu Zayd,[125] which first had to be decoded and verbalized before it could be passed on to the hearers. With the absence of the proclaimer, rearticulation came to take the place of the listening. The recitation of the community or of the single worshiper is an *imitatio* of the Prophet.

121. See the evidence of this in images and texts in Graf, *Moses Vermächtnis*.

122. Cf. chap. 7, 264–277.

123. On the problem of abbreviating the three monotheistic religions as "Abrahamic," see Nagel, "'Der erste Muslim'—Abraham in Mekka."

124. On "inlibration," see above, 92–95, and Madigan, "Gottes Botschaft an die Welt."

125. See Kermani, *Offenbarung als Kommunikation*.

Even as it makes use of the same verses, the Prophet *imitatio* implies an entirely new reading of the Qur'an. It de-historicizes the earlier message, since the divine communication, which had once been spoken in a defined historical time through the resumption of Prophetic time, the *illud tempus*, becomes a sacral recollection that removes the reciting hearer/speaker from time. Simultaneously, it restages the original scene of the genesis of Islam; the text thus becomes exclusively Muslim.

Contrarily, within the Qur'anic self-understanding, the divine message recorded on the "preserved tablet," from which the proclaimer receives his communications, was still perceived as universal, that is, it was destined for monotheistic believers in general. The "mother of the scripture," *umm al-kitāb*, most likely has its equivalent in the hypostasizing of the logos or wisdom as the first-created thing of God known from ancient Judaism; cf. Prov. 8:22–36. In that all creation is already recorded in the "original writing," it is coded "scripturally"—a Qur'anic conception that can be traced back to preceding Jewish speculations over the relationship between word/book and body, even if the acoustically realized word remains of prime importance for the Islamic conception of divine self-communication. What the American Kabbalah researcher Elliot R. Wolfson has claimed for the Jewish and Christian relationship between word and body can be extended also to Islam. According to Wolfson, both Jewish and Christian thought are based on a particular correlation of body and book/word,[126] but with a reversal of their respective emphasis, in a way that can be summarized as follows: "For Christians the body is the embodiment of the book, for Jews the book is the textualization of the body."[127]

Looking for an "embodiment of God's word" in Islam, one should not seek to find it in a "book" representing scripture, as presupposed in the concept of "inlibration," but rather in the living recitation of the Arabic Qur'an. This has its place in an organic "resonant cavity," which, as is appropriate for a ceremonial-acoustic performance such as Qur'an recitation, is fit to incorporate spoken word and cantilena. This "resonant cavity" is not to be sought in transcendence but rather, since spiritual and aesthetic experience are innate in the creation of man, in human nature itself.

126. Wolfson, "The Body in the Text."
127. Ibid. 482.

3

The Qur'an and History

3.1 History of Communicated Speech

3.1.1 The "Ahistorical" Qur'an

The consciousness of historicity is often perceived to be a discovery of European culture that is claimed to have been developed nowhere else independently. The Qur'an, whose central interest in timelessness is indisputable, seems to confirm this verdict. For many critics, it serves as a key example of indifference to history. This is the judgment of the historian of early Islam Fred Donner:

> The purpose of stories in the Qur᾿ān, then, is profoundly different from their purpose in the Old Testament; the latter uses stories to explain particular chapters in Israel's history, the former to illustrate—again and again—how the true Believer acts in certain situations. In line with this purpose, Qur᾿ānic characters are portrayed as moral paradigms, emblematic of all that is good or evil. Moreover, as stories, they are not imbued with much, if any, development—which is why they can appear as detached fragments. In this sense, the Qur᾿ān can be seen to be profoundly ahistorical; it is simply not concerned with history in the sense of development and change, either of the prophets or peoples before Muḥammad, or of Muḥammad himself, because in the Qur᾿ānic view the identity of the community to which Muḥammad was sent is not *historically*, but *morally* determined.[1]

This verdict by Fred Donner does not stand alone. Hans Zirker, author of two monographs on the Qur'an with a Christian-theological bent,[2] bemoans the lack of a linear conception in the Qur'an: "Revelations are in the Islamic view grantings from God that recurred in the past numerously and identically. They were meant to remedy the harms caused by men and to enable them to live according to God's directives. Accordingly, they are always isolated occurrences that indeed triggered historical consequences, but which cannot be integrated into an encompassing goal-directed history of revelation."[3]

1. Donner, *Narratives of Islamic Origins*, 84.
2. Zirker, *Christentum und Islam*; Zirker, *Der Koran: Zugänge und Lesarten*.
3. Zirker, *Christentum und Islam*, 68.

This negative judgment against any Qur'anic interest in history is not new.[4] In comparison with the two older monotheistic scriptures, it on first glance does appear plausible. Certainly, the Qur'an offers no sacred historical drama pursued through the great acts of creation, election, exodus, conquest, exile, and the hope of liberation, as does the Hebrew Bible, nor does it offer a goal-oriented history of proclamation and of the earliest believers, as does the New Testament. The canonized Qur'an begins famously not with the story of creation but rather, after an introductory prayer (sura 1), with a kind of dedication to the receivers, that is the community that is constituting itself, followed by narratives, legislation, and polemic (sura 2).[5] Above all—apart from the final partial corpus, the "final thirtieth," *juz' 'amma*,[6] that stands at the text's end—the suras that follow each other generally belong to different periods of emergence, and thus do not connect to each other with any narrative logic. Nor do the biblically inspired Qur'anic narratives follow the order of their biblical sequence; nearly all narratives occur more than once, not only in different versions but also in different contexts. Some narratives that take shape early follow one and the same striking model: a messenger of God preaches the message of the one God and of eschatological reckoning to his people, but meets with rejection and must experience the fatal punishment that falls on his people, while he himself is saved from catastrophe. Evaluating this narrative type to the exclusion of all others, scholars have often alleged to the Qur'an as such a cyclical view of history.[7]

But is the Qur'an wholly "ahistorical"? Are the earlier, pre-Qur'anic revelations that are recalled in the Qur'an truly "numerous and interchangeable"? Can one designate the messenger figures of the Qur'anic narratives universally merely as "moral models," that is, ideal types without development that are only of avail for the ethical message of the Qur'an? Above all, does the image of the proclaimer remain static, without change or development? This widespread impression in current research emerges if one reads the Qur'an post-redactionally, post-canonically, that is, as a document closed in itself, a composite of chronologically and theologically equivalent evidence, without registering the processes of change reflected in the language, style, and referentiality of the Qur'an. Narratives featuring the same actors displaying the same behavior must in this synchronic reading appear as historically irrelevant reiterations. This "holistic" approach—though without the concomitant negative valuation correlates with the perspective of the Islamic tradition itself, where the invariability of the image of the Prophets—indeed, the ideality of the prophetical type as such—possesses a dogmatically binding significance. Islamic theology's lack of interest in the

4. Cf. Neuwirth, "Qur'an and History."

5. Among these, an extensive story of creation is depicted in Q 2:29–39.

6. Cf. chap. 5, 166–170.

7. This assessment from Rudi Paret's influential essay "Das Geschichtsbild Mohammeds" (1951) is generally adopted by later scholars without further critical examination.

historical communication process—though not true without exception for the entire tradition—is not surprising. It is a consequence of canonization, which established an obligatory teleological reading, according to which the Qur'an reflects not the process of trial and error in the development of a socially consensual mode of thought but rather merely different manifestations of one and the same truth. This reading obscures the progressive self-reflection of the proclaimer and his community and their increasingly innovative exegetical treatments of biblical stories, which in Medina even lead to a kind of *counter-history* in the face of biblical history, a rewriting of biblical narratives that involves a reversal of their ideological thrust.[8]

In what follows, we intend to free the Qur'an from its perception as an authorially conceived "book" and reclaim it as an open-ended communication process occurring in history. The conception of the Qur'an as the homogenous scripture of Islam, which is suggested most persuasively by the Sira, will be flashed out. The value of a traditional reading oriented toward the Sira is not to be contested, tradition does however treat the Qur'anic genesis from the teleological viewpoint assumed by the later community, and therefore cannot illuminate the text *in statu nascendi*. The Sira must therefore be perceived not as a rival to the historical image, as evidence of a competing truth claim, but rather as a document of a distinctly new scriptural discourse. At the same time, what must be avoided is the eclectic perception upheld in Western research that identifies the Qur'an with the later canonized codex reading it—ignoring its non-chronological sura order and sacral coding—as a historical report, as if it were immediately evaluable as a document of the state of affairs in Mecca or Medina. Such a reading skips the step of a microstructural examination of the texts of the respective suras registering the topoi, formulas, and speech modes called for by the textual genre of the sura as such, which is required before the text can be evaluated for its historical information.

In addition, the current study does not share the skeptical premises that demand that the temporal and spatial coordinates of the Qur'anic emergence should be suspended; rather, we assume heuristically, despite the almost complete lack of explicit namings of place, the traditional scenes of Mecca and Medina.[9] Nothing compels us to view the milieu of the Qur'an as a culturally undeveloped space. Indeed, the cultural and social scenario of the peripheral Hijaz is only being explored by research; yet the literature that we already possess, in particular poetry and heroic prose narratives, justifies an image of a society whose verbal sensibilities and literary formation defy all clichés of an "empty Hijaz."[10] The

8. See chap. 11.

9. This heuristic position distinguishes the account presented here from the position of those skeptical scholars, many of whom no longer insist on the late dating of the Qur'an, but who continue to consider a shift in its localization, or treat it altogether as a purely literary creation; for example, see Hawting, *The Idea of Idolatry*, and Crone, "What Do We Actually Know about Mohammed?"

10. Montgomery, "The Empty Ḥijāz." Cf. also Noth, "Früher Islam."

extensive corpus of hero stories of the so-called *ayyām al-ʿarab*,[11] the "battle days of the Arab tribes disparately transmitted prose texts interspersed with poetry that report the tribal confrontations of sixth/seventh centuries, offers—despite the fact that it was written down only in retrospect—an authentic record of autochthonous nomadic culture, and provides convincing explanations of the social and ideological preconditions for the changes that set in with the Qur'anic proclamation. Despite the gaps in research that still exist, a rough image is already taking shape, allowing historians such as Robert Hoyland to state positively the compatibility of the known facts about the peninsula with the basic data of the Islamic tradition.[12] Peter Brown even claims that within the Arabic language area, the living heritage of Hellenism, which developed a universal nomenclature and iconography for the locally worshipped pagan divinities and united different cultural groups through the phenomenon of a shared verbal koine, was at least partially responsible for the fast success of Islam with its strongly universalizing tendency.[13]

Seen against this background Jaakko Hameen-Antilla's hypothesis, based on the stylistic closeness of the early Qur'anic proclamation to the ancient Arabic soothsayer speech, that Muhammad first worked on the peninsula as a wandering "seer" (*kāhin*), before settling down in Yathrib/Medina as a Prophet in the biblical style, proves anachronistic.[14] The Qur'an in its early parts is not monolithically ancient Arabic, but rather makes frequent recourse—as a glance at the intertextual inventories such as Heinrich Speyer's *Die biblischen Erzahlungen im Koran* (The biblical narratives in the Qur'an) evinces—to a multitude of Late Antique religious traditions, which it appropriates through creative repositioning. Even if we cannot generally name these traditions with any precision, they nonetheless call for an open, intertextual microstructural reading of the Qur'an that pays attention to the older traditions that resonate recognizably in the text. The text is thus to be perceived as polyphonic, as a conversation with other texts; it justifies its emphatic message—presented or the first time Arabic language through its nearness to the older traditions and grounds its authority not least in its participation in existing debates underway among the learned traditions of the two older religions.

11. A convincing depiction of the social significance of this literature is conveyed by Montgomery, *Vagaries of the Qasidah*. The *ayyām al-ʿarab* have been given very little scholarly attention since Bräunlich, *Bistām ibn Qais*, Caskel, "Ajjām al-Arab," and Meyer, *Aiyām al-Arab*. Al-Qadi, "La composante narrative," represents a newer study. A research project by Toral-Niehoff, Die Ayyām al-Arab als "Tribal History" der arabischen Spätantike, is currently being conducted at the Freie Universität Berlin.

12. See Hoyland, "New Documentary Texts and the Early Islamic State"; Hoyland, *Arabia and the Arabs: From the Bronze Age to the Coming of Islam*.

13. Brown, *The World of Late Antiquity*; cf. also Bowersock, *Hellenism in Late Antiquity*.

14. Hämeen-Anttila, "Arabian Prophecy." On this connection, see chap. 12, 424–430.

3.2 Two Manifestations of the Qur'an

If we do not accept to understand the Qur'an,[15] in conformity with much recent scholarship,[16] as a kind of apocryphon, as a mere rewriting and reconfiguration of biblical and post-biblical traditions, that is, as a written text conceived for readers and of random origin, we cannot avoid reflecting on the conditions of its emergence. It is not a matter of indifference whether a text designs a particular new formation of extant materials "for readers," or if rather these readers—as hearers—themselves participate in this reconfiguration. Some of the prima facie most compelling interpretations of single verses or passages[17] that result from the synchronic reading of the Qur'an as an authored text lose their persuasiveness once they are checked against the communication situation of the pre-canonic Qur'an, that is, the protracted "religious dialogue" occurring over time and involving a number of agents. To ascribe to the whole Qur'an the intention of "decentralizing and subverting earlier traditions,"[18] as occurs sometimes in recent American research, entails the assumption of an authorial intention that is not compatible with its character as proclamation. However many liberties a purely canon-referential interpretation may offer to the researcher, it is unwarranted in the case of the Qur'an, as long as it cannot be adapted historically to the proclamation process. It is not merely that synchronic readings go halfway.[19] They also implicitly contest the Qur'an's status as a founding document of a gradually formed communal consensus and thus the rank of the foundational document of a new religion—a methodological short circuit with ideological implications, arising from the essentialist perception of the Qur'an as a kind of biblical apocryphon.

It is an unmistakable fact that the early history of Qur'anic discourse went through two phases. These can be identified with some simplification as the phase that lasted up to the death of the Prophet, which was primarily oral, and the one belonging to the generation after him, which additionally relied on writing. But these two phases are rarely differentiated strictly either in the tradition or in later research, partly because of their close chronological sequence. Since this distinction relates not only to pure chronology and different media of communication, but also to different configurations of the text in the consciousness of the recipients, we will consequently distinguish in the following between "two Qur'ans,"

15. This section is based on previously published preliminary works, such as Neuwirth, "Eine europäische Lektüre des Koran."

16. See the methodologically insightful essay by Hughes, "The Stranger at the Sea"; similarly, Cuypers, *The Banquet*.

17. This also applies to Hughes's essay "The Stranger at the Sea" (where a later-achieved, critical picture of Moses is employed to explain an earlier text) and, most importantly, to Brown, "The Apocalypse of Islam," which adduces a Qur'anic position only reached in Medina through the involvement of Jewish exegetical principles, to explain a middle Meccan text.

18. Brown, "The Apocalypse of Islam," 87.

19. On the overall problem, see Sinai, "The Qur'an as Process."

the pre-canonic and the canonic text.[20] It is worth remarking that the Islamic tradition itself maintains a distinction between two different perceptions of the Qur'an, even if it does not apply the two concepts as terms relevant to religious-historical development. It distinguishes between the oral text, the recitation of the Prophet, *qurʾān*, and the written Qur'an codex, *muṣḥaf*, which was handed down through the centuries by tradition subjected to strict philological controls, until finally, it merged in the year 1925, into the form of a printed text.

The Qur'an codex lies before us as a "anthology" of individual texts, suras, the arrangement of which follows no chronological order, let alone any narrative logic. Its 114 suras are arranged according to a conceivably arbitrary criterion: their length, in descending order. But it is just this "raw form" of overall structure that fits poorly with the presupposition of skeptical researchers of a compilation of the corpus by anonymous scholars undertaking the construction of an Arabic foundational myth based on the sayings of a mythical prophet. The mechanistic representation of text reflected in the Qur'an codex would be quite astonishing to find within the later epoch assigned by skeptical researchers—the eighth century—a time from which we have artfully composed extant literary texts. But it fits unproblematically into the scenario suggested by the Islamic tradition: that of a "dealing with inheritance" practiced on the part of Qur'an collectors after the Prophet's death. Indeed, the heterogeneous masses of text that the redactors brought together from memory and from the transcripts of the companions of the Prophet (*ṣaḥāba*) can most plausibly be thought of as an unordered stock published without exterior intervention. The ancient canonic formula "You must add nothing and take nothing away" (Deut 13:1) was already deeply inscribed in the consciousness of the proclaimer, for whom the problem of the integrity of his proclamation had often been an occasion for troubling self-testing, as the Qur'an itself shows. Clearly, at the time of its proclamation the text was already sacrosanct as an "inspiration" (*waḥy*) or a "sending-down" from God (*tanzīl*). It is likely this perception of the protected character of individual texts that motivated the redactors to renounce every insertion on their side into the text, so that it emerged without any literarily ambitious formulation of its theology, such as could have recommended itself following the model of the biblical books. Abstaining from every semantic or chronological control over individual texts, the redactors however at the same time denied the reader any aid and support of their approaching the text—a serious shortcoming often bemoaned by outsiders. From the perspective of the redactors, such a renunciation of readability would have been acceptable, since at the time of the text's

20. Zwettler, "A Mantic Manifesto," also insists on a distinction between the "scripture" existing in codex form and its pre-canonical, previous "revelation." However, in our context the communication of the text to listeners should be at the fore in place of this distinction. The mantic quality of the oration should not be marginalized, as it forms part of the *persuasio* of the communication, the persuasion strategy.

first binding codification, a period following Muhammad's death by at most sixty years and perhaps as few as twenty,[21] the written form of the text was meant only as a control: through writing, the textual stock could be authoritatively delimited, and the ordering and the shape of the individual texts be fixed.[22] What was not fixed, however, was the exact articulation of the text, as the early scribal technique foresaw neither the representation of short vowels nor the differentiation of graphically identical signs for consonants.[23]

3.2.1 Muṣḥaf, a Ceremonially Framed Sacral Text

Regardless of the mechanistic sequencing of individual texts, the codex serves the formal expectations bound up in Late Antiquity with a scripture: that the most sublime "book" should have a beginning highlighted by special pathos and a correspondingly expressive end. In fact, the Qur'an text is embedded in a solemnly phrased frame that is clearly recognizable as such. The introductory unit, al-Fātiḥa, "the opening," is an exceptional text, not a sura in the strict sense; since it does not consist of God's speech to men, but is rather a prayer spoken by the community of believers, forming the religion's central communal prayer, comparable to the Christian Our Father.[24] The Fātiḥa, which opens the corpus as a sort of prooemium, serves as a petition for divine guidance in the ritual situation of approaching the scripture. The text is not chosen by accident: although the name al-Fātiḥa could indicate its function as an opening of the written corpus, it was clearly already in use in a scarcely less prominent opening role, namely as an entrance formula or introitus for the Islamic ritual of prayer, which should go back to the praxis of the Qur'anic community. With the Fātiḥa then, a liturgically central text of the community was chosen as an opening of the Qur'an codex.[25] Analogous to this also are the last two suras, which, despite the fact that they are introduced formally through the divine command *qul*, "Speak [the following text]," and thus are presented as divine speech addressed to the proclaimer, are also not conventional suras. In these texts, two apotropaic formulas that were arguably already common use—marked by the words *aʿūdhu bi-rabbi*, "I take refuge with the Lord . . ."—are adapted for a new function, to shield the Qur'an from the influence of demons. The positioning of suras 1, 113, and 114—which are lacking in the early Qur'an exemplar of Ibn Masʿūd, an early collection that preceded the canonized edition[26]—must apparently be attributed to the formal conceptions

21. Cf. chap. 4, 140–144.
22. Neuwirth, "Structure and the Emergence of Community."
23. Cf. chap. 4, 212–213.
24. Winkler, "Fatiha und Vaterunser."
25. Neuwirth and Neuwirth, "Sūrat al-Fātiḥa."
26. Nöldeke, *Geschichte des Qorans*, 1:108–110, identifies both of the last two suras as preexisting texts "adopted" in the Qur'an. On the absence of the suras in Ibn Masʿūd, see Jeffery, *Materials*, 20–24. On the editing the Qur'an, see chap. 4.

of the redactors of the so-called Uthmanic text, who were confronted with the task of fixing a *textus ne varietur*, a text with claims to bindingness. It is no wonder that a similar apotropaic formula—not recorded in the *muṣḥaf*—that is traditionally pronounced before the beginning of a Qur'an recitation, *aʿūdhu bi-llāhi mina l-shayṭāni l-rajīm*, "I take refuge with God from the accursed Satan," sounds like an echo of the two closing suras.

If one looks past these framing parts, what is yielded for the Qur'an is a "book block," at the beginning of which stands a kind of dedication of the corpus; the scripture is intended for those who share the belief in the oneness of God and fulfill three basic obligations (Q 2:1–5):

alif lām mīm
dhālika l-kitābu lā rayba fīhi
  hudan li-l-muttaqīn
alladhīna yuʾminūna bi-l-ghaybi
  wa-yuqīmūna l-ṣalāta
  wa-mimmā razaqnāhum yunfiqūn
wa-lladhīna yuʾminūna bi-mā unzila ilayka
  wa-mā unzila min qablika
  wa-bi-l-ākhirati hum yūqinūn
ulāʾika ʿalā hudan min rabbihim
  wa-ulāʾika humu l-mufliḥūn

Alif lam mim.
That is the scripture—no doubt is in it,
a right guidance for the God fearing,
who believe in the unseen and perform the prayer
and spend from that which we supply them,
and who believe in that which was sent down to you,
and who are aware of the life hereafter.
They are rightly guided from your Lord
and they are the blessed ones.

It ends with a concise formulation of the Islamic creed in sura 112, "the Pure Faith":[27]

qul huwa llāhu aḥad
Allāhu l-ṣamad
lam yalid wa-lam yūlad
wa-lam yakun lahu kufuwan aḥad

27. The sura is discussed in chap. 13, 477–480.

> Say: He is God, one
> God, the constant.
> He did not beget and was not begotten,
> and there is none equal to him.

The two more ancient scriptures commence and end quite differently: the Hebrew Bible begins and ends historically. At its beginning, we even find two reports about the creation of the world: "In the beginning God created the heaven and earth" (Gen 1:1), and "On the day when God created heaven and earth . . . God planted a Garden in Eden. . . ." (Gen 2:4, 2:8). Just as the oldest event of human history stands at the beginning, so at the end we find the chronologically most recent events in the history of the people of Israel, their return to the promised land: "As the word of God was fulfilled out of the mouth of Jeremiah, God awoke the spirit of Cyrus, and he had the following announced by mouth and by writing: so speaks Cyrus, the king of the Persians: God gave to me all kingdoms of the earth, the God of the heavens. He commissioned me to build Him a house in Jerusalem. Whichever of you how belongs to his people, let his God be with him! Let him go up!" (2 Chr 36:22–23.)

The New Testament is given a similar historical frame: The Gospel of Matthew begins with a genealogy of Jesus: "Book of the ancestry of Jesus Christ, of the son of David, of the Son of Abraham. Abraham begot Isaac" (Mt 1:1),[28] and the Gospel of John even begins with a reference to Gen 1:1: "In the beginning was the word, and the word was by God" (Jo 1:1). The New Testament ends with an eschatological announcement of the Second Coming of Christ: "He who testifies this, says: yes, I am coming soon. Amen. Come Lord Jesus!" (Rev 22:20).

Contrarily, the Qur'an does not take up history in its two ultimate positions. Rather, at the beginning it takes up scripture, *kitāb*, that is, the divine teaching, and at its end the image of God in distinction from that of the two older religions. It begins with three of the emblematic letter names (*alif lām mīm*) and ends with the word "one," *aḥad*. The redactors could have easily found a report of creation or a Qur'anic evocation of events from communal history, if they had intended to make the Qur'an recognizable as a "history book" of the new community with a setting of history in initial and final positions. The most likely explanation for the fact that this did not occur is the still undeveloped notion of a scripture, which prevented the proclaimer or his contemporaries from envisioning such a project of compilation.[29]

28. The Gospel of Mark begins with a quote from Isaiah: "The beginning of the good news about Jesus the Messiah, the Son of God, as it is written in Isaiah the Prophet: I will send my messenger ahead of you, who will prepare your way" (Mark 1); the Gospel of Luke begins with a historical localization: "In the time of Herod King of Judea, there was a priest named Zechariah, who belonged to the priestly division of Abijah; his wife Elizabeth was also a descendant of Aaron" (Luke 1).

29. See Madigan, *The Qur'an's Self-Image*; cf. chap. 2, 140–144.

The Qur'an after the death of the Prophet continued to be communicated orally, supported by the memory of the companions of the Prophet. The outcome of the first codification, an initiative that was—according to the tradition—prompted by state power, therefore was not the production of a continuously readable book, as in the cases of the Hebrew Bible or New Testament, but rather the production of what the word *qurʾān* alongside "recitation" and "reading" also signifies: a lectionary. The official Qur'an is a lectionary, a collection of pericopes, that is, a corpus of texts for the selection of liturgical recitations. The Qur'an in a unique way insists on its liturgical function—not only by virtue of its self-designation—while also maintaining its close connection to the other scriptures. William Graham has stressed that the recognition of scriptures beyond one's own, which in the West was first developed in the nineteenth century, is already evident in the Qur'an:[30] countless verses speak of the "scripture," *kitāb*, or the "scriptures," *kutub*, of other religions, a category that the Qur'an, although still oral, will also claim for itself by the end of its development. According to Graham, the Qur'an is the only scripture that identifies itself as such through its self-referentiality.

One should or course not imagine this "community of scriptures" of Torah, Gospels, and Qur'anic proclamation, sketched in the Qur'an itself, to be a kind of co-equal siblinghood valid for all time. As much as the text of the Qur'an stresses at length its essential compatibility with the other scriptures that it seeks to confirm, so too is the Qur'an valid within Islamic theology as the final legitimate scripture that perfects all others. Between the pronouncements of the Qur'an text and its later interpretation lies the break of canonization,[31] which effects a transformation in perception: the historical-dialogical character of the Qur'an as a religious conversation with and about others becomes, through canonization, turns into a divine monologue.

3.2.2 *The Pre-canonical Qur'an (Qurʾān)—Drama of Community Formation*

Yet before the text is solidified through codification and finally assumes the form of a binding codex, *muṣḥaf*, it is a drama, an interaction in flux between a proclaimer and his community. As Andreas Kellermann has pointed out, research has too often treated the texts assembled in the Qur'an "implicitly as a 'literary product' compiled by an 'author" in a fixed form."[32] Thus Theodor Nöldeke refers to the Qur'an as a book "the text of which is preserved for us quite unadulterated,"[33] and Carl Brockelmann and others automatically apply the concept of

30. See Graham, "Scripture and the Qurʾān"; Wild, "Why Self-Referentiality?"

31. On the implications of canonization, see Sinai, *Studien zur frühen Koraninterpretation*, 1–22; al-Azmeh, "Muslim Canon."

32. Cf. Geyer's review of Vollers, *Volkssprache*, cited in Kellermann, "Die 'Mündlichkeit' des Koran," 3.

33. Nöldeke, *Sketches from Eastern History*, 1–2, cited in Kellermann, "Die 'Mündlichkeit' des Koran," 3.

drafting in writing to the Qur'an.[34] In critical philology, the question of the "original text" of the Qur'an dominates, prompting the quest to arrive at the original sense intended by the Prophet, as well as the search for possible source texts and for the original "speech form" employed "by the author." Thus, the written version of the Qur'an is often viewed as a unity, and studied with the criteria of literature composed and received in writing, with no regard for the differing contexts, functions, and forms of the originally independent individual texts. In this, the Qur'anic language and style (or the "talent" of the author) are often denigrated in a trivial[35] and prejudicial way.[36] In this unquestioned assumption of literality and authorship, Kellermann sees an obscuring of the complex character of the Qur'an, which is equally oral and written; preferring to position the Qur'an in the "gray zone between a purely written and a purely oral literature,"[37] he therefore approaches the text text-linguistically. Although the present attempt to distinguish these two commingled manifestations of the Qur'an follows a more historical-traditional goal, it confronts the same necessity: to call into question the supposed written form of the Qur'an and its ascription to an "author."

In order to do justice to the text-generating interaction between the charismatic speaker and his community as it took shape, one should replace the conventional author-reader relation with a model borrowed from the theory of drama, which distinguishes between two levels of communication. There is on the one hand an "inner communication level," the "interaction drama" that plays itself out between the protagonists (the proclaimer and his community), which can be described by historical research;[38] here, dialogues emerge and a mass of rhetorical strategies are applied as a means of *persuasio*. This level is vaulted by the "outer communication level" occupied by the "I" or "we" speaker, it is manifest in the text and in the later readers/hearers of the Qur'an. In the that initiates the text corpus (Q 2:2), it can be demonstrated how distant the view of the Qur'an as a "textual result of a charismatic interaction" (Nicolai Sinai) is from conventional Islamic and Western approaches: reading the Qur'an as a homogenous, post-redactional corpus, as *muṣḥaf*[39] (the "outer communication level"), one has to translate the verse cited above (Q 2:2), *dhālika l-kitābu lā rayba fīhi hudan li-l-muttaqīn*, as "This [i.e., the Qur'an] is the scripture in which is no doubt, a right guidance to the God fearing"; reading it however as a testimony of the proclamation process, the "inner communication level," one will take *kitāb* to mean not the Qur'anic corpus, but rather the heavenly scripture reclaimed by

34. Cf. in detail Zwettler, *Oral Tradition*, 174, note 15.

35. Cf., e.g., Kopf, "Religious Influences," 48, cited in Kellermann, "Die 'Mündlichkeit' des Koran," 3.

36. Kellermann, "Die 'Mündlichkeit' des Koran," 3.

37. Ibid.

38. The further text-immanent level of communication, generated by rhetorical effects, in which a divine speaker turns to a Prophetic recipient—and occasionally also directly to the remotely addressed listeners—needs to remain outside our scope.

39. See Madigan, *The Qur'ān's Self-Image*.

the Prophet as a "template of revelation": "That is the [heavenly] scripture, no doubt is in it, a right guidance for the God fearing."[40] The text read in this way has been reconfigured from an already closed "book", the "Qur'an)"—present here and now—to an open text that is still on its way to closure. The canonic "mis-reading" of this important verse is not, however, arbitrary. If we set the Fātiḥa aside as an introductory prayer and look past the introductory letter names *alif lām mīm*, the verse presents the first pronouncement of the Qur'an. It can easily be comprehended that, understood in this sense by the redactors after the death of the Prophet, appeared as particularly suited for the beginning of the codex, where it can fulfill the function of an expressive dedication of what the Qur'an book that has become the substitute for the voice of the proclaimer addressing the already constituted community.[41]

3.3 The Conversation with the Older Traditions: Stations of Community Formation

Certainly, the pre-canonic Qur'an formally is almost consistently the speech of a divine "I" or "we" addressing the proclaimer—"you"; but, as in an overheard telephone conversation, the situation in which the conversation takes place can be reconstructed easily from the fragments of speech that are heard. In view of the plurality of actors that participate in this Qur'anic drama, the text becomes polyphonic; for alongside the addressed speaker Muhammad, individuals and groups of hearers are pictured as present in the text or at least spoken of in their absence. These persons and groups are for their part involved in debates that are not always explicitly divulged in the text, but without knowledge of which the innovativeness of the Qur'anic position remains obscure.

Let us take three simple examples: in the Qur'an, Jesus is identified as *ʿĪsā ibn Maryam*, "Jesus, Son of Mary." Since other prophets appear without genealogical distinction, such a reference should not be strictly necessary for Jesus. Clearly what is occurring is a "theological correction," a replacement, recognizable to the hearers, of the Christian title "Jesus son of God," a title that—being a clear confessional designation—did not fit with the new strict monotheism. Without this title—which is eliminated and reformulated for the hearers—Jesus can be accepted without problems among the biblical prophets by the universally oriented community. An even more striking parallel case is the *Basmala*, the wording of which, *bi-smi llāhi l-raḥmāni l-raḥīm*, "In the name of God, the compassionate merciful," is a clear reworking of the Christological formula of invocation "In the name of the Father and the Son and Holy spirit." Both the Qur'anic designation of

40. It should not be surprising that the translations usually undergird the distant deictic reference to the "scripture," which is presented as already existing, through renditions with "this is" (Paret).

41. Neuwirth, "Structural, Linguistic and Literary Features."

Jesus and the new coinage of an Islamic invocation formula, are samples of communal interpretive history. A further example would be the "preserved tablet," *al-lawḥ al-maḥfūẓ* (Q 85:22): in the Qur'an, unlike in the Hebrew Bible and the Jewish tradition, there is no mention of two tablets written exclusively for Moses's covenant with God, but rather of a single tablet preserved in heaven[42] as textual support of the revelation. This tablet, unlike the tablets of Moses, does not suffer destruction within history, but rather remains "preserved" in the transcendent realm. It also enjoys universal authority; contrary to the Jewish tradition, since it is not an elected people of God but rather all men who obtain the writing preserved on the tablet. Although this tablet is already known from the biblical apocryphon of the Book of Jubilees, the express qualification as "preserved" should be read as an intentional Qur'anic response to the biblical tradition.

A similar innovation emerges in the phrasing of the Islamic creed in sura 112, "The true belief," which has already been cited. Its opening verse, "Speak: God is one," *qul huwa llāhu aḥad*, is a free translation of the Jewish creed "Hear Israel: the Lord, our God, is One," *shemaʿ Yisraʿel adonai elohenu adonai eḥad* (Dtn 6:4), the key word of which "one," *eḥad*, still resounds in the Qur'an text in its Arabic shape, *aḥad*. This audible citation across linguistic borders underlines all the more clearly the Qur'anic turn—signalized through *qul*, "speak!," directed to all mankind—from a national to a universal cult.[43] It is interesting that this discovery has also been made in recent Turkish Qur'an research by Mehmet Paçacı,[44] but it is not attributed in his work to the innovation of the Qur'an but rather is seen as an indication of the continuity of local traditions. Paçacı sees in the "citation" not an engagement between the Qur'an and an individual older text but rather a manifestation of the monotheistic "Semitic religious tradition," which is presupposed by Paçacı to be a constant. The novelty of the Qur'an, the social handling and new theological formulation of older texts, thus remains obscured. One thus avoids the fundamental question of how far the Qur'anic communication process reflects the theological intentions of the community itself—for example, the intention to "counter" a tradition already firmly founded by the surrounding religions, in order to set up its own new formulation according to its developing theology. Investigations of the Qur'anic intertexts have so far not attempted to take into account the dialectical engagement of the community with older traditions. Yet the Qur'anic new formulations are, according to

42. This source of authority exhibits an affinity with the important divine book of accounts or registers the book of Jubilees (second century BCE), which also exists in a competitive relationship with Mosaic writing on the tablet. This intertext still remains relevant for the later period, where the divine "original" is denoted as *kitāb*, "scripture"; cf. chap. 8, 285–286.

43. See Sinai and Neuwirth, "Introduction"; cf. chap. 13, 472–475.

44. Paçacı, "Sag: Gott ist ein einziger." On more recent Turkish Qur'an theology overall, see Körner, *Revisionist Koran Hermeneutics*. While attempts at contextualization seem to be missing in Arabic Qur'an scholarship, they have been taken up with great enthusiasm in Iranian scholarly circles, especially within the Merkaz-e Adyan in Qom, as a lecture tour by the supervisor of the Berlin project Corpus Coranicum in 2007 demonstrated.

our hypothesis, stations within a communal formation, milestones along the way from a post-biblical syncretism to a Qur'anic theology of its own.[45]

If one does not deal with the connections between individual versions of respective themes received in the Qur'an, then what is historically new in the accentuations of the Qur'an remains unrecognized. The purposeful pronouncements of the Qur'an lose their pungency and their direction of impact to become monotonous to the outside reader. For the Muslim reader, who reads the Qur'an as a canonical text and as the founding document of an already established, exclusivist religion, the prophetic politics of universalization documented in the text belong to a history that is already decided, and thus is without great importance for the perception of the Qur'an. The aura of a victorious religion that surrounds the Qur'an, and its status as the immediate self-communication of God, do not encourage the reconstruction of its historical unfolding. The critical researcher will however recognize the "prophetic politics" reflected in the text as one of the discursive strategies that can help explain the wondrous success of the Qur'an in history.

In contrast to the fixed canonical codex, the pre-canonic Qur'an should be understood as the transcript of a communication process, an ensemble of texts that have their *Sitz im Leben* in a public and audibly pronounced performance (*qurʾān*). These performance texts document the results of theological debates carried out within this very community. It is not that the proclaimer "developed himself" as an individual (as conventional Western research sees it), but rather that debates in the community took shape. In this process a consensus emerges concerning particular messages; whose evaluations of individual figures therefore do not require justification when the texts are recited again by the proclaimer. This is clearly reflected in the figure of Satan, who first occurs as Iblīs, "Diabolos," in much the same sense of the Satan figure of the Book of Job, entertaining a dialectic relation to God and ambivalent in many respects, and who is later slips into the role of the New Testament Satan, as a manifestation of evil, the dualist opposite to God.[46] The community at this stage has agreed on an exclusively negative understanding of the figure in the sense of the Christian Satan.

Such a result of community formation can also be recognized in the stratagem of the clausula that becomes frequent in the middle and late Meccan periods, forms such as *inna l-llāha l-ʿazīzu l-ḥakīm*, "God is the powerful, the wise," which reflect a consensus reached by the community in their image of God as a ubiquitous power.[47]

Yet another striking textual characteristic can be added: textual corrections, which can occasionally already be observed in Mecca, but which become

45. See chap. 8, 278–282.
46. Neuwirth, "The Qur'ān, Crisis and Memory."
47. See chap. 13, 472–477.

frequent in Medina. As the community broadens and over time comes to include Jews among the hearers in Medina, certain recitation texts turn out to be in need of later revision and expansion. The Medinan expansions of Meccan suras, many of which were first studied by Nöldeke and Schwally, have frequently been treated as simple additions, evidence of later states of knowledge, or even as bothersome interruptions of the flow of suras, but rarely considered as evidence for the continual process of community formation.[48] Yet the "additions" clearly attest to new religious-political demands: the presentation of theologically significant episodes of Israelite salvation history time and again needed to be deepened discursively or to be revised. Such a revision was intended by the Medinan extension of the Meccan narrative of the Golden Calf in sura 20, where, following an initial recitation of the episode as an edifying story within a longer Moses cycle, a strong interpretive point is added to it in Medina. In its extended Medinan form, which in individual formulations evokes the Jewish Yom Kippur liturgy, it is reread through a new theologically significant interpretation, which accommodates the discourse of sin and guilt which in Jewish tradition is bound up with notions of history.[49]

3.4 History Discourse

3.4.1 *Jāhilīya: Attaching Taboo to the Pagan Way of Life*

The historical period in which Islam emerged is disputed in both Western and inner-Islamic research. We find a shibboleth in this period's frequent designation as *jāhilīya*, namely, "(time of) ignorance," a highly ambivalent concept in the Islamic tradition that has not been unanimously explained in Western research.[50] Aaron Hughes has investigated the concept's representation in recent research and has criticized the persistent perception of this period as "separated from Islam by a sealed border."[51] Etymologically, *jāhilīya* is a derivative of *jahl* ("rashness"), the antonym of *ʿilm* ("level-headedness"), and refers to excessive, heroic zeal,[52] so that *jāhilīya* came to mean a "time of barbarism."[53] In view of the Qur'anic equation of the *jahl* of the pre-Islamic heroes, their heroic passion, with religious ignorance, *jāhilīya* has been understood in the Qur'an in the sense of

48. Numerous later additions to the early suras were already recorded in the inner-Islamic tradition. Nagel attempted to show historic evidence for these additions They are, however, often not congruent with the additions established in critical scholarship. In order to identify later expansions, one has to adhere to Nöldeke's formal criteria and systematically subject alleged additions to the same historic examination as those of all other Qur'an texts.

49. Neuwirth, "Medinan Additions"; cf. chap. 10, 318–324.

50. Ultimately, see Rosenthal, *Knowledge Triumphant*, 31–35.

51. Hughes, "The Stranger at the Sea."

52. See Goldziher, "Was ist unter al-Gāhilijja zu verstehen?" Cf. also the discussion in Hawting, *The Idea of Idolatry*.

53. A different etymology is suggested in Chabbi, *Le Coran décrypté*, 28–29, which seeks to understand the word in the sense of an inaccessible space auguring calamity.

"(time of) ignorance."[54] The word occurs in the Qur'an no more than four times, always in the context of Medinan critiques of pagan emotionality or excessive forms of behavior. In European translations, *jāhilīya*—appearing as an abstract term because of its *-īya* ending—is generally reproduced neutrally as "paganism." The four Qur'anic *jāhilīya* verses are as follows:

> Then, after grief, he sent down to you safety and drowsiness,
> which overcame a group of you,
> indeed the people of another group
> were anxiously occupied with themselves,
> while they employed conjectures about God,
> as one kept doing in paganism [*jāhilīya*], and said:
> "Does something stand before us of the matter [for decision] (Q 3:154)
>
> Do you wish for yourselves the modes of decision of paganism [*jāhilīya*]?
> Who could better decide for people
> who are convinced than God? (Q 5:50)
>
> Remain (you women) in your house,
> do not show yourselves off, as one was accustomed to do in paganism [*jāhilīya*], perform the prayer. (Q 33:33)
>
> (Then,) when the unbelievers let the impetuousness of paganism [*jāhilīya*] penetrate their hearts,
> upon which God sent down his *sakīna* [inner peace]
> on his messengers and the believers
> reminding them of the word of fear of God.
> They deserved it truly and were worthy of it
> God has knowledge of all. (Q 48:26)

Although the translation of *jāhilīya* as "paganism" may appear fit at first glance, in the Qur'an the concept certainly had not yet acquired its later epoch-referential meaning, a sense that would presuppose the breakthrough of a new period that had not yet occurred at the time of the proclamation. The translation as "paganism" is only legitimate under the presupposition of a canonized Qur'an that has already "formed history," so that the time before the proclamation could be viewed as a "prehistory" that had already been overcome. But what did this word mean for the proclaimer and his community, who were not yet aware of this looming development? The only inner-Qur'anic explanation is due to Franz

54. Wellhausen, *Reste altarabischen Heidentums*, 71,n1, already saw a correlation between *jāhiliya* and the Pauline *agnoia*, the "days of ignorance" (Acts 17:30); so also Pines, "Jāhiliyya." This Christian term may in fact have been known and could have been transmuted into *jāhiliya*. But even if such a precursor was already available, the pathos with which the term is used in the Qur'an (esp. in Q 48:26) points to a different understanding: less in the sense of a temporal attribution than in a sense of an approach to life.

Rosenthal. He interprets the ending *-īya* as a plural rather than abstract ending, so that *al-jāhilīya* would mean in all instances "the unknowing ones," the "religiously stubborn"—in the Qur'anic context, a characteristic of the unbelievers. Yet, given the special emphasis with which the morphologically unfamiliar word is used in the cited verses, there seems "to be hidden a specific and more significant connotation."[55] Rosenthal is struck by the categorical devaluation of a clearly outmoded way of life, brought to expression by the word *jāhilīya*, and this recalls for him a similar categorical devaluation of a culturally nonconforming life mode encountered in post-exilic Judaism. His proposed solution[56] would be to understand *jāhilīya* as an echo of the Jewish concept of *galut*, Aramaic *galutha*, "exile," "diaspora," the articulation of which is similar to the new word formed from the root *j-h-l*, being identical in two consonants.[57] This calque, a neologism integrating elements from two languages, could according to Rosenthal have

> emerged at any time, since the usage of the widespread Jewish term does not necessarily presuppose friendly or close contact with Jews. It is easy to recognize the affinity between *galut* in the way in which it was understood by Jews and *jāhilīya* as the expression was likely understood by Muhammad. In the Mishna, Avot 5:9, it is said that exile comes into the world as a result of idolatry, unchastity (incest), and bloodshed. Exile is a punishment for these sins, which however are not thereby repaid. Exile remains therefore a situation in which these sins persist. . . . *Galut* thus stands for the same characteristics of barbarism, lack of morals, and ignorance in face of the true God that Muhammad criticizes in the *jāhilīya*.[58]

Thus understood, the neologism *jāhilīya* would confirm the strategy that can be observed already by the middle Meccan period, the linking of individual new ideas to special and additional authority through connections to already established religious discourses of the surrounding environment.

If one accepts this interpretation and pushes it yet further, the *galut* discourse that is central to post-exilic Judaism can hardly be overestimated as a counterpart to the perception of *jāhilīya*: by way of this connection of the situation of the unbelievers to the concept of an exclusion from salvation imposed by God, the division between believers and unbelievers could evoke the notion of a decisive point between epochs. In connecting itself through the keyword *jāhilīya* to a Jewish historical dichotomy according to which there exists a condition that needs to be viewed as absolutely negative and only used as a negative foil, not as

55. Rosenthal, *Knowledge Triumphant*, 33.

56. For prior clarifying suggestions, see the discussion in ibid.; cf. also Tamer, *Zeit und Gott*, 6.

57. Hebrew gimel, *g*, corresponds to the Arabic *jīm*, *j*.

58. Rosenthal, *Knowledge Triumphant*, 35, further underlines the connection of *jāhiliya* and *sakīna*, Hebr. *shekhina*, in Q 48:26, which also has a precursor in rabbinic literature, see *Avot de-Rabbi Nathan:* "As long as Israel commits these sins, the *shekhina* will stay far away from the Jews."

a historical time relevant in itself, the Qur'anic community laid the basis for the ostracizing of the prehistory of Islam. But reservations regarding Rosenthal's interpretation remain. It is striking that the community itself did not fully exploit the polemical potential of this distinction. Mentions of *jāhilīya* in the Qur'an are limited to no more than four pronouncements, all closely bound up to situation and context, and not at all programmatic.

The construct of *jāhilīya* was to prevail for only a short period. As is well known, the verdict against the "pagan" past suggested by the Qur'an held only for the first few Islamic generations, for whom *al-jāhilīya* may have signified a "an age of wrong belief, dominated by conflicting tribal interests and rivalries."[59] This position in the Umayyad and Abbasid periods gave way increasingly to a new evaluation, in which *jāhilīya* stood for a " past, where the Arabs were unified, in which the 'true' values of Arab ethnic identity were manifested, and even emphasized as against Persian values."[60] It was only with later epochs, when the Islamic religion was given top status as the uniting bond of society above and beyond Arabic nationality and culture, that the pendulum swung back in the other direction.

3.4.2 *Qur'an and Ancient Arabic Time: Qur'anic Answers to the Images of History in Poetry*

However insecure the boundaries of the preceding period might have been, it can nonetheless be asserted that the self-positioning of the new religious movement in the continuum of time was an important concern of the community from an early point. The entry into a history discourse indeed began long before an auxiliary construction for the demarcation was found in the name *jāhilīya*. It can even be claimed that the initial discovery of an irreconcilable conflict between pagan thought and that of the new movement had to do with a conflict between two incompatible understandings of time. In a recent monograph, Georges Tamer[61] has discussed the connection between the ancient Arabic perception of "all-consuming time," *dahr*, in the poetry, which is also reflected polemically in the Qur'an, and earlier Greek and Hellenistic conceptions. In doing so, he has brought to light an important "overlaying": the role of the Hellenistic Aion, who "turns the ages," being superseded by the working of the one God, whose disposition over time is occasionally equally expressed through the metaphor of turning. This trace should be pursued, since this paradigm shift does not exclusively consist in the replacement of a cosmic or mythical figure by the personal unique God. The Qur'anic engagement with the understanding of time of the

59. Drory, "The Abbasid Construction," 35.

60. Ibid.

61. Tamer, *Zeit und Gott*, 6. A new reflection on time in ancient Arabic poetry is offered in Dmitriev, *Das poetische Werk*, 129–139.

pre-Islamic poets does not only manifest itself in supersession or polemic, nor is it confined to descriptions of God's dealing with the times of day and their particular metaphors,[62] although such examples are particularly striking. The application of the new conception takes place above all in quite neutral, seemingly "non-discursive" contexts, which already imply the new understanding of time. Because this has to do with the predominance of eschatological thinking and the replacement of a cyclical understanding of time with a linear one, the argumentations are frequently embedded into eschatological contexts. Examples are found already in the early Meccan period, for example, in sura 95, "The Fig Tree," *al-tīn*:

wa-l-tīni wa-l-zaytūn
wa-ṭūri sīnīn
wa-hādhā l-baladi l-amīn
la-qad khalaqnā l-insāna fī aḥsani taqwīm
thumma radadnāhu asfala sāfilīn
  illā lladhīna amanū wa-ʿamilū l-ṣāliḥati
  fa-lahum ajrun ghayru mamnūn
fa-mā yukadhdhibuka baʿdu bi-l-dīn
a-laysa llāhu bi-aḥkami l-ḥākimīn

By the fig tree and the olive tree
by Mount Sinai
and this [*hādhā*] secure city.
We created man in the most beautiful form
and brought him down to the lowliest measure.
  But those who believe and do good,
  for them is their deserved reward.
What then [*fa-mā*] leads you still to lie about the judgment?
Is God not the most righteous judge?

The hymnic sura[63] is one of the earliest Qur'an texts to give poetic form to the new linear understanding of time. It begins with four oaths, which closer study reveals to contain an implied notion of time: a pair of types of tree (or fruit) are invoked, which figure as symbols of the divine abundance of creation, but also as trees/fruits emblematic of the Holy Land, thus referring to the biblical *topographia sacra*. What follows, also in pairs, is the naming of two places: Mount Sinai[64] and Mecca, which is recognizable from the deictic *hādhā*, "this." As the

62. Tamer cites Q 39:5 and Q 24:44 as convincing examples, *Zeit und Gott*, 209.

63. On structure, see Neuwirth, *Studien zur Komposition*, 230.

64. *Ṭūr sinīn* in place of *saynāʾ*, with the pronunciation *sinīn* compelled by the rhyme, is the Qur'anic Arabization of an Aramaic toponym; see Jeffery, *Foreign Vocabulary*, 184–185; the Aramaic *ṭūrā de-Sīnā*—the common name of Mount Sinai for Jews and Christians—appears in the Targum to the Song of Songs 8 as the site of the conveying the divine teachings, in juxtaposition with the Mount of Olives, *ṭūr zetāyā*, the site of the resurrection. Traditional juxtapositions like this (see Horovitz, *Koranische Untersuchungen*, 123–125) may resonate in the

parallelism with the place of revelation Sinai signalizes, Mecca is addressed likewise as a sanctuary, the sacral inviolability of which is elsewhere expressly highlighted (Q 106:4). The two oaths upon places combine two no longer completely parallel references to authority that are not wholly parallel, for while the apparition on Sinai, which is a frequent them in early suras (Q 79:15ff., Q 53:36, Q 87:19), is supported through a biblical narrative, the sacredness of Mecca is vouched for only by the local cult of the *rabb hādhā l-bayt*, the "Lord of this [holy] house" (Q 106:3).[65] Nevertheless, both constitute references to the divine self-communication in prehistoric times. A pagan, ancient Arabic convention of style, the oath cluster belonging to the discourse of the seer, is filled out with biblical references (fig tree, olive tree, Mount Sinai), and is thus reclaimed for a context that is biblically imprinted.

The oath pronouncement focusses as is frequent with the topos of the reprimand of man (cf. Q 75:3, 80:17, 86:5, 90:4, 91:6, 100:6), in an assertion of the weakness of "man," *insān*,[66] which here refers to an instability not to be blamed on man himself but rather to one dependent on the creator: after the achievement of physical perfection, man-falls prey to the frailty of age. Leaving the additional verse 6 aside the closing pair of verses, presents a general exhortation to the hearer, They compress what is said into an argument that draws the conclusion (*fa-mā*, "what then") of the logical necessity of the Final Judgment.

Involved in this construction are, first, the notion of primordial time reaching back to creation and the communication of divine teaching, then the limited period of human life, and then finally the eschatological time of judgment. In what relation do they stand together in the sura? There is no immediately evident logical-causal relation between the discursive elements suggested by the rhetorical question "What lets you still lie about the judgment?" The relation becomes clear only through the sequence of symbols,[67] already schematic in the early suras which starts with evocations of creation (here: figs / fig tree, *tīn*, and olive / olive tree, *zaytūn*), to be followed by references to divine self-communication (here: Sinai and Mecca), and which have to be understood as initial scenes arousing the expectation of corresponding concluding settings. Thus creation, which in verse 1 is evoked with the image of the trees, ends necessarily with the end of the created world, not alone with the death of the individual (verse 5), but more generally with the resolution of the cosmos in the final day. Equally, the divine self-communication/teaching highlighted with the Sinai reference in verse

Qur'anic oath cluster alluding to the covenant, verses 1–2. Evocations of Sinai as an emblem of divine self-revelation are found in the early suras (see Q 61), even before Moses's revelation was presented in narrative; on the Qur'anic stories of Moses, cf. Speyer, *Qoranische Erzählungen*.

65. Cf. on such authorization references chap. 5, 171–172.

66. On this topos, see ibid.

67. See Neuwirth, "Images and Metaphors." Cf. also chap. 5, 166–168.

2 necessarily requires the repayment of the pledge of knowledge through the accounting at the end of times. A mention of the final day, which indeed follows at the end of the sura (verse 7–8), has therefore already been anticipated by the hearer after the mention of creation and divine self-communication.

The sura closes with a suggestive rhetorical question about God's function as judge. It reverses the empirically grounded verdict about the negative fate of man hurrying to life's end (verses 4–5) introducing an element of God's active intervention: God cancels the end and grants to man a duration that goes beyond death. This reversal of the sentence of mortality is also implemented rhetorically: indeed, man sinks down to the "lowest measure" (literally: to the "lowliest of the lowly"), but God, who already at the beginning of times worked as creator and teacher, appears at the end of times as restorer of order, as judge of all judges[68]—the identical comparative construction in Arabic of both pronouncements (verses 5 and 8) underlines their comparably secure truth. God removes the power of cyclical time, according to which the end of mankind brings death, while he extends linear time back into preexistence (*khalaqnā*, "we created," verse 4) and forward into eternity (*dīn*, "judgment," verse 7). A "sacred historical time," an eschatologically determined term for mankind, has begun with this teaching. It runs in opposition to his natural created lifetime in a non-cyclical way, and thus softens the threat of the physical end given by the accomplishment of the cycle.[69]

3.4.3 Sura 55: Qur'anic Answers to Biblical Images of History

While the time discourse in sura 95 appears as an already achieved position embedded in a creation theology and does not seem to require explicit justification against other points of view, there are also Qur'anic attestations of historically specific positions taking shape before the ears of the hearers, so to speak, in contradistinction to existing models of thought. The example that is perhaps the most striking for its intertextuality is the early Meccan sura 55, which engages a widespread biblical text that is very prominent in the liturgy of the Jewish and Christian traditions.

The sura, celebrated in Islam as *ʿarūs al-qurʾān*, "bride of the Qur'an," can for its part be counted as one of the most poetic texts of the Qur'an. It presents a central theological point, the complete symmetry of the divine order of creation, not

68. On God's function as a judge, see Rippin, "God." God as judge is a common image in the Psalms: Psalms 67:5: "because you judge people with fairness"; Psalms 98:9: "because He comes to judge the earth; He will judge the world righteously; and its people fairly."

69. The formulation of exception in verse 6 is revealed to be a post hoc addition through the excessive verse length and the analytic construction. It expresses the audience expectations of a later period, when the faithful listeners desired to be excepted from the negative judgment on man through a general eschatological reassurance. The fact that these softening formulas collide semantically with the pronouncements of the sura and contrast with its poetic character through its formulaic-analytic style has been accepted only reluctantly; cf. chap. 5, 185–187.

only semantically but also grammatically, that is, morphologically, syntactically, and tonally. It begins with a short hymn (Q 55:1–4):

al-Raḥmān
ʿallama l-qurʾān
khalaqa l-insān
ʿallamahu l-bayān

The merciful
he taught the Qur'an
he created man
taught him understanding / clear speech.

The conveyance of teaching (verse 2) and the faculty for clear thought/speech (verse 4) on the one hand and of creation (verse 3) on the other are the two great themes of the sura. While the text is dedicated semantically almost constantly to creation or to its fulfillment in paradise, the secondary theme of teaching and clear speech[70] is unfolded less in argument than linguistically, by means of rhetoric. Balanced order is thus a characteristic of the signified, creation, as also of the sign itself, language. Since the recital of the Qur'an itself counts as the most sublime speech act, *bayān*, "clear speech," can be understood above all as an evocation of Qur'anic language, and the sura should be recognized as an exposition of the interworking of *khalq*, "creation," and *qurʾān*, "revelation, divine teaching." Two ideas invested in creation itself pervade the sura: the symmetrically balanced order that informs both the world, *physis*, and the medium of its hermeneutical understanding, *logos*. The morphological dual form that pervades the entire sura, though it is often judged pejoratively as merely ornamental in research, cannot be disparaged in its form and functionality.

We thus have a text that is almost philosophical, which sets itself outside of the communication scenario that is so frequently bound up with circumstances in other Meccan texts of this period. It is not merely that the frequent refrain, with its rhetorical questioning, is directed to the mythical dual group of men and demons rather than to the historical hearers.[71] In addition, the discursive thread of the sura itself moves outside of worldly reality. The first part (verses 1–13) summarizes the primordial work of creation, while the second part (verses 14–36) contrasts the creation of men and demons and refers to potential rebels among the demons, who would rebel against the order of creation within its cosmically determined limits. The eschatological ending (verses 37–78) recalls cursorily the "historical" liars (verse 43) but remains elsewhere devoted to the

70. *Bayān*, literally "making clear," "clarification," can refer to thought as well as its articulation. On the prologue to sura 55, see also chap. 2, 89–92.

71. See Neuwirth, "Images and Metaphors."

mythical ensemble of men and demons, who appear on the Final Day in the situation of the judgment, where they are granted their verdict and retribution. In this, the fate of the damned is only briefly glanced, while for the righteous the place of their otherworldly bliss is painted with a detail unknown elsewhere, employing a unique arsenal of stylistic means. This part, the double description of paradise, forms the actual climax of the sura, as we shall see. The life in the hereafter, occurring within a spatially imagined eternity, is the central theological point of the sura.

A number of shared ideas and formulations, chiefly the unique antiphonic structure of the sura, show that this text stands in an intertextual relation to Psalm 136, which is also an antiphonic text. In sura 55, we not only have an exegetical reworking of this psalm but also a new theological reading, a counter-text intended as such, that deals above all with the psalmic understanding of time and eternity and evaluates these anew. Already the characteristic that is most closely bound to both texts, the refrain, is not identical. In the psalm it is an assurance of providence, *ki le-ʿolam ḥasdo*, "for in eternity shall be his grace." In the Qur'an it takes the form of a rhetorical question with a triumphant tenor, directed to creation as a whole, both men and demons: *fa-bi-ayyi ʾalāʾi rabbikumā tukadhdhibān*, "Which of the signs of your Lord will the two of you two deny?" God's grace is here not a promise for eternity but rather a reality, which can be "read" out of the signs of creation.[72]

Both texts at first unfold semantically in close relation to each other, as their beginning parts treat creation. But then the sequence of thoughts of the sura turns away from that of the psalm, which engages in a detailed recollection of history. A number of divine interventions, acts of the annihilation of enemies, are enumerated, whose salvific impact on the addressed confirms the truth of the promise of divine providence that is pronounced in the refrain. Historical recollection as a warrant of divine promise, as assurance of providence, had also played a role at the start of the proclamation, when historical memory shared with the pagan Meccans could still be set forth (e.g., sura 105).[73] With the shift toward the eschatological future, and with the appearance of the proclaimer as a prophetic speaker in the strict sense, history presents itself in retrospect, in light of the perception of contingency now standing at the center, no longer as worthy of trust but rather as a sequence of episodes of human failure that have brought about divine acts of punishment.

Although sura 55 remains beholden throughout to the refrain structure given by the psalm, it develops into a counter-text in its crucial section: it sets a diametric opposite against the psalmic historical memory, offering a future projection and eschatological description that, following the principle that permeates

72. Cf. chap. 7, 264–277.
73. Ibid.

the sura of demonstration of symmetry, is further dominated by pairs. The figuration of the "two gardens," *jannatān* (verse 62), connected to two further gardens, is not, as some critics claim, a result of the compulsion of rhyme[74] but rather depends on a stylistic convention of ancient Arabic poetry that employs dual descriptions of place to express the vastness of space; *jannatān* signifies—as some native Arabic philologists have pointed out[75]—"gardens upon gardens, endless gardens." As an illustration of the two paradise descriptions that are unfolded in the sura, verses 46–61 and verses 62–78, we present the latter:

wa-min dūnihimā jannatān
  fa-bi-ayyi alāʾi rabbikumā tukadhdhibān
mudhāmmatān
  fa-bi-ayyi alāʾi rabbikumā tukadhdhibān
fīhimā ʿaynāni naḍḍākhatān
  fa-bi-ayyi alāʾi rabbikumā tukadhdhibān
fīhimā fākihatun wa-nakhlun wa-rummān
  fa-bi-ayyi alāʾi rabbikumā tukadhdhibān
fīhinna khayrātun ḥiṣān
  fa-bi-ayyi alāʾi rabbikumā tukadhdhibān
ḥūrun maqṣūratun fī l-khiyām
  fa-bi-ayyi alāʾi rabbikumā tukadhdhibān
lam yaṭmithhunna insun qablahum wa-lā l-jānn
  fa-bi-ayyi alāʾi rabbikumā tukadhdhibān
muttakiʾīna ʿalā rafrafin khuḍrin wa-ʿabqarīyin ḥiṣān
  fa-bi-ayyi alāʾi rabbikumā tukadhdhibān
tabāraka smu rabbika dhī l-jalāli wa-l-ikrām

And aside from these are two gardens.
  Which of the signs of your lord will the two of you deny?
Of thick green.
  Which signs of your Lord will the two of you deny?
Therein are two rich over-bubbling springs.
  Which of the signs of your lord will the two of you deny?
Therein are fruit trees, palms, and pomegranates.
  Which of the signs of your lord will the two of you deny?
Therein are young girls, good, lovely—
  Which of the signs of your lord will the two of you deny?

74. Nöldeke, *Geschichte des Qorans*, 1:30: "If for example in sura 55 there is mention of *two* heavenly gardens, two types of fruits, and two further similar gardens, one sees clearly that the dual form is used on account of the rhyme"—a passage that is taken over by Schwally unaltered in GdQ², 40. Nöldeke repeated his assessment in 1910 in *Neue Beträge zur semitischen Sprachwissenschaft*, 9: "Rhyme necessitates the heavy dual forms in sura 55."

75. See Neuwirth, "Symmetrie und Paarbildung."

With black eyes, shielded in tents—
  Which of the signs of your lord will the two of you deny?
Which no man or demon has ever touched—
  Which of the signs of your lord will the two of you deny?
Leaning on beautiful green cushions
Lying there on *abqari* tapestries.
  Which of the signs of your lord will the two of you deny?
Praised be the name of your lord, full of majesty and honor.

3.4.4 Sura 55: Qur'anic Answers to Historically Specific Aporias of Ancient Arabic poetry

The vision of the ultimate future in sura 55 is surprising in its closeness to worldly scenes. The striking references to civilization in the praising of paradise, verses 70–76, require an explanation. Josef Horovitz[76] has explained such references to material luxury as the "green cushions," and "*abqari* tapestries," and the presence of beautiful young women (verses 70–74) in relation to the contemporary appreciation of banquets, and above all the poetic descriptions of wine drinking. But sensory pleasure in a promised hereafter is in no way unique to the Qur'an. Early church fathers such as Irenaeus of Lyon (around 140–200) claimed that the interaction between the sexes will persist in paradise[77]. The paradise hymns of the Syriac theologian and poet Ephrem (306–373) although not explicit are also clearly erotically encoded.[78] But mere reference to literary models for individual images does not suffice to explain the particular interweavings of nature, eroticism, and civilization in the Qur'anic paradise. Indeed, ancient Arabic descriptions of wine drinking occur without reference to luxuriant nature, and Ephrem's paradise hymns are without references to civilization. Yet all three elements do play a central role within pre-Islamic poetry: in the *nasīb*, the nostalgic opening part of the ancient Arabic long-form poem (the qasida).

The paradise description in sura 55 is thus not only an answer to the psalmic presentation of the presence of God as lord of history that is expressed in Psalm 136. It is above all an engagement with late antique traditions that can be found in texts lying closer to the Qur'an in time. The references to Ephrem's paradise hymns are unmistakable, although these still require systematic study. But the sura is equally close to ancient Arabic scenes, though less to the poetic banquet scenes assumed by Horowitz than to the situation presented in the *nasīb*, the complaint of the poet on the ruins, the *aṭlāl*. For only this scenario makes recurring reference to the entire trio of nature, erotics, and civilization. Not only do

76. Horovitz, "Das koranische Paradies."

77. See McDannell and Lang, *Heaven*, 47–68, who contrasts the representative of the sensual pleasures of paradise, Irenaeus of Lyon, with the ascetic Augustine of Hippo (354–430).

78. See Beck, *Ephräms Paradieshymnen*.

beautiful young women play a role there, so do the luxury objects found in the paradise description, pillows and tapestries, which are among the accessories of the litters carrying the women of the tribe, among whom is found the beloved praised by the poet for her beauty, who disappears from his sight on the morning of parting. What is present in the paradise description are objects of longing of the ancient Arab poet as well. But above all, it is his poetic location, the space of earlier social interaction that is now desolate, that serves as the trigger for the poetic complaint of the past that has found an inverted image of the luxurious and festive scenario of the banquet in paradise. While the poetic banquet scenes merely depict a moment of temporary pleasure that also includes elements disapproved of by the Qur'an,[79] the *nasīb* scenario stands closer discursively to the Qur'anic paradise descriptions: the Qur'an takes up the poet's complaint of the past and transfers it—with clear reference to the *nasīb* topos of complaint about the loss of socially animated nature, erotics, and civilization—into a praise of immortality.

In sura 55 and Psalm 136 we have two contrasting texts about divine power and God's administering of care toward created beings. The psalm has to do with God's creation and preservation, and the election of his people throughout time and history. The sura pertains to creation and worldly preservation as well, but is substantially concerned with the restoration of lost communication and historical reflection. While the psalm sees the proof of the divine presence in the dramatics of salvation and annihilation, in the Qur'an it is the sensible order of creation that stands at the center, and of which the verbal presentation of the proclamation is itself the proof.[80] Putting it in a pointed way one might say: the sura has less to do not with historical memory as such than with hermeneutics.

The new Qur'anic reading of Psalm 136 thus marks a reversal of the direction of impact in history and inner-worldly time, in favor of eschatology and hermeneutics—God-man interaction consists primarily not in divine intervention in social-political life but rather in a sharing of signs, the verbal announcement of revelation, and the "figurative handwriting" of creation. This kind of self-referentiality is foreign to the psalm. But the Qur'an, the product of an age of rhetoric, is not confined to hymnic speech, but rather orchestrates, together with the praising of God as the creator and teacher, a depiction of the triumphant idea of verbal virtuosity reachable in Arabic, and thus implicitly praises the hermeneutic sensibility of the historical community of hearers.

79. The uninhibited speech (*laghwun wa-lahwun*) favored in that setting is a target of Qur'anic criticism, see Q 88:11, 78:35, 56:25, 19:62. Still, the cups, wine, and musk that are attributed to the banquet may be reminiscences of the poetic feast descriptions cited by Horovitz.

80. Neuwirth, "Form and Structure of the Qur'ān."

3.5 History in the Qur'an

3.5.1 *Al-Umam al-Khāliya: The "Lost Peoples"*

How does the Qur'an view the history that preceded the proclamation? In view of the "canonical process"[81] which is at work in the Qur'an and the plural discourses that develop in succession within it, the question must be addressed on several levels. At the beginning of the development stands the conception of the divine assurance of providence, which derives from divine care experienced on the personal level and intervention on the social level, as well as trust in the further preservation and caretaking of God.[82] But this discourse, which stands in the psalmic tradition and counteracts the ancient Arabic worldview with its notion of the "contested" and always threatened space, is superseded already in early Mecca by a discourse based on eschatological visions, which are typologically more Prophetic. In the center of this stands contingency, the reality of the order of nature that is revocable at any time, and which was previously celebrated as safe and supported by God. In this context, the punishment legends, the stories of the "past/lost/by-gone peoples," *al-umam al-khāliya*, and the "messengers" *mursalūn*, sent to them, who call out for a pure faith in unity of God but do not prevail, play a central role. Here the Qur'an presents, as Tarif Khalidi has put it, "a landscape where time is less a chronology than a continuum."[83] It is nonetheless a continuum in which mankind is offered a *kairos,* unique point in time to make a fateful decision.

The histories of the peoples of the peninsula who were obliterated by punishment due to their refusal to accept belief in one God have been treated in the exemplary study by Josef Horovitz.[84] They occur in the Qur'an above all in the early Meccan period, but are later called to mind again and again.[85] All of them must have been familiar to the hearers from oral tradition, as allusions to such legends occur also in ancient Arabic poetry.[86] As some of these legends are localized in the further surroundings of the community, their traces can serve as empirically founded instructions. The events reported in the stories ultimately reflect the situation of the proclaimer in his milieu and are meant to influence the decisions required in reality by the hearers. Empirically perceptible "archaeology" finds a theological interpretation in the Qur'an: ruins take on an explanation, supported by the senses, as monuments of human moral failure in history. Together, the

81. See the introduction, 22–25.

82. Cf. chap. 7, 244–247.

83. Khalidi, *Arab Historical Thought*, 8.

84. Horovitz, *Koranische Untersuchungen*; see also the study by Marshall, *God, Muhammad and the Unbelievers*, 39–115.

85. Wansbrough, *Quranic Studies*, 20–25, bases his theory of a later Qur'an compilation from separate, individual traditions inter alia on the frequent repetitions of these stories.

86. See Hoyland, *Arabia and the Arabs*, 223–224.

punishment legends give expression to the biblical perception exemplified by the tower of Babel, that hubris before God cannot be maintained.

Yet unlike the case in Gen 11, it is not alleged to *al-umam al-khāliya* that they intended, as did their arrogant predecessors, to make a name for themselves; rather, they simply behaved out of folly, out of arrogated "independence." The Qur'anic reference to the ruins of the predecessors goes beyond referring to an intended moralist lesson. The model *of al-umam al-khāliya* and its centrality can only be adequately explained if one sets it in the context of ancient Arabic poetry—concretely, if one connects it, as was proposed for the description of paradise, to the central motif of the *nasīb*, the description of the *aṭlāl*, the weathered traces of earlier encampments. The speech of the poet standing nostalgically before these ruins opens to an aporia that is even often made explicit, the question of the whereabouts of the inhabitants of the historical past, the *ubi sunt qui ante nos in mundo fuere*?[87] One might hold that the question that remains open in the poetry finds an answer in the Qur'an. Certainly, the earlier inhabitants of the peninsula are not identical to the poetry's vanished inhabitants of former settlements, who were forced to follow the climatically conditioned nomadic cycles of movement and to disband at the new year, thus abandoning their places and disrupting former amorous interactions, breaking their emotional and social bonds. But the standpoint of each of these respective observers is similar, as in both cases he stands before abandoned traces of former social life. Indeed, in the Qur'an the earlier occupants of the space have themselves brought about the necessity of their disappearance and obliteration, for, as the punishment legends clearly evince, they missed their chance to turn back, their *kairos*. The viewing of their traces in the Qur'an is thus not the trigger of individual melancholy, as in the poetry, but rather an incentive toward critical self-reflection concerning the fate of the collective.

The histories of destruction are not—as in the biblical histories of the destruction of the enemies of Israel—primarily proofs of the divine power to intervene in history, nor are they primarily divine assurances of God's continuous caretaking out of loyalty to an elected people; indeed, the histories mention no salvation of the community's forebears. Their positive message lies elsewhere. Punishment stories in the Qur'an are at the same time stories of the triumphs of those who remain steadfast. The godly messengers involved in the respective events, predecessors of the proclaimer, triumph even if their mission remains unsuccessful; they are saved through divine interference and—in a later phase—raised up to become part of the liturgical memory of the community, their names receiving a eulogistic epithet, such as *salāmun ʿalā Nūḥin*, "peace upon Noah" (cf. Q 37:79, 109, 120, 130). Through their persistence, the messengers

87. See Becker, "Ubi sunt qui ante nos in mundo fuere?"

convert the virtue of "bravery," *ḥamāsa*, which was practiced excessively and sporadically by the ancient Arabic hero, into "patience," *ṣabr*, mitigating but also extending it. *Ṣabr* becomes a "cardinal virtue" of the Qur'anic community; the punishment legends are therefore also exempla of patient persistence.[88] Even if this role of the godly messenger is only implied in sura 91, "The Sun," nonetheless the unnamed godly messenger stands implicitly in this sura as the typus of the patient man (Q 91:1–15):

wa-l-shamsi wa-ḍuḥāhā
wa-l-qamari idhā talāhā
wa-l-nahāri idhā jallāhā
wa-l-layli idhā yaghshāhā
wa-l-samāʾi wa-mā banāhā
wa-l-arḍi wa-mā ṭaḥāhā
wa-nafsin wa-mā sawwāhā
fa-alhamahā fujūrahā wa-taqwāhā
qad aflaḥa man zakkāhā
wa-qad khāba man dassāhā

kadhdhabat Thamūdu bi-ṭaghwāhā
idhi nbaʿatha ashqāhā
fa-qāla lahum rasūlu llāhi nāqata llāhi wa-suqyāhā
fa-kadhdhabūhu fa-ʿaqarūhā
fa-damdama ʿalayhim rabbuhum bi-dhanbihim fa-sawwāhā
wa-lā yakhāfū ʿuqbāhā

By the sun and the early morning
and the moon when it follows it.
By the day, when he lets it shine,
and the night when he covers it.
By the heavens and that which built it,
and the earth and that which spread it out.
By a soul and that which formed it
And gave it its disloyalty and its piety!
Blessed it the man who keeps it pure!
Woe to him who tramples on it!

The Thamud lied in their rebelliousness
when the wretched one appeared among them.
For the messenger of God said to them:
"God's camel, let her to drink"

88. Cragg, *The Event of the Qur'ān*, 158.

But they called him a liar and threw it to the ground.
Your Lord came over them for their sin
And made them the same as the face of the earth,
Without fearing the consequences.

The two-part sura prepares the way for the narrative with an eight-verse oath series (part 1: verses 1–8). Although this series seems from its content to have no reference to the punishment legends that follow, it offers the structural key for an interpretation that goes beyond the mere moralistic message. It consists entirely of contrasting or complementary pairs, so that the liturgical idea evoked by the naming of the prayer time of *ḍuḥā* (cf. Q 91:1, 79:29),[89] and thus a human participation in the divine unity, is first hidden by the wealth of opposites within creation: after the contrast in the cosmic domain of heavenly bodies (verses 1–4) and of heaven and earth (verses 5–6), which is at first conveyed neutrally, that is, shown without moral implications, the various contrary inclinations of man are thematized as part of the divine work of creation (verses 7–8). In that the opposite pairs can be read at the same time as mutual completions representing the divine work of creation in its totality, the ambivalent final oath verse *fa-alhamahā fujūrahā wa-taqwāhā*, "and gave it its disloyalty and its piety" obtains a positive connotation: "God has put into the soul [the choice between] disloyalty and piety." Only on account of this freedom can man choose for himself. But if the catalogue that becomes moral toward its end owes its impact above all to the contrast, it increases the tense expectation of the hearer for a breaking of the chain of contrasts, until finally opening into the oath pronouncement (verses 9–10). It contains a liberating exclamation of benediction over those who have made the right choice between the options of the relevant pair of contrasts[90] and an evocation of woe for the thoughtless ones.

The punishment legend that ensues in the second part (verses 11–15), the earliest Qur'anic example of this genre, is not an isolated moral narrative, but rather demonstrates the ambivalence of human creation evoked in the oath cluster in a concrete event. The story, which may have been in circulation in pre-Islamic times as a familiar local legend regarding a cultic sacrilege of the Thamudians (Thamūd),[91] obtains in the Qur'an a theological point. Here the offense, the sacrilegious slaughter of a consecrated camel, is presented in connection with the punishment-legend topos of rebelliousness against the messenger of God. The sacrilege is a hostile act against the messenger of God, who—probably in response to his sermon—is accused of lying (verse 14). Sacrilege and defamation are paid for with the destruction of the insubordinate people.

89. Cf. chap. 5, 172–173.
90. Neuwirth, "Images and Metaphors."
91. Bencheikh, "Iram ou le clameur de Dieu."

But at the same time, the legend is presented in service of an argument. It is an exemplum of the false choice between the contrasting possibilities offered in the oath statement: "Blessed is the man, who keeps it [the soul] pure! Woe to the man, who tramples on it!" (verses 9–10). For it attests the refusal of the purification of the "soul," *nafs*. This purification (verse 9) is no purely individual act; it is at once a contribution to the safeguarding of the structures of creation. For in view of the extensive and increasingly moralistic catalogue of contraries, the purification comes to seem like a liberating interference into the chain of contraries, which can only be broken if its ambivalence (verses 8–10) is canceled by the insertion of a positive position free of contrast.[92] This and the contrary decision are both eschatologically relevant, as both final calls aim toward the evaluation in the hereafter of those deciding in the here and now, who must decide (verses 9–10).

In that the legend demonstrates the failure to realize at the moment of decision, the *kairos*, initiated in the oath statement, which had been evoked again in the call of the messenger of God (verse 13), it throws a threatening light onto the situation of the hearers who refuse the message of the proclaimer, to whom a *kairos*, a chance for their own salvation, is opened.[93] At the same time, the persuasive power, *persuasio*, that stems from the creation-theological embedding of the legend makes possible an insight into the dimension of meaning attached to the acceptance of the message of the messenger, one that far exceeds the decision for one's personal well-being.

3.6 Prophetic Succession, Counter-History, and Chronological History

This early punishment-legend discourse, which is much more concerned with the theological anchoring of the delivery of the message than with concrete history, and from which linear historical perceptions cannot be gleaned, is to be distinguished clearly from a later conception that takes shape in the middle and late Meccan phases of the Qur'an genesis.[94] Here, a new paradigm is established, which redirects the focus from the abandoned settlements in the present environment to the area, familiar only through textual references, of the messengers of God of the earlier Jewish and Christian traditions. The new center, which also becomes the orientation point of the direction of prayer, is no longer the local but rather the "distant" sanctuary, the Temple Mount in Jerusalem. The biblical messengers of God are now thematized increasingly clearly as a succession of prophets, a firm sequence, which stems from Noah through Abraham, Moses,

92. Neuwirth, "Images and Metaphors."

93. The messenger's direct speech and the account of its disregard (verses 14 and 16) probably originally stood together, so that the sura would have ended with the destructions of the Thamudians in verse 15; see Neuwirth, *Studien zur Komposition*, 228–229.

94. Cf. chap. 8, 277–279.

and Jesus and finally reaches down to the proclaimer himself. Their activities not only fill out a scenario composed of a differentiated sequence of historical episodes, but also show a tendency toward chronological order. Their interactions reflect concrete social experience and show themselves to be suited to serve as representative examples for the behavior of the proclaimer and the community in situations of crisis and, even more often, to offer a key to the understanding of their own plight.[95] Here, we can no longer speak only of the projection of one's own contemporary experience against the image of the past, which was representative for the earlier discourse; on the contrary, it is the experiences of the past that becomes a model for the understanding of one's own present. The community, which now inscribes itself as a new people of God in the salvation history of the earlier ones, selecting the Israelites led by Moses as a model and assuming the prayer direction of Jerusalem, thus constructs a counter-history in the face of its own local tradition.

It must have been the diverse upheavals in connection to the wholly new situation in Medina that later introduced yet another turn in historical perception. In the Medinan period, salvation history was displaced from the Holy Land to the peninsula itself. Thus, the community left the biblical text world that it had shared with the older religious groups, which held the Holy Land as the core of its imagined topography. This was manifested outwardly in the changing of the prayer direction from Jerusalem to Mecca.[96] But above all, the change of direction is reflected Medinan narratives. The central protagonist now is no longer Moses but Abraham, who is set into relief as the founder of the Meccan sanctuary and originator of the pilgrimage. The Kaaba and its rites now obtain a new dimension of meaning from the perspective of the exilic community, and now require, since Mecca has assumed the rank of an exilic sanctuary, a clear localization in the new religious discourse characterized by Abraham's worship of God.

Abraham thus acquires diverse new functions, among which his building of the Kaaba and his founding of the pilgrimage take pride of place.[97] His appearance as builder of the Kaaba in Mecca is neither biblical nor vouched for by post-biblical traditions, but is all the same vested with biblical authority, as the Qur'anic report restages an Abraham-Isaac scenario that is unfolded narratively in the Jewish and Christian tradition but now links the story to Abraham and Ishmael.[98] The foundation of the Kaaba presents itself here on the one hand as an analogue to the consecration of the Solomonic Temple and on the other hand as corresponding to the establishment by Isaac and Abraham of the sanctuary on Mount Moria, the site of the later Jerusalem Temple. It follows the model of

95. Neuwirth, "Erzählen als kanonischer Prozess."
96. See chap. 9, 332–337.
97. Sinai, *Studien zur frühen Koraninterpretation*, 135–144.
98. See chap. 11, 401–404.

post-biblical retellings of the Abraham-Isaac story, but it alters it from a legitimation story for the election of the descendants of Abraham through Isaac into an etiology of the Arabian Meccan sanctuary, exchanging the persons of the heirs of Abraham: the forefather of the Arabs, Ishmael, takes the place of Isaac, who in Judaism heads the Abrahamic tradition.[99] The Meccan sanctuary is thus a foundation of Abraham, deemed to be universal, but which is bound up in salvation history to the forefather of the Arabs. Its cultic legend corrects, so to speak, the older versions of a sanctuary foundation involving Abraham and Isaac, so that here we can speak of a renewed Qur'anic *counter-history*, counter to the biblical story followed earlier.

Finally, in Medina some verses also refer to actual history—military victories and defeats, and confrontations waged with learned Medinan Jews. Although these historical memories describe these events as divine interventions, or at least as being achieved with God's help, they do not assume a form of presentation that would be suitable to mold the reports into a narratively coherent history to be preserved for all time in memory. What therefore remains remarkable—and here we agree with Fred Donner—is the fact that despite the increasing interest in history in the Qur'an, the events in which the community itself is involved at no point crystalize into a grand narrative[100] such as we can read in the Hebrew Bible or its emulation in the Gospels. The Qur'an reflects no sequence comparable to the biblical world drama,[101] as could be further developed in liturgy into an annual cycle of worship. A corresponding realization of history is thus also lacking in the finally fixed Islamic cult.

But one's own participation in history, with the entrance of the Qur'anic community into the world of communities equipped with scripture, which was achieved in Medina, was understood as an event of seismic dimensions: *law anzalnā hādhā l-qurʾāna ʿalā jabalin la-raʾaytahu khāshiʿan mutaṣaddiʿan min khashyati llāhi*, "If we had sent down this Qur'an on a mountain, you would see it falling and shattered from the fear of God" (Q 59:21).[102] Such a triumphant confirmation of the authority-giving revelation could hardly have been thinkable in the earlier stages of the Qur'anic development. It marks a caesura in the perception of one's own history.

In view of the still awaited historical conclusions that can only be gained through a microstructural diachronic reading, it must be surprising that the value of a chronological reading of the Qur'an is more often than not disputed or even relinquished by historians.[103] Certainly, one might agree with Marco Schöller's

99. Witztum, "The Foundation of the House."

100. Cf. chap. 9, 313–316.

101. Cf. chap. 6, 208–212.

102. Khalidi, *Arab Historical Thought*, 7. The verse is Medinan.

103. Rippin, "Muhammad in the Qur'ān"; see additionally the criticism in Marshall, *God, Muhammad and the Unbelievers*, 8–15.

assertion of the merely "accidental historicity of the Quranic pronouncement."[104] The Qur'an itself is not essentially interested in exterior chronology, but rather in the sense of what is presented. But even if the Qur'an stands particularly far from the model of a history book in comparison to the two other scriptures, and even if it speaks above all paraenetically and increasingly raises the claim to timelessness in the course of its development, it should be deemed all the more remarkable how clearly it gives information about the history of perceptions, as it relates stories from different perspectives, from varying dispositions of space and time. Although the Qur'an draws no continuous history of its past and present, still a history of the Qur'anic perspective, that is, of the changing view of world and self of the proclaimer and his community, can well be constructed in its rough outlines.

104. Schoeler, *Exegetisches Denken*, 8–15.

4

Redaction and History of the Text

4.1 History of Transmission up to the Uthmanic Redaction

In the dispute being waged at present in the media and in some polemical writings about Islam over the "authenticity" of the transmitted Qur'an,[1] skeptics increasingly focus on the relevance of unpublished manuscripts that putatively conceal revolutionary alternative forms of the Qur'an—as if the relevance of the text should stand or fall entirely on its early manuscript transmission. But the Qur'an text, which is intensively poetic and shaped to fit memorization, was not transmitted primarily in writing but above all orally—indeed, even the standard modern print edition of 1925 is based not on manuscripts but rather, as Gotthelf Bergsträsser has expounded in a thorough investigation, on oral philological tradition.[2] The scholarly storm surrounding the origins of the Qur'an, with its stubborn focus on manuscripts, thus comes to nothing. What it does demonstrate is exaggerated skeptical zeal, widespread in general vis-a-vis Islamic cultural achievements or claims which in this particular case casts doubts on the community's capacity to have achieved the unprecedentedly rapid collective agreement on a *textus ne varietur* for the Qur'an. As John Reeves has recently shown,[3] such ultra-rigorous standards could never be applied to the Hebrew Bible—where it has long been accepted that the Masoretic text, regarded canonical since the Middle Ages, is neither the oldest nor the best transmitted text. Yet no one would seriously throw doubt for that reason on the text of the Hebrew Bible questioning its "authenticity." Nor does the diversity of apocryphal gospels from the second century onward,[4] illuminated by international Bible scholarship in the modern period, undermine the canonical New Testament's status as an authoritative corpus. A glance at the much more transparent state of the tradition of the Qur'an not only shows that no comparable spectrum of competing traditions is involved, it moreover compels the insight that in the case of the

1. The chapter is an extended and revised version of an account in Neuwirth, "Der Koran." On the contemporary debates, see Burgmer, *Streit um den Koran*, 82–97; Ohlig, "Einleitung"; see also Marx, "Was ist eigentlich der Koran?"

2. Bergsträsser, "Koranlesung in Kairo."

3. Reeves, "Problematizing the Bible."

4. On the theological relevance of the Nag Hammadi findings, cf. Pagels, *Fünftes Evangelium*, and in general, Ehrman, *Lost Scriptures*, and Ehrman, *Lost Christianities*.

Qur'an we are confronted with only one single tradition, which seems in neither its oral nor its written transmission to have generated substantial variants. The accusations raised in early Shiite circles against Qur'an redactors, alleging that they suppressed alternative text forms, do not make up a valuable counterargument.[5] The arguments adduced in the Shiite sources—claiming that explicit mentions of persons from the Prophet's family have been eliminated in the canonical edition—are hardly convincing in view of the Qur'anic general tendency to leave contemporary individuals unnamed. Two short individual suras ascribed to Ubayy's codex have already been shown by Nöldeke[6] to be no more than epigonal imitations of short Qur'an suras.

Our emphasis on the reliability of the tradition that has come down to us with the Uthmanic text is not meant, however, to downplay the significance of manuscripts, on which we must rely, primarily for the accurate orthographic reconstruction of the oldest text forms. In view of the primacy of the oral transmission and the still little developed codicological research, the following summary presentation will sideline the issue of the manuscripts and deal primarily with the literary manifestation of the oral tradition.[7]

4.1.1 *The Qur'an at the Death of the Prophet*

Any attempt to reconstruct the first processes of collection after the death of the Prophet in the year 632 meets with problems in evaluating the reports of the indigenous transmitters. Though the individual hadith traditions contradict each other in personal and chronological details,[8] they share the zeal to highlight the miraculous, which is acknowledged as immanent in the Qur'an, to be equally involved in the initiative of the gathering of the Qur'an. Their presentation, according to which the corpus for the first Qur'an collection was carefully carried out under the supervision of the Prophet's scribe Zayd ibn Thābit under the reign of Abū Bakr (r. 11–13/632–634) or ʿUmar (r. 12–23/634–644), drawing from disparate fragmentary materials such as palm stalks, potsherds, shoulder bones, etc. and only secondarily from the memory of the hearers, cannot be maintained in view of the results of literary analysis and must therefore be considered a strong exaggeration.[9]

5. See Brunner, *Schia*; Brunner, "Einige schiitische Stimmen"; Amir-Moezzi and Kohlberg, *Revelation and Falsification*.

6. Nöldeke and Schwally, *GdQ*², 2:33–43.

7. An intensive examination of the script traditions, in continuation of an older, intermittently interrupted survey project, is underway in the Corpus Coranicum project. See "Handschriften," 267–273.

8. The various traditions are discussed in Welch, "Kur'ān," 404–409; cf. also Nöldeke and Schwally, *GdQ*², 1–27. See now also Motzki, "The Collection of the Qur'an."

9. Burton, *The Collection of the Qur'ān*, argued that the Prophet intended to make final edits himself and must have left behind a complete codex intended to be normative. The surviving accounts of a post-Muhammad edition have no real basis, but rather served to enable the *uṣūl*-scholars to ascribe the legal practices not supported by the vulgate text to the Koran, the first source of law. By appealing to auxiliary traditions—following Burton—these traditions would have been postulated for just this purpose. However, Burton does not sufficiently address the

For Theodor Nöldeke,[10] who first submitted the indigenous tradition to systematic critique, this exaggerated notion of fragmentedness offered a confirmation of his own image of the suras as often secondary, redactional compositions. Contrarily, the editor of his work, Friedrich Schwally,[11] in his analysis of the suras arrived at the conclusion that a large number of them should have received their final form already from the Prophet himself, though Schwally did not go so far as to see this as the norm. Nöldeke's reservation, repeated also in other works, against the sura as an originally intended unit remained decisive for research, despite Schwally's revision. Régis Blachère again adopted the theory of the secondary compilation of the suras in his *Introduction au Coran*[12] and repeated it in his *Histoire de la littérature arabe*.[13] Arthur Jefferey, who produced multiple summaries on the first collection of the Qur'an,[14] favored the view that the suras received their traditional divisions and composition only through the later redaction. Richard Bell, in his *Introduction to the Qurʾān*,[15] does assume a written fixing of a larger sura groups by the Prophet himself, and considers the written recording of all revelations within his lifetime possible, but assumes in many cases later reworkings by the Prophet himself or, more frequently, errant conflations of doublets and authentic textual materials by the redactors. According to his scenario the Prophet when reworking already proclaimed messages, replaced obsolete passages with revised versions, the new version being written on the back side of the old version, so that both versions were erroneously taken to be equal parts of the sura and accepted into the collection one after the other. Bell attempted by using typographical means in his Qur'an translation[16] to make recognizable this kind of putative secondary expansion of suras labelling them "doublets." According to his hypothesis as well, a large number of suras would have to be considered accidental forms or haphazard conglomerates of single revelations that were no longer recognizable in their original form. Focusing on the pre-redactional text, this problem can only be approached on the basis of literary-critical studies.[17]

fundamental issue, that the theory of abrogation does not only refer to controversial interpretations or to missing verses from the vulgate text, but rather is motivated to a much greater extent by contradictions in the Uthmanic text itself. His approach could only explain elements of the codex variations that are relevant legally, while the question about the emergence of merely stylistically or grammatically interesting variations remains unexplained; cf. Neuwirth's review of Burton, *The Collection of the Qur'ān.*

10. Nöldeke, *GdQ.*
11. Nöldeke and Schwally, *GdQ*², vol. 2.
12. Blachère, *Introduction au Coran.*
13. Blachère, *Histoire de la Littérature arabe*, vol. 2.
14. Jeffery, *Materials*, 1–18.
15. Bell, *Introduction*; see also Watt, *Bell's Introduction.*
16. Bell, *The Qur'ān Translated*; see also Nagel, "Vom 'Qur'ān' zur Schrift."
17. On the Meccan suras, see Neuwirth, *Studien zur Komposition.* On more recent studies, cf. chap. 5, 163–166.

All Islamic traditions agree that at the time of the death of the Prophet, the Qur'an did not yet exist as a closed official collection. That the Prophet had intended such for a long time was taken for granted in view of putative Qur'anic self-references, which Arthur Jeffery discussed in detail in *The Qur'ān as Scripture*. Since then, however, Daniel Madigan has shown[18] that these Qur'an texts require a different interpretation,[19] there being no evidence within the lifetime of the proclaimer for the ultimate goal of producing a distinct written scripture of its own. It is true that the proclaimer felt challenged by the liturgical readings of the "possessors of scripture" (*ahl al-kitāb*) of his religious milieu to equip the Arabic language speakers with similar liturgical texts for recitation, yet these texts were not meant to take the form of a closed book, but were rather to be communicated orally only. It is true that the term *qur'ān*, often adduced as evidence for the written-scripture-conception, which within the Qur'an designates "recitation," "reading," "text to be read," in its Syriac signifies counterpart means "lectionary" (*qur'ān* = *qeryānā*), yet at no phase of the Qur'anic proclamation does the word signify a written corpus. The seemingly unambiguous word *kitāb*, "writing," "book," "scripture," indicates throughout the Qur'an the transcendent writing, though excerpts from it had already assumed material form in the hands of the Jews and Christians. Indeed, criteria such as the structure and length of the middle and late Meccan verses, which are no longer easy to memorize, indicate that the proclamations must have at some point assumed written form for mnemotechnic support. It is plausible that already in the middle Meccan period the proclaimer took care to fix the individual communications in writing.

One indicator within the text itself suggests that it was already in the middle Meccan period, in the so-called Raḥmān-period, that is, the period in which the name of God "al-Raḥmān" becomes the norm, that the recording of suras had begun. An important hint is given in this period by the practice of introducing the suras with an invocation formula, the basmala: *bi-smi llāhi l-raḥmāni l-raḥīm*, "in the name of God, the merciful compassionate," which in view to its use of the term *al-Raḥmān*. assigns itself to the so-called-*Raḥmān*-period. That this formula, a radical reinterpretation of the Christian invocation of the Trinity "in the name of the Father and the Son and the Holy Spirit," should, like its Christian counterpart, have been used not least to introduce a piece of writing is apparent from a Qur'an verse that connects it to writing, namely, the quote from a letter sent from Solomon to the Queen of Sheba, which in the Qur'an is introduced by the basmala (Q 27:30). This attestation of the introductory function of the basmala may indicate that already in this period the suras to which the basmala was being added had obtained the form of written pieces in addition to their oral manifestation. If one agrees with the frequently drawn conclusion[20] that the

18. Madigan, *The Qur'an's Self-Image*.
19. See chap. 2, 76–80.
20. See Schoeler, "Schreiben und Veröffentlichen"; Nagel, *Medinensische Einschübe*, 113–127.

writing down of suras began in Mecca, one has to assume the systematic participation of writing in the process of the emergence of the suras—a decisive turn in the consciousness of the community that appears analogous, if incompletely so, to the transition from ritual to textual coherence of a society described by Jan Assmann.[21] The assumption of a consequent recording of the proclamations no longer must confront opposing arguments based on the assumption of the relatively undeveloped knowledge of writing in ancient Arabia. Already Nabia Abbott[22] had shown that among the contemporaries of the proclaimer, literacy should be assumed for a relatively wide circle of people.[23]

That parts of the Qur'an were memorized by numerous private persons for liturgical use, and that larger groups of suras were even committed to memory by official Qur'an reciters in Medina, is a fact well attested.[24] Thus, the written form receives the status of a mnemotechnic support for the oral tradition, functioning as templates for the purposes of teaching and learning. As such, written recordings were a necessary precondition for the preservation of the long verses of the Medinan suras. A structural analysis of the Meccan suras has shown that the inner logic of the sura compositions in this part of the corpus disproves the hypothesis of a genesis from broken fragments or the assumption of rows of duplicates.[25] We are thus confronted with the task of a new interpretation of the evidence, which also bears on the first Qur'an collection. Provisionally, the most probable theory seems to be that at the death of the proclaimer, the revelations received by this time had been fixed in writing, in the form of copies that had been established with his approval by some of his companions, although these forms were not submitted by the Prophet himself to a final redaction in the form of a codex. The ordering of the suras in a particular sequence—liturgically of secondary importance—cannot be assumed to have been fixed by this time.

4.1.2 The First Collections

The indigenous tradition assigns the first official redaction, carried out by one of the scribes of the Prophet, Zayd ibn Thābit, to the time of the first caliph, Abū

21. Cf. chap. 7, 279–282.

22. Abbott, *Studies in Arabic Literary Papyri*. See now Schoeler, "Schreiben und Veröffentlichen"; Stein, "Literacy."

23. Bell's assumption of a consequent written fixing of the text is thus warranted. Yet Bell takes the traditions about the disparate and small-sized writing materials too literally when he uses them as the basis for his explanation of similar Qur'anic passages—considered as doublets—due to having been written on the two sides of such small pieces of material. Indeed, as Grohmann, *Arabische Paläographie*, vols. 1–2, demonstrated, writing materials were widespread in ancient Arabia. Schwally, *GdQ*², already noted a tendency in the accounts about the writing materials to overemphasize the efforts of the early collectors. Especially for the long suras, the use of consistent writing materials like papyrus—cf. Endress, "Handschriftenkunde"—or parchment can certainly be assumed. Grohmann offers a great deal of evidence for the existence of these materials at the time of the Prophet; see now Schoeler, "Schreiben und Veröffentlichen."

24. Cf. Sayyed, *Die Revolte des Ibn al-Ashʿath*.

25. Neuwirth, *Studien zur Komposition*; cf. chap. 5.

Bakr, and claims that his successor, ʿUmar, also participated in it. Though the reports over this are obviously not free from bias,[26] an unofficial yet systematic collection of revelations undertaken by Zayd is probable; such early collections (*ṣuḥuf*, "leaves"; *maṣāḥif*, "codices"), which one should imagine as complete to varying degrees, are also attested for other companions of the Prophet (*ṣaḥāba*), and slightly divergent readings are transmitted from them.[27]

It is a specific feature of the Qur'an's textual transmission that due to the double existence of written and oral traditions, many orally transmitted textual variants are preserved in text-historical and exegetical literature. Important materials have been collected by Arthur Jeffery in *Materials for the History of the Text of the Qur'an*. With the expansion of the Islamic hegemony, three collections by the companions acquired the status of authoritative codices for reading in several of the new urban centers (*amṣār*): those of ʿAbd Allāh ibn Masʿūd (Kufa), Abū Mūsā al-Ashʿarī (Basra) and Ubayy ibn Kaʿb (Damascus). For the texts of Ibn Masʿūd and Ubayy, not only do we have transmitted readings, but we also have two slightly divergent lists of their contents and sequencing of the suras. Ubayy's Qur'an contains two short suras beyond the stock of the Uthmanic edition, whose original status as part of the revelations appears very unlikely given the concerns about vocabulary and phraseology raised by Schwally.[28] They may represent early prayers from the time of the Prophet, similar to the opening and closing suras of the Uthmanic edition (suras 1, 113, 114), which are excluded by Ibn Masʿūd from his collection.

That further text forms were also in circulation alongside the standardized codex has been shown by a new analysis of three early Umayyad fragments.[29]

4.2 The "First Official Qur'an Edition of ʿUthmān"

We are informed—though only incompletely—about the divergences between the old codices of the *amṣār* by the non-canonical readings that have reached

26. The assumption that all the traditions about the process of collecting the Qur'an go back to the eighth or ninth century was a hypothesis made in Wansbrough, *Quranic Studies*, who claimed that the individual revelations were not collected during the generation after the Prophet but were rather united with the corpus "Qur'an" over the course of the first two centuries. The Uthmanic redaction would thus belong to the realm of fiction, fabricated for the purpose of reproducing the model of traditions on the rabbinic redaction of the Mishna. In truth, the corpus itself, with its frequent modifications of a fixed group of topics, does not fit well with the notion of a redaction from the different traditions retaining "logia" of the Prophet achieved only later, during the emerging of the community; see chap. 1, 47–50, and cf. Neuwirth's review of Wansbrough, *Quranic Studies*. On the contrary, clear compositional rules can be substantiated for the literary character of the Qur'an, so that a kind of technically external explanation for the genesis must be eliminated. As precarious as the indigenous accounts may be individually, their portrayal of the course of events is still the most plausible explanation for the form of the text we have available to us today.

27. On the individual collections and the discernible relationships between them, see Jeffery, *Materials*; on the value of codices that can be traced back to "pre-canonical" interpretations, see 151–152. Atwan, *al-Qirāʾāt*, illuminates local Syrian traditions.

28. Nöldeke and Schwally, *GdQ*^{2}, 33–38.

29. Dutton, "An Umayyad Fragment"; cf. also the treatment of a further fragment in Puin, "Ein frühes Koranpalimpsest."

us, the *qirāʾāt shādhdha* or *shawādhdh*. The confrontations between the Syrian and Iraqi troops over the correct textual form, which are said to have occurred amid conflicts with the Armenians around the year 30/650–651, are reported to have motivated the official redaction triggered by the caliph ʿUthmān (r. 23–35/644–656), thus already presupposing significant differences between the texts. The varying forms of reading thus seem to have presented a danger for the early Islamic state that could only be averted through the standardization of the text.[30] According to the tradition, Zayd ibn Thābit was commissioned again, now in collaboration with three representatives of the Quraysh tribe, to produce transcripts from the codex which he had already compiled, which were to be sent out from Medina to the four most significant Islamic centers, Mecca, Damascus, Kufa, and Basra, thus replacing the codices of the *ṣaḥāba* that were locally circulating—a process that must have come to completion more gradually than the tradition about the old codices being destroyed by the order of ʿUthmān would suggest. The reports of resistance on the part of Ibn Masʿūd on the one hand and compliance on the part of Abū Mūsā on the other reflect a process of transition, which—depending on place—was completed either slowly or quickly from one reading tradition to another in these centers.[31] It is the five centers designated as *amṣār*, Medina, Mecca, Damascus, Kufa, and Basra, from which the later canonical readings derive the names of for the slightly divergent orthographies of their variants. Although the Uthmanic redaction cannot be safely verified historically, the term *rasm ʿuthmānī*, "Uthmanic consonantal script," has been adopted for the ultimately canonized consonantal form of the text, which also underlies the printed Cairene text edition that is standard today and on which the following presentation also relies.

4.2.1 The Sequencing of the Suras and the Sura-Opening Letter Groups

The three independent collections from which sura sequences have been transmitted, the Uthmanic text and the pre-Uthmanic codices of Ubayy and Ibn Masʿūd, display different orders. These differences notwithstanding, they follow a shared principle: putting the longest suras at the beginning, and then continuing in descending order to the shortest ones.[32] Hans Bauer succeeded in showing that the ordering of the suras according to their length was applied relatively strictly in all three versions, as long as this principle did not violate another priority: keeping together suras that already belonged together.[33] This consideration

30. See *GdQ*², 47–50. On the social-historical background and impact of the Uthmanic redaction, see Sayyed, *Die Revolte des Ibn al-Ashʿath*.

31. None of the pre-Uthmanian codices have reached us in writing; a few of the palimpsest sheets are still controversial as to attribution (cf. Bergsträsser, *GdQ*², 3:53–57, 97–100; Diem, "Geschichte der arabischen Orthographie. I, II, III, IV") or offer only very short excerpts of texts (see Dutton, "An Umayyad Fragment").

32. See Nöldeke and Schwally, *GdQ*², 63–68; Bauer, "Die Anordnung der Suren."

33. See now Dayeh, "Al-Ḥāwamīm."

is evident especially for suras whose text is preceded by individual letters or letter groups, Arabic *fawātiḥ* "(sura-) opening elements." This principle, of keeping together the suras with preceding letter names, is applied consistently in the Uthmanic recension, partially in that of Ibn Masʿūd, but not in Ubayy's Qur'an. A solution to the problem of the letters therefore would also shed light on the question of the original ordering of the suras.

The Islamic tradition treats the letters or letter groups that introduce the suras as integral parts of the revealed text, interpreting them as abbreviations of words or sentences with the function of sura names, or else as enigmatic demarcations by the Prophet for cosmic phenomena and the like. According to a third view, they represent the smallest elements of the language of revelation—an interpretation worthy of consideration, which is also taken up in arguments for the inimitability of the Qur'an.[34] In Western discussions,[35] we find the additional interpretation of the letters as redactional additions. This view, according to which the letters were carelessly allowed to stay and then penetrated into the recitation text, has little appeal in view of the care for textual integrity observed elsewhere in the early Islamic community.[36]

An observation already maintained in the commentary of Fakhr al-Dīn ar-Rāzī (d. 1209) is worthy of consideration: the beginning verses of those suras that are "coded" by a letter or letters almost always indicate their content as revealed word of God—this inner connection between letters or letter groups and sura types contradicts the assumption of the addition of the signs for merely technical redactional reasons. The signs must have been found extant already by the redactors at the start of the suras, since these redactors by grouping together with identically or similarly coded suras had to violate the principle followed elsewhere of ordering according to length. One should therefore consider a genetically close connection between the suras introduced by letters, an indication that they were perhaps treated by the proclaimer himself in his disposition of texts as belonging together. That the letters themselves were no accidental choice is corroborated by Alford Welch's observation[37] that most of the suras so introduced continue in the rhyme of the last-mentioned letter's name, and that the letters are identical with the fourteen (consonantal) letter forms of the Arabic (Kufic) alphabet, leaving out the fourteen further ones derived from them through additional signs. The

34. The traditional interpretations are discussed in Abd ar-Rahman, *Al-Iʿjāz al-Bayānī*, 127–139.

35. An overview is offered by Schwally, *GdQ*², 68–78 (up to 1908), Bellamy, "The Mysterious Letters," and Welch, "Kurān." See also the contributions on the problem gathered by Paret in Paret, *Der Koran*.

36. Nöldeke later rescinded his earlier interpretation, in *Orientalische Skizzen*, and affiliated himself with Islamic tradition, which aims to recognize in the letters clues to the divine, original text of the Qur'an. Meanwhile, Bellamy, "The Mysterious Letters," attempted to find abbreviations of the basmala in the letters. The unintelligibility of the symbols, which is already attested early on, does not agree well with the requirement that the letters are supposed to stand for a universally known formula. See the attempts to explain this in Hans Bauer, "Über die Anordnung der Suren"; Goosens, "Ursprung und Bedeutung"; Jeffery, "Mysterious Letters of the Koran"; Massey, "Letters of the Qur'an"; Massey, "Mysterious Letters."

37. Welch, "Kurān," 414.

conclusion here, that the *fawātiḥ* represent the Arabic alphabet, becomes plausible against the background of the high esteem attributed to the phenomena of writing, teaching, and clear speech.

4.3 The Imperial Project of ʿAbd al-Malik

If the historicity of the Uthmanic redaction is hard to verify, it is even harder to maintain the hypothesis of an essentially later compilation of the Qur'an. Manuscripts discovered in the 1960s, only later evaluated, have brought to light Qur'anic fragments that can be dated contemporaneously with, or even prior to, the rule of the Umayyad caliph ʿAbd al-Malik ibn Marwān (r. 65–86/685–705). These fragments remain unpublished but are known from non-comprehensive, scattered reports.[38] According to our current state of knowledge, they essentially attest to the textual form familiar to us today. Further, similarly ancient—but also incomplete—manuscripts preserved in the collections of various European libraries are now being studied in part by Francois Déroche.[39] This transmission develops historical contours thanks to unquestionable testimonies from early Islamic literature about the initiatives toward fixing a *textus receptus* in this period. Omar Hamdan describes an initiative of ʿAbd al-Malik to unify the differing Qur'an texts in circulation at his time, for which purpose a number of large-scale exemplary codices were produced.[40] Estelle Whelan has brought to light reports about scribal workshops, "scriptoria," for the production of codices.[41] It is possible to reconstruct from the philological literature the important measure of an orthographical reform during the time of ʿAbd al-Malik, which coincides approximately to the onset of the Kufic script, which comes to replace the earlier "Hijazi" or *māʾil* script.[42] Islamic tradition maintains that it was already the third caliph ʿUthmān (r. 23–25/644–655) who was responsible for the decisive standardization of the text, and that he was the first to produce an edition and publication of the Qur'an. In fact, some issues, above all the reports about a competition between the versions maintained by reciters from the circle of the Prophet and those of the newly binding text, undergird the assumption of an early complete collection. But even with the contrary assumption of such a final redaction carried out not before ʿAbd al-Malik, as Alfred-Louis de Prémare holds,[43] the date of the fixing of the Qur'an text draws quite near to the end of the textual production,

38. Puin, "Observations on Early Qurʾān Manuscripts in Sanʿāʾ"; Dreibholz, *Early Quran Fragments*. See also Leemhuis, "Codices"; Bothmer, "Architekturbilder im Koran"; Bothmer, Ohlig, and Puin, "Neue Wege."

39. On the transmission history, see especially Déroche, *Les Manuscrits du Coran*; Déroche, "Manuscripts"; Déroche, *La transmission écrite*; cf. also Leemhuis, "From Palmleaves to the Internet."

40. See now Hamdan, *Studien zur Kanonisierung*; cf. also Hamdan, "The Second Maṣāḥif Project."

41. Whelan, "Writing the Word of God."

42. Fraser, unpublished lecture, given at the Freie Universität Berlin on December 19, 2010.

43. De Prémare, "Abd al-Malik."

which is the death date of the Prophet. Even if one does not admit a redaction by ʿUthmān around 655, in no case could more than sixty years have passed between the conclusion of the text and its binding publication—a term that, despite the conclusions of de Prémare, is too short to assign adequate space for authoritative, targeted, and theologically relevant modifications of the text, let alone a new construction of an Arab myth of a "golden age under the rulership of the Prophet and his companions." At the time of ʿAbd al-Malik and the wars of expansion, Islamic history was already in full swing,[44] and Qur'anic texts were already the object of learned disputes being played out at the court of ʿAbd al-Malik.[45]

ʿAbd al-Malik's well-attested initiative to unify the writing of the Qur'an is referred to properly by Omar Hamdan as forming part of an "imperial project" that also included the Arabization of the chancellery and the minting of coins. Such a reform of orthography concentrated on the Qur'an should most probably be conceived of as occurring on the basis of an already constituted binding text. For the historicity of its emergence, we do not need to rely merely on reports but can also see evidence in the traces of vocalization and differentiation between consonants in the inscriptions in the Dome of the Rock that were carried out under ʿAbd al-Malik.

That building, which now stands as the most striking testimony of the "imperial project" of the caliph, shows in its inner ambulatorium a 240-meter band of inscriptions consisting almost entirely of Qur'an citations. This, the oldest Qur'anic document,[46] dating from the years between 690 and 700, has been analyzed by Estelle Whelan.[47] In agreement with Christel Kessler,[48] she argues for distinguishing between two separate inscriptions. She concludes: "With slight deviations, these Qur'an passages reflect the text that is familiar to us from the Cairene edition." She holds that the insertion into the Qur'an citations of the *basmala* and the repeated credo formulas (*shahāda*) is consistent with the image familiar elsewhere from inscriptions. The inscriptions in the Dome of the Rock offer an anthology of Qur'anic pronouncements about Christianity and the persons of Jesus and Mary in particular—both of whom are celebrated in Jerusalem by numerous magnificently decorated churches. It is the religious-political goal of the inscriptions to downgrade Jesus, who is celebrated in Jerusalem as the son of God, to his "Qur'anic dimension" as a mere servant of God, and to put the

44. Donner, *Narratives of Islamic Origins*, 84.

45. See van Ess, "Abd al-Malik and the Dome of the Rock."

46. At the same time, relevant works mention an epitaph from Cyprus from the year 650 containing sura 112; see Grohmann, *Arabische Paläographie*, 2:71, and Combe, RCÉA I, no. 5. This Qur'an document, possibly the earliest, has not been found to date, and appears to be first attested in the pilgrimage account of al-Harawī, *Kitāb al-Ishārāt* (personal communication by Jens Sauer).

47. Whelan, "Evidence." A photographic reproduction of the inscription is offered in Grabar, *The Shape of the Holy*, 92–99; an English translation can be found in ibid., 60. On the inscription text, see Neuwirth, "The Spiritual Meaning," and now Hoyland, "New Documentary Texts."

48. Kessler, "Abd al-Malik's Inscription"; see also Blair, "Date of the Dome of the Rock."

Prophet of Islam, who is highly honored in heaven and earth—as is pronounced in the verse Q 33:56, cited several times in the inscription—on equal footing with him. Whelan discusses further reports of Qur'an inscriptions in the main mosque of Medina that are no longer preserved and collects reports indicating the existence of a copyists' workshop in Medina prior to the rule of ʿAbd al-Malik.

The assumption that the Qur'an, transmitted above all orally in the various centers of the emerging realm, obtained a binding textual form consistent with the form and arrangement of the text as we have it, perhaps around 655 but at the latest in the reign of ʿAbd al-Malik around 690, can no longer be dismissed out of hand.

Of course, within these twenty or even sixty years, verses may have been manipulated, added, or eliminated; above all, there is no guarantee that all of the proclamations of Muhammad were preserved. There is a gray area here that cannot be illuminated. There are indeed some few elliptical textual units that are perhaps to be explained through the assumption of missing textual elements. "Non-canonical" readings, which are transmitted to us from some old pre-Uthmanic text traditions,[49] occasionally show slight deviations. Palimpsests that have recently come to light, which were found in the main mosque of Sanaa in the 1960s and are now finally being analyzed, promise insight into further divergences.[50] But revolutionary finds are not expected.

4.4 Text History

4.4.1 Early History of the Uthmanic Text

With the replacement of the early Qur'an exemplars of the Prophet's companions, the *ṣaḥāba*, in the new centers, *amṣār*, those text forms deviating from the Uthmanic text were not yet eliminated. The victory of the Uthmanic text was only guaranteed once it was recognized as the binding basis for the recitation. In the early stage of the development, in which oral tradition was dominant, the sensitivity for the exact reproduction of the text was not yet very developed; one simply eliminated linguistic and semantic offenses through slight textual alterations. Soon, however, two principles were established for the interpretation of the consonantal text: linguistic correctness, *ʿarabīya*, and compatibility with the consonantal text, the *rasm*, of the Uthmanic codex, the *muṣḥaf*—thus the language mastery of the Qur'an reader and instructor was considered the most important source of authority for the formation of the text.[51]

49. Jeffery, *Materials*.

50. They are currently being edited by Christian Robin, Paris, and Behnam Sadeghi, Stanford. Already published are Dutton, "An Umayyad Fragment," and Puin, "Ein frühes Koranpalimpsest."

51. See Beck, "Der uthmanische Kodex."

With the spread of Islam and the concomitant increase in demand for reciters and Qur'an instructors, the emphasis shifted from the oral transmission to the written text. In his interpretation of a text that was ambiguous in both its consonantal skeleton and its vocalization, the Qur'an reader initially was free to decide his interpretation of the ambiguous consonant signs, *al-ikhtiyār bi-l-ḥurūf*, and choice about vocalization, *al-ikhtiyār bi-l-qirāʾa*. But fixed schools soon took shape, where only the eclectic texts of renowned scholars were recognized, so that as a third criterion for the fitness of a reading now the principle of tradition took hold, that is, the transmission on the basis of a reliable chain of transmission, *isnād*. With increasingly firm adherence to the tradition, the guaranteed right to one's own critique warranted by the other two criteria became less perceived. Roughly contemporary with the renouncement of independent interpretation of the consonantal text, the non-Uthmanic variants were also relinquished: while it was only in the third/ninth century that legal scholars reached agreement about the cultic unfitness of all non-Uthmanic text forms, it was already in the second/eighth century that the complete victory of the Uthmanic text was achieved.

Textual history entered a new stage with the introduction of signs to differentiate between consonants and signs of vocalization—a measure probably adopted after the model of the Syriac and Hebrew Bibles, or simultaneously with the Christian and Jewish practice. While the differentiation of consonants began already in the first/seventh century, the vocalization by means of additional signs for short vowels,[52] initially only in words with competing possibilities of pronunciation, was introduced generally into the text from the end of the second/eighth century onward. In the third/ninth century, we find the introduction of a consistent *scriptio plena* for long vowels.[53]

The confrontation between advocates of a unified form of writing and transmitters who championed an exact preservation of the old consonantal form, the *rasm*, with all its orthographic arbitrariness, has been sketched by Edmund

52. The legitimacy of the entry of additional characters into the holy text was initially controversial; the ritual reservations are reflected in the consistent use of a different color of ink; see Endress, *Herkunft und Entwicklung*, 179; cf. also Gründler, *Development*. For examples beyond the literature mentioned there, see James, *Qur'ans and Bindings*, nos. 2, 3, 5, 7, 10, 12, 15, 16, 17.

53. On "orthography reform," see Blachère, *Introduction au Coran*, 75–102, where indigenous traditions are discussed and paleographic evidence is evaluated, but see now especially Endress, "Herkunft und Entwicklung," 171–181, and Hamdan, *Studien zur Kanonisierung*. On orthography generally, Bergsträsser, *GdQ*², 3:19–26, stresses the most important idiosyncrasies in the Uthmanian text. This fundamentally descriptive portrayal was expanded with a historical outline in Diem, "Geschichte der arabischen Orthographie. I, II, III, IV." An orthography of a pre-Uthmanic fragment is given in Bergsträsser, *GdQ*², vol. 3, 53–57. But see also Diem, "Geschichte der arabischen Orthographie. I, II, III, IV." On the idiosyncrasies of orthography of an Iraqi codex from the third century as against later ones, see Jeffery and Mendelsohn, "Orthography." On the orthographic characteristics of codices in the Hijaazi ductus, see Pretzl, *GdQ*², 3:254–256. Pretzl offers an overview of the indigenous literature on writing the Qur'an in *GdQ*², 3:238- 240. Pretzl himself also edited what is considered in Islam to be the standard work on Qur'an orthography, *Kitāb al-Muqniʿ* by Abū Amr al-Dānī (d. 444/1053).

Beck.[54] The conflict was decided in favor of the traditionalists, as is shown by the Qur'anic orthography used down to today, which is not thoroughly consistent.[55]

4.4.2 *Non-canonical Readings*

Due to the exclusion of the non-Uthmanic textual form of the recitation, the early "non-canonical" readings (*qiraʾāt shādhdha, shawādhdh*), which date back to the codices of the *ṣaḥāba*, had to rely entirely on an extra-Qur'anic literary transmission. Indeed, no longer recognized as part of a text for recitation (*qurʾān*) yet bearing substantially the same meaning, the non-canonical readings entered the commentary literature and, on account of their close relation to the *textus receptus*, were incorporated into Qur'an-specific philological works.

Bergsträsser, in the context of his collection of materials for the *Apparatus criticus zum Koran* (see under "Manuscripts"), published critical editions of the only two existing early collections of non-canonical readings known in his time, those in the *Mukhtaṣar fī shawādhdh al-Qurʾān min Kitāb al-Badīʿ* by Ibn Khālawayh (d. 370/980) and those preserved in the collection by the founder of scholarship on the Qur'an text, Ibn Mujāhid (d. 324/936), in excerpts preserved in the work of the grammarian Ibn Jinnī (d. 392/1001).[56] A further source, the *Kitāb al-Maṣāḥif* of Ibn Abī Dāwūd al-Sijistānī (d. 316/926), was edited by Arthur Jeffery.[57] Jeffery also supplemented Bergsträsser's Ibn Khālawayh edition with marginalia.[58] The relevant chapter from the *Faḍāʾil al-Qurʾān* by Abū ʿUbayd ibn Sallām (d. 224/838) has since been edited and evaluated by Anton Spitaler.[59]

Jeffery compiled an extensive collection of the scattered non-canonical readings available in his *Materials*,[60] the material of which is culled from twenty-seven early codices in total. But Jeffery neither notes the respective sources of the readings nor assesses their value; a major edition of the readings presenting all of this evidence envisaged by Jeffery could no longer be realized. On the other hand, in his collection of the variants of Ibn Masʿūd and Ubayy, Bergsträsser attempted to produce an assessment:[61] while the authenticity of the variants ascribed to Ubayy appears improbable to Bergsträsser, a major portion of the readings ascribed to Ibn Masʿūd seem in fact to go back to his codex. The question of whether these readings are closer to or further from the original proclamation than the canonical text has not been addressed. A much more negative picture is drawn by Edmund Beck for the readings of Ibn Masʿūd preserved in

54. Beck, "Der uthmanische Kodex."

55. Cf. the characteristics of the orthography of the official Qur'an of Cairo in Bergsträsser, "Koranlesung in Kairo"; on one of its special manifestations, see Spitaler, "Die Schreibung des Typus salāh."

56. Bergsträsser, "Koranlesung in Kairo."

57. Jeffery, *Materials*. The work is made easily accessible by Magermans, *Index*.

58. Jeffery, "Abu Ubayd."

59. Spitaler, *Fada'il al-Qur'an*.

60. Jeffery, *Materials*.

61. Bergsträsser, *GdQ*², 3:57–95.

the Qur'an commentary by al-Farrāʾ (d. 207/822).[62] The variants collected here appear for the most part to be secondary textual interventions complying with the explanations of particular grammatical phenomena upheld by al-Farrāʾ.

A narrower selection of non-canonical variants, or *shawādhdh*, namely, forms that are due to a punctuation or vocalization of the consonant text that is not compatible with the rules of classical grammar, has been collected by Karl Vollers in his *Volkssprache, Popular Language and Written Language in Old Arabia*.[63] He views these forms as representing the original textual form of the Qur'an. Even if this thesis itself has been rejected,[64] the work still shows that the transmitted dialectal variants contain sufficient authentic linguistic material to be valuable, if not for the Qur'an itself, then at least for Arabic linguistic scholarship. Comparable language-historical relevance can be presupposed for the dialectal variants that have come to light since then.[65]

4.4.3 *The Seven, Ten, and Fourteen Canonical Readings*

The history of the Qur'an text since the second/eighth century appears as a protracted process of standardization. The end of the first main phase is marked by the elimination of the non-Uthmanic text forms and the freely construed readings. In the next phase of the development, which begins in the early third/ninth century, in which the oral tradition again predominates, there is a new criterion applied to judge the reliability of the reading: the principle of the majority, *ijtimāʿ al-ʿāmma, ijmāʿ*, according to which a reading is only reliable when supported by the majority of readers. The *ijmāʿ* principle, which came to replace the tradition principle, further restricts the freedom of the reader and soon led to the standardization within each of the respective *amṣār*, and later between the *amṣār*. But a decision in favor of a particular textual form was still based on the critical evaluations of particular readers, that is, the established praxis consisted in *tartīb*, the linking together of readers of different origins, which in Bergstrasser's view would have led, had it continued unhindered, to the production of a more satisfyingly representative *textus receptus* than the version that has received nearly exclusive validity, if only very recently: Ḥafṣ ʿan ʿĀṣim (Ḥafṣ d. 180/796; ʿĀṣim d. 127/745).

Meanwhile, at the initiative of the Qur'an scholar Ibn Mujāhid (d. 324/936) in the year 322/934, seven readings, that is, seven transmitted versions of the entire Qur'an each based on one authority, were recognized as canonical, while all other forms of the recitation were excluded—a concession to the Qur'an schools

62. Beck, "Die Zuverlässigkeit"; Beck, "Die Ibn-Masʿūd-Varianten," nos. 1, 2, 3.

63. Vollers, *Volkssprache*.

64. See the review by Geyer and Nöldeke of Vollers, *Volkssprache*, as well as a detailed discussion in Zwettler, *Oral Tradition*, 117–121.

65. Spitaler, "Die Schreibung des Typus salāh."

loyal to the tradition principle (*taqlīd*). This constriction of the earlier freedom must have impeded the formerly free discussions of the Qur'an text. Ibn Mujāhid not only sought to work against the eccentric reading of individual passages but was also interested in legitimizing complete recensions of the Qur'an through chains of transmitters with respect to entire texts. The choice of the canonical seven readings (*al-qirāʾāt al-sabʿ*), one for each of the *amṣār* and three for Kufa, was not made arbitrarily, but rather confirms the prominence of individual recognized Qur'an authorities of the second/eighth century in the recitation praxis and in the schools operating at the time. Those selected were Nāfiʿ (d. 169/785—Medina), Ibn Kathīr (d. 120/738—Mecca), Abū ʿAmr ibn al-ʿAlā (d. 154/770—Basra), Ibn ʿĀmir (d. 118/736—Damascus), ʿĀṣim (d. 127/745—Kufa), Ḥamza (d. 156/773—Kufa), and al-Kisāʾī (d. 189/804—Kufa). The choice did not go unchallenged; the community understood the seven as an approximate and negotiable number allowing the unavoidable addition of other readings, and also developed systems of eight, ten, and finally fourteen readings.

In this process of Qur'an teaching, closed readings came to take the place of individual open types of reading. Ibn Mujāhid himself in his *Kitāb al-Sabʿa*[66] presented his treatment as a concordance of the seven parallel versions and thus laid the foundation for an extensive commentary literature, *ḥujaj al-qirāʾāt*, which provided grammatical reasoning, *taʿlīl*, for the individual readings of the seven and later also of the ten and fourteen readings. The oldest such commentaries are the *Kitāb al-Ḥujja fī l-qirāʾāt al-sabʿ* by Ibn Khālawayh (d. 370/987), the *Kitāb al-Ḥujja fī l-qirāʾāt* by Abū ʿAlī ibn Aḥmad al-Fārisī (d. 377/987), and the *Kitāb Ḥujjat al-qirāʾāt* by ʿAbd al-Raḥmān ibn Muḥammad Abū Zurʿa (d. 403/1013). The development of grammatical explanations was strongly advanced through close collaboration between grammarians and Qur'an readers at the court of the Hamdanids in Aleppo and, after the dispersal of this scholarly circle, shifted to the new center of Cairo. Here, it was also communicated to the two Maghrebian Qur'an readers whose works on the seven readings and the phonetic formation of the text, *tajwīd* (see pp. 155–156), would be decisive for the later period: Abū ʿAmr al-Dānī (d. 444/1053) and Makī ibn Abī Ṭālib al-Qaysī (d. 437/1045). With them, the science of reading ultimately became bound up with grammar as a propaedeutic science. In numerous supercommentaries, but especially the versification by Abū l-Qāsim al-Shāṭibī (d. 590/1194) titled *Ḥirz al-amānī wa-wajh al-tahānī*, al-Dānī's work on the seven readings, *Kitāb al-Taysīr fī l-qirāʾāt al-sabʿ*, was preserved in Qur'an teaching down to the present day.[67] The other approved systems received corresponding treatment. For the ten readings, Ibn al-Jazarī (d. 835/1431) wrote the decisive grammatical commentary, the *Kitāb al-Nashr fī l-qirāʾāt al-ʿashr*, whose numerous supercommentaries in the following period

66. Ibn al-Mujāhid, *Kitāb al-sabʿa*.

67. Cf. Neuwirth, "Koranlesung zwischen Ost und West"; Neuwirth, "Makī ibn Abī Ṭālib al-Qaysī."

provide the foundations for scholastic teaching. For the fourteen, Aḥmad al-Dimyāṭī al-Bannā' (d. 1117/1705) gives the standard explanation in *Itḥāf fuḍalā' al-bashar fī qirā'āt al-arba'ata 'ashar*.

Existing attempts to describe the seven readings have not gone beyond the general observation that the divergences are essentially of a phonetic kind.[68] A more exact description can be glimpsed through a "horizontal sectioning across the mass of readings" in the reading of one of the fourteen, al-Ḥasan al-Baṣrī (d. 110/728), undertaken by Bergsträsser.[69] Among the differences relevant for the assessment of the text of Ḥafṣ 'an 'Āṣim, which achieved success in the east of the Arabic world, the treatment of the *hamza*, the glottal top, deserves particular notice. Among the few dialectal interferences that can be presupposed for the Prophet himself is a more propulsive pronunciation or "lightening" of the *hamza*, which is reflected by the Qur'anic orthography. But the question of whether the *hamza* was pronounced by the Prophet himself or his Hijazi followers within verse contexts is not easy to answer.[70] It is certain that some rhymes written with *hamza* require the pronouncement of the sound, but others do not allow it. We cannot exclude the hypothesis that *hamza* in the Qur'an was originally as a rule articulated and lightened only where a rhyme required it. For the transmission, it is significant that the Iraqi readers, among whom 'Āṣim achieved validity in the east, are just those who realize the *hamza* most consistently.[71]

One can easily be led by the dominance of the Ḥafṣ 'An 'Āṣim reading in the Islamic east, and its increasing prominence even in the Maghreb since the 1925-printed Cairo *al-Qur'ān al-Karīm*,[72] to lose sight of the fact that it is only one of the seven canonical readings that are held as equally valid by the strictest Islamic orthodoxy. Correspondingly, the relation between the textual variants among the seven systems are not to be understood in the sense of *textus receptus* and variant readings.[73] If one wants to speak of a *textus receptus*, one should understand by this all seven readings and not any one of them, since in the classical period Ḥafṣ 'an 'Āṣim was by no means the most widespread text, but rather stood behind Abū 'Amr (d. 154/770) in the east and behind Warsh 'an Nāfi' (Warsh d. 197/812; Nāfi' d. 169/785) in the west. One must recall that there was not one uniform and unified text accepted everywhere, but rather a number of textual forms in usage side by side, and that the educated Muslim knew this and was brought up with an astoundingly productive freedom in dealing with his scripture. The

68. See Pretzl, *GdQ*², 3:186ff.

69. Bergsträsser, "Die Koranlesung des Hasan von Basra."

70. Neuwirth, *Studien zur Komposition*, 325–359.

71. Consequently, in the modern recitation of this reading, *hamza* is also realized in positions where it violates the rhyme scheme.

72. This edition and its philological foundation is described extensively in Bergsträsser, "Koranlesung in Kairo."

73. Paret, "Textkritisch verwertbare Koranlesarten," emphasized the necessity of utilizing textual interpretation for the explanation of problematic passages. It should be added that even seemingly unproblematic passages of a reading can appear in a new light through attention to textual variants.

projection of the notion of an official, unified text back into those highly creative times would equal a blacking out of one of Islam's greatest spiritual and cultural attainments and would be an enormous anachronism. The full scale of the liveliness and legitimacy of the discussions of the grammarians, commentators, jurists, and theologians is only to be understood against this background. The final aim must be to realize that Islam in its classical period found a solution for the problem of the textual uniformity of its scripture that was as pragmatic as it was elegant, and which linked tolerance in view of the unattainability of an absolutely uniform text to the legitimate need for unity in ritual, maintaining a high level of linguistic sensibility.[74]

The extensive task of evaluating the canonical and non-canonical readings according to stylistic and compositional criteria remains to be done. Tradition has sidelined the non-canonical readings on purely practical grounds, and thus left open questions about the respective "original" readings.[75]

4.5 Instructions for Qur'an Reading and the Controls of the Textual Form

4.5.1 *"Beautiful Pronunciation"*

The doctrine of "beautiful pronunciation" (*tajwīd*) of the Qur'an developed out of the comprehensive complex of ritual performance rules for Qur'an readers (*ādāb ḥamalat al-qurʾān*). They first received independent treatment in works of the fourth/tenth century, where they are represented according to purely linguistically/phonetically methods independently from the ritual aspects of approaching the Qur'an. They find their initial treatment in the didactic poem of Abū Muzāḥim ibn Khāqān (d. 325/937),[76] titled *al-Qaṣīda fī tajwīd*. In that work, varying ways of performance are characterized and diverse phonetical problems are dealt with utilizing the terminological apparatus of Arabic linguistics. The *Qaṣīda* was commented on by Abū ʿAmr al-Dānī, who also composed an independent *tajwīd*-textbook, *Kitāb al-Taḥdīd fī ʿilm al-tajwīd*. His work, as also the *Riʿāya fī l-qirāʾa* of his fellow Andalusian and contemporary Makī ibn Abī Ṭālib al-Qaysī, offers detailed compendia on the articulation sites of the consonants, the linking and doubling of the consonants, contraction, assimilation, the contextual use of case endings (*tanwīn*), and so on. In Abū ʿAmr al-Dānī, we also already find variations of vocalic pronunciation, such as the coloring of the *a* (*imāla*), the dropping of vowels (*sukūn*, the pause), *ishmām*, *rawm*, nasalization.

74. The following remarks are mostly based on an essay by the author, "Koranlesung zwischen Ost und West."

75. On the interpretations, see Pretzl, "Die Wissenschaft der Koranlesung." The newest summary is offered by Paret, *Kirāʾa*. A depiction of Qur'an instruction in modern times is conveyed in Bergsträsser, "Koranlesung in Kairo"; Cantineau and Barbès, "La récitation coranique"; and Kellermann, *Koranlesung im Maghreb*.

76. Sezgin, GAS 1:14.

These materials become fixed inventories added as propaedeutic components to the classical *qirāʾāt*-works on the foundations of pronunciation, *uṣūl*, which form the basis for the presentation of individual differences in pronunciation, *farsh al-ḥurūf*.

A special area of *tajwīd*, which already received theoretical discussion from the second/eighth century onward, is the teaching of the positioning of pauses in speech during performance (*waqf*).[77] The performance of longer verses required a structuring of the elements of discourse into smaller semantic units, which were most often preserved in the oral tradition, but which required express clarification in syntactically controversial cases. For the application of such pauses, several grades of necessity were distinguished, which are marked in the Qur'an exemplars with various symbols. A literary-critical investigation of the principles of this internal structuring of verses would add essentially to our knowledge of the indigenous reception of the Qur'an as a verbal work of art.

Also within the area of *tajwīd* falls the cantilena.[78] Only in recent times have attempts been made by Western researchers to write these with musical notation.[79] Meanwhile, in the Islamic world sound recordings of the Qur'an on cassettes and CDs are ubiquitous. This was initiated with the first complete recording by Shaykh Mahmud Khalil al-Husari, *al-Muṣḥaf al-Murattal*.[80] This recording, completed in 1962, is an acoustic counterpart to the Cairene Qur'an edition, insofar as the reciter chosen for the recording, al-Husari, possessing the status of *shaykh al-maqāriʾ al-miṣrīya*, represented the highest ranking representative of the Al-Azhar University on these matters. The sociological consequences of this influential recording for the tradition of recitation have been illuminated by Bernard Weiss.[81] The initiator of this collection of vinyl recordings, which was conceived as an official recording, Labib al-Saʿid (ʿAyn Shams University, Cairo), presented its principles and motives in a treatise that accompanied it.[82] The Qur'an recitations broadcast by many Arabic radio and television stations would offer the possibility of recording a diversity of different reciters and analyzing their types of performance (in collaboration with musicologists). Important findings on the musical and social significance of contemporary recitation practices[83] can also be gained from the recording of contemporary live Qur'an performances.[84] These are by no means always solo performances, but rather, as Andreas Kellermann has shown, are frequently organized as group recitations, especially in the Maghreb.

77. See Pretzl, "Die Wissenschaft der Koranlesung"; Pretzl, *GdQ*², 3:234–237.

78. On its artistic configuration in time see Talbi, "La qirāʾa bi-alḥān."

79. Bergsträsser, "Koranlesung in Kairo"; Cantineau and Barbès, "La récitation coranique"; and Kellermann, *Koranlesung im Maghreb*.

80. See Kellermann, "Die 'Mündlichkeit' des Koran."

81. Weiss and al-Saʿid, *The Recited Koran*

82. Al-Saʿid, *Al-Jamʿ al-ṣawṭī al-awwal*.

83. See now the overview by Nelson, *The Art of Reciting*.

84. An isolated example is offered in Kellermann's unpublished dissertation, "Koranlesung im Maghreb."

4.5.2 *Verse Counting*

The history of the tradition of verse counting, which goes back to the end of the first/seventh century, has been sketched by Otto Pretzl.[85] Since the middle of the second/eighth century, the discipline of the counting of verses has been transmitted as an auxiliary discipline alongside Qur'an reading; being bound up practically with the positing of pauses in reading (*waqf*) it remains the object of theoretical discussion. Reading pauses that are to be respected in performance—or to be avoided—are regulated within a separate discipline, *al-waqf wa-l-ibtidā'*, "the pausing and beginning again," which also has retained a slot for optional pauses in reading that are neither obligatory nor forbidden. The position of pauses in reading in some cases can decide between theologically relevant textual interpretations but is in general relevant only for the reciter as a guide to producing a desirable sensory experience of the text, accordingly they are marked in the text of the 1925 Cairene edition. The numbering of verses has been subject to greater interest among researchers. A detailed overview and critical evaluation of the individual works on verse numbering is given by Anton Spitaler at the start of his systematic presentation of the Islamic verse-numbering traditions, which are related to the five *amṣār*.[86] In the Cairene text, which reproduces the Kufic reading of Ḥafṣ ʿan ʿĀṣim, the verse numbering follows the Kufic tradition, namely, the presentation of al-Shāṭibī (d. 590/1194) in his work *Naẓīmat al-zuhr fī l-aʿdād wa-khtilāf ahl al-bilād*.[87]

With his compression of all the recognized verse endings recognized in the tradition into overview lists for each individual sura, Spitaler offered an important contribution not only to textual criticism but also to the comprehension of the indigenous understanding of form. For while Islamic tradition is primarily concerned with verse numbering, it is worthwhile noting that the fixing or non-fixing of the verse end entails a decision about the structuring of the text, which can be checked as to its validity through literary-critical criteria. The Qur'an verse as a rule bears a recognizable end marker in its final rhyme, but in some cases a sound complex suitable for rhyme closure also occurs within verses, and in some cases a rhyme does not correspond to the schema offered by neighboring verses, so that differences in the treatment of respective verse groups can emerge. The evaluation of the Islamic divisions and the principles that lie behind them is still in its beginnings, but a critical review of the verse divisions of the Meccan suras[88] has shown already that none of the Islamic systems reflects a consistent procedure of verse division, and that not even a consensus of the traditional systems

85. Pretzl, *GdQ*², 3:237f.

86. Spitaler, *Verszählung*.

87. See the explanation (*taʿlīqāt*) following the Cairo text; cf. Bergsträsser, "Koranlesung," 10, and Spitaler, *Verszählung*.

88. Neuwirth, *Studien zur Komposition*, 11–63.

can guarantee a "correct" division in agreement with the text's discernable literary structure. Rather, in the Meccan suras alone in at least twenty-one cases a verse ending must be asserted or dropped against all traditional dictates. The analysis of the text thus cannot blindly follow the privileged tradition, but must rather recheck all transmitted verse endings critically.

4.6 Manuscripts

The predominance of the oral as against the written tradition in Qur'anic transmission is unmistakable. Gotthelf Bergsträsser, though himself a pioneer of research in Qur'anic manuscripts, highlighted the value of scholarship based on orality, not overlooking however the necessity of evaluating manuscripts:

> One could almost go so far as to claim that it was only the spirit of the *'ilm al-qirā'āt* that could create such an edition [i.e., the Cairo Qur'an of 1925]: all European philological meticulousness and care toward collation would hardly have reached the nearly absolute accuracy that was achieved by the Egyptian Qur'an scholars thanks to their lifelong-practiced memory, their mastery of all details, and their religious reverence for the smallest items. While it is the ancient tradition that lives on in this most punctilious exactness, what is even more vividly alive are the signs of independent progress that goes beyond what is received from tradition. . . . We have to accept the difference in scientific approach, whereby the Islamic scholar takes as a basis the newest presentations and oral transmission, while our historical methods require reference back to the oldest reachable sources, the oldest manuscripts of the Qur'an itself and the oldest literature about its text. For a textual edition, the difference in result is less than one would expect. . . . We too, in an edition of the Qur'an text, could hardly offer anything other than the consonants of the Uthmanic Qur'an with reading signs following the recension of the Ḥafṣ 'an 'Āṣim; the number of places where our alternate evaluation of the sources would lead us to present this text differently would be slight.[89]

Yet this situation should not obscure the fact that for the recording of textual forms prior to the prevailing of the closed readings, we must rely on the earliest Qur'an manuscripts in addition to the non-canonical readings.[90] In order to determine the oldest reachable non-reconstructed form of the consonantal text, the Bavarian Academy of Sciences had conceived the project of a collection of photographs of the oldest preserved Qur'an manuscripts,[91] a project that, under

89. Bergsträsser, "Koranlesung in Kairo," 112.
90. On the script, see the standard work by Déroche, *Islamic Codicology*.
91. Bergsträsser, "Plan eines Apparatus Criticus zum Koran."

the title Apparatus criticus zum Qur'an, was supervised from the late 1920s onward by Gotthelf Bergsträsser himself. Following his death in 1934, it was carried forth by Otto Pretzl.[92] He set himself the goal of "determining through research in the Qur'an manuscripts themselves the oldest attainable non-reconstructed form of the consonantal text, and illustrating the textual history of the Qur'an in the earliest centuries through a critical apparatus of reading variants."[93] In 1938, relying extensively on codices from Istanbul collections, Pretzl issued a brief introduction to the problems and methods of research in Qur'anic manuscripts,[94] wherein he distinguished on paleographic grounds between three groups of codices, which on the basis of their information on orthography and verse divisions can be assigned with some certainty to particular branches of tradition.

Prior to this, the textual history of the Qur'an had been the subject of independent scholarly pursuits, which resulted in the well-known great collections of Qur'an manuscripts (above all in London, Paris, St. Petersburg, and Berlin) and which led to the first publications of manuscripts. A palimpsest whose underwriting (*scriptio inferior*) shows the Qur'an text in archaic ductus and whose upper layer (*scriptio superior*) shows a Christian-Arabic text was edited at the start of the twentieth century.[95] A substantial step forward in our knowledge of the manuscripts was achieved by the manuscript finds of Sanaa: there, in 1972 and 2007, in a false ceiling of the great mosque, numerous Qur'an manuscripts from quite different epochs were discovered, including some from the earliest period. Among the manuscripts that became known in 1972 was a palimpsest with a Qur'an text on both the superior and inferior surfaces.

Although manuscripts from the time of Muhammad do not seem to have survived, the oldest ones do reach back to the first Islamic century. One of these codices, which can probably be dated to before the time of ʿAbd al-Malik (r. 65–86/685–705), has been reconstructed to a great extent and analyzed by Francois Déroche.[96] Marcus Fraser dates several hundred fragments back into the first century.[97] Sergio Noja Noseda has made a number of early codices available in facsimile editions with facing transcription in the Naskhī script that is current today.[98] While all of the early codices that have come down to us are preserved in differing local varieties of the early Arabic monumental script ("lapidary," with its two variants, the Hijazi and the so-called Kufic ductus), the earliest Qur'an manuscripts are likely those unofficial documents that show a cursive that also occurs in a highly developed form in secular papyri from the first half of the

92. Pretzl, "Die Fortführung des Apparatus Criticus zum Koran."
93. Pretzl, *GdQ*^{2}, 3:247.
94. Pretzl, *GdQ*^{2}, 3:249–273.
95. Mingana and Smith Lewis, *Leaves from Three Ancient Qurâns.*
96. Déroche, *La transmission écrite.*
97. Fraser, unpublished lecture at the Freie Universität Berlin, December 19, 2010.
98. Noseda, *Les manuscrits de style Higazi*, vols. 1–2.

first/seventh century.[99] In the Hijazi script, also called *māʾil*, "leaning," due to its form, different scribal hands can easily be distinguished. It is a great merit of Marcus Fraser to have traced its development through comparison of the individual characters not only in manuscripts but also in dated coins and inscriptions from the first Islamic decades, and to have offered detailed documentation of the transformation into the Kufic ductus through an intermediary phase.

In the next phase, the Kufic script represents a calligraphically sophisticated scribal ductus, which Fraser associates with an orientation toward the Greek-Latin majuscule script; though the Kufic is not to be considered a new script, but rather a monumental development from the Hijazi script. Dated inscriptions allow us to date the beginnings of this calligraphically sophisticated script to the time of the third Umayyad caliph, ʿAbd al-Malik. The famous inscription on the inner side of the circular arcade (ambulatorium) of the Dome of the Rock in Jerusalem dates from the year 691; to the same period belong milestones with engraved inscriptions, which mention the rule of ʿAbd al-Malik. The beginnings of the Kufic script can thus be set at about sixty years after the death of the Prophet.

Less is known about the scribal workshops, the scriptoria, from which the oldest manuscripts originate. Estelle Whelan[100] has collected reports from historical sources about scriptoria in Medina. Marcus Fraser succeeded in deducing the sites of three centers of manuscript production from the paths of transmission of concrete codices: Sanaa, Fustat, and Damascus. He considers the future discovery of manuscript hoards on the peninsula to be possible—perhaps confirming the scriptoria in Medina that are mentioned in historiographical sources.[101]

In recent years, first datings of writing materials with radiocarbon analysis (carbon-14 methods) have been carried out for Qur'an manuscripts.[102] The research of textual history, which, apart from the identification of text variants, also undertakes the chronological assignment of all its textual evidence, is today inspiring hope thanks to international collaboration. Above all, Bergsträsser's project of the *apparatus criticus* to the Qur'an,[103] which was interrupted for a long

99. On the history of the development of the Lapidaris, especially of the Kūfī, see Grohmann, *Arabische Paläographie*, vols. 1–2; a short overview is offered in Grohmann, "Die Entstehung des Korans"; reproductions of old codices can be found in Abbott, *The Rise of the North Arabic Script*; Levi della Vida, *Frammenti coranici in carattere cufico*; Vajda, *Album de paléographie arabe*; Al-Munajjed, *Le manuscrit arabe jusqu'au Xe siècle de l'Hégire I*; Lings, *The Qur'anic Art of Calligraphy*; James, *Qur'ans and Bindings*. A detailed paleographic analysis of the Damascene Qur'an scrolls, which supposedly go back in some parts to the first century, is given by Ory, "Un nouveau type de mushaf"; synoptically, see Endress, "Herkunft und Entwicklung."

100. Whelan, "Writing the Word of God."

101. Fraser, lecture December 19, 2009.

102. See Bothmer, Ohlig, and Puin, "Neue Wege der Koranforschung"; Rezvan, *The Qur'an of Uthmân*; Dutton, "An Umayyad Fragment"; Dutton, "Some Notes."

103. The project was interrupted for a long time due to the archive being bombed in early 1945. Bergsträsser's collection of films and audio recordings on phonographic cylinders are, however, extant and have been handed over to the Corpus Coranicum project, as a permanent loan from the Bayerische Akademie der Wissenschaften.

time after Otto Pretzl's death in 1941, was taken up again in the year 2007 in a new form: the approximately 450 Agfa film rolls left by Bergsträsser are now being digitized as part of the Corpus Coranicum activities of the Berlin-Brandenburg Academy of Sciences and are being utilized for the systematic textual documentation that forms part of that research project. Other parts of the bequest of the Munich Qur'an Commission have now been partly examined and await evaluation in the coming years. Bergsträsser's conception of text-historical analysis proved groundbreaking for the activities of the academy, which in the coming years will realize Bergsträsser's research plan through the gradual publication of the photo collections long thought destroyed.[104] A French-German research project, Coranica, integrated with the Corpus Coranicum, has set itself the goal of providing an edition and scientific investigation of the oldest preserved Qur'an manuscripts—a task to which Sergio Noja Noseda had devoted himself for well over a decade, in collaboration with Francois Déroche and Christian Robin. Special attention should be paid here to the dating of the relevant manuscripts. The anticipated results should lay the groundwork for a history of the Arabic script and the evolution of Arabic orthography, the development of the distribution of text units within suras and so on. The goal of this research, which will be supplemented through the inventory of the oldest datable Qur'an citations in inscriptions on stone, coins, papyri, ornamental objects, textiles, and the like, is the development and publication of relevant materials for a systematic scientific edition of the text.

4.7 New Qur'an Editions and Translations

The spectrum of Qur'an texts available today is broad. Modern Qur'an manuscripts and lithographs in the Islamic east generally follow the tradition of Ḥafṣ ʿan ʿĀṣim, in the west that of Warsh ʿan Nāfiʿ, or, in Libya, of Qālūn ʿan Nāfiʿ (Qālūn d. 220/835). They have not been treated bibliographically. Lithographs of the Ḥafṣ over time text assimilated more and more to the standardized orthography of secular texts. The first printed Qur'an edition in the Near East backed this tendency with purist principles: in order to restore the Ḥafṣ text to its earliest orthographic form, the editors of the official Cairo Qur'an (*Qurʾān Karīm*, 1344/1925) oriented themselves strictly to the Uthmanic script; their edition represents a reconstruction of the early consonantal text on the basis of individual and relatively recent orthographic works. Since according to Bergsträsser's judgment the degree of exactness could scarcely have been heightened by the reproduction of older materials, the official Qur'an should be considered the best edition currently available. It is generally used as a basis in Western research and has

104. See Marx, "Ein Koran-Forschungsprojekt"; Marx, "Der Koran nach Agfa."

replaced the previous edition by Gustav Flügel,[105] which is based on no consistent Islamic tradition. While Flügel's edition should be considered fundamentally obsolete, his accompanying concordance is still valuable,[106] since in taking into account grammatical function words it goes beyond the concordance to the Cairo text by Fu'ad ʿAbd al-Baqi, *Al-Muʿjam al-mufahras li-alfāẓ al-Qurʾān al-Karīm.*[107]

Such a vast number of translations is now available into European languages that we can give no adequate account of them here. An overview of the earliest European Qur'an translations is offered by Arthur Jeffery.[108] Further translations into European languages are given in summary by Jeffery[109] and Rudi Paret,[110] and into (non-European) Islamic languages by J. Pearson.[111] The critical scholarly translations of Richard Bell,[112] Arthur Arberry,[113] Regis Blachère,[114] and Rudi Paret[115] still count as standard works. Paret's German translation has not been superseded by the newer and more readable editions of Adel Theodor Khoury[116] and Hans Zirker,[117] or by the outlandish one by Ahmad Milad Karimi.[118] All translations that have appeared in English from the start of the twentieth century down to today are discussed critically by Matthias Radscheit.[119] The most artistically valuable German translation, and the one that comes closest to the original in its linguistic attitude, is still the selection by Friedrich Rückert.[120] A new and dependable translation with artistic claims has been made available by Hartmut Bobzin;[121] a modern poetic version is expected from Stefan Weidner.

105. Flügel, *Corani textus arabicus*; see Bergsträsser, "Koranlesung in Kairo," 12–13.
106. Flügel, *Concordantiae Corani arabicae.*
107. Abd al-Bāqī, *Muʿjam.*
108. Jeffery, "Progress in the Study of the Qur'an Text."
109. Jeffery, "The Present Status of Qur'anic Studies."
110. Paret, *Vorwort zu Der Koran.*
111. Pearson, "Translations of the Kur'an."
112. Bell, *The Qur'ān Translated.*
113. Arberry, *The Koran Interpreted.*
114. Blachère, *Le Coran*, vols. 2–3.
115. Paret, *Der Koran: Übersetzung*, accompanied by *Der Koran: Kommentar und Konkordanz.*
116. Khoury, *Der Koran.*
117. Zirker, *Der Koran.*
118. Karimi, *Der Koran.*
119. Radscheit, "Aktuelle deutsche Koranübersetzungen im Überblick."
120. Rückert, *Der Koran, im Auszuge übersetzt*, ed. A. Müller. For criticism of some translations of the Qur'an, cf. Fischer, *Der Wert der vorhandenen Koranübersetzungen*, as well as Paret, *Der Koran*, which collects reviews of individual translations of the Qur'an.
121. Bobzin, *Der Koran.*

5

Sura Structures and Chronology

5.1 The Sura as Novelty

5.1.1 *An Unrecognized Genre*

A desideratum articulated more than thirty years ago remains unfulfilled: "The Qur'an has had a fate in Western research not dissimilar to that of early Arabic poetry: as historical, cultural, and grammatical-verbal evidence, it became the object of a scholarly literature that cannot be dismissed, but as that which it is in essence, as it was conceived of from the very beginning, that is, as liturgical discourse and text intended for recitation, it has scarcely ever been appreciated."[1] Indeed, in the time since then, research into ancient Arabic poetry has made significant progress, so that the "evaluation" of the poetry for historical or practical information is no longer the central pursuit, yet the Qur'an remains primarily a quarry for data of the most various kinds: the life circumstances of the Prophet, his ideological goals, the religious practices of his contemporaries, even their means of physical nutrition. But the perception of the Qur'an as a text existing in progress and reflecting a communal formation, which is always constructing anew its scenario of proclamation and having its primary *Sitz im Leben* in liturgical performance, has not prevailed and, with the proliferation of the skeptical approach, remains further than ever from the central focus of research.

If one wants to approach the liturgical Qur'an, the primary object of formal investigation cannot be the textual compilation of the Qur'an, but must rather be the unit that was intended by the Prophet himself as the formal medium of his proclamation: the sura. Although smaller thematic units may have emerged in connection to particular "occasions of revelation," *asbāb al-nuzūl*, what is relevant for literary-critical interrogation is not these external occasions for the handling of a theme but rather their formation and insertion into a composition. In this investigation, we will adhere to the unit of the sura as a heuristic basis—despite the tendency predominant in recent research toward atomizing or ignoring this form.

That the sura unit[2] must have belonged to the formal conceptions of Qur'anic discourse itself is attested externally by the oldest surviving Qur'an manuscripts,

1. Neuwirth, *Studien zur Komposition*, 1.
2. Neuwirth, "Sura(s)."

which already mark the sura beginnings and ends as we find them in the later canonized codex.[3] The name *sūra* (pl. *suwar*) is apparently first coined within the proclamation itself; it is reserved for the Qur'anic textual unit and is used nowhere for texts outside the Qur'an (before the modern period). Within the Qur'an, *sūra* signifies in the first instance a smaller textual unit of undefined extent. The word occurs first in the middle Meccan period, in the "challenge pronouncements," the so-called *taḥaddī*-verses, where opponents are challenged to bring forth a textual unit of the same sort: "Speak: so bring then a *sūra* like it, and call out to whom you can other than God" (Q 10:38, similarly late Meccan Q 11:13 and Medinan Q 2:23; cf. also Q 9:64, 86, 124, 127; Q 24:1 and Q 47:20). When exactly this textual unit became identified with the units distinguished as suras in the codex remains unclear, but the most probable etymology seems to indicate that what was initially intended was a short textual unit. It has long been assumed the derivation of the Arabic *sūra* from a Syriac *sūrtā*, "line," "line of writing,"[4] a connection now seems more likely with Syriac *shūrāyā*, "beginning," or, in a liturgical context, "introduction (of the reading of scripture by a psalm reading)."[5] The designation *sūra* would then in Qur'anic usage make reference to a textual unit that elsewhere is clearly liturgical, and which, similar to the older suras in ductus and extent, would be kept relatively short and poetic. What we now have as suras may have circulated early on under individual names similar to those used now, which pick up on either a beginning word of the text or an especially striking word from within it, although secure information on the earliest state of affairs is not available.[6] That different names remain in circulation until today for some suras show that the orally transmitted text was known well enough to guarantee that its individual texts could be recalled by the help of various key words.[7]

It seems that for some time the sura unit came to fulfill for the Qur'anic community the function of those liturgical reading pericopes known from the neighboring religions; that is, they corresponded to the *parasha* in Jewish worship and the pericope in Christian worship. But while within those traditions, the "excerpting" or pericopizing of the text for reading only occurred when the canonical text was already available in its entirety, the Qur'anic sura unit was from the beginning conceived as such and used as the object of a continuous performance praxis, a social frame of communication that is reflected clearly in many suras.[8] Thus, suras are not excerpts from a complete delineated text, but

3. This also applies to the manuscript finds of Sanaa; cf. chap. 4, 158–161; they reflect a clear differentiation between the suras, and in general follow the order of the suras in the dominant textual tradition.

4. Nöldeke, GdQ, 1:31; Jeffery, *Materials*, 180–182.

5. On this hypothesis, see Neuwirth, "Sūra(s)."

6. Occasionally, the Fātiḥa can be evoked in later texts with its concurrent name, *al-ḥamd*, as in sura 15; cf. Neuwirth, "Referentiality and Textuality."

7. On the names of the suras, see Kandil, "Surennamen," 44–60.

8. For detail on this development, see chap. 6.

rather elements of a communication that remained open-ended for a significant period. While Meccan suras as a rule clearly evince the character of intentional performance units, the long Medinan suras yield problems in this light. In view of the extent of time required for their performance, they can hardly have been intended as singular performances. But not all the long Medinan suras can be dismissed as secondary, redactional collections. In this sura type, which is no longer suited to performance in its entirety, one must consider a newly conceived aim, perhaps that of a biblical book. There is much to indicate that in Medina, the polythematic sura, tailored in length and ductus for performance,[9] is being superseded by other forms of proclamation, so that the neatly composed Meccan sura ultimately leaves the scene; it is largely for this reason that the unit "sura" has received little attention in inner-Islamic scholarship. Although the classical commentaries follow the sequence of suras, they focus their exegesis as a rule on individual verses and hardly ever sum up their exegetical results for an entire sura. The modern "literary commentary," the *tafsīr adabī*, also does not take entire suras as its basis.

If one interprets "sura" not as a kind of chapter heading but rather as the designation of a genre in the context of proclamation, it becomes evident that the genre "sura" has scarcely been adequately studied. For Richard Bell and Régis Blachère, who both studied the style and composition of the Qur'an, the sura does not stand as the central point, but rather the smaller compositional units from which they are composed. As against that, Theodor Nöldeke had based his chronology on the sura as a whole—without however taking an interest in the "sura" as a genre concept. A foundational contribution to the description of the composition of suras is offered only by Josef Horovitz, who in the frame of his treatment of Qur'anic narrative pays close attention to the appearance of formulas or coined expressions with introductory and concluding functions, and thus provides an important criterion for the demarcation of the individual building blocks of suras. It is only in recent times that analyses of suras have been undertaken,[10] in which the choice of the sura unit however seems to be pragmatically motivated—the sura is a clearly delimited unit—rather than driven by an interest in its literary form and function within the Qur'anic corpus—an approach from which only the much-studied exceptional case of the monothematic sura 12, "Joseph," is an exception. In what follows, the sura structures particular to the individual phases of the Qur'an's development will be presented briefly in

9. Cf. chap. 6, 255–229.

10. See Mir, "Coherence in the Qur'an"; Mir, "The Sūra as a Unity"; Mir, "The Qur'ānic story of Joseph"; Neuwirth, "Yusuf-Sure"; de Prémare, *Joseph et Muhammad*; Sells, *Approaching the Qur'an*; Sells, "A Literary Approach to the Hymnic Surahs"; Sells, "Sound, Spirit and Gender"; Sells, "Sound and Meaning"; Waldman, "New Approaches"; Zahniser, "The Word of God and the Apostleship of ʿĪsā"; Zwettler, "A Mantic Manifesto." Cf. also Neuwirth, "Sura(s)." See now also Schmitz, *Sure 2*, and Cuypers, *The Banquet*. A list of his interpretations of individual suras can be found ibid., 517.

their formal and thematic elements, and some new criteria will be drawn for the chronological attribution of the texts.

5.2 The Early Meccan Suras

5.2.1 *Overview*

In contrast to the already-established canonical codex, the pre-canonical Qur'an should be understood as the textual remnant of a communication process, and thus as an ensemble of texts that have their *Sitz im Leben* in a public or at least audibly performed recital (*qur'ān*). These individual texts are to be identified, at least for the Meccan period, with the suras. The suras equate to the "scenes" of the Qur'anic drama, so to speak, while the great "acts" are the discourses that developed one from the other, and which are debated within larger sura groups.[11] In the attempt to recognize the individual "scenes" of this drama, it is still a valid principle, 150 years after the first appearance of Theodor Nöldeke's *Geschichte des Qorans*, to divide the text corpus heuristically into three Meccan periods and one Medinan period—intending with "period" not chronologically determinable, absolute, or even relatively dated text sequences, but rather text groups distinguished by formal similarities and unmistakable shared discourses.

In Nöldeke's chronology, the first Meccan period includes suras 51–53, 55–56, 69, 70, 73, 75, 77–83, 85–102, 104–109, and 111–114: in essence, the so-called "last thirtieth" of the Qur'an, which down to today represents a partial corpus of suras used prominently in ritual prayer.[12] They are mostly short texts, at first monothematic, later also polythematic. They testify to an experience of consolation undergone by the person of the proclaimer, who is addressed as "you." Apart from the second-person address, which is an element introduced by the Qur'an, this consolation is conveyed in a style that is highly evocative of the Psalms, which are in fact paraphrased time and again.[13] This partial corpus, in which research has long attempted to uncover biographical allusions to the proclaimer's situation, should rather be considered as an Arabic expression of psalmic piety, as a microstructural reading shows. The early texts are text-referential rather than situation-referential; they do not yet always reflect the scenario of the speaker-hearer situation that will soon become ubiquitous. With Harris Birkeland, one can plausibly assume the earliest sura group to be the five suras (93, 94, 106, 107, and 108) that give expression to comfort, encouragement, and the assurance of providence.[14] Closely following is a number of suras that project the Final

11. On these discourses, see chap. 7–9.

12. On the overriding oral character of the Qur'an, see Graham, *Beyond the Written Word*; cf. also Nelson, *Art of Reciting*.

13. Neuwirth, "Psalms."

14. Birkeland, *The Lord Guideth*; now also Sinai, "Qur'ān as Process"; cf. chap. 7, 241–243.

Judgment in metaphors that often recall the Revelation of John, a vision of the future presented as shockingly close that radically redresses the erstwhile predominant cyclical understanding of time. Time is now extended linearly, back to an original beginning before the chronological time of man, reaching from the creation of the world and the first divine self-communication down to the end of human time: the dissolution of the created world, the judgment and the ensuing retribution. The new theologumenon of linear time, central for this early phase, wherein everything leads ultimately to a rendering account is instrumental for a decisive "turn" in the worldview of the Qur'anic community, toward an eschatological fulfillment of time, a turn that is decisive enough to give every human interaction a new, ethically relevant quality. But these "eschatological suras"—like the preceding ones—do not yet draw their authority from the reference to a divine speaker who has introduced himself as an actor. They rather make use of authorization strategies drawn from pre-Islamic sacral speech; such as clusters of oaths upon natural phenomena, and ultra-rhythmic, short speech units thus exploiting the almost magical power of language to project the foreseen apocalyptic events.

What in the early Meccan suras counts in consideration of the imminent judgment is not only ethically correct behavior but also ritual observance. Day and night are subdivided into sacral sections of time reserved for prayer, which are often evoked in the introductory parts. But the most important time-specific innovation is the introduction of eschatological prophecies. With their expressive and strikingly repetitious structures, these prophecies strongly mark the audible and rhythmic shape of the early suras. Their most important characteristics are the oath clusters and the so-called *idhā*-phrase-series—rows of sentences beginning with *idhā* "if (and when)," which conjure eschatological scenes at the beginning of a sura.[15] Unlike biblical oaths the Qur'anic oath clusters do not function as invocations of a supernatural power from outside of the text, but rather draw their authority from their very linguistic force. The value claim of the early suras is not yet grounded in an extratextual authority: one should speak here of a poetic rather than a theological truth claim.

The hymnic passages, characterized by parallelism, also follow a scheme of repetition. In their attitude of thankfulness for divinely guaranteed safety and preservation, they seem to form counterpoints to the eschatologically marked texts with their dreadful projections of punishment, yet the argumentation that accompanies them often leads similarly into eschatological trains of thought.

Toward the end of the early Meccan period, the consolations and exhortations, at first directed toward the proclaimer individually and positioned at the conclusions of suras, give way to a new mode to confirm the truth claim of the

15. See Neuwirth, *Studien zur Komposition*, 190–193; cf. below, 174–176.

proclamation now involving the collective of hearers: the "affirmation of revelation," which will become the prevailing form of sura conclusion in the following periods.

5.2.2 *Elements of Form and Semantics*

5.2.2.1 *The Sura Beginning*

Of the approximately thirty early Meccan suras, no less than fourteen begin with an oath or an oath cluster.[16] This observation invites a closer treatment of the oaths, firstly because typologically marked openings of literary compositions of a shared genre often carry significance for the overall structure that goes beyond their individual semantic value, as can be seen, for example, within pre-Qur'anic Arabic literature in the opening of the ancient Arabic qasida, the *nasīb*.[17] On the other hand, the Qur'anic oaths deserve attention since they are controversial in research: although the few available studies on the overall composition of early Meccan suras do not yet allow conclusive judgments as to the function of the introductory oaths, individual observations on these sura openings—supported by indigenous traditions that are by no means warranted—have spawned far-reaching hypotheses about the specific Prophet type of Muhammad. In particular, on the basis of the sura-introductory oath clusters, whose rhetorical structure is closely related to that of the pronouncements of the ancient Arabic seers and soothsayers, the *kuhhān*, some have arrived at the conclusion that the early suras might be seen as proclamations of this particular speaker type.[18] In this argumentation, a particular evidential power is assigned to the oath clusters, since these clusters display an "obscurity of sense, which is everywhere more implicated than executed."[19] In view of the insecure transmission of the few pronouncements of the *kuhhān* that have been traced up to now from other sources, the comparison itself cannot be verified. But it remains a desideratum to describe the types and forms of oaths and oath clusters in the Qur'an as to their function in the Qur'anic discourse.

It should be asserted at the outset that the discourse type "oath"—which taken in the strict sense consists of only the verbal part of an act made up of both words and particular symbolic gestures[20]—does not serve in the Qur'an as the

16. On the complex problems of Qur'anic oaths, see Neuwirth, "Images and Metaphors"; Neuwirth, *Studien zur Komposition*, 187–188; Robinson, *Discovering the Qur'an*, 102–103.

17. See Lichtenstädter, "Das Nasib"; Jacobi, *Poetik der altarabischen Qaside*; J. Stetkevych, *Zephyrs of the Najd*; S. Stetkevych, *The Mute Immortals Speak*; Montgomery, *Vagaries of the Qasida*.

18. This circular reasoning was expressed by Wellhausen, *Reste*, 135: "The most important documents for the style of the Kahin are the oldest suras in the Qur'an." Cf. further Watt, *Bell's Introduction to the Qur'an*, 77–79; Paret, *Mohammed und der Koran*, 24–25. Contrast the more reserved statement in Blachère, *Introduction au Coran*, 178–179. A new attempt has been offered by Hämeen-Anttila, "Arabian Prophecy," 115–146, which constructs a *kāhin's* career for the proclaimer of the Qur'an.

19. Nöldeke and Schwally, GdQ^2, 75.

20. On the type of oath in the context of religious speech, cf. Heiler, *Erscheinungsformen*, 311–314; Lehmann, "Biblical Oaths."

trigger for any magic effect or legal obligation, but is rather used exclusively as an artistic, literary means to produce an emphatic effect. With this in mind, one can give an account of its striking formal characteristics: first, the accumulation of oath formulae, which often form a kind of rhythmical startup for the suras, corresponding here to other types of stereotyped introductory clusters. That neither magical influence nor legal obligation is intended becomes evident from the simple verbal formulation, which is limited to the naming of the oath object ("by X") and the oath pronouncement, without any other immanent compulsion being expressed, usually phrased "*inna* X *la*-Y." Yet there are shared characteristics between the literary oaths of the Qur'an and genuine—that is, binding—oaths, first of all the particular relation between the two parts of the oath. Both types of oaths draw for their assertion on the reference not on phenomena of the everyday world surrounding the speaker but to phenomena of a different, in most cases hierarchically superior realm. Genuine oaths do this in order to summon these phenomena as guarantors or testimonies for the truth of the ensuing pronouncements, while literary oaths, on the other hand, employ enigmatic phenomena to give particular force to the unambiguity of their pronouncements. Between the oath cluster itself and the pronouncements that require underscoring lies a clear break not only syntactically but also semantically. As a rule it is only the ensuing section to which the oath cluster connects semantically providing it with a structural or iconic matrix ("Bildmatrix") for its pronouncements.

Three major groups of oath clusters emerge in the Qur'an: (1) oaths by animate beings or phenomena not named explicitly (*fāʿilāt* oaths, "tableaux"): suras 100, 79, 77, 51, and 37; (2) oaths by sacred sites: suras 95, 90, and 52; and (3) oaths by cosmic phenomena and times of the day and night: suras 93, 92, 91, 89, 86, 85—this last category also includes some oaths that occur within the interior of suras.[21]

5.2.2.2 *Oath Clusters as Tableaux*

There are five introductory oath clusters that do not name their oath objects with a distinct designation, but rather employ a metonymical use of the feminine active plural participle, identified in Arabic grammar as *fāʿilāt*. Not without ambiguity, the verbs employed in the oath clusters communicate the impression of swift and violent movement (Q 100:1–3: *wa l-ʿādiyāt ḍabḥā*, "by the fast runners")[22] or violent action (Q 79: 1–4 *wa-l-nāziʿāt gharqā*, "by the violently pulling"), contributing to a sensibly threatening tone. The frequent usage in the Qur'an of this participle form for the metonymical paraphrase of a catastrophic event, as for example *al-qāriʿa*, "the knocker" (as herald of a natural catastrophe, Q 101:1–3), gives additional frightening effect to the pronouncement, which

21. A discussion of all the oaths is offered in Neuwirth, "Der Horizont der Offenbarung."

22. Sura 100 is discussed in chap. 10, 359–362, and chap. 12, 428–434.

remains enigmatic in terms of its concrete accompanying circumstances. The *fāʿilāt* series, in that they draw up entire tableaux in order to illustrate an onrushing calamity through natural phenomena, can probably be best likened to a biblical seer vision. An example is Q 77:1–7:

wa-l-mursalāti ʿurfā
fa-l-ʿāṣifāti ʿaṣfā
wa-l-nāshirāti nashrā
fa-l-fāriqāti farqā
fa-mulqiyāti dhikrā
ʿudhran aw nudhrā
inna mā tūʿadūnā la-wāqiʿ

By those sent out in rows
Then violently roaring,
Then spreading out widely,
Then driving out from each other,
Then raining down reminding
Forgiveness or warning:
That which is threatened to you falls here.

The oath series (verses 1–6) draws a panorama of meteorological and natural phenomena, the stormy movement of which is translated finally into a verbal warning (verse 6), thus achieving a threatening introductory tone. One can imagine storms as the subjects of the movements referred to in this oath series, and the objects of *nāshirāt*, "spreading" and *fāriqāt*, "driving apart," are most likely rain clouds; both of these occur in a shared context also elsewhere (cf. Q 79:1–5). According to this interpretation in the sense of forward-driving rain clouds—which is suggested by the particular powers introduced only metonymically through qualification—the oath cluster evinces the immediately comprehensible image of a directed and continuous sequence of movement. What is surprising then is how, at the end of the series (verses 5–6), the rain clouds are supposed to have the ability of verbal articulation (*dhikr*, remembrance, *ʿudhr* "forgiveness," *nudhr*, "warning"). Does this tableau, the *fāʿilāt* forms of which are stereotypically bound up in the Qur'an with eschatological connotations, conjure up the events of the Final Day, as in suras 100[23] and 79? Or, in view of the connection of the movements of nature with verbal pronouncements, is it an illustration of the communication process of the Qur'anic message?

The oath pronouncement (verse 7) expresses explicitly the "coming down" of the events announced in the oath series—in the image of the rain clouds driving on the storm: *inna-mā tuʿādūna la-wāqiʿ*, "that which is threatened to you falls here." In view of the parallels, this threat is clearly eschatologically directed. Even

23. See the discussions of this sura, chap. 10, 359–362, and chap. 12 428–434.

if the oath series, with its storm-driving clouds (verse 1) possessing violent movement (verse 2) and destructive power (verse 4), does not function exclusively as a prefiguration of eschatological events and the loosing of creation, but rather at the same time reflects the dynamic of verbal communication between heaven and earth, still their morphological form in the *fāʿilāt* structure evokes unmistakable eschatological associations. The oath series thus persists in its double readability as an evocative nature tableau functioning as an apocalyptical harbinger, and a (super)natural image of the process of revelation. It is this ubiquitous subtext and matrix of images that remains present throughout the entire sura.[24]

5.2.3 *Oaths by Sacred Sites*

In addition to these *fāʿilāt* oath clusters, we find a small group of oath series upon particular sacralized sites (suras 95, 90, and 52),[25] which serve to evoke the existing knowledge of the hearers regarding the salvation historical meaning of the given sites that is only hinted at in the oath; for example, the naming of Sinai to evoke the revelation to Moses. These oaths not only serve as epitomized recollections of revelation recalling salvific acts of God but also form a kind of subliminal argument, even when no direct logical relation to the oath pronouncement obtains. In Qur'anic thought, divine care through self-revelation in history is tied to the exhortation for fit human action that will become clear on the day of reckoning—the oaths thus stand in service of an argumentation for the necessity and unavoidability of the Final Day. This progression of ideas is formed, for example, in Q 52:1–8:

wa-l-ṭūr
wa-kitābin masṭūr
fī raqqin manshūr
wa-l-bayti l-maʿmūr
wa-l-saqfi l-marfūʿ
wa-l-baḥri l-masjūr
inna ʿadhāba rabbika la-wāqiʿ
mā lahu min dāfiʿ

By the mountain
and a writing, inscribed
on parchment, unrolled.
By the much-visited house,
and the roof raised high,
by the roaring sea.
The punishment of your lord arrives,
none can avert it.

24. Neuwirth, "Images and Metaphors," 9–11.
25. Ibid., 13–18.

The oath series evokes two scenes of divine self-revelation: Mount Sinai and Mecca. Both are clearly recognizable as symbols, for they are bound to each other by two further elements of monotheistic emblematics: written down, "codified" writing, *kitāb masṭūr*, and "parchment," *raqq*, the material basis of writing. The two sites are named indirectly, as in sura 95: Sinai is named through the Aramaic term for mountain, *ṭūrā*, immediately recognizable as the holy mountain. Mecca or its sanctuary is evoked in its function as pilgrimage site, *bayt maʿmūr*. The holiness of both places is founded on the divine self-revelation that occurred historically on site, in which an obligation was imposed on mankind. In agreement with the conventions of early Meccan texts, the primordial divine self-communication (verses 1–4) is bound up with the idea of the beginning of creation, which in this symbolically laden context is evoked through two images culled from the cosmic arena: the firmament of heaven and the sea (verses 5–6). The conceptual combination of divine creation and teaching is, as elsewhere, the precondition for the idea of eschatological resolution and rendering account, so that with the naming of both an expectation is awoken in the hearers. Its fulfillment is not delayed, as in the two other suras that begin with the same sequence of creation teaching, suras 95 and 90, but rather the threat of punishment is immediately expressed in the oath pronouncement itself (verses 7–8).

5.2.3.1 *Oaths by Heavenly Phenomena*

The third and most extensive group of oath series are oaths by heavenly phenomena,[26] by times of day or, more frequently, night. These oaths stand in no direct, unambiguous connection to what follows immediately. They are neither projections of catastrophe nor expressions of the double thought-figure creation-teaching/dissolution of the cosmos-accounting, but rather often thematize times of prayer service, as Q 93:1 *al-ḍuḥā*, "the bright day," or Q 89:1 *al-fajr*, "the sunrise," and Q 103:1 *al-ʿaṣr*, "the late afternoon," which have to be assumed as prayer times by the early Meccan period.[27] References to the night can frequently be understood as references to the vigils of the proclaimer and his community. Moreover, these oath objects are often exploited hermeneutically: they are bound respectively to oppositional or complementary pairs, and in some cases bring out the ambivalent oppositionality of the elements of creation, as in sura 91,[28] or, in other cases, the balance of creation, which also implies the contradictory strife of human inclinations, as Q 92:1–4, 5–13:

wa-l-layli idhā yaghshā
wa-l-nahāri idhā tajallā
wa-mā khalaqa l-dhakara wa-l-unthā

26. Neuwirth, "Images and Metaphors," 18–28.
27. Rubin, "Morning and Evening Prayers"; cf. chap. 6, 215–217.
28. Cf. chap. 3, 132–135.

inna saʿyakum la-shattā
fa-ammā man aʿṭā wa-ttaqā
wa-ṣaddaqa bi-l-ḥusnā
fa-sa-nuyassiruhu li-l-yusrā
wa-ammā man bakhila wa-staghnā
wa-kadhdhaba bi-l-ḥusnā
fa-sa-nuyassiruhu li-l-ʿusrā
wa-mā yughnī ʿanhu māluhu idhā taraddā
inna ʿalaynā la-l-hudā
wa-inna lanā la-l-ākhirata wa-l-ūlā

By the night, when it covers everything
and the day, when it shines bright.
By Him, who created male and female.
Your striving is disparate.
He who gives and is God-fearing
and recognizes the most beautiful as true,
for him we ease his way to easiness.
But he who is greedy and proudly repellent
and lies about the most beautiful,
for him we ease his way to hardship.
His possessions will not help him when he plummets.
The guidance is only with us
and to us only belongs the first and last.

The oath series (verses 1–3) begins with the naming of the night, the time of the vigil,[29] which is bound by verse 2 to the oppositional pairing day/night. Then follows, as a further pair of contrasts, the naming of the two genders willed by the creator as such. These oppositions, immanent in creation, prepare the central pronouncement of the sura, the reality of the morally differing directions of human striving, with which the hearers are directly confronted in verse 4: "Your striving is disparate." The two elementary contrasting pairs of the oath series, day/night and male/female, prove to be the structural matrix for the "contradictoriness of the strivers" that is unfolded in the subsequent confrontation of the pious and the proud (verses 5–13). Verses 5–7 and 8–10 draw up a double image of the morally and liturgically approved and of those deficient in both respects, whereby the negative wing of the image (verses 8–10) is strengthened through verses 11–13 by a proportionally balanced extension (verses 11–13). The righteous behavior as well as the misconduct are twofold: they are manifest in social conduct (verses 5 and 8) and in belief/unbelief in the hereafter (verses 6 and 9). The punishment of

29. On the proclaimer's vigils, see chap. 2, 71–73.

the damned emphasizes the frailness of supposed human power, and once again refers the decisive oppositional pair, the here and the hereafter (verse 13), to God alone. (An additional second part of the sura follows, which again takes up the theme of the vigil that is evoked in the oath series.)

In addition to this characteristic of providing an image or structural matrix for the wider sura text, the inner dynamic of the oath series has been highlighted.[30] It results from the accumulation of parallel syntactical elements, which form a rhythmic buildup, and then shapes the hearers' expectations, through the amassing of image elements, into a resolution of the images into explicit proclamations. It is no accident that it is this type of expressive sura introduction from which the characteristic initial image of later suras finally developed: the writing, *al-kitāb*. The "writing" or the "scripture" is thus the only relic from among a complex ensemble of the manifold accessories of revelation originally comprising complex cosmic, vegetative, topographic, and cultic-social elements.

5.2.3.2 *Eschatological Scenes and Processes*

While oath clusters allude to eschatological events only in the case of the *fāʿilāt*-series, and there only indirectly, this eschatological reference is the rule in another type of early Meccan sura introductions: the *idhā*-phrase clusters, that is, the array of "if (one day)" phrases: it forms the first verse cluster of an ensemble that consists in total of three parts, comprising an "eschatological scenario," an "eschatological process," and a "double image" or "diptych."[31] Eschatological prophecies are introduced as a rule by short, linked rows of *idhā* . . . ("if one day . . .") followed by subject and predicate, which thematize the events of the Final Day, that is, the loosing of the cosmos and the waking of the dead (e.g., in Q 99:1–3, Q 84:1–5, and Q 77:8–11). They form an "eschatological scenario" that is continued by an "eschatological process," the display of human behavior on the Final Day. In some cases, the *idhā* sentences are not limited to natural or cosmic phenomena but include also preparations for the scenario of judgment, such as the erection of the throne, the blowing of the trumpets, and the opening of the books, as in Q 81:1–14:[32]

idhā l-shamsu kuwwirat
wa-idhā l-nujūmu nkadarat
wa-idhā l-jibālu suyyirat
wa-idhā l-ʿishāru ʿuṭṭilat
wa-idhā l-wuḥūshu ḥushirat
wa-idhā l-biḥāru sujjirat

30. Neuwirth, "Images and Metaphors," 31–32.

31. On the eschatological elements, see in detail Neuwirth, *Studien zur Komposition*, 190–193; Robinson, *Discovering the Qur'an*, 105–106.

32. Neuwirth, *Studien zur Komposition*, 221.

wa-idhā l-nufūsu zuwwijat
wa-idhā l-maw'ūdatu su'ilat
bi-ayyi dhanbin qutilat
wa-idhā l-ṣuḥufu nushshirat
wa-idhā l-samā'u kushiṭat
wa-idhā l-jaḥīmu su''irat
wa-idhā l-jannatu uzlifat
'alimat nafsun mā aḥḍarat

When the sun is rolled up
and the stars cease to shine
when the mountains are made to move
when the pregnant camels are left alone
and wild animals are herded
when the seas overflow
when souls are put in pairs
and the hidden is asked
for what sin she was murdered
when scrolls are unfolded
and the sky is removed
when hellfire is kindled
and the garden is brought near,
then a soul will know what it accomplished.

The two-part sura is filled out with two exactly equal parts of eschatology and polemic, respectively. The first part (verses 1–14) is made up of a single *idhā* cluster with following pronouncements. The cluster, consisting of twelve snapshot images, is unfolded in pairs. The first pair thematizes catastrophic cosmic changes of sun and stars (verses 1–2). What follows is a pronouncement about the earth, followed by its correlate, the sea (verses 3 and 6, which follow later due to a displacement of the verse). A further pair (verses 4–5) focuses on scenes of the Bedouin lifeworld, which is presented as a "topsy-turvy world": following the convincing interpretation of Nicolai Sinai, the pregnant camels, which are particularly valuable as livestock, are left unattended, and therefore come into danger, while wild isolated animals, which otherwise move on their own, are grouped into herds. This is followed by a depiction of humankind (verses 7–9), whose souls are re united with their bodies; in this restoration of mankind, carefully kept secrets come to light, as in the case of the guiltlessly murdered and buried newborn girl, who is introduced as an interrogator (verses 8–9)[33]—this too is clearly a Bedouin reference. It is only here that the preparation for the judgment

33. *Wa'd*, "burying alive," was practiced in impoverished Bedouin societies to dispose of unwanted female progeny.

begins, with the unrolling of the register of deeds (verse 10) and the raising of the curtain: the sky is "taken away," to clear the stage for the judgment (verse 11). Finally, the two places in which the blessed and the damned will make their stay are prepared or "brought near" (verses 12 and 13).

Following this highly dramatic *idhā* cluster, which is formed through such strong parallelisms and which is unique due to the featuring of animals not mentioned elsewhere in eschatological scenarios, the pronouncement is performed, limited to just one verse, consummating the significant pathos that has accumulated from the long preceding sequence. It is all the more emphatic because it yokes its word order chiastically to that of the preceding verses. While in the oath series the verb stood at the end and formed the rhyme, it now stands at the beginning and thus carries the stress of the verse; in this way, the thought of wisdom or insight obtains special emphasis: *ʿalimat nafsun mā aḥḍarat*, "a soul knows what it has accomplished" (verse 14). The cluster offers an impressive rhythmic buildup to the final pronouncement, which consists in the laying open of the knowledge of man about his earthly conduct. Beneath this, as a subtext, we can make out a polemical confrontation with the Bedouin world known from heroic poetry, which is inserted through the negative image of the buried girl.

In place of *idhā* we can also find *yawma*, "on the day when" (e.g., in Q 101:4–5, Q 79:6–7). The *idhā/yawma* clusters are followed formally by a sentence of the type "then only [occurs]," the so-called eschatological process, which imagines the psychic condition (Q 81:14) and behavior of man experiencing the apocalyptic situation and illuminates the division of mankind into groups of blessed and damned. Here, in place of a description, can also occur an exclamation of woe (Q 52:9–12) or an address to the damned (Q 52:13–16).

5.2.3.3 *Double Images, "Diptychs"*

The concluding descriptions of the hereafter that then follow bring into the picture the blessed who are granted paradise after the judgment and those who are damned to punishment in hell.[34] These elements are clearly divided into two corresponding parts. Introduced by stereotyped formulas such as *fa-ammā . . . fa-*, "as for the (x), the (x) are"; *wa-ammā . . . fa-*, "but as for the (y), the (y) are" (Q 101:6–7; 8–9, Q 92:5–7; 8–10) or *wujūhun yawmaʾidhin* X. . . *wujūhin yawmaʾidhin* Y. . . "Some faces on that day are X, other faces that day are Y" (Q 80:38–39; 40–42), they contrast the situation of the blessed in the gardens of paradise with that of the damned in hellfire. It is striking that both utopian images are heavily laden with metaphors, and together they form a double image, the parts of which show either exactly equal verses or proportional verse numbers to each other—so, for example, in the cited example: Q 92:4–7 and 8–10 together with 11–13. As such, they recall the contrasting images of the two scenes of the

34. Cf. chap. 7, 257–263, and chap. 12, 441–444, where a further example is discussed.

hereafter in early Christian iconography, and could be described as a kind of diptych. Not rarely, these diptychs include recollections of the earthly behavior of men. In these cases flashbacks follow that provide a justification for the verdict, but which occasionally may turn into direct attacks on the opponents of the proclaimer. They serve for the most part to enumerate vices that are to be avoided (cf. the "vice catalogue," e.g., in Q 75:31–33, Q 83:29–33) and virtues to be imitated (cf. the "virtue catalogue," e.g., in Q 51:16–19). Such descriptions of the lot of the judged in the hereafter and the virtue and vice catalogues may also occur unconnected to the double images. As an example of a double image with a flashback to the earthly behavior of the judged and a kind of vice catalogue, we present Q 69:19–24, 25–32, 33–37:

fa-ammā man ūtiya kitābahu bi-yamīnih
fa-yaqūlu hāʾumu qraʾ kitābiyah
innī ẓanantu innī mulāqin ḥisābīyah
fa-huwa fī ʿīshatin rāḍīyah
fī jannatin ʿāliyah
quṭūfuhā dānīyah
kulū wa-shrabū hanīʾan
bi-mā aslaftum fī l-ayyāmi l-khālīyah
wa-ammā man ūtiya kitābahu bi-shimālih
fa-yaqūlu yā laytanī lam ūta kitābiyah
wa-lam adri mā ḥisābiyah
yā laytahā kānati l-qāḍiyah
mā aghnā ʿannī mālīyah
halaka ʿannī sulṭānīyah
khudhūhu fa-ghullūh
thumma l-jaḥīma ṣallūh
thumma fī silsilatin dharʿuhā sabʿūna dhirāʿan fa-slukūh
innahu kāna lā yuʾminu bi-llāhi l-ʿaẓīm
wa-lā yaḥuḍḍu ʿalā ṭaʿāmi l-miskīn
fa-laysa lahu l-yawma hāhunā ḥamīm
wa-lā ṭaʿāmun illā min ghislīn
lā yaʾkulūhu illā l-khāṭiʾūn

He who is handed his register in his right hand will say:
"Here it is! Take my register and read it to me.
I thought I was to meet my reckoning."
He shall have a life of contentment
in a lofty garden
whose pickings are within reach.
"Eat and drink in good health,
because of your former deeds in days gone by."

And he who is handed his register in his left hand will say:
"I wish I had not been handed my register,
nor known my reckoning!
If only my death had been final! My wealth does not help;
My power has collapsed around me."
Seize him and shackle him,
then scorch him in hell,
then lash him in chains, seventy arms in length.
He did not believe in God, the most powerful,
and did not encourage the feeding of the poor!
So today here he has no friend
and no food but the dirty water of hell,
which only sinners drink.

Sura 69 begins with the announcement of a punishment, which is first exemplified by the fates of the destroyed peoples (verses 1–12). The second part of the sura (verses 13–37) is filled out eschatologically. The apocalyptic event is announced by a trumpet blast (verse 13); shakings of earth and mountains follow (verses 14–16). The splitting of the heavens (verse 16) opens the stage for the entrance of angels, who carry the throne of the divine judge, and the entrance of men who themselves will be judged. The assignment of the judged among the blessed or the damned (verses 19–37) is shown through the handing over of their register of deeds (*kitāb*, verse 19, 25), from which they take away their "accounting" (*ḥisāb*, verse 20, 25). The concluding double image of the judged first inserts the fate of the blessed (verses 19–24), to whom is granted the stay in a garden with ample fruits, accompanied by welcoming and appreciative speeches. The negative part of the double image (verses 25–32) depicts the punishment that is readied for the thoughtless, who are not prepared for the judgment: torture and hellfire. This part is expanded into an exhortation to the guards of hell and a flashback, so that the description of the damned occupies the doubled space of that of the blessed. The different treatments of the judged contrasted in this double image—the pleasantries of the blessed (gardens, rich meals, friendly speech) set against the excessive torment of the damned (chaining and penalty by fire, and finally nauseating meals) presuppose familiarity with earlier, more detailed descriptions. In this double image, belonging already to the end of the early Meccan period, we see a contrast above all of the inner attitudes of the blessed ones, who have directed their lives toward God's judgment, with that of the damned, whose disobedience to divine authority is connected to their neglect of social duties—this results in the end in satisfaction for one and regret for the other.

5.2.4 *Narratives: Lessons from History*

Early Meccan suras often refer back to abandoned sites that were apparently occupied in the past by prospering societies, whose downfall, manifest in the collapse of buildings and irrigation systems, is identified not as due to natural catastrophes but as punishment for the unbelief of the occupants and the rejection of the divine messengers sent to them (see for example Q 91:11–15, Q 85:4–8, Q 51:24–46). The places that remain behind in a demolished state, which in part appear as already familiar to the hearers, are presented as collective monuments, *lieux de mémoire*, illustrating an order willed by God, according to which human misbehavior attracts divine punishment and eventually also annihilation. Josef Horovitz, who investigated the Qur'anic stories according to historical, narrative, and linguistic criteria,[35] speaks aptly of "punishment legends." Here, we can make an elementary distinction between stories that are filled out with narrative details (in suras 105, 91, 79, 68, and 51) and mere evocations of stories presumed already familiar (in suras 85, 89, 69, 51, 53, and 73). Suras 89, 69, 51, and 53 present examples of the minimal form of the "list." It should be emphasized that longer narratives, often introduced with formulas such as *hal atāka ḥadīth* . . . , "has the news reached you of . . . ," are also assumed to be familiar, or at least suggested to be so. In these narratives, what occurs is less a communication than a re-presentation. Q 89:6–14 offers a narrative sequence:

a-lam tara kayfa faʿala rabbuka bi-ʿĀd
Irama dhāti l-ʿimād
allatī lam yukhlaq mithluhā fī l-bilād
wa-Thamūda lladhīna jābū l-ṣakhra bi-l-wād
wa-Firʿawna dhī l-awtād
alladhīna ṭaghaw fī l-bilād
fa-aktharū fīhā l-fasād
fa-ṣabba ʿalayhim rabbuka sawṭa ʿadhāb
inna rabbaka la-bi-l-mirṣād

Have you not seen how your Lord dealt with ʿĀd,
with Iram of the pillars,
who had no equal in the land
and with Thamud, who hewed into the rock in the valley,
and with Pharaoh the lord of the poles,
who were defiant in the land
and wrought so much havoc.
Your Lord poured out a flood of punishment over them.
Truly, your Lord is lurking!

The recollection of the punishment legends is preceded by an oath on liturgically relevant times (verses 1–5), to which this narrative follows immediately, in the position of an oath pronouncement. It develops—in continuation of the idea of the "relevant times" from the oath series—the idea of the fatefully decisive

35. Horovitz, *Koranische Untersuchungen*, 1–77.

time. Earlier societies, in full possession of the material signs of earthly greatness, did not recognize their decisive chance, their *kairos*, and fell to a divine verdict of punishment. Verses 6–14 bring together, under the theme of divine evaluation, the fates of three ancient peoples presented as defiant and destructive, as the formal introduction already announces (verse 6): *a-lam tara kayfa faʿala rabbuka bi*-X, "Have you not seen, how your Lord has dealt with X?" The retribution that overtakes them is pronounced in a metaphor: *fa-ṣabba ʿalayhim rabbuka sawṭa ʿadhāb*, "for your Lord poured out a flood of punishment over them" (verse 13). The addressed hearers (verses 17–20), standing in an equally decisive time, must keep in mind not to miss the assignment that is set to them.

It is striking that it is through the Qur'anic stories drawn from history, no less than the enumeration of great divine deeds in creation, that the value of "signs," *ayāt*, is measured. Equally to such enumerations, the stories point to his omnipotence, which also includes the power to awaken the dead. The narratives are thus involved, either explicitly or implicitly, in an argument about the theological point in dispute among the hearers: of the resurrection. This kind of embedding of the narratives into an argument, which later becomes frequent, in the early Meccan suras is not yet linked explicitly to the term "signs."[36] Instead, what occurs are introductory formulas of warning such as "Have you not seen. . . ," which prod the listener to think about the testimony of his eyes or his memory.

It should be emphasized that all the major narratives occurring in the early Meccan period are structured into halves, so that two equal main parts are yielded: in sura 79 six to six verses, in sura 51 seven to seven, and in sura 68 nine to nine. Apparently, the intended function here is as mnemotechnic aids for the reciter.

5.2.5 *Hymnic*

A distinction should be made between "pure hymns," that is, texts in which God is praised for His own sake out of man's feeling of dependency and gratitude, and those paraenetic texts in which the praise and admiration of God's omnipotence and deeds primarily offers a threat against the high-handed, or a "sign" and warning to men of understanding.[37]

One might regard sura 106 as the oldest nucleus of a pure Qur'anic hymn; the two similar sura beginnings Q 87:1–5 and 96:1–5 then appear as its direct extension. In both texts, the understanding of the liturgical word granted by God to man is expressed already as *qurʾān*. Q 87:1–8:

36. For discussion of the punishment legends, see chap. 3, 131–135.

37. See Neuwirth, *Studien zur Komposition*, 192–195; Robinson, *Discovering the Qur'an*, 109–110; Baumstark, "Gebetstypus."

sabbiḥi sma rabbika l-ʿalā
alladhī khalaqa fa-sawwā
wa-lladhī qaddara fa-hadā
wa-lladhī akhraja l-marʿā
fa-jaʿalahu ghuthāʾan aḥwā
sa-nuqriʾuka fa-lā-tansā
illā mā shāʾa llāhu
innahu yaʿlamu l-jahra wa-mā yakhfā
wa-nuyassiruka li-l-yusrā

Glorify the name of your Lord, the highest,
who creates and forms
who measures and guides
who produces the pastures
and makes them dark chaff.
We will have you read, and you will not forget
except what God wants
He knows what is in the open and what concealed.
We shall ease your way toward ease.

The sura begins with a call to the praise of God (verse 1), which then leads into a hymn (verses 2–5) composed of three parallel predicates introduced by *alladhī*, "who." God is praised as the Creator, who forms man, measures his upkeep, and guides him rightly. But God's life-giving attention, his bringing forth of spring pastures, provides no safety, for he lets the life of nature be erased again in the sequence of the seasons and thus, as one can adduce from ancient Arabic poetry, repeatedly shakes the society of the nomadic tribes brought together by the flourishing of nature in the winter and spring. God is also the lord of time, the cyclical natural sequence of which does not follow fate—as in ancient Arabic poetry—but rather God's will. The hymnic enumeration of the divine bounties thus ends in a remembrance of loss that is familiar from the poetry, but which has now been detached from its pessimistic thrust, in that it is divinely willed. After this accumulation of titles of power, the divine voice turns, as if to authorize the hymn, and promises communication to the proclaimer, that is, further divine communication: with verses 6–8, the hymn turns suddenly into a address of God to the reciter, to whom help in memorizing the received speech is ensured and salvation in the hereafter is promised. The promised safeguarding against forgetting (verse 6) underlines the preservation of integrity demanded for the transmission of the text. The partial taking back of divine assurance, added later in the form of a formula of exception, is perhaps based on an experience of the unsustainability of this project experienced in the intervening time.

On the other hand, those hymns that have a polemical function, the "polemical *ayāt*," are already discernible from their formal introductions. They begin, for example, with an emphatic prompting, *fa-l-yanẓuri l-insānu ilā* . . . , "Man should look to . . ." (Q 86: 5, Q 80:24), or more frequently with rhetorical questions such as *a-fa-lā yanẓurūna*, "Do they not see?" (Q 88:17), *a-lam najʿal*, "Have we not designed?" (Q 78:6, Q 77:25), or *a-yaḥsabu l-insān*, "Does man think perhaps" (Q 75:27). In one instance, the rhetorical question even precedes a formula of damning: *qutila l-insānu mā akfarah* "Damned be man, how unthankful he is!" (Q 80:17).

5.2.6 Encouragement to the Proclaimer and Polemic

As speeches of consolation, we can name above all the complete suras 94 and 93.[38] Two further verse groups console specifically about attacks from the unbelievers: Q 68:1–7, in which the end of the verse group is shored up with a doxology, and Q 70:5–7, which is held together by shared rhyme.

The calls that exhort the proclaimer to worship, recitation, and praise of God are located most frequently at sura endings and beginnings, such as in Q 52:48–49, exhortation to patience in Q 53:62, 56:74, 69:52, 73:1–4, 74:7, 87:1, 96:1–3, and 96:19; calls to proclamation in Q 51:55 and 52:29; calls to praise of God in Q 84:24, 87:9, 88:21, and 93:11.

Exhortations to patience, also already integrated into polemical pronouncements, are frequent, as in Q 51:54, 52:48, 68:8–9, 68:10, 68:48–50, 73:10, 74:7, and 86:17.

Some polemical elements carry clear formal markers. Pronouncements of woe according to the formula *waylun li-* . . . *alladhī* . . . , "Woe to . . . , who. . . ," occur for example in Q 107:4–7 and in 83:1–3, where a threat of the Final Day follows. In Q 83:10 and Q 52:11, *waylun* has the function of the direct introduction of eschatological verse groups, *waylun yawmaʾidhin li-l-mukadhdhibīn/kādhibīn*, "Woe on that day to the liars." In Q 51:60, *fa-waylun* introduces the closing verse.

As damning formulas, we find in Q 80:17 *qutila*, "Be damned," and in Q 111:1 *tabbat yadā*, "May the hands wither." In the last case, what follows is a mockery of the attacked that is closely derived from poetic models and concerns punishment with hellfire (*lahab*, "flame") (Q 111:1–5):

tabbat yadā Abī Lahabin wa-tabb
mā aghnā ʿanhu māluhu wa-mā kasab
sa-yaṣlā nāran dhāta lahab
wa-mraʾtuhu ḥammālata l-ḥaṭab
fī jīdihā ḥablun min masad

38. Neuwirth, *Studien zur Komposition*, 196, 200–201. Cf. also Robinson, *Discovering the Qur'an*, 109–110, 122.

Withered should be the hands of Abū Lahab! And he himself!
Of no use to him will be his possessions and what he has gained.
He will burn in a fire that flames high!
And his wife—carrier of firewood!—
Around her neck is a braid of palm fibers.

As August Fischer already recognized in 1937,[39] the sura represents an early Qur'anic example of ancient Arabic invective, *hijāʾ*. While other Qur'anic invectives aim at groups of opponents, in this sura the attack aims at an individual opponent, who is prominent enough to be harmed by the threatened loss of his legal capacity—the right hand is required for swearing. Though his identity remains unrevealed in the Qur'an, it must be a man who, along with his wife, is of noble origin, for the social downgrading of his wife that we meet in the text and which is not located only in the eschatological future but rather, as is suggested by the direct address, in the present imagination of the speaker indicates a privileged position for the couple. The reversal of the image of the neck of the woman hung with jewels, celebrated equally in ancient Arabic poetry and Hellenistic iconography alike, by the materially worthless and socially stigmatizing mark of a slave woman represents an attack on the private life of the couple.

Threatening speeches are recognizable through characteristic phrasings. Either attention is drawn to the disapproved by *a-raʾayta lladhī*, "Have you seen the one who" (Q 107:1–3, 96:9–18, 53:33–37), or God announces that he himself will take over their punishment: dharnī, "Leave to me" (Q 74:11–17, 73:10–18). The evil are warned of, *fa-lā tuṭiʿi l-mukadhdhibīn*, "So do not obey the liars" (Q 69:8), or *fa-tawalla ʿanhum* "So turn from them" (Q 51:54). Accusations are simply observed (for example in Q 105:1–2: "Do you see not, how your Lord . . .? Has he not . . . your cunning?), or more often strengthened with emphatic exclamations such as *kallā*, "no!" and *bal* "nay rather" (Q 89:17–20, 87:16–17, 82:9, 75:20–21).

The defense of the Qur'an performance against those who despise it represents a special case of polemic. These parts most often form the conclusion to a sura and show the following characteristic opening phrases: *fa-mā lahum lā yuʾminūn*, "What is with them that they do not believe?" (Q 84:20–23), *fa-mā li-lladhīna kafarū qibalaka muhṭiʿīn*, "What is with the unbelievers, that they stretch their neck to you?" (Q 70:36–44), *fa-mā lahum ʿani l-tadhkirati muʿriḍīn*, "What is with them that they turn away from the reminder? (Q 74:49–55), *fa-ayna tadhhabūn*, "Where are you going?" (Q 81:26–28), *a-bi-hādhā l-ḥadīthi antum taʿjabūn*, "Are you amazed by this communication?" (Q 53:59–61).

As positive counterparts to this, we find confirmations of the character of the revelation of the Qur'an, which are formulated more freely. The announcements

39. See Fischer, *Wert der vorhandenen Koran-Übersetzungen*. On *hijāʾ* in general, see van Gelder, *The Bad and the Ugly*.

of revelation—to be interpreted, with Nicolai Sinai, as its own category—explain the origin, authority, and function of the Qur'anic proclamation. They frequently show a "free-floating" pronominal reference to the Qur'an: *in huwa illā dhikrun li-l-ʿālamīn*, "It is nothing but a reminder to mankind" (Q 81:25–28; cf. 81:19–21, 80:11–16, and 51:23, 53:4).

5.2.7 *Initiating Questions*

A particular characteristic of Qur'anic argumentation is the employment of an "iniating question." Such questions phrased as *wa-mā adrāka mā* X, "What makes you know what is X?"—posed after mentioning a newly introduced concept or image X that is generally unfamiliar—serve to emphatically stress the novelty of the concept by means of a delay of the progression of discourse. What follows then for the most part is not a concise explanation, but rather a contextualization of the questioned word within eschatology. With the three exceptions of Q 86:2–3, 90:12–16, and 97:2–4, all the initiating questions refer to eschatology. Two initiating questions are found in the short sura 101 (verses 1–3, 4–11):[40]

al-qāriʿah
mā l-qāriʿah
wa-mā adrāka mā l-qāriʿah
yawma yakūnu l-nāsu ka-l-farāshi l-mabthūth
wa-takūnu l-jibālu ka-l-ʿihni l-manfūsh
fa-ammā man thaqulat mawāzīnuh
fa-huwa fī ʿīshatin rāḍiyah
wa-ammā man khaffat mawāzīnuh
fa-ummuhu hāwiyah
wa-mā adrāka mā hiyah
nārun ḥāmiyah

The knocker
What is the knocker?
What makes you know what is the knocker?
On a day when mankind will be like scattering moths
when the mountains will be like ruffled wool,
then he whose scales are heavy
will have a full life.
But he whose scales are light
his mother is the pit.
Do you know what that is?
Burning fire.

40. On this, see Sells, "Sound and Meaning."

With the repetition of the onomatopoetic *al-qāriʿa* three times in rhyme position, the catastrophe, which announces itself through knocking, is summoned. The first "initiating question,"[41] about its nature (verses 2–3), remains unanswered, but it awakens the expectation of a particularly relevant communication. An eschatological scenario is presented as an explanation (verses 4–5: two conditional phrases), drawing the apocalyptic tableau of a cosmos that is coming loose. The "knocker" is thus to be understood as a heralding of this event. The catastrophic event is demonstrated on the one hand by the disintegrating structure of human society and on the other hand by the collapse of landscapes that had seemed stable. Both similes not only shrink men to the measure of insects and turn mountains to formless masses but draw drastic images of a world turned upside-down: both the firmness of mountains and the aloofness of man in family groups are topoi of ancient Arabic poetry and figure in early Meccan suras as signs of the power of divine creation. The eschatological scenario leads into a scene of judgment (verses 7–9), represented by the twice-named symbol of the scales, which is given special highlighting through its position in rhyme, made possible only by a break of the rhyme scheme. After this, the just and the damned are submitted to opposing evaluations: while the just receive the unambiguous prophecy of a fulfilled life, the fate of the damned is at first kept hidden in fog by a threatening and enigmatic metaphor, until, after a second initiating question increasing the tension (verses 10–11), it is unveiled as hellfire. This second initiating question again first brings the procession of ideas to a halt by means of an especially important and yet ambiguous statement, in order to draw the hearers' attention. Its answer, as usual, is not an actual clarification of matters but rather a picturing of the consequences of the situation that was evoked.[42]

5.2.8 *Later Additions*

Additions to the early Meccan texts,[43] which originate in later periods, can have various functions and assume different forms. A frequent type is the mitigation of a verdict, a formal addition of the form *illā* X, "except X," or "but otherwise for X" (Q 103:3, 95:6, and 84:25: *illā lladhīna āmanū wa-ʿamilū l-ṣāliḥāti lahum ajrun ghayru mamnūn*, "except for those who believe and do good deeds, for them is unstinted reward"). Behind the exemptions seem to stand the attempts of

41. Neuwirth, *Studien zur Komposition*, 232.

42. Verse 9, *ummuhu hāwiya* (literally: "his mother is given over to the fall," so that *hāwiya* is to be understood as an adjective), can also be understood as a euphemistic paraphrase, meaning doom. Similarly, the metaphorical meaning of *umm* could possibly be "home, haven," so that *hāwiya* would then represent a neologism. The double meaning is probably intended. For the translation, which can only express one meaning, the more logically smooth rendition, "haven," is preferable. The unfamiliar appellative *hāwiya* is understood by Torrey, "Three Difficult Passages," as an Arabization of the Hebr. *howa*, "doom" (Is 47:11, Eze 7:26). The wording, however, appears rather as a Qur'anic ad-hoc creation, a neologism.

43. See Neuwirth, *Studien zur Komposition*, 201–203, and now Sinai, *Studien zur frühen Koraninterpretation*, 153–160.

the hearers to be explicitly excepted from the assignation to negative categories, which is a clear index of the repeated recitation of early Meccan texts in later phases of communal formation. On the other hand, a sura that sounds all too threatening can be made more bearable through conciliatory additions. An example is Q 70:1–7:[44]

sa'ala sā'ilun bi-'adhābin wāqi'
li-l-kāfirīna laysa lahu dāfi'
mina llāhi dhī l-ma'ārij
ta'ruju l-malā'ikatu wa-l-rūḥu ilayhi
fī yawmin kāna miqdāruhu khamsīna alfa sanah
fa-ṣbir ṣabran jamīlan
innahum yarawnahu ba'īdā
wa-tarāhu qarībā

A questioner questioned the imminent punishment
—nothing can keep it from the unbelievers—
from God the Lord of the ladders
to whom the angels and the spirit ascend
in a day that spans fifty thousand years.
So have patience for the time being!
They see it in the distance
but we see it quite near.

The sura begins with an actual question, about the point in time of the arrival of the threatened punishment (cf. Q 77:7; 69:15, 52:7–8, 51:5–6), which is then dismissed with the mere mention of its inevitability. The punishment is imposed by God, the "Lord of the ladders." If one understands this predication, which occurs only once in the Qur'an, in agreement with the threatening context (verses 5–7), then one would have to think of *ma'ārij* as the ladders knotted from fraying ropes in the Christian image tradition, across which those awakened from death go over the abyss into heaven, so that only the good are safe from falling into the abyss—a conception which is also reflected in the traditional Islamic *ṣirāṭ* image of a rope ladder stretched across an abyss, which occurs in later literature.[45] Without the addition of verse 4, the introductory part is a threat of judgment that seamlessly leads into an eschatological scenario (verses 8–18). The threatening tone is upheld in the rest of the sura, in which only a catalogue of virtues (verses

44. A detailed interpretation is offered in Sinai, *Studien zur frühen Koraninterpretation*, 154–156.

45. It is worth noting that both interpretations of the stepladder have found impressive iconographical manifestations: the slender stepladder, which gives passage to those awakened on doomsday and reaching to the redemptive "other side," is used as a means of threat both in Byzantine iconography and in later Islamic folklore (*ṣirāṭ*). As against that, Jacob's ladder, which is not explicitly mentioned in the Qur'an, symbolizes the connection between heaven and earth. It lives forth as an allegory for Mary in Byzantine iconography.

23–35) temporarily strikes a conciliatory tone.[46] It may have been that this dark mood was considered difficult to bear, and in any case it was supplemented with verse 4, which, with its extra length and citing of a number, clearly breaks the frame, and which replaces the image of the "testing ladder" with the conciliatory scenario. The insertion of the climbing up and down of angels, a later association, and the "spirit" *al-rūḥ*, causes the reinterpretation of the third verse from a threat of eschatological punishment into a proof of divine favor, in a similar formulation as the equally ambivalent *laylat al-qadr* in Q 97:4. The expansion in form to a two-part verse belongs to the middle Meccan period, in which verses of this length are frequent and where an entire sura (Q 37) is largely devoted to the angels. An encouragement to the Prophet closes the first part of sura 70. The exhortation to be patient that closes the first part (verses 5–7) flows into a polarizing statement, which makes the belief in the final day, "the punishment," a criterion for the distinction between a "we" binding the speaker and community and a "they" of the "others."

5.3 The Linguistic Form of the Suras

5.3.1 *Formal-Structural Elements: Rhyme*

One of the mediums of presentation that most strongly characterizes the linguistic register of the early Qur'an is the aural correspondence between discourse elements that exists between the ends of individual units of speech.[47] In Western Arabic studies, this is usually designated as "rhyme," although Islamic Qur'an studies reserves the term "rhyme," *qāfiya*, for poetry and for the Qur'an speaks simply of a "divider," *fāṣila*. In fact, Qur'anic rhyme follows its own formal rules that are independent from poetry. On the other hand, as Theodor Nöldeke already stressed,[48] the Qur'anic rhyme is not to be simply equated with the prose rhyme of *saj*ʿ, rhymed prose, in that the Qur'an, unlike *saj*ʿ prose, does not "rhyme" only identical consonants but also merely related and later even essentially different consonants. The evaluation of rhyme as exclusively ornamental, which, since Nöldeke, has long held sway, has obscured the fact that in a literary genre in which the rhyme changes, rhyme can be applied functionally as a medium of composition. In fact, in the Qur'an, the change of rhyme is not arbitrary, nor does it principally point to a secondary composition. A detailed description and classification of Qur'anic rhyme, presented in 1981, makes possible a secure evaluation of the rhyme structures in the Qur'an texts.[49]

46. Neuwirth, *Studien zur Komposition*, 213.
47. See in detail in Neuwirth, *Studien zur Komposition*, 67–115.
48. Nöldeke, *GdQ*, 1:37.
49. See the tables on the rhyme structure of the Meccan suras in Neuwirth, *Studien zur Komposition*, from 90.

As the means of rhyme change is applied more frequently and consistently in the early Meccan time than later, and often serves to produce particular rhetorical effects, it is worthwhile to illustrate the range of rhyme changes in the early Meccan suras through the example of Q 80:33–42:

Eschatological scenery (cosmic catastrophe):
fa-idhā jāʾati l-ṣākhkhah
Eschatological scenery (with reference to mankind):
yawma yafirru l-marʾu min akīh
wa-ummihi wa-abīh
wa-ṣāḥibatihi wa-banīh
Eschatological process:
li-kulli mriʾin minhum yawmaʾidhin shaʾ nun yughnīh
Double image—the good:
wujūhun yawmaʾidhin musfirah
ḍāḥikatun mustabshirah
Double image—the evil:
wa-wujūhun yawmaʾidhin ʿalayhā ghabarah
tarhaquhā qatarah
ulāʾika humu l-kafaratu l-fajarah

But when the Scream comes to pass,
that will be a day when a man flees from his brother,
from his mother and his father,
from his wife and his children:
each one of them that day will have something to preoccupy him.
Some faces that day shall be radiant
laughing, full of cheer;
and some faces that day shall be covered with dust,
laid with gloom.
These are the blasphemers, the dissolute.

The semantic structure is depicted in sound by rhyme bundles:

33	eschatological scenery (cosmic catastrophe: isolated rhyme)	āCCah[50]
34–36	scenery (with reference to men)	3(C)Cīh
37	eschatological process	3(C)Cīh
38–39	double image—the good	3CCirah
40–42	double image—the evil	3Carah

The closing part of the sura presented here begins with an eschatological scene (verse 33), which first names the appearance of the catastrophe that will deafen

50. C = consonant, 3 = any short vowel (a/i/u).

the ears, presented in a single verse in isolated rhyme, which possesses onomatopoeic force through its vowel form (long *ā*), supported by an intensified morphological form (doubled *kh*). What follows is a presentation of the catastrophic relations of the Day of Judgment, confirmed by the alienation of man from his closest genealogical relatives (verses 34–37), held together by an end-stressed rhyme in a shrill *-īh*. It pictures an overturned world, in which man flees from his closest kin. The scene is continued by a double image (verses 38–42), in which human beings are represented by their expressions, which are either joyful or saddened. The double image is held together by the slightly transferred antepenultimate rhyme, in which the happiness of the good is reflected in a rhyme form with light *i*, while a dark *a* in the same position correlates to the gloomily described expressions of the bad.

The composition of sense units supported by rhyme belongs among the Qur'anic innovations in relation to poetic language—it is something never attempted in ancient Arabic poetry, which is held together throughout by monorhyme. The sonic marking of semantic breaks supported by rhyme can be treated as characteristic for the early Meccan suras, even if not all breaks in thought are underlined with a change in rhyme. That phonetic elements are also exploited for the composition in other respects is stressed above all by Neal Robinson and Michael Sells.[51]

5.3.2 *Structural and Formal Elements: Verse Structures*

In view of the intermediary position of the Qur'an between poetry and prose, we should treat the suras on the one hand as sequences of verses and on the other hand as sequences of sentences; and to define the respective relations between these two elements in the frame of the individual suras, and in the frame of the respective stages of development. The Qur'an verse is of course not a constant quantity. Verses containing units smaller than a sentence occur alongside verses that extend over a long sequence of sentences. They also do not share rhythm or meter. What is shared by them all is only the end rhyme, even if the character of the rhyme changes markedly in the Meccan period. Occasional doubts about the originality of these verses are based on confusion of verse divisions and verse numbering. The division of verses is marked by rhyme position and should have already come to bear on the recitation by the proclaimer and his community. The particular marking of these rhymes in Qur'an manuscripts and their numbering as against that were first developed and recorded in the course of transmission.[52] The recording of verse numbers in the text was introduced by Western scholarship only later to easy references to text units in the written codex. There is

51. See Robinson, *Discovering the Qur'an*, 167–176; Sells, "A Literary Approach to the Hymnic Surahs"; cf. also chap. 12, 441–444.

52. On the age of this prosody, see Spitaler, *Verszählung*, 1–2.

a decisive difference in the status of "verse division" in the originally intended form of the suras and that in the prose books of the Old and New Testaments, which only later, in their Western tradition, that a different type of division and numbering was laid over the text like an external net.

The Arabic philological tradition rightly distinguishes between the Qur'an verse, with its special term, *āya*, pl. *āyāt*, literally: "sign (of God's power)"; the single verse of poetry, *bayt*; and the *qarīnat al-saj*ʿ, the speech unit of the rhymed prose of ancient Arabic seers and soothsayers. While the Qur'an verse of the early Meccan suras still reflects its origin from ancient Arabic *saj*ʿ, rhymed prose, that of the middle Meccan period shows a increasing tendency to establish a new, independent form, for which Arabic literature offers no analogue. The expression "rhymed prose" for the Qur'an is not felicitous, since the early parts are not prose, and in the later parts rhyme is only one of several important formal criteria.

Verses in the early Meccan suras display various structures. The minimal verse size is a single syntactic element, or several syntactic elements, which still do not form a full sentence, as for example *dhawātā afnān*, "with fruit pods" (Q 55:48), or *ka-amthāli l-luʾluʾi l-maknūn*, "like hidden pearls" (Q 56:23). As a rule, the verse contains a phrase or a sentence and is accounted then as an independent verse, such as *fa-ṣabba ʿalayhim rabbuhum sawṭa l-ʿadhāb*, "So your Lord poured down on them a flood of punishment" (Q 89:13). What follows as the next longest are two-part verses, consisting of two complete sentences, such as *fa-aqīmū l-wazna bi-l-qisṭi wa-lā tukhsirū l-mizān*, "So carry out the weighing rightly and do not cheat with the weight" (Q 55:9). These short structures, in which a rhyme is still clearly audible as an end signal, become rarer already in the middle Meccan period.

5.4 Defining Criteria of Chronology

5.4.1 *Authorization Strategies*

Nöldeke's chronology, his "sequences of development," was based in the first place on formal criteria such as verse structures, sentence structures, and verse lengths, but also on semantic reference points, with a view above all to the religious knowledge current among the proclaimer and his hearers, which is assumed to have increased in extent and precision over time. These criteria must be re-checked, however, in view of the frequently raised accusation of circularity, and must be supplemented.[53] As has been shown, in those text types described as early Meccan—such as the hymn, the oath cluster, and others—formal characteristics established for the early suras such as relative verse length, correspond to the semantic ones. In contrast, suras of the middle and late Meccan periods

53. See Sinai, *Studien zur frühen Koraninterpretation*, 59–96.

display semantically and formally different elements. Yet, additional criteria for chronological classification are demanded.

These can be deduced, for example, from the situation of the hearers reflected in the text. Who really were the first hearers of the early suras? The Islamic tradition, which imagines the pre-Islamic epoch as a time of "ignorance," *jāhilīya*, presents them as mostly pagan, and therefore biblically illiterate, while admitting the existence of some individuals close to Christianity or otherwise imbued with religious knowledge, as well as some learned Jews. Certainly, the observance of the Kaaba rites, which seems to have persisted until the cult reform of the Prophet and which can be deduced from the early suras, points to an audience that was not monotheist in the strict sense, not at least in terms of liturgical practice. But the proportion of Syriac-Aramaic loan words, and above all the echoes of monastic ideas in the Qur'an,[54] evince a familiarity not only of the proclaimer but also of the nascent community with biblical and post-biblical traditions.[55] In our view, those present at the Qur'anic performance, generally recorded as passive and uninvolved hearers, are to be understood—at least in part—as identical with the Qur'anic community taking shape. Their presence in the text can therefore be counted as an important index for the *Sitz im Leben* of a given sura, for its situation of proclamation. Are hearers presumed to be present in the text and eventually addressed directly, as it seems to be reflected in the suras recognized as early? Or are they rather to be imagined as absent, as later texts would suggest? Does the community manifest its presence through the insistence on defined positions, for example, by opposition to accept the harsh Qur'anic judgments against "men" in general, *al-insān*? Q 103:1–3 offers an example:

wa-l-ʿaṣr
inna l-insāna la-fī khusr
illā lladhīna āmanū wa-ʿamilū l-ṣāliḥāti
wa-tawāṣaw bi-l-ḥaqqi wa-tawāṣaw bi-l-ṣabr

By the late afternoon.
Truly, man is at a loss
Except those who believe and do good
and call each other to truth and patience.[56]

54. See Baumstark, "Gebetstypus." Although the hypotheses of Lüling, *Urkoran*, und Luxenberg, *Syro-aramäische Lesart*, which suppose a Christian origin of Qur'anic texts, are methodologically and historically unfounded, they do bring awareness to the often underestimated dimension of Christian cultural presence in the urban centers of the peninsula. However, pace Luxenberg, Christian knowledge was already prevalent and did not need to be mediated by the Qur'an.

55. Crone, "The Religion of the Qur'anic Pagans," identifies the Meccan enemies of the proclaimer, who in the Qur'an—albeit only in the middle Meccan period—figure as *mushrikūn*, as "pagan monotheists." See Hawting, *The Idea of Idolatry*. The differentiation between pagans and believing listeners, influenced by the Bible, needs to be explored further; cf. chap. 6, 203–208.

56. Cf. Q 95:4–6.

In such later additions of exceptions to the rule, something of the "canonical process" is reflected, stretching over the entire Qur'anic genesis: older communications are not cast to the side as closed, but rather undergo "further rewritings" clad in a new recitation, through revision and expansion, even if, in the case of the proclamation, this remains oral.

Further indices for textual development are provided by the increasingly differentiated authorization strategies of the texts. While at the beginning verbal authorizations are chosen and Qur'an texts are "legitimized" in their transcendent origin by their rhetorical reference to authoritative speech acts of earlier mantic speakers, as for example the oaths that were previously employed by seers, *kuhhān*, and hymnic formulas already current from the monastic tradition, at a later stage the self-reference of God in the form of "I" and "we" discourse becomes the standard from of self-authorization of a text. This new ubiquity of God as focus of a scriptural religion is reflected also in the later oath references. With the differentiation of the cult, which toward the end of the early Meccan period no longer revolves centrally around the rites of a sanctuary,[57] the references at the start of suras to holy sites and liturgically relevant times,[58] which occurred in the early oath clusters, fade into the background, giving way in the following period to the introductory mentions of scripture, *kitāb*.

5.5 Middle and Late Meccan Suras

According to Nöldeke, the middle Meccan suras are Q 15, 17, 18, 19, 20, 21, 23, 25, 26, 27, 36, 37, 38, 43, 44, 50, 54, 67, 71, 72, and 76; the late Meccan suras are Q 6, 7, 10, 11, 12, 13, 14, 16, 28, 29, 30, 31, 32, 34, 35, 39, 40, 41, 42, 45, and 46. Both stocks of texts are treated together summarily in what follows.

5.5.1 *New Sura Structures*

In contrast to the early Meccan suras, the claim to validity of the later texts is unambiguously grounded from the beginning in an authority external to the text. This new referentiality can be deduced most clearly from the changed function of the Qur'anic narrative and from a new prominence in the recitations of "(excerpts from the heavenly) scripture," *al-kitāb*. The turn toward this new self-understanding of the collective of hearers as a community authorized by scripture can be deduced from the middle Meccan sura 15, which for the first time shows the form of a communal prayer service, in which a reading from a written text, introduced as such, stands as the central, crucial part.[59] Also, in the same text, we find confirmation of the existence of a communal prayer, the Fātiḥa. The

57. Rubin, "Morning and Evening Prayers."
58. Neuwirth, "Images and Metaphors," 18–28 (for pagination see above)
59. Cf. chap. 6 and 7.

reproductions of biblical stories within suras now take on a liturgical function, marking the divine confirmation of God's work in history. In view of the growing interest of the community in the biblical inheritance as a part of their developing biblical-monotheistic identity, it is no wonder that the bulk of the middle and late Meccan suras, which have now developed into long prose texts, seem to reflect a monotheistic prayer service, beginning with an introductory appellatory section, that is, a hymnic, apologetic, polemical, or paraenetic introitus, and close with a section in a related genre, most frequently containing an affirmation of the character of revelation of the Qur'an. These framing sections have been compared with the supplication litanies of the church, that is, introductory and concluding responsories recited by a presbyter or deacon and responded to by the community.[60] The center of the monotheistic prayer service, as against that, and similarly of the fully developed sura of the middle and late Meccan period is made up of biblical recollections; in the case of the prayer service, this is a biblical reading; in the case of the sura, it is a story from the biblical narrative stock. With recourse to a concept coined by Jan Assmann,[61] one can describe the change in orientation of the community as a transition "from a ritual to a textual coherence."

5.5.2 *New Authorizations: Recited Excerpts from the Heavenly Writing (Kitāb)*

By the later Meccan suras, the oath clusters employed earlier as authorization have given way to mentions of the "scripture" By far the majority of the later Meccan suras begin with an emphatic evocation of the scripture, often preluded by an individual letter name from the Arabic alphabet or, more frequently, a combination of several letter names such as *nūn* or *kāf, ṣād, hāʾ, ʿayn, mīm*, etc. In these enunciations of letter names, the interpretation and function of which is disputed in both Islamic tradition and Western research,[62] we should most likely see an evocation of the "heavenly alphabet," the minimal units of the transcendent writing. This interpretation would also clarify why they are never used for early Meccan but only appear in the later suras. This incipit employing an introductory mention of writing, and referring back to *al-kitāb*, seems to indicate a new cultic function of the recited text, which is no longer conceived as an intermediate communication of a divine message through the proclaimer to the community, but instead is perceived concretely as a performance from the heavenly script thought to be preexistent and only realizable through recitation.

60. See Neuwirth, "Sūrat al-Fātiḥa"; cf. chap. 6, 215–217.

61. See Assmann, *Das kulturelle Gedächtnis*; Assmann, "Kanon und Zensur."

62. See the attempts at explanation by Hans Bauer, "Anordnung der Suren"; Goosens, "Ursprung und Bedeutung"; Jeffery, "The Mysterious Letters"; Bellamy, "The Mysterious Letters"; Massey, "Letters of the Qur'an"; Massey, "Mysterious Letters."

In the middle and late Meccan suras, furthermore, a new spatial framing of the message can be noted. The texts, which exhibit numerous biblical stories, expand the field of vision of the hearers, who are transferred in their imagination from their local environment into a far-off landscape, the Holy Land, which is familiar as the stage of the history of the spiritual forebears of the community, the Israelites. The introduction of the direction of prayer, the *qibla*, toward Jerusalem, should be viewed as an eloquent testimony of this general change in spatial orientation.[63] It was introduced at a phase of development in which a palpable expansion of the horizon among the nascent community was setting in, relating to both time and space, through the new focus on the biblical heritage. One could speak of the Jerusalem *qibla* as the gestural expression of a genuine experience of having reached new spiritual horizons. Two fundamental novelties created a new self-understanding of the community: the newly achieved convergence of the Qur'anic proclamation with the scriptures of the two other monotheistic religions, and the simultaneous adoption of the *topographia sacra* of the earlier religions. The community was now to be among the receivers and bearers of scripture and to take part in the recollection of salvation history as it was conveyed through the medium of scripture. Through the gesture itself, the direction of prayer toward Jerusalem indicates this new connection between the Qur'anic community and the older religions. It is not surprising that the Qur'anic references to the Meccan sanctuary and its rites as safeguards of social coherence—references that occurred several times in the introductory parts of the Meccan suras—are now replaced by stereotyped evocations of the scripture, *al-kitāb*. The scripture now counts as the most significant shared spiritual possession, a spiritual space that supersedes the symbolic power of real space.

5.5.3 *Reduction of Rhyme and New Verse Structures*

The great majority of verses of the later periods include several phrases or periods. With respect to their length, verses in the late Meccan period would correspond to whole verse groups of the early Meccan period. The increasingly complex thought structures in these discursive texts require more complex hypotactic constructions in place of the parataxis that dominated early on, so that analysis has to respect a complex internal structuring of the verses (through parallelism, antitheses, coordination and subordination of clauses). In the case of these complex suras, the colometric approach, based on the "colon," the breath unit, as a basic overarching category for the description of verses proves appropriate.[64] It is evident that in these text a rhyming verse ending no longer is sufficient on its own as a means of structuring, since the respective preceding

63. See Neuwirth, "Erste Qibla"; Neuwirth, "The Spiritual Meaning of Jerusalem."
64. A colometric analysis was undertaken by the author in *Studien zur Komposition*. For this approach in general, cf. Norden, *Die antike Kunstprosa*; as well as Lausberg, *Rhetorik*. 65. Cf. also chap. 13, 472–477.

rhyme can no longer be recalled after the long and complex statements that has followed it. Indeed, the verses that simply end in the now frequent sounding -*ūn*/-*īn* can no longer to be understood simply as "rhyme verses." Rather, what makes the correspondence between the late verses is the entire end colon, that is, the entire final breath unit, which is at most a formula, or at least a sentence standing isolated from its verse context. This sentence, which concludes the verse and in many cases does not take part semantically in the main line of the statement, offers an interpretive addition to the pronouncement, or presents metatextually the spiritual world as looming behind the earthly one, frequently referring to God's omnipotence as a source for all earthly events. A "closing clausula" has thus taken the place of rhyme.[65] The examples in the Qur'an are innumerable; an clausula that comments on the pronouncement preceding it within a verse is: *mā khalqukum wa-lā baʿthukum illā ka-nafsin wāḥidatin inna llāha l-samīʿu l-baṣīr*, "The creation and the awakening of you all is as that of a single being; God is the hearing, the seeing" (Q 31:28). The argument for the reality of the Final Day, proffered from an inner-worldly perspective, is strengthened and imbued with greater authority by reference to the transcendent God watching over mankind.

An often repeated objection to Qur'anic form, which has—particularly in the circles of historically oriented scholars—raised doubts about the actual shared origin of the short poetic texts and the more prosaic long ones, is the lack of general stylistic coherence. Certainly, the verse structures and the amplitude of their cola, that is, the breath units united into one verse, vary over the periods of development, often even within single suras, while the sequences of themes for their part offer a turbulent picture. However, on the basis of thematic criteria, supported by the control of the syntactic and morphological connections existing between the verses, the middle and late Meccan suras can be explained as holding to firm compositional schemes, which in the middle Meccan period are frequently confirmed by changes of rhyme at the joints of the composition. That the short early Meccan suras are not yet based on similarly schematic plans is easily understandable. Yet from the earliest point onward there is a binding principle at work, which becomes dominant for the later compositions: to construct the suras out of clearly proportioned building elements. Already in the suras of the early Meccan period, one can frequently find small units formed symmetrically in relation to each other, while other verse groups also occur that stand in contrast to one another in a 1:2 proportion. In the middle and late Meccan period, it is a common phenomenon for there to be proportions between at least two of the three main parts and between verse groups determined by content. These proportions between building elements, typical for the character of the Meccan suras, have not been sufficiently

65. Cf. chap. 13, 472–477.

clearly recognized up to now.[66] They could not be recognized, because the necessary precondition for their identification, the critical checking over of the traditional verse divisions, had not been carried out, while the checking of the verse endings, for its part, must be based on study of rhyme and verse structures. This work has now been completed for the Meccan texts.

5.6 Medinan Suras

5.6.1 *Overview of the Medinan Developments*

5.6.1.1 *Oratory Suras*

The Medinan suras are Q 3–5, 8–9, 22, 24, 33, 47–49, 57–59, 60–61, 63, 66, 98, and 110. They can be grouped roughly into short, frequently monothematic "oratory suras" (sura 22, 24, 33, 47, 48, 49, and 57–66) on the one hand and "long suras" (suras 2–5, 8, and 9) on the other. An important development impacting the understanding of scripture that was achieved in Medina is the new relationship between the heavenly scripture and proclamation: while in Mecca, *qur'ān*, performance conditioned by situation, and *kitāb*, excerpt from the heavenly scripture, were kept clearly distinct from one another, the two become difficult to distinguish in Medina. Now, while texts about often ephemeral communal affairs are recorded in performances of "(excerpts from the heavenly) writing," the recitation of the proclaimer becomes wholly identical with the excerpts of the *kitāb*, the heavenly scripture. The fact that Qur'anic community has achieved its entrance into salvation history is reflected in new texts that involve an address to the community, the members of which are directly approached with formulas such as *yā ayyuhā l-nās*, "O people!" At the same time, the Prophet takes on a new aura in these suras. Designated as *al-nabī*, the proclaimer is no longer a mere mediator of the message but now enters into the text itself. He is personally addressed by God with the formula *yā ayyuhā l-nabī*, "O Prophet!"[67] (Q 33:22); he becomes an actor who works synergetically with the divine personage; and is thus mentioned in the combination *Allāhu wa-rasūluhu*, "God and his Prophet" (Q 33:22). This development reaches its culmination in sura 33, with the establishment of the proclaimer as an intermediary figure: *inna llāha wa-malā'ikatuhu yuṣallūna 'alā l-nabīyi yā ayyuhā lladhīna āmanū ṣallū 'alayhi wa-sallimū taslīma*, "Truly God and his angels pray for the Prophet, O believers, pray for him and wish him well" (Q 33:56). But the verse could also perhaps be read declaratively: "O believers, say about him, 'God bless him and give him peace,' " in which case the formula of

66. The valuable observations on individual suras in Müller, "Die Propheten in ihrer ursprünglichen Form," were not yet sufficiently proven, and so were not widely received.

67. See Bobzin, "The 'Seal of the Prophets.' "

blessings that later became obligatory would have already been institutionalized at the time of the Prophet.

The Medinan suras have not yet been investigated as to their structure, so here only a rough overview of their forms and liturgical implications can be given. What is new is a type of sura—following quite distinct formal rules—in which the historical memory so extensively avoided in the late Meccan suras is further put to flight, now in favor of oratorical prophet speech. A group of suras that has been brought together to form a small partial corpus (22, 24, 33, 47, 48, 49, 57–66), perhaps already before the redaction, consists of an address to the community, the members of which are addressed directly. These suras, which in some cases (59, 61, 62, 64) are introduced by hymnic introductory formulas reminiscent of the Psalms, such as *sabbaḥa li-llāhi mā fī l-samawāti wa-l-arḍi*, "All that is in heaven and on earth shall praise God" (Q 57:1), can only be understood from their composition as address. For the most part they deal with an isolated theme, often a point of political-social controversy, or eventually an issue having to do with the privileges and terms of respect reserved for the household of the Prophet. The person of the proclaimer is now no longer a mere mediator of the message, but rather works synergetically with the divine person.

The suras of this type mark a new transformation of form: they are structurally homogenous, devoid of the variety of "classical" composition elements used in the beginning of the older suras, such as hymns, catalogues of virtues, and confirmations of revelation, or the classical contents of the middle section, such as historical reminiscence or historical reflection and concluding topics such as revelation polemic or confirmation of revelation. In contrast, their structure is seemingly quite simple: a rather stereotyped hymnic introduction is followed immediately by the exposition of the subject of the speech, in the style of the rhyme-clausula speech. The "oratory sura" is only rarely artfully constructed. The sura has now become an address styled by simple cultic devices.

5.6.2 *Long Suras*

With the long suras, we are no longer dealing with units meant for performance. In this sura type, with the authorization as suras of text masses that have grown purely through accumulation, the development arrives at a new stage: the majority of the long suras (Q 2–5, 8, 9)[68] dispense with any overall composition; they no longer attest to transparent composition schemes. Apart from their conventional introduction, they function rather as catchalls for

68. Examples of certain secondarily merged long suras are suras 2, 3, 4, 5, 8, and 9. The fact that it is worthwhile to search for underlying structures in these suras was demonstrated by Zahniser, "Guidance and Exhortation." In order to contextualize the results, there must be a search for a communal usage, a *Sitz im Leben*, for the presupposed intentional long form. This step is not possible for researchers who proceed simply from Muhammad's "authorship"; see, e.g., Schmitz, *Sure 2*; Cuypers, *The Banquet*.

isolated verse groups related to classical topoi, now supplemented by quite specific statements, such as calls to battle and historical reminiscences. The collection of the individual elements into the transmitted long suras is difficult to date. A compilation of the long suras as we have them only in the course of the redaction in some cases cannot to be excluded, but they could just as well have been compiled before the redaction. Some of these long suras might simply have been scattered "stores" of verse groups long held to be suited for further expansion, which however in Medina were no longer considered for a reworking to achieve the shape of the conventional compositions. In this period, the orientation toward scripture was no longer warranted primarily by the memory shared with the Israelites, the Banū Isrāʾīl, but rather was bound up with the activity of the Prophet himself. The current form recited in liturgy, therefore, is no longer the complex sura with the salvation historical memory at its center, but rather the "oratory sura." It is not to be rejected outright, however, that a formal intention also lies behind the long suras. If what has been demonstrated with high probability for sura 3[69] should turn out to be applicable also to other long suras, then these texts should best be compared to entire biblical books.

The community's shift of interest from largely cultic concerns to religio-political and social interests is reflected in new formulas of authorization. Although directives—mostly affecting the cult but also ethical rules such as the Ten Commandments, Q 17:23–39—are occasionally given already in Mecca, these directives take on a new form in Medina. In one case, a Medinan instruction lightens a stricter Meccan one: in place of the instruction to hold vigils lasting long times of night, which was directed to the proclaimer in the early Meccan sura 73 and expressed in short *sajʿ* verses (1–3), a legislation to the people follows in Medina, presented in prose, which contains a lightening of the collective obligation for vigils, in the extension of the sura, verse 20. But as a rule we encounter directives whose obligatoriness is underlined through a reference to the transcendent source, such as *kutiba ʿalaykum*, "It has been prewritten for you" (Q 2:183–187), or *farīḍatan mina llāhi*, "as an obligation laid down by God" (Q 9:60).

A further new element of Medinan suras is the reports about events occurring contemporaneously, whether these are events experienced by the community or events staged by them, such as the battle of Badr, 2/624 (Q 3:123); the battle of Uḥud, 3/625 (Q 3:155–174); the expulsion of the Banū Naḍīr, 3/625 (Q 59: 2–5); the siege of Khaybar, 7/628 (Q 48:15); the expedition to Tabūk, 9/630 (Q 9:29–35); or the later so-called farewell sermon of the Prophet, 10/631 (Q 5:1–3). Since

69. Zahniser, "The Word of God and the Apostleship of Isa"; cf. also Neuwirth, "Mary and Jesus."

these reports no longer display a prominent literary form, it is not surprising that, in contrast to the situation in Judaism or Christianity, where biblical stories are crystallized to form a kind of mythical drama, no "grand narrative" arose on the basis of the Qur'an. A meta-historical overall picture of the genesis of Islam was first constructed only later, through the inclusion of a mass of non-canonical traditions, through the Sira.

6

The Liturgical Qur'an

ON THE DEVELOPMENT OF CULT AT THE TIME OF THE PROCLAMATION

6.1 The Ancient Arabian Preconditions

The worship of God reflected in the Qur'an[1] in its peculiar relation to pre-Islamic Arabian religiosity, which is most frequently described as henotheism, is a central theme of traditional overview presentations on the emergence of Islam.[2] These treatments generally describe the transition to monotheism as a civilizing step of progress away from the earlier pagan period, at times even as a historically predetermined development. Islamic tradition adapts a similar view. It combines a strongly negative evaluation of pre-Islamic cultic practices with a rigorous disqualification of the pre-Islamic period as a whole, considering it a "time of barbarism" or a "time of ignorance," *jāhilīya*, a period that gave way, with theological necessity, to the more illuminated epoch of Islam.[3] But why not turn the tables and perceive the pre-Islamic past as a time of flourishing? Such a perspective would be justified by literary history: from the perspective of the polycultural classes of the Umayyad and Abbasid periods, the *jāhilīya* represented an epoch of spiritual freedom and limitless creativity, displaying exemplary character and great educational worth for the new educated elites.[4] This "secular" perception of pre-Islam inspired the intense activities of collection and editing carried out by philologists, genealogists, and connoisseurs of poetry, who not only compiled collections of highly artistically developed poetry but also supplied an extensive mass of narrative literature providing plots and dialogues full of brilliant elements. The tribal past of the Arabs, despite its Islamic condemnation, is far better documented than that of other ethnicities, even if this evidence largely still awaits assessment. The pre-Islamic Arabian Peninsula is just now being discovered as an object of Late Antiquity research.[5]

1. This chapter is an extended and heavily revised version of the essay "Vom Rezitationstext über die Liturgie zum Kanon."

2. Watt, *Muhammad at Mecca*; Paret, *Mohammed und der Koran*; Bobzin, *Muhammad*; Cook, *Der Koran*.

3. Cf. chap. 3, 119–125.

4. Drory, "The Abbasid Construction."

5. Montgomery, "The Empty Ḥijāz."

Western researchers who share in the valorization of pre-Islamic literature often do not accept the claims of the "underdevelopment" of the pre-Islamic period that are made in the Islamic tradition. Yet they assume—not without teleological reasoning—a kind of decadence in the pagan religion, which seemed to herald a predetermined breakthrough toward monotheism. This conception of decadence was rejected by Ludwig Ammann in his revolutionary 2004 monograph *Die Geburt des Islam* (The birth of Islam). For him, ancient Arabian paganism, with its adherence to tribally binding rites, was in no way vanishing at the time of Islam's genesis. Rather, if one broadens one's view from rites to other forms of collective self-expression, then paganism's vitality becomes clearly recognizable: this anthropocentric pagan culture does not solve the problem of coping with contingency through cult alone, but does so equally through a kind of division of labor between ritual, practiced religion and a kind of poetry distant from the cultic realm but aware of the problems of the time. Thus, rites serve to cope with acute situations of emergency, while poetry poses decisive life-philosophical questions, solving them for its audience through the formulation of specific sequences of thoughts that are exemplified time and again within the moment of poetry performance. Going beyond Ammann's claims, one can see here a substitute liturgical function of poetic performance, in which the audience shores up its own central values and goals by listening to a familiar sequence of evocations of prototypical scenes.[6] Andras Hamori has brought these observations, also touched upon by Renate Jacobi[7] and Gottfried Müller,[8] to a point: "Already in the sixth century, before the coming of Islam, these poems, rather than myths or religious rituals, served as the vehicle for the conception that sorted out the emotionally incoherent facts of life and death, and by the sorting set them at the bearable remove of contemplation. Qaṣīda poets spoke in affirmation of a model they shared; their poetry tended to become a shared experience, all the more as the affirmation was through the replay of prototypal events which the model so successfully charted."[9]

Ammann, who integrates the poetry into the religious thought of pre-Islam, attempts to illuminate the development of cult reflected in the Qur'an in light of the pre-Islamic religious situation, which in his view formed a basis to which "foreign" concepts were then added only secondarily. In his own, distinctly sociological, phrasing, he clarifies that his "reconstruction of the Meccan phase of the revelation . . . assumes that the sources of meaning (available to the Meccans) served as points of reference for searches after new meaning, which could lead

6. Cf. chap. 12, 444–447.
7. Jacobi, *Studien zur Poetik der altarabischen Qaside.*
8. Müller, *Ich bin Labid.*
9. Hamori, *The Art of Medieval Arabic Literature*, 22.

to the further development of accepted meanings and the adoption of foreign options of sense."[10]

Crucial here is the "endogenous dynamic,"[11] that is, the processes of change that results from within the ancient Arabic situation itself. For Ammann, then, the development in worldview occurs first and primarily in the consciousness of the Prophet Muhammad, who is considered as the main actor, a person whom he sees, similarly to Jacqueline Chabbi,[12] as deeply rooted in the tribally organized world of the pagan Meccans, and who in his view was individually motivated to no small degree by his peculiar biographical conditions, to question the religious routines of his society. Unlike the Islamic tradition, however, which assigns Muhammad a comparably unique role as a religious individual,[13] Ammann (although closely clinging to the Prophet's vita) describes the career of the Prophet as in no way historically pre-determined, but rather as an unforeseeable breakthrough.

In the following, some of Ammann's observations will be submitted to a "Qur'anic cross-check," so that, inter alia, a more strictly defined liturgical development will come into focus, while the *ḥajj* and the social interactions connected to it will be sidelined.[14] Indeed, in the first instance, the Qur'an is a liturgical text and at the same time a document of its own reception and of the formation of a community. Its self-referential approach to its own performance throws light on the identity construction of the community that occurred simultaneously with the genesis of the Qur'an. The following presentation is more narrowly limited than Ammann's, but must diverge from it, since the Qur'an itself allows no conclusions about the personal development of the proclaimer, who must therefore recede into the background.

Such a systematic interrogation of the Qur'an in relation to the development of cult was already attempted in 1980 by Fazlur Rahman,[15] who also drew, however, from the Sira, and therefore, like Ammann, foregrounds the person of the Prophet as a lone actor. This focus is problematic, since the Qur'anic text indicates a much more complex scenario; it is filled with actors who are already familiar with those sense directives that Ammann treats as "foreign," namely,

10. Ammann, *Die Geburt des Islam*, 35.

11. Ammann, *Die Geburt des Islam*, 89, sets his observation into a wider context: "The cultural frame of the Arabian Peninsula can be seen as a dynamic balance between the Bedouin and peasant-urban forms of life. Our admittedly speculative thesis is that this also relates to poetry and religion, as complementary references of orientation. If we concede a diachronic sense to the discourse of a "Heldenersatzreligion" (poetry serving as a substitute for religion) and "Ersatzgedicht der Frommen" (the Qur'an serving as a substitute of the poem for the pious), then we may state that Bedouinization favors the deconstruction of cult, i.e., secularization, while settlement favors the building up of cult, i.e., desecularization.

12. Chabbi, *Le Seigneur des Tribus*.

13. See Khalidi, *Images of Muhammad*.

14. See Hawting, *The Development of Islamic Ritual*.

15. Rahman, *Major Themes in the Qur'ān*. Marshall, *God, Muhammad and the Unbelievers*, examines the shifting perception of unbelievers solely on the basis of the Qur'an; see 18–19.

those produced by the encounter with Jews and Christians. In other words, the exchange with bearers of "foreign" traditions that triggered such revolutionary developments for Ammann is already underway in the Qur'an, but not as a conversation with outsiders—rather, this exchange takes place among pluriculturally educated hearers. Certainly the Qur'anic message became sharper over time and adopted increasingly complex arguments, but if we follow the text, we see that this does not occur at a stage in which the proclaimer "comes to consciousness, perhaps through comparison with Christian and Jewish Arabs, of the rift between theory and praxis, between the imposition of formulas and one's own acts; and the routine, as soon as it falls victim to reflection, appears as meaningless or not sufficiently full of meaning."[16] Following the Qur'an, we must reckon with a greater number of people in Mecca already possessing a strongly distinct Jewish/Christian religious identity, who were also not untouched by ancient Arabic poetry. It will be argued here that these "preformed" hearers have to be assumed as already involved in the formation of the message, at least on a preparatory level, even if their development into a community first gets underway through the charismatic appearance of the proclaimer and the early recitations, for which he alone is responsible.[17]

6.1.1 "Precarious Monotheism"

Ammann describes pre-Islamic religion quite conventionally as henotheism—that is, "a form of situational and therefore short-term monotheism,"[18] in which a high god, elevated from the world and concerned with primordial but not daily interests, holds sway above a greater pantheon. Patricia Crone,[19] on the other hand, would see the "unbelievers"—whom she would identify for the whole Qur'an as *mushrikūn*, or "associators"[20]—as "pagan monotheists," who scarcely distinguish themselves from the believers. She convincingly locates the Qur'anic image of the *mushrikūn* within late antique religious history, and identifies the Qur'anic unbelievers as representatives of a kind of worship of God known from the Greco-Roman context, in which a highest god, acknowledged as such, is

16. Ammann, *Die Geburt des Islam*, 36.

17. The biography of the Prophet condenses to a minimum the monotheistically educated contemporaries of the Prophet, in order to exalt the proclaimer and transform him into a figure that inevitably unleashed revolutionary developments through his Prophetic gift.

18. Ammann, *Die Geburt des Islam*, 26–27: "A worshipper or a group of worshippers turns in a state of emergency principally to one single deity—he asks, hopes for, and expects everything from him; the mentioning of other Gods is thus excluded."

19. Crone, "Religion of the Qur'anic Pagans."

20. The word *mushrikūn* only becomes terminological in the late Meccan period; at first *sharīk* and *shurakā'* occur as commercial metaphors for the act of assuming partners, as in Q 68:41 (end of the early Meccan period). *Shirk* is only documented five times in total, each time in a late Meccan context. In order to avoid anachronism, a study of the repudiators of the Qur'anic message would have to first discuss the earliest mentioned form of Meccan polytheists, namely, "the deniers," *al-mukadhdhibūn*. Hawting's interpretation in *The Idea of Idolatry*, which assumes a later compilation of the Qur'an, is problematic in that it dismisses the chronological data.

evoked in some situations directly, but as a rule only through instances of mediation: "There can, of course, be no doubt that the widespread identification of local and foreign deities (a process formerly known as syncretism) and the increasing prominence of the One testify to a radical transformation of paganism. But to pagan monotheists, the one and the many coexisted instead of competing. The input of Biblically derived monotheism was required in order for the many to be seen as illegitimate."[21] But what is the benefit of this terminological correction by Crone, put forward as a plea for a new classification of the *mushrikūn*? What are the differences, with respect to the direct worship of God or that carried out through intermediaries, between the "two monotheisms," that of the deniers, *mukadhdhibūn*, later *mushrikūn*, and that of the proclaimer and his community? Are these differences in fact insignificant in substance, a mere shibboleth between the adherents of different cult practices?

6.1.2 *"Firmly Fixed" Monotheism?*

In order to make these differences perceptible, Crone's plea for a contextualization of the *mushrikun* within Late Antiquity should be extended to those who would become the "pure monotheists," the proclaimer's hearers. For it is they who first perceive the *mushrikun* as such, who first construe them in a polemical way. This construct shows an interesting development: the polemical application of expressions using the root *sh-r-k*, which is clearly a commercial metaphor, begins at the end of the early Meccan period, as the community increasingly orients itself toward written religious traditions. *Sharīk*, "partner," and *mushrik*, "one who takes a partner," refer here, and very often later, to the "partners" of the criticized group itself: the *mushrikūn* are those who attract "partners," *shurakāʾ*, in their "business with God." The perspective is thus not directed toward God, but rather toward the unbelievers themselves: *am lahum shurakāʾu fa-l-yaʾtū bi-shurakāʾihim*, "Or if they have partners, let them bring their partners!" (Q 68:41). At the same time, the partners are associated with a nearness to God: *am lahum ilāhun ghairu llāhi, subḥāna llāhi ʿammā yushrikūn*, "Or do they have a God other than God—he is exalted above that to which they ascribe partners!" (Q 52:43). The theologically explosive perception that is documented here for the first time, that the opponents not only have partners but also ascribe this to God, becomes virulent in a later period: *wa-yawma yaqūlu nādū shurakāʾiya lladhīna zaʿamtum*, "On the day when he said to them: 'Call my partners here, whose existence you have claimed'" (Q 18:52, also Q 16:29, Q 28:62, 74).[22] Josef Horovitz

21. Crone, "Religion of the Qur'anic Pagans," 181–182.

22. Horovitz, *Koranische Untersuchungen*, 61, states: "This variance could be based on the fact that Muhammad intentionally employs *sharīk* playfully, or that he was confronted by the existing term *mushrik* and was unsure of its explanation. . . . Perhaps Muhammad took this significance already from South Arabian usage. On the other hand, the Arabic term recalls Jewish *shittef* in the special significance of 'associating something/someone to God,' as in [BT] Sukka 45b: *ha meshattef shem shamayyim we-dabhar aḥer neʿeqar min ha-ʿolam*."

considers it possible that we should see here a conscious playing on both registers of meaning, and points to a similar usage of a commercial metaphor in a South Arabian inscription and in the Babylonian Talmud: "Whoever associates (*meshattef*) something else with the God of heaven, is excluded from the coming world" (bSuk 45b). The key term "associator," which is first introduced in Hebrew, takes on an ironical coloring in the Qur'an through the association of a "company" between men and God, into which they have now contracted partners. In other places, however, the notion is taken more seriously theologically. The two usages of *mushrik/shirk* are intertwined, and the thought of an eternal punishment for "God associators" is difficult to imagine without the already existing rabbinic discourse about the "part played in the future world," which we see expressed in the Talmudic parallels. The adoption of this meaning of *shirk* as "God association," which begins in the middle-late Meccan period, fits well with the tendency in this phase to authorize Qur'anic statements through precedents in the written religions.

The dependents of the proclaimer are not simply monotheists on the Jewish or Christian model, but rather become such in the course of their engagement with their nearby and more distant milieu. What distinguishes them—according to the Qur'anic evidence—from the "deniers" and later "associators" is their orientation toward writing. Their worship is toward a God manifesting himself in writing, to whom one can draw near through liturgy—a concept of God that is quite obviously foreign to the "deniers." The successive formation of a polemical designation for the opponents is an exemplary case of this process of gradually occurring self-construction of the believers.

We should thus assume heuristically that we have before us in the hearers of the proclaimer in Mecca persons who already possess a religious formation, who, through their cultural "hybridity," their nearness to several traditions, show themselves to be products of Late Antiquity. Several earlier critical presentations have instead viewed these "preformed hearers and speech partners" as informants,[23] that is, preferred to see them as actors indifferent to the process of communal formation, from whom the proclaimer has extracted knowledge in order to then pass this information on to his listeners in the form of revelations: a short-circuited interpretation of the diversity of traditions reflected in the Qur'an. If one really assumed, as is frequent in traditional Qur'an research, that the proclaimer turned to Jews and Christians present in the city in order to widen his biblical knowledge and that these figures were prepared to teach him, a grotesque picture would emerge:[24] one would then have to imagine the proclaimer

23. Nöldeke, "Hatte Muhammad christliche Lehrer?"; Lammens, *Fatima*; Goitein, "Mohammad's Chief Teachers," and recently especially Gilliot, "Les 'informateurs'"; Gilliot, "Informants"; Gilliot, "Zur Herkunft"; Gilliot, "Authorship of the Qur'an."

24. Rahman, *Major Themes in the Qur'ān*.

as a constant seeker of information, and assume that the community forming around him took no active role in the development of new collective identity documented in the Qur'an.

But such an acquisition of traditions obtained by a single individual within the "pagan horizon" is unlikely, particularly because the Qur'an from the start assumes important theological aspects to be familiar or at least immediately comprehensible. Already the oldest suras reflect the awareness, shared between the proclaimer and a growing number of the hearers, that binding divine messages have occurred previously, in proximity to the new performance, and with shared transcendent sources, so that this new text is no longer subject to human intervention and already guaranteed referentially through the commandment "You must add nothing and take nothing away." Even if this text is not recognized from the beginning as a scripture in its own right, nevertheless it is recognized early as an oral communication *from* a transcendent script, as a scripture reading (*qurʾān*).

From around the middle Meccan period, the original heavenly writing, recognized as the source of earthly manifestations of scripture, moves into the center of the community's interest. Here, a similar development can be seen for the Qur'anic community as that which Jan Assmann has described for the passing of entire cultures from illiteracy to the use of writing.[25] In the case of this community, no new introduction of technical means of writing took place—this would already have been familiar to some hearers, while others remained without it; rather, what came about was consciousness of the crucial meaning of a *heavenly* and all-inclusive script, which opened a new view of the world and, above all, opened the space of cultural memory. It is not that one learned to write, but rather that one realized that God writes. He conveys knowledge that reaches the audience orally but is authorized through writing. Even if this development does not coincide exactly with what Assmann meant by the passing from memory culture to writing culture, still we find reflections of some of his most important conclusions in the Qur'an. Assmann proceeds from the assumption that "at the stage of pure memory culture, cultural memory coincides extensively with what circulates within the group of sense. It is only with writing in the strict sense that there is the possibility of self-sufficiency and greater complication of this outer level of communication. Only now does a form of memory take shape that goes beyond the horizon of the sense communicated and transmitted in a previous age and exceeds the region of communication, just as the individual memory exceeds that of consciousness."[26] Assmann speaks here of a "society's passing from ritual coherence to textual coherence."

25. Assmann, *Das kulturelle Gedächtnis*, 87ff. The purely technical procedure of the recording of texts, which Nagel, *Medinensische Einschübe*, 113–127, assigns to the late Meccan period, is not adequate as an explanation of the new, scripturally referential paradigm.

26. Assmann, *Das kulturelle Gedächtnis*, 22–23.

In the emerging community, one can indeed see a gradually achieved "textual coherence." Alongside the newly discovered central concept of the writing activity of God or his scribes, we can note also the codifying activity undertaken by certain individuals in the community—if one assumes, quite plausibly on the basis of the text itself, that the writing down of the suras had begun already in the middle Meccan time, during the so-called Raḥmān period,[27] that is, when the name al-Raḥmān becomes frequent.[28] These assumptions are based generally on the mere frequency and prominence of the term *kitāb*, "writing," in texts of this period; but the Qur'anic use of writing is not fully captured by these mentions of writing, where it is perceived only in the sense of a mnemotechnical aid—yet researchers like Richard Bell, and more recently Tilman Nagel, have drawn far-reaching conclusions from this.[29] What we see here is a complex process: in the case of this particular transition to written culture, codification does not replace memorization and oral performance, but rather the performance texts live on in a cultic frame through the medium of a living recital, while further texts are subjected to the same mode of performance. In terms of the arena of performance, no substantial transformation takes place. What is gained, rather, is a new consciousness of participation in a scripture, together with the perception of proximity to typological precursors, a consciousness that, with its discovery of a new time-space framework derived from the salvific historical past, effects a change in the text's rhythm and its linguistic and literary forms. As will be shown, the genesis of the Qur'an deserves a revision with regard to this new aspect. It now appears as a gradual transformation of a community of listeners, changing from a group held together by shared rites and short recitations, that is, ritual coherence, to a new community entrusted with scripture and applying the technology of writing to preserve the portion of scripture that has been given to them, that is, textual coherence. This transformation shows its results most significantly in the context in which Qur'an recitation took place as living recital, that is, in cult. Given the impossibility of tracing the early development of cult through non-Qur'anic sources, we must rely on the text of the Qur'an alone for its reconstruction.

6.2 Cult and Canon in Islam

In view of the unparalleled rapidity with which the emergence of the Qur'anic corpus took place and the swift subsequent appearance of an authoritative codification (Gregor Schoeler speaks rightly here of the "publishing" of the Qur'an),[30] a second process that occurred in parallel to this might slip from view all too easily,

27. Cf. chap. 8, 290–292.

28. Cf. chap. 4, 141–143.

29. The assumption by Nagel, *Medinensische Einschübe*, of a systematic construction of a scripture for the Qur'an, has been shown to be untenable by Madigan, *The Qur'ān's Self-Image*.

30. Schoeler, "Schreiben und Veröffentlichen." On the particular attempts at reconstruction of the textual history, cf. chap. 4.

namely, the formation of a comprehensible living recitation, whose *Sitz im Leben* is Islamic liturgy and obligatory worship, with its central prayer ritual of *ṣalāh*. It should be stressed here that what took place is not merely the formation of two modes of "publication" but also the development of two Qur'anic spheres of influence and affect—which would later become separate institutions, in the forms of teaching and cult. The orally recited Qur'an is an immediate cultic practice, that is, a performance and a communication, not an objectifying textual study. The question of the relation and interaction between writing and cult in the several stages of development prior to the fixing in writing or institutionalization has only been sporadically touched upon in scholarship.[31] A history of Islamic cult, on the model of the standard work for Judaism by Ismar Elbogen,[32] has never been produced and is hardly to be expected. Instead, we have only isolated individual studies, which, despite the useful collection by Gerald R. Hawting,[33] still offer no comprehensive picture.

In what follows, the Qur'anic text itself will be investigated for indications of the interaction between scripture and ritual. In addition, we will seek to investigate the status of the cultic practices documented in the Qur'an. On the other hand, the suras or sura parts, recognized as intended unities, are to be investigated using genre criticism for their possible function as liturgical speech realizable within a cultic frame.[34] In view of the lack of basic preliminary work on the Medinan suras and the prevailing uncertainties in their periodization, our present examination will be cursory and will not go beyond a preliminary sketch. Nevertheless, it is worthwhile to establish a method that responds to John Wansbrough's call for a form-critical analysis of the Qur'an, but does not renounce the attempt to evaluate the particular literary indications of a progress achieved in the development of the cult.

The thesis that there was a concurrent and interrelated formation of ritual and scriptural canon, which we suggest existed from the very beginning, is not suggested by the static relationship between cult and canon that was ultimately established in Islam. Namely, if one looks at the two complexes of "Qur'an" and the "official, or obligatory, Islamic prayer service," *ṣalāh*, from the perspective of the functions assigned to them in the Sunna, and which remain valid in the religious life of Muslims, then one gets the impression of an interaction that was quite intense in places but that on the whole is limited. Certainly, the prayer service devotes a prominent position to the Qur'an: the daily prayer and the ending

31. See especially Baumstark, "Gebetstypus"; Goitein, "Prayer in Islam"; Denny, "Islamic Ritual."

32. Elbogen, *Der jüdische Gottesdienst*. In the time since, both high religious festivals have received considerable sociological and religious-historical attention; see Denny, "Islamic Ritual"; Roff, "Pilgrimage"; Nabhan, *Das Fest des Fastenbrechens*; but the historical and phenomenological approach represented in Wellhausen, *Reste*; Goitein, "The Muslim Month of Fasting"; and Wagtendonk, *Fasting in the Koran*, has not been exhausted.

33. Hawting, *The Development of Islamic Ritual*; the volume contains no analysis of a text applied in ritual.

34. For the Meccan suras, see Neuwirth, *Studien zur Komposition*; there is still no systematic examination of the Medinan texts.

part of the Friday prayer service include the recitation of short Qur'an passages in several places, and the sermon makes recourse to individual verses; but the prayer services are not centered on scriptural reading; rather, ritual concerns are given priority. On the contrary, prayer services have always been scheduled around preestablished times of day, and to that extent are cosmically oriented. They call for strictly regulated ritual provisions[35] and for most of their durations require that prescribed physical positions are rigorously adhered to,[36] which leave no doubt in substance as to their ritual character. Even where recitation from the Qur'an is obligatory, in the mostly short reading sections (*qirāʾa*) at the start of the first and second prayer sequence, *rakʿa*, usually these are taken from only a delineated, partial Qur'anic corpus. Since the Friday service adopts the prayer ritual as its final part but does not allocate a place to an extensive Qur'an reading, the situation there is similar. Thus, in official cult, the Qur'an is represented either by short suras or sura excerpts; thus, its more extended forms are no longer represented as liturgical units in official cult.

The structurally integral elements of the Qur'an have their liturgical place, rather, in occasions of private piety, such as in the extensive recitations on the individual days of Ramadan, when the Qur'an is divided up into thirty parts, each to be read on a single day, and in the observance of important rites of passage such as circumcision, marriage, and the obsequies for the dead—none of which is recitation prescribed for in the Qur'an itself. Complete longer suras are listened to in private houses and cemeteries, but not in obligatory prayer or the Friday collective prayer services, which were the cultic frameworks that included obligatory Qur'an reading from an early period.

That this state of affairs represents the endpoint of a process of development will become apparent once we look at those complex suras, which, on the basis of formal criteria, can be proven to have been intended by the proclaimer as self-contained units of recitation. They belong primarily to Theodor Nöldeke's middle and late Meccan periods,[37] and thus for a long time proved formative for the shape of the sura, until finally giving way to either a simple monothematic structure or a long sura no longer displaying a clearly structured composition. The structure of the complex middle and late Meccan suras—characterized by narrative passages framed by strongly formulaic appellatory or dialogic introductory and concluding passages—seems to indicate that the entire text would have been recited in a single public setting. But the public recitation of such a complex text sequence in its entirety, which would have been the norm during the Meccan period of the Prophet's ministry, was no longer the prevailing practice

35. On the primarily ritual nature of the Islamic prayer service, see Graham, "Islam in the Mirror of Ritual"; Denny, "Islamic Ritual."

36. It is remarkable that the later "pillars of prayer," *arkān al-ṣalāh*, fixed in legal literature, more often than not refer to postures, but not to verbal articulations by the person praying.

37. On the structures of these suras, see Neuwirth, *Studien zur Komposition*, 238–333. Cf. also chap. 5, 192–196.

in the Medinan period. As exceptions to this, we can name the *tarāwīḥ* evening prayers during Ramadan, which in some traditions call for a complete recitation, *khatima*, of the Qur'an, in which a thirtieth of the Qur'an, a *juz*ʾ, is given a public recitation on each day. This resembles the later "thirtieths" that also contain complete suras.[38]

It hardly needs to be stressed that in this situation, which does not allow for more extensive units of meaning, there are no prescribed pericopes for Friday or holiday services that invite the presentation of theologically indispensable passages from scripture. This state of affairs is significant. What formed the backbone of cult in the other two religions—the recollection of the foundational events of salvific history condensed into a cycle of scriptural readings throughout the year—is missing in Islam. In Judaism, this scripturally aided remembrance is intensified by accompanying prayer formulae and hymns that together serve to conjure up the great drama of Israel's history with God: the election of the Israelites as God's chosen people, their exodus, their settling down in the Promised Land, their exile, and the anticipation of the Messiah.[39] In the Christian tradition, the commemoration is celebrated in the reading of the scripture in the Eucharist, epitomizing the two great stages of Christ's ministry and his redemptive sacrifice.[40] These forms of commemoration have no equivalent in the Islamic cult.

A comparable commemoration does take place within Qur'an recitation, which is most frequently embedded in the prayer ritual, where it is not episodes from salvific history, however, but rather the original scene of Islamic religious genesis itself, the onset of revelation through the Prophet Muhammad, that is re-enacted. This commemoration takes center stage, so to speak, in place of the progress of salvific history, and equally small-scale is its performance, which cannot be bound to a liturgical course of the year. No Friday service recalls those parts of inner-Islamic sacred history that could be considered milestones in the foundation of the new religion, such as Muhammad's visions reflected in the Qur'an; his dream journey to the Jerusalem temple, *masjid al-aqṣā*; the *hijra*; his shocking victory over the overpowering enemy in the battle of Badr; or the reform of the pilgrimage rites. We do not find service elements that recall explicitly the individual phases of inner-Islamic, let alone pre-Islamic and mono-theistic, sacred historical memory. This development will become virulent only later; it is, however, founded in the genesis of the Qur'an.

38. This practice of the *tarāwīh* is not the standard everywhere. The author experienced it in the Mohammad Al-Amin Mosque in Beirut, but not in the Umayyad Mosque in Damascus or the Fatih Mosque in Istanbul.

39. The perception of a sacred historical memory already institutionalized in cult is strongly attested in Zobel, *Das Jahr des Juden*, 11–12. Rosenzweig's classic formulation from 1921 (*Der Stern der Erlösung*, 369), "What the Jew possesses as an event in the annual turn of the seasons, the immediacy of all individuals to God in the complete society of all to God, he no longer needs to acquire in the long passage of world history," has been studied in its cultural-historical implications by Assmann, *Politische Theologie*, 112.

40. On the early theology of Sunday, see Klinghardt, "Sabbat und Sonntag."

Two remarkable particularities thus need to be explained: on the one hand the complete lack of institutionalized recollections of salvific history[41] through the year, carried out in cult, that is, in Qur'an performance, and on the other hand the relinquishment of the original type of sura whose structure had been that of a complex liturgical unit that included a narration. Both particularities stand in close relation to each other, as the following synopsis of textual and cultic development will show.

6.3 Emergence of a Liturgy

In our summary of cultic and textual development, let us turn first to the oldest suras, which do not yet introduce the central theme of salvific historical narrative.[42] We should investigate them for traces of a social frame for the recitation, and pursue also the question of cultic orientations shared between the proclaimer addressed as "you" and his hearers. Only with a rough conception of the immediate shared cultic praxis of all those reached by the Qur'anic recitation can we come to recognize the change that would divide the new identity of the "believers"[43] from the ancient Arab identity. The early suras, and the debates carried out in them, offer a viable path for this. For, proceeding from the fact that the proclaimer addressed as "you" did not present his message in private missionary work in a free sermon style, but rather presented it to his hearers in his cultically styled "Qur'anic" speech, one must see the people addressed or mentioned in the plural grammatical forms in the text as real persons from his environment, before whom or in whose surroundings the performance takes place. One must also identify the forum of the public debates reflected in the suras with the scene of their liturgical performance. The text is thus a supplementary writing to the proclamation itself. If one draws conclusions without recourse to the Sira, the Qur'anic scenario consists of the proclaimer ("thou") alongside the hearers addressed as "you." In addition, there are absent adherents, "you," or, more frequently, opponents, "they." The proclaimer enters as a messenger with a message that has perhaps already been formed beforehand; that is, he enters into "a space that is distended in time and space."[44] But he may also perform his message spontaneously. These two possibilities of text genesis are only clearly distinguishable in cases where the recitation itself responds to accusations or behaviors of the group imagined as present ("you" or "they") or, meta-textually, makes commentary pronouncements about what has already been performed.

41. Contrary to that, modern sermon handbooks for proclamation do follow the annual sequence of Fridays but do not reflect the course of Islamic salvific history at all.

42. With the exceptions of suras 51 and 79, the early Meccan texts do not contain Prophet narratives; the same is true of the middle Meccan material, apart from suras 50, 67, 72, and 76.

43. *Āmana* only becomes a term in middle Meccan usage, but from an early point the group around the proclaimer already identified itself through collective practices and convictions.

44. Ehlich, "Text und sprachliches Handeln."

Are there recognizable insights and convictions shared by the speaker and parts of the hearership that unite them into a community of identity? Following roughly the process of Assmann, who coined the phrase "cultural memory" as an abbreviation for the complex interaction of cultural identity and reference to the past, we will first discuss the question of the significant space recognizable in the suras. "Significantly, place plays the primary role in collective and cultural mnemotechnics, the culture of memory. . . . Memory culture operates by the setting of signs into natural space. Even, and especially, entire landscapes can serve as the medium of cultural memory. They are then not so much accentuated through signs and monuments, but rather elevated as a whole to the rank of a sign. . . . It is a matter of topographical 'texts' of cultural memory, of a 'mnemotope.' "[45] Let us now look to the Qur'an.

6.3.1 Mecca and Rites of the Shrine as Central Memory Figure

It is hardly surprising that Mecca and its sacred area, *ḥaram*, appear as the central mnemotopes in the early Meccan suras.[46] Mecca is frequently represented among the places that recur in the thirty-two typologically early suras. Outside the two narrative historical recollections (suras 105 and 106) that commemorate the repulsion through divine intervention of an aggressor from the shrine, that is, from the *ḥaram* foundation given by God to the Quraysh,[47] Mecca is evoked as a symbolic site in the context of oaths introducing the suras, as the theater of the theophany, whose only equivalent is Mount Sinai: twice Mecca occurs in this position in connection to the foundational site Sinai, indicated deictically as *hādhā l-balad al-amīn*, "this secure city" (Q 95:3), or as *al-bayt al-maʿmūr*, "the house of God visited [by pilgrims]" (Q 52:4). Mecca is thus not introduced through its quotidian place names, but rather through a cultic circumlocution: as a settlement attached to a sacred area and a pilgrimage site. A third time, again in an oath context, a coded mention of Mecca is connected to the foundation of social life as such, Q 90:1–3.

At the same time, the *ḥaram* of Mecca must be presupposed quite concretely as the theater of social interaction: above all, the site of the rites accomplished there, although this is not made explicit in the Qur'an,[48] and an explicit naming of the Kaaba is entirely lacking. Cultic instructions to the speaker, such as *fa-ṣalli li-rabbika wa-nḥar*, "So pray to your Lord and sacrifice" (Q 108:2), designate those cultic behaviors that have their natural place in the shrine in combination with sacrifice, which Uri Rubin has documented for the surroundings of the Kaaba; namely, these are the *ṣalāh* rites. Q 96:19 records the element of prostration,

45. Assmann, *Das kulturelle Gedächtnis*, 59–60.

46. On the ritualistic functions of the holy site, see Rubin, "The Kaʿba."

47. See chap. 7, 244–247.

48. The Islamic tradition is unanimous here; on the reconstruction of the cultic situation, particularly in reference to the area of the sanctuary reserved for sacrifice, see Rubin, "The Kaʿba."

sajda, that belong to *ṣalāh: fa-sjud wa-qtarib*, "So throw yourself down and come nearer." In the same sura position, namely, at the end, we see elsewhere exhortations to the proclaimer to conduct another practice that is akin to prayer, the cultic recitation: *wa-ammā bi-niʿmati rabbika fa-ḥaddith*, "The grace of your Lord, proclaim it!" (Q 93:11), *fa-dhakkir innamā anta mudhakkir*, "So remind, for you are a reminder!" (Q 88:21), *fa-sabbiḥ bi-smi rabbika l-ʿaẓīm*, "So praise the name of your Lord, the powerful" (Q 56:96). In Q 52:48–49 (*wa-sabbiḥ bi-ḥamdi rabbika ḥīna taqūm / wa-mina l-layli fa-sabbiḥhu wa-idbāra l-nujūm*, So give praise to your Lord, when you stand up [or: when you stand in prayer], / and of the night and by the decline of the stars"), there is even mention of an established time for vigils: the nighttime until the fading of the stars.[49] Here, it is best to assume a ceremonial utterance in private space. Similar exhortations occur elsewhere only at the beginnings of suras: *iqra bi-smi rabbika lladhī khalaq*, "Recite in the name of your Lord who created" (Q 96:1); *sabbiḥi sma rabbika l-aʿlā*, "Praise the name of your Lord, the High (Q 87:1); *qum fa-andhir / wa-rabbaka fa-kabbir*, "Rise up and warn / and praise the loftiness of your Lord [or: say a 'God is great' over your Lord]" (Q 74:2–3); *qumi l-layla illā qalīla / . . . wa-rattili l-qurʾāna tartīla*, "Stand throughout the night, except for a short time / . . . and perform the reading in clear recitation" (Q 73:2–4). That the recitation that is required here should be seen in close connection to the *ṣalāh* ritual is documented by the short catalogue of virtues that calls for *ṣalāh* and hymnic recitation: *qad aflaḥa man tazakkā / wa-dhakara sma rabbihi fa-ṣallā*, "Prosperity to him who purifies himself / and praises the name of his Lord and prays" (Q 87:14–15), and by the fact that in the context of a Qur'an recitation (Q 53:59: *a-fa-min hādhā l-ḥadīthi taʿjabūn*, "Do you wonder at this speech?"), we find the statement *fa-sjudū li-llāhi wa-ʿbudū*, "Throw yourself down before God and pray to him" (Q 53:62). Clearly, for the proclaimer and his dependents, the two belong together: performed or heard recitation and *ṣalāh* rites. Since no indication is given of any scene apart from Meccan cult, we are to imagine the old and new prayer service first in a shared context, a thesis that is supported in traditional history by the (reconstructed) notion that the prayer times were at first identical and the rites were accomplished together.[50]

6.3.2 *Critique of the Behavior of Cult Participants*

What speaks in favor of this claim above all are the critiques of individual cult participants. The critical references to cult behaviors become increasingly frequent and more detailed, and they are set into a frame that unites the pagan Meccans and the new cult participants, so that on the basis of the Qur'anic evidence we can

49. If *ḥīna taqūmu* is to be understood as a reference to a prayer ritual, then praise of God would be imposed in this prayer and in this vigil.

50. Rubin, "Morning and Evening Prayers."

assume the Kaaba rites to have been initially shared. We find objections to a lack of seriousness, and to both ritual and ethical laxity: *fa-waylun li-l-muṣallīn / alladhīna hum ʿan ṣalātihim sāhūn / alladhīna yurāʾūn / wa-yamnaʿūna l-māʿūn*, "Woe to those who pray / who take their prayer lightly, / who want to be seen / and who refuse to give help," where the same people are condemned for ethical and ritual laxity (Q 107:4–7). Going further, there are condemnations also of the handicapping of dependent persons in cult (*a-raʾayta lladhī yanhā / ʿabdan idhā ṣallā*, "What do you think of he who hinders / a servant when he prays?" Q 96:9–10), or even the refusal of the ritual altogether: *qālū lam naku mina l-muṣallīn*, "They say: we were not among those who pray" (Q 74:43), and *fa-lā ṣaddaqa wa-lā ṣallā*, "He did not recognize [the message] as true nor did he pray" (Q 75:31). Cultic omissions are rebuked, in analogy to the *ṣalāh* context, and also in connection to a recitation performance, alongside the omission of postures of humility: *wa-idhā qīla lahumu rkaʿū lā yarkaʿūna / . . . fa-bi-ayyi ḥadīthin baʿdahu yuʾminūna*, "If it is said to them: bow on your knee, they do not bow. / . . . In what message after this would they believe?" (Q 77:48–50), or disrespectful laughter in place of being moved emotionally: *a-fa min hādhā l-ḥadīthi taʿjabūn / wa-taḍḥakūna wa-lā tabkūn / . . . fa-sjudū li-llāhi wa-ʿbudū*, "Do you wonder at this speech / and laugh rather than cry? / . . . Throw yourself down before God and pray to him!" (Q 53:59–62). The *ṣalāh* rite, which in some of these cases appears to form part of the recitation of the proclaimer already in the early period clearly consists of the physical gestures of humility that later Islamic cult established as obligatory: *sajda* (Q 53:62), *rakʿa* (Q 77:48), and *qiyām* (Q 73:2). But we learn nothing about which prayer texts are pronounced here. It is important that the prayer rites mentioned in the Qur'an, Q 107:4 and Q 108:2, are nowhere distinguished unambiguously from the ancient Arab ones; it is clearly the inherited form, with the elements *rakʿa, sajda*, and *qiyām*, that is to be conceived as the frame for the recitations. Its exclusive mention at the beginning or end of the sura may refer to an introductory or closing function of the rite within the liturgical service developing in connection to the recitations.

If one takes into account that the proclaimer views his opponents as among the cultically lax hearers, that he bemoans their lack of respect in regard to his own liturgical contribution (the recitation), and that those who follow him in their prayer are exposed to the mockery of these same opponents (Q 83:29), then one can find here further evidence for an initially established cultic community shared between the proclaimer and his Meccan compatriots in the shrine. Shlomo Dov Goitein also presupposes an already existing pre-Islamic prayer rite, which the new community continues to follow—without, however, observing the "reform" of the cult initiated through the additional liturgical element of recitation.[51] This reform, which has not been noted in the research up to now, is an

51. In a letter from February 18, 1962, Goitein wrote the following to Paret, who wanted to date verse Q 107:4ff. to the Medinan period: "In reference to the ṣalāt of the Meccans, I believe that this expression familiar to Christians

important developmental step in both the Qur'an genesis and the formation of the community.

6.3.3 *The Ritually Determined Prayer Times and Their Reform*

Particularly in those parts of suras that receive emphasis through oaths, we find confirmation of the centrality of the rites as "memory figures," mnemotopes, in yet another sense, in relation to the medium of time. That is no surprise, since ""memory figures" must be actualized at a particular time. The contents of the recollections are connected to time both through the attachment to primordial or extraordinary events and through the periodic rhythm of references to memory. The calendar of holidays, for example, reflects a collectively lived time."[52] The daily sequence of times of day (structured by sacred times reserved for divine service) is the microstructure corresponding to the macrostructural calendar of holidays. Some of the times of the day that were later fixed for prayer occur quite early, and indeed emphatically, in oath contexts, clearly carrying great weight for the symbolic function of the oaths: *ʿaṣr*, "late afternoon" (Q 103:1); *fajr*, "sunrise" (Q 89:1, 74:33, 52:48); and *ḍuḥā*, "bright day" (Q 93:1, 91:5).[53] Oaths sworn by the nightly vigil time, *layl* (Q 91:4, 92:1), are also linked to a liturgically relevant time. Uri Rubin has been able to distill from the wealth of traditional materials the fact that in ancient Arabic cult, a morning prayer (*ḍuḥā*) was current, while the afternoon prayer (*ʿaṣr*) was perhaps introduced by the proclaimer himself in Mecca. For all other prayer times, he can find no ancient Arabic evidence.[54] Accordingly, for the times mentioned in the oaths, at least apart from *ḍuḥā* and *ʿaṣr* (Q 103:1), the adoption of an early Meccan praxis is probable. We also find an oath upon the consecrated period of ten days, *al-ayyām al-ʿašr*, "the ten days" (Q 93:2), which perhaps indicates the beginning of the *ḥajj* period.[55] In this emphatic echo of liturgically relevant times, we see a possession of signs shared between proclaimer and his hearers, which in part refer to cosmically determined times relevant to the rites of the Kaaba.

What becomes usual in the more complex suras, the clear assignment of ritual acts of divine service to particular sacred times, is already foreshadowed in the early suras: in the closing verses of sura 52, we find the following call to hold off on prayer at the break of day: *fa-sabbiḥ bi-ḥamdi rabbika ḥīna taqūm / wa-mina l-layli fa-sabbiḥhu wa-idbāra l-nujūm*, "So praise your Lord, when you stand up

and Jews was already used for the superficial cult of the pagans. Muhammad was indignant that his countrymen did not take their own cult seriously. At the beginning of his career, Muhammad himself believed in the numen of his home city"; see Paret, *Koran: Kommentar*, 525. Cf. Goitein, *Studies in Islamic History and Institutions*, 88; Birkeland, *The Lord Guideth*, 85.

52. Assmann, *Das kulturelle Gedächtnis*, 60; cf. Assmann, *Das Fest und das Heilige*.
53. Rubin, "Morning and Evening Prayers."
54. Ibid.
55. See Wagtendonk, *Fasting in the Koran*.

[or: when you stand in prayer], / and at night, and at the fall of the stars" (verses 48–49). Here a morning prayer and vigils seem to be called for, wherein the time of morning prayer is to be identified with *fajr*, "sunrise," rather than *ḍuḥā* "the bright day." According to Rubin, the *fajr* prayer replaces the pagan *ḍuḥā* prayer, the latter of which had as its model the Jewish *shaḥarit* service. Accordingly, already in the early Meccan period, the community possesses two prayer times no longer shared with the Meccans. Whether one should presuppose an orientation to Jewish cult, as Rubin suggests, or rather one toward monastic worship—also responsible for the vigils referred to so intensely in the Qur'an (Q 73:1–5, 20; 74:2)—so that with *fajr* and *ʿaṣr* we have an adaptation of *orthros* and *hesperinos* rather than *shaḥarit* and *minḥa*, we cannot here decide. What is important is that the worship of the proclaimer grew out of liturgical practices of the Meccans and first went its own way through gradual alteration of the prayer times.

If we revisit the early suras while bearing in mind their function as complements to the prayer rites, as we have sketched above, their ancient Arabian elements no longer appear stylistically surprising. The technique of the oath introduction, a continuation of the *kāhin* style of oration, or the stereotypical *idhā* series[56] of the eschatological sura beginnings, and indeed, the entire *sajʿ* ductus with its short constituents, is based on the repetition of the same formal elements in the same position; one can thus interpret them as a translation of the ritual performance, which is equally reliant on repetition into linguistic expression. It is in light of their close association with the Kaaba rites—attested from the very beginning—that the unique form of the early suras must be understood. This aspect may equally provide an explanation for the fact that these suras, and these suras alone, constitute a partial corpus reserved in a special way for the *ṣalāh* ritual down to the present day.[57]

6.4 Cultic and Textual Development in the Middle Meccan Period

6.4.1 *Al-Kitāb as Nucleus of Divine Self-Communication*

If one acknowledges the close relationship between the central memory figure of the *ḥaram* rites and the particular form of the earliest suras, which seem to integrate themselves smoothly into these rites, then one must assume a different frame of emergence for the longer and formally more complex structured suras: they must derive from a new state of the development of the cult. Our

56. Cf. chap. 5, 174–176, and Neuwirth, *Studien zur Komposition*, 188–189.

57. The "final thirtieth of the Qur'an," *juz' ammā*, is taught first in traditional schools. Mastering this partial Qur'anic corpus, which is mostly made up of early Meccan suras, is considered a sufficient requirement for the necessary readings on ritual prayer; cf. Neuwirth, "Der Koran—Mittelpunkt des Lebens."

investigation then turns from the short suras to those compositions that take narratives of the past as a new and central theme.

If one asks about this group, which, to simplify for our purpose, will be designated "history suras"—which generally begin with a reference to their origin from writing[58]—what is the central memory figure that anchors them in time and place and seeks also to trace the indications of circumstance and performance framework of the suras, then quite a new picture emerges. In place of the spatial and temporal references to rites at the emphatic sura beginnings and the heightened sura endings, we find a direct mention of the writing (*kitāb*), or, more rarely, of the recitation text (*qurʾān*).[59] Only three of the complete twenty-two history suras begin without direct reference to writing. All six of the suras of this type that still contain an opening oath evoke mentions of divine writing rather than any reference to spatial and timely ritual.[60] But in these suras, the oaths themselves are quickly superseded by a solemn deictic introduction that now becomes the rule, beginning demonstratively: "that is the writing" (*dhālika l-kitāb*),[61] or else beginning with a nominal phrase consisting of a single word—"it is a writing" (*kitābun*).[62] These introductions remain frequent until the end of the Qur'an genesis. Remarkable also is the employment, which now becomes frequent, of one or an ensemble of letters, which occur mostly in addition to an evocation of writing, and are most likely to be understood as sacral correspondents or "intonations."[63]

6.4.2 *Formation of Liturgies and Scriptural Pericopes*

The recourse here to writing, since there was no corpus of written Qur'anic text for the later Meccan suras to draw upon, most likely refers to an entity beyond a concrete book. This entity may be taken to be the heavenly scripture that was

58. "History suras" that lack an introduction with reference to scriptural elements are the suras 21, 23, 54; the two suras that contain a doxology *in nuce*, suras 25 and 67, constitute an exception. In services in Jewish and Eastern Christian worship, scriptural reading is also preceded by a doxology.

59. The relationship between them is controversial in scholarship. The stipulation made by Nagel, "Vom Qur'an zur Schrift," 165, seems to be strongly dominated by an idea of Muhammad as an author, whose individual shift in consciousness is seen as responsible for the significant developments in the Qur'an: "Thus the development of the concept of 'writing' in the Qur'an may show to us the stages of the routinization of the Prophetic experience granted to Muhammad. In the end Islam shows itself to be a religion based on the legal provisions that go back to the 'scripture.'"

60. The introductory oaths to suras in which "scripture" and the *qurʾān* are found: Q 36:2, 50:1, *qurʾān*; Q 37:3, *dhikr*, "exhortation"; Q 38:2, *qurʾān dhū dhikr*, "reading with the admonition"; Q 43:2, 44:2, *kitāb*.

61. Deictic reference to "scripture," *dhālika l-kitāb*, "This is the scripture," or more often: *tilka āyātu l-kitāb*, "These are the signs of scripture," introduce suras 2, 10, 12, 13, 15 26, 27, 28, and 31.

62. The introductory verses refer to the scripture by means of monopartite nominal sentence, Q 7, 11, 14, *kitābun*; similarly suras 32, 39, 40, 41, 54, and 46: *tanzīl l-kitāb*, "[this is] a sending down of the scripture"; sura 19: *dhikru raḥmati rabbika*, "[this is] a reminder of your lord's compassion"; and sura 24: *sūratun anzalnāhā*, "[this is] a sura, which was sent down to us." However, one can also read these verses as appellatory: "A scripture!" and so forth.

63. But cf. the explanation attempt that goes in another direction in Paret, *Der Koran*.

made available for recitation, *qur'ān*, and remembrance, *dhikr* (Q 19:2.51), from which texts are now "sent down" in spurts.[64] According to the middle and later Meccan suras, to receive the "writing" is a distinction that had already been bestowed on earlier messengers; yet the proclaimer does not have knowledge of these texts from books, but rather from oral communications. What unites the various receivers of writing is not the vouchsafed identity of the respective corpora that emerge and whose identity would scarcely be possible to check across the language barriers, but rather the consciousness concomitant to the high valuing of the symbol of writing, that there exists in the transcendental realm one comprehensive, integral text that only requires that it be sent down, proclaimed, and arranged into suitable form for divine service, and subsequently subjected to exegesis to make it accessible to mankind. The fact that the text in its entirety was not at the disposal of the proclaimer but was only conveyed to him as fragmentary recollections does not contradict this. In this "excerpting" of writing into the Arabic language, which is occurring here for the first time, we can see a process analogous to the pericopizing of entire works, which was a common practice among Jews and Christians.

Such a narrative pericope from the heavenly writing stands—in close analogy to the Jewish and Christian service,[65] where the central element is a reading from the Torah or Gospel—in the center of the cultic sura recitals performed in Mecca. Surrounding this scriptural reading, the *dhikr*, which consists above all of recollections of history, we find hymnic, polemic, and revelation-confirmatory elements, so that a structure emerges for the entire recital that can be understood as a reprise of a Jewish or Christian liturgy. It is remarkable that different Prophet histories and individual biblical figures are expressly identified as "recorded in the writing," while other Qur'anic topoi, such as polemic, are presented without reference to writing, but rather in commentary form, as in, "If they say . . . , then say . . . " "Divine origin" is thus not to be taken in this phase as wholly synonymous with "excerpt from the heavenly writing." Even if eventually the Qur'an—as its name *qur'ān* (a loanword from Syriac, *qeryānā*, "lectionary, pericope, reading") already seems to suggest—will become, after the death of the proclaimer, its own pericope book for the extraction of texts for cultic recital by Muslims, during the proclamation itself the individual recital texts are constituted heterogeneously, namely, out of a narrative excerpts from the heavenly writing, to which are added verse groups of various liturgical and discursive genres as framing elements.

64. For a discussion of scriptural evocations, see Madigan, *The Qur'ān's Self-Image.*

65. Both Jews and Eastern Christians know of pericope books, apart from their biblical codices: *tiqqun soferim* and *evangelistarion*, which present decontextualized daily liturgical reading portions for practical, oral usage.

6.4.3 Easing of Forms and New Mnemotechnic Supports

The recourse to "writing" indicates an expansion of consciousness that can hardly be overestimated: First, the sacred topography that was confined up to that point to Mecca is widened to include the homeland of earlier messengers, so that the Holy Land comes forth as a particularly blessed region.[66] Second, the temporal setting of the message has been extended into the distant periods of salvific history, and, what is more, the speaker's entrance among the group of those who received messages from a writing that is only ever released in spurts, above all the Israelites, was to transform the new community into a people of God related to them. In the end, this entails nothing less than the adoption of the *memory* of the Israelites as their own memory,[67] the crossing over into the Israelites' tradition and thus a necessary distancing from the Meccan identity that was preserved above all by rites. It is remarkable that this new orientation is also expressed gesturally in the prayer service, namely, in the adoption of a direction of prayer that is no longer locally determined but rather suggested by sacred history. The new theological quality of this adoption of a prayer direction, involving not only ritual but also an act of memory, has not yet been perceived sharply enough.

6.4.4 Gestural Orientation in "Textual Space": The Direction of Prayer toward Jerusalem

The alignment toward Jerusalem—in place of the cosmic orientation to the east that was current up to this point[68]—makes gesturally manifest, so to speak, the profound change that took place in the early community in the middle Meccan period, and which we have attempted to discuss in analogy to the transition from a ritual to a textual coherence developed by Jan Assmann.[69] After the early phase, in which the new proclamation still stands in the frame and context of the Kaaba rites, we observe in the Qur'anic community a kind of conversion process, namely, the change from an ancient Arabian orientation based on oral ancestral traditions to a biblical one based on writing. The biblical stories that were previously evoked at most in short allusions now come to the foreground in the middle Meccan period. The protagonists of the early historical narratives are at first equally figures from the Arabian Peninsula and biblical figures, but over time the Arabian figures become less prominent than the biblical figures, and the Holy Land itself enters the scene in place of the local Arabian one. The biblical sacred-historical past that replaces their own historical memory now forms a "text world" in competition with reality, approached in prayer through the physical

66. On evocations of the Holy Land in the Qur'an in detail, see Neuwirth, "The Spiritual Meaning of Jerusalem in Islam"; cf. also chap. 8, 287–289.

67. Cf. Assmann, *Das kulturelle Gedächtnis*, 40–42.

68. Or to the front of the Kaaba, as Rubin assumes, "Kaʿba," 319–320.

69. Assmann and Assmann, "Nachwort," 272. Cf. chap. 8, 285–287.

gesture of facing the prayer direction and in cultic recitation—both practices that are already familiar in the surrounding monotheistic traditions.

One example among many for this new orientation is offered by the history of the Jerusalem temple, which is told in Q 17:4–7;[70] following the suras 106, 95, 90, and 52, there is no more reference to the Meccan sanctuary, with the one exception of a short evocation in Q 29:67: *a-wa-lam yaraw annā jaʿalnā ḥaraman āminan wa-yutakhaṭṭafu l-nāsu min ḥawlihim*, "Do they not see that we have set up a secure sanctuary, while the people around them are robbed?" The only middle Meccan exception is the reference to *al-masjid al-ḥarām*, the "holy place of worship," in Q 17:1, which serves however to place Mecca into a tense relation to Jerusalem. The verse[71] speaks of a night rapture of the proclaimer from the "sacred" to the "far[thest] place of worship," *al-masjid al-aqṣā*:

> *subḥāna lladhī asrā bi-ʿabdihi laylan mina l-masjidi l-ḥarāmi ilā l-masjidi l-aqṣā alladhī bāraknā ḥawlahu li-nuriyahu min āyātinā innahu huwa l-samīʿu l-baṣīr*
>
> Praised be He who led his servant out at night from the sacred place of worship to the far[thest] place of worship, around which we have blessed, in order to show him our signs—He is the hearing, the seeing.

This verse reflects the replacement in the middle Meccan period of the local sanctuary orientation toward the Israelite sanctuary in Jerusalem, a step that goes much further than a mere change of ritual praxis. The change in emphasis marks a new phase in the development of worship, which is manifest in new forms. The suras no longer show poetic speech in the tradition of ancient Arabic *sajʿ*, but rather develop as biblical "readings" narrative texts that are framed by dialogic (hymnic, polemical, or apologetic) elements. The suras not only break the frame of a verbal supplement to a given ritual but also show themselves liturgically and stylistically to have outgrown their old frames: in their structure, they are reprises of older forms of worship, and, in their diction, they clearly make reference to Jewish-Christian formal language.[72] At the same time, the technique of the narrative section requires the length of individual verses to be expanded, in order to differentiate the various narrative levels through hypotaxis and more complex sentence formations. What emerges is the pluripartite Qur'an verse containing more than two cola, which is no longer easy to memorize, especially as its monotone conclusion at the end of the final clause offers very little help for memory. From this period on, it seems that the codification of the new compositions has been taken care of. The more

70. Neuwirth, "Erste Qibla."

71. Q 17:1 is discussed in chap. 8, 287–289. Cf. also, on its relevance as proof of the Prophet's succession to Moses, chap. 11, 408–412.

72. Baumstark, "Gebetstypus."

complex structure of the verses, in which rhyme no longer offers mnemotechnic help, almost requires this step. In the Qur'an, then, we do not find an "invention of writing"—what we can observe, rather, in the reorientation to the *kitāb* (the "writing") is a transition toward a technique of memory through writing. This technique, which is bound up with the transcendent original image of writing, now becomes a kind of exterior storage that flanks memorization.

6.4.5 The Clausula

As the stereotypically formed final clause now replaces the end-verse rhyme, this entails not only a stylistic and mnemotechnical change of form but also a change in the intended function of the Qur'an text.[73] With the new form—prose discourse consisting of interspersed recollections of God, evaluations, and admonitions of behavior—we see the creation of an effective stylistic medium for the sacral encoding of discourse, as well as a remarkably flexible theological means of binding inner-worldly affairs to the transcendent God. The verse-end clausulas are not simply end markers of a complex semantic-syntactic verbal unit; they are also, and above all, paraenetic pronouncements about what is presented in the main text, meta-textual reminders of the source of the discourse, God himself, or at least his admonitions and valuations. Q 12:23 offers an example:

> *wa-rāwadathu llati huwa fī baytihā ʿan nafsihi wa-ghallaqati l-abwāba wa-qālat hayta laka qāla maʿādha llāhi innahu rabbī aḥsana mathwāya innahu lā yufliḥu l-ẓālimūn*
>
> She coveted him, the one in whose house he [Joseph] was, she locked the doors and called: "Come here." He said: "God forbid, He is my Lord, who has made my stay beautiful." Sinners do not prosper.

The clause "Sinners do not prosper," a negative evocation of the benediction *qad aflaḥa man tazakkā*, "Blessed be he who purifies himself" (Q 97:14),[74] introduces a new, transcendent, reference and turns the speech of Joseph from the inner-worldly connection—a trick of his Lord would be an act of ungratefulness—toward the transcendent. Not only Joseph's speech but the entire report of the verse is commented upon: following the norms established by God, what awaits the violator is loss, despite any external gain.

Thus, already in the middle Meccan period, numerous pronouncements make a direct or indirect appellatory point by means of the self-descriptive clausula, which opens up a theological discourse that transcends the level of the report. Qur'anic salvific history itself is here turned to cultic address and takes on an appellatory character.

73. Cf., for more detail on the form and function of the clausulas, chap. 5, 195–196; on its text-strategic efficacy for theological messages, cf. chap. 13, 472–477.

74. Similar calls for blessing are found in Q 91:9 and Q 23:1.

It is notable that the texts, at least in the middle Meccan period, use devices beyond the clausula to facilitate their own memorization, often through mnemotechnical assistance, by employing fixed proportions between individual parts of suras.[75] This seems to indicate also that the longer texts were entrusted to a circle of individuals capable of cultic recitation. For the use of these individuals, who would have been active also in the absence of the proclaimer, the symmetrical proportions would have offered a welcome mnemotechnic aid. The oral tradition remains the primary form of the text's preservation, as we can see from the scriptless reading out within *ṣalāh*, which is maintained down to today.[76]

6.4.6 *A New Temporal and Spatial Situation*

As has been shown, this change of form coincides with the community's move away from the former times of day determined for ritual. In fact, in the history suras, cultic directions appear for the observance of the morning and evening times, but no longer as symbolically loaded oath objects, however, and rather to signal recommended prayer times. That is easily understandable, since these rulings are innovations: in place of the familiar prayer time of *ḍuḥā*, shared with the Meccans, is the time of *fajr*:[77] *wa-sabbiḥ bi-ḥamdi rabbika qabla ṭulūʿi l-shamsi wa-qabla ghurūbihā*, "Give praise to your Lord before the rise of the sun and before it goes down" (Q 50:39). We find mention of these same two prayer times also in Q 11:114 (*wa-aqimi l-ṣalāta ṭarafayi l-nahāri wa-zulafan mina l-layli*, "Hold the prayer at the two ends of the day and across a phase of night),[78] where in addition a vigil is also intended. Q 17:78–79 speaks of an evening prayer (*ʿaṣr*) and of a recitation at the time of *fajr*, attesting to the fact that rites and recitation were already combined in the middle Meccan period. In addition to this, a vigil is also further recommended (Q 17:78–79):

> *aqimi l-ṣalāta li-dulūki shamsi ilā ghasaqi l-layli wa-qurʾāna l-fajri inna qurʾāna l-fajri kāna mashhūdā*
> *wa-mina l-layli fa-tahajjad bihi nāfilatan laka ʿasā an yabʿathaka rabbuka maqāman maḥmūdā*

> Perform the prayer when the sun declines, until the night darkens. And the recitation of the sundown, truly, this recitation will be witnessed!
> And stay awake at night amid the recitation, as an additional service, so that perhaps your Lord will raise you up to an honorable place.

75. See the scheme of composition in Neuwirth, *Studien zur Komposition*.

76. Cf. Graham, "Islam in the Mirror of Ritual"; Graham, *Beyond the Written Word*; Kellermann, "Die 'Mündlichkeit' des Koran."

77. The fact that this prayer was already evoked in the early Meccan period indicates that it existed early on alongside the *ḍuḥā* prayer, which it would later come to replace.

78. Rubin, "Morning and evening Prayers," 121–122.

We see that the only prayer preserved from the early Meccan period is the *ʿaṣr* prayer, which, like the *fajr* prayer, was not a pre-Islamic Meccan rite according to Uri Rubin's research. Although one should assume for these prayers that a recitation practice was integrated into the rites, it is in no way certain that these also included the new, longer suras; rather, one can imagine the continued use of the short suras for these rites.

In favor of their persisting role in cult, we can state on the one hand the observation that many early Meccan suras undergo a reworking in this period and are adapted to a new situation, in which the hearers desire to find their image affirmed in the cultic texts. They seek now, for example, to be excepted from the "reprimand of mankind" as ambivalent creatures that is so often pronounced in the early Meccan period (as for example *wa-l-ʿaṣr / inna l-insāna la-fī khusr*, "By the late afternoon! Truly, man is at a loss," Q 103:1–2), so that additions are now made to the recitation through formulas such as *illā lladhīna āmanū wa-ʿamilū l-ṣāliḥāti wa-tawāṣaw bi-l-ḥaqqi wa-tawāṣaw bi-l-ṣabr*, "except those / who believe and do good deeds and are inspired toward truth and patience" (Q 102:3). But above all, the later suras themselves have taken on so much complexity that they can no longer be imagined as "verbal accompaniments" to a rite, but seem rather to require their own separate performance frame.

A further centrally important innovation occurs at this point: the middle Meccan sura 15 confirms the existence of a newly introduced prayer formula, the Fātiḥa, Q 1:1–7,[79] in which the "we" form—which, in contrast to the "thou" style of the other suras, exhibits a reversal of the relation between speaker and receiver—presupposes the real existence of an ensemble of worshipers, a new cult society. The Fātiḥa can be dated approximately, and belongs to the Raḥmān period.[80]

bi-smi llāhi l-raḥmāni l-raḥīm
al-ḥamdu li-llāhi rabbi l-ʿālamīn
al-raḥmāni l-raḥīm
māliki yawmi l-dīn
iyāka naʿbudu wa-iyāka nastaʿīn
ihdinā l-ṣirāṭa l-mustaqīm
ṣirāṭa lladhīna anʿamta ʿalayhim
ghayri l-maghḍūbi ʿalayhim wa-lā l-ḍāllīn

In the name of God, the compassionate, the merciful.
Praise be to God, the Lord of the worlds,
the compassionate, the merciful,
the king of the day of judgment.

79. See Neuwirth and Neuwirth, "Sūrat al-Fātiḥa."
80. Cf. chap. 4, 142–144.

It is you we serve, you we call on for help.
Lead us to the right way,
the way of those you have shown grace to,
not those toward whom you are angry
and not those who go astray

The Fātiḥa, because of its constant use both within and outside of worship services, has been compared with the Christian Our Father,[81] with which it shares some structural characteristics (invocation, universal then individual pleading, evocation of positive and negative forms of divine intervention). But at the same time, it also resembles the Christian introductory to the prayer service, the Introitus—with which it shares an initial position, "opening" the Islamic prayer.[82] Without being able to decide between these two functions, it should be noted that in the Fātiḥa, which is also acknowledged as an addition within the Qur'an (Q 15:87), we now find a text that supplements the available elements of the service (the rites and scriptural recitation),[83] adding a crucial element, namely, the communal prayer. With the new availability of this, a distinct cult is already created *in nuce*, going beyond recitation supported by rites.

In view of the prayer times that are no longer shared with the pagan Meccans, it is questionable whether this extended prayer service still occurred by the Kaaba. The Qur'anic text gives no indication of its location. What suggests the increasing exclusiveness of an audience already won over by the message is the observation that we no longer find dramatic scenes involving the opponents as protagonists. Rather, the increasingly polemic passages in these later suras often refer to disputes already past or simulate arguments still to come;[84] that is, they follow the scheme "If they say, then say" (*qul*). In view of the simultaneous exhortations to recitation and prayer[85] that now become firm elements of the sura conclusions, recitation seems to have continued to form part of the prayer rite. Yet we need to assume that the longer sura readings should have obtained additional frameworks of their own.

6.5 Cultic and Textual Development in the Late Meccan Period

To sketch the development of the further Meccan suras, which are similarly complex but of a stronger polemical character and which widely dispense with

81. Winkler, "Fatiha und Vaterunser."
82. See Neuwirth and Neuwirth, "Sūrat al-Fātiḥa."
83. See Neuwirth, "Referentiality and Textuality."
84. Radscheit, *Die Koranische Herausforderung*, thus concludes in favor of the subsequent construction of such scenarios. However, his hypothesis presupposes an authorial origin of the Qur'an, and thus does not consider arguments based on the interactions between proclaimer and hearers that are reflected in the text.
85. See the analysis of suras in Neuwirth, *Studien zur Komposition*.

narrative[86] would require preliminary analytical work giving specific treatment to the structures of argument, far beyond of the scope of the present study. In lieu of this, an attempt will be undertaken on the basis of a single sura to gain some insight about the liturgical *Sitz im Leben* and hearership of the late Meccan suras. Sura 29, "The Spider," Al-ʿAnkabūt, which is addressed indirectly to its hearers (*a-ḥasiba l-nāsu . . .* ?, "Do the people perhaps believe . . . ?," verse 2), confronts central communal problems from the very beginning: a crisis is underway, which resulted from disappointment about the half-heartedness of some people initially counted among the believers, who then became apostates (verse 10). The entire beginning part (verses 1–13) gives the impression of an experience of *fitna*, a divine testing (*fatannā*, verse 2), in which creed alone does not count, but rather the "hearts of men" will be tested (verse 10). The crisis is aggravated by the fact that under the difficult conditions of the conflict with the unbelievers (verse 12, *alladhīna kafarū*, verse 48, *al-mubṭilūn*), a new quality of loyalty is required, which, in the case of differing religious orientation within families, even displaces the authority of parents (verse 8), so that the necessity of honoring one's parents, which had already been preached in the Decalogue (Q 17:23), must now be rewritten. In this situation of rigorous self-restriction, we find the first introduction of the image of *jihād, athlon*,[87] that is, inner struggle (verse 8, and again finally verse 69). What is striking is the nearly complete relinquishment of direct address to those present, which is only lifted in the case of the controversial exhortation to possibly show one's parents disobedience (verse 8).

Despite this introduction, which clearly displays the form of a speech, the sura goes on in a conventional way. In the usual position of the sura's middle part, the Prophets Noah (verses 14–15), Abraham (16–27), and Lot (29–35) are recalled, introduced simply through the formula *la-qad arsalnā . . .* , "We have sent down already . . . ," so that Abraham's sermon against idolatry, including the derivation of God's power to resurrect from his power of creation, carries over topoi from the sermon of the proclaimer in remarkable ways. Then follow reminiscences of the fates of the peninsular Arabian peoples Madyan (verse 36–37) and Thamud (verse 38), and finally those of other stubborn unbelievers (verse 39), whose punishments are recalled in a litany-like catalogue (verse 39). In all this, what is striking is a new, paraenetic point of emphasis: instead of creating tension by pursuing the narratives to their climax, their paraenetic points (such as Lot's wife having to stay behind as punishment) are unveiled from the beginning. The series of narratives is concluded by a parable (*mathal*), introduced explicitly as such, whose educational value is highlighted again at the end (verse 43): the

86. For the sequences of themes in the late Meccan suras 6, 10, 13, 16, 28, 30, 32, 35, 39, 41, 42, 45, and 46, see the analysis in Neuwirth, *Studien zur Komposition*, 290–313.

87. The conception of *jihād*, as struggle in application of the affairs of God, precedes the idea of violent *jihād*. A monastic Christian ideal (*athlon*) may be reflected here, such as is present in 1 Tim 2:5.

construction of "auxiliary deities" is just as incapable of carrying a load as the web of the spider (verses 41–43). Apart from this parable, placed emphatically at the conclusion of the historical recollections, nothing is new in this part of the sura—the narrative section can for that reason be explained best as the fulfillment of already established expectations of the hearers, who anticipate finding in the center of the performance salvific historical recollections—just as is the custom in Jewish and Christian services where readings from biblical history occupy the center.

The announcement of the final part (verse 44) is, on the other hand, liturgically striking, amounting to an emphatic signal that is almost an exclamation: *khalaqa llāhu l-samawāti wa-l-arḍa bi-l-ḥaqqi inna fī dhālika la-āyatan li-l-muʾminīn*, "God created the heaven and earth in truth, and in that is a sign for the believers." The verse is not linked semantically to what follows and serves with its great cosmic reference solely to signal a new beginning, whereby attention will be aroused. In this function, it recalls above all the hymnal formula with which the community in the synagogue accompanies the relocating of the Torah scroll in the shrine: *hodo ʿal ereẓ we-shamayim*, "His majesty is over the earth and the heavens." Without considering a direct derivation, the parallel shows the rhetorical efficiency that a cosmic reference can have for the introduction of a new part of a prayer service. As in the majority of the Meccan suras, the final part begins with a consolation of the Prophet confirming the transcendent origin of the message (verses 46–49). The concluding polemic in the "they" form aims at apparently absent opponents, who would concede to God creation (verse 61), preservation (verse 62), and even occasional rescue from danger (verse 65), but do not grant worship to him alone, although their privileged social situation as neighbors of the Meccan sanctuary (verse 67) should be a clear sign to them. The conclusion entails an exhortation to *jihād*, to militant, if at this stage still nonviolent, commitment in the cause of God.

That the Qur'anic *ecclesia militans* that is reflected here stands in close relation to its Christian interlocutor is evident, not only from the recognized necessity to conduct disputes with the "people of scripture" in a conciliatory way (verse 46: *wa-lā tujādilū ahla l-kitābi illā bi-llatī hiya aḥsan*, "Do not dispute with the peoples of the scripture, except in a friendly way"). It follows that disputes are already underway. The community recognizes the scriptural revelations of the others, some of whom are perhaps even present among the hearers: *fa-lladhīna ataynāhumu l-kitāba yuʾminūna bihi wa-min hāʾulāʾi man yuʾminu bihi*, "Those to whom we have given the writing, believe in it, and also among those here [some] believe in it" (verse 47). The community recognizes the God of all of them as one and insists at the same time on the genuineness of the revelation to the proclaimer. The argument seems to be carried out constructively; the turning toward the Christians is clearly no momentary event. Rather, a number of references to the New Testament point to an already existing exchange, an appropriation of the forms of Christian forbearance of adversities. Most striking are the references to the carefree "birds among the heavens" (Mt 6:26), which recur in the Qur'an generalized to "animals" (verse 60), and to the "apartments in the house of the Lord," which become the apartments of paradise (verse 58), and finally the predictions from Mt 16:28, Mk 9:1, and Lk 9:27 that some contemporaries will "not taste death, before they have experienced the lordship of God on the earth"—a prediction that is reformulated in the Qur'an into the universal statement that "every soul will taste death" (verse 57).

Although in its rhetoric and its unfolding of numerous arguments the sura is clearly an address, it is not a direct confrontation with the fickle or the unbelievers; it no longer presupposes a scenario occupied by hearers of different provenance, but rather comments from an elevated position on a public addressed neutrally as "you," while maintaining a concern about their belief and nonbelief and the kinds of behavior required by them. Despite these evocative traces of a sermon, the sura is nonetheless oriented toward liturgy: it still follows the three-part scheme known since the middle Meccan period, which reflects the reading of scripture in the middle, and in which the confirmation of revelation in the closing part is announced to the hearers through a clear signal. Although formally a dialogue—interrupted only a single time (verse 8)—between God and proclaimer, the sura itself recalls a collective experience: already in the rhetorical question at the beginning, *a-ḥasiba l-nās*, "do the people believe," reminds one of earlier introductory formulas for the expression of disapproval of a false view, *a-yaḥsabu l-insān*, "does man believe" (Q 75:3.36, 90:5, 7, 104:3). Even if the text avoids direct approach to the hearers or addressees, there is still a clear connection between speaker and hearers given through inner-Qur'anic textual references. The sura thus reflects a liturgical reading before a hearership already familiar with the Qur'anic discourse, which now begins to open itself up to the "people of the scripture," while renouncing ever more harshly the non-monotheistic unbelievers.

While sura 29 still preserves the old tripartite structure with historical recollections in the middle part, the majority of the late Meccan suras (eleven of twenty suras)[88]—which are structurally no longer clearly tripartite—no longer entail any narratives. Their place has been taken by the historical reflections or the yet more clearly paraenetically oriented parables, *amthāl*, a classical monotheistic textual type—indeed, a topos of the sermon. But the late Meccan suras remain polythematic. The step toward a monothematic sermon, which is yet to come in Medina, does not occur in Mecca.

Cult, insofar as it concerns the praise of God embedded in a prayer context, seems to have expanded: not only are the two morning and evening prayer times confirmed, but a midday prayer, *ẓuhr*, and a late evening prayer, *'ishā'*, are also

88. Lacking a narrative are the suras 13, 16, 28, 30, 32, 35, 39, 40, 41, 42, and 45; those with narratives are suras 6, 7, 10, 11, 14, 29, 31, 34, and 46. See Neuwirth, *Studien zur Komposition*, 290–313.

emerging: *fa-subḥāna llāhi ḥīna tumsūna wa-ḥīna tusbiḥūn / wa-lahu l-ḥamdu fī l-samawāti wa-l-arḍi wa-ʿashīyan wa-ḥīna tuẓhirūn*, "Praised be God when you come in the evening and in the morning, to him is due praise in the heaven and earth, in the late evening and when you come in the midday" (Q 30:17–18).[89] The recitation is also now preceded by a formula for the avoidance of mischief, *aʿūdhu bi-llāh mina l-shayṭāni l-rajīm*, "I take refuge with God from the cursed Satan": *fa-idhā qaraʾta l-qurʾāna fa-staʿidh bi-llāhi mina l-shayṭāni l-rajīm*, "If you recite, then utter the formulas: I take refuge with God from the cursed Satan" (Q 16:98).

6.6 Cultic and Textual Development in Medina

6.6.1 New Sura Types and Their Sitz im Leben

Medinan suras can be roughly grouped into the short, frequently monothematic "oratory suras" (22, 24, 33, 47, 48, 49, 57–66) and the long suras (2–5, 8, and 9). As a development important for the understanding of scripture, we find in Medina a new relation to the heavenly scripture and the proclamation: while in Mecca *qurʾān*, situationally conditioned performance, and *kitāb*, excerpt from the heavenly writing, were held clearly separate from each other, the two become difficult to distinguish in Medina. We now find texts about occasional, ephemeral communal matters within the performances of "excerpts from the heavenly scripture"; thus, the *qurʾān*, the recitation of the proclaimer, becomes identical with the excerpts from the *kitāb*, the heavenly scripture. In tune with the Qur'anic community's entrance into salvific history that is thus attested, we find new texts, consisting of an address to the community, whose members are directly addressed in formulas such as *yā ayyuhā l-nās*, "O people." At the same time, the Prophet appears with a new aura in these suras, which in some cases (suras 59, 61, 62, 64) are introduced by stereotyped hymnal introductory formulas that evoke the Psalms. Designated as *al-nabī*, he is no longer the mere mediator of the message but has now moved to stand beside the text. Only now does he bear the name "Muḥammad" (Q 3:144, 33:40, 47:2, 48:29), which should be understood as an honorific title, "the Praised." He is addressed directly by God by the formula *yā ayyuhā l-nabī*, "You Prophet,"[90] and becomes an actor who works in synergy with the divine personage and is mentioned in the combination *Allāhu wa-rasūluhu*, "God and his messenger."

Closely linked to the proclaimer, a number of locations now appear, called *masājid*, especially the *masjid al-ḥarām* in Mecca. The entire cult is now organized

89. Hawting, "Introduction," xvii, discusses the finally established three daily prayers; in contrast see Horovitz, "Terminologie des islamischen Kultus."

90. See Bobzin, "The 'Seal of the Prophets.'"

around this old center,[91] which is perceived explicitly as the original place of the rites.[92] The rites of the pilgrimage are accorded late recognition as a legacy of the *masjid al-ḥarām*, which now, as a result of a longstanding Meccan tradition recognizing Abraham as its founder,[93] is recognized also as the natural foundation of the new religion, which in its other aspects, however, is much more indebted to the legacy of Moses.[94] It is notable that the change of the direction of prayer, *qibla*, in Medina, just like its initial introduction,[95] once again displays an element of the particular consideration accorded to the psychic situation of the proclaimer and, implicitly, of the community.[96]

The suras of this period mark a new transformation of form: they are structurally homogenous and dispense with the multiplicity of "classical" compositional elements of the older suras (e.g., the characteristic beginning and closing elements of hymn, catalogue of virtues, and revelation introduction; the classical middle sections with historical recollection or discussion; and the closing revelation polemic and confirmation). The new oratory suras display a comparatively simple structure: a mostly stereotyped hymnic introduction is followed immediately by the exposition of the subject, in the form of a speech showing end rhyme. The "oratory sura" is only rarely carried out artfully; it has become a ritually stylized address, a new form achieved through comparably simple means.

The emergence of a sura type without a distinctive composition indicates a shift in emphasis toward the end of the development. There seems no longer to be expectations of firmly structured liturgies. Polythematic compositions, with their attendant complex discourses often discharged on different generic levels, are replaced by a simple form. The sura has now approximated itself to the genre of the sermon. The proclaimer has come to feature beside the text as a representative charged with socially and politically relevant duties, and addressed personally with the title *yā ayyuhā l-nabī*, "You Prophet!" The similarity to the form of address later familiar in the Friday sermon is not accidental: it is at this period

91. With the single exception of Q 17:1, all Qur'anic references to *al-masjid al-ḥarām* are Medinan and therefore occur in the context of debates surrounding the rights of the Prophet and his community: Q 2:144, 150 *qibla* shift; Q 2:191 declaration of war; Q 2:217 remembrance of the expulsion of the faithful from the Kaaba cult; Q 5:2 invocation to respect the Meccan cult symbols; Q 8:34 indictment of the expulsion of the faithful from the Kaaba cult; Q 9:7 pact with the *umrat al-qaḍā'*; Q 9:19 assessment of the *siqāya* and *'imāra* duties; Q 9:28 expulsion of the faithful; Q 22:25, Q 44:25 judgment of the expulsion of the faithful from the Kaaba; once, in Q 5:96–98, pilgrimage regulations are discussed.

92. The *qibla* shift from Jerusalem to Mecca becomes binding with Q 2:144–150.

93. See Rubin, "Hanifiyya and Ka'ba"; cf. Sinai, *Studien zur frühen Koraninterpretation*, 135–160.

94. See Goitein, "Prayer in Islam." A clear testament to Moses's function as a prototype of Muhammad is traditionally offered by the establishment of the Jerusalem *qibla* in sura 17; see Neuwirth, "Erste Qibla," where Muhammad and Moses are compared several times.

95. The connection between the first establishment of *qibla* and the night journey of the proclaimer to Jerusalem is also established in the traditional exegesis; cf. the evidence in Duri, "Jerusalem in the Early Islamic Period."

96. Cf. chap. 9, 334–337.

that the Friday service was first institutionalized.[97] The Qur'anic mention of its establishment occurs in the context of a defense of the proclaimer as an Arabian prophet, a "messenger from within your midst," Q 62:1–5, who is contrasted expressly with those Jews who possess the Torah but do not understand it. As it is in the context of this confrontation that a day of gathering, *jumʿa*, is introduced, it might be concluded—though without explicit evidence—that the intention here is to establish an opposing model to Shabbat.[98]

It is noteworthy that native "proto-Islamic" history is touched upon, but never unfolded narratively.[99] This prefigures a momentous development: not only the renunciation of general monotheistic historical memory but also the relinquishing of the community's "proto-Islamic" historical memory as a backbone of the prayer service. The person of the proclaimer himself stands increasingly as the focal point. The generally highly formulaic introductions of these suras may indicate their recitation at the beginning of a longer ceremony, which, given the absence of conventional sura endings at this stage, may have most likely been concluded with a following prayer ritual.

With the second Medinan sura type, the "long sura," the discrepancy between the textual unit sura and the pericope designed for recitation within a cultic frame, which had occasionally already arisen with the longer late Meccan texts, becomes the rule. Given their length, the long suras as such could no longer serve a cultic function. But since even the shorter Medinan suras, being for the most part monothematic, no longer fit the older complex model, the expectation of the hearers for a complex prayer service presenting salvific historical memory in the form of a narrative from the biblical traditions as its centerpiece, seems to have faded away. It is no surprise, then, that the Islamic prayer service in its ultimately fixed form includes no performance of complete suras, but only short pieces inserted into the rites.

6.6.2 *Medinan Additions*

We find an important index of the continued recitation of older suras during Muhammad's ministry in Medina in those texts that can be identified as additions to Meccan suras.[100] They serve precisely to actualize the older texts that

97. See Q 62:9; see also Goitein, "Friday Worship," Becker, "Zur Geschichte des islamischen Kultus."

98. See Goitein, "Friday Worship." A non-canonical reading of *jumuʿa* (Q 62:9) makes the chronological framework of the new day of worship explicit: the Aramaic borrowed word, *ʿarūbā*, "eve," points to a day of preparation for Shabbat, apparently concretely to a Friday market, see ibid.

99. An example of the few verses that reflect the fateful event of victory at Badr is Q 8:41–44; see Wagtendonk, *Fasting in the Qur'an*. Here, an event is interpreted mythically in detail, point by point, but is still not condensed into a mythical story. The verses clearly aim at the evocation of a memory presumed to be living among the hearers.

100. Hence what is intended here is not the Medinan additions accounted for in the tradition, which Nagel, *Medinensische Einschübe*, collected and discussed, but whose criteria for identification still need to be checked. This has more to do rather with verses that stand out for formal and text-logical reasons, thus indicating a Medinan interaction scenario.

were still in use, but that required concretizing or modification in light of new communal developments. This became a means, for example, for the expression of the increasingly demanding life circumstances of some members of the community, who as tradespeople or fighters could no longer dedicate themselves to protracted vigils. Q 73:1–4, with its exhortation valid within the early Meccan period, *yā ayyuhā l-muzzammil / qumi l-layla illā qalīlā / nisfahu awi nquṣ minhu qalīlā / aw zid ʿalayhi wa-rattili l-qurʾāna tartīlā*, "You, wrapped one, / stand through the night / half the night or somewhat less / or somewhat more / and perform the reading in clear recitation," is thus extended by a Medinan closing verse, mentioning the groups to be exempted explicitly, which lightens the strict command for them: *fa-qraʾū mā tayassara minhu*, "So recite what comes easy to you from him/it" (Q 73:20). Similar lightenings are attached also to the cultic instructions concerning the Ramadan fast, which was first issued in Medina: Q 2:187 cancels the obligation of sexual abstinence for the nights of Ramadan implied in Q 2:185.

But the additions also reflect interactions across the borders of the community, to which the recitation responds. In the early Medinan period, a new group of hearers appears on the stage, if not in reality, then at least virtually: the Medinan Jews. Jews appear as believers (Q 2:62, 5:69, 22:17), or in other places they are confronted with the requirement of accepting the new message (Q 4:162). In some Qur'anic texts, they belong to the "peoples of the writing" (Q 3:113–114) and obtain assurances of a doubled reward in view of their belief in their own revealed writings and the Qur'an (Q 28:52–54).[101] But the full significance of their presence only becomes clear by means of a Qur'anic strategy that seems to presuppose Jewish hearers: older Qur'anic texts are extensively reworked, and thus adapted to the expectations of a more complex Medinan listenership. Textual analyses show that some biblical narratives that were already formulated in Mecca were subjected to a revision in Medina, and thus gained theological dimensions that clearly relate to Jewish biblical exegesis.[102] In the case of the story of the Golden Calf,[103] which is told in the Meccan period in Q 20:84–99, and again in Q 7:142–156, the additions, which appear clearly as such through their stylistic form, make distinct reference to a contemporary Jewish exegetical reading of the Exodus text.[104] Divine wrath—which is not a theme in Mecca, where human repentance brings about immediate forgiveness—now enters the community's horizon of knowledge, most probably as a result of disputes with Jewish scholars. A new theological reflection is required, which disputes the image of God predominant in the rabbinic tradition from Exodus 34:6–7, the so-called thirteen

101. Rubin, "Jews and Judaism"; Rubin, *Between Bible and Qur'an*.
102. Neuwirth, "Meccan Texts"; cf. chap. 9, 318–324.
103. See Hawting, "Tawwābūn."
104. Neuwirth, "Meccan Texts."

attributes, which plays a central role in the atonement ritual of the day of repentance (Yom Kippur). The extensive "correction" of the understanding of the previously narrated Moses story may be a tribute to Jewish hearers, who in the early Medinan period are clearly assumed to be among the proclaimer's audience.

Examples such as the development of the story of the Golden Calf can illuminate the debates that would have played out between the Jews and the new community. Both groups set out to become competing exegetical trustees of the same heritage and thus into rival interpretative communities. Medinan additions, as such, were conceded early on to exist by the Islamic tradition,[105] but have still not been submitted to systematic study as to their implications for the Qur'anic process of communication. Observations on the different Qur'anic readings of the story of the Golden Calf suggest the successive development of a discourse of guilt and atonement, which over time came to involve the new community and the Medinan Jews, before these became the target of serious Qur'anic polemic.

That such interpretive "corrections" of stories or faith positions that were initially presented without religious political implications, but which were required by the new situation of dialogue, became commonplace in Medina is attested by the intake of Jewish creeds in the Qur'anic horizon. In the short sura 112, we even witness an offer of consensus to the Jewish hearers, while the Nicene Christian confession of divine sonhood is rigorously paraphrased in the sense of a negative theology, so that a clear negation is offered to the Christians.[106] The new forms of the community's religious credos that emerge, above all the creed formulated in sura 112, may have arisen out of the debates with Jewish interlocutors, just as the Fātiḥa was due to inner-community reflection over Christian forms of worship circulating within the area.[107]

This kind of emergence of cultic forms from the negotiation of Jewish traditions, which is typical for the Medinan context, is reflected in a particularly strikingly mode in the shaping of the two high feasts that were institutionalized during the Medinan period. The Ramadan month of fasting, typologically a repentance festival, clearly developed out of the nucleus of the ʿAshūrāʾ fast, an adaptation of the rites of the Jewish day of atonement, Yom Kippur.[108] Shlomo Dov Goitein succeeded in finding clear traces of the Yom Kippur liturgy, above all the repentance litany, in Q 2:186, a verse that forms part of the Ramadan legislations of Q 2:183–187. But what is striking above all is a close connection to the role of Moses in salvific history, reflected in the etiology of Ramadan, which is founded on the reception of the *furqān*, "the deliverance / delivering decision" (Q 2:184). Just as Moses received the scripture and the deliverance, *furqān* (Q 2:52), so these

105. Nagel, *Medinensische Einschübe*, 113–127.
106. Cf. chap. 13, 477–480.
107. Neuwirth, "Sūrat al-Fātiḥa."
108. Goitein, "The Muslim Month of Fasting"; cf. also chap. 9, 410–415.

two distinctions are also granted to the Prophet, who not only received the scripture, the Qur'an, but also like Moses was able to deliver his community thanks to divine intervention from the greatest danger—namely, in the battle of Badr, which is evoked in Q 8:42–43. These distinctions are remembered in Ramadan.

While the Ramadan month of fasting, which is marked strongly by liturgy, is linked in no small measure to older liturgical models such as the repentance liturgy cited by Goitein,[109] the pilgrimage festival, although closely related typologically to the Jewish pilgrimage for the Feast of Tabernacles (*ḥag ha-sukkot*), presents itself rather as a reform of ancient Arabian rites. In the case of the pilgrimage, which had already taken shape in pre-Islamic times, and which seems to be a pure festival of the change of seasons,[110] a salvific historical interpretation was provided. It focuses on the person of Abraham, which in the local tradition was already linked to the Meccan sanctuary, and refers the duty of the pilgrimage—Q 22:27–29—back to him. At the same time, it is he who in a prayer—Q 2:127–129—predicts the appearance of a Prophet of writing, and thus the emergence of verbal worship at the Kaaba. The Abraham connection works in two ways: on the one hand, it is directed against the Jews' claim of special godliness in recognition of the piety of Abraham—Abraham's demand for the privileges for his descendants, Q 2:124, is decided negatively—and, on the other, it establishes an opposing tradition, which claims that the first son of Abraham, Ismail, the forefather of the Arabs, participated synergetically, in place of the biblical Isaac, in the founding of the sanctuary by Abraham.[111]

6.6.3 *Summary*

With the appearance of the long sura, there arose for the first time a discrepancy between the textual unit of the sura and its oral performance in a ritual setting: the long suras as such are too long to serve a cultic function within a single service. For the *ritual* part of the prayer service, short suras or verse groups are required; in the *service* part, the sermon-like "oratory suras" proved more suitable for the liturgically framed communications. Thus, the need for a complex form of verbal service involving polythematic compositions such as were common in Mecca was no longer present. In addition, the short Meccan suras, which continued to be recited, fulfilled an important liturgical purpose. Whether because sufficient structured performance texts already existed by that time or because formal emphases other than the liturgical became more important, in the Medinan sura types we no longer see the response to an expectation of a complex prayer service developed around salvific historical memory at its center.

109. Ibid.

110. Wellhausen, *Reste*.

111. Cf. chap. 11, 394–395. On the foundation of the holy site, see especially Witztum, "The Foundations of the House"; Sinai, *Studien zur frühen Koraninterpretation*.

New forms, which no longer constitute a literary genre, such as citations of legislation, which are unfamiliar in terms of their genre and structure, replace the old compositions. This turn toward simpler forms initiates the path toward the erosion of the literarily through-composed sura. Once individual texts could be excerpted from the long suras without particularly violent intervention, it was only a short step to the pericopizing of the Qur'an, which would later become common in Islamic worship: the excerpting of texts for recitation from the longer suras based solely on considerations of the desired content or extent. Whether or not this praxis goes back to the time of the Prophet's ministry, in any case the Qur'an contains, in the "compromise form" of the long sura, the formula for the dissolution of its own compositions.

6.7 From Qur'an to Islamic Cult

The simplicity of Islamic cult in its finally fixed form, the fact that both the daily *ṣalāh* and the Friday service focus on the ritual rather than verbal expression of the worshipper, has challenged scholars time and again. Shlomo Dov Goitein[112] attempted to explain this, above all, assuming that this format served the needs of an audience that took shape in Medina after the wars of conquest, which had scarcely any previous religious formation. A simple ritual would have met the needs of this new audience. The new believers required a simple cult. Eugen Mittwoch[113] and Carl Heinrich Becker,[114] who both investigated the structure of the Friday service, also considered the conditions after the first wave of conquest to have been decisive in its formation. Becker recognized clear reflections of a Christian liturgy in the Friday service, while Mittwoch finds Jewish liturgical reflections instead. The Friday service, it is true, can only be explained in the details of its final form by its encounter with the cultic forms of the two older religions. But if we follow the evidence of the Qur'an itself, both substantial elements, the sermon on the one hand and the *ṣalāh* at the close of the ceremony on the other, already stem from an intrinsically Qur'anic (in the case of the *ṣalāh* even pre-Qur'anic) development. Thus, the decisive question remains unanswered: Why is the final form of the verbal service in Islam comparably plain—why is it not closer to the Jewish-Christian structure, that is, a typologically more diversified form of worship?

The development sketched earlier makes the whole problem appear much more complex. After all, what was described is a move from simpler to more complex forms, from a cult determined by ritual in the beginning to one determined by verbal service in later Mecca, which in the end becomes once more

112. Goitein, "Friday Worship."
113. Goitein, "Friday Worship."
114. Becker, "Zur Geschichte des islamischen Kultus."

simplified, still in the lifetime of the Prophet, resulting in a combination of ritual and a sermon-like oration.

Let us once more recapitulate the hypotheses presented here regarding the development of canon and ritual: The pre-Islamic *ṣalāh* rites at the Kaaba were adopted as the framework for the liturgical recitation of the Qur'an, which constituted the initial stage of a verbal service. The new practice was dignified and legitimized through its performance in a particular, revered space and at specific times of day that were considered to be auspicious. The early suras verbally imitate, so to speak, the basic pattern of the rites, translating the fast and rhythmical repetition of gestures into verbal linguistic forms, repetitive rhymed prose. But the practice of a shared cult of the pagan Meccans and the nascent community did not last long; the believers soon relinquished the customary prayer times, and thus oriented themselves more closely to biblical models. Formally, the recitation texts developed beyond their ritual frames, constituting, from the middle Meccan period, text ensembles that clearly recall in structure the monotheistic prayer services. The consciousness of participating in a "scripture" into which the stream of relevant tradition merged, opened their eyes to history, and furthermore allowed them to assimilate as their own the memory of the followers of the two older religions, who were already living in a scriptural culture. This new orientation manifested itself in the new genre of the "history sura," which can be understood as a reflection of the Jewish and Christian verbal service, in which the salvific history of the Banū Isrāʾīl, and especially the leadership of Moses, plays an essential role. History, or, in the late Meccan suras that do not contain narratives, the interpretation of history, is clearly the backbone of these suras, which were composed of paraenetic exhortation and narrative with a view to being recited. The "scripture," as the emblem of the transcendent God and with it the consciousness of a stream of tradition that had incorporated the individual's experience of a divine power exerted in history, which now finds its first expression and pronouncement in Arabic, asserts a new conception of time. This concept of time is no longer cyclical and predetermined, but rather linear and open to human intervention. Perception expanded not only into times past but into the faraway space of the other recipients of scripture, whose ritual center was even adopted as the *qibla*. Thus Jerusalem took the place of Mecca, which for the community had evolved into a space of inner exile.

Later, the more the proclaimer came to occupy a position of authority alongside the text with the aura of a divinely authorized dignitary, and the more the community approached the models of the older faith communities, the more urgent it became to interpret the present through sermon-like paraenesis. In Medina, the resetting of the ritual center adopted from the "other" religions by the community's own inherited local sanctuary and the readopting of the pilgrimage that is so significant from pre-Islamic ritual practices indicate the erosion of the erstwhile significance of the memory inherited from the Banū Isrāʾīl.

All these developments are linked to the change in orientation from a verbal service in the Jewish and Christian vein to more ritual forms of service. The emphasis on Abraham's founding of the rites endowed the emerging community with additional weight as against the piety of the Banū Isrāʾīl and their Jewish and Christian heirs, which had been considered in Mecca as exemplary and had found expression in the complex "history suras." But not only their particular figures of memory that had become ambivalent through the real history of events but equally the community's own experiences were henceforth denied narrative exposition. The emerging "scripture" indeed undergoes a completion, and the collation of even isolated groups of verses was taken care of in the long suras. However, the last phase of Qur'anic genesis was not exploited to mythologize past experience of achievement; its purpose was not to fix historical recollection, but rather to interpret the present through oral proclamation and to provide reassurance of divine guidance in the future. The two tenets are pursued and documented by the oratory suras.

The short *ṣalāh* suras, closely connected to the rites, have accompanied the entire process (some, like Q 78:20, even undergo Medinan expansions); they thus shaped the post-Qur'anic notion of the pericope, the text selection suited for prayer consisting of a short verse group that was easy to memorize. As for the notion of the sura, which for the proclaimer of the Qur'an had been a significant organizing factor for the composition of recitation units intended as such, little remains beyond its relevance for Qur'anic philology, as a historically inherited textual demarcation, without notable practical consequences for the reception.

If we find the suras, in spite of all this, appearing in the final text canon as distinct units marked by the basmala, this fact does not reflect the practice contemporary to the final redaction, of the liberal use of the Qur'an as a book of pericopes. On the contrary, it directly acknowledges the claim to canonicity raised by the transmitted shape of the Qur'an that had evolved long before. It is true that a continuous text oriented transparently according to the history of creation and the development of the monotheist faith did not evolve—after all it was not a theological school that determined the conclusion of textual growth and its definitive ordering, but rather external circumstances. However, while the textual stock extant at the time of the final redaction was arranged into a corpus according to external, even mechanical criteria, it is impossible to overlook the signs of an elementary care employed to create a consummate scripture: the Qur'an is opened by a "proem"—the Fātiḥa, a text that does not belong to the genre of the sura—and is concluded by a kind of colophon, with the apotropaic gestures of the two last suras, 113 and 114. The actual corpus thus begins[115] with the evocation

115. The fact that the first and final two suras were taken up in the Koran is thanks to the redaction based on the Uthmanic textual material alson, as the suras lack in the reports about the pre-canonical codex of Ibn Masʿūd; see Jeffery, *Materials*, pg. 23. Cf. ch. 3, pg. 109–113.

of writing followed by a short Islamic catechism: *alif lām mīm dhālika l-kitābu lā rayba fīhi hudan li-l-muttaqīn*, "Alif lam mim. That is the scripture—no doubt is in it—a right guidance for the God-fearing" (Q 2:1–2), and ends with a text that, like its liturgical model, the Shemaʿ Yisraʾel,[116] has compressed the confession of God's unity—both as a statement and as an emphatic motto—into the most urgent formula possible: *qul huwa llāhu aḥad*, "Say: he is God, one!" (Q 112:1).

The question, raised by Ludwig Ammann, about the exogenous or endogenous dynamic in the formation of cult is answered differently in our survey of the Qur'an than in his work: the development of cult is surely not to be explained through the pagan and the pre-Islamic alone, even if one gives due consideration to the "taking over of foreign forms." The sura structure, which for some time reflected the shape of Jewish/Christian service and which was gradually formed in accordance with these services, should have been due to a living experience of such services, not to mere hearsay about them. One should therefore assume already for the Meccan periods the presence of a hearership that was formed in monotheism. For them, we should presuppose that the Lord's Prayer or the service Introitus, the Christian equivalents to the Fātiḥa, was certainly already a part of their religious formation, as was the wording of the Jewish credo Shemaʿ Yisraʾel, which is audible in sura 112, familiar to the Medinan hearers. The oscillation between different forms of service, at first determined by ancient Arabic rites, then the dominant three-part monotheistic worship of the suras of the middle and late Meccan period, and finally the refocusing on ritual in Medina, where the ritually determined performance of the *ḥajj* is reestablished—all this does not indicate a development initiated by "foreign patterns of meaning" but rather a continuous negotiation of forms of worship within the community itself, which joined interlocutors of diverse provenance and orientation, to construct a shared identity.

116. On the text cf. chap. 13, 477–480.

7

Stages of Communal Formation in the Early Meccan Period

7.1 Communal Engagements with Local Traditions: Successively Pursued Discourses

If one assumes that the Qur'an is a document of a communal formation, and that it thus exhibits important phases of inner-communal debate, then one should seek to understand the proclamation as it developed through the sequence of theological, ethical, liturgical, and other discourses that engaged the early community. But how can this sequence be determined? Attempts at a diachronic reading of the Qur'an up to now have been based on the Sira,[1] which sketches a broad panorama of the proclamation, without however including the communal engagement with older religious cultures into its scope. As a rule, however, the Qur'an was assumed to be a closed scripture, so that researchers limited themselves to surveying anthologically documentary evidence on individual themes,[2] without asking questions of development. It is true, even in the present attempt to read the Qur'an diachronically and without exegetical backing, as a communication process against the background of the traditions preceding it, that one enters into necessary compromises. Indeed, the chronology that is chosen as a starting point, which has been worked out in critical research, relies for its most basic data (e.g., the time spans of the proclamation, the two milieus of communal formation, the *hijra*) on the Sira tradition, it thus remains hypothetical to some degree.[3] But the probability of this chronology itself, and of the theses derived from it, is bolstered fundamentally once investigations into the individual discourses can substantiate a clear sequence, or indeed an irreversible development.[4]

In relation to this sequence of discourses, the early Meccan development can be divided heuristically into a number of phases, which will be given in overview. In the foreground initially stand ideas such as consolation of the Prophet and the

1. Cf. Watt, *Muhammad at Mecca*; Watt, *Muhammad in Medina*; Paret, *Mohammed und der Koran*; Cragg, *The Event of the Qur'ān*.

2. Cf. Rahman, *Major Themes*; Jomier, *Bible and the Koran*; Jomier, *Great Themes*. Exceptions are Robinson, *Discovering the Qur'ān*, and Marshall, *God, Muhammad and the Unbelievers*.

3. The sura sequence constructed by Nöldeke, on the basis of preliminary work by Weil, is based on a critical examination of the Islamic exegetical tradition, see Nöldeke, *GdQ*, 1:58–234; cf. chap. 5, 163–168.

4. See now the theoretical reflections on the possibilities for reconstructing the chronology in Sinai, *Studien zur frühen Koraninterpretation*, 59–74.

divine promise of loyalty, "assurance of providence," formulated in texts that rely to a large degree on psalmic models. But in the same early Meccan period, other texts already reflect the prophetic vocation of the proclaimer, which imposes on him the special office of warning of the Final Judgment, bringing to the fore the prospect of a "withdrawal of providence," the apocalyptical loosing of the cosmos and the judgment in the hereafter. These short early Meccan texts standing in proximity to each other operate with similar formal means. Orienting themselves primarily to the needs of the individual pious man embodied in the exemplary figure of the proclaimer, they quickly become the liturgical inventory of the community members at large, who continuously recall the texts already extant in their own ceremonies of recitation.[5] Thus, for this early phase, the two discourses of "consolation"/ "assurance of providence" and "prophetic warning of the judgment," can be seen as the lowest common denominators of the communal debates. Both discourses make use of topoi: in the consolation, these often refer back to the Psalms, while in the case of the warning of judgment they evoke Christian-monastic sermon topics,[6] reformulating these in an innovative way. They construct new image complexes, which not only bring together exclusively biblical or post-biblical traditions but also integrate the local social experience transmitted in the indigenous ancient Arab society. This applies especially to the descriptions of the hereafter—thus for example, a central Bedouin virtue, excessive generosity with hospitality at its center, is subverted into the counter-image of the entertainment of the damned, introduced by cynical toasts with nauseating meals in hell.[7] Also, the reflections over the "peoples gone by," *al-umam al-khāliya*, which since John Wansbrough have been adduced as evidence for the presence of older monotheistic topoi in the Qur'an,[8] are not merely biblical reminiscences in the Qur'an, but rather display a reinterpretation of a motif treated in ancient Arabic poetry, which ultimately gives form to the Late Antique *ubi sunt* complaint against transitoriness.[9]

A third discourse revolves around a particular creation theology, the interpretation of creation as a sign system of God. The praise of creation is indeed already a topos of the Psalms, but in the Qur'an it is repurposed into an argument in the debate about God's omnipotence and power to resurrect. The early Meccan suras develop an elaborate new, epistemically oriented interpretation of creation, to which the later suras will refer time and again. One could certainly cite further relevant themes in the early Meccan suras, for example, the "reversal" of the conception of time from a cyclical to a linear, eschatologically directed time—a

5. This persistent continuation of use can be deduced from the later inserted expansions of many early suras; cf. chap. 6, 231–233.

6. Andrae, *Person Muhammads*; Andrae, *Ursprung*; Andrae, *Mohammad*.

7. Cf. chap. 5, 176–178.

8. Wansbrough, *Quranic Studies*, 21–27.

9. Becker, "Ubi sunt qui ante nos in mundo fuere."

debate that was carried out not for its own sake but rather as a part of the greater discourse about judgment. The attempt undertaken here to pursue discourses following each other in sequence intentionally restricts itself only to the most apparent developments.

To ground this method of the definition of dominant discourses, which developed their own concomitant formal structures, one can refer to a new practice in biblical scholarship, which speaks in this context of "rhetorolects": "With the help of three literary genres, biographical-historical gospels, letters, and apocalyptics," the New Testament scholar Vernon K. Robbins writes, "the Christians of the first century wove six socio-rhetorical discourse forms, wisdom miracles, prophetics, sufferings of death, apocalypse, and creation, into a discourse form capable of connection, which would become canonical for the Christians of the Mediterranean world. . . . In the socio-rhetorical model, every particular discourse represents a "rhetorolect," which constitutes itself through particular topoi, discourse figures, and formulas."[10] If one adapts this model to the Qur'an, then it is the discourses we have cited—consolation and assurance of providence, warning of the judgment, and reflection on the signs of God in creation and scripture, followed by additional discourses in the middle and late Meccan time—which would each form a rhetorolect. As in the model of biblical scholarship, here too it is the recognition of the topoi, discourse figures, and formulas bound up with the discourse that makes it possible to explore the epistemic potential of the respective rhetorolects/discourses. But in contrast to this example, in which the rhetorolects stand next to each other as elements of a corpus composed in writing, in the diachronic investigation of the Qur'an we are dealing with the development of the individual discourses out of the ones that precede them.

7.2 Psalmic Piety

7.2.1 Consolation

The thesis that the Qur'anic development can be understood as a sequence of differing theological, ethical, liturgical, and other discourses that captivated the proclaimer and community should be slightly modified for the beginning phase. The early Meccan suras do not make much reference to communal issues and, viewed formally, are in the earliest phase dialogues between God and an exemplary pious man[11]—addressed directly in second-person informal address, very much in the style of individual psalms, where the complaint of the godlessness of the opponents and the divine consolation experienced by the psalmist stand at the center. The suras 93, 94, and 108 have been rightfully designated "suras of

10. Robbins, Newby, "Prolegomenon," 31.

11. On attempts to identify the oldest suras, see primarily Birkeland, *The Lord Guideth*; see also the review in Paret, "Leitgedanken." See also now critically Sinai, "Qur'an as Process."

consolation."[12] Characteristic for the text strategies applied in this phase is sura 93, *al-ḍuḥā*, "the Bright Day":

wa-l-ḍuḥā
wa-l-layli idhā sajā

mā waddaʿaka rabbuka wa-mā qalā
wa- la-l-ākhiratu khayrun laka mina l-ūlā
wa-la-sawfa yuʿṭīka rabbuka fa-tarḍā

a-lam yajidka yatīman fa-awā
wa-wajadaka ḍāllan fa-hadā
wa-wajadaka ʿāʾilan fa-aghnā

fa-ammā l-yatīma fa-lā taqhar
wa-ammā l-sāʾila fa-lā tanhar
wa-ammā bi-niʿmati rabbika fa-ḥaddith

By the bright day.
By the night when it settles.

Your Lord has not abandoned or disdained you.
The last will be better for you than the first.
Your Lord will give to you, and you will be content.

Did he not find you an orphan and shelter you?
Did he not find you going astray and guide you?
Did he not find you in need and enrich you?

The orphan you must not aggrieve,
the beggar you must not revile,
and the grace of your Lord, proclaim it!

The short text does not stand alone typologically. It follows the typical scheme for the consolation suras (suras 93, 94, and 108):[13] experience of divine worship (missing in suras 94 and 108), followed by recollection of a lack, culminating in a promise of fulfillment or a summoning to divine services.[14] The time *al-ḍuḥā* mentioned at the start, "the bright day," is not to be understood purely chronometrically, but rather represents time employed liturgically. For with the initial evocation of the daylight, we find an evocation of a time of day at which, according to Uri Rubin, prayers were made,[15] both in pagan cultic practice and during the early phases of the communal development—a type of worship to

12. Sinai, "Qur'an as Process," 428.
13. Cf. chap. 5, 180–182.
14. On these suras: Neuwirth, "Images and Metaphors."
15. Rubin, "Morning and Evening Prayers."

which the sura stands in close relation in content, awakening through recitation (*fa-haddith!*) the remembrance of received consolation, and thus constituting an expression of thanks. The night which comes to an end with the onset of light is mentioned as a second phase of time, it was perhaps spent in vigils (see Q 73:1–4, and cf. Q 92:1–2, 91:1.4, 89:1.4, 81:17–18, 74:33–34). The psalter refers also to such times as relevant to worship, such as Ps 119:55 ("I have remembered thy name at night"), Ps 119:62 ("At midnight I rise to praise you") and Ps 119:147 ("Already at dawn I rise and call"). A resonance in sura 93 of the experience of prayer exercises is suggested by the pronouncement following the oaths (verses 3–5), through which a new consciousness is reached. An apparently tormenting apprehension has been dissipated: "Your Lord has neither abandoned nor disdained you." This too is a psalmic topos: "For he has not disdained and loathed to have mercy on the poor" (Ps 22:25). Consolatory expectations are raised: "The last will be better than the first for you," and these expectations culminate in the hoped-for condition of spiritual fulfillment: "Your Lord will give to you, so that you are satisfied"—a thought that has its parallel in the Psalms, although without eschatological connotation: "He will give to you what your heart wishes" (Ps 20:5).

What is more, the subject of the paraenetic remembrance in verses 6–8 is an earlier achieved passage from a state of lacking to one of fulfillment. The benefactions thus received obligate one to engage in corresponding behavior toward others. Harris Birkeland has attempted to place the sura biographically into the vita of the proclaimer.[16] His position—presented as in agreement with the Islamic tradition[17]—is certainly not to be dismissed out of hand, but his detailed identification of the individual pronouncements of the sura with concrete biographical stages of the proclaimer—an orphan's fate, liberation from low social standing through rich marriage, and so on—carries the danger of narrowing the significance of the text. For the recalled life situations of lack and the consoling declaration of the persisting nearness of God also recall verses from the Psalms,[18] a text corpus whose importance as a model is reflected throughout the entire sura. For example, one can compare to Q 93:9–1 a Psalm of thanks (Psalm 9), the fourteenth verse of which even contains the thought figure of the obligation of "further telling" about the received benefaction: "Lord, be gracious to me, see my misery, lift me up out of the torrent of death, so that I may tell of all your glorious deeds" (Ps 9:14). The psalmically stamped Qur'an text not only aims to convince through the voice of the speaker but also promises validity as a liturgical text for other pious men.

16. Birkeland, *The Lord Guideth*, 37.

17. Raven, "Sira and the Qur'an."

18. Rippin, "Desiring the Face of God," also assumes a topos here, but he does not contextualize his assessment within the Qur'anic proclamation, assuming rather a later compilation of the Qur'an that doesn't undergo any development.

The closing verse, taking up the task of drawing the consequences of the personally experienced right guidance—just as verse 9, on the orphans, illustrates consequences out of verse 6. Verse 10, on the poor, which illustrates the consequences from verse 8, shows the way in which divine right guidance (*hudan*, verse 7) will be given to others: through recitation: *wa-ammā bi-niʿmati rabbika fa-ḥaddith*, "And the grace of your Lord, proclaim it!" Thus, the circle closes. The summons to liturgical recitation at the close refers back again to the experience of night and morning worship that was evoked at the start, with the vigils and *ḍuḥā* prayer. To accept the point that a real-life situation of the proclaimer is depicted here does not exclude consideration of the psalmic text referentiality. The sura integrates important psalmic topoi of the worship of God but is also an expression of a wholly new experience that, as near as it comes to that of the psalmist, also creates its own distinct kind of assurance out of eschatological expectations (verse 4).

It is interesting that this text, with its social references to a context shared with the pagan Meccans, also draws on local rhetorical strategies. In order to authorize his already markedly monotheistic pronouncements about the nearness of the personal God, the proclaimer makes use of ancient pagan Arabic stylistic means for the production of authority: he employs formally the oath series characteristic of the ancient Arabian seer,[19] of which the first object, the morning prayer time, appeals to the cultic practices of the community, including present pagan hearers. Without this introduction, the text could appear to be a personal inner monologue of a pious man or of the proclaimer, but through the oath it obtains a cultic coding that creates a virtual connection to other participants in cult.

7.2.2 *Assurance of Providence*

Alongside these individual addresses stand some that are already collective. They appear above all in two complete suras, 105 and 106, which, like the consolation suras, still primarily have the character of an exhortative appeal, and thus do not yet set out to invalidate the objections of opponents that will later become so striking, and that first emerge from the threat of the Final Judgment that is tied up with the Prophetic calling of the proclaimer. Gottfried Müller has recently pointed to the relevance of these suras for the developmental history of the text, claiming that the message of divine caretaking must proceed necessarily the message of the judgment: "To stipulate the point of departure in the thought of the threat of judgment would be problematic in that God, who shows himself inimical in the threat, must first have manifested himself as caring. Before God retreats, he must have been there, to be experienced in his presence; he must have been recognized in his initiatives that embrace mankind."[20] Müller connects this

19. Cf. chap. 12, 437–440.
20. Müller, "Die Barmherzigkeit Gottes," 342.

divine assurance with an already existing covenant with God: "The initial point is not the nothing of man before the being and totality of the Deity . . . , but rather the covenant, in other words, the Qurashite federation, which understood itself as a covenant with God, as *ḥums*, and which establishes the covenant communication with God in the form of an historical account. . . . The Qur'anic relationship to God constitutes itself in the idea of election."[21] Suras 105 and 106 will be briefly presented:

Sura 105, *al-fīl*
a-lam tara kayfa faʿala rabbuka bi-aṣḥābi l-fīl
a-lam yajʿal kaydahum fī taḍlīl
wa-arsala ʿalayhim ṭayran abābīl
tarmīhim bi-hijāratin min sijjīl
fa-jaʿalahum ka-ʿaṣfin maʾkūl

The Elephant
Do you not see what your Lord has done to the people of the elephant?
Did he not make their scheming into error,
and send upon them flocks of birds
and throw against them stones of burned clay
and turn them into eaten grass?

In the center of the sura is the annihilation of an aggressor who remains unnamed, in all his military power,[22] introduced as testimony of the omnipotence of the personal God worshiped by the proclaimer (*rabbuka*, "your Lord"). While the wording of the text might indicate nothing more than an exemplary divine punishment, a central event of local Meccan history is addressed here, which for the hearers apparently does not need to be connected explicitly to Mecca. On the basis of the numerous ancient poetic citations gathered by Josef Horowitz that attest to the defeat of the Abyssinian army commander Abraha, it should be assumed "that already in pre-Islamic times in Mecca, the narrative of a train of Abyssinians accompanied by an elephant was widespread, and the Islamic tradition rightly referred sura 105 back to this."[23] The short Qur'anic text thematizes an event of great significance: Uri Rubin,[24] who reconstructed the course of the Abraha campaign from the traditional literature, was able to show how the defeat that is evoked here, of Abraha, who had to retreat from Mecca empty-handed, was a turning point for the position of the Meccans on the peninsula, who due to this event could first establish themselves as the protecting power of a cultic center and dispense with the contracts with other tribes that had previously been

21. Ibid., 342–346.
22. On the historical background, see Kister, "Campaign of Ḥulubān," and Shahid, "People of the Elephant."
23. Horovitz, *Koranische Untersuchungen*, 96–98.
24. Rubin, "Īlāf."

vital for assuring their livelihood. This background restores the historical dimension to the modest evocation of the event.

Yet the event is not simply reported in the sura but receives a new interpretation: with the entrance of God (*rabbuka*, "your Lord") into the role of the main actor of the narrated story; the local tradition about the event is raised to an incident of salvation history serving to prove the omnipotence of the one God as the Lord of history. The closing verse works in a particularly expressive way, through its contrast between the approaching aggressors with their majestic elephant and the traces that finally remain from them, which are as void as chaff or "eaten grass."

The salvation historical incorporation of local tradition is made even more plausible through the recourse to a psalmic topos: also in Ps 37:1, the image of becoming null and void is depicted in the pastoral metaphor "Wither like the green of the herb;" cf. also Ps 58:7, with its language of "withering like the grass on the road." With the appeal to the significance of the event, recognized by both the believers and the other listeners, local history is reclaimed as part of salvation history.

This sura is followed by a further recollection of divine benefactions bestowed on the home city of the proclaimer.

> Sura 106, *Quraysh*
> *li-īlāfi Quraysh*
> *īlāfihim riḥlata l-shitāʾi wa-l-ṣayf*
> *fa-l-yaʿbadū rabba hādhā l-bayt*
> *alladhī aṭʿamahum min jūʿin*
>   *wa-āmanahum min khawf*
>
> Because of the relief of the Quraysh,
> their relief from the winter and summer caravan trains,
> they should serve the Lord of this house
> who guards them from hunger and protects them from fear.

This syntactically extraordinary sura beginning has provoked varying interpretations, which can only now be settled due to the investigation of the historical background by Uri Rubin.[25] *Īlāf (Allāh)* is employed in some poetic instances[26] as a verbal noun in the sense of "grant of security, protection of God," and thus divine relief (from worries and fears). In the sura, *īlāf* is to be understood correspondingly,[27] where "relief" can indicate either caravan journeys

25. Rubin, "Īlāf." Rubin's study established the claim, based on its own criteria, that sura 106 together with the preceding sura should make up an integral text, yielding the translation for the beginning verses "So that the Quraysh bring together their summer and winter caravans."

26. Kister, "Mecca," 108.

27. The text has long been interpreted in scholarship as a trade agreement between the Meccans and the surrounding tribes, who arranged a winter expedition to Yemen, Abyssinia, and Iraq and a summer expedition to Syria; thus Birkeland, *The Lord Guideth*, 123; Kister, "Mecca," 121; alternatively, Crone, *Meccan Trade*.

that have become superfluous on account of the general recognition of the sanctuary after the defeat of the Abyssinians or the new possibility to travel unmolested. The following simple sequence of ideas is thus yielded: an instigation of liturgical practices is derived from the memory of having been granted social privilege, further strengthened by two divine benefactions named in the closing verse: material preservation, and the inviolability and therefore safety of Mecca, guaranteed by the sacral aura of the sanctuary (cf. Q 95:3).[28] The sura, which culminates in an appeal to keep the cultic allegiance of the Meccans (verse 3: "they should serve . . . "), refers to what is familiar to the hearers: their privilege, recognized across tribal boundaries, as residents of a sanctuary. But what is evoked here is not familiar in its entirety; rather, a decisive new thought is suggested: the God worshiped in the Kaaba ("the Lord of this house") is brought together as one with the personal God of the proclaimer, who is also the Lord of history. It is not new cultic services that are required in verse 3, but rather the recognition of the power of the one God that extends into the social life of the collective.

It is these very early suras, which derive the confidence in God's providence from history, that are most closely related to the history psalms. It is striking, as will be demonstrated, that in later texts of the Qur'an, history is seen from a wholly different perspective.

7.3 Excursus: Are the Early Meccan Suras Biographical of the Prophet?

Gottfried Müller assigns the texts presented here to a "pre-prophetic" phase. They give the impression of "a history, which understands itself as a history in rise, a leading out, a liberation, from a past history, out of which man draws his hope and confidence." In opposition to this stands the "actual Prophetic speech of the proclaimer," with which "the area of the told or tellable history is left behind."[29] Müller, along with other researchers,[30] sees this change accomplished in sura 96, which is the first revelation according to tradition, and which is read as a Prophet's initiation. In order to be interpreted in this way, and Müller's reading here is no exception, the sura must be placed within the narrative frame given by the Sira/Prophetic biography, where Muhammad experiences a vision in a cave on Mount Ḥirāʾ, in which he is exhorted to recite or "read" from a writing unrolled before him. The scenario follows the model of the biblical calls to prophethood (one can compare for example Is 6:6–8 or Is 1:6–9), where the

28. This external perspective on Mecca as a place of privilege associated with prestige and respect is evinced also in ancient Arabic verse by Müller, "Die Barmherzigkeit Gottes," 346.

29. Müller, "Die Barmherzigkeit Gottes," 357.

30. Bobzin, *Koran*; Paret, *Muhammed und der Koran*.

"novice" first declares himself not to be capable to receive the call and is then given the assignment again with greater emphasis until he accepts it.

But this "hagiographic" presentation in the Sira contradicts the unambiguous statements of the Qur'an text. The notion that this scenario is reflected in the beginning verses of sura 96 is to be entirely excluded on several grounds. That sura 96 is constantly adduced as evidence of the calling to prophethood can be explained linguistically—from the etymological closeness between the designation of the message as *qur'ān* and the two imperatives that begin the sura, *iqra'*, "read out!, call out!" But precisely this opening formula, with its exhortation to cultic recitation, takes up a psalmic topos (cf. Ps 149:5 "Let them praise the name of God," cf. also the self-exhortation to praise in Ps 9:3 "I shall sing, Most High, your name"). Above all, the progress of the sura is incompatible with the interpretation in the sense of a prophetic initiation. Nothing in the sura recalls prophetic speech of the future. It belongs rather to the texts that give expression to gratitude.

What is new here, however, is that the text does not deal with a personal liberation (as in sura 93), or a salvific event affecting the collective (as in sura 105), but rather with the reception of scripture: in that participation in the divine scripture (verse 4) stands as the authority behind the act of the recitation, the sura documents a new position for the proclaimer: he, who on the basis of the previously recited eschatological texts already has opponents among his hearers (verses 9–14), can—emboldened by the scriptural authorization of his proclamation—meet them with self-consciousness. In light of the prophetical biographical interpretation, which simply ignores the progression of the sura in verses 6–19, it is of value to look more closely at the sura:

Sura 96, *al-'alaq*
iqra' bi-smi rabbika lladhī khalaq
khalaqa l-insāna min 'alaq
iqra' wa-rabbuka l-akram
alladhī 'allama bi-l-qalam
'allama l-insāna mā lam ya'lam
kallā inna l-insāna la-yatghā
an ra'āhu staghnā
inna ilā rabbika l-ruj'ā

a-ra'ayta lladhī yanhā
'abdan idhā ṣallā
a-ra'ayta in kāna 'alā l-hudā
aw amara bi-l-taqwā
a-ra'ayta in kadhdhaba wa-tawallā
a-lam ya'lam bi-anna llāha yarā

kallā la'in lam yantahi la-nasfa'an bi-l-nāṣiyah
nāṣiyatin kadhibatin khāṭi'ah
fal-yad'u nādiyah
sa-nad'u l-zabāniya

kallā lā tuṭi'hu wa-sjud wa-qtarib

The Clot
Recite, in the name of your Lord who created,
created man from a clot.

Recite, for your Lord is most bountiful
who taught with the pen,
taught man what he did not know.

And yet man is intemperate,
he thinks himself sufficient.
But to your Lord is the return.

What about the one who forbids
a worshipper as he prays?
Do you think he is guided right?
Does he command to piety?
Do you see he cries lies and turns away?
Does he not know that God is watching?

No!
If he does not stop, we will seize him by the forelock,
a lying, sinful forelock.
Let him summon his group,
We will summon the watchmen.

No! Do not obey him,
prostrate yourself, draw near!

The beginning part (verses 1–5) starts with an exhortation to worship[31] (as in Q 87:1–6), followed by a hymn in praise of God's power of creation and his initiation of mankind into the wisdom of revelation. The address "recite!" at the opening of the hymn itself, like "praise!" (*sabbiḥ*) in sura 81, is to be understood not as directed to an individual but universally, and corresponds in this function to *halleluyah*, "God be praised," which frequently occurs at the start of Psalms, which is similarly imperative. The conception of divine communication of wisdom as an act of generosity ("the generous," verse 3) belongs in the context

31. On the social parameters, see the attempt at reconstruction in chap. 6, 201–204.

of such psalmic exclamations as "I see the heaven, the work of your fingers, moon and stars, which you fix: what is man, that you think of him, the son of man, that you take him as yours?" (Ps 8:4–5), although in the Psalms, communication of wisdom itself does not belong to what is granted by God. The hymn that follows in the sura is composed in a particularly artful way. It stresses the two central thoughts of creation and teaching, through the stylistically striking figure of concatenation: verses 1–2 take up the word *khalaqa*, "create," in the prominent rhyme and again in the beginning position of the ensuing verse, while verses 4–5 put *ʿallama*, "teach," into corresponding focus. The exhortation *iqraʾ*, "recite," or "read" from verse 1 is taken up again anaphorically in verse 3. Such artful figures, which in the assumption of a text intended for silent reading would halt the procession of thought, presuppose the situation of a public reading.

It is not to be overlooked that the two divine benefactions taken as motivations for the recitation, creation and teaching, are set into a close relation by a stylistic highlighting with identical stylistic means. Their shared naming at the sura's beginning—as also in other early texts such as sura 95—form part of an argument for a new understanding of time. Divine creation and teaching mark the beginning of an eschatologically conceived, linear progression of time. Unlike in the cyclical model, it is no longer the beginning and end of man's lifetime that compose the two end-points of time's progression, but rather the primordial creation and the Final Judgment; time is now filled with eschatologically oriented divine teachings, for which account will be rendered on the Final Day. Man stands henceforth in an ethical responsibility. Even if the mentioning of God's scriptural wisdom, generously shared with mankind, stands in this text in no unambiguous relation to the communicated message, it still vouches for an association made by proclaimer and hearers already in early Meccan time, between authorized wisdom and scripture,[32] the participation in which entails ethical obligations.

What follows in the second part (verses 6–8) is a reprimand of man, whose high pride stands in sharp contrast to his humble origins from a clump of clotted blood (verse 2, *ʿalaq*). The reprimand also applies to the rejection of divine teaching by man, who would see himself as "independent" of God's generosity (Q 96:3 *al-akram*). The denial of divine creation and teaching does not, however, free him from his dependency, as the closing part demonstrates. With verses 9–14, the situation of prayer and perhaps also of recitation is made present: someone present disturbs the worship of a weaker fellow worshipper. The scene, occurring perhaps during the recitation, is commented upon at once: question is put ironically as to the ethical value of the authority of the apparently powerful opponent. A threat closes the scene, through God's comprehensive view into the event—this

32. Cf. Sinai, "Qur'ānic Self-Referentiality"

too is a psalmic topos (cf., for the perception of God as seeing and hearing, Ps 94:9: "He who plants the ear, should he not hear, He who forms the eye, should he not see?" or Ps 64:6: "They say: who sees us?"). The passage is characterized stylistically by its challenging questions, taken up again anaphorically in verses 9, 11, and 13: *a-raʾayta* . . . , "Have you seen . . . ?," or: "What do you think of . . . ?"

Although invectives and hindrances in worship are also not infrequent in the Psalms, here one can assume, in view of early Meccan treatments of the prayer situation elsewhere (Q 108:2; 107:5–6; 87:15; 75:31; 70:23, 34),[33] an imitation of lived reality, which then merges into a flash-forward to the Final Day in the following threat of punishment (verses 15–18). The threat appears first as a threat of social exposure through bodily disgrace, and recalls the punishment of "haters" that stands also at the end of the text in Ps 21;13: "Yes, you should seize them on the shoulder, with your knitting you should bind them together to their faces."; but it shows itself in the course of the sura to be eschatological: the wanton one is seized on the day of judgment by his forelock (as also in the later texts Q 55:41 and Q 11:56), apparently in order to be thrown into the fire. Sarcastically, he is encouraged to call his comrades for help, who will then be opposed by the "watchers," who remain enigmatic and therefore all the more threatening. This part of the sura is also directed to present hearers, and is therefore formed linguistically in a particularly artful way: verses 15–16 stress—again through concatenation, that is, through the repetition of the rhyme word in the beginning words of the following verse—the forelocks standing in for the person of the wanton one, symbolizing his social privilege, and by which his debasement is then confirmed.

The you-address (*lā tuṭiʿhu, iqtarib*, "do not obey him!," "draw near!") at the sura's end, Q 96:19, which refers back to the concrete scenario of the sura, may be directed expressly to the proclaimer. In favor of this notion, that here we do not have wholly text-referential speech, but rather reference is made to lived reality, we can cite the prayer situation introduced realistically in the sura. The final call, an exhortation with following call to worship, takes up again the call to recitation that stands at the sura's beginning.

What now remains of the traditional linking of the sura with a prophetic initiation? On the basis of the stringent thought sequence of the parts I and II, which build on each other, and their stylistic concatenation, we certainly cannot assume a secondary compilation. One cannot simply sever the parts of the text that follow on the call to recitation, and which do not thematize a mythic original scene, but rather an everyday situation. The resumption in the second part of the rhetorical figure of concatenation, which is characteristic of the first part, is further evidence for the unity and coherence of the parts. The sura thus belongs

33. Cf. chap. 6, 213–215.

to that type, which already reflects interactions between speakers and hearers—it thus cannot be the first instance of the proclamation. Here, as in other suras such as Q 104, in the tradition and in the Western research that follows it, prophetic biographical data have been derived from the Qur'anic text, which are then used with a circular logic to interpret the Qur'an.

7.3.1 . . . or Are the Early Suras Universal Testimonies of Psalmic Piety?

The early suras show structures that initially recall religious poetry; they contain meditations and self-reflection that, if they were not dressed in the you-form of inspiration, could represent the inner monologue of an exemplary pious man. In many cases, therefore, no certain judgment can be made about whether they refer primarily to the psychic situation of the proclaimer, or are primarily text-referential. But, in terms of method, it is never justified to import life information from the Sira into the sura text. We are on firm ground only where suras reflect their own reception through hearers. Early Meccan suras—already sura 96—become polyphonic texts, in which likeminded hearers as well as the proclaimer's opponents come to speak. Evocations of the hearers, which are too concrete to be understood text-referentially as biblical topoi, can be taken as depictions of the historical scenario of proclamation.

But the Qur'anic references to the Psalms are so numerous[34] that there can be no doubt that the Psalms had an inceptive formal molding effect on the Qur'an. As is known, the Psalms—unlike what is to be supposed for the Qur'an—are an expression of a rural society. It would be difficult without the Psalms to explain how images from farming (e.g., the fruit-bearing tree as image of the righteous), or from the vegetative cycle (the sprouting and then withering of grass as an image of the temporality of mankind), which dominate in the Psalms, should come to appear in the Qur'an. But in the Qur'an, the blessings of nature serve, somewhat differently from in the Psalms, as exhortations to human gratitude. Also, figures of thought such as the obligation to praise God derived from experienced benefactions, the merely putative power of man to hide his deeds before the view of God, the ongoing divine testing of man, but also God's showing him the way, are characteristic for both text corpora. In both, there is much language related to waking and praying at night, and of steadfast holding to the personally recognized truth of divine power in the face of a majority of deniers/liars. The ambivalence of man, his susceptibility to hubris and self-deception,[35] are present to the speakers of both text corpora. But above all, the psalmist and the proclaimer of the Qur'an are closely related in their emotional beholdenness to the nearness of their personal God, his face turned toward them.

34. First proven in Speyer, *Die biblischen Erzählungen im Qoran*, 447–449.
35. See Cragg, *The Event of the Qur'ān*, 95–109.

The psalter as a partial corpus of the Bible appears recognizably and explicitly in the Qur'an from an early point. Already the middle Meccan sura 17:55 mentions a scripture belonging to David named *zabūr* (Q 17:55; Q 21:105; Q 4:163). The Psalms thus stand as their own scripture, in a strict sense, alongside the Torah given to Moses (*al-tawrāh*) and the Gospel connected to Jesus (*al-injīl*)—without however being given status as an authoritative predecessor of the new proclamation. For certain particular pronouncements, the Qur'anic text appeals explicitly to the Psalms: *wa-la-qad katabnā fī l-zabūri min baʿdi l-dhikri anna l-arḍa yarithuhā ʿibādiya l-ṣāliḥūn*, "We have written in the Psalms—after praise: our righteous servants shall inherit the earth" (Q 21:105). The wording recalls Ps 37:29: *ṣaddiqim yireshu areṣ*, "the righteous shall inherit the earth." But the Psalms are present more as a liturgical typus than as a concrete text-form, so that for wide parts of the Qur'an text one can speak of a psalmic intertextuality. This is not difficult to explain: a liturgical piety imprinted by the Psalms is to be presumed as present within the Syrian church, which stretched into the region of the Arabian peninsula,[36] and particularly so in monastic circles, and it could have even had formative effects on members of the Qur'anic community.[37] Since there is no evidence for Arabic translations of the Psalms in the pre-Islamic period,[38] one must assume an oral, and ultimately also non-Arabic tradition for the communication of the Psalms to Arabic-speaking recipients. The explanation put forward in recent research of the designation "sura," which had never been adequately understood, as an "introductory psalm-recitation" would fit well with this intertextual presence of the Psalms in the early Qur'an: according to this thesis, *sūra* would be connected to the Syriac word *shūrāyā* "beginning," which in a liturgical context means, "the introduction of a reading by Psalm recitation."[39] Individual verse groups of the Psalms, which were in use in Christian services as liturgical "between-texts," may have become known by this term in relation of their function in worship, so that the early suras, similar to the Psalms, might have appeared as Arabic equivalents to these sorts of text. An already established Syriac liturgical concept would then have triggered the designation of a novel Qur'anic conception.

It would be inadequate, however, to simply see in the early Qur'an a replica of the Psalms. Although the earliest suras, still corresponding to a personal divine-human dialogue, are often praises or complaints similar to the Psalms, the eschatological expectation of the discourse gives a decisive new emphasis, whereby Psalm references are recast in the form of arguments.[40] Also, as comes out of the

36. Toral-Niehoff, "The ʿIbād in al-Ḥīra."
37. Griffith, "Christians"; Griffith, "Christian Lore and the Arabic Qur'an."
38. Schippers, "Psalms."
39. Brockelmann, *Lexicon Syriacum*, 488.
40. See chap. 13, 466–468.

examples of suras 105 and 106, a significant role is played in the early proclamation by the consciousness of the native sanctuary tradition, the significance of Mecca, and the historical memories connected with Mecca, and the relevance of ritual times. If these ideas also gradually fade into the background in the later Meccan period, they still remain as references, and reappear at the end of the development in Medina as a fundamental level of an increasingly complex perception of the sacred.

7.4 The Prophetic Office of Warning of the Judgment

7.4.1 A New Image of History

Yet there is a serious divergence between the early suras and the liturgical language characteristic of the Psalms: the clearly divergent image of history. For, although views back into history are frequent throughout the Qur'an, the perspective adopted toward this history, aside from the providential suras 105 and 106 on Mecca, is clearly pessimistic. A sequence of ancient peoples of the peninsula whose settlements now lie in ruins but still attest to their previous greatness, have fallen prey to collective annihilation—a divine punishment for their insubordination against the messenger sent to them to proclaim the unity of God, a punishment that they themselves have brought on themselves. But as much as these narratives, with their stereotyped character, recall psalmic catalogues of history, in which we find lists of God's acts of retribution against various enemies of the elected people, so strikingly do they lack the dimension of salvation that is central to the Psalms. Although the warner comes from among them, the divine infliction of the older peoples remains—unlike for the enemies of Israel—without salvation historical impact on any especially privileged people; the hearers of the proclamation are not "inheritors" of those saved in history. The emphasis of the "punishment legends" is thus different from that of the history Psalms. While the biblical references to history emphasize the saving acts of God in divine interventions that are proofs in themselves of his timeless loyalty and thus give rise to trust in a salvific future under God's covenant, the Qur'anic reports, insofar as they do not occur within the providence discourse of Mecca, remain without such promise. Certainly, they demonstrate divine justice, which punishes the sacrilege of rejecting the faith in one God with destruction. In that they also stress the survival of God's servants, they can also obtain implicitly a promise of loyalty from God, but they stand primarily to demonstrate divine power: the earthly punishment is above all an anticipation of the punishment awaiting all sacrilege at the Final Judgment.

In addition to their prominent tone of thanks and recurring praise of God in hymns and exhortations to praise, the early suras have yet another side: the threat of an inner-worldly catastrophe and of the Final Judgment. One could designate this double manifestation of divine working in rabbinic language God's *middat ha-raḥamim* and *middat ha-din*.[41] Gottfried Müller sees here the decisive turn in the early Meccan development: the

> opposition of two literary forms—the narrative report taken from one's own history, and the Prophetic proclamation transcending this history—is highly relevant. It affects . . . above all the experience of God Himself, who in the former has the trustworthiness of the originator of the people's and tribe's history, and in the latter unfolds the threat of death and thus . . . calls for a quite different kind of creed, the creed of one God, whose power and working can be deciphered . . . only once this threat has been realized. A creed that not only implies a partial improvement, but leads the way to an actual conversion.[42]

The question that arises in view of the approximately equal part played in Mecca by hymnic and eschatological suras, which of these two came first, thanks or the fear of the Final Day,[43] was answered by Harris Birkeland in favor of thanks, but this has met with little response in research. With Tor Andrae,[44] one can explain both the two basic contrasting attitudes in the suras equally by reference to the monastic piety of the time, where both fear of punishment and praise of God are central liturgical themes. Nonetheless, that Birkeland has named an important development in the genesis of the Qur'an by setting the consolation suras first becomes clear by way of Müller's thesis of the substantial novelty of what is given with the Prophetic speech. It is noteworthy that the two sura types are differentiated in a strikingly clear way: the positive "praise suras" extensively apply linguistic devices from monotheistic liturgical language that had long ago been introduced, attested by a wealth of Syriac loan words that were apparently already current in Arabic, while the depictions of the cosmic catastrophe draw not only lexically but above all stylistically and structurally on the ancient Arabic models of seers and soothsayers. Somewhat different is the dispersal of such coinages in the depictions of paradise and hell, already both well-known from monastic piety. Here, in the descriptions of paradise, we find Syriac-Christian conceptions alongside the predominant ancient Arabic features, while in descriptions of hell almost exclusively ancient Arabic images are employed.[45]

7.4.2 *The Loosing of the Cosmos and the Trial of Mankind*

It is in connection to the announcements of the judgment that the most rhythmically turbulent and phonetically striking suras take shape. Here, as nowhere else,

41. Grötzinger, "Middat ha-din."
42. Müller, "Die Barmherzigkeit Gottes," 358.
43. Birkeland, *The Lord Guideth.*
44. Andrae, *Mohammad.*
45. See chap 3, 125–127, and chap. 5, 176–181.

we find series of parallel conditional sentences (protasis) introduced with *idhā*/ *yawma* "if once / on the day when," arranged one after another, so that a massive tension is built up that is released only with the main clause, the apodosis, which closes the series. The semantic tension corresponds to the syntactic tension: only after the protasis has presented the loosing of the cosmos, mostly in a movement from above to below, can the apodosis introduce the turn that is so fateful for mankind, either consoling or utterly destroying: The scenario then splits into two contrasting parallel scenes, in which the blessed and the damned are exhibited in two diametrically opposite situations, presented against each other in a "double image."[46] An example is sura 84:1–6, 7–15, 16–25.

Sura 84, al-inshiqāq

idhā l-samāʾu nshaqqat
wa-adhinat li-rabbihā wa-ḥuqqat
wa-idhā l-arḍu muddat
wa-alqat mā fīhā wa-takhallat
wa-adhinat li-rabbihā wa-ḥuqqat
yā ayyuhā l-insānu innaka kādiḥun ilā rabbika kadḥan fa-mulāqīh

fa-ammā man ūtiya kitābahu bi-yamīnih
fa-sawfa yuḥāsabu ḥisāban yasīrā
wa-yanqalibu ilā ahlihi masrūrā
wa-ammā man ūtiya kitābahu warāʾa ẓahrih

fa-sawfa yadʿū thubūrā
wa-yaṣlā saʿīrā
innahu kāna fī ahlihi masrūrā
innahu ẓanna an lan yaḥūrā
balā inna rabbahu kāna bihi baṣīrā

fa-lā uqsimu bi-l-shafaq
wa-l-layli wa-mā wasaq
wa-l-qamari idhā ttasaq
la-tarkabanna ṭabaqan ʿan ṭabaq
fa-mā lahum lā yuʾminūn
wa-idhā quriʾa ʿalayhimu l-qurʾānu lā yasjudūn
bali lladhīna kafarū yukadhdhibūn
wa-llāhu aʿlamu bi-mā yūʿūn
fa-bashshirhum bi-ʿadhābin alīm
illā lladhīna āmanū wa-ʿamilū l-ṣāliḥāti
lahum ajrun ghayru mamnūn

46. Cf. the discussion of structural idiosyncrasies in chap. 5, 176–179.

The Splitting

I
When the sky is split,
and heeds to its Lord and is fit.
When the earth is distended,
and heaves and leaves what is in it,
and heeds to its Lord and is fit:
Man!
You press to your Lord struggling and will meet him.

He who is given his record in his right hand
he will be given an account that is light
and go to his people in joy.

He who is given his record behind his back
he will call out for doom
but be scorched by the blaze.

He was joyful with his people,
he thought he would never return.
But his Lord indeed could see.

No, I swear by the dusk!
By the night when it fills!
By the moon when it is full!
You will rise stage upon stage.
Why do they not believe,
and when the recitation is recited do not bow?
Those who do not believe cry lies.
God knows better what they gather,
so give them news of a terrible punishment
    except those who believe and do good,
    they have a reward unstinted.

An eschatological scenario of five verses, introduced by *idhā*, "when, once," occurring twice, opens the sura, describing the changes in heaven and earth, respectively. The heavens break open, the earth is leveled, and the human life-world is extinguished (verses 1–5). Both heaven and earth are personified and involved in mythical actions—the heavens flee and subject themselves to God, while the earth empties itself like a woman giving birth, in order to subject it-self similarly to God. In place of the elsewhere frequent description of the reaction of mankind to the dissolving of the cosmos ("the eschatological process"),[47]

47. For the demarcations and configurations of the individual thematic sections, cf. chap. 5, 174–180.

an address follows with a consoling tone to man, to whom the long-sought encounter with his Lord is announced (verse 6). As the following double image (verses 7–15) shows, this takes place on the Day of Judgment. The judgment scene itself is skipped over, and the immediately ensuing double image shows first the blessed, then the damned after their judgment has been carried out, the outcome of which is recognizable in the mode they receive their accounting. The ancient Near Eastern conception, frequently adduced in early Meccan time, that the divine scribes record the deeds of men,[48] is reified here in the form of concrete writings or books handed to the judged. In place of the elsewhere frequent assignment, ultimately oriented to scenes such as Mt 25:41ff, of the judged into people of the right and people of the left, it is now the concrete right or left hand into which the reckoning is handed. The beatific wage of the pious and the woes of the wicked are here indicated only through the joy of the pious (verse 9) and the distress of the frivolous (verse 11). As is frequent in the early suras, the two parts of the double image are equally proportioned. Verses 10–15 stand in a 1:2 relation to verses 7–9, the negative image being expanded through a flashback explaining the error of the condemned. Their downfall is due to their careless way of life and their frivolous disregarding of the message of judgment, without social accusations being made against them beyond the rejection of the central statement of belief of the proclaimer.

The second part (verses 16–25) begins with a threat, emphatically introduced by two oaths upon the phases of the night, which evoke a development that remains enigmatic and undefined (verses 16–18),[49] followed in verse 19 by an equally undefined exclamation of threat directed to the listeners who are imagined to be present. In a speech in which the opponents are now imagined as absent (verses 20–22), a rhetorical question follows about the reason for the denigration of the recitation and the slander against the proclamation. The closing threat of punishment (verses 23–24), dressed in an assurance encouraging the proclaimer of the omniscience of God, is done at the direction of God himself. With the last verse (verse 25), easy to recognize by its syntax as a later addition, a further assurance of freedom from punishment is pronounced for the believers, who at this later phase apparently must have already been confirmed as a community standing in God's favor.[50] The sura—without the addition—is proportioned: 6:9:9, and is thus well suited mnemotechnically for the use of worshipers in the early, ritually oriented community.

48. See Jeffery, *The Qur'ān as Scripture*.

49. See Neuwirth, " Images and Metaphor"; cf. also Kandil, "Schwüre in den Mekkanischen Suren."

50. For the additions, cf. chap. 5, 185–187.

7.4.3 The Banquet in the Hereafter

The central element of Prophetic discourse about the future, eschatological foresight, is more complex. Alongside the "eschatological scene," the presentation of the successive collapse of the cosmic structures it includes the "eschatological process," the reaction of the humans to this event, as well as the judgment itself, where, in the image of measurement or weighing, the deeds of mankind recorded in a register book are examined. Scales and accounting books are the visual images of this process of reckoning. After this, the judged are led forward to their retribution in the hereafter, in a place indicated only vaguely, given no particular location in the familiar cosmos, neither the heavens nor an inferno underground. The "places" of the judged present themselves rather through depictions of particular social interactions. It is striking that their two manifestations, the humiliating punishment and the honoring reward, are both framed through the image of the banquet. The two images belong closely together; they are similarly structured and often set in relation to one another through identical or proportional dimensions, so that the notion of the double image or diptych, commonly used for Christian iconographical representations of paradise and hell, easily comes to mind. Among the numerous examples, we present the eschatological part of sura 78,[51] Q 78:17–20, 21–26, 27–30, 31–36:

inna yawma l-faṣli kāna mīqātā
yawma yunfakhu fī l-ṣūri fa-taʾtūnā afwājā
wa-futiḥati l-samāʾu fa-kānat abwābā
wa-suyyirati l-jibālu fa-kānat sarābā

inna jahannama kānat mirṣādā
li-l-ṭāghīna maʾābā
lābithīna fīhā aḥqābā
lā yadhūqūna fīhā bardan wa-lā sharābā
illā ḥamīman wa-ghassāqā
jazaʾan wifāqā

innahum kānū lā yarjūna ḥisābā
wa-kadhdhabū bi-āyātina kidhdhābā
wa-kulla shayʾin aḥsaynāhu kitābā
fa-dhūqu fa-lan nazīdakum illā ʿadhābā

inna li-l-muttaqīna mafāzā
ḥadāʾiqa wa-aʿnābā
wa-kawāʿiba atrābā

51. The beginning portion of the sura is discussed in chap. 13, 466–470. On further double versions, cf. chap. 5, 176–179.

wa-kaʾsan dihāqā
lā yasmaʿūna fīhā laghwan wa-lā kidhdhābā
jazāʾan min rabbika ʿatāʾan ḥisābā

The day of separation will be a date appointed,
a day when the trumpet will be blown, and you will come forth in droves,
when heaven will be opened and become apertures,
when mountains will be leveled and become a mirage.

Hell lies in wait
final destination for transgressors
staying there for eons.
They taste there no coolness or drink,
only boiling water and filth.
A worthy payment.

They expected no reckoning,
cried lies upon lies at our signs.
We reckoned everything in a writing.
Taste!—we will give you nothing more but torment.

For the pious there is a place of retreat,
gardens and vines,
beautiful companions,
a cup overflowing.
In it they hear no idle talk or lies.
A reward from your lord, a gift that is due.

In the two-part sura,[52] an image is first drawn of creation in paradisiacal dimensions, as a protected world offering security. But this very assurance shows itself in the second part of the sura to be deceptive: the security promised crumbles to dust in view of the power of God before the inner eye of the hearer. The eschatological part (verses 17–36) begins with a ringing confirmation of the irreversibility of the date of judgment, and then brings the horn of judgment itself into the picture, drawing a scene of judgment that evokes a theater piece (verses 18–20): the "curtain of the heavens" rises, and the actor, that is, the addressee himself, enters the stage. The scene proceeds in a detailed double image (verses 21–36), which recapitulates the earthly behavior of the damned in flashbacks. Indeed, the triumph of the punishing God over the unbelievers who doubted the Final Day proceeds further, it goes beyond the withdrawal of earthly safety and the leading into hell: in their evaluation, presented in fast-forward, the judged are confronted in a cynical way with a "world turned upside down," a hell (*jahannam*) in which

52. See Neuwirth, *Studien zur Komposition*, 217.

hospitality is perverted into torture, and entertainment into the serving of revolting dishes, without an end to their stay in sight. The malevolent address with *dhūqū*, "taste," stresses the travesty: the host is "generous," even in the excessiveness of his entertainment, staging the meal as social interaction. But the host has changed this into its perverse opposite, a scenario of the denial of life's essentials: "You taste no cool drink!" (verse 24); excrement and hot water is forced on the guests—a perverted image of the excessive hospitality of the ancient Arab hero and the negative image of the true divine hospitality in paradise.

The punishment hits them due to their earthly failure to take the message of judgment seriously. The following expansion of the diptych of the damned into a catalogue of vices (verses 27–30), concluded by a cynical closing imperative (*dhūqū*), corresponds to the equally cynical commentary on the fate of the liars in the hereafter in verses 22 and 26. The granting to the good contrasts with the emotionally charged speech about the bad; to them, aside from paradisiacal sensory pleasure, is also promised "peace from chatter and lies" (verse 35), that is, freedom from the chief nuisance in the experience of the proclaimer. As retribution, they are offered not only the "full cup" known from the Psalms (Ps 23:5, *kosi rewayah*), but also young beautiful companions—wholly in agreement with the conceptions of the hereafter among certain early Christian authors.[53] With this image, the sura could have been concluded.

Attached to this text, however, is a further scene, which is linked syntactically to the closing scene of the original text structure, and is thus conceived of as a continuation, Q 78:37–40:

rabbi l-samāwāti wa-l-arḍi wa-mā baynahumā
al-raḥmāni lā yamlikūna minhu khiṭābā
yawma yaqūmu l-rūḥu wa-l-malāʾikatu ṣaffan
lā yatakallamūna illā man adhina lahu al-raḥmānu
wa-qāla ṣawābā
dhalika l-yawmu l-ḥaqqu
fa-man shāʾa ttakhadha ilā rabbihi maʾābā
inna andharnākum ʿadhāban qarīban
yawma yanẓuru l-marʾu mā qaddamat yadāhu
wa-yaqūlu l-kāfiru yā laytani kuntu turābā

Lord of the heavens and earth, and what is between them,
the merciful, they cannot address Him.
On the day when the spirit and the angels stand in rows
they will not speak, except one permitted by the
merciful, who speaks rightly.
That is the day of the truth

53. On Irenaeus of Lyon, see for examples McDannell and Lang, *Heaven*.

and who wishes can take refuge with the Lord
We have warned you of a nearing punishment,
a day when man will see what his hands put forth,
when the blasphemer will cry, "I wish I were dust."

The heavenly court with the angels does not belong to the paradise scene that has just been presented, but rather refers back again to the preparation of judgment. The presentation of the court, added in the middle Meccan Raḥmān period,[54] reflects a strictly hierarchical order, in which only restricted freedom of speech exists, so that not even the angels are permitted to perform their intercessions. In view of this overwhelming and exclusivist manifestation of the court, the despair of the sinner, who wishes death for himself, is all the more comprehensible. The addition, discernible from its verse structure, is not (as is elsewhere frequent) a consoling-softening one, but further adds alterity to the scenario of the hereafter.

The Qur'anic paradise has been treated in a seminal study by Josef Horovitz,[55] in which he attempts to show, by way of numerous poetic parallels, that the heavenly banquet refers back to actual experiences, or at least to frequent experiences drawn from ancient Arabian banquets: "In the early period he [the proclaimer] was intoxicated by luxurious scenes to which he himself may have been an eyewitness in wine taverns, or which were familiar to him from the descriptions of the poets, whose setting he now moves to the abode of the blessed."[56] But Horovitz does not derive this paradise exclusively from ancient Arabic precedents: "The traits from which the image is composed are of quite different origins; Jewish-Christian reminiscences mix with presentations of pagan goings-on. And even this national Arab element shows itself to be thoroughly marked by foreign impact; already the many foreign words in the descriptions of the heavenly banquets recall the high degree to which the material culture of the environment in which Muhammad lived was indebted to the surrounding lands."[57] But Horovitz's naming of possible precedents does not sufficiently describe the intertextuality here. The Qur'anic paradise stands in a yet more complex connection; certainly, it corresponds to psalmic ideal conceptions ("You set before me a table in the view of my enemies, you anoint my head with oil and give to me fully," Ps 23:5), just as it corresponds to images of the hereafter in Christian penitential sermons.[58] But it is above all a picture drawn in opposition to the situation of crisis always present in ancient Arabic poetry.[59] One can see in the Qur'anic descriptions of paradise a radical reversal of the existential experience of loss that is expressed in the *nasīb*, the first part of the *qaṣīda*. The emptying of the world of aesthetic form, of social

54. Cf. chap. 5, 192–195, and chap. 8, 282–285.
55. Horovitz, "Das Koranische Paradies," 1–16.
56. Ibid, 15–16.
57. Ibid.
58. Andrae, *Mohammad.*
59. Cf. chap. 3, 128–131, and chap. 12, 444–447.

interaction, and sensory pleasure that is bemoaned there, its barrenness of material culture, is countered in the Qur'anic paradise by a promise of restitution.

The ancient Arab poet, who before the entrance of the Prophet, was the speaker of his society in the introductory section of his poem bemoans the nearly washed away traces, the *aṭlāl*, of earlier settlements in a now desolate place. Nature presents itself to him as bleak and repellent; it offers no answer to his question of *ubi sunt*,[60] of the whereabouts of those whose social life once animated that space. The scenario is a dumb mirror of his own transience. All culture, all human achievements, fall prey to time or become overgrown,[61] as it were, by cyclically renewing nature: the only testimony to the living spaces and the social order of the former inhabitants of the place are weathered traces of habitation—a loss that reflects itself also personally and individually: the former relation of the poet to his beloved is broken, and conviviality, joy in life, and refined ways of interaction in a materially luxurious habitat, which is especially bound up with the world of women, all this has vanished since the fragrant caravans of the women have departed, their image being effaced and turned—as the poet Labīd expresses it—"into a mirage." But just as the traces of human culture are transitory in the poet's perception, so are the phenomena of nature eternal. In the words of the poet Labīd:

balinā wa-mā tablā l-nujūmu l-ṭawāliʿu /
wa-tabqā l-jibālu baʿdanā wa-l-maṣāniʿu[62]

We pass away, but the rising stars do not.
Fortresses and mountains remain when we are gone.

Time can do nothing to nature; it is intransitory, *khālid*, or it renews itself timelessly in a cyclical way. Mankind on the other hand is eaten away by time, which is personalized as *al-dahr*, "fate."[63] This perception of the overwhelming of man and his culture by nature is countered by the Qur'an. God himself takes over the role of fate and frees man from his transience, redefining the time of man. Time now extends from the creation of the primordial world and the simultaneous creation of the power of understanding / clear speech, *bayān*, (Q 55:4) in man, down to the end of the world, when, after the loosing of the cosmic structures on the Final Day, man must redeem the original pledge of divine instruction. Time extends even beyond that. For after the judgment, an infinite eternity begins, which the Qur'an dresses in the spatial conception of paradise. Not in sura 78 but indeed in a sequence of other suras, among which sura 55 is especially striking,[64] what is

60. On this philosophical motif popular in Late Antiquity, cf. Becker, "Ubi sunt qui ante nos in mundo fuere."
61. See S. Stetkevych, *The Mute Immortals Speak*, 8–54.
62. Ibid.
63. See Georges Tamer, *Gott und Zeit*, 99–102.
64. Cf. chap. 3, 123–125.

given to man is not only the biblical promise of eternally lush and fruit-bearing nature but also of material luxury: "green pillows on fine carpets," "upholstery covered in brocades," and above all the presence of beautiful young women—all objects of nostalgic longing for the ancient Arabic poet who in reality was confronted with the desolate condition of his space and the ruins of a lost civilization. Paradise is a space in which man is no longer delivered to nature but finally retrieves that which is bemoaned as lost: the former cultural "dressing," that is, aesthetic culture, again bound up with the presence of women, and even courtly luxury in the eternal banquet of the hereafter.

The presence of women does not need to be attributed exclusively, as Horovitz assumes, to the association with poetic banquet scenes. The question of the presence or absence of sexuality in the hereafter was a major topic and long controversial in patristic literature. Voices for the continuation of worldly intercourse stand alongside voices pleading for a purely spiritual hereafter.[65] The inversion of the *nasīb* scenario through the admission of eroticism in paradise thus corresponds to a conception also disputed elsewhere in Late Antiquity, that of a sensually fulfilled afterlife. It is important to note that nature, which in the *nasīb* is threatening and defies the questioning of man, is thus retooled as a backdrop of a banquet. Nature is immortalized on its seasonal apex of pleasantness in springtime and allowed to remain blooming and fruit-bearing forever. Culture, social communication, and refined lifestyle are salvaged from the transitory to the eternal; the previously ambivalent eternal nature is tamed; it is raised to a new status: to serve as the luxurious life-giving backdrop of eternal feasting. The Qur'anic paradise is a counter-world, based on both ancient Arabian and biblical conceptions.

7.5 Reflection on the Signs of Scripture and the Signs of Creation

7.5.1 *A Qur'anic Theology of Signs*

Gottfried Müller had identified a radical innovation in the Prophetic speech of the proclaimer about the future, which brought about a "new tradition, a tradition of significant 'signs.'"[66] Such a sign theology can in fact be demonstrated. A striking trait already of the Meccan suras is the close relation between a "natural theology" and a particular theory of knowledge—based at once on language and insight. The closeness to the discourse of later biblical wisdom literature, such as Ecclesiastes or the Wisdom of Solomon, comes to mind, texts in which

65. See McDannell and Lang, *Heaven*, 47–68, who contrast the doctrine of Irenaeus of Lyon (ca. 135–202) on the sensual pleasures of paradise to those of the ascetic Augustine (354–430).

66. Müller, "Die Barmherzigkeit Gottes."

the order underlying all affairs of the world is demonstrated in both nature and in examples from salvation history.[67] This relation is most evident in those Qur'anic mentions of creation that take the form of series or clusters of individual details of creation, often introduced explicitly as "signs"; "*āyāt of creation*." As is already suggested by the etymology of the Arabic word *āya* (pl. *āyāt*; Syriac *āthā*, "miracle signs, written signs, letters"),[68] the creation *āyāt* signify something beyond themselves constituting with their inherent reference function, a Qur'anic textual type of its own.[69] They serve hermeneutically to prove the presence and omnipotence of God. But the designation of the Qur'anic passages naming the phenomena of creation as *āyāt* is not derived from the early suras, but is rather extrapolated from later texts such as the late Meccan citation *wa-fī khalqikum . . . āyātun / wa-fī khtilāfi l-layli wa-l-nahāri . . . āyātun . . .*, "In your creation . . . are signs / and in the change of day and night . . . are signs" (Q 45:3–4). The early texts rather put forward arguments with the same train of thought but without naming the concept *āya*, as in *fa-jaʿala minhu l-zawjayni l-dhakara wa-l-untha / a-laysa dhālika bi-qādirin ʿalā an yuḥyiya l-mawtā*, "He made them as two sexes, the male and female / is he not able to revive the dead?" (Q 75:39–40). The designation *āya* itself is not yet frequent in the early Meccan period, occurring only ten times, and referring in those instances to obvious "signs," that is, phenomena that engender wonderment, such as destroyed settlements of earlier peoples (Q 51:37, 54:14), an eclipse of the moon (Q 54:2), or even esoteric signs given to the Prophet (Q 79:20, 53:18). Only once do we find a sign of creation marked as *āya: wa-fī l-arḍi āyātun li-l-mūqinīn*, "Upon the earth are signs for the convinced" (Q 51:20).

7.5.2 *Core Concepts of the Qur'anic Creation Discourse*

7.5.2.1 *Sign—āya*

Nevertheless, already in the early Meccan period, there is a pronounced sensibility for the sign character of the communicated message itself, the *āyāt* that are "recited": *idhā tutlā ʿalayhi āyātunā qāla asāṭīru l-awwalīn*, "When our signs are recited to him, he says: fables of the ancients" (Q 83:13; cf. also Q 90:19, 78:28, 74:16, 54:42). *Āya* is thus used from the beginning in the two meanings of a textual sign (Greek *stoicheion* or *logos*) and a sensory, physical sign (Greek *semeion*). Thus, the designation *āya* is in no way confined to creation-specific textual units; but is used in general to mean a shorter textual unit of the Qur'an not defined in extent.[70] Thus, from the outset, a deictic-paraenetic function is acknowledged for the recitation texts. It is striking that the identification of the two types of

67. Kugel, *The Bible as It Was*.

68. The word also occurs in ancient Arabic poetry with the meaning "way marking," cf. Imru' al-Qais, 65:1; see Ahlwardt, *The Divans*, 160. In its concise meaning, which also occurs in Christian Arabic poetry (see Dmitriev, "An Early Christian Arabic Account," 355–366), it can only be explained as a loan word.

69. Neuwirth, *Studien zur Komposition*, 180, 195–196.

70. Neuwirth, "Verse(s)."

āyāt as equally "readable" signs manifesting themselves on the one hand in the recited text and in the other hand in creation itself, making it an "understandable text," remains implicit in the early suras—with the only exception of Q 51:20. Apparently, it had not yet developed into a reflexively perceived object of theology, as it was to be formulated exemplarily, for example, in the already cited verses Q 45:3–6. But in view of the argumentative evidence and the explicit identification of creation and signs in Q 51:20, one can already assume an epistemic implication of the Qur'anic descriptions of creation for the early suras.

It is worthwhile to recall briefly the biblical precedents: the Hebrew Bible stages signs very dramatically. Moses receives God's writing signs, the tablets, which are written by God himself (Dtn 4:13), or at least dictated by God (Ex 34:28). Micha Brumlik has thus noted that "the Hebrew Bible in one of its crucial statements, namely in Ex 3:14, has God indicate his name as 'I will be that which I will be.' In addition, God states . . . in Ex 33:23–38 that living men cannot catch sight of what he is. . . . The . . . God who eludes any perception of his, whose . . . presence cannot be represented in the image—i.e., in a pictogram or hieroglyph—because of its abstract processionality, could only be made known in the frame of a writing that depicts spoken language"[71]—an image of God that, as Brumlik formulates, perhaps "is based on writing, or more precisely, is even based on the combinatorics of the alphabet." A nearness of God's self-manifestation to the signs of writing/revelation has survived in the Qur'an, even if the form of the letters was not at first of interest and the two "writings" of God were at first perceived separately, until the word *āya* finally became a homonym for both and the letter names acquired a highly visible position at the start of suras.

7.5.3 The Conjunction Khalq—Qur'ān, Creation—Recital

This epistemic implication of the Qur'anic "creation signs" has been pointed out often in the research.[72] But a phenomenon closely bound up with the epistemic dimension, yet going beyond it, has been widely neglected: the connection made frequently and explicitly in the Qur'an between the creation of man and his fitting out for divine instruction, and thus his faculty to acquire knowledge in face of the divine works.[73] Consequently, only the trajectory reaching from the establishment of creation down to its loosing at the end of times was perceived,[74] not however the equally existing trajectory stretching from the primordial instruction of man to his rendering of the pledge of knowledge. It is not to be overlooked

71. Brumlik, *Schrift, Wort und Ikone*, 17.

72. Petersen, "Creation," 429; Graham, "The Winds"; Dmitriev, "An Early Christian Arabic Account," 252–256; Schimmel, *Die Zeichen Gottes*, 272–275.

73. Cf. chap. 3, 119–121.

74. Petersen, "Creation," 479–480, even claims a cyclical concept, without noting the double reference to creation and instruction . This double trajectory of tension was first demonstrated for the structure of suras beginning with an oath; see Neuwirth, " Images and Metaphors "

that a number of early suras in prominent citations, mostly at the beginning, a double-naming: mention the primordial creation, preceded by a naming of divine revelation or instruction of men. The evocation of divine teaching can also occur indirectly, such as through the mention of a site of revelation considered emblematic, such as Mount Sinai. What is not immediately evident in its theological implication due to mere juxtaposition becomes clearly recognizable once reference to divine communication or teaching is replaced or expanded by the mention of human language or capacity for reason,[75] as in Q 55:1–4, *al-raḥmān / ʿallama l-qurʾān / khalaqa l-insān / ʿallamahu l-bayān*, "the merciful. / He taught the *qurʾān* / he created man / he taught him clear understanding [or: clear speech]." That this double naming is no accident is clear from its function in the field of tension that exists between protology and eschatology. Both initial settings, primordial creation and teaching, correspond to a double final position, related in the same text: the loosing of creation on the Final Day and the call to the redemption of the token of learning in the ensuing judgment. If one looks for what is innovative in Qur'anic thought, it is worth referring to this double trajectory in creation theology.

7.5.3.1 *Judgment—dīn*

The idea of theodicy is already central in the early suras. What is assessed and requited in the judgment, *dīn*, is at first generally named as "good" and "bad," *khayr* and *sharr* (Q 99:7–8).[76] Since the negative element here appears calculable, almost measurable, it does not yet touch on the problem of "evil."[77] It often refers concretely to the fulfillment or neglect of social duties (Q 69:34), as emerges from the numerous flashbacks to the social practice of the sinners. But just as often, we find language related to the failure to "read" the divine signs in creation (Q 75:31) or to the disregard of the textual signs communicated in the reading (Q 75:33, 68:15.45). What is central here is thus not only compensatory justice toward men but also the staging of God's sovereignty expressed in his office of judge (Q 95:8)—an office that is invested with all the paraphernalia of ancient Near Eastern rulership and juridical dignity. Thus, we find the symbol of the scales, already prominent in the biblical context (Q 101:6–8), and also the throne of the judge (Q 1:4, 81:20, 85:15). This grandly staged office of judge has an extension in his hospitality, expressed through exuberant generosity toward the pious, and in his equally excessive abuse—his inverted hospitality toward the evildoers in the afterlife utopias of paradise and hell.

Despite this predominance of the divine actor, the Qur'anic *dīn* is not part of an apocalypse. It is not the end of an eon that stands imminent in the worldview

75. This goes unnoticed in Heemskerk, "Speech."

76. On the ethical terms, see Izutsu, *Ethical Terms*.

77. Schmidt-Biggemann, "Vorwort," 9: "Evil is not the simple negation of good—the negation itself would be too easily predictable: evil in even when personified displays the fascination of utter unpredictability."

of the early Meccan suras, but rather God's call for accountability. We find no predictions of battles of the end times, as in the apocalypses of the Jews and Christians, but only divine intervention, no taking to account of peoples, but rather of the individual man. The Qur'an sketches an eschatology in which the emphasis is on the extension of this world into the next. This new worldview, which is developed in the early suras, on closer inspection turns out to be centered on creation: paradise as the idealized projection of the world and hell as its perverted reflection play central roles. What is at stake is not only the communication of the imagined closeness of the end of time (Q 78:40, 70:7) but equally the establishment of a new linear progress of the world, which stretches from a double beginning in creation and instruction to a double ending, in the loosing of creation and the rendering of the pledge on judgment day. It is above all this newly established field of tension that distinguishes the Qur'anic eschatological view of the future from an apocalyptic imagination. It is a field of tension in which man can establish a meaningful life, shielded from the terror that strikes entire peoples that we find in the extremely violent apocalyptic scenes that characterize especially the Revelation of John. It is not a question of which side of power the individual is on, but rather of how he conducts himself individually.

Thus, paradise—which occupies a broader space in the Qur'an than hell—is by no means the place of return from the earthly exile which had been initiated by the expulsion from the Garden of Eden, as one might expect in analogy to Christian conceptions. The earthly manifestation of creation is no accursed site of suffering and punishment, but rather shows itself to be clearly and essentially related to paradise.[78] In this, it also distinguishes itself clearly from nature as reflected in the worldview of the pre-Islamic poet, for whom the environment is not immediately accessible, but which rather must be retrieved through heroic deployment.[79] The "world" is distinguished from the paradise of the afterlife less by its faultiness than by its contingency, its security that is revocable at any time, which it preserves for man only for a time; compare the early Meccan texts Q 104:3 and 90:5. Creation in the Qur'an is not primarily a reality but above all a "text" that carries in itself divine teachings. Thus, it should be no surprise that the Qur'anic descriptions of creation are primarily oriented not toward actual nature but rather equally to "literature," that they are not primarily reality-referential but rather equally text-referential.[80]

Josef van Ess has outlined the impact of the Qur'anic perception of creation on later Islamic theology:

78. On the depiction of the human habitat, see sura 78; cf. chap. 13, 466–468.
79. Müller, *Ich bin Labid*; cf. Neuwirth, "Geography."
80. Cf. the discussion of the description of creation in suras 78 and 55 in Neuwirth, "Psalmen."

> In relation to inanimate creation, God's absolute disposal is obvious. . . . Indeed, the world has its order, but it is not the ordering of a cosmos. The order for him who sets it, namely God, is not binding. . . . In the Muslim view, God does not speak through nature but rather from beyond it. It is—one might say—theologically absent, it is not a power that man could give himself over to; it has no emotional value. 'Mother nature' cannot be translated into Arabic: the Muslim is not a protector of nature. . . . The idea that the wastes, the mountains, the forests, are creation, and therefore might have meaning in themselves, does not occur; creation has its sense either in relation to man, in that he draws benefit from it and thanks God for it, or in relation to God, in that his power is manifest in it. God and man are the coordinates of the theological system. *Tertium non datur*. The Islamic theologians do not proceed from cosmogony as did the Greeks or, in a certain sense, even the medieval scholastics; they do not seek the first principle of nature, they write no commentaries on Genesis.[81]

One could hold that the Qur'anic creation theology already prefigures this development, but we must not overlook the expressions of joy inherent in the God-given inhabitability of the world that is evident in many verses, as in Q 78:6–16.

7.5.3.2 *Name—ism*

Among the insignia of power of the creator belongs his sublime name, *ism*. Already three times in the early Meccan period, "the name" is set in an immediate context to creation: God's name, as that of the creator, becomes the object of praise: *sabbiḥi sma rabbika l-aʿlā lladhī khalaqa fa-sawwā*, "Praise the name of your Lord, the exalted, who created and formed" (Q 87:1–2); *iqraʾ bi-smi rabbika lladhī khalaq*, "Recite in the name of your Lord, who created" (Q 96:1); *tabāraka smu rabbika dhī l-jalāli wa-l-ikrām*, "Praised be the name of your Lord, in majesty and magnanimity" (Q 55:78).[82] As in biblical usage, we also find the "face," *wajh*, of God in place of his name: *kullu man ʿalayhā fān wa-yabqā wajhu rabbika dhū l-jalāli wa-ikrām*, "Everything upon it is ephemeral, but the face of your Lord full of majesty and generosity remains" (Q 55:26).[83]

To read here a simple circumlocution of the naming of God in consideration of his transcendence, a hedging against anthropomorphic conceptions of God, is inadequate, in that the hymnic predications of God in the early suras anticipate the later nominal coinages such as *al-khāliq*, "the creator." These—conceptualized

81. Van Ess, "Islam," 124–126.

82. Likewise, mentions of the name of God without reference to creation come up in the exhortations to praise in Q 56:74, 73:8, 87:15.

83. Cf. the early Meccan verses Q 92:20 and 76:9.

as God's "beautiful names," *al-asmā' al-ḥusnā*—will become an emphatically presented topic in the Qur'an. The unpronounceable name of God, we might say, has become a name that is pronounceable in many forms, to be summoned in different situations. This becomes most evident in the Medinan sura 59, where verses 23–24 strongly remind of the so-called thirteen attributes, *shelosh 'esre ha-middot*,[84] in a verse from Exodus, which for its part became decisive for the Jewish theology of names, Ex 34:6–7:

> The Lord, the Lord God, merciful and gracious, longsuffering, and abundant in goodness and truth, keeping mercy for thousands, forgiving iniquity and transgression and sin, Who will by no means clear the guilty; visiting the iniquity of the fathers upon the children, and upon the children's children, unto the third and fourth generation.

In the Qur'an, a less ambivalent image of God is drawn, in the Medinan verses Q 59:22–24:[85]

> *huwa llāhu lladhī lā ilāha illā huwa*
> *'ālimu l-ghaybi wa-l-shahādati,*
> *huwa l-raḥmānu l-raḥīm*
> *huwa llāhu lladhī lā ilāha illā huwa*
> *l-maliku l-quddūsu l-salāmu l-mu'minu*
> *l-muhayminu l-'azīzu l-jabbāru l-mutakabbir—*
> *subḥāna llāhi 'ammā yushrikūn*
> *huwa llāhu l-khāliqu l-bāri'u l-muṣawwiru*
> *lahu l-asmā'u l-husnā*
>
> He is God, there is no God but He.
> Knower of the unseen and the seen, the merciful, the compassionate.
> He is God, there is no God but He,
> the king, the holy, the peaceful, the faithful,
> the preserver, the almighty, the overwhelming, the sublime.
> Exalted be God beyond what they associate.
> He is God, the creator, originator, the giver of forms,
> His are the most beautiful names.

One can see in the term "beautiful names," and the decidedly positive predications of God, an answer to the ambivalent biblical combination of names promising grace or punishment in Ex 34:6–7, even if the concept of "beautiful names" occurs already in the middle Meccan period, before the encounter with learned

84. Cf. chap. 9, 318–322.
85. For a Qur'anic rereading of the verse Ex 34:6–7 in the Qur'an, see chap. 9, 322–324.

Jews that is presupposed in Medina, in Q 20:8 and 17:110, both times in the context of a controversy triggered by the introduction of the name al-Raḥmān, and in Q 7:180. Indeed, the name of God is already strikingly frequent in the Qur'an in Meccan times. Although the Qur'anic name theology has not yet been set into relation with the Jewish and Syriac-Christian name theologies that developed before it,[86] it is already quite apparent that in the Qur'an the highest value is assigned to the power that emanates from the name of God. According to the Medinan verse Q 2:31, God teaches Adam all names, which also must imply the name of God. And not only does the Qur'anic text itself deal in the middle Meccan period with the distinction between the empowered names of God and the names, empty of authority, merely coined by man, as in Q 53:23: *in hiya illā asmāʾu sammaytumūhā antum wa-abāʾukum*, "They [the three ancient Arabian goddesses] are only names that you coined, you and your fathers." Above all, it must not be overlooked that from at least the middle Meccan period, the units of recitation, the suras themselves, take on the introduction *bi-smi llāhi l-raḥmāni l-raḥīm*, "In the name of God the compassionate the merciful," a formula that gives primacy to the notion of God's ability to be named and evoked by man at the beginning of all further utterance. The name of God, his verbal self-manifestation, thus appears as a linguistic means of bridging the distance from his creation and his transcendence.

7.5.4 Recognizing, Knowing for Certain, Looking, Seeing versus Lying without Belief, Telling Lies: ʿIlm And Kufr

The human capacity and readiness for the knowledge to be derived from creation is expressed at first in positive terms, *ʿalimat nafsun*, "then a soul recognizes" (Q 82:5), *āyātun li-l-mūqinīn*, "signs for them who are sure in their knowledge" (Q 51:20), or in the form of an exhortation, *fa-l-yanẓur*, "man should then look" (Q 88:17; cf. *a-lam najʿal lahu ʿaynayn*, "have we not made him two eyes?" Q 90:8).[87] Franz Rosenthal assumes that behind the Qur'anic expression *ʿilm al-yaqīn*, "certain knowledge" (Q 102:5), is the Christian theological term *he gnosis tes aletheas* (Syriac *idaʿtha de-shrārā*, "the knowledge of the truth"), an observation that requires support through further citations.[88] But the idea of the readiness for knowledge is expressed far more frequently in a negative way. The denial of the signs (*kadhdhaba*),[89] or the lack of recognition (*kafara*)

86. Some of the ideas developed later in Sufism are very close to the Jewish ones: Schimmel, *Die Zeichen Gottes*, 279, points out, "The fact that Ibn Arabi 'beheld' in his vision the letter h, because h is the last and most essential letter in the name *Allāh*, which refers to his *huwiyya*, his ipseity." Manifestations of God in letters were already common in earlier Jewish mysticism of Late Antiquity; see Scholem, "Der Name Gottes."

87. In contrast, the root *ʿ-q-l* does not occur in early Meccan texts; on the significance of *ʿ-q-l* in the Qur'an, see Kermani, "Verstand."

88. Rosenthal, *Knowledge Triumphant*, 22–28.

89. *Kadhdhaba* in the early Meccan period, often refers to judgment, in addition to signs of earlier messages as well as creation (as in Q 79:21 *fa-arāhu l-āyāta l-kubrā / fa-kadhdhaba*, "He showed him the greatest signs. But

in face of them, is among the accusations raised most frequently in the early suras. Both are explicitly linked with *āyāt* as the key hermeneutical object (*kafara bi-āyātinā*, "He was not insightful in view of our signs," Q 90:19; *kadhdhaba bi-āyātinā*, "He denied our signs," Q 78:28; cf. also *kallā innahu kāna li-āyātinā ʿanīdā*, "Indeed no! he was defiant against our signs," Q 74:16). The refusal to read the *āyāt*—whether they pertain to creation or are of a textual nature—is occasionally bound up with an opposite demand raised by the unbelievers for an unambiguous "scripture," *kitāb*, or "outspread pages," *ṣuḥuf munashshara*, (Q 74:52), while the early Qur'anic texts in this phase do not yet present themselves as *kitāb*, but rather as *tadhkira*, "reminder," in reference to a heavenly textual or earthy "readable" writing of creation.

This connection of *kafara*, "to be unbelieving," to the hermeneutical discourse surrounding the *āyāt* invites a rethinking of Toshihiko Izutsu's classification[90] of the concept of *kufr* and its derivatives among the ethical conceptualizations of the Qur'an. Izutsu understands *kafara* in the sense of *kāfir niʿma* "to be ungrateful," in agreement with the meaning that would prevail later in dogmatics. According to him, it is thus above all an ethical fault that underlies the Qur'anic concept of unbelief. This deduction is problematic, since the Qur'anic verb *kafara* should be derived from *kufr*—a loan word from Syriac, which already denotes "unbelief."[91] The verb is firmly established already in this abstract terminological sense in early suras,[92] behind which there may be assumed a faded etymological significance of "to cover."[93]

But the theological technical term is by no means adopted with all its connotations from Christian usage, since Christian matters of belief are not of direct concern in the early Qur'an. What, then, are the objects of "unbelief" in the Qur'an? As the early usage of *kafara* shows,[94] a concrete object is already envisaged: in the two earliest citations, it is the *āyāt* that are referred to as the object of *kufr*, either explicitly or implicitly: *wa-lladhīna kafarū bi-āyātinā hum aṣḥāb al-mashʾāma*, "Those who are unbelieving of our signs are the people of the left hand"

he denied them"; cf. also Q 78:28); particularly relevant for this context is the refrain *waylun yawmaʾidhin li-l-mukadhdhibīn*, "Woe to the deniers!" in a creation *āyāt* series, Q 77:24–28.

90. Izutsu, *Ethico-Religious Concepts*. This interpretation is criticized by Ghassan Masri, (personal communication), whose call to focus on the epistemic dimension of the Qur'anic *kufr* concept is taken up here.

91. Jeffery, *Foreign Vocabulary*. Nonetheless, the discovery of such a "loan word" does not suffice. Griffith, "Christian Lore and the Arabic Qurʾān," 115–116, classifies such "borrowed words" as calques. "Syrianisms are words or sentences in the Arabic language of the Qur'an, which evoke a Syriac expression that lies behind them. They are thus 'calques' or 'loan translations' from Syriac into Arabic. . . . What is Syriac in the Qur'an is no longer Syriac, but in the best case is a 'Syrianism' in Qur'anic Arabic. . . . The Qur'an, which marks out a new hermeneutic horizon, integrates every originally Syriac element in its Arabic diction in the frame of significance that this language has constructed."

92. See verses, such as Q 73:17, 51:60, 68:51, 70:36, 84:22, 85:19, 70:2, 74:10, 86:17, 80:42, and 83:34.

93. This pre-terminological meaning is common to the Semitic languages, but is already "overlaid" in Syrian and Hebrew with theological signification.

94. The verb occurs seven times in early Meccan texts, six times in the participle form.

(Q 90:19), *qutila l-insānu mā akfarah / min ayyi shay'in khalaqah*, "Cursed be man, how unbelieving he is! / From what material has he been created?" (Q 80:17–18). In the other citations where the meaning "to show unbelief" is expressed by *kafara*, there is no reference to a concrete object of the unbelief, but here too we can assume an analogous unbelief in regard to the signs of creation or texts. The denial of opinions of belief is also expressed by the verb *kadhdhaba*, where along-side the reference to *āyāt* (*kadhdhaba bi-āyātinā*, "He declared our signs as lies," Q 78:20) we also find language related to the denial of the judgment. In any case, following these observations, we should rethink the exclusive assignment of the Qur'anic *kufr* idea to an ethical conceptualization. The parallelism of the usage of *kafara* and *kadhdhaba* and the twice-occurring explicit connection of *kafara* with *āyāt* give the concept an unmistakable epistemic dimension.

7.5.4.1 Homonymy: Āya, "Miracle Signs"/"Written Signs"

One can speak then of a close linkage—becoming more explicit over time—of divine "creation" (*khalq*) and divine "communication" or "teaching" (*qur'ān, ta'līm*), manifest in the simultaneous equipping of man with *physis* (*khalq*) and *logos* (*qur'ān* or *ta'līm*), and in the structure inherent in creation (*khalq*) that is recognizable through reason (*bayān*) due to its immanent comprehensibility. A field of tension emerges, occupied by the divine creator; creation, which itself shows a hermeneutically effective structure; and man, endowed with ability for reason and speech, who through the application of his faculty of understanding/language is able to "learn" (*'alima* in Q 82:5) and to "recognize" (*ayqana* in Q 51:20) creation as God's manifestation. In contrast to the denial of these signs or communications, we find expressions of "recognition" or giving thanks (*shakara* in Q 56:70).[95]

The gifts given to man in language and reason thus converge. This Qur'anic interpretation of the human faculty of knowledge, which is not equally apparent in the two older scriptures, can most plausibly be explained through reference to Neoplatonic philosophy whose integration into theological discussions had already been achieved by Syriac thinkers. Adam H. Becker points to a widely attested tradition according to which God used letters in order to create the world. He ultimately deduces this from the polysemy of the Greek word *stoicheion*, which can mean both "element" and "letter." This equivocity becomes productive in Syriac theology. Thus, the plural of the Syriac word for "sign," *āthwāthā*, which may stand behind Arabic *āyāt*, is derived from the singular *āthūthā*, which itself means both: "element" and "letter sign." but is also related to the more broadly connoted singular *āthā*, which means "sign" or "miracle sign," and above all reproduces the Greek *semeion*, for example, in the Syriac translation of the New Testament (Peshitta), where it indicates the

95. See Rosenthal, *Knowledge Triumphant*, 19–28.

signs that Jesus worked (Jo 2:11–18).[96] This same equivocity is constitutive for the Qur'an.

7.5.5 Late Antique Backgrounds

After this short survey it is useful to turn back once more to the Late Antique preconditions of the Qur'anic creation theology. Letters, signs, and names are equally introduced in the Late Antique *Sefer Yesira*[97] as an integral part, or even as instruments, of creation, they play a somewhat less prominent role in the Qur'an: "signs" are homonyms for details of both text and creation; the "name" is thoroughly de-semiotized through the fanning out of the one unpronounceable name into the plural *asmāʾ al-ḥusnā*; from the middle Meccan period, letters occur no longer as signs but as the signified itself, while also signifying beyond themselves through their transcendent reference,[98] they finally, in the late Meccan period come to occupy the opening positions of suras. The Qur'an stands closer to Syriac-Christian theology than it does to Jewish mysticism.

Here, the observations of Adam Becker on the Syriac theory of creation deserve attention: "The focus on what we say about something in a discussion of how we 'comprehend' and 'investigate' it seems to derive from the Neoplatonic practice of drawing an explicit connection between words, things, and concepts. Neoplatonic texts regularly conflate these three very different ontological modes. In the prolegomenon to his commentary on the *Categories,* Ammonius explains that commentators in the past have disagreed as to whether the *Categories* treats words (*phonai*), things (*pragmata*), or concepts (*noemata*). He resolves this dispute by suggesting that all the three positions are correct in part."[99] About the Syriac theology that arises from this ambiguity, Becker writes, "Stemming from ambiguities in the use of the Greek *logos*, the relation between words for 'speech' and 'reason' in Syriac would have contributed to his confusion: *meltā* means 'word,' 'speech,' or 'reason.' "[100] This can also be applied to Qur'anic Arabic: *āyāt*, considered linguistically, are texts (passages of the Qur'an); considered semantically, they are details of creation; and if considered theologically, they are ultimately signs received in creation that, if "read," yield a distinct textual understanding in parallel to revelation.

96. Becker, *Fear of God*, 131, explicitly emphasizes the relationship to *Sefer Yesirah*; cf. to a related Greek treatise, cf. Bandt, "Vom Mysterium." The remarkable double meaning of *āya* in the Qur'an, in the sense of text sections of undefined extent, and of visible signs, exhibits the same ambiguity. Peters, "Creation," 174, adopts the internal Qur'anic marking of individual verses as *āya*, but this meaning is most likely post-Qur'anic.

97. See now Herrmann, *Sefer Jezira*.

98. The problem of the so-called ciphers, *ḥurūf muqaṭṭaʿa*, is still unexplained; the presumption that isolated appearance of letters at the beginning of individual suras involve the invocation of letter names seems to be the most plausible; cf. chap. 5, 193–194.

99. Becker, *Fear of God*, 134–135.

100. Ibid.

Here, Becker attributes a central significance to the Syriac theologian Ephrem (306–373), according to whose theology God nears men through language and reveals himself to them through nature. While the Neoplatonists, through whose mediation the Syriac theologians received Aristotle, treated language as a necessity conditioned by human corporality, Becker stresses that for the Syrians, language became a means for the solution of the problem of God's radical transcendence: "Ephrem of Nisibis, the great Syriac poet of the fourth century, emphasized in particular that God is unknowable in his essence. According to Ephraem, God bridges the ontological and epistemic distance between himself and his creation through the various acts of self-revelation. Two of these . . . are the differing symbols which he has scattered over all of creation, and his self-dressing in a garment of names. Ephraem founded an entire theology of names, through which God 'attracts' to himself human language in order to be knowable."[101] This statement could be applied without adaptation to the Qur'an—thus a synopsis of Ephrem's theology in relation to the Qur'an, and a detailed comparison between them is an urgent desideratum.

101. Ibid.

8

Stages of Communal Formation in the Middle and Late Meccan Periods

If the early Meccan suras already show a nearness to the prayer praxis of the two more ancient religions[1] and trace paths in sign theology that were already traveled by Syriac theologians, it should be no surprise that the discourses that developed soon afterward also developed in close contact to biblical and post-biblical traditions, even to the degree of constituting a *counter-history* to the inherited ancestral tradition of the community. One can see this step, accomplished in the middle Meccan phase, as the entrance of the community into the "successors of the Israelites," their self-identification as a new people of God standing in the Mosaic tradition and claiming participation in monotheistic salvific history. The key element of this sacred history is the conception of divine self-communication through "scripture," having both earthly and heavenly manifestations, and which can be either codified or oral. The central idea of God's mercy, which in the middle Meccan period is recorded in the name of God "al-Raḥmān," "the compassionate," which becomes frequent in this period,[2] refers not least to this self-communication through writing, perceived by the proclaimer as an act of generosity (Q 96:3–4):

iqraʾ wa-rabbuka l-akram
alladhī ʿallama bi-l-qalam
ʿallama l-insāna mā lam yaʿlam

Recite, your Lord is the most generous
who taught you with the pen,
taught man what he did not know.

1. Rubin, "Morning and Evening Prayers," brings together the evening prayer Ṣalāt al-ʿAsr, as delineated by the pagan Meccans, with the Jewish Minḥa prayer; and Ṣalāt al-Fajr, the sunrise prayer, with Shaḥarit. Likewise, this could also be reminiscent of the Christian equivalents, Orthros and Hesperinos; cf. Horovitz, "Terminologie des islamischen Kultus."

2. Although the name al-Raḥmān already comprises an established designation for God in South Arabian (see Robin, "Himyar et Israel"), a continued influence of the sense of "mercy" should be assumed for the Qur'anic usage.

The new consciousness is reflected in one sense semantically and theologically, through the new focus on biblical prophet narratives and their contextualization within the communal reality in agreement with a newly emerging worldview. But the new consciousness shows itself equally through a "liturgical reform," so that what emerges is a new sura form that depicts structurally a monotheistic service revolving around the reading out of biblical stories: this three-part composition takes shape in the middle Meccan period.[3] In the late Meccan period, this three-part formal schema with narrative at its center is maintained in some instances, but in other cases is replaced by a form that is more thoroughly discursive. The sura then moves beyond this increasingly loose portrayal of a prayer service and takes on elements of the Late Antique homily, employing traditional paraenetic forms such as the allegorical story or parable.[4] This textual genre, made widespread by the Gospels, becomes representative of the late Meccan suras and serves as the medium for the critique of several Christian traditions that are theologically problematic for the community; above all, it enables a new, narratively dense dressing for thoughts that could only be represented previously through abstract argumentation.

In addition to the three discourses already traced for the early Meccan suras—consolation and assurance of providence on the one hand and prophetic warning of the judgment and sign theology on the other—some discourses that appeared later must also be investigated. In the center of the middle Meccan development stands the self-construction of the community as a new people of God, through recourse to biblical and post-biblical traditions and, bound up with this, liturgical innovation in the development of a structured prayer service. That this progress in communal formation brings with it an exegetical process of exclusion and the replacement of central earlier traditions, that is, a demythologizing and new myth foundation, becomes particularly clear in sura 19, "Mary," in which the complex Christian traditions about Mary and Jesus are negotiated anew. As a third middle Meccan discourse, we can name the anti-pagan polemic in disputes over concrete objects of belief, which can also be demonstrated in sura 19. In the late Meccan period, when the standard form of the tripartite sura gives way to a looser structure better suited to sermonizing, a fourth discourse emerges in the development of new homiletic instruments, above all the parable or simile. This "emblem of prophethood," still little noticed in Western research, becomes an important medium for the authorization of the message in the later parts of the Qur'an.

3. See chap. 5, 192–193.
4. On homiletics, see Berger, "Antike Rhetorik"; cf. 498–501.

8.1 From Real World to Text World: The New People of God

8.1.1 The Election of the Community in Preexistence

A goal of the Qur'anic proclamation since the entrance of the proclaimer into the role of Prophet is the warning (*andhara*, "to warn," Q 19:97) of the judgment, the reminding (*dhikr*, Q 81:27) of God's power and working in nature and history; his medium is the recitation, the reading (*qurʾān*, Q 75:17–18), which is the approach to the one God through liturgy. Already in the early period, the praxis of prayer is an important act that establishes identity;[5] indeed, it is only through the achievement of an elementary prayer service going beyond the ritually embedded short recitations that the community first enters into a new phase in the formation of cult, and at the same time a new stage of self-reflection. A turn toward this state emerges strikingly in the middle Meccan sura 15, where individual elements of the prayer service are given explicitly by name. In the same sura, the community also receives the confirmation of its election in preexistence, and is explicitly addressed as the receivers of sacred-historical messages. A connection to the older monotheistic groups, who have already made the earlier Israelite sacred history their own and now go further down the path of the Israelite people of God, is thus announced. Sura 15, which can be considered the locus classicus for this turn, will be presented in short here.[6]

The tripartite sura[7] is one of the earliest to feature a biblical story in its middle part. The beginning section (verses 1–48) begins with a "sacral intonation," the naming of three letter names *alif lām mīm*,[8] followed by the confirmation that what is to be recited is an excerpt, namely, "an ensemble of signs from the heavenly writing," *āyāt al-kitāb*, and at the same time "a clear reading," *qurʾān mubīn*. The transcendent storage and the pronouncement in the word in the here and now are two complementary mediums of the "writing." A polemical conjecture, *rubbamā yawuddu lladhīna kafarū law kānū muslimīn*, "Perhaps the unbelievers would like to be ones who submit" (verse 2), opens into an exhortation to the proclaimer to leave them to their superficial and sensually oriented life (verse 3). Then follows a polemical confrontation with the opponents about the origin of the message, wherein their obstinate refusal in face of the earlier divine acts of annihilation is indicted as particularly frivolous: they express doubt about the transcendent source of inspiration of the proclaimer and challenge him to bring forth the angel that he claims as the bringer of the message (verses 5–9). A consolation of the proclaimer follows: prophets are always mocked, God himself

5. Cf. chap. 6, 208–212.
6. A detailed analysis and interpretation of the sura is offered in Neuwirth, "Referentiality and Textuality."
7. Neuwirth, *Studien zur Komposition*, 264.
8. On this structural element, see chap. 5, 193–194.

puts this attitude in the hearts of the unbelievers, and even miracle signs will not remove unbelief from the world (verses 10–15).

Then, as counterpart to the polemic, a hymnic verse group follows (verses 16–18), which adduces *visible signs*. God is praised in the form of first-person plural predicates, first as the creator of the heavens, which not only are "ornamented" toward visual perception but are also protected against demons who attempt to overhear the divine wisdom[9]—an implicit argument against the demonic source of inspiration alleged for the proclaimer (verse 6). The following praise of the luxurious outfitting of the earth (verses 19–25) delivers a further argument for God's power, which is also capable of waking the dead.

The narrative that then follows (verses 26–48) could already be considered part of the narrative second section, but it also continues the ideas of creation from the beginning section, now broadened to the primordial creation of men and demons, and continues to treat the demons, whose disempowerment is now exemplified in the central figure of Iblīs/Diabolos.[10] This episode, which will be taken up time and again subsequently in the Qur'an, is here expanded into a scenario of the election of the community occurring already in preexistence. The introductory verses of the narrative *wa-la-qad khalaqnā l-insāna min ṣalṣālin min ḥamāʾin masnūn / wa-l-jānna khalaqnāhu min qablu min nāri l-samūm*, "Truly, we created man from a clump of moist clay / and the demons we created earlier from flaming fire" (verses 26–27) cite almost verbatim a statement on creation from the early Meccan sura 55, where it is repeated almost fifty times in a refrain calling demons and men to their debt of gratitude.[11] In sura 15, the statement acquires a new function: it names the potential of conflict that inheres in God's treatment of Satan, which now unfolds in relation to the earthly fate of man. For Iblīs, who is counted among the demons/*jinns* because of the more sublime material of fire from which he is created, is superior to man, who is created out of clay, yet man is preferred by God. Upon being commanded to fall down before the first man alongside the angels, which are also reckoned among the *jinn*, Iblīs refuses, offering the plausible argument of his preferable origin: *qāla lam akun li-asjuda li-basharin khalaqtahu min ṣalṣālin min ḥamāʾin masnūn*, "He said: I will not prostrate before a mortal, whom you have created from a clump of moist clay!" (verse 33). He is expelled from the garden, but then assumes a task that is fundamental for Qur'anic theodicy, that of testing man through acts of temptation, *la-uzayyinanna lahum fī l-arḍi wa-la-ughawwiyannahum ajmaʿīn*, "I will beguile them with beauty on the earth, and lead them all astray" (verse 39).

9. On this mythical concept, cf. Hawting, "Eavesdropping."

10. Iblīs, from the Greek, *diabolos*, is identified in later suras with Satan, *al-shayṭān*; see Neuwirth, "Qur'ān, Crisis and Memory."

11. Neuwirth, "Psalmen"; cf. also chap. 3, 127–131.

The function fulfilled by Iblīs of the examiner that stands by God's side, or of "prosecutor" of the creatures, which is familiar not only from the book of Job but also from an extensive ancient Near Eastern literature, is not a negative "demonic" role, but rather the role of assistant in support of divine justice. The corresponding figure in Job has been called "trickster," one "who attempts to intervene in creation and do something other than that which the creator God does."[12] Indeed, Iblīs is conciliatory, and even allows an exception from his target group: *illā ʿibādaka minhumu l-mukhlaṣīn*, "but not your true servants" (verse 40). The agreement of God shows that Iblīs does not yet figure as absolute evil, as he will in the later Qur'an, but rather still oscillates in his value: *qāla hādhā ṣirātun ʿalayya mustaqīm / inna ʿibādī laysa laka ʿalayhim sulṭānun illā mani ttabaʿka mina l-ghāwīn*, "He said: that is for me a straight road! You have no power over my servants, except for over those who are beguiled and follow you" (verses 41–42). God's servants—that is, as one sees in due course, the Qur'anic community—are thus excepted from the temptation by Iblīs.

The narrative, which opens with an announcement of judgment, is the first of seven Adam-Iblīs stories told in the Qur'an.[13] Above all, this is the first sura in which the term *ʿibādī*, "my servants," is introduced in the sense of "my community." That the "servants" protected from Iblīs are identical with the new community is shown by their lowly social position, which is depicted as a consequence of their earthly good deeds in resistance to Satanic temptations—a reversal of the worldly canon of values, which now makes the underprivileged social position of the community a sensible sign of their religious privilege.

Not only is this community elected already in preexistence, it is also the present receiver of divine blessings, namely, communications from the heavenly writing performed by the proclaimer. Two such biblical narratives now appear in the adjoining second part (verses 49–84), the "reading section" of the prayer service that is reflected in the sura. Namely, the term "my servants" has just been introduced (in verses 40 and 42), and these "servants" then become the addressees of a reading: *nabbiʾ ʿibādī annī anā l-ghafūru l-raḥīm / wa-anna ʿadhābī huwa l-ʿadhābu l-alīm / wa-nabbiʾhum ʿan ḍayfi Ibrāhīm*, "Announce to my servants that I am the forgiving, the merciful / that my punishment is the painful punishment / and tell them about the guests of Abraham" (verses 49–51). What follows is the first narratively unfolded biblical story in the Qur'an. It reports the meeting of Abraham with the messengers of God near Mamre (verses 52–60), and proceeds to the announcement of a son to the aged Abraham as evidence for God's "mercy," *raḥma*, and then turns to the adjoined (verses 61–74) narrated destruction of the inhabitants of Sodom as evidence of his punishing justice, *ʿadhāb*.[14]

12. Colpe, "Aus der Geschichte des Teufels," 70–75.

13. Neuwirth, "Qurān, Crisis and Memory."

14. On the development of the Qur'anic story of Abraham, see now Sinai, *Studien zur frühen Koraninterpratation*, 57–149.

The still-palpable traces of the catastrophe of Sodom give rise to the association of other peoples of the Arabian Peninsula, namely, *aṣḥāb al-ayka*[15] and *aṣḥāb al-ḥijr* (verses 78–84), whose cities have also been destroyed.

The third part (verses 85–99), like the first one, is directed in appellation to the proclaimer. It begins with an emphatic self-affirmation of the creator, which, here and in other suras, signals a new dramatic act of the prayer-service drama[16]: *ma-mā khalaqnā l-samawāti wa-l-arḍa wa-mā baynahumā illā bi l-ḥaqqi*, "We have not created the heaven and earth and what is between them except in truth" (verse 85).

It is among the subsequent exhortations, advice on conduct, and consolations to the proclaimer that close the sura that we also find the verse that, uniquely in the Qur'an, confirms the new existence of a text corpus available in addition to the Qur'an, namely, the Fātiḥa: *innā ataynāka sabʿan mina l-mathānī wa-l-qurʾāna l-ʿaẓīm*, "Truly we have given you seven [verses] for repeating, and the glorious reading" (verse 87).

8.2 From Mecca to Jerusalem: New Liturgical Forms

8.2.1 *The Fātiḥa*

The traditional critical arguments in favor of the identification of *sabʿan mina l-mathānī*, the "seven for repetition," or literally "seven repeated," with the Fātiḥa, do not need to be rehearsed in detail here.[17] That only this could be intended comes out clearly from the chronological position and from the form of the sura in which the mentioning of the Fātiḥa is embedded. If it were in fact true, as the majority of the critical researchers assume in opposition to the unanimous Islamic tradition, that the "seven *mathānī*" indicate seven repeated legends of punishment,[18] then one must essentially give sura 15 a later date, since in the early Meccan period seven such legends were not yet available. Furthermore, the reference to only seven such Qur'anic narratives, which would then be quite unmotivated, would scarcely justify such a triumphal mentioning of the *mathānī* as a text corpus *in addition* to the Qur'an (*wa-l-qurʾān*). But the decisive observation here is that the Fātiḥa itself, of which the individual elements are "cited" in several middle Meccan suras, are evoked frequently, namely, with no fewer than seven mentions, so that we can assume a very close connection between the two texts.[19] This means that the self-perception of being a community distinguished through

15. The name can now be geographically located; see Puin, "Leuke Kome."

16. On this introductory topos, cf. the parallels in Neuwirth, *Studien zur Komposition*, 264–266, and chap. 2, 80–89, as well as chap. 6, 227.

17. Neuwirth, "Sūrat al-Fātiḥa"; cf. also Sperl, "The Literary Form of Prayer."

18. On the punishment legend hypothesis, see Rubin, "Prophets and Prophethood"; Horovitz, *Koranische Untersuchungen*; Paret, *Mohammed und der Koran*.

19. See a list of evocations of the Fātiḥa in sura 15, in Neuwirth, *Studien zur Komposition*, 340f

divine election and possessing recited excerpts from the heavenly book is bound up with the new consciousness of having another important liturgical text available in addition to the Qur'an recitation. A communal self-consciousness belongs together with a viable structure of prayer service. With the Fātiḥa, we now find an element that, unlike the recitation of the suras, grants a voice to the community itself. One can see here something corresponding to the Christian Our Father[20] or, even more so, a re-forming of what stands in at the start of the Christian service as the Introitus; Q 1:1–7:[21]

bi-smi llāhi l-raḥmāni l-raḥīm
al-ḥamdu li-llāhi rabbi l-ʿālimīn
al-raḥmāni l-raḥīm
māliki yawmi l-dīn
īyāka naʿbudu w-īyāka nastaʿīn
ihdinā l-ṣirāṭa l-mustaqīm
ṣirāṭa lladhīna anʿamta ʿalayhim
  ghayri l-maghḍūbi ʿalayhim
  wa-lā l-ḍāllīn

In the name of God, the compassionate the merciful.
Praise be to God, lord of the worlds,
the compassionate the merciful,
the king of the day of judgment.
You we serve and You we call on for help.
Lead us to the straight road,
the road of those You have shown grace to,
  not that of those you show anger to
  and not that of those who go astray.

That the Fātiḥa, although clearly an oral prayer text, has been seen in research up to now as a part of the Qur'an, as one of the revelations/proclamations, and not as a parallel text that was affixed to the codex redactionally as a kind of prooemium, can be explained by the dominant view of the Qur'an as a fixed written text and not a liturgical performance text that relies on further complementary texts. Indeed, the early Islamic tradition itself attests to the fact that the Fātiḥa does not belong to the corpus of suras, in that it discusses controversially its connection with the bismillah, the invocation formula *bi-smi llāhi l-raḥmāni l-raḥīm*, "in the name of God the compassionate merciful."[22] In the dominant text form of the Kufic tradition,[23] the bismillah—uniquely in the Qur'an—is not an opening

20. Winkler, "Fatiha und Vaterunser."
21. Neuwirth, "Sūrat al-Fātiḥa."
22. Neuwirth, "Sūrat al-Fātiḥa," 348.
23. Cf. chap. 4, 149–155.

credit, but rather a first verse of the sura. This is how one arrives to the number seven—given in sura 15—for the *mathānī*, the "repetition verses," and at the same time one can confirm that the basmala was indeed recited with the sura in cultic practice. In the case of the Fātiḥa, the text tradition of the Qur'an and the cultic tradition transmitted in the schools of law diverge.[24]

A perspective founded in the history of liturgy is adopted by Anton Baumstark, who, in the context of his attempt to classify the Qur'anic formulas of divine worship typologically, succeeds in reconstructing a monotheistic "genealogy" for the Fātiḥa as a central prayer formula. According to Baumstark, in formulation and structure it resembles an ancient Christian worship, the so-called doxology of the Greek daily prayer, which corresponds to the Gloria in Excelsis of the Latin mass—which, like the Fātiḥa, is a central part of the daily observed liturgy, but not of the scripture.[25] Functionally though, there is a closer parallel to Jewish-Christian service openings. As has been shown,[26] in cultic practice the Fātiḥa is even today not bound up with the bismillah in certain rites. The beginning of the prayer ritual would then be—in agreement with other service-introductory formulas—*al-ḥamdu li-llāhi rabbi l-ʿālamīn*. Transferred in the Qur'an into a universal-monotheistic diction, this corresponds to the doxology with which, for example, the Chrysostom and Basil liturgies begin: "Praised be the kingdom of the Father and the Son and Holy Spirit, now and always for all eternity." In both liturgies, the Qur'anic and the Byzantine, we have before us a hymnal incipit, which in the Fātiḥa is continued by two multipartite predications (verses 2 and 3). In the Greek liturgy, it fills a complex sentence, which together with the immediately following antiphonic *kyrie eleison*, "Lord, have mercy," includes all elements that are expressed in the first part of the Fātiḥa: the praise, "praised be," *al-ḥamd*; the reference to the rulership over the present and eternity, "now and always for eternity," *rabbi l-ʿālamīn*[27] (verse 2); the idea of mercy, "have mercy," *al-raḥmān al-raḥīm* (verse 3); and finally the eschatological "kingdom of the father," *mālik yawm al-dīn* (verse 4). Similar parallels can be detected in the second part of the Fātiḥa, to the litany of supplication connected to the hymn, so that the assumption can be maintained that the Fātiḥa stands as a service introduction in the tradition of older service beginnings, alongside the hypothesis represented by Winkler[28] and Goitein,[29] that the Fātiḥa is an Islamic Our Father. It may have fulfilled both functions from the beginning, that of Introitus and that of communal prayer.

24. See Spitaler, *Verszählung*, 31; on the problematic see Neuwirth, "Sūrat al-Fātiḥa," 335.

25. Baumstark, "Gebetstypus im Koran," 242–248.

26. Neuwirth, "Sūrat al-Fātiḥa."

27. While "Lord of the worlds" is understood in a few cases in the Qur'an as "Lord of the inhabitants of the worlds," it is analogous to the concept of "Lord of the world and eternity" familiar to the older traditions.

28. Winkler, "Fatiha und Vaterunser."

29. Goitein, "Prayer in Islam."

8.2.2 "Scriptural Reading" as Center of the Middle Meccan Sura

Contemporary to the introduction of the Fātiḥa as communal prayer, the suras show from the middle Meccan period an almost stereotyped three-part structure of appellatory beginning part, narrative middle part, and appellatory closing part,[30] a structure that also underlies the Christian prayer service, where prayer and prayer litany precede a scriptural reading standing in the center, to which dialogic parts, further prayer litanies and credo formulas, follow. The sura itself seems in this period to reproduce such a multipart service.[31] This progress in the prayer form, the outdoing of the previous cult dominated by rites, is thus due to two new characteristics, the new structure of the sura and the availability of a mandatory extra-Qur'anic text, the Fātiḥa. It coincides with the self-perception of the community as an elected people of God.

It is striking that narratives in the late Meccan suras are often referred to expressly as elements of the scripture, *al-kitāb*. This writing is conceived as unchanging and comprehensive, and it preserves a stock of knowledge codified by heavenly scribes (Q 80:11–16)[32]—perhaps a Qur'anic adaptation of the idea, dominant in the book of Jubilees, a Jewish apocryphal writing from the second century BCE, of the heavenly register,[33] an idea already common in ancient Near Eastern writings. The narrative communications from the heavenly scripture are at first distinguished from less universal elements such as, for example, debates over ephemeral matters of the community. The ceremonial function of the biblically inspired narrative is underlined by introductory formulas such as *wa-dhkur fī l-kitāb* . . . , "mention in [the excerpt of] the writing . . ." (Q 19:16). In a later phase, in Medina, as the particular form of the message communicated to the community is already itself treated as constituting scripture, that is, as the matters of the community are recognized as part of sacred history, entire suras figure as manifestations of the *kitāb*.[34]

By far the majority of the later Meccan suras begin with an emphatic evocation of the scripture, often introduced through an "intonation," the naming of an isolated letter of the alphabet or a combination of letters.[35] These evoke the heavenly "writing source," a reference that was not yet required in the early suras. This incipit seems to indicate a newly achieved cultic function of the recited text, which is no longer conceived as the immediate communication of divine messages to

30. Neuwirth, *Studien zur Komposition*, 264–266.

31. This thesis still requires systematic verification based on liturgical-historical considerations. But it seems to be heuristically useful to set into relief the linking of the development of cult and that of the text corpus.

32. Cf. chap. 4, 77–79.

33. Jeffery, *Qur'an as Scripture*.

34. Sinai, "Qur'anic Self-Referentiality."

35. The so-called isolated letters, *ḥurūf muqaṭṭaʿa*, are not to be understood here as editorial additions, but rather as a means of expression already introduced by the proclaimer. Their origin and meaning are unresolved; cf. chap. 5, 193–194.

the community, but rather as a performance of the holy writing that is thought to be preexistent and only capable of being realized in performance.

8.2.3 *Orientation to Jerusalem, Center of Israelite Sacred History*

The middle Meccan suras attest to a new spatial framework for the message. These texts, which contain numerous biblical stories, show an expansion of the historical horizon of the hearers, who are carried beyond their local environment into the distant landscape of the Holy Land, *al-arḍ allatī bāraknā fīhā*, "the land that we have blessed" (Q 21:71), which is familiar as a setting for the history of the "spiritual forebearers" of the community, the Israelites. The introduction of the direction of prayer, *qibla*, toward Jerusalem is an eloquent testimony of this general change in spatial orientation. The process that culminates in this new ritual orientation can be roughly made plausible through use of the categories of ritual and textual coherence, which were introduced by Jan Assmann.[36] The biblical stories, which before appeared only in brief allusions, now enter the foreground in middle Meccan times, so that the protagonists of the early historical narratives, figures from the Arabian Peninsula, give way to biblical figures, and the Holy Land itself enters as the backdrop in place of ancient Arabia. One example among many is the story of the Israelite temple itself, which is told in Q 17:2–8,[37] while in middle and late Meccan times there is hardly any more mention of the Meccan sanctuary. The biblical sacred-historical past, which is set in place of the inherited indigenous historical memory, now forms a "text world" in competition with reality, which can be approached in prayer through the physical gesture of the direction of prayer.

The measure of application of this first direction of prayer is not attested in the Qur'an, nor is the Islamic tradition unanimous on it,[38] but it is generally presupposed to have held for the Meccan period in the most recent research. But above all, the assumption of the prayer direction toward Jerusalem is clearly reflected in a Qur'an verse (Q 17:1), which depicts a "night journey" of the Prophet to the "far[thest] place of supplication," *al-masjid al-aqṣā*:[39]

> *subḥāna lladhī asrā bi-ʿabdihi laylan mina l-masjidi l-ḥarāmi ilā l-masjidi l-aqṣā lladhī bāraknā ḥawlahu li-nuriyahu min āyātinā innahu huwa l-samīʿu l-baṣīr*
>
> Glory to him who carried his servant by night from the sacred *masjid* to the furthest *masjid*, whose precincts we have blessed, to show him our signs. He is the hearing, the seeing

36. Cf. Assmann, *Das kulturelle Gedächtnis*, 87–103; cf. chap. 6, 208–212.
37. Neuwirth, "Erste Qibla—fernstes Masjid?"
38. Duri, "Jerusalem."
39. The verse is discussed in terms of the history of cult in chap. 6, 220–222; cf. the abrogation of Jerusalem as the direction of prayer, chap. 9, 334–337.

The enigmatic verse can only be understood in light of Qur'anic conventions of paraphrase (*al-masjid al-ḥarām* = Mecca; *alladhī bāraknā ḥawlahu* = the Holy Land).[40] The term *ʿabd*, "servant (of God)," is not reserved exclusively for the proclaimer but, in view of its origin here, must have been coined to describe him. The verb *asrā*, "travel at night," is mostly used in the Qur'an to indicate the exodus of Moses.[41] A geographical name for the place of destination does not occur, but the reference to the "far[thest] place of worship" is clearly comprehensible in view of the new focus on biblical history, and the qualification "whose precincts we have blessed" refers elsewhere in the Qur'an to the Holy Land. The "far[thest] place of worship" is thus not only the name of the sanctuary but also an indication of its location in relation to the Kaaba.

But what does this verse of the Qur'an have to do with the direction of prayer toward Jerusalem? The verse, isolated from its narrative progress by its hymnic reference to the experience of the Prophet,[42] speaks cryptically of a journey by the proclaimer who, at his place of destination, will see "signs" *āyāt*—an evocation of earlier visions reported in suras 53 and 81, which also culminate in the vision of signs.[43] The reference to Exodus that resonates with the verb *asrā*—the nightly exodus of Moses (Q 20:77, 26:52, 44:23),[44] conceived as happening at night, is phrased analogously—indicates further the experience of a miraculous liberation. That the "exodus" of the proclaimer in Q 17:1 is not accomplished physically but rather should be interpreted metaphorically, is yielded from the Qur'anic image of the Prophet, who is not granted a facility for miracles. The most important thing conveyed by the verse is the liberation experienced by the proclaimer, in analogy to Moses, through God's action, his "exodus" from a scene of compulsion and his participation in a particular God-man communication.

If one presupposes that the direction of prayer toward Jerusalem was already introduced at the time of the proclamation of the verse, then one can understand the journey as an imagined extension of the gestural assumption of the direction toward Jerusalem. The Islamic tradition offers the interpretation of a dream vision, which followed immediately after the nightly prayer.[45] The vision as a miraculous completion of the prayer would fit well with Jerusalem as place of destination, which according to the Jewish tradition is the target of prayer par

40. Neuwirth, "Spiritual Meaning of Jerusalem." Attempts to identify a heavenly Jerusalem, as is undertaken by Busse, "Jerusalem in Muhammad's Night Journey," are not convincing, as they do not take into account the direction of prayer, and above all because a verse in the same sura (17:93) vehemently denies the possibility of a journey to heaven for the proclaimer; see also now Rubin, "Muhammad's Night Journey."

41. *Asrā*, "to set forth at night," occurs twice in the Qur'an to describe Lot's nocturnal flight: Q 11:81 and 15:65. It describes the Exodus three times: Q 20:77, 26:52 and 44:23.

42. A story of the Jewish Temple follows, without reference to the transfer of the servant of God mentioned here.

43. There the Prophet is equally referred to in the third person singular. The Sira thus associated the visions with the nocturnal journey. See van Ess, "Vision and Ascension."

44. Cf. chap. 11, 408–411.

45. Al-Ṭabarī, *Jāmiʿ al-Bayān*, vol. 15, 3.

excellence. Since the Babylonian exile, the temple was considered not only the center of the world but also the place where all prayers converge, in order to rise toward God.[46] The Jerusalem temple is defined from the beginning, according to Solomon's prayer of dedication (1 Kings 8:23–53), as a collection point for all prayers, even and especially from worshipers in exile; it could also, for that reason, be the geographical orientation for prayer for the new believers attached to biblical tradition. With this direction of prayer, the early community of the proclaimer gives symbolic expression to their belonging to the biblical tradition. At the same time, the orientation toward Jerusalem represents a clear turning point against the privileging of Mecca that was stressed frequently in the early Meccan period (Q 90:1, 95:3, 105, 106). While in the early suras only Mecca receives mention by name (apart from Sinai), one finds in the later Meccan suras up to the *hijra* scarcely any more reference to Mecca, aside from Q 17:1, where Mecca is contextualized with the Jerusalem temple. Instead, the Promised Land is introduced as the space in which the biblical prophets acted. Suras of this period culminate in the often-repeated appeal to follow examples going back deep into the history of the "spiritual forefathers," the Israelites. Jerusalem, represented through its temple, is the center of the space delineated by the scripture of the *banū Isrāʾīl*. All prayers gravitate toward the direction of Jerusalem as their natural directional goal.[47]

8.2.4 Ambivalences: Jerusalem and the Christian Symbolism of Its Temple

Jerusalem was not unknown to the hearers of the Qur'an at this time. The sixth-century mosaic maps of Madaba,[48] one of the representations of Jerusalem that is chronologically closest to the Qur'an, shows the Christian city with the Anastasis church at its center, while the area that the Qur'an often thematizes, namely, the Temple Mount, is only represented by its eastern outer wall or its gate. The monuments to which the Qur'an refers, the Solomonic temple or its successor, the Herodian temple, no longer belong to the existing buildings of the city represented on the map. They are not only architecturally absent but already obsolete in the Christian perception of Jerusalem, from which the pre-Christian history is excluded. But it is just these sites that are the object of the Qur'anic memory, which is further acted out in the assumption of the direction of prayer to the *masjid al-aqṣā*.

Yet the Qur'an does refer to the inter-testamental, "original" Christian Jerusalem, but not without taking up a critical position toward it. The Qur'an

46. Cf. Wensinck, *The Ideas of the Western Semites*.
47. Neuwirth, "Erste Qibla."
48. See Küchler, *Jerusalem: Ein Handbuch*, especially the chart, 1268–1269.

indeed locates several narratives known from the New Testament or the Apocrypha in Jerusalem, where the Jerusalem temple is spoken of as a vaulted building similar to a palace, *miḥrāb*, which perhaps could also be interpreted as a partial area of the temple covered by a canopy, as is found on Byzantine icons. Sura 19, "Mary," discusses the priest Zachariah, who works in the temple (*miḥrāb*) and prays there for the appearance of an heir[49]—a prayer whose fulfillment introduces a quite different history from the tradition of the Gospels. The Qur'an—and possibly also already an exegesis preceding it that was hostile to allegory—here not only "corrects" the report of Luke but equally negotiates the early Christian interpretation, according to which inter-testament figures such as Zachariah mark the transition of the temple cult into a church cult. According to the early Christian interpretation, the church, allegorically embodied as Mary, "inherits" the temple, represented by its priest. The Christian (apocryphal) tradition has Mary thus grow up under the care of Zachariah in the temple[50]—a symbolically significant detail, which the Qur'an (in sura 3, "The Family of Amram") adopts as a narrative element, but without the implicit interpretation of the Christian tradition. In that the Qur'an accepts the childhood of Mary in the temple but does not treat this allegorically as a sense paradigm for the church but instead as merely a local narrative frame, it "corrects" the Christological reading of the history of Mary; it "dulls" its symbols,[51] which are reinterpreted in the Qur'an into realities, details of an individual life of the saint Mary. The Qur'anic story of the temple as *miḥrāb* thus sets itself against Christian traditions. Its Christological symbolism, which has no place in the worldview of the community, is eliminated from the Qur'anic image of Jerusalem, while central Christian characters are de-allegorized and retrieved in an event-historical connection.[52]

As against that, what is spoken of in the report about the fate of the Jewish temple, that is, the Solomonic and then Herodian temple, which is referred to in 17:4–7, is not a *miḥrāb* but rather a *masjid*, "place of worship." This terminological difference raises the question how closely these two traditions were bound up with one another in the consciousness of the community, a question that can scarcely be answered in view of the primarily paraenetic interest of the two references to the temple. It remains worthy of note that in Q 17:1 it is the manifestation of the temple as *masjid*, reflecting Israelite-Jewish tradition, not its conception as *miḥrāb* tied up with Christian sacred history, that is given primary place. It is the Jewish temple, *al-masjid al-aqṣā*, which for the community

49. The figure is formed in the Qur'an with reference to Luke 1:5–25; the miraculous birth of the son is not connected with Zachariah's encounter with the angel, but rather with his prayer.

50. On the textual and iconographic traditions, see Marx, "Mariology in the Qur'an."

51. The Medinan sura 3 makes this clear: the priest Zacharias—who in the liturgical tradition figures symbolically as the last representative of the temple cult—is entrusted with the care of adolescent Mary, who symbolizes the church. This relationship, which illustrates the succession temple-church in Christian tradition, is constricted in the Qur'an to a simple guardian-ward relationship.

52. Cf. chap. 10, 354–356.

is clearly held as the center of the Holy Land, toward which the worshipper supplicates and toward which also the proclaimer was transferred in his spiritually achieved exodus, his "night journey."[53]

8.3 Mythical Narrative, Biblical History, and Qur'anic "Corrective": Mary and Jesus

8.3.1 *Sura 19—A Raḥmān Sura*

How are the biblical stories in the Qur'an, which take on such a central position from the middle Meccan period, to be read? How do communal confrontations enter into the narratives? Although the groundwork for the recognition of their less narrative than exegetical reading was laid by the works of Heinrich Speyer and Josef Horovitz, few detailed studies of specific stories in light of preceding exegetical traditions have been undertaken, and even fewer place the respective stories in the context of an inner-Qur'anic development.[54] This is true also for one of the biblical-Qur'anic stories that is most frequently discussed in the research (Q 19:1–40), the narrative of Mary and Jesus.[55]

It is initially striking that, notwithstanding the numerous Christian traditions reflected in the Qur'an,[56] the figure of Jesus himself is not very prominent in the Qur'an. At his first appearance, he does not figure independently but rather as an accompanying figure in a story about his mother, and remains closely bound up to her. The Qur'anic Jesus, ʿĪsā, bears the matronymic Ibn Maryam, "son of Mary," obviously a polemically motivated "overwriting" of his Christian title "Son of God," and this already signals his exclusively inner-worldly role in the Qur'an. The story of his life is not told coherently, but individual reports are scattered throughout the entire Qur'an,[57] without crystalizing into a coherent vita, as for example in the case of Moses.

The story of Mary in the Qur'an is extraordinary also in other respects. It includes the announcement of her motherhood, her delivery of Jesus, and

53. The Sira tradition on the development of the Prophet's journey replaces *al-masjid al-aqṣā* with *bayt al-maqdis*, Hebrew *bet ha-miqdash*, which is related to the Jerusalem temple. In the context of the direction of prayer, the Sira speaks of al-Shām, Syria, thus employing the purely geographical term. *Qibla* corresponds to the Jewish *kawwana*, the direction and intention of prayer. The etymological reference of *qibla* to the "fore," the holy site in front of the person praying, evokes Psalms 16:8 *shiwwiti YHWH le-negdi tamid*, "I have set the Lord always before me," which is used in places of prayer as an inscription pointing in the direction of Jerusalem.

54. On the current state of scholarship, see chap. 1.

55. On the image of Mary and Jesus in the Qur'an, see Robinson, "Jesus," and Stowasser, "Mary"; cf. also Parrinder, *Jesus in the Qur'an*; McAuliffe, "Chosen of all Women"; Schedl, *Muhammad und Jesus*; Zahniser, "The Word of God"; Neuwirth, "Mary and Jesus"; Bauschke, *Jesus im Koran*; cf. also chap. 9, 324–332.

56. Cf. Andrae, *Ursprung*, Griffith, "Christians and Christianity"; McAuliffe, *Qur'ānic Christians*; Busse, *Die theologischen Beziehungen*; Robinson, *Christ in Islam*; Bauschke, *Jesus im Koran*; Suhrmann, "Early Islam"; and Lawson, *Crucifixion*.

57. Jesus (ʿĪsā) is named nineteen times in the Meccan suras; the only extensive discussion of his role is found in suras 19 (verses 1–33) and 43 (verses 47–65); short reminiscences occur in Q 21:91, 23:50, and 42:13.

later—in a Medinan text—even her own birth, and the particular emphasis is always put on Mary's dignity as mother of a prophet, while her ritual and sexual purity are so central that no significant interaction with other (human) protagonists is attributed to her. This particular representation of the two figures opens the question of their interpretation for the Qur'anic community.

Mary and Jesus occur for the first time in sura 19, Maryam, "Mary," one of the so-called Raḥmān suras.[58] These suras, which total seven,[59] and which on formal grounds should be assigned to the middle Meccan period, set in place of *rabb*, "Lord," which was frequent as the name of God up to that point, al-Raḥmān, "the merciful." Later, al-Raḥmān is in turn replaced by Allāh—a development the background of which has not yet been adequately explained,[60] as the partial corpus of the Raḥmān suras still awaits a full study. For sura 19, at least, a close relationship emerges with a further Raḥmān sura that engages—though without narrative—similar points of contention, above all the role of God as father: namely, sura 43, "The Splendor." In the Meccan suras, this debate is not yet carried out with Christians, but rather with pagan opponents.[61] In that the communal reception of sura 19 is recorded in the somewhat later sura 43, whose readings in turn triggered latter additions to sura 19, the view of the two suras together will shed some light on the detour-rich process of the Qur'anic proclamation, and should attest to a continuously sharpening communal consciousness around the social and theological potential for conflict embedded in biblical stories.

8.3.1.1 Formation and Later Growth of Proclamation

In terms of structure, sura 19 presents an exceptional case, in that it begins straight away with a "scripture reading" or biblical narrative, without an argumentative introductory part and introduced only by the giving of theme *dhikru raḥmati rabbika ʿabdahu Zakarīya*, "reading from the [or: a recollection of the] compassion of your Lord to his servant Zachariah." The first part (verses 1–65) is a narrative unfolding of the story of Zachariah and his late-born son John (1–15), then the story of Mary and Jesus (16–40), then finally a series of short reports about further prophets (41–65). A second section of the sura follows (66–98), in

58. See Nöldeke, *GdQ*, 1:121. The Fātiḥa is also among the Raḥmān suras, which in Q 15 is presupposed to already be in cultic use. The name of God, al-Raḥmān, remains present in the text through the use of the bismillah, whose position as preceding the texts of all the suras should have been fixed already during the proclaimer's proclamation. Additionally, the bismillah seems to point to an early adoption of writing as a mnemonic aid.

59. These are the suras 19, 20, 21, 25, 36, 43, and 67, plus sura 1, *al-Fātiḥa*.

60. The solution proposed by Al-Azmeh, "From Alexandria to Bagdad," which—following the model of Old Testament source analysis—ascribes the use of the various names of God to a conflation of traditions with different names of God that were joined retroactively, is not convincing in view of the interrelations between the suras.

61. Mary and Jesus receive central attention in the Medinan sura 3: "The House of Amram," *Āl Imrān*, a text that shows traces of an intensified theological exchange with Christians, but without taking a polemic position on particular Christian dogmas; Buhl, "Zur Koranexegese." These kinds of polemics occur in later reminiscences, especially often in sura 4, in contexts that are not embedded in narratives.

the place of the "sermon" that would be required by the prayer service structure after the "reading"; with thirty-two verses, it is exactly proportional to the narrative section that is twice its length.[62]

The sura stands out for its poetical shape; its verses of middle length bear the striking rhyme in *-īya* or *-ayya*,[63] which does not appear elsewhere in the Qur'an, and which in the sermon section, from Q 19:75 on, is lightened to a looser but still marked rhyme scheme.[64] The individual narratives are not simply sequenced one after another but linked according to shared motifs, such as the parent-child relationship, which is treated three times (and reflected negatively once in the polemic against the fatherhood of God), or shared patterns of behavior such as the repeated muteness or silence of protagonists. The narrative/reading part of the sura owes its solemn tone not least to unfamiliar poetic formulations, as in Zachariah's description of himself, which, apart from a strikingly expressive metaphor,[65] also takes up a poetic convention of syntax:[66] *innī wahana l-ʿaẓmu minnī wa-shtaʿala l-raʾsu shayban*, "My bones have grown weak and my hair is white" (Q 19:4). In addition, we find tropes such as paronomasia (*tajnīs*), as for example in verses 23, 79, 83, and 84; parallelism (verses 15, 20, 30–31, and 33); and a chiastic construction (verse 13)—in sum, these are phenomena that indicate a relatively early composition, as Nöldeke already assumed.[67]

This impression of a particularly artful composition is disrupted, however, by a verse group (verses 34–40) that follows immediately on the story of Mary. It bears the simple rhyme of later suras, *-ūn*/*-īn*, and introduces the name of God Allāh in place of al-Raḥmān. Even more striking is the over-long[68] and prosaic verse 58, which closes the narrative sequence and in its content shows itself to be an insertion of a Mary story from Medina.[69] These kinds of expansions of the text are not mere additions or glosses to a text established in writing, as they have been understood in previous research, but rather they demonstrate the continuous liturgical usage of the sura, which made it necessary to adapt the text to the newly achieved insight into the theological implications of what is narrated.

62. Neuwirth, *Studien zur Komposition*, 269; on the verse divisions, see ibid., 93.

63. On Qur'anic rhyme, see Neuwirth, *Studien zur Komposition*, 65–123, and chap. 5, 187–189.

64. Nöldeke's argument in *GdQ*, 1:130, for a later dating of this second part, grounded in this observation, is not convincing.

65. The formulation *ishtaʿala l-raʾsu shayban* does not appear in a concordance of ancient Arabic poetry; cf. Arazi and Masalha, *Concordance*.

66. Analytic expressions like *al-ʿaẓmu minnī* in place of the simple *ʿaẓmī* are characteristic of poetic Arabic; see Bloch, *Vers und Sprache*.

67. Nöldeke, *GdQ(2)*, 130.

68. Instead of the usual two to five, this encompasses a whole of seven short units of speaking, so-called cola. (A colon normally refers to a simple phrase matching a unit of breath; on colometric analysis of the Qur'an, see Neuwirth, *Studien zur Komposition*, 117ff.)

69. The verse is also recognized by the Islamic tradition as a later addition; see Nagel, *Medinensische Einschübe*.

8.3.1.2 Verses 1–33—A "Reading" about Zachariah and Mary

As in the Gospel of Luke (Lk 1:5–25), two miraculous birth stories are set in parallel in sura 19: that of John, called Yaḥyā in the Qur'an, and that of Jesus, who remains unnamed within the story. Sura 19 begins with a scene localized in the Jerusalem temple: the priest Zachariah prays there for an heir, one to carry on his office. His request is fulfilled, but the son, John, will not carry on his priestly office, but rather will be a prophet like Zachariah himself. But what stands in the center of the early Christian reading of the story of Zachariah and Mary is not thematized in the Qur'an: the turn in church history. With this turn the temple cult as such comes to a standstill, and the church appears as its successor, which is symbolized in the allegorical exegesis by the person of Mary.[70] It is onto Mary as an image of the church that the inheritance of the temple is transferred; this is an idea that pervades the Syriac liturgical tradition, but which remains wholly excluded in the Qur'an, even if a number of traces remain to indicate it. It is difficult to decide whether the Qur'anic presentation—which differs both from the thrust of the Gospel of Luke, which binds the two miraculous births together in order to establish John in the image of the "precursor" of Christ, and from the liturgical tradition, which employs Mary allegorically as heiress of the temple cult—corresponds to a "corrective" produced by the community itself, or whether the story was already widespread in this anti-typological and anti-allegorical reading. In any case, verses 1–33 represent an independent new formation; Q 19:1–15:

> Kaf hā᾽ ʿayn ṣād
> A recalling of your Lord's mercy toward his servant Zachariah
> When he called out to his Lord a secluded call.
> He said: My Lord, my bones have grown soft, my head is aflame with white
> And in calling to you Lord I have never been miserable.
> I fear my kinsmen after me and my wife is barren.
> So give me some kin from you, to be my heir and the heir of the house of Jacob, and make him pleasing to you, my Lord.
> O Zachariah, we give you news of a boy whose name is Yaḥyā, we have never given this name before him.
> He said: Lord, how can I have a boy when my wife is barren and I have reached an age of impotence?
> He said: So has your Lord spoken: It is easy for me, I created you, before you were nothing.
> He said: Lord, give me a sign.
> He said: Your sign is that you will not speak to the people for three full nights.

70. On the Christian-messianic traces in the Qur'anic story of Mary, see chap. 10, 365–368.

> So he came out from the sanctuary to his people and signaled to them to glorify God in the morning and evening.
> John, take the scripture with strength,
> we granted him sound judgment as a child
> and tenderness from us, and purity, and he was pious,
> Dutiful to his parents, not arrogant or disobedient.
> Peace be upon him the day he was born, the day he dies, and the day he is brought back to life.

Unlike in the report of the Gospel, the Qur'anic narrative does not bind both stories to a single event. They are linked less as elements of the same divine plan than through analogous motifs: the miraculous birth of a child and the temporary speechlessness of the father/mother. John is gifted to the aged Zachariah and his infertile wife, while Mary's son is born without the participation of a male partner. Both figures remain mute for a limited time. The priest Zachariah, who works in the temple, *miḥrāb*,[71] experiences the muteness imposed on him for three days as a sign of God's truthful intent to work the wonder promised to him. He inspires others to speak: his community should praise God in the morning and evening (verse 11).[72] Mary is also compelled to remain mute, in order to guard against the consequences of her socially taboo delivery out of wedlock. Her newborn child will speak in her place. Her muteness for its part works a wonder. Both stories carry a similar miraculous outcome: in the story of Zachariah, a voice speaks, perhaps from the angels, directly to the newborn John and prophecies to him his future. In the case of Jesus, the corresponding words are placed—no less miraculously—into the mouth of the infant itself in the first person. Both the son of Zachariah and the son of Mary are destined to become prophets. They will have access to the scripture (Q 19:12, 30), be gentle, and show reverence for their parents (verses 14 and 32). Zachariah's son is granted special tenderness, *ḥanān*—a play on words that seems to go back across linguistic borders to his original name, Yoḥanan (verse 13). Both are given the obligation to give alms, *zakāh* (verses 12 and 31), and are honored with a formula of blessing (eulogy) that is added to their name.

Notwithstanding these commonalities, Mary's story is more complex than that of Zachariah—above all, because it clearly discards allegorical interpretations and reshapes mythical motifs. This appears already in the annunciation episode, Q 19:16–21:

71. The temple is called *miḥrāb* only in a Christian context (Q 19:11; 3:37, 39; 3:37). It appears elsewhere as *masjid* (Q 17:1ff.).

72. This praise of God occupies the place of the hymn, which according to Lk 1:67–79 is spoken by Zacharias himself and which is in ecclesiastical liturgy part of the morning praise of the Benedictus. It has its equivalent in Luke's Mary hymn, the Magnificat (Lk 1:46–56), which is recited in the evening. The Qur'anic insistence on both liturgical times "mornings and evenings" for the recitation of the praise of God may possibly reflect an already existing Christian tradition. On the history of both psalms, see Flusser, "The Magnificat."

And Mary in the writing, when she withdrew from her people to an eastern place.
She took up a veil between her and them
and we sent to her our spirit, which appeared to her as a shapely man.
She said: I take refuge from you in the compassionate, if you are pious.
He said: I am a messenger from your Lord to give you a pure boy.
She said: How can I have a boy when no man has touched me, and I have not been wanton?
He said: your Lord said this: it is easy for me. We will make him a sign for the people and a mercy from us—and it was a matter ordained.

When the divine spirit, *rūḥ*, comes near to her, Mary has already withdrawn from her kin to an "eastern place," *makān sharqī* (verse 16). What appears in the Qur'an to be an arbitrary localization is the result of the de-allegorizing of a Christian tradition, related to the symbolic interpretation of Mary as the temple. The closed eastern gate of the temple, the closing of which was decreed by God himself according to Ez 44:1–2, will only be opened by the Messiah according to Jewish and later Christian tradition. The early church (Hieronymos, Ambrosius) rendered this prophecy to Christ and thereby Mary as his virgin bearer: *solus Christus clausas portas vulvae virginalis aperuit. Haec est porta orientalis clausa . . .* " "Christ alone opened the closed doors of the virgin womb. That is, the locked eastern gate [of the temple]."[73] In the Qur'an, Mary is still connected with the eastern place, but, now detached from that symbolism, it becomes rather a topographic detail, a station on her way to the wastes in which she will give birth.

She hides herself from her kin,[74] when the spirit comes near to her in the form of a beautiful youth—not an angel, as in Luke. Paying no heed to her defenses, he reveals himself to be a divine messenger and unveils his assignment, to give her a "pure boy."[75] There is no word at this phase of the narrative about Mary's divine election. At the startling announcement of a pregnancy, she receives—unlike in Luke—no clarification, but the message is limited instead to the mere reference to God's omnipotence, which was already adduced to dispel Zachariah's doubt in verse 9. Only at the end of the story is the promise given that the child will become a sign for mankind and an example of divine mercy.[76]

73. See the testimonies from Ambrose and Jerome in Dettinger, "Beiträge," 33. The allegory is primarily established liturgically. On the allegorical dimension of the Mary figure and its Qur'anic traces, cf. chap. 9, 365–367, and Marx, "Mariology in the Qur'an."

74. "She shielded herself with a veil / with a curtain in front of her" could be a reminiscence of the Mary story in the proto-Gospel, where Mary weaves a curtain for the temple. In the Qur'an this detail was severed from the symbolic temple tradition and transferred into a "pragmatic" narrative element.

75. A textual variant transmitted by Warsh, *li-yahabaki*, "so he may give you," makes God himself instrumental in the event.

76. The episode is summed up again in a somewhat later text, which de-personifies the spirit, portrayed as a life-giving power that induces Mary's pregnancy: *wa-llatī aḥsanat farjahā fa-naffakhnā fīhā min rūḥinā wa-ja'alnāhā*

Mary's otherworldly, liminal situation reaches its climax with the experience of birth itself; Q 19:22–33:

> So she carried him and withdrew with him to a distant place. Pains of labor came to her under the trunk of a palm.
> She said: I wish I had died before this and was completely forgotten.
> He called out from beneath her: do not be sad. Your Lord has made a brook to flow beneath you. Shake the trunk of the palm toward you and it will drop soft fresh dates. Eat and drink and feel soothed, and if you see any person, tell them: I have vowed to the compassionate a fast, and will not speak a word today to any human being.
> And she came to her people, carrying him.
> They said: Mary, you have done a terrible thing!
> Sister of Aaron, your father was not bad man, nor was your mother wanton.
> She pointed to him.
> They said: How do we speak to a child in his cradle?
> He said: I am God's servant. He brought me the writing and made me a Prophet, and made me blessed wherever I may be. He charged me with prayer and almsgiving as long as I live, and to be dutiful to my mother. And he did not make me arrogant and miserable. Peace be upon me the day I was born, the day I die, and the day I am brought back to life!

Coordinates of time and space are lacking in the mythical story; the scene of the birth is not Bethlehem during the Herodian census but a "secluded place," *makān qaṣī*. As labor overtakes her, she flees to the trunk of a palm.[77] The tree shows itself immediately to be miraculous. A voice becomes audible from below—that of the child or an angel. It grants her courage, and a brook opens beneath her as the tree gives fresh dates. She also becomes safe from persecution, since her son will speak for her, while she herself withdraws from the conflict by a vow of silence. The promise is fulfilled; the newborn gives himself as a prophet and—avoiding every claim to divinity—acknowledges himself as servant of God. He attests, like the angel to John/Yaḥyā before him, only his particular divinely endowed distinctions.

Here the story breaks off, without the religious-historical dimension of the event being treated. In the center stands the miracle worked by God's omnipotence, that is, his *raḥma*, mercy, which, as the etymology of the word *raḥma* from *raḥm*, "womb," already attests, has a natural affinity with the areas of life defined

wa-bnahā āyatan li-l-ʿālamīn, "And she who safeguard her shame, we breathe our spirit into her and make her and her son into a symbol for mankind (Q 21:91).

77. The tree is introduced with a definite article, as it is apparently known to the listeners.

as feminine. The story of Jesus in the Qur'an is embedded from the very beginning in the story of his mother.

8.3.2 *The Text as Conversation between Differing Traditions*

While the report about Zachariah hews closely to Lk 1:8–25 and 1:57–80, the story of Mary, who remains passive, stands essentially closer to the apocryphal Protevangelium of Jacob.[78] This text, of great influence in Late Antiquity, depicts chiefly the image of Mary, whose identity as the daughter of Joachim and Anna, two saints of the church, goes back to this writing. The image of Mary in the proto-gospel is clearly different from that of Luke. It knows no self-conscious fiat, "Let it be" (Lk 1:38), the assent of Mary treated as so important in the later Mariology of the eastern churches. Also lacking is the Magnificat (Lk 1:46–56), Mary's praising of the power of God that overwhelms all. What is stressed rather is her ritual purity, later her virginity[79]—she is held apart from mankind already during her earliest childhood and then raised in the temple, which she only leaves as an adolescent.

Also in the Qur'anic version of sura 19, Mary is more the medium of a divine plan than its courageous protagonist. In this birth story, she seems to be transfigured into a mythical personage, who is saved from death by a miraculous palm. The episode, which is lacking in Luke and in the proto-gospel, clearly recalls the story of Hagar and Ismail from Genesis 21:9–21, where an angel shows Hagar the saving palm and well. But, as Suleiman Mourad has shown, the episode also has a Christian parallel in a further apocryphal gospel, Pseudo-Matthew,[80] compiled between the sixth and eighth centuries.[81] This apocryphon sets the palm miracle in connection to the flight of the holy family to Egypt. The context is conceivably different: in Pseudo-Matthew, it is an experience in which Joseph, Mary, and the child, who at this time is capable of action, take part, while in the Qur'an it is the delivery of a feminine figure isolated from all human interaction. Mourad attempts, however, to produce a plausible connection, for which he must adduce further ancient texts.

Mourad is able to show that the connection of the palm to the divine personage in the case of the Mary-Jesus story is not unique. In Greek mythology, the palm is connected to the cult of Apollo, and there is a sanctified palm at the temple of Apollo at Delos. Its honoring goes back to the legend of Apollo's birth,

78. For a dating of the Gospel of James to around 160 CE, see Berger and Nord, *Das Neue Testament*, 1319–1333; Hock, *The Infancy Gospels*; Schneemelcher, *Neutestamentliche Apokryphen*, 277–290.

79. On the role of virginity, see Foskett, *A Virgin Conceived*. In the Qur'an, the centrality of her virginity is demonstrated not only in sura 19 but also in the proclamation in Q 21:91, where Mary isn't referred to by name but rather by her honorific, *wa-llatī aḥṣanat farjahā*, "she who safeguard her shame." This predication evokes a liturgical encomium of Mary in the celebratory liturgy of the Dormition of the Mother of God: *fī mīlādiki ḥafiẓti l-batūlīyata wa-ṣuntihā*, "In childbirth, you protected your virginity and kept it."

80. Schneemelcher, *Neutestamentliche Apokryphen*, 306–308.

81. Mourad, "From Hellenism," 207.

according to which his mother, Leto, gave birth at the trunk of a palm tree. Leto, fleeing from the wrathful Hera, took refuge on the secluded and rocky island of Delos, where she gave birth to Apollo under a palm on the bank of the Inopus River. Mourad, who traces the reception of the story through Greek and Latin literature, arrives at the conclusion that

> in any case, the palm tree story in Qur'an 19.22–24 is an obvious reworking of Leto's labor in the Greek tradition. It is about a distressed pregnant woman (Leto/Mary) who seeks an isolated place (Delos/a remote spot), sits by the trunk (Greek: *premnon*, Arabic: *jiz'*) of a palm tree next to a river (Inopus/stream), and delivers a holy child (Apollo/Jesus). . . . The alm tree story in Pseudo-Matthew seems to be an obvious later reworking of the version that found its way, in concise form, into the text of the Qur'ān. It preserves the second element, namely the palm tree miracle, but deletes the association of the birth-place of Jesus with the palm tree. The canonical gospels are almost silent about the circumstances of the birth of Jesus. All that is known comes from Luke 2.1–20, which mentions nothing about Mary's labor other than the following: 'While they were there [in Bethlehem], the time came for her to deliver her child. And she gave birth to her firstborn son and wrapped him in bands of cloth, and laid him in a manger, because there was no place for them in the inn.' It is not unlikely, then, that some early Christians, ignorant of the Gospel of Luke or unconvinced by it, circulated a story that was meant to describe the circumstances of Mary's labor and delivery. . . . A possible group might be the Christian community of Najrān, in West Arabia, who used to worship a palm tree before converting to Christianity. Changing the Leto/Apollo palm tree story to fit Mary/Jesus would have permitted them to keep part of their belief, yet give it a Christian tone.[82]

Their connection of the palm story with Mary would then—according to Mourad—have as its model both the Qur'anic version and the apocryphal version from Pseudo-Matthew.

Whatever roads the transference may have taken (Mourad does not go beyond hypotheses), according to Mourad the Qur'anic Mary carries traits of the presentation in the Protevangelium of Jacob, and those of a local Arabian birth story. The integration of the palm in this story harmonizes with the ancient Arabian adoration of the tree as a symbol of feminine beauty.[83]

Despite her virgin birth, the Qur'anic Mary is therefore very distant from the role she plays in the Christian tradition, where she is connected to historical sites

82. Mourad, "From Hellenism," 213. A recollection of Greek mythology can also be recognized in the Qur'anic images of the virgins in Paradise; see Saleh, "The Etymological Fallacy."

83. See Rückert, *Amrilkais*, 23; Neuwirth, "Das Gedicht als besticktes Tuch," 116.

and events, and above all possesses an individual personality. And she is just as distant from the early Christian allegorical tradition. The traces of her symbolic connection to the temple, which resonate in her address as "sister of Aaron" (verse 28) or her flight to an "Eastern place," remain without function.[84] Symbols are reinterpreted into narrative elements—a reduction that is balanced out by a new form of myth creation, opening new dimensions of meaning. Thus, sura 19 is, at least to a greater degree than any other Qur'an text, bound up with feminine associations.[85] Already the name of God "Raḥmān," which occurs in this sura sixteen times, that is, more frequently than in any other sura, is derived from a root that immediately denotes the female womb, *raḥm*. Correspondingly, two narratives of the sura revolve around motherhood, and the most important one even around a mother's delivery. The word *raḥma*, "compassion," another derivative of the same root, is first introduced in sura 19, and occurs twice, in verses 2 and 21, and a third instance (verse 13) is paraphrased with *ḥanān*, "empathy, mercy." The sura orchestrates this femininely connoted virtue, while also putting forth an aural-etymological connection between the created sphere, occupied not least by Mary presented as mother, and the transcendent sphere, where al-Raḥmān, "the compassionate," holds sway.

8.3.3 *The Unexpanded Sura: A Hagiographic Image of Jesus*

The child Jesus, who speaks in Q 19:30 on behalf of his mother, names himself a "servant of God," *ʿabd Allāh*. The statement is not to be understood in the sense of an anti-Christological confirmation of his purely human nature, but rather follows other self-pronouncements that are transmitted by other Prophets (cf. Dtn 5:34, Neh 10:29, Rev 15:3).[86] The "scripture" (Q 19:30) granted to Jesus corresponds to the specific Qur'anic conception not of four gospels *about* Jesus but rather a revelation given to him himself, which is treated as of equal rank to the Torah and Qur'an.[87] Jesus's statements about the received blessing (verse 31) and its proper benedictory formula (verse 33) recall Luke 11:27–28.[88] The mention of the death of Jesus (Q 19:33) may ultimately, in view of the middle Meccan verse group Q 43:59–61 in which Jesus figures as "sign of the [final] hour,"[89] count not

84. On this de-allegorizing tendency in the Qur'an, cf. also chap. 9, 365–368.

85. A dissertation on the gender aspects of the story of Mary and the "gendered speech" used there was completed by Husn Abboud in 2008 at the University of Toronto ("The Qur'anic Story of Mary"). A translation of it into Arabic is available: Abboud, *Qissat al-Saiyida Maryam fī al-Qur'ān*.

86. Busse, *Die theologischen Beziehungen*, 127.

87. Griffith, "The Gospel in Arabic," discusses in detail both of these perceptions of the Gospel, against the backdrop of the still missing Arabic translation of the Gospels at the time of the Qur'an's emergence; see also, Griffith, "Gospel."

88. Busse, *Die theologischen Beziehungen*, 128.

89. Instead of the canonical Qur'anic reading, *ʿilmun li-l-sāʿati*, "knowledge about the hour," Jesus's qualification should rather be read as *ʿalamun li-l-sāʿati*, "sign of the hour." The non-canonical interpretation is ascribed to Ikrima; see Jeffery, *Materials*, 173.

as a historical event but an eschatological one. For, according to the Qur'anic presentation (Q 4:157–158), Jesus did not die on the cross but was instead raised up to heaven.[90] According to later Islamic hagiography, he will return at the end of times and defeat the Antichrist, and only then will he die. This popular conception, which is evoked in Q 43:61, can also be presupposed for sura 19. In its essential part, the sura treats Jesus not as a figure acting in time but rather as an icon of pure piety—exceeded in this only by his mother.

8.4 Anti-Pagan Polemic

8.4.1 Politicization of the Image of Jesus: Early Polemics against Jesus as Son of God

It is surprising that in a later addition to the story of Mary and Jesus, Jesus is bound up with theological doctrines. He no longer remains limited to the rank of a servant of God, entrusted with the two essential imperatives of love of God (symbolized through prayer [*ṣalāh*]) and love of man (symbolized through the giving of alms [*zakāh*]), which were attributed to him in the original form of the sura. In the commenting verse group Q 19:34–40, he becomes a theologically disputed figure with a firm motto (Q 19:36, taken over from Q 43:64), frequently repeated in later suras, which remains connected to him also in Medina (Q 3:51, 5:117): "God is my Lord and your Lord, serve him. That is the right way." In slightly modified form (in Q 21:92 and 23:52), this carries echoes of the first command of the Decalogue (Ex 20:2–23),[91] which is cited by Jesus at the end of the temptation story (Mt 4:10): "You should worship God, your Lord, and him alone" (Ex 20:3). This uncompromising confession of the unity of God excludes, according to Qur'anic understanding, a father-son relation between God and Jesus. The verse group 19:34–40, appended to the story, thus indicates a state of reception in which the recitation of the largely mythical Mary-Jesus story was already supported by discursive commentaries.

> This is Jesus son of Mary: a statement of truth about which they dispute.
> It is not for God to take a child—Glory to Him! When he determines any matter, he merely says "be," and it is.
> God is my Lord and your Lord, so serve Him,
> This is a straight path.
> But the sects fell into dispute among themselves. Woe to those who do not believe in the spectacle of a terrifying day.
> How well they shall hear, how well they shall see, on the day they come before us! But the wicked today are plunged in manifest delusion.

90. See Lawson, *Crucifixion*.
91. Busse, *Die theologischen Beziehungen*, 133.

Warn them of the day of regret, when judgment is passed, they are inattentive and do not believe
We will inherit the earth and what is upon it, and to us they will return.

Right at the beginning of the commentary, the child, unnamed up to that point, is identified. In addition to his name, ʿĪsā, he bears the matronymic Ibn Maryam, "son of Mary,"[92] which is easily recognized as an overwriting of the Christian title "son of God." With this "official" introduction of the person of Jesus, the mythical discourse is left behind and the figure obtains political relevance, which plays a role in the social reality of the community. For Jesus son of Mary / ʿĪsā ibn Maryam is no longer only a sign of divine compassion (verse 21), but rather the object of dispute (verse 34). He is followed by an opposing group, which clearly assigns Jesus to a pantheon[93]—an insinuation that is disputed by the argument that God can create everything immediately through his word, and therefore does not need to bear a child (verse 35). Jesus refers to himself—in the slogan taken over from Q 43:64—as *servant* of God (Q 19:36). The person of Jesus is not only an object of dispute in the present but was also this in the past, where a schism came about after his death (verse 37). These statements about Jesus are not yet polemics against Christian beliefs, but rather, as a comparison with sura 43 shows, they still stand in the context of the confrontation with pagan opponents.

8.4.2 *Mutual Coinage of Two Texts: Suras 19 and 43*

The two closely related suras, 19 and 43, both dealing with Jesus, clearly developed in dispute with each other. Sura 43 shows itself already as later than sura 19, through its new self-authorization, its triumphal beginning[94] that proclaims the Arabic dressing of the message. A similar indication is made by the excerpt of a citation from sura 19 in sura 43, the final verse of which (verse 89) transfers Abraham's reaction to his father's idolatry from sura 19 (verse 47) verbatim to the proclaimer. Both say to the idolaters, or the pagan opponents, "farewell," *salām*. But the most significant step forward that sura 43 shows in comparison to sura 19 is the new sovereign position that the proclaimer adopts against the insinuation that God might have children. In sura 19 (verses 88–91), he reacts while emotionally overwhelmed to the shocking insinuation, Q 19:88–91:

And yet they say: "The Merciful has taken to himself a son!"
You have uttered a thing most terrible
The heavens shake when you mention it,

92. This association only appears once in the New Testament (Mk 6:3), whereas Jesus is elsewhere associated only with Joseph (Lk 3:23, 4:22; Jo 1:45, 6:42). Both of Jesus's genealogies go through Joseph (Mt 1;1–17) or begin with him (Lk 3:23–38); cf. Bauschke, *Jesus im Koran*, 22.

93. See verse 88. In Q 19:80, Ibn Masʿūd reads the collective *wild* instead of the individual *walad*; see Jeffery, *Materials*, 59.

94. See Wild, "An Arabic Recitation."

> The earth splits apart,
> The mountains stagger and collapse,
> When they ascribe a son to the Merciful.

But in sura 43, verse 81, he has gained the sovereign status of a superior dialogue partner:

> Say: If the merciful had a son, I would be the first of his worshippers.

In sura 43, the central theme is polemic against the worship of several divinities occurring in various forms, whether in the form of adoption of feminine divinities as angels (Q 43:15–22) or in blind adherence to the ways of the father, which Abraham refuses in exemplary fashion (Q 43:26–28). In this context, we also see Jesus's status as child of God, a theme that the pagan opponents take up eagerly, Q 43:57–58:

> And when the son of Mary is adduced as an example, behold, your people are loud in protest, and say: What! Are our gods better, or is he? They adduce his example only in order to argue. Indeed, they are a people fond of dispute.

This does not refer to the Christological problematic but rather to the ranking of Jesus among the pagan pantheon, in analogy to the "daughtership of God" that is thematized in sura 53, which the pagan opponents themselves claim for their goddesses. "Are our gods better, or is he?" (Q 43:58)—with this challenging question, the pagan Meccans signal their leveling of every special status of Jesus. In the end, though, Jesus himself obtained the word in order to establish unity, yet he himself set loose the disintegration of his community into sects (*al-aḥzāb*); Q 43:63–65:

> When Jesus came with evident signs, he said: I come to you with wisdom, and to make clear to you some of what you differ about. Be pious before God and obey me. God is my Lord and your Lord, so worship him, for this is the straight path.
>
> But the sects among them fell into dispute—woe to the wicked from the torment of a painful day!

It is not only that sura 43 is based on the older sura 19—in contrast, the polemical addition in sura 19 is also due to the Jesus-polemic from sura 43. Thus, Q 19:37 is almost identical with Q 43:65; the immediately preceding statement of Jesus in Q 19:36 corresponds in turn almost precisely to Q 43:64. But above all, the discussion in Q 43:57–65 provides a situational grounding for the full naming of Jesus, and thus makes the establishment of Jesus's servanthood to God comprehensible as a logical answer to an argument, while the corresponding information about Jesus in sura 19 is introduced abruptly and stands in no logical context within the narrative. The verse group Q 43:57–65 shows itself to be the model for the stylistically isolated and argumentatively context-free verse group Q 19:34–40. Their addition to sura 19 seems to have become necessary, after the later sura 43 uncovered the polemical potential that was linked to Jesus in confrontation with the pagan Meccans. Every new recitation of the originally poetically told story of Mary and Jesus was now exposed to challenging questions; defensive argumentative strategies were required—even if the unique poetic composition in the Qur'an was broken up by these practical-discursive insertions, and the "recitation" lost some of its ceremonial quality.

Sura 19 in its unexpanded form shows hardly any interest in the nature of Jesus. It does not revolve at all around Jesus, whose birth story says much less about him than it does about his mother. It is first in sura 43[95] that ʿĪsā ibn Maryam enters the stage as a significant religious-political figure, but still without Christological symbolism, as an object of dispute among the pagan Meccans, who bring him into the debate as a rival to their divinities, and the new community, who accept no family of Gods. After he has become the object of dispute, he later enters into a new religious-political role in sura 19, in order to dispel any suspicion that the son of Mary could be accepted by the community as the son of God.[96] The polemical verse group documents the disputes with pagan opponents that had become a daily event in middle Meccan times, disputes no longer having to do with simple belief and unbelief but with concrete points of contention. The new situation required that potential for eventual conflict had to be treated in references to sacred history, so that in some cases a disambiguating position had to be taken up through "commentary."

8.4.2.1 *Further Prophet Stories*

The polemical-explanatory verse group Q 19:34–40 interrupts a series of prophet stories. One among them—also about a father-child relationship—is closely linked to the Zachariah-Mary story, namely, the confrontation of Abraham with his father (Q 19:41–50). As an obedient son, Abraham dissuades his father from idolatry but must become resigned to his choice and part with him peacefully: *qāla salāmun ʿalayka*, "He said, farewell" (Q 19:47). Like Mary, who left behind her kin, he renounces the genealogical bind, in order to enter into a transcendent bond. The sequence of Prophet narratives proceeds with a story about the close relation of Moses to God (verses 51–53) and a brief mention of Ismail (who does not appear here as Abraham's son, verses 54–55) and Idrīs (verses 56–57). The narrative part of the sura closes with an isolated direct speech

95. It is only mentioned three more times in the Meccan suras, twice in the context of other messengers (Q 42:13, Abraham, Moses, and Jesus; Q 6:85, Zacharias, Jesus, and Elias). In Q 23:50, Jesus is figured with his mother (*ʿĪsā bnu Maryam wa-ummuhu*); all references are late Meccan.

96. These findings are corroborated further through the contextualization of sura 19 with Q 43:16–29; see Neuwirth, "Imagining Mary—Disputing Jesus."

of the angels (verse 64), who confirm that they are entirely dependent on God's instructions—an implicit rejection of their status as the daughters of God, which was disputed in detail in some early suras.[97] The closing verse of the first part of the sura is an encouragement to the proclaimer to carry his service of God patiently forward.

8.4.3 *A Later Discourse? The Prophetic Succession*

But before this "end credit" to the narrative part, the narrative sequence is brought together in a confirmation of the special status of the Prophet—with a verse that in turn attests to a later new reading of the sura, Q 19:58:

> These are, of Prophets, the ones on whom God bestowed his blessings from among the progeny of Adam, from those we carried with Noah, from the progeny of Abraham and Israel, and from those whom we guided and elected. When the verses of the merciful are recited to them, they fall down in prostration and weep.

The idea that certain prophets form a group belonging together is wholly foreign to the context of sura 19. Not only do we lack the term "prophets"—in the plural *nabīyūna, anbiyāʾ*—but the whole concept of a divine project of prophecy, embodied in different figures legitimized by genealogy or election, stands outside the horizon of Meccan prophetology. It first becomes relevant in Medina, where it is closely connected to the depiction of the holy family or the House of Amram, the *Āl ʿImrān*.

At the time of the proclamation of the unexpanded sura 19, the community had no knowledge of the high value that accrued to the family of Mary and Jesus as founders of the Christian tradition in the Medinan period, a ranking that, as the relevant sura (sura 3), "House of Imran," shows, was only rivaled by the founders of the Abrahamic, that is, Jewish tradition.[98] But after the Christians standing in the tradition of Mary and Jesus are recognized as elected—God elected among men Adam and Noah, the House of Abraham, and the House of Amram (*Āl ʿImrān*), Q 3:33—they can no longer be missing from the list of the privileged and had to be added into the early suras as well. The addition in Q 19:58, required by the Medinan discourse of Prophetic succession, legitimizes the family of Mary, who are no longer recognizable through genealogy but rather through her pure preservation and chastity: "And such as those that we have rightly guided and elected, if our signs are recited, they fall down in prostration and weep." The later raising of the Christians into the rank of the elected shows that the sura was

97. The angels already played a role in a late Meccan addition to the early sura 53; her status is a matter of controversy in Q 43:19, a text that is closely related to sura 19. They also appear in the Raḥmān sura 21 (verses 26–29), where they are presented as entirely subordinate to God. For further religious contexts for the angels and their disputed responsibilities, see Schäfer, *Rivalität*.

98. Neuwirth, "The House of Abraham."

interpreted in retrospect in terms of the history of the emergence of Christianity, and must therefore have been adapted in its repeated recitation at Medina to the newly achieved communal self-positioning in view of the Christians.

8.4.3.1 *The Polemic-Paraenetic Sura Part—"Sermon" and Conclusion*

The final part of the sura (verses 66–98) first argues against unbelief about the Final Judgment (verses 66–77) and complains of the lack of respect for the Qur'an performance (verses 73–74). It next addresses the fleeting value of wealth and progeny (*walad*) and their worthlessness in face of the judgment (verses 75–80). The main thrust, however, is the assumption of divinities (*āliha*) in addition to God (verses 81 and 87). It is in this context that the unbelievers are mentioned, with the pronouncement *ittakhadha l-Raḥmān waladan*, "The merciful took on a child" (verse 77). This is not an evocation of the Christian dogma of Jesus being the son of God, but rather, in view of the use of *walad* for progeny in general, a polemic against the pagan pantheon, in which the highest God possessed progeny. The saying could allude to the daughters of God, which were claimed by the unbelievers (Q 53:19–21).

The second part of the sura reverses the positive image of the parent-child relation that is central in the first part, in that it displays the blasphemous character of the projection of such a relationship onto God. The short confirmation of revelation, which concludes the sura, again shows the tension, so characteristic for the sura, between muteness (verses 10 and 26) and speech (Q 19:3–4 30.48.52) that is "understandable" and "hearable":

> We made it easy on your tongue to give tidings to the pious, and to warn a people who harbor malice. How many generations before you we have destroyed! Do you perceive any one of them, or hear from them a sound? (Q 19:97–98)

8.5 New Homiletic Instruments: Morality Speeches and Parables/Likenesses

8.5.1 *An "Emblem of Prophethood"*

In the late Meccan suras, we see a gradual transformation of the earlier suras, which were structured on the model of a prayer service, into complex compositions, in which the individual parts recall sermons. A means of presentation of this homiletically marked sura part is the likeness/parable. The Qur'anic moral likenesses and narratives, of which many appear at first glance to be related to Gospel texts, are, despite extensive collections of the materials,[99] still largely unresearched. Above all, their position in the Qur'an as a new hermeneutical

99. See Lohmann, "Gleichnisse im Koran"; Sister, "Metaphers und Vergleiche"; Buhl, "Vergleichungen."

element has not yet been illuminated. The Qur'anic designation *mathal* seems to have become a technical term at a certain point, a term that named an exegetical pragmatics, and perhaps also a reference to the parable speeches of the older religions.[100] It is this linking of the *mathal* to the development of the community and the developing prophetic self-understanding that still awaits description. Illustrative stories, which are similar to a likeness or parable but not named as *mathal*, occur already in one of the last early Meccan suras, and at numerous points in middle Meccan suras. On the other hand, the parable narrative, intended explicitly as *mathal*, develops first in the late Meccan period and remains a striking characteristic of Qur'anic speech throughout the Medinan period.

The Qur'anic *mathal*, intended as such,[101] could be termed an "emblem of prophethood"—to employ a term coined by John Wansbrough. Wansbrough, who based his form-critical studies on the observation that the Qur'an adopts fundamental elements of biblical prophet speech, includes among the "emblems of prophethood" the employment of great themes such as revelation, exile, and promise,[102] but the parable or likeness also deserves to be mentioned here, as it is typical of both prophet speech and also, perhaps primarily, the speech of wise men. Although the specific narrative-paraenetic form of the parable or likeness occurs also in "profane" literary genres, including ancient Arabic poetry, its striking presence in certain biblical books—above all the "Solomonic corpus" of wisdom (Song of Songs, Proverbs, and Ecclesiastes)—led it to become a distinguishing mark of biblical speech, which, as is known, was in later times set wholly as an equal to prophetic speech. Thus, it is no wonder that the form of the parable among the hearers of Jesus inspired wonderment as prophetic speech: "Since Jesus has accomplished this speech [the Sermon on the Mount in parables], the people were shocked at his teaching, for he taught them as one who possessed power [*hos exousian ekhon*], not like their book teachers" (Mt 7:28–29).[103] The form of the parable was not therefore considered immediately equivalent to the speech of the "exegetes," but rather was considered a charismatic privilege, a symbol of power of the prophets[104]—despite the problem of it being not immediately comprehensible.

Parable discourse seems to have been perceived with more skepticism in roughly contemporary Jewish circles. Haggai Ben-Shammai indicates a low appreciation of it, which rabbinic discussions considered "of low literary value" and

100. An analysis of the biblical Hebrew text type, *mashal*, is offered in Haggai Ben-Shammai, "Parable and Simile."

101. For examples of unmarked parable speech, cf. chap. 10, 363–365.

102. Wansbrough, *Quranic Studies*, 53–84.

103. Cf. also Mt 13:10–17: "The disciples came to him and asked, 'why do you speak to people in parables?' He replied, 'Because knowledge of the kingdom of heaven has been given to you; whoever does not have. . . . In them is fulfilled the prophesy of Isaiah, who says: "You will be ever hearing but never understanding; you will be ever seeing but never perceiving." ' "

104. This observation is thanks to an unpublished lecture by Michael Marx, given at Princeton in 2009.

"obscure in expression."[105] He cites here the preface to the midrash collection on the Song of Songs (*Shir ha-Shirim Rabba*), which sought to justify the use of parables not only in the Song of Songs but throughout the Solomonic corpus. The frequent use of the disparaged parable is said in these writings to provide valuable service in the exploration of the deeper sense of the Torah. This valuation is itself founded through parable or likeness: the use of parable is like the use of a torch (by itself worthless), which even a king will use when he must use it to search for a (valuable) lost pearl.[106]

But the parable is not only controversial in the rabbinic context. Also in the case of the Qur'anic parable, the opponents of the proclaimer were struck by the lowliness of the objects with which the parable operates—an accusation that is addressed apologetically in the Medinan verse 2:26:

> God shies not from drawing a likeness even from an insect, or else anything large or small. Those who believe know it is the truth from their Lord. Those who disbelieve say: "What did God intend by this likeness?" God thereby leads many astray, and guides many. But the dissolute alone he leads astray.[107]

If this apology grants some room for an ambivalence toward *mathal* as a means of persuasion, still it draws the triumphal claim of the positive usefulness of the new strategy of *mathal* employed by the proclaimer—regardless of the fact that this strategy does not hit its mark with the unbelievers, Q 17:89:

> In this reading we have elucidated to mankind every sort of likeness, but most people will assent to nothing but unbelief.[108]

Though the consciousness of the hermeneutical achievement of the *mathal* on the part of the community stood against its rejection by the unbelievers, the introduction of this speech figure should be recognized as an important stage of the Qur'anic rhetorical development.

8.5.1.1 The Posing of Questions from Biblical Scholarship versus Qur'anic Questions

Older research, which treats the morality speeches and parables in the Qur'an in isolation from their wider sura contexts, is marked strongly by Bible scholarship. Adolf Jülicher's work *Die Gleichnisreden Jesu* (The parable speech of

105. Ben-Shammai, "Parable and Simile."

106. Ibid, 160.

107. The same provocative question is posed in Q 74:31 by the unbelievers, a Medinan addition, which does not relate to parable speech, but rather to a situation where the unbelievers assume an assertion they fail to understand to be a scornful text type.

108. Cf. also Q 30:58. "We have propounded for men in this Qur'an every kind of likeness: But if you bring to them any sign, the unbelievers are sure to say, 'You do nothing but speak vanities.'" Cf. Q 39:37.

Jesus)[109], which appeared around the turn of the twentieth century, has proven fundamental; in this work, the author pleaded for a veritative, "literal" interpretation of the parables that were previously read so often allegorically. According to Jülicher's long-influential interpretation, parables—in opposition to allegory, which addresses the "knowing"—are directed to those who must still be illuminated, who are guided to recognize the familiar in what appears initially as strange. Parable discourse juxtaposes an image part and an object part (which often remains implicit), and these two are linked by a central thought (*tertium comparationis*). Parable discourse serves to illustrate this thought within an apologetic or ethical message.

A renewed interest in parable, bringing Jülicher's work to bear on the Qur'an,[110] was reflected first in Hartwig Hirschfeld's study *New Researches in the Composition and Exegesis of the Qoran* (1902),[111] which emphasizes the rhetorical and apologetic function of the parables.[112] Further studies followed applying the same approach,[113] but even the most detailed study, by Theodor Lohmann (1955),[114] remains limited to the recognition of the parables' mental statements. Lohmann fails in his attempt to treat the respective *tertium comparationis* in the often fragmentary Qur'anic *mathal* structures, just as he is misled in his expectation to find immediate dependencies of the parables on Christian or Jewish tradition.[115]

A newer approach is emerging, as biblical scholarship and research in parables in recent decades has moved away from the earlier dichotomous distinction between veritative and allegorical speech, and thus put the focus on the "parable as expanded metaphor." Accordingly, Hannelies Koloska no longer merely sets the biblical and the Qur'anic into historical relation, but rather focuses above all on the formal language of the Qur'anic *mathal*.[116] Instead of seeing in the parables of the Qur'an the illustration of abstract ideas or concepts, she focuses on the parables as narratives, "which in turn represent an event."

Nevertheless, literary-critical questions must be supplemented with historical ones. For as essential as knowledge of the methodologies of biblical studies remains for Qur'an research, it is certainly not always sufficient to adequately

109. Jülicher, *Gleichnisreden*.

110. An investigation of the Qur'anic *mathal* by Hannelies Koloska is in progress; an overview of her research is offered in summary here.

111. Hirschfeld, *New Researches*, 83–101.

112. Hirschfeld, *New Researches*, 83–84, attempts to explain longer parables as historical occurrences, with the help of commentary.

113. Buhl, "Vergleichungen"; Sister, "Metaphern und Vergleiche"; Speyer, *Die biblischen Erzählungen im Qoran*, 426–438.

114. Lohmann, "Gleichnisreden Muhammeds."

115. Ibid., 285. Ben-Shammai's new study, "Parable and Simile," goes a bit further, concentrating on the *tafsīr* reception.

116. Koloska's still unpublished investigation employing form-critical criteria arrives at a rough classification into comparison, metaphor, parable, and allegory.

describe Qur'anic phenomena. The Qur'an is not least an exegetical text, which views traditions from neighboring cultures critically, and through negotiating them adapts them to its new worldview. In view of this dynamism of the proclamation process, the old questions—allegory or not? connection to the parables of the Gospels?—do not become obsolete but remain of significance. A purely synchronic reading of the Qur'an would ignore the complexity of the Qur'anic references—the successively negotiated older traditions and the changing position of the hearer toward these traditions. Such a reading would miss the fact that Qur'anic engagements with the problems disputed in the milieu of the Qur'an genesis are at the same time stages of communal formation. Self-referential Qur'anic mentions of the availability of parables, such as Q 17:98 and 30:58, indicate the significance that the community itself attributed to this text type previously not known in Arabic in this formation. What function do parables fulfill in the Qur'an?

8.5.1.2 Examples of Qur'anic Parable Speeches

The Qur'anic parable narratives that are named explicitly as *amthāl*, "likenesses," occur as a rule within biblical reminiscences. Although the textual type as such could already carry Christian associations in view of its frequency in the Gospels, the Qur'anic likenesses are in no way homogenous and do not necessarily refer back to the New Testament.[117] Some likenesses take up thematic references to the Psalms, while structurally recalling the likenesses of the Gospels: Q 14:24–27 evokes Psalm 1 but is expanded into a dichotomous statement:

> Do you not see how God draws a likeness: a goodly word is like a goodly tree; its roots are firm and its branches reach the sky.
> It brings forth its nourishment at every turn, by its Lord's leave.
> And God draws likenesses for mankind, so perhaps they will reflect.
> And the likeness of an evil word is like a bad tree uprooted from the ground; it has no bed.
> God gives strength to the faithful with speech unchanging in the present life and the hereafter, and he leads the wicked astray. God does what he wills.

The reference that spawns this image is clearly the tree simile from Psalms 1:3: "He will be like a tree, planted in water courses, that gives its fruit at the right time and whose leaves do not wither." In the Qur'an, however, it is not man but rather the "good word" that rises like a tree and bears fruit. On the other hand, the bad word is like a useless and unsteady tree. Although it is not said whose word is meant here, the "good word" seems to be identical with the firm speech

117. For Qur'anic recourses to parables in the Gospel, see Lohmann, "Gleichnisreden Mohammeds"; for further references, see Wansbrough, *Quranic Studies*, 242.

of God, while the bad word brings with it the error-inducing speech of seducers of all kinds. The qualities of the tree made evident individually are no longer transferable to the word but are more probably to be understood as "narrative excess" of the expanded metaphor, increasing their suggestive power. The *tertium comparationis* is firmness and vital power. That in the Qur'an it is not men but the word that is spoken of as a tree—an attribution that from a pragmatic viewpoint is not very evident as an object part[118]—is best explained by the Qur'anic restraint toward the exaltation of man; the transference of the image to God's word may be thought of as a "corrective" of the psalmic elevation of man.

A further likeness from the same sura takes up an image from Psalms 1:4 ("The ungodly are not so, but like the chaff that the wind drives away"):

> The works of those who do not believe, they are to be compared with ash, blown by the wind on a stormy day.
> They have no power over that which they have earned.

In the psalm, the opponents of the righteous are described, who in contrast to the high and firm tree are like chaff lying on the ground. In the Qur'an, it is again not men but rather abstract ideas that are employed as the "object part": it is the deeds of the unbelievers that the wind blows. In both texts, the construction of the ash/chaff comparison through the depiction of a stormy day strengthens the intensity of the idea of the nullity of the wicked and the deeds of the unbelievers.

A narrative from the middle Meccan period (Q 36:13–32) modifies a simile from Mt 21:33–44:

> Strike for them the likeness of the people of the town, when messengers arrived.
>
> We had sent them two but they called them liars, so we backed them with a third, and they said: we are messengers to you.

As in Matthew, here too a simile is related about the sending of prophets. While in the Gospel a country scenario is chosen as backdrop, a vineyard, with symbolic connotations already in a Christian context, whose workers are warned by the owner of the vineyard through messengers to hand over the harvest, the Qur'an speaks of a city to which messengers are sent. In both likenesses, the messengers are Prophets sent to mankind but rejected by them and threatened with death or even killed. While in the Gospel, there is a gradual buildup—first the messengers fall victim to the attacks of the wine gardeners, then the son of the owner himself—in the Qur'an the event unfolds according to the model of the punishment legends: the messengers are derided in a disputation, and it is not they who are killed but rather an unknown person who hurries to help and gives

118. Cf. Mt 12:33, in the context of speech, and cf. Lk 6:43.

a sermon of warning. The two likenesses, with their similar outward plots, follow clearly divergent directions. While the Gospel likeness focuses on the steadfastness of God that leads to the sacrificing of his own son to prepare men for God's kingdom, and thus ends with the murder of the son of the vineyard owner by the criminal wine farmer, in the Qur'anic parable there is only an allusion to martyrdom (Q 36:26), and even this relates only to an outsider who will be repaid for his sacrifice. The Qur'anic story has "redirected" the narrative from the theologically decisive position of a Christ parable to a parable of the sending of prophets. The victim sacrifice thus remains an interlude—the Christological parable of the Gospel is "de-allegorized" and thus theologically softened.

In the same realm of images—of power/powerlessness—are the comparison and compared in the *mathal* of Q 16:76, which shows no reference to the Gospels, but is rather derived from the Qur'anic confrontation between belief and unbelief itself:

> God strikes a likeness of two men: one is dumb, with no power over anything, a burden to his guardian. Wherever he sends him, he brings back nothing good. Is such like one who commands justice and is set upon a straight path?

Here, the standard rhetorical question about the equality of a rightly guided person and an unbeliever is formed into a likeness. The detailed depiction of the object of comparison makes it possible to project the drastic situation of the powerlessness of a deaf person, who exercises useless abilities, onto the unbeliever as "deaf to the message," enslaved by earthly life and doing only useless things. In contrast to them stands the hearing and thus understanding of the rightly guided one, who is himself empowered for right guidance. The rhetorical questions, which elsewhere remain abstract, gain significantly in density and memorability through the narrative depiction enabled by parable discourse.

Parable speeches in the Qur'an—as far as they are marked expressly as *mathal*—in general do not allow for allegorical interpretations, but instead reshape bold metaphors and allegories of the predecessor traditions into simple stories, so that one can speak of a "myth corrective": as the examples presented here show, the likenesses soften the "exalted" perceptions of man that are incompatible with the Qur'an (Q 14:24–27), and implicitly decrease the strength of Christologically laden older texts (Q 36:13). But other Qur'anic likenesses free themselves entirely from the relation to predecessor texts and apply the technique made available by this type of "narrativizing" of thought to an immediate world of experience (Q 16:76). Unlike some parable speeches not marked as *mathal*,[119] all of these likenesses remain in the realm of veritative speech.

119. Cf. chap. 10, 360–365.

On the one hand, parable discourse seems to be a textual type specifically suited to prophets—one can think of the Ezekiel vision of the rotten bones, which is controversial as to its status as parable discourse in Jewish exegesis;[120] but on the other hand, it appears, as the preface to the midrash on the Song of Songs shows, to be the ideal medium of the wise man or, according to a later view, the Prophet, for the exploration of the deeper sense of the scripture. In the Qur'an, the text type of the likeness, which arises in the middle Meccan period and is soon applied programmatically, is in one sense an element of mantic speech, in that God himself strikes the likenesses. But at the same time, it is an object of dispute and a means of persuasion among believers and unbelievers. Clearly, it quickly wins the consensus of the community, as it develops into a characteristic trait of the late Meccan suras, remaining at the same time a target of the mockery of the unbelievers.

The Qur'anic likeness still awaits systematic research, in which the observations of Daniel Boyarin and David Stern on rabbinic parables will require careful consideration.[121]

120. Ben-Shammai, "Parable and Simile," 167–169. Jesus's listeners in Mt 7:28 also contrast his manifestly Prophetic speech with that of the scribes; see above, 306–307.

121. In accordance with Stern, *Parables in Midrash*, and Stern, "Rhetoric," Boyarin explores a non-allegorical meaning of the parables in rabbinic literature; see Boyarin and Stern, "Exchange on the Mashal."

9

Stages of Communal Formation in Medina

9.1 The Turn of Exile

The decisive turn that was achieved by the proclaimer and community with the *hijra* and the configuration of a political entity in Medina is reflected clearly in the early establishment of the date of the *hijra* as the beginning of the Islamic calendar. "Up until the migration to Medina, Muhammad and his dependents were *objects*, even according to the Muslim view: victims, born of a historical context that they wanted to alter but could not, they only become the *subjects* of defined historical developments after the *hijra*, subjects who would set new standards for their nearer and further surroundings that would ultimately take on world historical dimensions."[1] The transition from activity that was above all kerygmatic to activity that was also political and ultimately even military is described in detail in the Sira,[2] and is also reflected in the Qur'an text itself. But the event of the *hijra* itself is only evoked vaguely in the Qur'an,[3] and never reported concretely. This silence about the *hijra* may be based on the fact that it was perceived as an act of "turning away" (*hijra*) from their opponents,[4] as a flight, enforced on the adherents of the Prophet whose ambivalent and perhaps even humiliating circumstances in no way predicted its future aura of a world-historical event paradigmatic for later generations of believers. The *hijra* is not focused in the Qur'an as a triumphant, history-making event, as Patricia Crone has shown with clarity.[5] What does appear in the Qur'an, however, is the new situation into which the community entered by way of this event: the Medinan interaction scenario stands out clearly, through novel politically programmatic declarations[6] and legally binding

1. Noth, "Früher Islam," 11–12.
2. See the analysis in Ammann, *Die Geburt des Islam*; Nagel, *Medinensische Einschübe*; Rahman, *Major Themes*; Donner, *Narratives of Islamic Origins*; Donner, *Expansion and the Islamic State.*
3. This occurs most distinctly in Q 9:40, where *hijra* is not mentioned but rather, in its place, *idh akhrajahu lladhīna kafarū*, "when the unbelievers expelled him."
4. This usage in the Qur'an is not yet terminological, but see the early Meccan instruction to the proclaimer: Q73:10: *wa-ṣbir ʿalā mā yaqūlūna wa-hjurhum hujran jamīlan*, "And be patient over what they say and avoid them with gracious avoidance."
5. The gradual development of the concept of *hijra* occurs in post-Qur'anic Islam, where it initially stands for the divinely ordained flight of the Prophet and his earliest followers to Medina, and later for the "emigration" of Muslim fighters to the garrison-cities—the Prophet's emigration, thus standing as a model for militarily motivated emigration; this is traced in Crone, "The First-Century Concept of Hijra."
6. For example, Q 3:79 on the question of authority and Q 22:39–30 on the justification of the struggle.

instructions[7]—often underlined in their irrefutability by references to their transcendent source, such as "It is (already) written for you," *kutiba ʿalaykum* (Q 2:183), or "as a duty imposed by God," *farīḍatan min llāhi* (Q 9:60)—from the Meccan context, where comparably rigorous and specific rules were not yet necessary.

Even family relationships become regulated within the community for the first time in Medina (Q 4:24–25, 35, and 65:6). Here, Albrecht North stresses the

> very concrete restrictions of traditional male dominance. This occurred, decisively, above all in relation to financial regulations. Thus, the dowry of the man became the possession of the woman after marriage, no longer the possession of her family or, more precisely, of the male part of this family. She could now obtain wealth through marriage and have disposal over this—with a fair division of property. Even if she possessed a lesser share than her male guardians, she could still inherit from . . . her relatives and her husband. . . . Also, divine revelations now governed the traditional forms of polygamy, clearly to the benefit of women of the Muslim *umma*. What was intended was not to grant males surplus enjoyment of sexual pleasures, but the enforcement of the man's duty to provide, also financially.[8]

Even if the equality before God promised to women (Q 33:35) is not fully reflected in the rules for practical interaction with them, nevertheless the rules for divorce and for adequate provision represent an important step of reform.[9] But above all, we can point to an elevation in the accepted image of women. "This entailed an essential 'atmospheric' change in the relation of the sexes to each other . . . , so that man and woman become viewed in principle with absolute parity in their quality as believers; a situation in which such a fundamental leveling of the gap between the sexes could take place did not exist up until then, and its creation can justifiably be called revolutionary."[10]

The new situation of the proclaimer and his community in Medina is marked by various conflicts with tribal, religious, and personal opponents, as the Qur'an itself documents.[11] Such engagements, which in a number of cases were carried out violently (above all, the military actions against Mecca and further cities or tribes of the peninsula) dominate the entire period of his ministry in Medina. The interaction scenario also becomes more complex: Since also qasida poets,

7. Likewise Q 2:186; on the institutionalization of fasting, cf. Goitein, "The Muslim Month of Fasting"; Q 4:11 and passim on inheritance; cf. Kimbler, "The Quranic Law of Inheritance"; Q 9:60 and passim on giving alms; cf. Dutton, "Zakāt."

8. See Noth, "Früher Islam," 51–52.

9. See Watt, *Muhammad at Medina*, 272–289; cf. also the feminist discussion in Barlas, "Women's Readings."

10. Noth, "Früher Islam," 51. The comparative contextualization of this reform alongside early Christian reconsiderations of gender relations still awaits being done. See Boyarin, *A Radical Jew*.

11. See Noth, "Früher Islam," 52–57.

who in the tribal society were responsible for the public representation of collectively relevant incidents, now enter into the debates and incite a confrontation between attackers and defenders of the new movement, for a while new public speakers—remaining however outside the Qur'an—appear on the stage alongside the proclaimer. These conflicts that break out between the proclaimer and the poets are not always solved verbally but in some cases escalate to violence. There are some texts extant by some of the poets involved in this, which—unique in view of the otherwise missing evidence on the immediate environment of the proclaimer—provide profane "para-texts" that aid in the reconstruction of several events that are merely alluded to in the Qur'an. In particular, four poets as Agnes Imhof has shown are decisive in this: Labīd ibn Rabīʿa, Ḥassān ibn Thābit, Kaʿb ibn Zuhayr, and Kaʿb ibn Mālik.[12] These poets through their new images of God and understandings of society, which are different from those of the ancient poetry offer unique insights into the gradually developing religious changes in the circles around the proclaimer.

In addition, there is another important new element within the Medinan suras: the reporting of contemporary events, above all military confrontations in which the community becomes involved or that it has itself triggered, such as the Battle of Badr, 2/624 (Q 3:123; 8:41–44), the Battle of Uḥud, 3/625 (Q 3:155–174), the expulsion of the Banū Naḍīr, 3/625 (Q 59:2–5), the siege of Khaybar, 7/628 (Q 48:15), and the expedition to Tabūk, 9/630 (Q 9:29–35). However, these reports are not narrative depictions of great historical moments, but rather are dressed in isolated verse groups that stand in a wider paraenetic or polemical context. Yet, in one unique case, a later recollection of an event of salvation, the Battle of Badr, which evokes the precedent of the exodus of the Israelites,[13] seems to suggest that a consciousness of having experienced an event of salvation historical dimension had arisen (Q 8:41–44):

> On the day of decision [*yawma l-furqāni*], the day when the two hosts met—God is powerful over everything.
> While you were on the nearer side [of the valley]
> and they were on the farther side, with the riders beneath you.
> Had you made an appointment,
> you would surely have failed to keep the appointment.
> But [this happened] so that God might bring about
> a matter already decreed,
> and so that those who were to perish would perish
> after a clear proof [had been given]. God is the hearing, the knowing.

12. Imhof, *Religiöser Wandel*.

13. *Furqān*, which is used in verse 41 to indicate "saving," also designates the saving of Moses through the Exodus; on the analogy to the Badr exodus see Marshall, *God, Muhammad and the Unbelievers*, 136–138.

When God showed them to you in your sleep [*fī manāmika*] as few—Had
he showed them as many,
you would have lost heart and you would have differed over the matter.
But God saved you. He knows what is hidden in the hearts.
When he showed them to you, as you met, few in your eyes,
and made you few in their eyes,
so that God brought about a matter already decided.
And all matters return to God.

This text, which enacts an important communal-historical memory through clear references to Exodus, indicates for the first time and uniquely a kind of mythicization of history, which would be required for a salvation historical great narrative: God himself has driven the struggling parties into the decisive confrontation through an illusive visual representation. Yet, although the "saving decision," *furqān*, which is described here as miraculous, belongs to the foundation legend of the fasting month of Ramadan,[14] this Qur'anic report assumes no outstanding place in the sura.[15] The purely occasional character of the recourse to chronological history makes it amply clear that the historically relevant events in Medina had not yet been brought together into a grand narrative comparable to Jewish or Christian salvation history.

9.1.1 *Formal Innovations*

It is not only thematic innovations that characterize the Medinan texts, however; also, and above all, structural and text-strategical innovations mark these suras. Suras in Medina take on new literary structures; individual sura models such as the "oratory sura," possessing particular structural characteristics, now attest to the political role of the proclaimer.[16] Above all, a new polyphony develops in the suras, in that for the first time they now address a confessionally mixed public.[17] The texts clearly show that the proclamation takes place, at least temporarily, in the presence of Jewish hearers, as the argument enters into "current" Jewish debates. This opens new thematic horizons and causes earlier pronouncements to be submitted to a checking for discursive suitability in face of the new expectations being raised by a pluricultural public, which now entails also educated Jewish hearers. This challenge not only leads to the discovery of problematic implications of earlier reported stories, but also triggers new reflections on the proclamation itself, not only on its relationship to earlier scriptures

14. Cf. chap. 11, 417–418.

15. The beginning of the account is not clearly signaled in the transmitted form of the text, but the account is triggered by the associations of the military order.

16. Cf. chap. 5, 196–198.

17. A reconstruction of the political field of forces, shaped also by the Jewish tribes, is offered in Lecker, "Muhammad at Medina."

but also on its very hermeneutic valence, that is, the question of its clearness or ambiguity. The proclamation thus reaches a new level of self-reflection. We also see a new challenge emanating from an aspect of theology that had not yet been a topic before: Christology. Without entering positively into the Qur'anic discourse, Christology becomes a spur to reflections on the ambiguity inherent in revealed speech, even including acknowledgment of the possibility of paradox in God's word.[18]

The compositional stringency that seems to be maintained in some of the so-called long suras, which Michel Cuypers[19] has attempted to show in a monograph on sura 5, must still be checked. The hypothesis should not mislead us into looking at the Medinan texts as having been already fixed in writing and freed from any historical proclamation situation. Such an interpretation underplays the inner-Qur'anic shaping of the suras and reduces the complex proclaimer-hearer interaction to a monologue, or even a post-Muhammad recording of thought figures culled from biblical books, especially Deuteronomy, and transferred to the Qur'an. The situation of transmission is in fact much more complex. A reading of the suras as a written fait accompli may seem at first view to be less hypothetical than a diachronic reading, but such a reading in fact applies presuppositions that neglect both the oral character of the Qur'anic text and its conversation with contemporary traditions, thus obscuring the genesis of a religion reflected in the Qur'an.

The perceived plurality of claimants to interpretive monopoly over "the (heavenly) scripture" in Medina also led to a new definition of one's own placement into salvation history. A "re-conversion" takes place: departing from their loyalty to the biblical Banū Isrāʾīl that had taken root in Mecca, the new community constructs its own, more strongly locally anchored salvation historical past, though not without holding on to biblical paradigms. Above all, the state of exile, which was earlier experienced spiritually rather than physically, is now restaged in present reality; the center of exilic nostalgia, earlier on Jerusalem, is now transferred to Mecca, which becomes the new crystallization point for ritual prayer. Likewise, the actual necessity of struggle comes to be reflected in categories aligned with biblical precedents—involving a confrontation with the Christian phenomenon of martyrdom, which was ubiquitously negotiated in Late Antiquity.

Without claiming to present all the relevant discourses that may have moved the Medinan community, in what follows we will discuss five problem fields that have been given little attention in research up to now. They manifest themselves in the Medinan period for the first time, where they occupy so prominent a position that their significance for the formation of the community is unmistakable: the

18. Neuwirth, "Mary and Jesus."

19. Cuypers, *The Banquet*, and Schmitz, *Sure 2*, examine a complete long sura as to the circumstances of its composition as an intended unit; cf. Robinson, *Discovering the Qur'ān*, 196–223, and Smith, "Structure."

Jewish theologumenon of God's wrath; the perception of a possible ambiguity of the word of God, which is suggested by the paradoxes of Christology; the reflection on two central genealogies, the Abrahamic and the Aaronite, the latter including the "Holy Family"; the construction of a new centrality for Mecca; and, finally, the relation of the community of belief to struggle and martyrdom. A further related discourse from this period, the universalizing of key texts and credo formulas from rivaling religious groups, will be presented in chapter 13, "The Rhetorical Qur'an."

9.2 The Discovery of God's Wrath

The self-awareness of belonging among the bearers of a safeguarded tradition, which was reached by the community of believers in Mecca, undergoes a stress test when the "official" inheritors of those biblical traditions themselves appear on the stage and raise their own claims to interpretive monopoly. The Qur'an texts, which already in late Mecca had taken on increasingly polemical coloring in the confrontation with pagan opponents, thus adopt an even sharper tone. This becomes especially clear in the Medinan "extensions," the "continuations of narratives" and reworkings of Meccan discursive texts (the so-called Medinan additions), which give a new theological thrust to the texts already in circulation, and in so doing often give them a new religious-political point. This strategy of "politicizing" the proclamation, which can best be explained through the situation of competition with the other religions, is one of the clearest indices for the textual genesis out of debates with bearers of different traditions.

We can see an example of this in the story of the Golden Calf (Ex 32:15–35), which is first told in the Meccan sura 20, "Ṭaha," with a purely edifying intent, even suggesting the excusability of the major sin of idolatry. This story undergoes an updating in Medina. It takes on a new interpretive point, which can no longer be derived from the biblical predecessor text, but rather reflects the tone and even part of the wording of the theological interpretation that the story of the Golden Calf had taken on in Judaism already in the pre-Talmudic period.[20]

The narrative of Moses as messenger of God and leader of his people was told numerous times in the Meccan suras, yet without much attention being paid to the episode of the Golden Calf. Only in two of these texts does the event figure prominently. It first appears in the rather early middle Meccan sura 20, a text that is almost entirely dedicated to the life of Moses,[21] and again in the late Meccan verses Q 7:142–156. In both texts, Medinan additions are inserted

20. See in detail Neuwirth, "Medinan Additions?" On the Jews of Medina, see Lecker, *Muslims, Jews, and Pagans*; cf. also the older study Wensinck, *Muhammad and the Jews of Medina*.

21. It is told in Q 79:15–26 (early Meccan); 37:114–122, 20:10–99, 26:10–67 (mid Meccan); 40:21–55, 28:1–46, 10:75–93, and 7:103–156 (late Meccan). With the exception of Q 7:103–156 and 2:54ff., all the versions of the story are discussed in Neuwirth, "Erzählen als kanonischer Prozess."

to retrospectively endow the episode with a theological point that focuses on God's wrath.

In sura 20, the episode occupies the last part (verses 87–99) of the life of Moses, which is narrated in detail, and which, apart from an introductory passage (verses 1–9), fills out the entire sura (verses 10–99). The narration takes a particularly empathetic approach to the Moses figure, stressing his intimate relationship with God and dispensing with the reproaches for his occasional faults, which we find in later texts, above all Q 26. The presentation remains purely narrative; the text refrains from adopting any particular theological position. Not even the report about the Golden Calf[22] is allowed to darken the positive image. It is restricted to the basic facts: the episode begins with the point that God himself tells Moses that a divine trial has occurred that his people have failed to pass (verses 83–85; cf. Ex 32:7)—a strikingly undramatic beginning for the historically momentous story. In the unexpanded form of the sura, the story also dispenses with such momentous points as the giving of the tablets,[23] the foundational event of the election of the Israelites, after which the Israelites' violation of the covenant with the sin of idolatry comes as the scandalous counterpoint. Thus, in the unexpanded sura, what is lacking is just what, from the Jewish perspective, forms—in Daniel Boyarin's words—one of the two "high points of the *Heilsgeschichte*."[24] The other key point, the miraculous crossing of the Red Sea, is equally marginalized, being only briefly summarized (verses 77–79). Thus, those very events that are the triggers of significant discussions in the rabbinic tradition are either marginalized or wholly left out of the Qur'anic presentation of the sura *before* its expansion.

When Moses turns to his people after his encounter with God, he himself becomes witness to their idolatry. The blame for this grievous sin, however, is not placed on members of the community (even Aaron is exonerated as Moses's representative), but on a figure unknown in the biblical account, named al-Sāmirī,[25] who has apparently mixed among the Israelites as a stranger. The strategy to downplay the enormity of the transgression by assigning blame to a "foreign" actor recalls the later midrashic narratives of the story,[26] which freely introduce other figures in order to exculpate the Israelites. The stopgap figure, who is named only by his *gentilicium* al-Sāmirī,[27] is accused of having seduced the people, against the will of Aaron, into producing the idol. Moses thus turns his anger on al-Sāmirī, who, much like Iblīs, the seducer par excellence, is cursed and expelled. The story that ends with the unexpected scenario of reconciliation instead of divine retaliation, concludes with a praise of God's uniqueness (verse 98).

22. For exegetical explanations of some problematic details, see Hawting, "Calf of Gold."
23. Cf. Fishbane, *Sacred Attunement*; Heschel, *Heavenly Torah*.
24. Boyarin, "The Eye in the Torah," 534.
25. Horowitz, *Koranische Untersuchungen*, 114–116.
26. Speyer, *Die biblischen Erzählungen im Qoran*, 327–332.
27. For an explanation, see ibid., 329–330; Horowitz, *Koranische Untersuchungen*, 14–16.

The story in sura 20, which as a whole is dedicated almost entirely to the Moses cycle, can thus be classified as a hagiographic account, unrelated to any particular theological discourse.

It should then be all the more surprising that theological reflections that are in striking contradiction to the reconciliatory tendency enter into the story in verses 80–82. They are given in the form of an address, which is easily recognizable by its particular rhetorical shape as a Medinan addition[28] that interrupts the narrative. This address warns the Israelites, Banū Isrāʾīl, to beware God's wrath, in a tone that is no longer empathetic but instead severe and threatening. The addition is placed in the caesura between the very short account of the people's exodus (Q 20:77–79)[29] and the story of the Golden Calf (Q 20:83–99). (The additional verse group Q 20:80–82 is in italics):

> And we revealed to Moses [saying], "set out at night with my servants and strike for them a dry path in the sea, not fearing to be overtaken nor dreading anything."
> Then Pharaoh pursued them with his troops and so they were overwhelmed by the water.
> Pharaoh thus led his people astray and did not guide them rightly.
>
> 80 *"Children of Israel, we have delivered you from your enemy*
> *and we made a covenant with you on the right side of the mount,*
> *and sent down to you manna and quails.*
> 81 *Eat of the good things we have provided you with* [a],
> *but do not be excessive in this,*
> *so that my wrath will not descend upon you* [b].
> *Those upon whom my wrath descends will be ruined* [c].
> 82 *I am indeed forgiving to him who repents,*
> *does good deeds, and is rightly guided."*

In verses 80–82, the event of the granting of the Torah, which was not yet reported in the sura but which plays a crucial role in Jewish tradition, is added and made into the basis of a warning, alongside the miraculous nourishment through manna and quail. The verses shift the speech from the report into a direct address, which provides an additional argument for the status of the verses as an

28. On the Medinan additions, see Nagel, "Medinensische Einschübe." His examination is limited to the documentation and interpretation of accounts offered in tradition, which however only cover a fraction of the actual additions that have been identified by critical scholars since Nöldeke. The additions established here and in sura 7 are not presented in Nagel's list of those parts of Meccan suras that are traditionally considered as Medinan additions.

29. This passage on what is from the Jewish perspective (see Boyarin, "The Eye in the Torah," 534) the central event, the crossing of the Red Sea, could have been added later as well, together with the direct address, to meet the expectations of Jewish listeners looking to find reference to the main event of their salvation history. However—unlike for verses 80–82—there is no compelling reason to adopt the reading of this as a later addition.

addition. The formula *yā banī Isrāʾīl*, "Children of Israel!" cannot be an address to the historical Israelites spoken by Moses, since this occurs nowhere in the Moses stories; they are much more likely to form part of the sermon of the proclaimer himself,[30] in analogue to the contemporary Medinan verses Q 2:40, 47, and 122, and thus to be aimed directly at the progeny of the Israelites, the Medinan Jews, among the hearers. But reference to the historical Israelites is implausible above all because of the content of the address itself. The warning to the addressees "to exceed not," which extends the immediately preceding exhortation to "eat of the good things," can best be understood as aimed at excessiveness in the respecting of dietary laws. Such an excess, which would lead to the segregation of its followers from the larger community and thus to social polarization, would be irrelevant for the historical Israelites, but becomes significant in the context of a shared living situation among differing religious groups, as we find in Medina. The content of the address to the Israelites as such thus already makes it probable that, as in sura 2, contemporary Jewish hearers are being addressed.

There is also a theological argument that, above all, corroborates this interpretation: the thematization of divine wrath. Although the addition evokes episodes that were left out of the unextended original narrative and therefore required a supplement (God's covenant at Sinai and his providing the Israelites with divine sustenance),[31] the commentary does not just refer to the warning against excess but also hints already at the worship of the idol, which will be reported immediately after. It culminates in a threat of divine wrath that is directly linked to the guilt-sin discourse around the worship of the Golden Calf, a wrath that can only be avoided through repentance, belief, and good deeds. This is an idea that had not been addressed in any Meccan texts up to that point.[32]

9.2.1 A Central Scriptural Verse: Its Jewish and Qur'anic Readings

The introduction of the idea of God's wrath[33] in the context of the adjoining story of the Golden Calf is no accident. On closer inspection, verses 82b–83 show themselves to be an allusion to a particularly momentous scriptural verse, the locus classicus for the idea of guilt and atonement in the Jewish tradition

30. While the Banū Isrāʾīl are mentioned multiple times in the Meccan suras, they are directly addressed only in the Medinan period in Q 2:40, 47, 122 and 61:6. This never occurs in the voice of Moses; the conveyer of the speech to them in Q 2:40, 47, and 122 is in fact the proclaimer himself, and those addressed are exhorted to recognize the Qur'an. This means that in these contexts, it is not the historic Israelites but rather the Medinan Jews who are addressed. As an exception, the late Medinan verse 61:6 could be mentioned in which the address does occur in the historic past. Here, Jesus is the speaker, announcing the coming of the proclaimer.

31. For the form of the Qur'anic summary report, it is most probably references such as *Mekhilta de-Rabbi Ishmael* and *Sifre Devarim* that should be considered (personal communication by Dirk Hartwig).

32. Cf. with Boyd, "Sin and Grace."

33. Apart from Q 20:81b.c., the word occurs in Mecca only once again in the same sura (verse 86), where the same formulation, *(fa- /an) yaḥilla ʿalaykum ghaḍab(ī/un min rabbikum)*, "so that my wrath comes down on you from me/your Lord," is used. This sentence again interrupts the otherwise factual account. It could in turn be a later addition to emphasize the new idea of the wrath of God see Neuwirth, Medinan additions.

as such,[34] which also belongs to the immediate context of the biblical story of the Golden Calf, Ex 34:6–7. God's image as both wrathful and forgiving has its most expressive form in the divine self-description that is revealed to Moses when, after the event of the Golden Calf, he is given the new set of tablets. It displays what Jewish tradition has labeled the "thirteen attributes," *shelosh ʿesre ha-middot*, of God, which all connect with (justified) wrath (*middat ha-din*) and mercy (*middat ha-raḥamim*), and which have assumed a prominent position in Jewish liturgy from an early period. Ex 34:6–7:[35]

> And the Lord passed by before him, and proclaimed:
>
> YHWH, YHWH, a gracious and merciful God, forbearing and rich in grace and fidelity, who preserves mercy for the thousands, forgives guilt, wickedness, and sins, but does not allow one to go unpunished,
>
> but who rather visits the guilt of the father unto the sons and descendants down to the third and fourth generations.

The verse figures prominently also outside of the Bible, particularly in the liturgy of the Jewish Day of Atonement, Yom Kippur. There, the relapse into idolatry is recalled as the exemplary case of sin of the Israelites overall,[36] through an "anthology" of Bible verses, among which Exodus 34:6–7 is evoked several times.[37] In view of the fame of these verses and their prominence in Talmudic discussions, they can be presupposed to have been part of the knowledge store of the Jews of Medina as well. At the very least, the Medinan Jews' observance of the festival day itself stands beyond question, as it provides the only convincing explanation for the practice of fasting on the Day of Atonement that was also upheld at this time by the Qur'anic community in Medina.[38] One should therefore assume that the two final verses of the Medinan addition (Q 20:81–2) are an echo of this Bible text, which is so central for the wrath discourse.[39] Thus, a verse of scripture enters the picture that seems most likely to have been brought into the conversation

34. Cf. Lindqvist, "Sin at Sinai."

35. The significance of the thirteen attributes for the act of atonement is documented in the Babylonian Talmud in Rosh ha-Shana 17b: " 'It is written: and the Lord went past him and proclaimed.' Rabbi Yohanan said: 'If this paragraph had not been written, it would be impossible to express it, since the text teaches us, that the Holy—blessed be he—wraps himself, like a *shammash* who is reciting the prayers for a congregation, and in revealing the right order of the prayers to Moses, he said to him: Whenever Israel sins, let them pray to me in your manner, then I will forgive them' " (personal communication by Dirk Hartwig). On rabbinic theology, cf. Schechter, *Aspects of Rabbinic Theology*, and Urbach, *The Sages*.

36. See bT Sanhedrin 102a: "There is no calamity struck onto Israel, without it being connected to the sin of the Golden Calf."

37. This observation is based on the contemporary structure of Yom Kippur liturgies documented in the traditional prayer books, *makhzorim*. The dating of liturgical textual forms in Judaism is difficult to determine (see Elbogen, *Der jüdische Gottesdienst*), but the high significance of the verse already in rabbinic discussions suggests a long tradition of liturgical use.

38. Goitein, "The Muslim Month of Fasting."

39. Its position in the Qur'an not after but rather immediately before the story of the Golden Calf should not be problematic in view of the later insertions that also elsewhere do not always follow their reference texts exactly.

theologically by the Medinan Jews. It is evoked this way in the Qur'an in order to reach the actual "bearers" of the discourse of guilt and atonement "in their own language." A striking reinterpretation of the thirteen attributes has however taken place in the Qur'anic version, which equally focuses on the notions of forgiveness (*ghafur*, "forgiving," verse 82) and wrath (*ghaḍab*, "wrath," verse 81 b and c). Yet the biblical threat of a divine retaliation over generations is alleviated into a punishment inflicted only on persistent transgressors—a "theological corrective" that corresponds to the image of God that had already achieved consensus in the community: God is free of emotional affects, and even his wrath does not distract from the power of the decisions he has already issued. Either transgressions of his commandments will be atoned for through repentance, or the transgressors will fall victim to eschatological damnation. Despite this softening, a threat prevails in the additional verses: the wrath of God can only be met through remorse and repentance (*man tāba*, "he who repents," verse 82).

This interpretation of the text, in the sense of a wrath discourse introduced retroactively into the story of Moses, is strengthened by a similar recourse to the thirteen attributes, again through a Medinan addition, in a further telling of the story of the Golden Calf in the late Meccan sura 7 (verse 142–156).[40] In both cases, the addition of an idea drawn from an identifiable biblical text possessing additional weight through its liturgical and/or discursive presence in the Jewish tradition serves a religious-political goal in the Qur'an. In sura 20, one can speak of a "politicizing" of the sura, which had been religio-politically neutral in its original form. The reference to Ex 34:6–7, a text that in the biblical context directly follows the granting of the new set of tablets, is drawn into the context of atonement for idolatry as it had been in the Jewish tradition, the Yom Kippur liturgy. At the same time, it is connected pragmatically to an admonition to the contemporary Jews that is relevant for the community, namely, not to follow too closely those legal instructions that would separate them from the customs of their surroundings. A conversation with the inheritors of the Bible text has begun, in which we can read a plea for integration—a plea that is raised in "their own language," that is, with reference to texts and exegetical contexts of their tradition.

A systematic reading of the Medinan additions to the Meccan suras tracing their rabbinical and occasionally also Christian intertexts thus remains an important desideratum. As the cases that have been detected so far already show, the Medinan texts reveal a substantially new relationship to the preceding traditions, in that they no longer employ older texts and traditions paraenetically, as was the practice in Mecca, but rather now grant them a new discursive dimension: Medinan texts reflect the engagement with the theological positions of learned representatives of

40. Neuwirth, "Oral Scriptures."

the older religions, and thus reflect a conversation between religions. New actors now enter the process of the communal formation of consensus and contribute to it, deepening or modifying the earlier presentations of episodes from Jewish salvation history that now require revision. The Qur'an, still dynamic in the course of the proclamation, thus reveals itself as a polyphone text that often questions itself, whose differing voices have not yet received nearly enough attention.

9.3 The Discovery of Ambiguity in the Divine Writing

9.3.1 *Ambiguity of Scripture and Its Feminine Metaphors*

Around the same early Medinan period, when the discussion of the Jewish guilt-atonement problem was introduced in the additions to suras 20 and 7, Christian traditions also found new reflections in the proclamation. A particularly complex case of this, Q 3:1–64, is worth treatment at some length here.

Sura 3 offers a new reading, enriched by a number of details, of the story of Mary and Jesus, which was already narrated in sura 19.[41] Here too, as in the revision of the Moses story, we observe a "politicizing" of the old story: what appears to be a further narrative development of the story of Mary already told in Mecca is de facto a new religious-political interpretation. To explore the situational meaning of the narrative, its setting in the life of the community, as well as its role in the genesis of the Qur'an, we must look not only at the narrative (verses 33–64) but also at its prologue (verses 1–32). The prologue and the narrative that follows it connect the two great themes of the sura: the question of the hermeneutic valence of scripture as either clear or ambiguous, and the new perception of religious legitimacy that is accessible outside of the Israelite patriarchal tradition. While the latter idea is thematized in the beginning verse of the narrative (verse 33), the sura's prologue is devoted to the former idea, the plurality and possible ambiguity of scriptural meanings, right from the beginning (verse 7). This verse would later become the locus classicus for the uneven hermeneutic valence of Qur'anic verses, and would also feature prominently in the debate about the authority of interpretation (divine or human?). It is preceded by several verses that are relevant for its interpretation (Q 3:1–7):

> Alif lam mim.
> God, there is no God except him, the living, the lasting!
> He sent the scripture down to you in truth,
> confirming what came before it,
>   and sent down the Torah and the Gospel,[42]

41. Neuwirth, "Imagining Mary—Disputing Jesus"; cf. chap. 8, 294–296

42. The Gospel, *injīl*, which is understood in the Qur'an as a single scripture and not a plurality of Gospels, is mentioned twelve times, always in Medinan verses; aside from the verse at hand, it always appears in Qur'anic

before, as a guidance to mankind
and he sent down the saving decision [*furqān*].[43]
Those who do not believe in the signs of God,
they stand before an intense punishment.
God is almighty, vengeful.
Nothing is hidden from God on earth or in heaven.
It is he who forms you in the womb as he wills,
no God except him! He is the powerful, the wise.
It is he who sent down the scripture to you.
There are verses in it that are clear [*muḥkam*],
they are the mother of the scripture,
and others that are ambiguous [*mutashābih*].
Those in whose hearts is vacillation, they follow what is ambiguous [*mā tashābaha*]
in striving to raise doubt [*ibtighā'a l-fitna*]
in striving to interpret it [*ibtighā'a ta'wīlihi*].
But no one except God knows its interpretation.
Those strongly grounded in knowledge [*al-rāsikhūna fī l-'ilm*] say:
"We believe in it, everything is from our Lord."
But no one takes heed, except those who understand.

Verse 7 allows two basic interpretations,[44] since the syntactical referent of the expression *al-rāsikhūna fī l-'ilmi*, "those firmly grounded in knowledge," in verse 7, is open. If one reads it, as in our translation, as the beginning of a new sentence, the prerogative of interpretation would be reserved for God; if one understands it as part of the exception and reads "No one but God knows its interpretation, and those firmly grounded in knowledge," the approach to interpretation would be open to both, God and the learned. Both readings are formally possible, and have been treated differently among the Sunna and Shia.

But is this verse truly concerned centrally with the authority to practice interpretation, as recent research oriented toward the reception history of the Qur'an would have it? Or is it concerned rather with the nature of the revealed texts themselves, whose problematics are here reflected anew? The verse is in no way self-explanatory within the Qur'an: the concession of a hermeneutic ambiguity in scripture[45] should be surprising in view of the numerous previous

debates, and nowhere else in the introduction of a sura topic. *Injīl* is usually associated with *tawrāh*, the Torah. See Griffith, "Gospel," who does not seek, however, to fit the mentions of the Gospel into the Qur'anic discourse.

43. For an explanation, see chap. 11, 417–418.

44. See Gilliot, "Exegesis of the Qur'an, Classical," 99–100; cf. also McAuliffe, "Text and Textuality," which presents the inner-Islamic exegetical position. On the hermeneutic implications of the verse, see Madigan, *The Qur'ān's Self-image*, and—in response—Rubin's review of Madigan, *The Qur'ān's Self-image*. Additionally, see Wild, "Self-Referentiality."

45. Cf. Kinberg, "Ambiguous"; Kinberg, "Muḥkamāt and Mutashābihāt."

self-declarations of the Qur'an as a clear (*mubīn*) scripture (cf. Q 12:1 and Q 26:2: *tilka āyātu l-kitābi l-mubīn*, "those are the signs of a clear scripture," and Q 43:2: *wa l-kitābi l-mubīn*, "by the clear scripture!," etc.). Why, then, should there be verses that are ambiguous? The appearance of this category cannot be explained through reference to the Meccan experience of the proclaimer and his hearers; it remains unresolved as long as one approaches it in isolation from the new discursive challenges in Medina.

In fact, older intertexts loom large in the verses: the perception that verses of scripture have more than one meaning is not unheard of in the older religions. In Jewish tradition, the identification of different meanings of scriptural text units as "faces of the Torah" (*panim shel ha-tora*) formed part of exegetical practice since the Tannaitic period (ca. second century CE). That experiences with the Jews stand in the background of sura 3 is suggested also by the word *al-tawrāh* in Q 3:3 to designate the scripture given to the Jews,[46] whose indigenous Jewish name appears here for the first time. The exegetical perception of scriptural texts as being liable to more than one understanding, which was an everyday perception in Jewish interpretation, and which can be presupposed to have been known to the Medinan Jews, thus seems to be reflected in the Qur'anic verses at hand:[47] an innovation that can hardly be overestimated for the self-understanding of the community. What occurs here is an opening of scriptural discourse toward exegesis that was not dared before, and which research has not yet examined in terms of its emergence and its *Sitz im Leben* among the community.[48]

It is an opening that, as Q 3:7 shows, was accompanied by insight into an already existing praxis of interpretation, named *taʾwīl*,[49] which equally points to exegetical activity and professionalism. This concept could be a new discovery in the Qur'anic discourse, although the word appears already, with less theoretical foundation, in reference to the praxis of dream interpretation in the story of Joseph, Q 12:36–37 and 12:99–101. According to its etymology, *taʾwīl* seems to

46. It occurs five times in sura 3; in the other four places, it stands in an explicit polemic against the Banū Isrāʾīl, targeting the Medinan Jews or the People of the Scripture, respectively. The introduction of the naming is noticeable, since previous references were always to *kitāb Mūsā*, "The Scripture of Moses"; cf. Adang, "Tawrat." The naming echoes Jewish usage, since Christian Arabic gives prevalence to "the Law," adopted from the Septuagint translation, *ho nomos*, *al-nāmūs*. The announcement of revelation in verse 3, with its reference to the internal Jewish usage, implicitly raises the claim of the Qur'anic revelation standing on the same level with the proclamation to the Jews.

47. See especially bT Sanhedrin 34a and bT Shabbat 88b, as well as Numeri Rabba 18:2, on the "seventy faces of the Torah" (personal communication by Dirk Hartwig). For the concrete rabbinic background, see Stern, "Midrash and Indeterminacy"; cf. also Boyarin, "The Genealogy of Indeterminacy."

48. An early exegetical genre, which investigates the ambiguity of Qur'anic lexemes that emerged from their different contexts, is labeled *mutashābih al-qurʾān*, "ambiguous issues in the Qur'an," or *al-wujūh wa l-naẓāʾir*, "the faces (= Hebr. *panim*) and their equivalents." The recognition of the fait accompli of ambiguity in versions of scripture, which is so prominent in the Jewish tradition, does not find its first reflection in the commentary, as Gilliot, "Exegesis, Classical," assumes, but rather is already reflected in the Qur'an.

49. *Taʾwīl* is apparently a more complex practice of interpretation, to be distinguished from *tafsīr*; cf. Q 25:33, from the Hebrew *pesher*, "literal interpretation."

indicate a "reference back to the first," or, in short, a deduction, and it is likely that this form of interpretation was a technique practiced among Jewish scholars. While in the case of *taʾwīl* an identification with a non-Arabic technical term is difficult, such an identification does suggest itself positively for the two qualifications of verses introduced in Q 3:7 (*muḥkam*, "clear," and *mutashābih*, "ambiguous"). They may ultimately go back, albeit through intermediaries that cannot be identified, to the Aristotelian antinomy of *amphiboles*, "ambiguous," and *pithanos*, "clear."[50] Here we see a group of new, hermeneutically relevant concepts, whose appearance might be explained by the hypothesis of an exchange of ideas between the community and the Jews of Medina, who had access to such techniques.

9.3.2 The House of Abraham and the House of Amram

Such an explanation, which merely posits an exchange with the Medinan Jews, is not sufficient, however, since it would isolate the prologue from the narrative that stands at the sura's center, which attests to the simultaneously increased presence of Christian elements in the early Medinan discourse of the community. The narrative that stands in the center of the sura relates to the Christian foundational myth: it focuses on the story of the mother of Mary, and of Mary as the mother of Jesus. As the two women, together with Jesus, who appears in a later part of the narrative, make up the *Āl ʿImrān*, the House of Amram,[51] or the Holy Family in Christian understanding, they form a counterpart to the *Āl Ibrāhīm*, the House of Abraham. With these figures, the House of Abraham is countered for the first time by a genealogical group of equal rank, which is equally elected (Q 3:33–34)[52]:

inna llāha ṣ̣ṭafā Ādama wa-Nūḥan
wa-Āla Ibrāhīma wa-Āla ʿImrāna ʿalā l-ʿālamīn.
dhurriyatan baʿḍuhā min baʿḍuhā min baʿḍin
wa-llāhu samīʿun ʿalīm

God elected Adam, Noah,
the House of Abraham, and the House of Amram above all men.
A progeny one from another.
God is hearing, seeing.

50. Cf. Bonitz, *Index Aristotelicus*.

51. Cf. the explanation in chap. 10, 365–368.

52. The term *Āl Ibrāhīm*, like *Āl Imrān*, is unique in this place and does not recur further in the Qur'an. Both designations thus have been developed for this particular context, where they enter a dialectic relation. But while the Abrahamites and their family story are well known from older proclamations, the Āl Imrān were only occasionally evoked up to that point—in sura 19, Mary and Jesus are mentioned without being labeled Āl Imrān.

The story of Mary and her mother, who remains nameless and who vows to consecrate her unborn child to the service in the temple, based on events that are related in the Proto-Gospel of Jacob, presents a counter-model to the family history of the Abrahamites. Not only are their most important actors women, but it is also strikingly explicit in its gender-specific physical detailing—"in my womb," Q 3:35; "I have given birth," Q 3:36; "a female one," Q 3:36. After the birth of a daughter rather than the expected son, the mother fulfills her vow to give her child over to the temple all the same. She herself names the child Maryam, Mary, in the absence of the father, who never appears in the story. Unlike the Protevangelium, no man is involved in the story—if for a moment we ignore the parallel story of Zachariah, who plays no active role in the story of Mary. Even Jesus, Mary's son, does not counter this imbalance in what follows, since his modest appearance in public and his refusal to exercise patriarchal authority (he does not give legislation, but rather alleviates earlier laws) show him also to be a counter-model to the Prophets from the firmly established House of Abraham. We can thus see a characterization being sketched of the House of Amram, the Christian Holy Family, that is named explicitly in the introductory verse, setting them in contrast to the House of Abraham, which receives equal mention. The striking emphasis on female actors and their conditions, especially the act of giving birth, has its reverse image in the characteristics of the male protagonists of the stories about the House of Abraham, which is based on the masculine genealogy of Abraham, Isaac, Jacob or Israel, and Joseph and distinguishes itself through unconditioned faith in God, readiness for sacrifice, pure belief in God's unity (Abraham), and the communication and preservation of the Prophetic family inheritance (Joseph). This parallelization, which occurs here for the first and only time in the Qur'an, setting the House of Amram against the House of Abraham, makes the "Holy Family" into an unmistakable competitor with the Jewish tradition. It is certainly not by accident that they appear now, and for the only time, in competition with them.

Let us turn now back to the prologue, to the still-open problem of the newly awakened attention to the ambiguity of verses of scripture. The imagery of the relevant verse, Q 3:7, strikes the reader as charged with gender associations: the professionalism of the anonymous interpreters who are lambasted for their obsession with interpretation is depicted surprisingly with gender-specific metaphors: they are condemned for their endeavor, literally their "desire" *ibtighāʾ*, to awaken doubt, or more literally "discord" or "temptation," *fitna*.[53] While these

53. Although *ibtighāʾ* refers mostly to spiritual goals in the Qur'an, such as the face of God and his pleasing, it can also refer to desire, Q 13:17. Considering the presence of the root, *b-gh-y*, in the term *baghīʾ*, "harlot," in the context of the story of Mary (Q 19:28), there could also be a sexual connotation here. Against the background of the often-spiritual goals of *ibtighā* in the Qur'an, its usage in the context of *fitna* appears to be especially subversive. *Fitna*, "temptation, divine test" (the word also connotes "straying from the right path, struggle within the community"), is usually a divine strategy in the Qur'an for testing peoples' faith. One agent of *fitna*, although not mentioned specifically in this connection in the Qur'an, is woman; cf. the Hadith *mā taraktu baʿdī fitnatan asharra*

ambiguous verses seem to trigger dealings with scripture that resemble dubious sexual relationships, clear verses stand in a legitimate genealogical relationship to the "mother of scripture," *umm al-kitāb*. Against this background, the behavior of the unbelievers appears not only as hyper-skeptical but also as "morally suspect," since they exploit the ambiguity of the text in search of *fitna*. In this light, the qualification of the heavenly reference text as the mother of scripture, *umm al-kitāb*, deserves new attention, as it conflates two discourses. the masculine, power-informed discourse related to the vertically achieved "sending down" (*kitāb, tanzīl*) on the one hand and the more submissive female discourse related to maternal conception and reproduction, *wad*, on the other.[54]

The gendered image of the *umm al-kitāb*, Q 3:7, is preluded by the preceding verse's reference to procreation, which anticipates the hermeneutical engagement with the *āyāt muḥkamāt* and the *āyāt mutashābihāt*, Q 3:6:

huwa lladhī yuṣawwirukum fī l-arḥāmi kayfa yashāʾu
lā ilāha illā huwa l-ʿazīzu l-ḥakīm

It is he who forms you in the wombs how he wishes.
No God except him, he is the powerful, the wise.

While this verse could be read outwardly as a pronouncement about God's power of creation and omniscience, it may also be read as a statement about giving birth and motherhood. There is an implicit correspondence between the antagonism of two kinds of scriptural verses and two stages of prenatal development, since God creates the child in his mother's womb, while its gender remains indeterminate. The unborn child remains "ambiguous," *mutashābih*, until its birth; only God knows its nature. Mary's mother is unaware she is carrying a female child and thus pledges her to the temple. It is a matter left to God, in which form what is hidden will come to light—both in motherhood and in the sending down of scripture. It is striking that in both cases a feminine "temporary storage" is employed: the "mother's womb" in sexual reproduction and the "mother text" in the sending down, in revelation.

Since the process of revelation involves a—positive—female agent, the *umm al-kitāb*, for the sending down of the scripture, it is only logical that the aberrant interpretive acts of the skeptics should be presented in gendered categories

ʿalā l-rijāli mina l-nisāʾ, "I did not leave behind me a more harmful temptation for men than women"; see Wensinck, *Concordance*, 5:63. The hadith is quoted in Saleh, "Woman," 128.

54. The image of the "mother of scripture" also seems to reflect earlier perceptions. It contains an echo of a hermeneutic category familiar from rabbinic scholarship, according to which a safely transmitted reading of a Bible text "has a mother" in the scripture itself: *yesh em la-miqra*, while a reading that only survives in its consonantal structure is a reading that has a mother in tradition, *yesh em la-masoret*; see bT Sukka 6b and passim and the discussion in Bacher, *Die exegetische Terminologie*, 1:119–120. Horovitz, *Koranische Untersuchungen*, 65 rejects the Jewish intertext—unjustifiedly—because it does not harmonize with the Meccan mentions of *al-kitāb*. The Qur'anic reuse of earlier-coined concepts does not however follow strict rules in general.

as well that evoke feminine associations: their desire (*ibtighāʾ*) for the disturbance of order, for *fitna*—an expression that seems to evoke the feminine power of temptation.[55]

9.3.3 *The Theological Context of "Ambiguity": Christology*

Finally, let us turn back to the question of what might have been the trigger for this new interest in the ambiguity of texts in the Qur'an. Although the terms *taʾwīl*, *mutashābih*, and *muḥkam* point to professional exegetes in general, who are most likely to be sought among the Medinan Jews and whose interpretations may have irritated the community, Q 3:7 is not merely an occasional polemic. The consciousness of the existence of both clear and ambiguous verses opens a new theoretical horizon. In the Jewish context, it is true, this perception is current, having given rise to an entire exegetical tradition. Nevertheless, to explain Q 3:7 entirely through an exchange with the Medinan Jews fails to do justice to the rhetorical structure of the sura and its purposeful cross-references. As the introductory verse of the narrative (Q 3:33) makes clear programmatically, there is an intentional equalizing of the Christian and Abrahamite traditions. In addition, we find a detailed narration of the story of the Holy Family for the only time in the Qur'an (Q 3:33–64), which sketches a Christian counter-model to that of the families of the patriarchs and prophets of the Abrahamites. The feminine presence that comes out so strongly in the narrative reaches back into the prologue, where in verses 6 and 7 the ambiguity in the contexts of motherhood and of the sending down of scripture are set in parallel. It also gives hermeneutical coloring to the situation of those "strongly grounded in knowledge" and those "who have trepidation in their hearts," who, measured by the social rules for behavior between the sexes, adopt either legitimate or offensive behavior toward scripture.

The problem of ambiguity and clarity is not only a hermeneutical problem but also a theological one. In the extra-Qur'anic religious traditions, it is bound up in particular with the person of Mary, in whom virginity and simultaneous motherhood are "unclear," and even capable of raising doubts. Reading the much discussed verse 3:7 contextually, not in isolation from the wider progress of the sura, as is too often done, one has to connect the two sources of authority: the authority of the Jews, based on long established exegetical praxis, and the new Christian authority, which is based on a softening of the fiction of unambiguity, as suggested by the behavior of its founding figures. On this point, it is helpful to look at a central liturgical text of the Eastern Church tradition, which can be dated into the sixth century: the Akathistos Hymn,[56] a hymn to the Virgin Mary. Mary herself appears here as an object of contradictory perceptions. To the

55. The problem of gendered speech in the Qur'an has received little attention to date; see Barlas, "Women's Readings," and Abboud, *Qissat al-Sayyida Maryam*.

56. It is based on a series of older Mary homilies; cf. Peltomaa, *The Image of the Virgin Mary*.

believers, she is a "clear," *anamphibolos*, symbol of belief, but to the unbelievers she is "ambiguous," *amphibolos*, and a cause of irritation.

> *Chaire ton apiston amphibolon akousma,*
> *chaire ton piston anamphibolon kauchema*

> Rejoice, you who are ambiguous for the unbelievers,
> rejoice you who personifies the unambiguous pride of the believers![57]

In this text, it is not the "mother of scripture "but the "mother of the incarnate Word" that is praised as a clear object of belief. Ambiguity appears solely before the eyes of the unbelievers.[58]

Without attempting to establish a direct relationship between individual traditions on the basis of such an isolated testimony, it is worthwhile to pursue this trace. In doing this, we can take up a suggestion by Nasr Hamid Abu Zaid,[59] who sketches an alternative scenario for the ambiguity discourse to that of the debates with the Medinan Jews. Abu Zaid assumes that the focus of the ambiguity debate was not the problem of exegetical praxis (*taʾwīl*) as such, but rather a particular theological issue perceived as ambiguous, namely, Christology. This interpretation is appealing, not only in view of the centrality of Christian traditions reflected in the sura but also in view of another consideration: both the prologue and the narrative part of the sura introduce new discourses. The prologue opens a rhetorical-hermeneutic discourse about the ambiguity of scripture, while the narrative part opens a genealogical discourse. In particular, verse Q 3:7 focuses on ideas that fit well into the rhetorically and philosophically informed Christological debates. It is true that the Qur'an text does not make explicit the idea that triggered the debate about the admissibility of interpreting the ambivalent verses, yet this trigger can be deduced from references in the sura itself. Traces of the Christological paradox are found already in the prologue, where the image of the "mother of scripture," *umm al-kitāb* in Q 3:7, with its connotations of gender, is preluded by a reference to motherhood (Q 3:6), which evokes the ambiguity of the still unborn child, expressed in *kayfa yashāʾu*, "as he wills." "It is he who forms you in the wombs how he wishes. No God except him, he is the powerful, the wise." The divinely willed fact of the ambiguity offered to men, which is illustrated here, is relevant not only for the story of Mary—the

57. The (undatable) Arabic translation of the hymn does not employ the pair *mutashābih* and *muhkam*, but rather (*khabar*) *yaltabis*, "knowledge that is unclear," and *lā yushawwihuhu ltibās*, "knowledge that is not blurred by ambiguity."

58. An extensive discussion of the possible Christological implications of the Qur'an text is offered in Neuwirth, "The House of Abraham."

59. Abu Zaid, in a lecture at the the summer academy of the Institute for Advanced Study, Berlin, entitled "Literary and Historical Approaches to the Bible and the Qur'an," given in September 2007 in Istanbul. His interpretation is based on Sira accounts, which refer to the Christians of Najran, who according to tradition were the audience of Q 3:53, while the interpretation offered here forgoes this reference.

conception and birth of Jesus is above all ambiguous, an extreme case of the "as he wills," *kayfa yashā'*, since he is conceived without the participation of a human father, and his divine/human nature stipulated in Christian theology defies any expectation of clarity. If one sees the stories of birth that stand in the center of the sura in the context of the Mariological/Christological liturgical traditions, marked by the ensemble of "ambiguity-loaded motherhood" (Q 3:6, 34ff.) and the "ambiguous word of God" (Q 3:7), then we can give credence to the claim that it was the problematics raised by Christology that provoked this thematizing of the ambiguity of verses of scripture.

Accepting support from the Sira, one could locate this interpretation easily within a specific situation in the Medinan proclamation.[60] In our investigation, however, which is based on Qur'an texts exclusively, we cannot proceed beyond hypothetical assumptions. What can be assumed with probability about the communal-historical status of the prologue and narrative of sura 3 is that in the early Medinan period an attempt was made, which was not later pursued further, to undermine or at least counterbalance the authority of the Abrahamite tradition, and thus also defy its actual heirs who possessed scripture and exegesis, the Medinan Jews, through the projection of another historically powerful genealogical group, the Christians. In this reflection on the genealogy and fates of the Christian founding family, the ambiguous and even paradoxical must have been striking. The insight newly discovered in Medina, that scripture could also contain unclear truths of belief withdrawn from immediate understanding, may have helped to make the difficulties of Christology graspable. The Christological paradox, which was *Ioudaiois men skandalon, ethnesin de moria*, "a point of anger for the Jews and a folly for the heathens,"[61] was not taken up among the Qur'anic truths of belief, but it seems to have entered the horizon of the community at least for some time.

9.4 From Jerusalem Back to Mecca

9.4.1 *Medina*

In the change of the direction of prayer, *qibla*, from Jerusalem to Mecca, we can see a decisive ritual and religious-political innovation that took place soon after the *hijra*. This reform signals one of several religious-political shifts in loyalty carried out by the community in Medina. The often-repeated explanation of this step as a consequence of the so-called break with the Jews[62] is not supported by Qur'anic texts.[63] In general, we should be predisposed to think that a turn in

60. On the exchanges with the Christians of Najran, see the commentary on sura 3; cf. Irfan Shahid, "Najrān"; cf. also Nebes, "The Martyrs of Najrān."

61. 1 Cor 1:23.

62. Watt, *Muhammad in Medina*, 202–204; Watt, *Muhammad. Prophet and Statesman.*

63. See Rahman, *Major Themes*, 131–149; cf. Marshall, *God, Muhammad and the Unbelievers*, 148.

prayer toward a direction that is not suggested cosmically (such as the east in the non-Jewish monotheistic praxis) but rather directed toward a historically charged space, expresses a deep affiliation to that place, so that one can speak here of an exilic longing—particularly if this place, as it was for the Babylonian Jews and as it was again for the believers in Medina, was the initial homeland. To merely assume political opportunism would not do justice to this situation. Tilman Nagel has convincingly argued that the migration of the proclaimer and his dependents took place without their safety being initially guaranteed, so that it amounted to a flight, which could only succeed thanks to the existing relationships of neighbor protection warranted by the *jiwār* structure, a network of relations of mutual protection.[64] One should thus conceive of the resettlement from Mecca to Medina not as an option that was temporarily condoned but as an exile whose term could not be foreseen,[65] and which imposed high moral demands on the migrants. That the community risked a military conflict with the Meccans only one year after the *hijra* could only have been possible because the commitment of the believers to the newly formed society of emigrants that obligated them to extreme exertions, was much more rigorous than had the loyalty requested in Mecca. The newly demanded exertion is reflected in the stereotypical formula designating the emigrants as *alladhīna hājarū wa-jāhadū*, "those who emigrated and are striving" (Q 2:218; 8:72, 74, 75; 16:110), often extended with the unambiguous *fī sabīli llāh*, "in the way of God," that is, "in battle" (e.g., Q 22:58). From this exilic perspective, Mecca takes on a new position; it becomes the object of conflict, the place from which the believers were wrongly driven, whose elite must therefore engage in struggle (Q 22:39–40): "Permission is given to those who fight because they are wronged. God is surely capable of giving them victory. Those who were driven out of their living places without right, because they said 'Our Lord is God . . .'" Even if the moment of emotional loss is not itself thematized, the social and mental situation of exile is nonetheless unmistakable: Mecca is the center of collective memory. It is therefore no surprise that, according to tradition, soon after the Battle of Badr, in the second year after the *hijra*, a change in the direction of prayer to Mecca was proclaimed, with a text that echoes the foundational biblical text on the establishment of a direction of prayer, which had also arisen out of a situation of exile: 1 Kings 8:23–53.

64. See Nagel, *Medinensische Einschübe*, 128–137; similarly, also Ammann, *Die Geburt des Islam*.

65. Cf. Cragg, *The Event of the Qur'ān*, 129; Donner, "The Historical Context." Nagel, *Medinensische Einschübe*, attempts to reconstruct the Medinan situation of the community on the basis of Qur'anic evidence. The work is an important contribution to reconstructing the historical environment of the Qur'an, despite the ill-founded literary-critical thesis claiming that the cases of supposed Medinan additions gathered by Ibn ʿAbd al-Kāfī are in fact of Medinan origin.

9.4.2 *Jerusalem*

The Meccan direction of prayer was not the first to be adopted by the Qur'anic community. Already during the Meccan period, the community adopted a historically determined direction of prayer: toward Jerusalem.[66] The orientation toward Jerusalem—in place of the otherwise frequent cosmic orientation toward the east—was merely one symbolically expressive sign of a profound change that was taking place in the middle Meccan period among the early community. If the adoption of the former *qibla* toward Jerusalem had been a turning point for the community striving to integrate the Holy Land into the new mental map of their *topographia sacra*, the Medinan change of the direction of prayer was of no less momentousness, marking an important signal of a new orientation. It shows that just as the longing for Jerusalem had earlier reached far beyond the scope of the real world, now Mecca became a similar site of exilic longing. It is worthwhile to look closer at this act of revision of the previous great symbol of identity, which first permitted the environment of Mecca to be perceived as a new "Holy Land," and to transfer central prerogatives of Jerusalem to Mecca.[67]

9.4.3 *Mecca*

The new regulation of cult can be dated to the year 2/624, that is, just after the stress test of the Battle of Badr that had been successfully passed by the community. Not differently than a millennium earlier among the Jewish exilic community in Babylon, it was the reflection on their own origins that laid the basis for the exiles' self-assertion. As in the prayer for the dedication of the temple, which in the book of Kings is articulated by Solomon (1 Kings 8:23–53), the Qur'an text unit that is decisive for the reform of the direction of prayer also seeks to establish the new *qibla* as an exilic direction of prayer, Q 2:142–145:

> The ignorant among the people will say,
> "what caused them to turn away from their former direction of prayer,
> toward which they used to turn?"
> Say: "to God belongs the east and the west.
> He guides whom he wills toward a right path."
>
> We have made you into a community of the middle,
> so that you may be witnesses for the rest of mankind,
> and so that the messenger may be a witness for you.
> We established your former direction of prayer,
> so that we could distinguish between those who follow the messenger
> and those who turn on their heels.

66. See chap. 8, 282–284.
67. Cf. Neuwirth, "The Spiritual Meaning of Jerusalem."

It was indeed a hard test except for those whom God guided.
God would not allow your faith to be in vain.
He is the all-caring, the merciful.

Surely, we see you turning your face in the heaven.
Now, we will turn you in a direction that will satisfy you.
Turn your face toward the sacred place of worship;
and wherever you are turn your faces towards it.
Those who have received the scripture certainly know
that this is the truth from their Lord.
God is not unaware of what they do.

If you went to the people who received the scripture
with every kind of proof, they will not follow your direction of prayer,
nor will you follow their direction of prayer.
Even among themselves, they do not follow one direction of prayer. And were you to follow their desires, after all the knowledge that came to you, surely you would be one of the evil-doers.

The "spiritual exile," which once caused the Meccan community to turn toward Jerusalem, the crystallization point for the prayers of the exiled, has now given way to an actual exile, a consciousness of being excluded from Mecca and its cult center. The reminiscence of the Solomonic establishment of the direction of prayer in Q 2:145, "wherever you may be," gives expression to this exilic character. The directing of prayer to Mecca obviously met with opposition, as the text shows. The relinquishment of the long-practiced orientation toward Jerusalem was found to be a difficult task (verse 143), giving rise to a controversy with the Jews. This step could be associated with a feeling of uncertainty on the part of the Prophet himself. It should be understood less as a gesture of turning away from the Jews, to whom continued adherence to their direction of prayer is conceded (Q 2:145), than as a new implementation of an established biblical model for coping with exile,[68] which is undertaken with the awareness that it will cause a polarization of those "to whom scripture has been given," who obviously are irritated by this step.

In what follows, Mecca takes on further distinctions, prerogatives that had once been granted to Jerusalem. Just as it is said in Isaiah 2:3 that Jerusalem is the place from which divine teachings issue ("For from Zion the teachings [*tora*] will go out and the word of the Lord from Jerusalem"), so now Mecca is given as the status of the origin of scripture and wisdom, according to a prophecy that

68. Rahman, *Major Themes*, 132–149. Nagel's interpretation of the change of the direction of prayer to Mecca, *Medinensische Einschübe*, 144–148, does not pay due respect to the theological dimension of the abrogation of the direction of prayer, nor does it consider the exilic aspect or attend to the construction of Mecca as a "New Jerusalem."

stems from the same early Medinan period, which is articulated by Abraham, Q 2:127–129:

> When Abraham and Ishmael began
> to raise the foundations of the house, they prayed:
> "Our Lord, accept this from us.
> You are the hearing, the knowing.
> Our Lord, grant us to submit to you [*muslimūn*],
> and make of our posterity a community
> that submits to you [*umma muslima*].
> Guide us in our rites and pardon us.
> You are indeed the pardoner, the merciful.
> Our Lord, send them a messenger from among themselves
> who will recite to them your verses,
> to teach them the scripture and the wisdom, and to purify them.
> You are truly the mighty, the wise.

With the Qur'anic proclamation, this prophecy has been fulfilled, and what is more, since Abraham founded the rites of Mecca and also implored for their completion through verbal prayer service, which is brought about by the proclaimer, the rank of greatest antiquity falls to Mecca. Not to be the most recent foundation but to be the most ancient sanctuary is what matters. Mecca can now claim this rank, eclipsing Jerusalem, which was first provided with the Temple by Solomon, Q 3:96:

> *inna awwala baytin wuḍiʿa li-l-nāsi*
> *la-lladhī bi-Bakkata mubārakan wa-hudan li-l-ʿālamīn*

> The first house of God which was made for the people,
> is that in Bakka [= Mecca],
> as a blessing and right guidance for the world.

Further distinctions of the Jewish Jerusalem come to Mecca through Abraham: after verses Q 37:99–113, particularly verse 102, had localized the important event of the "binding" of the son, Abraham's "Aqedah," in Mecca, it is no surprise that the later Islamic tradition continues to reclaim this event for Mecca, or for a place in the surroundings of Mecca. This approach to the event, which is not essentially dissimilar to that of the Christian tradition, which had moved the event from the Temple Mount to Golgotha, confers on Mecca a further decisive prerogative of Jerusalem, namely, to be the founding place for the special status of Abraham's descendants, now understood as his spiritual descendants.[69] Thus Jerusalem now retreats behind Mecca in the Qur'an. Later tradition indicates the relationship to

69. See Schechter, *Rabbinic Theology*, 170–198; cf. also chap. 11, 398–400.

be an overlapping sequence of ranks: Jerusalem is "the first of the two directions of prayer," *ūlā l-qiblatayn*, but only "the second of the two places of worship," *thānī l-masjidayn*. Already in the Qur'an, Mecca obtains the rank of a new Jerusalem.

9.5 Qur'an and Martyrdom

9.5.1 Dangerous Vicinity to Myth

The Medinan community soon became a warrior society, whose mission in struggle, *jihād*, is evoked in numerous verses.[70] The warrior ideal is not anchored in salvific history, however, and is bound up with none of the previous messengers with the one exception of the biblical king Saul. It is also notable that the newly introduced concept of *jihād* in the Qur'an is not at first understood as a military activity but initially represents an ascetic ideal of self-mastery, the control of egoistic urges, entirely in the sense of a spiritualized *athlōn*, or "contest, effort, struggle," as evoked in the late Meccan text Q 29:6, 69. This connotation of the control of the self still adheres to the concept as it later becomes a designation of military struggle, Q 61:10–11:

> O believers, shall I point you to a commerce
> that will save you from a painful torment?
> That you believe in God and his messenger
> and exert yourself in God's way [*tujāhidūna fī sabīli llāhi*]
> with your possessions and your life.
> That is the best for you, if you are understanding.

But the duty incumbent on the emigrants to exert themselves in battle is indicated more frequently by the word *qitāl*, "battle," which was already frequent before Islam. The interchangeability of these terms shows that *jihād* as such is not a struggle for a religious cause but rather refers to the military operation on behalf of the affairs of the new community, the community of belief. In this context the merit bound up with military operations of the believers for the survival of the community is often dressed in the economic metaphor of exchange, which promises great profit in the hereafter (Q 9:111):

> God has bought from the believers their lives and their wealth
> in return for paradise.
> They fight in the way of God [*yuqātilūna fī sabīli llāh*],
> they kill and are killed.
> That is a true promise from him in the Torah,
> the Gospel, and the Qur'an.

70. On all this, see now the fundamental study by Horsch, *Tod im Kampf*; cf. also Firestone, "Jihād."

As Silvia Horsch has shown,[71] the transformation in the understanding of struggle that manifests itself here stands "in connection to the founding of a genealogy based on scripture, in opposition to the genealogy based on tribal descent of the pre-Islamic period. Through the promise of reward in the hereafter for battle in this world, this understanding of struggle toward the end of the development is made apparent as an inheritance from the predecessor monotheistic religions. Struggle is thus set into a religious tradition; it no longer serves for the winning of honor for the tribe as in the pre-Islamic period."[72] Albrecht Noth summarizes: "An essential component of the tribalist form of life in Arabia at that time, struggle, which was already placed on the positive side of the scale of values, now becomes sublimated into '*jihād* in the way of God,' a highly esteemed religious merit, and it is only in this that the Islamic innovation consists."[73]

But there is a verse whose interpretation of struggle goes well beyond what is manifest here, a meritoriousness founded in religious loyalty.[74] This passage, which is often quoted in later Islam as evidence for the existence of a Qur'anic ideal of martyrdom, is as follows (Q 3:169–170):[75]

> Do not think that those who have been killed in the way of God are dead.
> No, they are living with their Lord and provided for.
> They rejoice in what their Lord has given them of his bounty,
> and they eagerly expect those who stayed behind to come after them: no fear shall overcome them! They shall not grieve!

Is martyrdom then already a Qur'anic ideal? Do we find the concept of martyrdom in the Qur'an? In view of the prominent position that martyrdom possesses in Christian tradition, one would expect traces of this discourse in the Qur'an. On the other hand, it is equally possible that the community taking shape around the proclaimer might have rejected and excised individual ideas current in the debates that took place in their environment, or might have remained silent about them or reshaped them to the point that they are not identifiable in their familiar significance. One such example seems to be the Christian martyrdom discourse, which is amply documented in Late Antiquity, but which does not seem to have put down roots in the Qur'an.

Assuming the peculiar Christian concept of martyrdom to be self-evident, research up to now has continuously given a negative answer to the question

71. Horsch, *Tod im Kampf*.

72. Ibid., 107.

73. Noth, "Früher Islam," 57. On the Prophetological implication of fighting, see Marshall, *God, Muhammad and the Unbelievers*, 117–138.

74. Heavenly reward is also promised to those killed in battle elsewhere in the Qur'an, without, however, implying particular nearness to God: "And do not say about those who are killed in the way of God, 'they are dead.' Rather, they are alive, but you perceive it not" (Q 2:154).

75. This highly daring, indeed unique verse is still frequently cited to sanction Islamic martyrdom and can be found in obituaries and on posters of young men who died in military conflict.

of a concept of martyrdom in the Qur'an.[76] Overview presentations on Islamic martyrdom, such as that by Etan Kohlberg, assert the absence of a martyrdom concept in the Qur'an. The numerous Qur'anic examples of the term *shahīd/shuhadā'*,[77] which would later come to mean martyr, should mostly be understood in the juristic sense of "witness/witnesses," even if, as Silvia Horsch has recently argued, in certain cases such as Q 3:140 an explanation in the sense of "martyr" cannot to be excluded:[78]

> If you have been afflicted by a wound, a similar wound has afflicted the enemy. These are battle days we alternate among mankind, that God may know those who truly believe and may receive some of you as witnesses, martyrs [*shuhadā'*]. God does not love the wrongdoers.

This verse, read as a testimony about Qur'anic martyrdom, would however not entail anything beyond the close connection between being wounded or suffering death in battle and the divine acceptance of the fallen. The special status that the Islamic martyr will enjoy later due to his extraordinary eschatological distinction is not addressed here.

But this is different in the verse cited above (Q 3:169), which in tradition provides the Qur'anic locus classicus for Islamic martyrdom as such. Though the verse contains no explicit designation of the martyr as *shahīd/shuhadā*,[79] one cannot dispute the fact that this verse is unique in the Qur'an, that no other verse among those that speak of the necessity of struggle conveys a comparably close connection between struggle, violent death, and nearness to the divine. Can this verse, then, serve as a reference text for Islamic martyrdom *avant la lettre*, as is often assumed? How does it relate to the concepts of martyrdom current in the other religious traditions?

On this point, we will first take a glance on Late Antique—that is, Christian—martyrdom, which was likely known to the Qur'anic community. Late Antique martyrdom—roughly speaking—derives its tension from the combination of three components: bearing witness, sacrifice, and mimesis/succession.[80] All three problem areas are treated in the Qur'an; an overview of their respective configurations in the Qur'an should therefore help to clarify the relationship of the Qur'anic proclamation to Christian martyrdom on the one hand and the Islamic martyrdom that developed later, which put death in battle at its center, on the other.

76. Noth, "Früher Islam"; but see now Horsch, *Tod im Kampf.*

77. Kohlberg, "Shahīd"; somewhat less rigidly, Cook, *Martyrdom.*

78. See the Qur'anic evidence of *shahīd/shuhadā'* in Horsch, *Tod im Kampf*, 15–17.

79. This category does occur in the Qur'an, though only by its name, in the context of schematic enumerations of the pious dead of earlier generations.

80. Cf. the definition of Frutaz, "Märtyrer," 128: "Martyrs of the Divinity of Christ and His Religion," quoted by Horsch, *Tod im Kampf*, 30.

9.5.2 *Bearing Witness?*

The idea of bearing witness can be considered the essential backbone of the early community, and is a trait already developed in the Qur'an. The confession of faith, the *shahāda*, "I witness that there is no God except God, and I witness that Muhammad is God's messenger" (*ashhadu an lā ilāha illā llāh wa-ashhadu anna Muḥammadan rasūlu llāh*), is sufficient to attest to a person's belonging to Islam. Its first part is Qur'anic, and is pronounced by God himself in a Medinan text (Q 3:18):

shahada llāhu annahu lā ilāha illā huwa
wa-l-malāʾikatu wa-ūlū l-ʿilm

God witnesses that there is no God except him,
and the angels and those grounded in wisdom witness this.

In many places, God appears as the witness of theological truths.[81] But above all, the covenant with God in preexistence, the so-called *ʿahd a-last*, which is fundamental and which in the Qur'an replaces the Mosaic giving of the tablets, consists of a bearing of witness.[82] Instead of the Israelites standing before Mount Sinai, it is all of mankind that is called to witness (Q 7:172):

When your Lord took out
from the loins of the sons of Adam their progeny,
and had them bear witness for themselves:
am I not [*a-lastu*] your Lord?
Then they said, "yes, we witness it" [*shahidnā*].
This we did, so that you will not say on the day of resurrection:
"we were not aware of this beforehand."

This original scene of bearing witness, which occurs in preexistence,[83] figures as the Islamic Sinai event, so to speak, but it consists not in the giving over of divine written signs but rather in an oral testimony. "To witness," *shahida*, is a central Qur'anic concept, which alongside its frequent usage in a strict juristic sense is used frequently to undergird the truth claims of monotheism. On the other hand, it does not occur where we might perceive a martyrdom scenario, as in a scene in Q 26:47–51, in which Pharaoh announces the execution of a number of magicians whom Moses had converted to monotheism. Their assertion of belief before their death, *āmannā*, "we believe," is apparently regarded as a more significant

81. He also attests to the second pronouncements of the later creed: *wa-yaqūlu lladhīna kafarū lasta mursalan qul kafā bi-llāhi shahīdan baynī wa-baynakum wa-man ʿindahu ʿilmu l-kitāb*, "Those who have disbelieved say, 'You are not a messenger.' Say, 'Sufficient is God as witness between me and you, and whoever has knowledge of the Scripture.'"

82. Cf. chap. 11, 408–415.

83. See Hartwig, "Urvertrag"; cf. also Obermann, "Koran and Agada."

testimony of faith than their death. It is scarcely surprising, then, that in none of the Qur'an verses that mention the merit of death in battle do we find language related to witnessing. The researcher of mysticism Fritz Meier has drawn a far-reaching conclusion from this: "The Muslims who fell in battle had nothing to bear witness to. The word *shahīd*, martyr, has a Christian flavor to it."[84] One could say more cautiously that in Islam, and above all in the Qur'an, the verbally articulated witnessing of the unity of God has a decisive rank. An explicit confession of faith in addition to an offering of physical self-sacrifice was at no time required of a Muslim martyr.

9.5.3 *Sacrifice?*

The relationship of the Qur'anic community to the second constitutive element of Christian martyrdom, sacrifice and sacrificial death, is ambivalent. Islam treats blood as essentially impure, while in Judaism it is accounted also as impurity detergent, and as a means of atonement.[85] Indeed, the sacrifice of animals is prescribed in the Qur'an, as in the Hebrew Bible (Q 22:36),[86] but the Qur'anic instructions do not follow biblical models and instead stand in the tradition of the Meccan pagan pilgrimage cult, whose external form they continue to uphold.

But the continuation of pagan sacrifice should not obscure the essential ambiguity that the Qur'an ascribes to animal sacrifice. The abolition of public sacrifice in the course of the Christianization of the Roman Empire three hundred years before Islam had paved the way for new forms of worship as a means of individual redemption, such as prayer, fasting, and alms. This "end of sacrifice" is reflected also in the Qur'an, where animal sacrifice is endowed with an entirely new meaning contrasting with the pagan rites of sacrifice: first of all, the ancient Arabian sacrificial rite is sublimated into an act of emulating the model of Abraham. Insofar as the entire institution of the pilgrimage or *ḥajj*—originally a rite marking a seasonal turn—is reinterpreted in terms of salvation history in the Qur'an, that is, referred back to the biblical Abraham—perhaps in agreement with older locally transmitted traditions—its climax, the ceremony of sacrifice (*ʿīd al-aḍḥā*), in which a ram or other animal is to be slaughtered, obtains the rank of an Abrahamic foundation. Its accomplishment by the Muslim worshipper thus becomes an *imitatio* of Abraham. The meaning of sacrifice for the Qur'an is limited to this complex. Not a symbolic configuration of meaning but rather the fulfillment of a divine command in imitation of a religious predecessor figure is to be imagined as the backdrop of Islamic sacrifice, according to both the Qur'an and orthodox belief. One can thus speak justifiably of a demythologization of

84. Meier, *Almoraviden*, 712–713.

85. Maghen, "First Blood."

86. As in Judaism, the "Noahide laws" apply also in the Qur'an, meaning the ban on spilling blood (Q 2:30, 84) and the ban on humans consuming blood (Q 2:173, 5:3, 16:115, 6:145); Islamic tradition also adopted the practice of kosher butchering.

sacrifice already with reference to the Qur'an. While the words spoken by Moses in his rite of expiation on the Day of Atonement, "this is the blood of the covenant" (Lev 16:10–16), are reconfigured in the Christian tradition within the institution of the Eucharist (Mk 14:23–24), they remain without reception in the Qur'an and in later (Sunnite) Islam.

Unlike in the biblical context, in the Qur'an sacrifice has no expiatory effects. This difference is not a mere ritual detail, but marks a decisively softened position vis-à-vis the treatment of blood and sacrifice as means of atonement in comparison with Judaism and Christianity. The biblical claim to an expiatory or purifying power for blood in the ritual context, as is expressed in the institution of Yom Kippur, Lev 16:10–16, which later becomes a theologumenon of the Christian church, in the Qur'an is unambiguously negated.

In the Qur'an, one can claim without exaggeration that the very idea of sacrifice is lacking: the spilling of the blood of sacrifice for atonement is not considered. It is however not simply passed over in silence, but is consciously excluded or "silenced." Not only is the proscribed sacrifice for the *ʿīd al-aḍḥā*, the "sacrifice festival," emptied of all mythical function, but such a function is explicitly negated, as Q 22:36–37—reminiscent of Biblical cult-critical pronouncements—says:

> The sacrificial animals we have assigned for you to be part of the rituals of God. Much good you have in them;
> so mention God's name over them as they stand in line.
> When they are fallen over their sides,
> eat of them and feed the humble and the beggar.
> That is how we subjected them to you, that you may be thankful.
> Their flesh and blood will not reach God, but your piety will reach him. Thus he subjected them to you, that you may glorify God for guiding you. And announce the good news to those who do good.

Sacrifice is thus reduced to an expression of fear of God—quite in the sense of the admonitions of the ancient Israelite Prophets, who called for piety rather than sacrifice. At the same time, sacrifice is a restaging of the sacrifice of Abraham, whose near-sacrifice of his son, redirected into an animal sacrifice, is localized according to the Qur'an not on Mount Moriah but in the Meccan sanctuary.

9.5.4 Negation of a Redemptive Model

In view of this lack of any recollection of the biblical institution of sacrifice in the Qur'an, the comparison of Christ to the scapegoat or the sacrificial lamb, whose blood redeems the sins of the community in the Yom Kippur ceremony, could not have entered the horizon of the early believers. The Qur'an, which already downgrades the blood of the sacrificial animal religiously to a *quantité negligeable*, thus distances itself from a tradition that was foundational for the predecessor religions. Consequently, the image of Christ suffering on the Cross[87] is replaced in the Qur'an by the image of Jesus teaching. There is no self-sacrifice of Christ. Jesus, who like all the other Prophets that appear in the Qur'an suffers repercussions from his unheeding people, is ultimately saved, like all Prophets in the Qur'anic schema, by divine intervention. He is raised to heaven, from where—according to later tradition—he will return to defeat the Antichrist. Jesus does not suffer on the cross, but another takes his place and dies there. His role is that of a proclaimer of the belief in unity and that of a caller to unity.

The idea of sacrifice thus has no place here: according to the overall optimistic outlook of the Qur'an, the world is not condemned; Adam's lapse does not mark the fall of man but merely forms an episode, since guilt can be atoned for case by case through repentance. A "second Adam" to erase the guilt of his precursor is not required, since there was no "first Adam" who took guilt upon himself. The privileged model of the believers is thus not Christ elevated for the accomplishment of his self-sacrifice; the role of model falls rather in the end of the Qur'anic development to a counter-figure, Abraham, the most "myth-resistant" figure among the biblical Prophets or patriarchs.

9.5.5 The Rededication of the Sacrifice: Abraham as Sacrificer and Model

As the Qur'an integrates the animal sacrifice into the rites of pilgrimage established by Abraham, Abraham becomes the founder of the Islamic sacrifice—insofar as one can speak of such in view of the minimalized status of sacrifice. The post-Qur'anic Islamic tradition, which condenses the ritual *ḥajj* ceremonies into a sacred drama to be reenacted by the pilgrims, raises this particular rite to the rank of the commemoration of Abraham's near-sacrifice, Aqedah, of his son.

Can the "binding of the son," the Aqedah, Abraham's preparedness to sacrifice his son out of utmost self-dedication to God then be regarded as a Qur'anic figure of thought? A glance at sura 37 shows that the Qur'anic reading of the Aqedah departs from the biblical presentation in its particular thrust and instead, in agreement with a Midrash tradition, remains devoid of any mythologizing dramatics: Abraham does not have to pass through the self-negating act of sacrificing his only son, but instead a social interaction between father and son is staged, and the son—informed about the divine command—shows himself ready to serve as the obedient victim.[88] The enactment is hardly begun when it is then broken off, since God himself frees the "bound one," offering an animal victim as his substitute. Thus the figure of the Aqedah, the binding of the son, although it is received in the Qur'an and its second, salvific part is restaged annually as the climax of the *ḥajj*, cannot be linked to the discourse of martyrdom. With

87. Cf. Lawson, *Crucifixion*, 26–42.
88. See chap. 11, 391–395.

the Qur'anic reinterpretation of the Abraham model, a previously revolutionary model is replaced by one that conforms with norms.[89]

9.5.6 *Martyrs on the Christian model?*

No bloody bearing of witness, no redemptive sacrifice, no imitation of a redeemer who breaks all norms—the Qur'an is thus a scripture with a strongly demythologizing tendency. Nonetheless, a topos of Islamic martyrdom did arise later, which was linked closely to death in battle on the one hand and an eschatological distinction for the fallen on the other. Fading out the demanding parameters set by Christian martyrdom, the uniquely emphatic verse Q 3:161 appears to mark a break in the Qur'an's otherwise hermetically sealed paradigm of almost absolute restraint from mythologizing, above all from the mythologizing of rites involving blood. The exceptional status of the fallen in the hereafter attested in this verse clearly falls outside of the dominant eschatological frame of the Qur'an, according to which all the dead will be awoken only on the Last Day. The fact that this *avant la lettre* description of martyrdom in its later form as *shahāda* is not distinguished as such seems to indicate either that during the Medinan period of proclamation self-denying operations were called for, without there being a theologically reflected concept of martyrdom behind them yet, or that associations with the Christian veneration of martyrs that figured most prominently were shunned. In other words: figurations of martyrdom are already present in the Qur'an,[90] but a clear concept of martyrdom had not yet been worked out, and there was obviously a reluctance to develop one. The once-established connection between violent death and privileged rank in the hereafter, which is the focus of Q 3:161, was, however, well-suited to paving the way for the integration of a mythical image of martyrdom into the thought of the early Islamic community: once violent death was recognized as a way of obtaining nearness to God, the biblical paradigm of the exchanging of sacrificial blood for divine favor, which had been banished from the Qur'an, was able to enter into Islam subcutaneously, as it were, and the verse could be read as an *avant la lettre* testimony for Islamic martyrdom. Certainly, the difference between the perception of the fallen warriors *in* the Qur'an and *after* the Qur'an remains significant.[91] Islamic tradition sacralizes martyrs on the battlefield already in this world, furnishing them not with redemptive blood, but with a related change of substance: the martyr's blood becomes musk that eliminates the impurity of the corpse—thus no washing

89. Ibid.

90. It is to Horsch's credit that she opened this particular venue of thought, in Horsch, *Tod im Kampf.*

91. Wensinck was not totally unjustified in putting the verse into the context of hero worship in antiquity. Thus the Islamic martyrs featured by the author of an early martyr treatise, Ibn al-Mubārak, are clearly modeled on heroes of antiquity. See Saleh, "Woman," 128.

of the dead body is required. Visible blood possessing magical faculties, an anathema in the Qur'an, thus becomes the God-pleasing emblem of the martyr. Yet the blood remains without function for the expiation of the collective, quite in the sense of the Qur'an. The Islamic martyr remains limited theologically to the status of the typus of the individual exemplary pious figure, even if he does possess special claim to reward in the hereafter.

10

Qur'an and Bible

10.1 Similarities, Dissimilarities

10.1.1 Biblical Narrative—Qur'anic Drama

The relationship between the Qur'an and the Bible[1] is not easy to define. Already in their literary form, the two seem to be distant from each other: unlike the Bible, the transmitted Qur'an is not a text to be read continuously. It does not narrate chronologically structured salvation history running from creation down to the time of the recording of the text, as is true *grosso modo* for the Hebrew Bible, where a "world drama" unfolds with the acts of creation—election—Exodus—settling in the land—exile—promise of redemption. The Qur'an sketches no comparably grand picture of history, although it likewise assigns a prominent place to the creation of the world and the history of the elected people, and although the Qur'anic community already at an early point understood itself as a new people of God led by a prophet akin to Moses. Also unlike the Hebrew Bible, it offers no spectrum of narrative, prophetic, poetic, and wisdom texts clearly assigned to individual books, but rather combines differing types of text into the new genre of the "sura," which is represented by the Qur'an alone. Neither does the Qur'an follow, in the style of the Gospels, the life and work of a divinely dispatched charismatic proclaimer and his founding of a community down to his death and the conclusion of his ministry. Although the Qur'an is the decisive document for the Islamic community's formation and reclaims for its proclamation a speaker endowed with divine inspiration, it offers neither a history of the community nor a biography of its proclaimer. Instead of laying out a salvation historical past, it rather summons up the eschatological future in its early texts, and in its later parts debates the implementation of the scripturally based monotheistic order of society in the present.

Concerning its diction, however, the Qur'an is indeed oriented to biblical models of speech; even more, it is wholly "prophetic speech." For what in the case of the Hebrew Bible was only achieved exegetically in retrospect, the reinterpretation of all parts of the corpus into one prophecy[2] grounded in inspiration, in

1. This chapter concentrates on questions that have already been treated in Bible scholarship but have not yet been posed for the Koran. The internal Koranic development of the community's perception of the Bible is discussed elsewhere; see chaps. 8 and 9, as well as chap. 3, 116–119.

2. See Kugel, "Poets and Prophets."

the Qur'an is already presupposed from the start: the Qur'an not only claims the status of prophetic speech but also, through the second-person address maintained throughout the entire text, shows itself to be mantic speech displaying, in its poetic texts and to a lesser degree also in its narrative texts, the structural characteristics of appellatory[3] persuasive speech. But since the text also displays dialogical patterns, often even citing speech and counter-speech, the Qur'an in its pre-canonical form should not be classified generically as narrative,[4] as for example the Pentateuch and the historical books of the Bible, but—in view of the fact that the exchange of the speaker with hearers begins early on and persists until the end of the proclamation—it should rather be regarded as drama.

"Drama" in the case of the Qur'an is certainly not precisely identical with the familiar fictional genre. For in the Qur'an we are confronted with a particular form of drama, which for the most part does not allow the protagonists to speak directly, but rather occasionally cites their speech and more often only refers to it; thus, it is a drama that is "presented" by an observer, who not only speaks but rather is also himself involved in the drama. The Qur'an is the "I" and "we" speech of a speaker perceived as transcendent, toward a "you" that is within the world, the proclaimer, who in turn addresses a hearership—even if this communication scenario is not yet entirely complete in the earliest suras. The voice of the "I" or "we" speaker, which jolts the drama, does not come from the stage itself, but rather from the "offstage" of the transcendent. Indeed, it is this voice that—once the address is translated into proclamation, that is, as soon as the speaker turns with the received message to his hearers—takes prominence, commenting on the acceptance or rejection of the message.[5] Above all, it is the voice of the decisive actor in the drama itself: God is the speaker, and at the same time takes part in what is reported as an actor. This multilayered scenario of communication and interaction, which drives the dialogical aspect of prophetic speech to its utmost limit, can be counted as the most decisive formal characteristic of the Qur'an, and it has no correspondence in the Bible.

In view of this particular communication situation, the Qur'an is never truly similar to biblical writings, even if in the different phases of its genesis it comes very close to particular partial corpora. Thus, in its early phase, it corresponds most fittingly in its form to the Psalms.[6] Like the Psalter, the early Qur'an consists of short, concisely formulated verses in poetic language, which, like the Psalms, formulate praises of God and prayer, as well as the complaint of an exemplary pious figure. In both corpora, the structure of the verses fits their purpose of

3. The term "appellatory" is introduced by Bühler, *Sprachtheorie*, who classifies language into the categories of description, pronouncement, and appellatory speech.

4. On the narrative technique of the Bible, see especially Alter, *Biblical Narrative*, and Alter and Kermode, *Literary Guide to the Bible*, and now also Sternberg, *Poetics of Biblical Narrative*.

5. See chap. 6, 214–216.

6. See Neuwirth, "Psalmen"; cf. chap. 7, 241–245.

being recited, arguably with cantilena. The later suras, on the other hand, are not only more complex thematically but also are composed of different types of text with their respective topoi and formulae. Examined according to their sequences of themes and genres, they are no longer comparable to biblical texts, but rather to a liturgical text ensemble. This becomes particularly clear in the tripartite middle Meccan suras, with their sequence of appellatory introductory part—narrative—appellatory closing part, corresponding to the sequence of liturgical elements of a monotheistic service, which begins and ends antiphonically and includes a narrative "reading" at the center.[7] Only toward the end of the development do further forms occur recalling biblical precedents, for example the Medinan "oratory sura," which evokes biblical prophetic speeches, and the "long sura," which seems to correspond to an entire biblical book.[8]

10.1.2 Exegetical Thrust

Yet these similarities, traceable on the surface, are relativized through an attitude that dominates the entire Qur'an and that is unthinkable of in the biblical books: the exegetical bias. According to self-referential pronouncements in the Meccan suras, the Qur'an will not bring something new, but rather dress in a new language what has already been proclaimed earlier, in order to reach a language community to which earlier revelations had not arrived: "to warn a people, whose fathers were not warned, so that they are heedless" (Q 36:6). This is expressed even more clearly in the Qur'anic claim to *tafṣīl al-kitāb*, "the exposition (according to situation) or interpretation of the (heavenly) scripture," which is expressed for example in Q 10:37: "This reading is not simply contrived without God's intervention; rather, it is the confirmation of that which was before it, and an exposition, *tafṣīl*, of the scripture [*tafṣīl al-kitāb*], in which there is no doubt, by the Lord of the Worlds."[9] Thus is set forth not only as a paraenetic but also an exegetical thrust, which manifests itself particularly in the reformulation of older traditions. Biblical narratives are not told for their own sake, but rather with a special exegetical interest, whose narrative mode—often bemoaned as elliptical—is grounded in this selective interest.

This elliptical form, however unwieldy it may seem to the modern reader, is justifiable in the Qur'anic context, since the contents must have been familiar to the hearers at least in rough form. Nicolai Sinai notes here that

> above all early Qur'an texts, in which no extended narratives occur, . . . were received well within an extra-Qur'anic horizon of knowledge. The fact that the Qur'an in the process of its proclamation . . . gives more fully

7. See chap. 6, 217–218.
8. See chap. 6, 229–232.
9. See Sinai, "Qur'ānic Self-Referentiality," cf. chap. 2, 76–80.

> detailed descriptions of the persons and events concerned indicates that this extra-Qur'anic horizon of understanding was to be replaced successively by an inner-Qur'anic horizon—i.e., the co-existence of complementary versions within a text corpus recognized across the community as canonical. The Meccan Qur'an texts thus selectively appropriate the horizon of understanding of the hearers, which was originally external to the text, not only in order to control it in its theological-moral implications but also to standardize it within the Qur'anic community.[10]

The same paraenetic bias that underlies the multiple narrations of the same stories is also effective in the rewriting of psalm texts, which the Qur'an reshapes from pure hymns into didactic argumentation: here too, we observe a normalizing of the theological-moral implications of the texts. Man does not praise God as the creator, as he does in the Psalms, but rather God himself recalls his acts of creation to man, thus obligating man to exalt him exclusively. Even when the Qur'an later steps out of the construction of mere succession and of a primarily interpretative relation to the earlier messages by taking on a radically new direction through the transfer of theologumena from the history of the Israelites and the Holy Land to the homeland of the Prophet and the Arabian Peninsula, even this large-scale new identity construction remains an exegetical project. If in the early parts of the Qur'an individual biblical and post-biblical texts are negotiated exegetically—one thinks for example of the calling of Moses, which receives a Qur'anic "continuation" through Muhammad's vision in sura 53[11]—the later parts of the Qur'an mirror the progression of an exegetical appropriation and integration of entire biblical discourses that take on a new value in the Qur'an. Understood in this way, the establishment of the prayer direction toward Mecca, for example, reflects a reconsideration of the prototype of the Solomonic dedication of the temple. Similarly, the reformation of the Kaaba cult in the Qur'an reflects the biblical-Prophetic, but above all post-biblical, devaluation of sacrifice in favor of the fear of God that is alone regarded as decisive.[12] That the treatment of biblical and post-biblical references is often clothed in the form of an argument is not surprising; the Qur'anic message emerged at a time when massive amounts of exegetical literature was produced in the surrounding milieu, which was to impart to the individual religious traditions their exclusive character.[13]

10.1.3 *What Should Be Compared?*

It may be just this dissimilarity that has blocked systematic comparative research between the Bible and the Qur'an up until now. All available reference

10. Sinai, *Studien zur Koraninterpretation*, 83.
11. Cf. chap. 2, 68–71, and chap. 11, 405–408.
12. Cf. chap. 9, 341–342.
13. Cf. chap. 13, 453–457.

works[14] contextualize the Qur'an with individual books of the Bible, not however with the entire text corpus. The problem of the similarity or dissimilarity of the two text corpora in their status of great traditions has not been recognized; collected volumes with the explicit theme of the Bible and the Qur'an[15] though often appearing to offer promising programs remain concerned only with accidental shared characteristics. Even the most thorough and comprehensive collection of biblical and Qur'anic themes, Heribert Busse's indispensable reference work *Die theologischen Beziehungen des Islams zu Judentum und Christentum* (*Islam, Judaism and Christianity: The Theological and Historical Affiliations*; 1991), which follows on Heinrich Speyer's encyclopedic work *Die biblischen Erzählungen im Qoran* (Biblical narratives in the Qur'an; 1935), systematically compares biblical stories with their Qur'anic counterparts, it remains stuck with the hierarchic relation between biblical "sources" and their Qur'anic "reworkings," without pursuing the theological significance of the particular Qur'anic reception of the Bible.[16] More recently, Hans Zirker has given an important spur to the synoptic treatment of biblical and Qur'anic theological positions, but his works are based on a synchronic treatment of the Qur'an text and show no interest in the progression of the negotiation of older traditions by the proclaimer and the community.[17]

The lack of a systematic comparison of the Bible and the Qur'an, both as literary texts and as evidence of changing theological conceptions, can best be explained by the failure of many researchers to put the Qur'an and the Bible on the same level. The reason for this should be sought in the still-current notion of the epigonality of the Qur'an.[18] The verdict of epigonality, according to which the Qur'an has selectively "taken over" narratives and ideas from the books of the Bible or post-biblical tradition,[19] obscures the full correspondence between the Qur'an and the two partial corpora of the Hebrew Bible and New Testament, which as the founding documents of their respective religions in unique a way provide the mythical-metaphorical subtext for the thought and language of their societies.

14. Thus, both of the most recent encyclopedias on the Koran, McAuliffe, *Encyclopaedia of the Qur'ān*, and Amir-Moezzi, *Dictionnaire*, make reference to biblical books but do not contain articles about the hermeneutical relation of the Koran and the Bible. The introductory works Robinson, *Discovering the Qur'ān*; Paret, *Mohammed und der Koran*; Bobzin, *Koran*; and Cook, *Der Koran*, are also little concerned with these relationships.

15. Reeves, *Bible and Qur'an*, is limited—with the exception of a single paragraph—to evidence on common contents, terms, and literary types; its major focus is Koran exegesis rather than the Koran itself. The title of the collection of essays edited by Seale, *Qur'an and Bible*, is misleading; it is a collection of heterogeneous works specific to the Bible, the Koran, and Islam, respectively. The articles on biblical subjects in McAuliffe, *The Cambridge Companion*, and Rippin, *The Blackwell Companion to the Qur'ān*, do not go beyond individual observations on particularities.

16. Busse, *Die theologischen Beziehungen*. Thyen, *Bibel und Koran*, is limited to the comparison of thematically similar biblical and Qur'anic texts.

17. Zirker, *Der Koran: Zugänge und Lesarten*.

18. See the numerous testimonies in Wild, "Schauerliche Öde"; cf. also Neuwirth, "De-mythifying Islam," as well as the introduction, 12–17.

19. The image introduced by Geiger (see chap. 1, 37–40) still characterizes most notions of the Qur'anic relationship to older traditions.

This perception of the "aura" of the scriptures stands and falls with the recognition of their particular referentiality—either transcendent or worldly—and, bound up with that, with the hermeneutic register to be employed in their reading. Thus the question of the comprehensibility of a layer of meaning beyond what is said according to the literal sense becomes inescapable also for the textual understanding of the Qur'an. The meta-historical dimension of speech that is claimed in the Qur'an from the very beginning, and which manifests itself in specific textual strategies, has generally received no attention in research up to now.

For the literary-critical handling of this dimension, the reflections of the literary critic Northrup Frye on the referentiality of the Bible are illuminating. Frye has labeled the Bible the "great code."[20] He studied the "biblical encoding" of premodern Western literature through numerous examples, showing how this "encoding" arises not only from the veritative, "literal" reading of biblical texts but frequently from their symbolic reading, which is achieved in the Christian context through the means of typology and allegory.[21]

The Bible reflects different forms of the treatment of language, which, according to Frye, require different readings. Frye reads the biblical text as a document of successive stages in the development of consciousness. The first, "poetic/metaphoric" stage is typical of a phase in societal development where poetry is the main source of cultural knowledge, not least because verse aids the preservation of memory in a mnemotechnically most effective way. The thought figure of metaphor that is operative here, with the structure "X is equal to Y," allows one to speak about the numinous forces immanent in the world, which were identified in ancient Near Eastern societies with deities and mythical beings, as is still evident from numerous texts of the Hebrew Bible. [22] Even if the origins of the Bible date back to this first "metaphoric" phase of language, the greater mass of biblical texts already shows evidence of a divide between poetic and dialectical thought. They belong to Frye's "phase of metonymy," in which the conception of a transcendent God moves into the center of the world's order. "Metonymic" then denotes a sort of analogical thought and writing, in which the verbal expression "is used *for* something" (X stands for Y), that *per se* eludes the direct verbal mode of expression. Here, in analogy to Plato's parable of the cave, an invisible world makes its appearance as the a decisive reference behind reality, so that many statements must be read metonymically, that is, as referring in their deeper sense to the transcendent.[23] This "religious reading" being suggested, according to Frye, by parts of the Hebrew Bible, becomes a universal principle for the later

20. Frye, *The Great Code*.

21. The search for forms of "rewriting the Bible" has now caught on; see Boitani, *The Bible and Its Rewritings*.

22. See Fishbane, *Biblical Myth*.

23. See Bruns, "Midrash and Allegory." Bruns emphasizes (637) that the hermeneutic techniques of allegory, so central for Bible readings, were established practices in Greek thought long before the development of grammar and rhetoric; see in detail Curtius, *Europäische Literatur*, 210–220.

Christian-theological reading of the text, according to which a full understanding of the Bible must rely on an interpretation going beyond the literal sense.

In the third phase—called "descriptive"—the individual subject interprets the speech by means of his own sensory experience of the objective world. Here, the criterion of truth is derived no longer from the inner stringency of the argument but from the extratextual sources of description. The dominant figure of thought now is a kind of comparison, "X is like Y"; a "true" verbal structure is therefore one that is "as that" which it describes. This mode of thought, which—applied to individual areas of daily life—coexists alongside the other two and is thus reflected already in descriptive passages of the Bible as well, becomes a prevailing principle of reading only in modernity. It is only since the eighteenth/nineteenth century that texts start to do without a symbolic interpretation "exceeding" the meaning of the words.[24] This attitude to the text, which places the literal sense in the foreground, goes back to a rigorous application of the historical-critical method, which "frees" the Bible from theology in order to understand it exclusively through its historical context.[25] However irreversible this development may be, according to Frye it does not permit to disrespect the diverse hermeneutical registers of the biblical texts and submit them as a whole exclusively to a descriptive reading which does not concede to the word any "power beyond its literary meaning."[26]

Frye's reflections raise questions that concern the Qur'an as well; for what Frye bemoans about the tendencies of the Bible reading that were dominant in his time, for the Qur'an is downright the rule: it is read not only in research but also in contemporary inner-Islamic (orthodox) reception, as simply veritative, regardless of its poetical-metaphoric or metonymic-allegorical implications.[27] In principle however, the possibility of a poetic-metaphorical and even allegorical reading, proffered for the Bible by Frye, needs to be considered for the Qur'an as well.

Frye's model, developed on the basis of Western Bible reception, is unmistakably marked by Christian theological and philosophical tradition. The applicability of this model to the Hebrew Bible in its early Jewish reception (at the time after Philo of Alexandria) is currently contested,[28] even if modern Jewish readings frequently follow the model established in Western literary history. So, for example, Robert Alter concedes to the Hebrew Bible—quite in tune with Frye's observation of the oscillation of biblical texts between several hermeneutic registers—a *double canonicity*. By this he means the status of the Bible as both

24. Frye, *The Great Code*, 3–30.

25. On the implications of this revolutionary development, see Reiser, *Bibelkritik und Auslegung*, 1–4.

26. Frye, *The Great Code*, 19.

27. This does not apply universally to the inner-Islamic exegetic tradition, which also recognizes various modes of "spiritual" (*bāṭinī*) exegesis.

28. Boyarin, "The Eye in the Torah."

an aesthetically standard-setting literary document and a theologically canon-forming religious one, which is then correspondingly received in this double manner. As Alter shows, the same biblical books that were later allegorized for discussions of doctrine or—as in the case of Song of Songs—already were allegorized for their inclusion in the canon equally fulfilled the function of a literary model for later Hebrew poetry, in which they were received for their exemplary style and imagery—in absolute independence from aspects of their transcendent significance.[29] Frye's challenge to look at the gradual process the of successive updatings within the Hebrew Bible itself that eventually produced the later complete corpus, in terms of an oscillation between different hermeneutic registers, is taken up today by biblical scholars such as James Kugel.[30] Jewish and Christian exegetes are now demanding new reflections on the knowledge potential implicit in typological and allegorical reading.[31]

10.2 Looking for Allegory and Typology in the Qur'an

10.2.1 Reservations: Christological Implications of Allegorical and Typological Readings of the Bible

As its etymology already indicates, allegorical thinking is grounded in the premise that words can have meanings that say something "other" than what is suggested by their literal sense. Allegory does not appear initially as a characteristic of exegesis, but often takes part already in the production of the text. One can think here of the parable delivered to David by the prophet Nathan (2 Sam 12:1–4), of the one single sheep of the poor man that the rich cattle-holder reclaims for himself—an allegory for the wife of Uriah whom David had taken possession of unjustifiably. Allegory appears most often in the form of narrative, as an interaction between actors that signifies something beyond itself and employs its narrative strategies to persuade of the truth of a particular message. The "true" significance of an allegory thus only reveals itself through the explication of its "double sense."[32]

The exegetical principle of practicing allegory, *allegoresis*, has its roots in scripture. Already the Jewish religious philosopher Philo of Alexandria made extensive use of it. Its Christian practice, goes back to Paul, who explicitly speaks of "allegory" (Gal 4:24), and employs it to interpret central biblical statements in a Christological vein.[33] One of the first church fathers, Origen, in the third

29. Alter, *Canon and Creativity*, 1–61.
30. Cf. Kugel, *The Bible as It Was.*
31. On this, see the introduction.
32. Frye, *The Great Code*, 85.
33. The three Pauline texts Ephesians 5, 1 Corinthians 10, and Galatians 4 are considered the fundamentals for the allegorical interpretation of the Christian tradition; see Wilken, "In Defense of Allegory," 200.

century, already makes it the basis of an elaborate apparatus of biblical explanation. Christoph Dohmen points to the philosophical origin of this exegesis, namely, Platonic anthropology, which distinguishes between body, soul, and spirit. For Origen, "the Bible not only has a body—that is the literal sense, the surface level of the text, which everyone can immediately *see*—but also a soul, i.e., a still deeper sense, which reveals itself through allegorical interpretation."[34] The allegorical interpretation, which as a rule is applied to the Old Testament, postulates "figurative" meanings in places where the text would also allow meaningful veritative readings. It is just this cooptation of the text for purposes outside of the text that makes allegorical interpretation problematic for the Jewish tradition. Daniel Boyarin points to this difficulty when he claims that "allegory presupposes a particular ontological and political positioning, a platonic longing for the unambiguous and unchanging, which is foreign to Rabbinic literature, and especially to the Midrash."[35] This is particularly clear for Boyarin in the contrast between two frequent traditional text types: the parable, where a Midrashic reading proceeds structurally from the abstract to the concrete, and Christian allegorical readings, which proceed from the concrete to the abstract.[36]

Related to the allegorical reading, but not identical to it, is typology.[37] Understood in its simple pre-terminological sense, typology is likewise not initially the discovery of exegetes, but rather is already detectable in the Hebrew Bible, where figures and modes of behavior show typological correspondences to each other. So, for example, Aaron's production of the Golden Calf shows itself as the typological precedent for the later cultic schism in the Northern Kingdom, in which golden bulls will play a role.[38] But in its theologically amplified, "technical" significance, typology is anchored in the Christian tradition, which understands it above all as the rediscovery of Old Testament configurations in the New Testament, which are identified as pre-stampings or "types" of so-called antitypes, that is, of persons and events in the life and works of Jesus. For Origen, this typological reading goes beyond a mere feedback of New Testament events into a divine salvific project that reaches back far into history. The particular figure of thought that motivates Origen, according to Daniel Boyarin, is an element of logos theology: "If the logos in its incarnation is God-man, then, in the view of Origen, the incarnation of the spirit in holy scripture is also divine-human. In this tradition, hermeneutics is an attempt to reach beyond the sensible text to its non- sensible meaning."[39] It is just this Christological context, which is difficult to ignore, that makes typology problematic for Jewish exegesis. The fact that

34. Dohmen, *Die Bibel und ihre Auslegung*, 47–48.
35. Boyarin, "The Eye in the Torah," 546–547.
36. Ibid.
37. Frye, The Great Code, 85.
38. Frye, *The Great Code*, 83.
39. Boyarin, "The Eye in the Torah," 548–549.

the two text corpora of the Bible stand in a typological relation to each other for Christian theology and that the Christian reading of the Hebrew Bible is animated decisively by its typological "translation," implies an unmistakable downgrading of the Hebrew Bible, which is demoted from a self-referential scripture to a collection of reference texts for the New Testament. Frye recognizes in the New Testament a "densely woven web of allusions to the Old Testament, often in the form of direct or nearly direct citations."[40] Not only individual statements but indeed entire mythic paradigms are reproduced typologically.[41]

10.2.2 *Questions on the Qur'an*

The widely divergent modes of approach to allegory and typology in rabbinic Judaism and Christianity, respectively, raise the question of to which tradition the Qur'an stands closest. As the Qur'an builds historically on the exegetical practices of Antiquity and Late Antiquity and looks back in particular to the growth of Christian teaching as an ensemble of anti-types to the stories and thought figures of the Hebrew Bible, it is worthwhile here to seek out traces of typology and allegory, that is, symbolic interpretations of the concrete narrative sequence of a biblical story, and the underpinning of non-biblical, "original Qur'anic" speech through transcendental subtexts as strategies for the communication of a theological message. Biblical intertextuality in the Qur'an has been seen up to now above all in the resumption of narrative plots and individual ideas;[42] indeed, in 1977, John Wansbrough already addressed the Qur'an's typological recourses to the Bible through his identification of so-called emblems of prophethood.[43] Heribert Busse offered a first concrete contribution to the recognition of typology in the Qur'an in his article *Herrschertypen im Koran* (Ruler types in the Qur'an), which appeared in 1979.[44] Busse succeeds in clarifying several typologically significant relationships between biblical figures in the Qur'an, which up to that point had been construed as due to misunderstanding precisely because they deviated from the biblical model. Busse still worked with a "simple" concept of typology, that is, one that is not theologically charged, which allowed him to uncover the interaction so frequently presented in the (early) Qur'an between contrastive negative and positive characters—for example, the stubborn unbelieving peoples and the persistently proclaiming messenger—in terms of "typology," as a predecessor scenario for the conflict of the proclaimer and his

40. Frye, *The Great Code*, 79.

41. An exemplary case—represented by the Gospel of Luke—of adopting the liberation story of the book of Exodus as a typos that is restaged in later history as its antitype has recently been presented in a study by Schiffner, *Lukas liest Exodus*; reaching results that are also relevant to Qur'anic references to the Gospels.

42. Speyer, *Die biblischen Erzählungen im Qoran*, collects traces of typology in the Qur'anic narratives without classifying them.

43. Wansbrough, *Quranic Studies*, 53–84.

44. Busse, "Herrschertypen im Koran"; cf. also, for a discussion of the work, chap. 11, 384–385.

overbearing opponents.[45] Though this has more to do with the identification of schematic precedents for Prophetic history than the unearthing of theologically relevant prefigurations, Busse nonetheless has succeeded to identify an important Qur'anic textual strategy. But reading the Qur'an as an authorial work, he does not explore the *function* of biblical configurations that accrues to them only in the course of the Qur'anic development. Thus, it goes unnoticed that the two sanctuary histories of Jerusalem and Mecca serve the goal developed in Medina, to construe Mecca as a new Jerusalem.[46] Likewise, the Moses typology, by which the Qur'anic community understands itself as a new people of God under Prophetic leadership,[47] remains unrecognized as the central part of a new Qur'anic Exodus paradigm. Even more limited to occasional observations, whose theological potential is not realized, are the contributions of individual researchers who in recent times have interpreted the biblical reminiscences in the Qur'an[48] but have not perceived the Qur'an as a new post-biblical proclamation that progressively inscribes itself typologically into a paradigm given earlier by the Bible.

The problem of typology was recognized more clearly by Gustav von Grunebaum, who already in 1960 raised the question of its role in early Islamic literature, though without focusing on the Qur'an. Rather, he laid his finger on the lack of typology in the exegesis of the Qur'an, where it would have suggested itself to him on the basis of the fundamental commonalities between the Bible and the Qur'an:

> Both Christians and Muslims proceed from the basic premise that biblical facts predict the coming of Christ or Muhammad, but only Christianity reads the *prefiguratio* of events, as they are reported in the New Testament, to be true through the *dicta et gesta* of the Old Testament. . . . David as typus of Jesus, his victory [as] a *victoria figurata et mystica* of the *victoria vera Christi*, the incident with Bathsheba and Uriah as *praefiguratio* of Jesus wresting the church from Satan or the Jewish people, or Christ sacrificed in Abel, the church symbolically presented in Noah's Ark . . . this mode of treatment has no systematic counterpart in Islamic *ta'wīl*. . . . Although the relatedness between the Qur'an and the older Bible is not so close as that between the Old and New Testaments, a typology would indeed have been expedient, e.g., in the comparison of the fate of the earlier prophets with that of Muhammad.[49]

45. Busse assumes that the Prophet developed "an independent typology, whether animated by the Christian Biblical interpretation or not"; see "Herrschertypen im Koran," 58–59.

46. Cf. chap. 9, 332–337.

47. Cf. chap. 8, 279–282.

48. Samir, "The Theological Christian Influence"; Reynolds, "Reading the Qur'an as Homily." Exceptions are provided by Mourad, "Mary in the Qur'an," and Witztum, "The Foundation of the House."

49. Von Grunebaum, "Die Erfahrung des Heiligen," 110n4.

Certainly, the concept of *praefiguratio* is lacking in the Islamic tradition, but not only can we frequently discern the phenomenon of the schematization of sacred historical figures brought to light by Busse, we can equally trace instances of theologically significant typologizing. Von Grunebaum simply looks for the parallel in the wrong place. For it is not the commentaries on the Qur'an that form the counterpart to the Christian exegesis of the church fathers but rather the Qur'an itself, which, no less a post-biblical text than the referred-to exegesis, presents an interpretation of biblical traditions. What is striking here is the formation, missed by van Grunebaum, of the earlier prophets on the model of Muhammad, as well as his self-presentation on the model of Moses and later of Abraham.

Certainly it is hard to overlook the fact that in the Qur'an we generally do not encounter theologically charged typology, but rather schematization. The reported events of various earlier peoples in the early suras, which take a catastrophic end in the punishment stories; the harassment of the righteous by powerful opponents; the final victory of the men of God: all these display a similar structure to the position described by the proclaimer for his own community, but they are cases of precedents willed by God rather than actual salvation-historical harbingers of what happens to the community. Thus, what is missing is the teleological tension immanent in the "hidden sense," which in the Christian view makes identifiable "David as typus of Jesus, his victory as a *victoria figurata et mystica* of the *victoria vera Christi*"[50] ("the secret pre-form of the true victory of Christ.")

Aside from this teleological dimension, one can in at least two cases reclaim for the Qur'an a typological relation: namely, between the proclaimer and his predecessor figures, Moses and Abraham.[51] both of whom are clearly depicted as his models in the Qur'an. Abraham and Moses come close to the status of prefigurations of the proclaimer, in that their stories as they are told in late Meccan and Medinan times merge with that of the proclaimer himself. Thus, for example, when Moses's reception of the tables of law is reported the focus—without formally marked transition—turns to the proclaimer who is exhorted to preserve "the most important of it" (Q 7:145).[52] The working of these two biblical figures and that of the proclaimer are linked through a theologically significant relation, even if this is less teleologically oriented than the typological relations extant between the Old and New Testament figurations that are reclaimed in the Christian tradition.

50. Ibid.

51. De Prémare attempts to prove a typological relationship between the Prophet and the figure of Joseph in *Joseph et Muhammad*. But in de Prémare's portrayal, the relationship of both figures does not go beyond similar external life circumstances and an identical monotheistic message. It is worth mentioning, however, that a theologically charged Joseph-Muhammad typology was instrumental in the development of the new religious movement of the Babis in the nineteenth century; see Dehghani, *Messianismus und Märtyrertum*.

52. Neuwirth, "Medinan Additions," 71–93.

10.3 Allegories in the Qur'an?

10.3.1 Visions of the Future

There is a sequence of early Meccan suras that begin with accumulations of images, which clearly are not to be understood veritatively; nor are they simply metaphors for something empirically known but rather signify something unknown, indeed supernatural. They are frequently located in the oath clusters at the beginning of suras, upon which, after an in-between part with instruction to the hearers, an explicit eschatological pronouncement often follows. A particularly striking example is Q 100:1–5:[53]

wa-l-ʿādiyāti ḍabḥā
fa-l-mūriyāti qadḥā
fa-l-mughīrāti subḥā
fa-atharna bihi naqʿā
fa-wasaṭna bihi jamʿā

By the snorting runners
striking sparks with their hooves
daring to attack in the morning,
they throw up dust with their steps,
and penetrate into the middle of crowds.[54]

Here, in the ancient Arabic *sajʿ* style, is depicted a tableau of enigmatic phenomena captured in fast forward-driving movement, which in view of their qualities—instead of names of the objects their qualifications that are put forward metonymically—need to signify horses and riders. Yet, what is intended are clearly not any horses/riders known from the history of the Qur'anic community.[55] Even if one treated the riders as a general image derived from empirical experience to indicate unknown, quickly approaching phenomena,[56] still a dimension of significance would remain unnoticed, one that is unmistakably evoked by the morphological form of the named phenomena: the participles in feminine plural (*fāʿilāt*) of verbs denoting violent movement throughout the Qur'an are bound up with eschatological associations.[57] It is in this grammatical form that a number of Qur'anic neologisms occur, all signifying catastrophic phenomena of the loosing of the cosmos at the end of time. That these remain

53. Neuwirth, "Images and Metaphors."

54. The German translation of this sura by Friedrich Rückert, *Koran*, 469 is particularly suggestive. On the text, see also chap. 12, 431–434.

55. Individual later commentators argue—anachronistically—for the possibility that what is at stake are the riders making a raid (*ghazwā*) active during Muhammad's campaigns. Ibn Qayyim, *Al-Tibyān*, reviews the pertinent attempts at explanation; cf. Neuwirth, "Images and Metaphors."

56. As also in Neuwirth, "Images and Metaphors."

57. See chap. 5, 169–171.

enigmatic in view of the indirect naming and must be filled in by the imagination of the hearers leads some commentators to put forward an "Islamic explanation," and to see in the "runners" angels appearing on the Last Day—although this interpretation is not compatible with the horse description that is maintained across the entire verse group.[58] The tableau, which describes the breaking out of warriors into an attack on an enemy tribe, should rather in accordance with the *fāʿilāt* forms be interpreted eschatologically. The horses/riders are then to be understood—no differently from the apocalyptic riders of the Revelation of John (Rev 9)—as omens of catastrophic events at the end of time. Here, the concept of allegory seems justified, since the presented image—the proclaimer presents it like a vision unfolding before his eyes—makes reference to an insensible world. Although not in conventional narrative form but rather in the form of oaths, a story is nonetheless told that, put into the categories established by Boyarin, employs the technique of dressing the abstract in the concrete in order to convince the hearers of the truth of a message. It is noteworthy that the short sura itself solves this allegorical enigma at its close. In sura 100 first an exhortation to the hearers follows in the form of a rebuke of man, verses 6–8:

inna l-insāna li-rabbihi la-kanūd
wa-innahu ʿalā dhālika la-shahīd
wa-innahu li-ḥubbi l-khayri la-shadīd

Man is obstinate against his lord
and is himself testimony of that,
and fervently he loves profit.

Only then is the eschatological interpretation of the oath series unveiled, verses 9–11:

a-fa-lā yaʿlamu idhā buʿthira mā fī l-qubūr
wa-ḥuṣṣila mā fī l-ṣudūr
inna rabbahum yawmaʾidhin la-khabīr

Does he then not know, if what is in the grave is brought alive
and that which is in the heart is uncovered,
that nothing then remains hidden to your Lord?

The tableau of riders from the oath series fades out, just when the actual raid—the invasion into the camps, the frightening of the opponents surprised in sleep in the early morning, the searching out and overturning of all containers—is to take place. The image that was thereby "arrested" is taken up again in the closing, but it is unraveled and reset into an expressly eschatological context: just those

58. See Neuwirth, "Images and Metaphors."

images that are suppressed in the oath series are now unfolded, with eschatological application: It is the sleeping dead that are awakened, and their innermost things, their remembrance of guilt, are turned outward. God himself turns out to be the performer of the raid announced in the oath series. The enigmatic phenomena that in the oath series are shown approaching at a threatening pace are none other than the harbingers of the waking of the dead and the judgment.

While in the speech of biblical prophets, monumental images are often depicted that reach across wide space, those Qur'anic allegories in the early suras, which in view of their ancient Arabian seer(*kahin*)-style come closest to biblical prophetic texts, remain limited to short blending of images. These always aim at one and the same object: the loosing of the cosmos on the Final Day. Here, not dissimilar from the prophecies of Ezekiel for instance, language itself plays a major role. It is language that generates that enigmatic-threatening atmosphere, which arises from the oath series. Several characteristics—the structure of syntactical repetition that recalls the performance of rites, the extensive use of neologisms that often remain mysterious being, formed according to the precedent of poetic metonymy, and phonetically the use of memorable rhyme, which accommodates each semantic unit in a mold of its own—all these distinguish the allegorical Qur'anic images as something new, for which biblical speech, despite occasional overlaps, provides no direct precedent.[59]

10.3.2 Allegorical Narratives in the Qur'an?

Another complex that also remains unresearched is the Qur'anic parable narratives, whether or not they are marked as parables expressly with the term *mathal*.[60] They stand in a complex tradition, since parables already occur in ancient Arabic poetry,[61] but play an especially prominent role in rabbinic discussions, and above all in the Gospels. Daniel Boyarin has insisted on their non-allegorical character, both for the rabbinic parables and also for those of the New Testament.[62] The assumption of an allegorical dimension for the Qur'anic parable speeches, carrying forward this tradition, does not therefore immediately suggest itself. Yet it is those parable-like narratives in the Qur'an[63] that are not termed *mathal* that do seem to permit an

59. As parallel cases we could name Q 77:1–6 and 79:1–5. These are to be distinguished from oaths upon places and things that had already acquired additional symbolic meaning in the earlier traditions, such as *al-ṭūr*, Q 52:1 ("The Mount"); *ṭūr Sinīn*, Q 95:2 ("Mount Sinai"); *al-tīn*, Q 95:1 ("The Fig Tree"); or *al-qalam* Q 68:1 ("The Pen"). These too cannot be read meaningfully in an exclusively veritative way. But although the evocation of Mount Sinai does not indicate the mountain as such invoking instead a particular scenario of origins, and although the naming of the fruit tree is less about actual means of nutrition than an evocation of a place of salvation-historical significance, and although the naming of the writing pen presents not the artifact but rather the complex of transcendent scripture, these condensed references should be seen as evocative keys for allegory rather than as examples of allegory itself.

60. Some examples are discussed in chap. 8, 305–313.

61. See Wagner, *Grundzüge I*, 98, 164.

62. See Boyarin's review of Stern, *Parables in Midrash*, 126.

63. On the stories explicitly labeled as *mathal*, see chap. 8, 310–313.

allegorical reading. This applies, for example, to the narrative of the "owners of the Garden," *aṣḥāb al-janna* (Q 68:17–33). This narrative seems, like the punishment legends, to aim at the critique of certain forms of behavior among contemporaries, without however limiting itself to an admonishing message. Despite the detailed presentation of the false behavior of the "owners of the garden"—who are punished since they did not pronounce a praise of God nor respect the common-law custom of giving the surplus harvest to the poor—it seems above all to be a parable about the illusive, merely apparent reality of the earthly world. For the "testing" proclaimed in the introductory verse refers not only to moral failures but to a fundamentally "wrong thinking," the consequence of which, the real loss, therefore only becomes recognizable in the hereafter. What is required in the Qur'an is the recognition of the reality of a spiritual world beyond the sensible one: the "garden" proves to be a "fleeting" possession, whose availability is revocable from one moment to the next. Read in this way, the narrative presents a reminder of the contingency of the earthly world, fitting into Daniel Boyarin's definition of allegory as an ultimately Platonic figure of thought, which interprets mutable figures metonymically and thus replaces them with corresponding unchanging and therefore "true" figures of the transcendent world. Q 68:17–32:[64]

> We are testing them, as we once tested the owners of the garden.
> When they swore they would harvest its fruit the next morning but failed to say, "If God wills."
> A disaster from your lord struck the garden as they slept
> and by morning the garden was as if stripped clean.
> As they rose up, they called out to each other:
> "go early to your fields if you intend to cull their fruit,"
> and went off whispering:
> "No poor man is to enter upon you today."
> And they hastened at once in the morning.
> When they saw the garden, they said, "We have lost our way,
> No, we are ruined!"
> The most reasonable of them said, "did I not tell you to glorify God?"
> They answered, "Glory be to our Lord, we were doing wrong "
> So they turned upon each other, in mutual reproach.
> They said: "Woe to us, we have done terrible wrong,
> But maybe our Lord will give us something better in exchange,
> we turn to our Lord sincere in will."
> Such is our punishment,
> but the punishment of the hereafter is far more grievous,
> if only they knew.

64. Boyarin's review of Stern, *Parables in Midrash*, 126.

The word *al-dunyā*, "the earthly world," does not occur, but it transpires that the here and now is no more than a weak reflection of the "other world," *al-ākhira*, as the closing verse shows (verse 33). As Frants Buhl, and after him Heinrich Speyer, detected, the narrative recalls Luke 12:16–20, where there is also language of a rich man wrongly imagining himself and his possessions to be secure. The Gospel story is not only "reversed" in the Qur'an by the eschatological closing (in Buhl's view a weakening of its effect),[65] but it also evokes the contingency of what exists through the references to gardens and vegetation.[66]

This projection of a hidden world (*ghayb*) standing behind the inner-worldly scenario (*shahāda*) is found elsewhere in the Qur'an as well. Indeed, the later mystical antinomy of *ʿālam al-ghayb* / *ʿālam al-shahāda*, "the hidden world" and the "apparent world," is not yet detectable, *ghayb* remaining closed to humans outside of the circle of the Prophets, but God is ever clearer presented as the omniscient ruler of both realms, as *ʿālim al-ghayb wa-l-shahāda*, above all in the late Meccan and Medinan periods (Q 32:6; 23:93; 64:19; 62:8; 59:22; 4:95, 105). Knowledge of what is hidden, secret[67] is already a theme early on (Q 53:35, 52:41), always in the sense of what is not accessible to man.

The double-facedness of the world, where the sensible scenario corresponds to a hidden other that lies outside the present and is therefore unknowable, is an explicit theme in at least one instance: in a (middle Meccan) riddle-story, which comes to an allegorical point: the meeting of Moses with an unnamed wise man,[68] identified by tradition with the figure of Khidr, a "servant of God," *ʿabd Allāh* (Q 18:64–82). In the narrative, Moses associates with the wise man in order to learn from him. The wise man, who anticipates the incapacity of the "novice" for deep insight, first tries to reject him: "How can you preserve patience with me, if you do not have full knowledge of it [wisdom]?" (verse 68). Taken in under the condition that he demand no explanations, Moses becomes three times the witness of morally objectionable or incomprehensible actions by the wise man. The tension increases with the delay of the solution of the riddle, which Moses demands twice in vain, heedless of the forbidding (verses 71, 74, and 77). Finally, when Moses prepares to ask for the third time, the wise man forestalls him: "This is the parting between you and me" (verse 78). The striking behaviors that are now interpreted, show themselves to be not symbolic at all, but rather thoroughly bound up with a purpose, though charged theologically. The wise man justifies every action by the

65. Buhl, "Mathal."

66. Speyer, *Die biblischen Erzählungen im Qoran*, 434. See also the interpretation of the story as an ethical allegory in Mir, "Language," 104–105.

67. See Izutsu, *The Structure of the Ethical Terms*; Rahman, *Major Themes*.

68. On the tradition-historical preconditions of the story, whose protagonist can only be related to the biblical character of Moses by assuming intermediate typological linkings, see Horovitz, *Koranische Untersuchungen*, 141–143, and Wheeler, *Moses in the Quran*. An important plea for the consideration of allegorical dimensions in sura 18 is expressed in Hughes, "The Stranger at the Sea," which is, however, primarily concerned with other stories in the sura.

argument that the road to a better future must be paved: his damaging of a ship was meant to prevent its confiscation (verse 79); his killing of a young man was to prevent his suspected mistreatment of his parents (verses 80–81); his building of a wall in the inhospitable settlement should help to keep secret a treasure that should only come to light with the coming to age of its possessor (verse 82). The problematic actions serve to promote the breakthrough of a future that is still invisible for the human observer.

But as concise as the explanations are, they leave the "novice" with serious open questions, on the one hand about divine providence, which—in quite an antinomian way—can be manifest in criminal (or unreasonably charitable) actions, and on the other hand about the freedom to break recognized norms of behavior in order to permit the coming of a better future. Though the story ends with a logically convincing disclosure, its formula of parting *hādhā firāqu baynī wa-baynik*, "This is the parting between you and me," verse 78 affirms the existence of ultimately unbearable paradoxes of earthly life, and implies the verdict of man's incapacity to await patiently the explanation lying in wait in the "hidden," *ghayb*. The story, which was read by later readers as testimony for the provisionality and contingency of the earthly world,[69] could be interpreted as a Qur'anic allegory, in which the "apparent world," *ʿālam al-shahāda*, and the secret one, *ʿālam al-ghayb*, are projected onto each other as inextricable. It demonstrates the deceptive reliability of appearances.

Even if we could add more instances of the appearance of allegory in the sense of the insertion of a counter-world valued more highly in a Platonic sense, still they would remain exceptional phenomena in the Qur'an. Indeed, in the genesis of the Qur'an, the two most important preconditions for allegorical discourse are lacking: a deep rooting in Platonic thinking and above all a practical necessity of reinterpreting scenarios of previous salvation history regarded authoritative but are no longer were compatible with the new worldview. Since the Qur'anic discourse successively grows out of debates over earlier traditions, thus eliminating already in the course of the process of its proclamation those theologumena that were deemed obsolete, occasionally also "overwriting" them with new ones of its own, it copes with the predecessor traditions in a relatively uncomplicated way. Here we need only recall the decided but inconspicuous elimination from the Qur'anic horizon of the idea of sacrifice central to the two predecessor traditions, which was accomplished during the proclamation itself.[70] A wholly different situation had obtained for the New Testament and early Christian theology, which built on the biblical tradition as a whole and therefore had to reform the sense

69. Later literary authors have seen here a reminder of transience, such as Muhammad Abū l-Qāsim al-Ḥarīrī (446–512/1054–1122), who puts into the mouth of his last maqama's protagonist, in a scene when this character says farewell to his pupil, the following words: *ijʿali l-mawta nasba ʿaynik fa-hadhā l-firāqu bayni wa-baynak*, "Keep death always in front of your eyes, for this is the parting between me and you," striking a concluding note to their lifelong relationship; see Neuwirth, "Adab Standing Trial."

70. See chap. 9, 326–332.

paradigm or the predecessor traditions that was decisive for salvation history in in a way that allowed to maintain their dimension of significance within the new readings, but adapting them to new functions. The changed configuration of sacrifice—from temple cult to the ritual of remembrance of Christ's self-sacrifice, demonstrates this most clearly. It is this theologically challenging confrontation of an authoritative predecessor tradition that above all requires the strategies of allegory and typology. The Qur'an is confronted with no corresponding requirement for allegorizing a predecessor tradition. Contrarily, it confronts the fait accompli of the allegorizations already carried out in the Christian tradition. It is thus less Qur'anic allegorizations than the Qur'anic handling of already extant allegory that can throw light on its exegetical hermeneutic. Certainly, the most eloquent example of how the Qur'an deals with a large-scale Christian allegory already during its genesis is offered by the Qur'anic story of Mary, which—following the discussion of the figure of Mary provided in chapter 8, will now be reviewed under the aspect of de-allegorization.[71]

10.4 "De-allegorizations"

As an inter-testamental figure, Mary occupies the space of transition between two great paradigms: temple cult and church. She was given increased theological significance, since the Council of Ephesus in the year 431, as the mother of God, the "God-bearer" (*theotokos*).[72] Already in earlier theology, she was considered an allegory for the church, and as such implicitly the "heiress of the temple." The great allegory, which turns a sacred historical figure into the universal symbol of a new religion, is manifest in numerous liturgical texts of the Greek and Syriac churches.[73] In the work of Ephrem of Nisibis (306–373), whose poems find frequent echoes in the Qur'an, Mary stands as a typos or allegory for the church: insofar as the church is the embodiment of Christ, the mother of the individual body of Christ is mystically the mother of all of the members of his mystical body.[74] At the same time, the curse that bears down on the earth is contrasted with the blessing of Mary's body: "Just as the bodies, which themselves have sinned, must die, and the earth, their mother, was cursed, so because of this body, since it itself is the church, is the earth blessed from the very beginning. For the earth is the body of Mary, the temple, which received the seed."[75]

71. The character of Mary was discussed in the previous chapters with a focus on her mythical configuration as relevant for the forming of the community in Mecca, and in the context of the election of the Christian holy family as a counterbalance to the Jewish concept of Abraham's family, as relevant for the forming the community in Medina. See also Marx, "Mariology in the Qur'ān."

72. On the manifestations of this new dogma in architecture, see Bieberstein, "Zum Raum wird hier die Zeit."

73. See also the evidence in Marx, "Mariology in the Qur'ān"; cf. also Murray, *Symbols of Church and Kingdom*, 142–150, and Beck, "Die Mariologie der echten Schriften Ephräms"; see also chap. 8, 294–300.

74. Murray, *Symbols of Church and Kingdom*, 144.

75. Maries, *Hymnes de S. Ephrem* 4.15, quoting Murray, *Symbols of Church and Kingdom*, 145.

The linking to the church at the same time establishes a connection to the Jewish temple, which was "superseded" by the church, and whose last representatives are accordingly imagined as interacting with the first representatives of the church. Inter-testamental figures that belong to the foundation history of Christianity—such as Zachariah, the father of John the Baptist, and Mary the mother of Jesus—are therefore localized within the temple itself, either in the canonical Gospels, as applies to Zachariah (Luke 1) or in the apocrypha (the Proto-Gospel of James) as applies to Mary. But it is only Mary who beyond that enters into an allegorical relation with the temple and church.

If one reads the Qur'anic stories of Mary[76] carefully, they reflect both images of Mary: that of Luke—the hagiographic—as well as the allegorical. The latter is evident above all in the address to Mary as *ukht Hārūn*, "sister of Aaron" (Q 19:28), and correspondingly as *bint ʿImrān*, "daughter of Amram" (Q 66:12). This naming that had long been taken as a mistaken identification with the Biblical M has been recognized in recent times as a typological assignment—Mary is addressed by God, as was Miriam, the sister of Aaron, and is thus her antitype.[77] This reading has again been corrected by Suleiman Mourad[78] in favor of an allegorical understanding. In fact, both these designations of Mary seem to carry weight; since regardless of the differing precursors of the Mary texts in sura 19 (middle Meccan; reference to Luke) and suras 3 and 66 (Medinan; reference to the Proto-Gospel of James), Mary is linked from the beginning to an Aaronite genealogy. The relevant verses—in chronological sequence—are:

> Sister of Aaron, your father was not an evildoer,
> nor was your mother wanton. (Q 19:28)
> When the wife of Amram said:
> "My Lord, I pledge to you what is in my womb,
> You alone are the hearing, the knowing." (Q 3:35)
> Then too there is Mary, daughter of Amram, she who guarded her chastity; and we breathed into her of our spirt,
> and she put her trust in the words of her Lord
> and was devout. (Q 66:12)

What does the allocation of Mary to the house of Amram, and thus to the family of Aaron—Amram is Aaron's father—entail for the hagiographic-veritative or allegorical image of Mary? As Mourad has emphasized, on the basis of this allocation Mary belongs to the priestly line of Aaron, the founder of the Israelite

76. See Neuwirth, "Icon of Piety—Trigger of Dispute"; Neuwirth, "The House of Abraham."

77. Similarly Tottoli, "Imran," and Busse, *Die theologischen Beziehungen*. On Mary in general, see Stowasser, "Mary"; however, her article is not interested in inner-Qur'anic development.

78. Mourad, "Mary in the Qur'ān"; Mourad, "Qur'anic Stories about Mary and Jesus," cf. also Henninger, "Spuren christlicher Glaubenswahrheiten."

sacrificial cult. But the theological implications of this assignment remain obscure if one reads it, as Mourad does, as merely an honorary designation of genealogy that serves to emphasize the scandalous aspect of Mary's delivery out of wedlock which in the eyes of her contemporaries, who would expect special observance of the law on the basis of her belonging to the temple amounts to a transgression that endangers her life.[79] But if one sets it, on the other hand, into the context of the Mary-church allegory, Mary's connection to the Aaronite temple cult, which is superseded by the church cult, takes on theological significance. The temple also plays a role elsewhere in her story: she is localized in Q 19:16–33, explicitly in the Temple, named as in the preceding story of Zachariah (Q 19:2–15) *miḥrāb*.[80] While the Gospel of Luke has Zachariah serve in the Temple but has Mary receive the annunciation of the birth of Jesus in a private house in Nazareth, Mary appears in the Qur'an from the beginning in the Temple, in agreement with the Proto-Gospel of James. While this can be understood veritatively from the pseudo-James tradition of Mary's childhood in the Temple, a further reminiscence springs to mind, comprehensible only as an allusion to Mary as the allegorical Temple: the echo of a messianic temple prophecy going back ultimately to Ezekiel, pertaining to the locked east gate of the temple area that will only be opened by the Messiah.[81] Q 19:16 seems to refer to this east gate: "And mention [in the reading] the writing of Mary, when she withdrew from her people to an eastern place." The explanation is already presented in chapter 8: Mary, given her allegorical connection to the church in the Christian tradition, stands also for the temple, through the east gate of which God will return to the city according to a prophecy of Ezekiel (Ez 44:1–2). The locked gate—which in the Christian interpretation illustrates the virginity of Mary—will be opened by the coming of the Messiah or, in Christian typology, by the birth of Christ as the Messiah.[82] If this interpretation is reflected in the Qur'an only in a vague detail, the insertion into the story of an "eastern place" belonging to the temple shows that the Temple references go beyond the genealogy linking Mary to Aaron.

Yet, the Temple references are not fit at all for a reconstruction of Mary's allegorical person. Rather, they attest a tendency to re-interpret allegorical texts veritatively. Mary is not the temple, she *dwells* in the temple; it is not her delivery of the Messiah that binds her with the "eastern gate," but rather she takes

79. Mourad, "Mary in the Qur'an," 165–166, on Q 19:28.

80. In this context the Temple is designated by the word *miḥrāb*, unlike at points where the Jewish Solomonic temple (or its successors) is mentioned as the "prayer site," *masjid*, par excellence (Q 17:1, 7). *Miḥrāb* is an expression that denotes a structure involving arches or covered by a canopy (Q 19:11, 3:37–39); see Neuwirth, "Jerusalem"; Neuwirth, "Erste Qibla."

81. On the history of the eastern gate of the Temple, see Küchler, *Jerusalem: Ein Handbuch*, 180–204; cf. chap. 8, 294–300.

82. See O'Shaughnessy, *Meaning of Spirit in the Koran*, 54, quoted after Paret, *Der Koran. Kommentar*, on Q 19:16. On the architectonic restructuring of the so-called Golden Gate, with respect of this Mariological concept, see Küchler, *Jerusalem: Ein Handbuch*, 180–204.

herself to an eastern place that is no longer defined. A de-allegorizing tendency has materialized here; whether this occurred already in pre-Qur'anic traditions circulating around Mary or first through treatments in the community cannot be determined with certainty. But Mary is not a biblical figure like others, whose significance is based on her social role alone; rather she becomes in a unique way, as is shown in chapter 8, the object of a Qur'anic myth foundation.[83]

10.5 Considerations on Qur'anic Prophetic Speech

10.5.1 On the Appellatory Character of Qur'anic Discourse

The Qur'an shares a number of textual genres with the Bible. The peculiarity that they are not distributed over different books, containing, for example, narrative, Prophetic speech, wisdom sayings, hymns, and the like rather occur in short, often minimally small text units and often appear in new ensembles, is one of the most marked Qur'anic distinctions from the Bible. Paul Ricœur identifies five distinct literary "poetics" for the Hebrew Bible[84]—prophetic, narrative, prescriptive, sapiential, and hymnal.[85] Although these could be identified easily within the Qur'an as well, in view their markedly different focuses as Vernon Robbins and Gordon D. Newby have justifiably argued.[86] they are little promising for the Qur'an.[87] What seems more fruitful for a comparison is the approach of socio-rhetorics, which focuses on the power of oral speech and rhetoric in the Bible. According to Robbins, "With the aid of three major literary modes—biographical-historiography; epistles; and apocalypse—first-century Christians interwove six sociorhetorical modes of discourse—wisdom, miracle, Prophetic, suffering-death, apocalyptic, and precreation discourse—into a distinctive, dynamic, and multivalent mode of discourse that became canonical for Christians in the Mediterranean world. . . . In sociorhetorical interpretation, each discourse represents a 'rhetorolect', which is construed through certain topoi, discourse figures, and forms."[88] Although a procedure of "discourse description" notably similar to this model has been carried out already in our sura analyses above,[89] nevertheless its one-to-one application to the Qur'an, namely, under the presupposition of identical discourses in the New Testament and Qur'an, will not lead much further.

Rather, what must be insisted upon is a significant distinction between Qur'anic and biblical speech, which also affects the transferability of such a

83. Cf. chap. 8, 290–300.
84. Ricœur, *Biblical Interpretation*, 75–85.
85. Robbins and Newby, "A Prolegomenon."
86. Ibid., 29.
87. Ibid., 29.
88. Ibid., 31.
89. Cf. chap. 5.

model. In the case of the Qur'an, not only are there prophetic speeches in a strict sense predictions of a disastrous or blessed future, but also, from a certain phase onward, in which the proclaimer has assumed a prophetic habitus, all other kinds of text become part of a comprehensive prophetic message. This means that all of them are subject to the same appellatory force[90] that marks prophetic speech and accordingly go beyond pronouncements of particular semantic contents, being not just narrative or hymn but also testimonies of the speaker that these speeches are the word of God, presented before hearers who must be won over by this testimony. The reclamation of prophetic speech also for descriptive genres such as narrative or poetic ones such as hymns is no Qur'anic innovation, but rather goes back to the model of early biblical exegesis.[91] But while this assignment of the status of prophetical speech to most biblical books, belonging to quite different text genres, is first made in retrospect, the Qur'an is prophetic speech in a "programmatic" sense; throughout, it consists of "address" to hearers, and thus also makes use of particular stylistic strategies.

Northrup Frye has contextualized the prophetic speech habitus with other biblical forms: "Prophecy . . . is geared to the future as wisdom is to the past. . . . Such prophets, though 'called' by God and invariably claiming to speak with the voice or authority of God, are no longer simply ecstatics . . . they are rather people with what seems to be an open channel of communication between the conscious and the unconscious."[92] Prophets distinguish themselves from other biblical speaking figures above all through their deep perception of a crisis. The task laid open to them, to lead a way out of this crisis, generates the force that is so strikingly articulated in language. If this force is not manifest immediately in the Qur'an, and there are also counterexamples of a great number of early verses that thematize trust in God (suras 106 and 96) and hope for spiritual fulfillment (sura 73), still already in the early Meccan suras, the vision of the future that is marked eschatologically in the Qur'an and that recalls biblical Prophet speech is dominant.[93]

If Northrup Frye contrasts the typus of the wise man, who appeals to the past, with that of the prophet, who speaks about the future, this should not give the impression that the two speaker types are mutually exclusive. Precisely in view of the particular speech of the proclaimer, which is both prophetic and interpretive of scripture, the historical classification of the two speaker types offered by James Kugel is helpful as a corrective.[94] Kugel notes that the typus of the prophet had already been replaced in the late books of the Bible by that of the wise man, who strives to interpret the already extant parts of the scripture. Concomitant with

90. The term is used in the sense of Bühler, *Sprachtheorie*, who differentiates the categories of description, pronouncement, and appellatory speech.

91. See Kugel, "Poets and Prophets."

92. Frye, *The Great Code*, 125–127.

93. Cf. chap. 7, 254–264, and Müller, "Die Barmherzigkeit Gottes."

94. Kugel, *The Bible as It Was*, 17.

the emerging authority of the scripture, the spontaneous speech of prophecy is relinquished. This historical development is apparently not true however for the Arabian Peninsula, where prophetic speakers still appeared in the seventh century and mantic speech was still alive. That the image of the "wise man" as a mere interpreter after the biblical model did not evolve may be related to the lack of an available biblical text in writing. Yet, the characteristic attributed by Kugel to the wise man of the Hellenistic period is all the more relevant for the proclaimer, who with the Qur'an does not articulate exclusively spontaneous prophetic speech, but rather for long stretches also interprets biblical and post-biblical traditions. The proclaimer cannot be adequately described by either of the two categories; rather, he represents both speaker types in one person. What would appear in the biblical milieu as an anachronism is still a living reality in Late Antique Arabia,[95] and can even be embodied within a single person.

10.5.2 *Qur'anic and Biblical Scenarios*

It is only to be expected that in the prophetic speech of the proclaimer a typological and image-specific model comes to the fore that is similar to that of the biblical prophets. In fact, in its eschatological parts the Qur'an comes distinctively close to biblical prophet speech, although the great visions of the biblical prophets have come to be replaced by the short sura-introducing tableaux of the oath series, which orient themselves stylistically to the ancient Arabic models of the seer speech. Apocalyptic visions such as that of the "valley of the rotting bones" in Ezekiel 37 have their Qur'anic counterpart in oath series such as Q 100:1–5 on the suddenness of the awakening, or Q 82:1–5 on the loosing of the cosmos. What Daniel Weidner says about biblical prophetical speech—"It is speech performance in the most eminent sense of the word, is performance with apocalyptic power, which at the same time must rely on being pronounced in the weak voice of the prophet"[96]—is true also for the Qur'an, and was certainly recognized by the proclaimer himself. If for Jeremiah the "word of the Lord is like a fire, like a hammer that smashes the stone" (Jer 23:29), so the Qur'anic perception of the power of the word is no less violent. Thus Q 59:21 says: "If we had sent this Qur'an down onto a mountain, you would see it humbled, shattered by the terror of God." Just as in the Bible, in the Qur'anic context the speech owes its impressing power to poetic text strategies—an immanent potential for conflict—which in both cases, after the discovery of the theologically normative character of the scripture, requires a demarcation between prophecy and poetry,[97] which in the case of the Qur'an already occurred during the genesis of the text itself.[98]

95. On Musaylima, Muhammad's "counter-Prophet," see Eickelman, "Musaylima."
96. Weidner, "Literatur und Antiliteratur," 174.
97. See Kugel, "Poets and Prophets."
98. Cf. chap. 12, 419–420.

The external circumstances also do not seem dissimilar: the fortunes of the biblical prophets are in full accordance with that of the proclaimer of the Qur'an. As in Ezekiel, who in several passages describes the situation of his prophetic utterances (e.g., in Ez 8:1, 14:1, 20:1, 33:31), scenarios are repeatedly described in the Qur'an that demonstrate an initial interest as the hearers come to listen to the Prophet, and then a lack of participation and even rejection of the word of God by those "striving for profit." One can compare, for example, Ez 33:30–32:[99]

> As for you, son of man, the children of your people are talking about you beside the walls and in the doors of the houses; and they speak to one another, everyone saying to his brother, "Please come and hear what the word is that comes from the Lord." So they come to you as people do, they sit before you as My people, and they hear your words, but they do not do them; for with their mouth they show much love, but their hearts pursue their own gain. . . . And when this comes to pass—surely it will come—then they will know that a Prophet has been among them.

with Q 78:1–2:

> What are they asking each other about?
> About the great tidings
> About which they dispute.

And Q 70:36–37:

> What is it with the unbelievers stretching their necks towards you
> And banding together from the right and left?

And—as evidence of resignation in view of the impossibility of converting the deniers—Q 88:21–24:

> So, exhort, you are only an exhorter;
> you are not supposed to dominate them;
> except for him who turns away and disbelieves;
> Him God will punish in the most terrible way.

The problem shared by the prophets is not only hermeneutical but also aesthetic and "artistic." Like Ezekiel, the proclaimer of the Qur'an for his early hearers was a kind of poet, who spoke in parables and images—an insinuation against which he defended himself energetically. Harold Fisch even sees in the case of Ezekiel a causal connection between the artistic form of his speech and his reception as a poet or bard: "He is both poet and Prophet, and that other, "artistic" kind of relation between text, author, and reader, shows itself as unavoidable. Namely, the

99. See Fisch, "Prophet und Publikum," 175–186.

more vehemently Ezekiel protests against the role of poet, the richer and livelier his language and images become. He seeks to ban his public, but without their presence his words would resound in empty air. He must fascinate them with his words, but the fascination of his words does not escape him."[100]

The proclaimer of the Qur'an also is aware of the verbal force of his speech, which can be compared throughout to that of the biblical prophets. The challenge to the opponents, to bring forth texts of equal worth, is pronounced several times (e.g., Q 11:13, 2:23). Indeed, one could argue that the power of prophetic language even served for a long time as the means of authorization of the individual sura performances. But there is a major difference: for the proclaimer of the Qur'an, it is essential for surviving survival keep aloof from the image of the poet who fascinates by his language. His rejection of the poet connection must be all the more energetic, since it would open the possibility of a dubious origin for the message which would be associated with the notion of inspiration from the demons/*jinn*, which is responsible for poetic speech.[101] Since he not only speaks to principally inclined or uncommitted hearers but is also confronted by decided opponents, he requires ever new authorizations for his speech; the fervent speech gestures of the early suras are thus soon transformed into modes of rational argumentation.[102]

Despite the differences, the shared characteristics remain overwhelming. Qur'an research can thus learn theoretically from research into biblical prophetic texts. Thus the relationship between Bible and literature recognized by Harold Fisch would be worth considering for the Qur'an as well: "The rhetoric of the biblical texts consists . . . in [the fact] that it lays out and problematizes its own rhetorical means. It works with literary means, but revokes it at the same time and negates it. The first 'intention' of the biblical text is the destruction of the 'aesthetic distance' assumed by its readers; as Erich Auerbach said, the Bible attempts to 'compel' its reader. . . . Thus, it draws monumental images, and then demonstrates them further in the next step, because its hearers and readers do not understand the images, but cannot be freed from them."[103] This necessity of the destruction of "aesthetic distance," which must have set in with the habituation of the hearers to the expressive oath series, may have been decisive for the stylistic paradigm shift that took place in the middle Meccan period, where the form of the ancient Arabian seer speech is relinquished and the suras start to appear in a rhythmic prose quite new in Arabic literary tradition—still prophetic speech but without the pathos that distinguished the early suras and their structural composition.

100. Fisch, "Prophet und Publikum," 176.
101. Cf. chap. 12, 424–430.
102. Cf. chap. 5, 192–194.
103. Fisch, "Prophet und Publikum," 173–174.

10.6 Considerations on Qur'anic Narration

10.6.1 Lived Reality or Biblical Text World?

In the Hebrew Bible, central figures of the topos of the exemplary pious man such as Abraham, are flanked by a number of persons with heroic character traits, who behave largely autonomously rather than always being led by a divine power. Although they do not act entirely independently from the divine will or providence, key biblical figures do bear heroic traits: above all Moses and David, but also more episodic figures such as Samson, Ehud, or Judith and Esther. In comparison to this, we hardly find any heroic figures in the Qur'an. Also missing are the heroic protagonists of the local Arabian legends, who do figure in the Qur'anic punishment legends, but who remain always anonymous,[104] stigmatized as wrongdoers and opponents of the messengers of God, with no distinct character of their own. The situation is similar in the cases of biblical figures that resurface in the Qur'an, who rarely take on the dimensions of autonomously acting heroes. Some, such as Noah,[105] receive no consistent presentation at all, while others such as David and Solomon are not embedded within stories stretching over an adequately long span of time to undergo a recognizable character development, but rather appear episodically in quite different connections. The native Arabian messengers of God Hūd, Ṣāliḥ, and Shuʿayb, on the other hand, do not act autonomously, but remain throughout performers of the divine will, playing almost identical rolls. If one excludes Moses (Mūsā),[106] Abraham (Ibrāhīm),[107] and Joseph (Yūsuf),[108] one must agree with the judgment pronounced by Jaroslav Stetkevych, that the Qur'anic narrative figures do not reach a degree of significance that would allow the reader to connect them with heroes, in the sense of those key figures "that are found in the related literary structures and symbol systems from the Epic of Gilgamesh through the Hebrew Bible, down to Homer and Virgil."[109]

Yet such a negative evaluation of the Qur'anic narrative figures in contrast to the Biblical ones offers little explanation.[110] Such a position, which would take the applicability of the "Bible as literature" approach to the Qur'an for granted, would raise unjustified claims for the Qur'an. This approach, developed in the 1980s, proceeded from the conviction that a focus "on the psychology of the figures [gives the Bible] a unique dynamic and vivacity, through which the interpretive approach draws the scholarly reader into the text, which in the theological or

104. On the reconstruction of ancient Arabian myth, see J. Stetkevych, *Golden Bough*, ix.
105. Cf. chap. 11, 385–391.
106. Neuwirth, "Narrative as a Canonical Process."
107. Sinai, "Qur'ānic Self-Referentiality"; Neuwirth, "The House of Abraham."
108. Neuwirth, "Yūsuf-Sure."
109. J. Stetkevych, *Golden Bough*, ix.
110. Ibid.

historical search for meaning has been lost."[111] It was especially Robert Alter's book *The Art of Biblical Narrative*[112] that reignited the debate over the literary qualities of the Bible and that, with unique "flair for the nature of the literary creative process of the Bible, pushed it back under the pen of its authors."[113]

But is Qur'anic narrative really to be classified within the narrative genre? In the case of the Qur'an, not only does the question of authorship represent a serious problem, in that for the proclaimer no continuously maintained intentional presentation can be assumed, but rather, what is more, the repeated narratives of the same plot are underlain by principally different intentions. Above all, the goal of *delectare*, to entertain, only rarely, most likely perhaps in sura 12, "Joseph," comes to the foreground ahead of teaching, *docere*. Robert Alter's interpretation of the literary techniques in the Bible as tools "to make the liveliness of artistic intuition literarily effective, and so to enable the production of pleasure in the text as an adventure of life,"[114] can thus not be applied to the Qur'anic narratives. This is because, on the one hand, the eschatologically oriented Qur'an in its early parts strives to draw in its readers with emphatic paraenetic speeches toward new self-reflection: they should "test themselves," in order to prepare themselves for the Final Day. On the other hand, the biblical narratives are never to be assumed as exact models for the Qur'an, since they may not have been known to the community in their original narrative form, but rather through oral transmission, or in the form of later re-narrations. The problem of the different readings of scriptures needs however—once one widens the perspective beyond the Hebrew Bible—be situated on a deeper level than suggested by Hans Peter Schmidt, according to whom it is the first requirement of the new "Bible as literature" approach to revive "what was almost entirely sunken behind the Jewish and Christian overemphasis on norms and morals, namely, the joy in the biblical text and the desire to raise again its background questions."[115] One could respond that a reading oriented toward religious ideas can be equally thrilling; a glance into Midrash literature shows a degree of enthusiasm among the rabbinic exegetes of the Bible that scarcely pales next to the joy of discovery in the "Bible as literature" research, although among these exegetes the linking of the Bible to "lived reality," which is reclaimed by modern researchers, is not a parameter of evaluation. The primary degree of reference for the Midrash is not reality but the world of the Bible text itself, so that historically conditioned theological and moral questions take on an important rank. One must rather ask whether the one-sided decision in favor of reality referentiality as a parameter of value for literature, which is today so dominant, and so intolerantly opposed to other readings, is not for its part also

111. Schmidt, "Von der Kunst," 31.
112. See also Alter and Kermode, *Literary Guide to the Bible*.
113. Schmidt, "Von der Kunst," 31.
114. Ibid., 32.
115. Ibid., 31.

historically conditioned, and whether it is not an attribute of a contemporary secular evaluative attitude. This interpretation is suggested by Schmidt himself, when he recognizes Robert Alter as one of the most influential comparatists, not only because "his close textual readings made the enjoyment of the biblical text experienceable even for the most unabashed sincerity of Western man, but [also] because his investigations of the Bible as a literary work par excellence presented and brought to new light the literary capacities of man and the literary constitution of the West, because great literature is not only expression but rather is also always a means for gaining knowledge of self and world, as well as a fictional way out of these."[116] Modern secular reality referentiality here stands in opposition to premodern non-Western religiously bound text referentiality.

In both Midrash and Qur'an, the orientation to authoritative texts and their norms outranks the immediate orientation to lived reality. The author of the most important reference work on the object, Heinrich Speyer,[117] already indicated for the numerous narrative texts in the Qur'an an orientation not directly to the Bible, but rather to the exegetical literature, and thus brought them into connection with didactic-Midrashic contexts rather than purely narrative ones. But Speyer's valuable collection of Qur'anic intertexts from the Midrash and from homilies has still not been evaluated, since he did not provide analysis of the particular forms of reinterpretation that the biblical and post-biblical traditions undergo in the Qur'anic narratives. But it is evident that already the Late Antique receptions of the Bible evince the very form of paraenetic reinterpretation that is reflected in the Qur'an. In wide parts of post-biblical traditional literature, and also in the Qur'an, dramatically formed biblical narratives with psychologically sensitive personal characterizations are transformed into didactic homiletic presentations—with theological messages placed in the foreground. Reading the Qur'anic narratives with appropriate expectations, one should center one's view less on deviations from putative biblical models than on the particular interpretive strategies of typology.

10.6.2 Cyclical or Historical-Linear Narration?

Qur'anic narration has until now been approached almost exclusively on the basis of the text as a continuum. The Qur'anic presentation of typologically related stories of prophets, with their similar or even identical messages, characteristic of the early suras, has led research to the conclusion that "the Qur'anic narrative" as such attests to a cyclical conception of the transmission of revelation. Rudi Paret's essay *Das Geschichtsbild Mohammeds* (The historical image of Muhammad), which, proceeding from the punishment legends, draws conclusions for the entire Qur'an without further differentiation, still holds sway in

116. Ibid., 33.
117. Speyer, *Die biblischen Erzählungen im Qoran.*

research.[118] Although Josef Horovitz, in his groundbreaking study on Qur'anic narrative, held strictly to Nöldeke's periodization and attempted to trace a linear development of the narratives that only putatively constitute doublets of one another, later researchers gave up chronology and went so far as to argue against there being any development in the Qur'anic presentation of prophets and messengers of God, apart from the addition of narrative details. Above all, it was contested whether the Qur'an has any serious interest in history such as is attested in biblical narrative texts. Fred Donner[119] does not stand alone in his assessment when he finds no development in the Qur'anic narratives, seeing rather the depiction of a moral pattern.

Even if we do not find a consecutive, linearly constructed conception of history in the early parts of the Qur'an, it is all the more important to observe the approaches toward a conception of history in the later texts. Gerhard Böwering has spoken of a "time atomism" that underlies the Qur'anic presentation of history, a view of history "that is typological in nature, and concentrates on the history of the prophets."[120] So, for example, the myth of the first transgression of man, the story of Adam (Genesis 3), does not serve in the Qur'an[121] to introduce history as an unforeseeable and unambiguous process of interaction between God and man. The story of Adam according to his view offers instead an example of the "anthropological constant" of human susceptibility to temptation and seduction. In fact, the lapse of Adam in the Qur'an, aside from his banishment from the garden, has no serious consequences for the fate of mankind, let alone for the perception of a new epoch of interaction between God and man. The myth, which is first introduced at a late stage of the Qur'anic development and is retold in differing contexts, serves primarily to express the evolving insights of the community into the nature of evil, and is less an origin myth than a progression in a debate about evil. The primarily exegetical interest in the phenomenon of the transgression overlaps here with the interest in the "explanation," central for the biblical tradition, of the history of humanity. It should be all the more surprising, then, that at the end of the Qur'anic development, in the latest version of the narrative in the Medinan text Q 2:30–38, we can recognize a contextualization of the story of Adam within the communal present, and thus a politicization of the narrative:

118. Paret, "Das Geschichtsbild Mohammeds," 218, basing his verdict on the punishment stories, arrives at the following conclusion: "If one wanted to characterize his [i.e., the proclaimer's] image in history, one could say that he did not envisage the course of world history in the form of a line that leads—though with occasional ups and downs—straight from the beginning of the human race to his time, but rather in the form of a spiral or a chain, on which a number of circularly shaped figures are connected to each other, which can be made to overlap at will." This sentence is explicitly affirmed by Busse, "Herrschertypen im Koran," 56–80.

119. Donner, *Narratives of Islamic Origins*, 84.

120. Böwering, "Chronology," 319–320.

121. Neuwirth, "The Qur'ān, Crisis and Memory."

And remember when your Lord said to the angels:
"I shall appoint a deputy on earth," and they answered:
"Will you place therein one who sows discord and sheds blood,
while we sing your praise and glorify your holiness ?"
He said: "I know what you do not." (Q 2:30)

The story of Adam's election before the angels, which has already been told in several earlier versions, takes on a political dimension in this text for the first time. Adam will be sent down as a representative of God in the world, regardless of the ruinous and violent actions foreseen for him by the angels. The primordial figure Adam is thus rehabilitated in history. That men, "you," are already designated in some earlier texts as "representatives [of God?]" or as "successors [of the angels] on the earth,"[122] *khalāʾif al-arḍ* (Q 6:165), *khalāʾif fī l-arḍ* (Q 10:14; 35:29), or *khulafāʾ al-arḍ* (Q 27:62), and that Adam here also represents man in general as an original father, does not detract from his assignment here as successor or representative. The election of Adam in sura 2 eclipses the preceding pronouncements about the role of mankind, in that it for the first time broaches the issue of Adam's rulership and reveals its ambivalence. It also departs in its tone from the biblical presentation. On first glance, one could understand the assignment of Adam as ruler as a resumption of the biblical act of granting power to men from the first report of creation, Gen 1:26–27;[123] but the Qur'anic version does not unconditionally assert the human appointment to rulership, equally problematizing man and making him the object of controversy; thus the angels foresee future disaster and attempt to prevent his being sent down. It is the historical time of the proclaimer, in which this prediction is already reality, that interferes with the narrative.

Adam obtains directives (*kalimāt*) for his mission in the world and is assured the safety of his descendants (*hum*, "them"), who—if following the right guidance announced for the future—will be met with no threats: the narrative, which first reports the instruction of Adam in the names of things (cf. Gen 2:28) and subsequently the transgression brought about by Satan's temptation, ends with strengthening assurances, which in the closing verses (Q 2:37–38) even seem to take back the hardships announced in the biblical report to the first men.

With the divine sending down of Adam as ruler to the world, human political power is legitimized, an understanding of the important verse Q 2:30 that proved so suggestive that the dynasty of the Umayyad Marwanids deemed it appropriate to introduce the figure of Adam into their iconography of rulership:[124] Adam is depicted in the throne hall of the Umayyad residence at Quṣayr ʿAmra as the "type of the ruler," whose image is placed above the throne of the caliph. In the context of the proclamation, the pericope Q 2:30–38 appears to be an expression

122. The interpretation is tentative.
123. Cf. Heath, "Creative Hermeneutics."
124. Fowden, *Studies on Hellenism*, 139.

of the perception of a salvation historical turn: it shows that the primordial project of God's "representative on the earth" sent down into the world with Adam, has in the current moment, in view of the newly constituted community who is now capable of representing the divine will, entered into a phase in which it can be politically realized in a way pleasing to God.

The Qur'anic story of creation, which already in its earliest version had adopted, through the displacement of the "fall" from the person of Adam to Diabolos/Iblīs, a beginning different from the biblical reports of creation, and which by marginalizing the transgressive act of the first human couple had in its later presentations radically alleviated the fatal character of the biblical primordial events, undergoes in its final version yet another departure from the biblical predecessor. In that it establishes an optimistic/confident view of man in the face of the doubt of the angels, in claiming that man's rulership is adequate to fulfill God's plan, it displays to the new community a testimonial of recognition as worthy bearers of a human order pleasing to God.

The fact that the Qur'an as a Late Antique text is less narrative than discursive, and that it is concerned not with salvation history told in chronological sequence but rather with the negotiation of theological concepts and paradigms, is indisputable. But it is also undeniable that in the course of the development, an increasing consciousness of the fulfillment of biblical history in the community's immediate present takes shape. Epoch formation is manifested in the Qur'an not *in* biblical history, but rather *after* it, in its restaging in the history of the community.

11

Biblical-Qur'anic Figures

11.1 Actors and Interaction Scenarios

11.1.1 Prophetology of the Qur'an—Hagiography of Exegesis

The Qur'anic scene is occupied by numerous figures, most of which have a biblical prehistory. As main figures of a story, we find Adam, Noah, Abraham, Lot, Joseph, Moses, and Pharaoh as the antagonist of Moses, Mary, and Jesus, and as a mythical figure Iblīs, later identified with Satan. Other figures make only minor appearances, such as David and Solomon, the Queen of Sheba, the wife of Potiphar, Azar, the father of Abraham, Goliath (Qur'anic Jālūt), Saul (Qur'anic Ṭālūt), and as an allegorical figure related to salvation history, Alexander the Great (Qur'anic Dhū l-Qarnayn, "the one with two horns"). Others again are introduced merely as exemplars of some striking moral behavior, such as excessive hubris (Haman, Korah) or with the purpose either to complete a genealogy (Isaac, Jacob), or to revise it (Ishmael). There are also marginal figures represented only by name, such as Idrīs, Dhū l-Kifl, and Luqmān, as well as protagonists who remain nameless such as the son of Noah and the wives of Adam, Abraham, Noah, and Lot. Finally, there are some isolated figures that equally remain anonymous but whom we can assign with probability to certain biblical predecessors, such as Nimrod, briefly inserted into a scene with Abraham. Representing the local Arabian prophet histories we find extra-biblical messengers of God such as Hūd, Ṣāliḥ, and Shuʿayb, who are assigned to particular unbelieving peoples, ʿĀd, Thamūd, and Madyan, respectively; the only individual negative figure from the punishment legends located in the Arabian Peninsula is Tubbaʿ.

What is striking about these characters is first of all their different origins, the coexistence of biblical protagonists with local Arabian figures and even a third genre, Late Antique personages connected to the Alexander legend. What is also hard to ignore is a certain hybridity of many of the characters. Indeed, the biblical origin of the majority of them does not always warrant an unambiguous biblical character, for more often what we find is a dense overlapping of the biblical stratum with later dimensions of meaning that had accumulated in the long post-biblical history of the tradition. What further distinguishes them from their biblical predecessors is their hermeneutical function: all Qur'anic figures play a part in a new collective prophetology that gradually takes shape. They are therefore not simply protagonists of narratives but are also embedded in arguments in support of a new, differentiated model of divine-human communication. This discursive status of the figures obscured only a short time later, in the first post-Qur'anic centuries when the figures, loosed from their argumentative connection, become the isolated protagonists of prophetic legends, *qiṣaṣ al-anbiyāʾ*, which transform the paraenetic narratives of the Qur'an by filling in often sensational narrative details into an edificatory literary genre, thus producing a corpus of narratives that far outstrips the Qur'anic narratives in its attraction as entertainment.

Earlier research in this field concentrated on the Qur'anic development as such. In his work *Koranische Untersuchungen*,[1] Josef Horovitz placed all the Qur'anic figures into the wider pre-Islamic context; reconnecting them to their biblical, post-biblical, and ancient Arabian prehistory. His *Untersuchungen* is an exemplary work that not only evaluates the available literary and epigraphic evidence in the different languages of the peninsula but also draws important historical conclusions from the linguistic forms of proper names, applying the methodology of comparative Semitics.[2] Going beyond this, Furthermore, Horovitz, in the first part of his work,[3] constructed a typology of the Qur'anic narratives, in which the largely schematic "punishment legends" take first rank, while narrative types elaborated later also occur. As against that, the detailed presentation of *Die Biblischen Erzählungen im Qoran* (*Biblical Narratives in the Qurʾān*) by Heinrich Speyer is oriented above all to the history of tradition: the work contextualizes the Qur'anic narratives with rabbinic and Christian-apocryphal writings, though without setting these findings into relief with their new Qur'anic reading. Contrary to Horovitz's work, which sketches a Qur'anic prophetology, Speyer's work is primarily a collection of materials, whose evaluation remains a desideratum.

Such an evaluation has still not been produced after seventy years, not least because of the lack of recognition of the fact that the Qur'an stands in a Late Antique, pluricultural discourse, thus distinguishing itself substantially in terms of genre as a paraenetic text from the narrative literature provided by Islamic tradition that reflects the reception of the already canonized Qur'an. It was John Wansbrough who viewed Qur'an and Sira as contemporaneous, thus opening the door to their undifferentiated synoptic treatment. While Horovitz and Speyer took the Qur'an as such into view, in recent times Qur'anic narratives are regularly illuminated through the "stories of the prophets," the *qiṣaṣ al-anbiyāʾ*[4] that developed later in the inner-Islamic tradition—an anachronistic approach, which also characterizes the numerous studies on individual figures that have since

1. Horovitz, *Koranische Untersuchungen*, 78–155.
2. Cf. also Horovitz, *Jewish Proper Names*.
3. Horovitz, *Koranische Untersuchungen*, 1–77.
4. Cf. Tottoli, *Biblical Prophets*.

appeared.[5] Through recourse to this *qiṣaṣ* literature, which was first codified around a century after the Qur'an, figures that are often only sketched schematically in the Qur'an can be made malleable, and thus they draw nearer to their biblical models. But this perspective not only entails leveling their specific Qur'anic form but also obscures their theological statement, which in the Qur'an is in no way identical to that in the Bible. Loosed from their Qur'anic argumentative context, the stories lose their direction of impact which is often a critique of earlier tradition; they become elements of an edificatory literature devoid of theological tension. Unlike in the Qur'anic narratives, which reflect and negotiate the knowledge circulating in the Hijaz, the reports collected in the *qiṣaṣ* literature are based on a systematic collection accomplished by scholars in the century after the Qur'an, in order to bring together as completely as possible all the available biblical and post-biblical traditions—centrally, the so-called Isrāʾīlīyāt.[6] They are evidence of an age in which the knowledge of Jewish-Christian traditions, due to mass conversion, was already founded on a new, broad basis, drawing not least on written sources.

But it is not merely surplus knowledge but above all quite a different approach to knowledge that separates these later generations from the Qur'anic community. Qur'anic discourse adapts reports about prophets to various debates concerning the community in the present, and thus employs them homiletically and argumentatively. This functionality stands in the center of the interest of a few scholars, who base their work exclusively on the Qur'an in isolation from the *qiṣaṣ* literature. Studies in this vein are available so far on Adam,[7] Abraham,[8] Moses,[9] Joseph,[10] Saul,[11] and Mary and Jesus.[12]

11.1.2 Punishment Legends

Research into the biblical-Qur'anic figures thus remains in its infancy, and all too rarely have the figures been brought into focus in their argumentative context or in relation to the evolving tension with their biblical predecessors.[13] A first

5. On Adam: Schöck, *Adam im Koran*; on Abraham: Firestone, *Abraham-Ishmael Legends*; on Moses: Wheeler, *Moses*; on Solomon and the Queen of Sheba: Lassner, "The Queen of Sheba." This tendency is also apparent in a number of articles in the *Encyclopaedia of the Qurʾān*; cf. Schöck, "Adam and Eve"; Schöck, "Moses"; Brinner, "Noah"; Firestone, "Abraham."

6. Cf. Tottoli, "Isrāʾ ıliyyāt"; see also Albayrak, "Qurʾānic Narrative and Isrāʾīliyyāt."

7. Neuwirth, "Qurʾān, Crisis and Memory"; on Satan: Bodman, "Stalking Iblis"; Sinai, *Studien zur frühen Koraninterpretation*, 86–93.

8. Nagel, "Der erste Muslim"; see especially Sinai, *Studien zur frühen Koraninterpretation*, 97–160; cf. also Bauschke, *Abraham*.

9. Goitein, "Ramadan"; cf. also Neuwirth, "Erzählen als kanonischer Prozess."

10. Neuwirth, "Yūsuf-Sure."

11. Walid Saleh, "King Saul."

12. Neuwirth, "Mary and Jesus"; Neuwirth, "Imagining Mary—Disputing Jesus"; Marx, "Mariology in the Qur'an"; Bauschke, *Jesus im Koran*.

13. Promising new beginnings are offered in the works of Sinai, *Studien zur frühen Koraninterpretation* (for Abraham); Witztum, "The Foundation of the House" (for Abraham and Ishmael); Marx, "Mariology in the Qur'an"

breakthrough was achieved with the model of the "punishment legends," to assess the topos of the *umam khāliya*, the "by-gone peoples," which Josef Horovitz described as independent narratives in various manifestations, as parts of a narrative series, or as mere evocations. In Horovitz's view, these are stories that proceed according to a shared pattern in which an insubordinate people disregards a messenger's call to the belief in one God and is therefore obliterated by a catastrophe. These descriptions differ substantially from the biblical reports of the annihilation of ancient peoples, in that they do not document God's care for a privileged "elect" people—the events have no salvific or providential effect for the new elect people, the Qur'anic community. Their positive aspect lies elsewhere; Horovitz emphasizes "The reverse image of the downfall of the disobedient peoples is the salvation of the messengers of God who have warned them."[14] It is this second point of the stories, that is bound up to the fate of the proclaimer himself, who, as the occasional use of identical arguments shows, recognized in the earlier messengers of God, who pursued their message despite threatening situations, predecessors of himself. Since most of these narratives feature biblical figures, it is their biblical pattern of thought that appears more obvious than their extra-biblical intertextuality:

> The history of the cities of the earlier times has become for him [the proclaimer] exclusively the object of religious contemplation, and the method that he applied to evaluate the traditions of his own people and that of others, recalls the approach followed by biblical writers, for example, the redactor of the Book of Judges, who in a schematic way explains the wars of the Israelite tribes with their neighbors: they did what was evil in the eyes of God, who therefore gave them over to the hands of their enemies, until finally, through their supplication, he sent them a savior (Jdg. 2:11, 2:7, 3:12, passim; cf. 1 Sam 12:7–15). If Muhammad again and again holds up the fate of earlier peoples to his countrymen as a warning example—one notes also the formula *fa-l-yanẓurū kayfa kānat ʿāqibatu l-mukadhdhibīn*, "so let them see what was the end of the deniers"—it can only be with the intention to warn them of a similar fate to that which others have suffered while living on earth, not only punishment in the afterlife: the obliteration of their city and its population, a fate that will be spared only to the messenger of Allah and his dependents. The fact that Muḥammad always speaks of the fate of cities (*qurā*) of the earlier time . . . shows that in forming his narratives he was thinking of his hometown Mecca, the "mother of the cities," *umm al-qurā*, Q 42:5, Q 6:92.8, cf. also *al-qaryatān*, Q 43:30, meaning Mecca and Taif.[15]

(for Mary). They take account not only of the biblical foundations but also of the figures' successive development in the rabbinic and homiletic literature of Late Antiquity.

14. Horovitz, *Koranische Untersuchungen*, 15.
15. Ibid., 30.

But our view should spread beyond the reality of the proclaimer. Indeed, the topos of the *umam khāliya* is rooted in a wider local Arabic tradition. The reference to topography, the emphatic viewing of the lingering traces of destroyed settlements and the nostalgic underlining of their unique glory, equally evokes the powerful model of the ancient Arabian perception of destroyed campsites, and thus the nostalgic beginning part of the qasida, the *nasīb*. In the innumerable poetic instances of bemoaning over the *aṭlāl*, the "abandoned campsites," we are dealing not only with places from the personal experience of loss of the individual poet, but rather this topos highlights subliminally, and occasionally concretely,[16] the no longer inhabited remains of earlier civilization.[17] In that the Qur'anic presentation tells or retells the "lost histories" of such cities—in the cases of the peoples of ʿĀd and Thamūd, pre-Qur'anic stories about tragic heroes have been reconstructed[18]—the mute ruins reclaim language and meaning. The question *ubi sunt qui ante nos in mundo fuere* ("Where have they gone who were in the world before us?") is so-to-speak "answered."[19]

This far-reaching second implication of the stories may be less relevant for their moral message, but it demonstrates all the more strongly the affective power of the Qur'anic hermeneutic, to take up poetic challenges and rethink the aporias opened by the poetry, and even to offer solutions for them. As against these punishment legends, whose schematic pattern is often wrongly ascribed to the Qur'anic narratives as a whole, Horovitz distinguishes a more elaborate and more strongly history-oriented form of narrative, the "stories of prophets and men of God":[20] "In the center of the Qur'anic narratives, even when they are not punishment legends, we almost always find a prophet, a messenger of God, a pious man. The Qur'anic prophetology can thus be identified as the central part of Muḥammad's image of history."[21] This will be examined in what follows.

11.1.3 Ruler Typologies

Thus, while Horovitz attempts to keep the progressive history of the proclamation in mind, Heribert Busse[22] in his article "Herrschertypen im Koran," "Ruler types in the Qur'an," consciously departs from a diachronic reading. He pursues striking connections of motifs that were already recognized by Horovitz in more detail,[23] and thus reveals an important narrative principle, which he terms

16. Horovitz, "Terminologie des islamischen Kultus," points out several verses of complaint motivated by dilapidated palace architecture by the Umayyad poet, Ibn Qays al-Ruqayyāt.

17. See Montgomery, "The Empty Ḥijāz"; Neuwirth, "Geography"; cf. also chap. 12, 444–447.

18. J. Stetkevych, *Golden Bough*, Bencheikh, "Iram ou la clameur de Dieu."

19. See chap. 3, 129–131.

20. Horovitz, *Koranische Untersuchungen*, 32–44.

21. Ibid, 44.

22. Busse, "Herrschertypen im Koran"; cf. also Neuwirth, "Myths and Legends."

23. Horovitz, *Koranische Untersuchungen*, 8–9.

"typology"—flashing out however, the theological implications that adhere to this term in biblical scholarship.

> As biblical figures, we find "Pharaoh and Nimrod of legend, who both declare themselves gods, the one as the antagonist of Moses, the other as the antagonist of Abraham; David and Solomon, who unite kingship and prophethood in their persons; the Queen of Sheba in connection with the Solomon story; Joseph having fled to Egypt, who grows into a prophet and in some sense a ruler; and Saul (*Ṭalūt*), who is proclaimed king by Samuel at God's prompting. . . . From the Alexander romance, enriched with biblical elements, comes the narrative of *Dhū al-Qarnayn*, the "two horned one," who travels the whole world and calls for belief. To South Arabia belongs *Tubbaʿ*, mentioned briefly only twice in the Qur'an (Q 44:37, 50:14) is; he rejects the message of God and perishes together with his people. We thus have the following ruler types: prophet-kings (David, Solomon, *Dhū l-Qarnayn*, Abraham, and Joseph), God-kings (Nimrod, Pharaoh, and possibly *Tubbaʿ*), and finally Saul, a king installed by a prophet, and the queen of Sheba who turned from paganism to right belief. . . . He [the proclaimer] contrasts the devotion of the prophet-kings, their wisdom in judgment, their building activities, and their universal rulership, which even ranges so far as to include the cosmos, to the corresponding negative qualities and forms of behaviors of the God-kings. In central positions we find on the one side Solomon and on the other side Pharaoh. What is required is to uncover the typological schema.[24]

Busse's approach is useful above all for those texts where the information on a Qur'anic figure is too limited to allows us to elicit the function of that figure's occurrence from the context, for example, for such rarely named and barely recognizable figures as Haman (Q 40:36–37, 28:38–42), Korah Q 28:76–82, 29:39), Nimrod (unidentified: Q 21:67–69, 2:258), or for the phenomenon of the tower tomb/palace building, which occurs not only with Pharaoh but also with Solomon, where it serves to delude the queen of Sheba. But as a primary approach to the Qur'an, this focus on schematic correspondences, Busse's "typology,"[25] is problematic; for it obscures the view to the microstructural formation of figures and their narrative function,[26] and, what is more, it obscures their gradual development in the course of the Qur'anic proclamation. Busse's conscious relinquishment of chronology leads him to the untenable assumption

24. Busse, "Herrschertypen im Koran," 58.

25. Cf. chap. 10, 354–355.

26. In relation to Saul, Saleh, "King Saul," has been able to show that he takes on the function of a model in a particular communal situation, in which Prophethood is complemented with political authority through the power of rulership, so that the proclaimer becomes the representative of rulership *and* warriorhood, eclipsing the functions of Moses, who does not appear as a warrior.

that the proclaimer follows a firm, unchanging thought pattern through his entire ministry, according to which "names, qualities, and behaviors of persons of salvation history [are] almost arbitrarily interchangeable. Muhammad seeks to elicit the typus, developing an independent typology, whether inspired by the Christian biblical interpretative tradition or not."[27] That this view leaves no room for the possibility of the negotiation of differing prophet traditions that were available to the community but rather assumes an exclusive role of the proclaimer as author clinging to an identical position across the entire text must be considered as a major weakness.

Although the Qur'an is "a book of the working of a prophet in the world"[28] rather than a work of history, it is an astoundingly revealing mirror for the perception of history. It documents an interest in salvation historical persons that follows less a linear development of their vitae than the line of their progressive exegetical "increase in meaning," which is achieved through the undergirding of what is historically reported about them with theologically important post-biblical traditions, or through the evocation of the figures' significance for the contemporary situation of the proclaimer himself. This multilayered character of the presentation cannot be observed from the very beginning. It shows itself clearly only in the successive formation of individual prophets, from whose synopsis—as Horovitz already showed programmatically—a Qur'anic prophetology can be read out. In the following sketch, particular attention will be paid to the gradual exegetical development of the figures through reference to the stories which grew up around them in post-biblical tradition.[29]

11.2 Noah—His Qur'anic Development

11.2.1 Noah in the Qur'an

Stories about Noah/Nūḥ and the flood were familiar to the Qur'anic hearers not only from the oral tradition but also from poetry[30]—apparently stripped, however, of their salvation historical interpretation in the sense of a renewal of the world (Gen 6:5–8). The flood stories connected to Noah[31] occur in the Qur'an similarly emptied of symbols, and demythologized in a way that recalls the Qur'anic story of Adam, which did not permit a reading as a myth of origin for the attainment of human self-responsibility. Although the events around Noah are recognized as having occurred at a time *before* those of all other messengers

27. Busse, "Herrschertypen im Koran," 58–59.

28. Ibid

29. In order to make the chronological relation immediately clear, the period of origin for the pertinent texts, indicated by I, II, III (= first, second, and third Meccan periods) and (M = Medina), precede the verse citations.

30. Horovitz, *Koranische Untersuchungen*, 146. Cf. also Hirschberg, *Jüdische und christliche Lehren*.

31. Speyer, *Die biblischen Erzählungen im Qoran*, 84–115; cf. also Abdel Haleem, "Story of Noah."

after Adam (Q I (=early Meccan) 53:53, I 51:46, II (=middle Meccan) 50:12), the Flood seems to be without relevance as a salvation historical new beginning, or as an end marker of the primeval, antediluvian epoch of direct divine intervention in creation that would be succeeded after Noah by the stories of the patriarchs.[32] Correspondingly, the Flood and the Ark have no mythical-allegorical dimension, but are reduced in the Qur'an to mere instruments of individual punishment or salvation.

Yet the narrative undergoes a clear and discernible development, so that the figure of Noah is significant for more than one of the Qur'anic discourses that evolve out of each other. It is first relevant for the early Meccan discourse of prophetic warning, which focuses primarily on the visualization of the peoples obliterated by punishment (*umam khāliya*). This function of Noah is foreign to the biblical report but plays a role in the rabbinic and patristic reception.[33] Later, Noah underpins the middle Meccan discourse of communal self-construction as a people of God standing in the tradition of biblical predecessors, where Moses ranges as the most direct model but is preceded by other exemplary figures. Finally, in Medina, Noah gains yet another significance, first in the genealogy discourse as the founder of a succession of prophets that culminates in the person of Muhammad and, at the end of the Qur'anic development, as a predecessor of the Prophet in his function as universal lawgiver.[34]

11.2.2 *Noah—Proclaimer and Survivor of a Divinely Imposed Punishment*

Noah occurs in the earliest suras together with the ancient Arabian messengers of God, who fail in their effort to call their peoples to the belief in one god. His story, which reaches back into the primordial times of salvation history, is told as the opening of a series of punishment legends, wherein the stories of ʿĀd, Thamūd, Lot (Lūṭ), and the people of Pharaoh (Firʿawn) follow, each being closed with the same refrain (verses 16–17), Q II 54:9–17:

kadhdhabat qablahum qawmu Nūḥin
fa-kadhdhabū ʿabdanā
wa-qālū majnūnun wa-zdujir
fa-daʿā rabbahu annī maghlūbun fa-ntaṣir
fa-fataḥnā abwāba l-samāʾi bi-māʾin munhamir
wa-fajjarnā l-arḍa ʿuyūnan

32. Kugel, *How to Read the Bible*, 78.

33. Ibid, 72–73.

34. Noah's profile does not emerge if one pursues the texts about him through a purely synchronic reading of the Qur'an, as in Brinner, "Noah." Neither can the "traditional-historical context of the Qur'anic portrayal of Noah" be illuminated merely through the collection of isolated Christian traditions on Noah, as attempted by Goßmann, "Noah im Koran."

fa-ltaqā l-mā'u 'alā amrin qad qudir
wa-ḥamalnāhu 'alā dhāti alwāḥin wa-dusur
tajrī bi-a'yuninā jazā'an li-man kāna kufir
wa-la-qad taraknāhā āyatan fa-hal min muddakkir
fa-kayfa kāna 'adhābī wa-ndhur
wa-la-qad yassarnā l-qur'āna li-l-dhikri
fa-hal min muddakkir

Before them the people of Noah cried lies,
They denounced our servant as a liar.
They said: "one possessed," and he was frightened.
So he called his Lord: I am defeated, so help me!
So we opened the gates of heaven with flooding water;
And caused the earth to gush with springs
and the waters converged in accordance with a decided decree
and we carried him on a ship of planks and nails
that coursed under our eyes, as reward for one who had encountered unbelief.
We left it as a sign. Is there someone who recalls?
How then was my punishment!
We eased the recitation for recollection.
Is there one who recalls?

The story narrates—at first view no differently than the Bible—the catastrophe of the Flood imposed by God as punishment for human corruption. But in the Qur'an, it is not the frivolity, the socially manifest wickedness of men, that causes God to regret their creation and leads to the drastic step of their obliteration (Gen 5:5–8). In the Qur'an we find no near total annihilation of mankind—such a dramatics would be alien to the Qur'anic presentation. While the biblical report and its mythical parallels, such as the Epic of Gilgamesh and the Deucalion Saga,[35] aim toward a radical renewal of mankind, in the Qur'an, prophetology is put into the foreground: men, concretely the society in which Noah appears as a proclaimer, meet punishment for their unbelief and their intimidation of the servant of God—crimes that also brought about the downfall of other "earlier peoples." So it is no wonder that, although the description of the flowing together of the waters suggests a cosmic scale, the annihilation of the frivolous is not the central theme in this early sura, but rather the miraculous saving of the messenger of God aboard an apparently scantily timbered ship (verse 12), which glides smoothly under God's direction across the violently stirred waters (verse 13). The ship—whether materially or as an idea—is to be received as a

35. This parallelization already occurred among Hellenized Jews; see Feldman, "Josephus' Portrait of Noah," 44.

warning sign (verse 17). The conciliatory tone predominates, for as severe as the punishment—which is here only implied—is, the warning is easily available in the "reading whose recollection is made easy." The story does tell of a threatening punishment for the frivolous, but above all relates a message awakening hope, a message that is "made easy" in the reading.

A little later, Noah's story fills out the entire sura 71. As in the cases of the other punishment legends, the emphasis is now on the annihilation of the insubordinate people, but this people is still not equated with all of humanity.

After a few cursory mentions (Noah is apparently a figure familiar to the hearers), he appears in a detailed story (Q II (= middle Meccan), 54:9–17, II 71:1–28). This narrative, which departs radically from the biblical report, places him in a situation that is strikingly similar to that of the proclaimer himself: Noah is not only being denigrated as one possessed, as in Q I (= early Meccan) 54, or someone inspired by demons (Q II 54:9, II 23:24), but is also despised for the fact that he does not win distinguished followers but only those in a socially low position (Q II 26:111). He sermonizes to his people about belief in one God (Q II 71:1–28) in the style of the proclaimer, reminding his hearers of the divine attributes and the requirement of repentance (Q II 71:10), which has become urgent in view of the impending judgment (Q II 71:18). But he is rejected, and his people insists on the worship of pagan divinities that are given by name (Q II 71:23–24)—a crime that is already laid on them in the rabbinic tradition.[36] Noah ultimately despairs and complains his sorrow to God, as in sura 54 he prays for the punishment of the people (Q II 71:21.26, Q II 26:117–118). His prayer is heeded, not simply with divine intervention but also with divine encouragement: it is announced to him that the frivolous will be drowned and will fall victim to the punishment of hell (Q II 54:15). Noah's story thus should serve as a sign (*āya*; Q II 54:15, Q II 26:121). He is further honored though a formula of blessing, "peace to Noah among men," *salāmun ʿalā Nūḥin fī l-ʿālamīn* (Q II 37:79) and taken up among the model figures from the biblical tradition. The text thus follows those of the exegetical traditions which accept Noah's righteousness (Genesis 6) without restrictions. This runs against the rabbinic tradition (Genesis Rabba 30:9, 32:6), which tended to downgrade Noah, the original father of the non-Jewish peoples, who were called "sons of Noah" because they were bound only to the commandments given to Noah.[37] Louis S. Feldman has seen in the rabbinic relativizing of Noah's merits a reaction to his reception in the church as a typus of Christ.[38] The thoroughly positive Qur'anic image of Noah does not enter into these debates but is oriented rather to Noah's immediate significance for the contemporary believers: with the formula of blessing, which defines the nature of

36. Speyer, *Die biblischen Erzählungen im Qoran*, 101.
37. Ibid., 96.
38. See Feldman, "Josephus' Portrait of Noah," 44.

the communal handling of Noah, now raised to a model figure to be collectively honored, his story is interwoven with the history of the nascent community.

Although Noah appears again in the lists of the ancient Arabian warners, to which he belongs beginning with the early Meccan punishment and judgment discourse (Q II 38:12–14, III=late Meccan) 14:9), the circumstances and dimensions of the catastrophe that he is elected to survive come more clearly into view with time. In the middle Meccan discourse of the construction of communal identity as a new people of God in Q II 37:75–79, his story is connected with the story of Abraham, who also confronts his unbelieving people, alongside other episodes of the history of the Israelites (Banū Isrāʾīl); he thereby becomes a member of the biblical tradition that is being newly adopted for the Qur'anic community.

11.2.3 Noah—Marker of a Turn in Salvation History

But it is not only through these events, which distinguish themselves from other acts of salvation as the realization of a divine plan (Q I 54:14), that Noah acquires new relevance; it is also thanks to the new orientation to scripture, to the *kitāb* of the Israelites, which emerges in the Late Meccan discourse. The changed perspective, according to which the prophets now appear as a succession, gives each of them his own significance, that at the same time affects the Qur'anic community oriented to its model. This change shows itself clearly in the detailed version of the Noah story in Q III 11:25–49. Noah now takes on the double task of building the ship (*fulk*; Q III 23:22) and selecting the pairs of animals (Q III 23:27). The cosmic dimension of the Flood is now recognizable for the first time, and salvation is staged as a new beginning. Noah is now distinguished as the messenger of "the generation that we pulled across the water" (*dhurrīyat*[39] *man ḥamalnā maʿa Nūḥ*, Q III 17:3; cf. II 19:58). It is part of the salvation history of the Banū Isrāʾīl, which the Qur'anic community has incorporated in this period into its own understanding of history.

Noah's sermon is quoted in detail; it shows him—in spite of his connection to the fateful flood—as a predecessor of the proclaimer, who for his part had already in the late Meccan period come to the insight that the unbelief of the pagans should be due to the divine will (Q III 11:34), and therefore would be inevitable. Noah is comforted in his despair by the divine request to take the believers and a pair of every creature (Q III 11:40) into the saving ship.

Only now is a son of Noah introduced, a negative figure who, though not reaching the degree of condemnation of the biblical son of Noah, Ham, will not adopt his father's belief in one God and must drown despite Noah's attempt to intercede for him with God (Q III 11:45–46). Noah gives up his son and thus

39. *Dhurrīya* denotes progeny in the sense of the inheritors of a charismatic role and does not necessarily indicate physical progeny.

gives up the preservation of his genealogical relations, in order to strengthen his transcendent relation—a decision before which the individual believers in the late Meccan period (Q III 29:8) also stand. Speyer attempted to find models in rabbinic tradition for this figure, who shares with Ham the negative reputation. But more likely this figure represents the actual conflicts between believers and unbelievers, which at the time of the proclamation of the sura were shaking inner-familial structures.

Noah obtains divine blessing not only for himself but for all peoples to come (*umam*, Q III 11:48). The ship ultimately drops anchor before Mount Jūdī,[40] which is localized in Arabia (Q III 11:44). Now too we see the first mention of Noah's long life span: already before the "Flood" (now termed for the first time as *ṭūfān*, Q III 29:14), he lived 950 years among his people—a specification that is perhaps meant to illustrate the grotesque situation of the pious man patiently but hopelessly proclaiming the belief in one God.[41] Without reference to a narrative, finally there is mention of Noah's wife; she figures as a negative example of a prophet's wife, alongside the baselessly punished wife of Lot (Q M 66:10–12).

11.2.4 Noah—Opener of a Succession of Prophets

Still in the Meccan period, Noah is recognized in what is from the Qur'anic perspective perhaps his most significant role: as the initiator of biblical prophecy (Q III 6:84). Alongside this, he is a model for the proclaimer, in that the prescriptions that go back to him, the "Noahide commandments," are also laid out for the proclaimer and the Qur'anic community: *sharaʿa lakum mina l-dīn mā waṣṣā bihi Nūḥan wa-lladhī awḥaynā ilayka*, "He has defined the religion for you, which he has also laid out for Noah, and which we have inspired to you" (Q III 42:13). Here, he appears as the first lawgiver, who, with a non-codified "natural law" so-to-speak undermines the barrier erected by the Mosaic legislation of Jewish law, and therefore rises to the rank of a model of the proclaimer for the "transconfessional community" of the proclaimer."

As in the cases of other biblical figures, Noah's image is "politicized" in the Medinan period; that is, his mention is inserted into a religio-political argument. He now appears no longer as a warner, but rather as a biblical Prophet, and, what is more, an axial figure, who divides past human history from the new "post-diluvian" chain of generations, so that now his achievement of reestablishing the human race after the Flood finds at least implicit recognition (Q M = Medinan) 3:33–34; Q M 19:58 = Medinan addition). In that religiously based genealogy takes on a central significance in Medina, as the Jews claim

40. On localizing the landing site of the ark on a mountain in Arabia, see Speyer, *Die biblischen Erzählungen im Qoran*, 107.

41. In ibid., 93, Speyer refers to a Midrashic parallel, which also expresses the lengthiness of the unsuccessful sermon in numeric categories.

primacy by way of their privileges as "successors of Abraham," Noah, together with Adam, and especially the House of Amram, *Āl ʿImrān*, the Christian holy family, form a counterbalance to the successors of Abraham that dominate the Medinan scene (Q M 3:1).[42]

In yet a later period, when there was no longer a standing political necessity to "balance out" the successors of Abraham through figures outside of the Jewish tradition, Noah and his successors again become mere salvation historical predecessors of Abraham and his descendants (Q M 52:26, M 4:163). At the same time, attempts are made to unite the biblical and Arabian messengers of God in one and the same succession of prophets (Q M 22:42–44, M 9:70). Finally, at a period when the Prophet himself is raised to the rank of the biblical prophets (*anbiyāʾ*) and all prophets are counted as participants in a shared covenant—*wa-idh akhadhnā mina l-nabīyīna mīthāqahum wa-minka wa-min Nūḥ*, "At that time, when we sealed a covenant with the prophets, so also with you and with Noah" (Q M 33:7)—Noah is the first among them, followed by Abraham, Moses, and Jesus, and closing with Muhammad himself.[43] The sequence is to be understood as a succession of prophets, and not as a biological genealogy, even if the Islamic tradition later fits them into genealogically oriented family trees.

Noah's Qur'anic career then culminates in his role as opener of a succession of prophets and as a lawgiving prophet. His elevation to the "forefather" of prophet generations is superior to his biblical role, scarcely noted in the Qur'an, as the forefather of the new humanity after the Flood. At the same time, at the end of the development, Noah has grown out of the role of the patient messenger of God proclaiming in vain, the righteous man of the local Arabian history. What was already his determining dimension in the Christian tradition—his initial position in a historically structured sequence of covenant partners of God, as the giver of pre-Mosaic law—also makes up his particular significance for the Qur'anic community in the late proclamation.

11.3 Abraham—His Qur'anic Development

11.3.1 Genealogical Paternity versus Transcendent Bond

Abraham,[44] who at the end of the Qur'anic development holds first rank among the prophets as the founder of the "original monotheism" foundational to Islam, accompanies the Qur'anic proclamation from the very beginning. Elements of his story are obviously known already to the hearers, since he occurs as a mere

42. Neuwirth, "The House of Abraham."

43. On this succession, which conforms to the standard sequence of Prophets in Christian theology, only prefixing Adam to this series and leaving the final position unoccupied, see Samir, "The Theological Christian Influence, who, however, does not acknowledge the Qur'anic reinterpretations.

44. On his Qur'anic career in the Meccan suras, see now Sinai, *Studien zur frühen Koraninterpretation*.

name (Q I 87:19) before any account of him is given. Early on, he is associated with a virtue that already adheres to him in the Bible (Neh 9:7–8): loyalty, faithfulness, Q I 53:37: *wa-Ibrāhīma lladhī waffā*, "and Abraham, who preserved loyalty." He becomes the protagonist of a typologically diversified story, which is dispersed among Qur'anic texts ranging from the earliest period to the very end of the Qur'an's emergence. The chronological sequence of Abraham-references is Q I 53:37, II 37:83–98, II 19:41–50, II 21:51–73, II 26:69–86, III 29:16–27, III 43:26–27, III 6:74–84, III 14, M 60:4.

Abraham's first merit is not, as in Gen 12:1–5, his decision to leave his father's house and homeland, in order to follow the call of God to "go forth" (Gen 12:1). In the Qur'an, Abraham has a pre-history in his original homeland. There, he confronts idolatry, a biographical detail that is equally recorded in the Book of Jubilees and the Testament of Abraham.[45] He does so by attacking the idols of his father and successively also those that are displayed in public (Q III 6:74–84, II 19:41–50, II 21:57–58, II 26:16–27, II 37:93); attempting, as he does in the Midrash,[46] to demonstrate their nullity rationally. A death penalty imposed on him for this is foiled through divine intervention (Q II 21:68–69, II 37:97–98, III 6:74–84, III 29:24). It is this experience, the rejection of idolatry, that causes him—as is laid out in one of the first Abraham stories—to emigrate from his homeland, which remains unnamed.[47] Spurred by his father (*uhjurnī*, "Leave me," Q II 19:46), who rejects him on account of his defense of idolatry, he seeks to accomplish a *hijra*, a "secession" from father and homeland, in order to encounter God in a new land, where he aims to establish a new clan (Q II 19:48–49, II 21:71, III 29:26). The earliest pericope on this, Q II 37:99–109, is briefly presented here:[48]

wa-qāla innī dhāhibun ilā rabbī sa-yahdīn
rabbi hab lī mina l-ṣāliḥīn
fa-bashsharnāhu bi-ghulāmin ḥalīm
  fa-lammā balagha maʿahu l-saʿya
  qāla yā bunayya innī arā fī l-manāmi
  annī adhbaḥuka fa-nẓur mādhā tarā
  qāla yā abati fʿal mā tuʾmaru
  sa-tajdunī in shāʾa llāhu mina l-ṣābirīn
fa-lammā aslamā wa-tallahu li-l-jabīn
wa-nādaynāhu an yā Ibrahīm
qad ṣaddaqta l-ruʾyā innā ka-dhālika najzī l-muḥsinīn
inna hādhā la-huwa l-balāʾu l-mubīn

45. Speyer, *Die biblischen Erzählungen im Qoran*, 131.
46. Genesis Rabba 38:19, quoted in ibid., 135–136.
47. In the Book of Jubilees and in Philo, idolatry, or star worship, is the motivation for his emigration.
48. On this text, see now Sinai, *Studien zur frühen Koraninterpretation*, 117–120.

wa-fadaynāhu bi-dhabḥin ʿaẓīm
wa-taraknā ʿalayhi fī-l-ākhirīn
salāmun ʿalā Ibrahīm

He said: I will go forth to my Lord, He will guide me.
My Lord, give me one of those who are righteous!
So we gave him news of a boy with forbearance.
  When he reached with him (i.e. Abraham) the age of doing the circumambulation,
  he said: "My son, I saw in a dream that I will sacrifice you.
  What do you think?"
  He said: "My father, do what you are ordered,
  you will find me, God willing, one of the patient";
when they both had submitted,
and he had thrown him on the forehead,
then we called him, "Abraham,
you have fulfilled the vision,
  so do we reward those who do good."
This is the clear testing.
We ransomed him with a great sacrifice,
and for those who come later we left upon him: "peace be upon Abraham."

Abraham's principal great merit is his readiness to sacrifice his son. The short pericope was told first more concisely, without the indented verse 102 which was added only in Medina: Abraham leaves his father, the idolater, and emigrates trusting in divine guidance. His prayer for a son is heard—a thought that originally segued directly into the sacrifice (verse 103), which is at the center of this episode, the "testing story." Although the victim is substituted thanks to divine intervention, the sacrifice is to be understood as a "clear test" (*balāʾ*, verse 106, compare Gen 22:1)—an idea also stressed in Haggadic literature.[49] Abraham's passing of the test entitles him to an honorific eulogy; from now on his name is linked with the formula *ʿalayhi l-salām*, "Peace be upon him." The story is clearly not meant to supply initial information about a crucial episode of salvation history, but rather to present a paragon of exemplary piety, relevant enough to merit resonance in the liturgical praxis of the present.

Perhaps it was Abraham's all too rigid obedience to God in this example that in Medina called for an explanation. In any case, the story, documenting a high degree of paternal cruelty, was subsequently expanded by means of a prose insertion, verse 102. This insertion provides an explanation involving the agreement of the son, who, asked for his consent, now volunteers himself for sacrifice—in

49. Isaac's contribution to his own sacrifice can already be found in Josephus; cf. Kugel, *The Bible as It Was*, 175ff. For further testimonies, see Witztum, "The Foundation of the House."

agreement with a Midrashic interpretation.[50] The Qur'anic reading differs decisively in its thrust from the biblical presentation of the Aqedah, "the binding," in Gen 22:1–19, by not allowing for a unilateral act of sacrifice: Abraham does not resolve upon the sacrifice by himself, but rather is supported by the decision of his son. As a result, and quite in accordance with the Midrash, an act of self-destruction is turned into a joint virtuous deed of father and son.[51] Obedience to God no longer transcends what man can bear, and its meritoriousness is moreover enhanced by the synergy of father and son.

There is not much here to recall the emphatic biblical "Go forth." Yet by turning away from his father and turning toward "his lord" ("I will go forth to my lord [*rabbī*], he will guide me," Q II 37:99), Abraham breaks exemplarily with the genealogical paradigm replacing it by a religious one. During the middle Meccan period, the Qur'anic community performs the same movement and exchanges its genealogical forefathers for spiritual predecessors. The development is heightened further in the late Meccan period, when some must even renounce their own genetic kin (Q III 29:8). Although the middle Meccan grounding of the physical *hijra* of Abraham is not linked with the later *hijra* of the community, it constitutes a model for the desirable behavior of believers in a situation of religious oppression by unbelievers, a behavior that may extend as far as renouncing one's own tribe. In the Qur'an, it is the destruction of the old order exemplified by Abraham that is the precondition for the setting up of a new one. The narrative of the destruction of the idols, which involves a rational argument, already familiar from Midrash,[52] raises Abraham to the level of a hero of cultural renewal.[53]

11.3.2 *Abraham as Cult Founder*

In view of the fact that the Qur'anic community gave no special status to the progeny of Abraham,[54] it is unsurprising that Abraham, whose name appears already in the earliest suras (Q I 87:19, I 53:37), never occurs as the progenitor of the Israelites. Rather, he is a model of exemplary piety, which includes unconditioned obedience and readiness to sacrifice even that which one holds most dear. Right at the beginning, Abraham appears in the Qur'an as the epitome of unconditional trust in God. Honored by a visit from supernatural messengers,

50. Cf. Speyer, *Die biblischen Erzählungen im Qoran*, 164–166.

51. This synergy of the father and son becomes a typological prefiguration of Christ's self-sacrifice willed by God the Father; see the attestations in Kugel, *The Bible as It Was*, 177.

52. Firestone, "Abraham"; Speyer, *Die biblischen Erzählungen im Qoran*, 134–140.

53. A different model of dealing with a religious opponent is the debate, thematized as an option in Medina, where Abraham conducts an argument with an anonymous, unbelieving ruler (Q 2:258–260), a scenario familiar already from apocryphal literature, but this occurs only in the Medinan period; see *Die biblischen Erzählungen im Qoran*, 140–142.

54. The privileged status of the Israelites as the people of God is nevertheless acknowledged; see, for example, Q 17:70; 2:47, 122.

who announce the birth of a son to a man who is already at an advanced age (Q I 51:24–30), he believes in the announcement despite its improbability.[55] In the same story, he negotiates with God over the fate of the people of Lot (Q III 11:74–75; cf. Gen 18:1–20) but ultimately acquiesces to God's decision and rejection of Abraham's intercession.

The most important event is the Aqedah, the "binding" (Gen 22:1–19), Abraham's sacrifice of his son, which he readily undertakes (Q II 37:99–113), and which is only averted at the very last moment by divine intervention.[56] This event, however, does not take place in the Holy Land, but rather in the surroundings of Mecca or within the Meccan sanctuary,[57] which recent research assumes to have been associated with Abraham already at the time of the Qur'an's emergence.[58] This sacrifice remained closely tied to Abraham and Mecca in post-Qur'anic Islamic worship as well. It is re-enacted at the local sanctuary down to the present day in the form of the sacrificial rites of the annual pilgrimage, which are etiologically grounded in this Qur'anic story.

That the sacrifice story,[59] which foregrounds the notions of genealogy and sacrifice, also contributes significant weight to the corroboration of patrilineal thought is not only a result of later development. According to M. Elaine Combs-Schilling, this myth of sacrifice at once contains and strengthens the significance of patrilineal bonds:

> Transcendence comes because, as told in the Qur'ān, the Prophet Abraham had to deny his own father in order to remain faithful to the one God. . . . Yet the Qur'ān also reinforces patrilineality by portraying the ultimate sacrifice that God demands of humans as the sacrifice of the most precious tie on earth—the father's link to his male child—the fundamental patrilineal connection. The myth of sacrifice ennobles that bond over all others. So at the same time that the Qur'ān underlines the limits of patrilineal affiliation . . . , it reinforces patrilineality, for it was the father in connection with the son that made for connection to the divine and won for father and son—and by extension all of humanity—long life on earth and eternal life thereafter.[60]

In view of his unique role in the biblical discourse of sacrifice, it is hardly surprising that in the Medinan period Abraham is connected with the introduction

55. On the pre-Qur'anic exegetical traditions of this story, see Speyer, *Die biblischen Erzählungen im Qoran*, 148–150.

56. See ibid., 164–166.

57. This is reflected in the Qur'anic Aqedah story, which seems to reflect the background of a pilgrimage rite; see Firestone, "Abraham."

58. Nagel, "Der erste Muslim"; see more recently also Nagel, *Muhammad. Leben und Legende.*

59. Delaney, *Abraham on Trial.*

60. Combs-Schilling, *Sacred Performances*, 57–58.

of the pilgrimage, which culminates in the performance of the sacrificial rites at Mina. It is he who makes the first call for pilgrimage, the *ḥajj*, Q M 22:26–27:[61]

> When we prepared for Abraham the site of the temple:
> "You are not to associate anything with me,
> and to purify my temple for those who circumambulate
> and those who stand and pray,
> and for those who kneel down and prostrate!
> And call out to people to go on pilgrimage,
> they shall come to you on foot,
> and on all kinds of lean riding animals,
> which shall come, from all the distant valleys."

Abraham's function as a founder of cult can hardly be overstated in its significance. A middle Meccan text already paves the way for the connection of Abraham to pilgrimage, through the contextualizing of the sacrificial event with the ancient Arabian rite of the "circumambulation," *saʿy* (Q II 37:102; see p. 392–393), here presupposed as already being a common practice. Abraham's being charged with enjoining people to perform the pilgrimage, made explicit in Medina (Q 22:26–27), lays the basis for the reinterpretation of the pilgrimage as a whole as an act of imitation of Abraham, which can be discerned already in early Islam. Following the example of Abraham, the pilgrims accomplish his (intended) sacrifice. The Abrahamic sacrifice, which prefigures the Islamic sacrifice, *aḍḥā*, the slaughter of a sacrificial animal obligatory for every pilgrim in Mecca, became a ubiquitous theme even of popular pictorial representation. That this is not a sacrifice in the biblically established sense of vicarious atonement[62] does not detract from its significance in Muslim piety.

11.3.3 Not "Father of Peoples"; "Paragon of Humanity"

In terms of religious politics, the significance of Abraham comes into view for the first time with his prayer for Mecca, communicated in a late Meccan sura (Q III 14:35–41). Abraham—so the prayer starts—has settled his progeny in Mecca, indirectly expressed as "in a valley without plant growth," and prays for their preservation and religious right-guidedness. Although Abraham's prayer transfers the most important activities out of their biblically attested milieu, the Holy Land, and into the Arabian Peninsula—and in so doing also inserts the son Ishmael, who is marginal in the Jewish tradition—the text does not show any polemical bias against the heirs and representatives of the older traditions. With Tilman Nagel,[63] it may be assumed that Abraham traditions, which connect him

61. See Sinai, *Studien zur frühen Koraninterpretation*, 144.
62. See chap. 9, 341–342.
63. Nagel, "Der erste Muslim"; see also Nagel, *Muhammad: Leben und Legende*.

with Mecca and the Meccan shrine, were already widespread on the peninsula before Islam. Biblical stories according to his thesis were already integrated into the local traditions at the time of the emergence of the Qur'an text. The Qur'anic reference to local history here attests to the community's new recollection of the local tradition, a shift in focus that was required in order to confront the pagans' insinuation that the believers had distanced themselves from the "paternal tradition." Nicolai Sinai, who has thoroughly analyzed the "Mecca pericope" (Q 14:35–41), comes to the conclusion: in that this pericope introduces Abraham into local Meccan history (probably through a processing of existing presumptions, which for us must remain diffuse), it rudimentarily "bridges the gap between the contemporary reality of the community and an imagined *counter-history*."[64] This gap had opened up since the middle Meccan period, through the construction of a close relationship of the community to Israelite salvation history.

No polemical tones can be read into this connection of Abraham to Mecca, which antedates the *hijra*. It is only later, in the central Medinan Abraham text (Q M 2:124–129), that not only does the genealogical Abraham-Ishmael lineage enter into the foreground, but the privilege of Abraham's progeny through Isaac is also explicitly denied. The text begins with a promise to Abraham, who is to be held up as a model, *imam*, for mankind generally, in recognition of his faithfulness even to the point of sacrificing his son—a promise that is immediately followed, however, by a divine restriction of favor: the clear rejection of a privileged rank of Abraham's decedents through Isaac conceded to them in Jewish tradition on the basis of the "dignity of the fathers," *zekhut avot*,[65] that is, by virtue of their genealogical descent, Q M 2:124:

> When Abraham was tested by his Lord through words
> that he then fulfilled.
> He spoke: "I want to make you an example for mankind."
> He spoke: "Also people from my descendants?"
> He spoke: "My covenant does not include the frivolous!'

In the Qur'an, the raising of Abraham to the rank of a universal model, *imāman li-l-nāsi*, "a model for mankind" is plainly clear. The divine intent to make this distinction public is found in the Jewish tradition as well, where the reinterpretation

64. Sinai, *Studien zur frühen Koraninterpretation*, 131.

65. This distinction of the progeny of Abraham stems from the promise of blessing, which follows in Genesis on the divine recognition of Abraham's faith: "Through your offspring all of the peoples of the earth shall be blessed, because you have heard my voice" (Gen 22:18). On this, see Aurelius, "Durch den Glauben gehorsam"; see also Schechter, *Rabbinic Theology*, 170ff. The Qur'anic retraction of the "merit of the fathers," *zekhut avot*—which is also attested by Speyer; see *Die biblichen Erzählungen im Qoran*, 169, and Sinai, *Studien zur frühen Koraninterpretation*, 138ff.—is all the more striking, since the "testings" (Q 2:124) that mentioned immediately beforehand, which Abraham underwent, are understood in Jewish tradition as actions by which he brought about the privileged status for his offspring; cf. Pirqe Avot 5:3.

of the biblical wording of Gen 22:12, "Now I know that you fear God," into the causative "Now I have made it known to all [that you have fear of God]," is attested in the Book of Jubilees, and it then has further iterations in the rabbinic tradition.[66] The promise of salvation to Abraham's progeny, following on divine recognition in Gen 22:18, is however turned down in the Qur'an in the address of God to Abraham (Q M 2:124).

The denial of this privilege in the Qur'an is interpreted by Nicolai Sinai in terms of religious politics:

> While in the Qur'anic version [of the sacrifice] Abraham's deed is valued merely as an individual merit [cf. Q II 37:105, 108–113], according to rabbinic conception it produced a collective salvific effect whereby the Medinan Jews could shore up their superiority against the Qur'anic community. Moreover, the *zekhut avot* idea was apt to neutralize the Qur'anic appeal to conversion. If God's forgiveness by the power of Abraham's zekhut, his readiness to sacrifice his son, is assured even for the renegade descendants of Abraham, and if the Jews are Abraham's descendants, there would exist no need for them to recognize the Qur'anic revelations out of fear of God's wrath. . . . It is very likely that this is the reason that Q 2:124, the "sacrifice pericope," is supplemented by an inversion of the promise of salvation that follows the sacrifice of the son according to Genesis.[67]

11.3.4 *The Synergetically Erected Shrine: Ishmael instead of Isaac*

What then follows in sura 2 is the requirement of Abraham and Ishmael, who enter together into sura 14, to purify the temple of God for the participants in cult (verse 125). After a petition by Abraham for the safety and the preservation of the residents (verse 126), there follows the great prayer for consecration of the Kaaba (verse 127), said by Abraham and Ishmael during their erection of the foundation walls of the Kaaba, which reminds in some details of the prayer for the consecration of the temple by Solomon, 1 Kings 8:14–61.[68] It culminates in a plea for the perfection of the Meccan worship, which in the form given by Abraham consisted only of the pilgrimage rites and the postures of humility required for prayer, but which is now to be complemented by a verbal liturgy. This specific petition is a *vaticinatio ex eventu* in the Qur'an, a prayer that had already found fulfillment with the onset of Muhammad's ministry, Q M 2:127–129:[69]

66. Cf. Kugel, *The Bible as It Was*, 172–173.
67. Sinai, *Studien zur frühen Koraninterpretation*, 140.
68. Neuwirth, "The Spiritual Meaning of Jerusalem in Islam."
69. On the idea, represented elsewhere in the Qur'an, that earlier scriptures had prophesied the coming of Muhammad, see Lazarus-Yafeh, *Intertwined Worlds*, 41–49, and McAuliffe, "The Qur'ānic Context."

wa-idh yarfaʿu Ibrāhīmu l-qawāʿida min l-bayti wa-Ismāʿīlu
rabbanā taqabbal minnā innaka anta l-samīʿu l-ʿalīm
rabbanā wa-jʿalnā muslimīna laka
wa-min dhurrīyatinā ummatan muslimatan laka
wa-arinā manāsikanā
wa-tub ʿalaynā innaka anta l-tawwābu l-raḥīm
rabbanā wa-bʿath fīhim rasūlan minhum
yatlū ʿalayhim āyātika wa-yuʿallimuhumu l-kitāba w-l-ḥikmata
wa-yuzakkīhim innaka anta l-ʿazīzu l-ḥakīm.

When Abraham began to erect the foundations of the temple, he and Ishmael [prayed there]:
"Our Lord, accept [our prayer, or: our sacrifice] from us!
You are the hearing and the seeing.
Our Lord, let us be submitted to you [*muslimīna*],
and make from our descendants a community submissive to you [*umma muslima*].
Guide us in our rites, and forgive us!
You are the one who forgives, the merciful.
Our Lord, send them a messenger from their midst,
to recite Your signs/verses to them
and teach them the scripture and the wisdom and purify them.
You are the powerful, the wise.

Neither the event of the erection of the Kaaba by Abraham and Ishmael nor their prayer is biblically grounded. Nor are they however a Qur'anic ad hoc construction, as has long been assumed in research, but rather, as Joseph Witztum[70] has convincingly shown, they constitute a Qur'anic restaging of the complex Late Antique vita of Abraham. In order to demonstrate this, Witztum contextualizes both the building activity of the two patriarchs (verse 127) and the prayer spoken by them with rabbinic and Christian traditions. While in the Qur'an we are faced with the building of a shrine, in the previous traditions it is instead an altar that is discussed: already Josephus has Isaac participate in the building of the altar on which he will be sacrificed.[71] It is this building whose erection the son is most strongly highlighted in the Christian traditions, as various Syriac and Greek homilies of the fourth and fifth centuries show which interpret the event in a Christological vein: father and son, the "wise architects of belief," together build the altar on which the redeeming sacrifice of the son will be offered. It should have been the Christological relevance of the father-son synergy that triggered

70. Witztum, "The Foundations of the House."

71. Ibid., 29. Further rabbinic sources quoted by Witztum are mostly drafted later than the Qur'an; see ibid., 30, note 32.

the promulgation of the altar topos in the Christian tradition, while Jewish traditions about the building of an altar after Josephus can only be traced back to the period after the emergence of the Qur'an.

In the Qur'anic reception, the idea of the altar is marginal; here, we are primarily dealing not with sacrifice but with the building of a concrete shrine, in which no sacrifice will be offered, but which will instead serve for the verbal worship of God. Abraham's following prayer is missing in the Christian texts; as it is in the Jewish tradition; Witztum can only refer to prayers spoken by Abraham alone, which relate not to the distant future, as in the Qur'an, but rather to Abraham's coping with the shocking situation of sacrifice. In the prayer, we should probably see not a recourse to Late Antique Abraham traditions as much as the expression of a new perception of the Meccan shrine. For the prayer can best be understood as a prayer for the "sanctity of the Kaaba" derived from the prayer for the sanctity of the Jerusalem temple (1 Kings 8:14–61, especially verses 33–34 and 55–58), a prayer which moreover should involve the son Ishmael, now acting in synergy with his father in the founding of the shrine.

If one takes into account the structural similarities of the three modes of a father-son synergy discussed in Late Antiquity, all engaged with the erecting of the respective shrine, then Ishmael takes part in the Meccan founding of the Kaaba, just as Isaac took part in the founding of the Jerusalem sacrificial site on Moriah or, according to the allegorical homilies, Christ in the founding of the sacrificial site of Golgotha. In the Qur'an, however, this father-son synergy lacks the mythic dimension, which in the other two traditions is culled from the weighty theological concept of sacrifice.

11.3.5 *Mecca Inherits Jerusalem*

The innovative attribution of the erection of the Kaaba to Abraham *and* Ishmael, their prayer together for the sacral integrity of the Kaaba, has further implications. It is a station on the way of the supersession of Jerusalem, previously so central for the community, by Mecca. Nicolai Sinai remarks: "Against the background of the erection of the Jerusalem temple on the site of Abraham's sacrifice, the invocation *ittakhidhū min maqāmi Ibrāhīma muṣallan* (Q M 2:125) could have originally had the meaning 'Take up the place in which Abraham stood, *when he wanted to accomplish the sacrifice of the son*, as a place of prayer!' . . . ; for with the emphatic identification of the sacrificial place as the Kaaba, Jerusalem has already been replaced by Mecca." An additional reference to Jerusalem is offered by the part of verse 125 that immediately precedes this invocation ("And when we made this temple into a place frequented by mankind, a sanctuary") where, with Josef Rivlin, one can see an allusion to Is 56:7—"for my Temple [*beti*] is called a house of prayer for all people."[72] Above all, Q M 2:129, on the coming

72. Sinai, *Studien zur frühen Koraninterpretation*, 142.

of a Prophet of scripture, must be read as evidence for the successive emerging of a cult which upholds the preeminence of Mecca over Jerusalem:[73] in Abraham's prayer, the important privilege of Jerusalem to be the original place of scripture and the liturgy of the word, are transferred to Mecca: what in Is 2:3 is true of Jerusalem ("For from Zion will come forth teaching and the word of God from Jerusalem") should now apply to Mecca, where with the arrival of Muhammad, the proclaimer of scripture and God's word that Abraham had prayed for, has appeared. With the participation of Ishmael, the progenitor of the Arabs, in the foundation of the shrine, a further step in the Arabizing of the cult is achieved.

The verses Q M 3:96–97 finally make clear the seniority of Mecca's sanctuary over that of Jerusalem, justified by Abraham as founder:

> The first temple, which was built for men,
> is that in Bakka [=Mecca],
> as blessing and right guidance for all the world.
> In it are clear signs,
> the place in which Abraham stood, whoever enters it is safe.

Mecca is thus "the first temple of God," that is, the older shrine with respect to Jerusalem, because it goes back all the way to Abraham. One could also claim: Mecca is the original Jerusalem. In this process of the "biblicizing" of Mecca, its cult, and its history, no figure is as deeply involved as Abraham.

11.3.6 The Abrahamic Covenant

In verse Q M 2:130, the covenant of Abraham, apparently considered as already established in fulfillment of the prayer, is declared the new and ideal collective identity:

> *wa-man yarghabu ʿan millati Ibrāhīma llā man safiha nafsahu*
> *wa-la-qadi ṣṭafaynāhu fī l-dunyā*
> *wa-innahu fī l-ākhirati la-mina l-ṣāliḥīn*
>
> Who would willfully abandon the covenant of Abraham,
> unless he wanted to make a fool of himself?
> We chose Abraham in this world,
> and in the hereafter he will be among the righteous.

The covenant of Abraham, *millat Ibrāhīm*, named after the biblical covenant of circumcision, Hebrew *berit mila*, is still ambiguous in the Qur'an: on the one hand *milla*,[74] borrowed from the Hebrew, means God's biblical covenant with Abraham

73. Neuwirth, "The Spiritual Meaning of Jerusalem in Islam."

74. On other interpretations, see Horovitz, *Koranische Untersuchungen*, 62–63; Jeffery, *Foreign Vocabulary*, 268–269; Ambros, *A Concise Dictionary*, 259. The lexeme *milla* already takes on the meaning of "community" during the Qur'anic development; see Q II 38:7. It occurs seven times in the Medinan suras, referring in all cases but one to Abraham: Q III 16:123, III 12:37–38, III 6:161.

delineated by circumcision, but at the same time it also designates the community of Muhammad, which now reconstitutes itself on the model of the Abrahamic covenant and identifies itself through the self-designation *millat Ibrāhīm*, "Abraham's covenant (community)," as a successor to the Abrahamic tradition.

This gradual appropriation of the figure of Abraham signifies at the same time its dissociation from the Jewish tradition surrounding it. For just when Abraham developed into a prototype of the new believers, *al-muslimīn* (Q M 2:135–136), he was also installed as the founder of the rites of the Arabic pilgrimage, which culminate in the slaughter of a sacrificial animal. To reclaim Abraham for a local praxis that must have been foreign to post-temple Judaism, which no longer permitted animal sacrifice, meant to distance him from the post-biblical foundations, which had previously been shared by the community and the neighboring Jewish groups. Indeed, the aspect of sacrifice, which in later Islam becomes the most visible marker of Abraham in popular religion and art, is not dominant in the Qur'anic image of Abraham, but rather ranks as a part of his earlier role as founder of monotheism *before* the revelation of scriptures. It is moreover an entirely demythologized sacrifice, as Q M 22:36 attests. Yet Abraham's function as the founder of the Meccan rites reveals a basic new reflection of the Qur'anic community regarding their relationship to Abraham and the traditions connected to him.

11.3.7 Abraham as "Righteous among the Peoples"

Abraham is not only the figure that transfers the decisive symbols and issues of belief from the Holy Land to Arabia but also the biblical figure that by the end of the Qur'anic development holds a unique position as having been active *before* the two great religions, and thus outside of them. Abraham takes on a symbolic character; he is a universal figure, who goes back before Judaism and Christianity. Q M 3:65–68:

> You people of the scripture, what do you dispute concerning Abraham, when both the Torah and the Gospel
> were first brought down after his time? Do you not understand?
> . . . .
> Abraham was not a Jew or a Christian.
> He was rather a god-pleasing *ḥanīf* [i.e., a servant of God from among the peoples].
> He was no idolater.
> The men who stand closest to Abraham are those who have followed him and this Prophet and those who believe!
> God is the friend of the believers.

The qualification *ḥanīf*, which is paraphrased as "servant of God from among the peoples," is Abrahams's designation at the end of the Qur'anic development.

What does the Arabic *ḥanīf*[75] mean? The Syriac word *ḥanpā*, from which it derives, means "heathen," or "one standing outside of established religion." In pre-Islamic poetry, however, *ḥanīf* occurs designating an ascetic who practices his worship alone. If one takes these two together, then *ḥanīf* bundles together independence from the established religions and exemplary piety, both characteristics of the Qur'anic Abraham. This increase in momentum of the figure of Abraham is no accident. He enters the stage at a time in which the image of the proclaimer himself is being formed anew. The erstwhile apostle, the "messenger," *rasūl*, in Medina has changed into a biblical "Prophet," *nabī*,[76] who places himself in the succession of prophets from Adam through Noah, Abraham, Moses, and Jesus. What is more, the proclaimer is not only a prophet from the biblical tradition but at the same time a prophet from a counter-tradition. Toward the end of his career he takes on the title of a *nabī ummī*, a "Prophet from among the peoples," Hebrew *navi me-ummot ha-'olam*.[77] *Ummī*, a calque, a new coining made up of more than one language, is on the one hand a derivation from the Arabic *umma*, "community," and on the other hand a transmission of the Hebrew *ummot ha-'olam*, "non-Jewish peoples." and forms the adjectival counterpart of *ḥanīf*, reserved almost exclusively for Abraham. This revaluation of the "peoples," who from the Jewish perspective were excluded from the privileges of the elect people, is connected to Abraham already by Paul,[78] as it is in the Qur'an. Gal 3:6–10 reads:

> Abraham trusted in God, and believed in him. This was credited to him as righteousness. Therefore know that those who are of faith are the sons of Abraham. And the scripture, foreseeing that God would justify the Gentiles through faith [i.e., if only they believe], announced beforehand to Abraham: "in you shall all nations be blessed." So those who are of faith are blessed along with Abraham, the man of faith.[79]

In the Qur'an, the revaluation of the "peoples" extends to those outside Judaism *and* Christianity who exalt the one God, and from among whom came the proclaimer himself, *al-nabī al-ummī*, "the Prophet from among the peoples," Q M 7:156–158:

> I shall write my mercy for those who are pious . . . /
> for those who follow the messenger,
> the Prophet from among the peoples [*al-nabī al-ummī*],

75. Rubin, "Ḥanīfiyya and Ka'ba."

76. Bobzin, "The Seal of the Prophets."

77. On the development of the word *ummī*, see Horovitz, *Koranische Untersuchungen*, 52–53, and Horovitz, *Jewish Proper Names*, 46–47.

78. I owe thanks to Friedmann Eisler for important insights regarding the Pauline conception.

79. Translation follows the English Standard Version (ESV).

whom they find indicated among them in the Torah and the Gospel,
who bids them to the good, and forbids them what is reprehensible,
who makes licit to them good things and forbids them bad things,
and takes away the oppressive obligations and chains that lie upon them. . . . / Speak: "O mankind, I am the messenger to you all
from God [*rasūlu llāh*], the ruler of the heaven and earth,
no God but him.
He grants life and gives death.
So believe in God, his messenger [*rasūlihi*],
the Prophet from among the peoples [*al-nabī al-ummī*],
who believes in God and his words, and follow him!"

Alongside the "Prophet from among the peoples," the "believers from among the peoples"—*al-ummīyūn*—are equally part of the salvific plan. Q M 62:1–2 encapsulates this development:

Glorifying God is all that exists in heaven and on earth,
the king, the holy, the powerful, the wise.
It is he who among the peoples [*al-ummīyūn*] has raised up a messenger [*rasūl*],
who reads to them his verses and purifies them
and teaches them the scripture and wisdom,
though they were previously in manifest error.

Here a revaluation of a descent "from among the peoples," which was already asserted by Paul, is repeated once again. The Prophet and his community are not simply "illiterate," or even "unlettered," as the qualification *ummī* is often understood. This understanding would be contradicted by his call "to teach the scripture and wisdom." *Ummī*, "from among the peoples," reflects rather the perception of a status outside the recognized religions, a perception that in Judaism was meant to be disparaging, but that was inverted into an honorary title.

Abraham, who in the Pauline conception already served an exemplary function, takes on an even richer role in the new model of the Qur'anic community: he becomes the actual founder of the new religion taking shape, which the proclaimer only comes to complete. Abraham—not Moses or Jesus—is for that reason the only biblical referent in the daily prayer of the community, which contains a short litany that brings together Muhammad and Abraham:

Allāhumma ṣallī ʿalā Muḥammadin wa-ʿalā Āli Muḥammad
ka-mā ṣallayta ʿalā Ibrāhīma wa-ʿalā Āli Ibrāhīm
wa-bārik ʿalā Muḥammadin wa-ʿalā Āli Muḥammad
ka-mā bārakta ʿalā Ibrāhīma wa-ʿalā Āli Ibrāhīm

God, bless Muhammad and the House of Muhammad
as you have blessed Abraham and the House of Abraham
And give salvation to Muhammad and the House of Muhammad
As you have given salvation to Abraham and the House of Abraham.

11.4 Moses—His Qur'anic Development

11.4.1 Moses's Calling—The Visions of the Proclaimer

A central historical development that runs parallel to the genesis of the Qur'an is the process of the proclaimer's becoming a prophet. To assume a role already shaped by eminent predecessors, is an act of self-authorization and at the same time an essential step to connect the community to biblical tradition.[80] The proclaimer was able to clearly perceive in the image of Moses, as though through a burning glass, the psychological contours of a prophet's becoming—the spiritual movement toward the transcendent God, the feeling of insufficient strength in the face of the task, the ambivalence between the obligation to familial lineage and the necessity of breaking with it, the experiencing of fear and overcoming it, and the power for patient persistence in a situation of humiliation. Thus, in the reflection of the life of Moses, the proclaimer experienced his own development as a divinely guided event.

Moses is evoked as the receiver of the Torah already in very early suras: *wa-l-tīni wa-l-zaytūn / wa-ṭūri Sinīn / wa-hādhā l-baladi l-amīn*, "By the fig tree and by the olive tree, / by Mount Sinai / and this secure city" (Q I 95:1–3); *wa-l-ṭūr / wa-l-kitābi l-masṭūr / fī raqqin manshūr / wa-l-bayti maʿmūr*, "By the Mount / and by the scripture, written down / on parchment unrolled / and by the visited house" (Q I 52:1–4). In these oaths, Moses's reception of the scripture is hinted at, which occurs as a divine self-manifestation in an especially distinguished site. Although the event of the giving of the Torah, together with Moses's deliverance of the Israelites through the Exodus from Egypt, is the most significant event in Moses's career in the Bible and in Jewish tradition, the earliest narrative testimonies of Moses in the Qur'an follow a different line. Moses occurs first as a warner, sent not for the liberation of his people but to convert an unbelieving ruler, Pharaoh. Indeed, Moses, unlike the other warner figures of the early suras, is ideally prepared for his task. He has experienced a call, in which he could hear the voice of God himself in a sanctified place (*bi-l-wādī l-muqaddasi Ṭuwā*, "in the sanctified valley of Ṭuwā," Q II 20:12), which instructs him to worship him alone and, reflecting early Meccan circumstances, to perform the ritual prayer

80. On Moses in the Qur'an, see Neuwirth, "Erzählen als kanonischer Prozess," and Wheeler, "Moses." Wheeler, however, bases his interpretation of the Moses texts on the exegetical tradition. The title of his monograph, *Moses in the Qur'ān*, is somewhat misleading in that it only deals with the story cycle of sura 18.

(verse 14). After an introduction given in an almost amicable tone to the performance of two magical tricks, which he will employ at Pharaoh's court (cf. Ex 4:3–7), he is dispatched to approach Pharaoh. Only through this authorization and after having been freed from fear—Moses prays *ishraḥ lī ṣadrī*, "Widen my breast," verse 25—does he assume a position from which to fulfill his public task. Like Moses, the proclaimer himself had experienced a deliverance, a "widening of his breast" (*a-lam nashraḥ laka ṣadrak*, "Have we not widened your breast?" Q I 94:1), before the beginning of his public proclamation.

Moses is a typological precursor of the proclaimer. Indeed, further shared characteristics cannot be overlooked, even if the two diverge from each other in important details: not unlike Moses, the proclaimer is also granted a personal encounter with God and experiences a vision[81] in which he sees God himself sitting upright on his throne: *dhū mirratin fa-stawā / wa-huwa bi-l-ufuqi l-aʿlā*, "Great in prestige he sat erect, enthroned / on the highest horizon" (Q I 53:6–7). While the site of the vision here remains open, the second vision of the proclaimer takes place, like Moses's meeting with God, in a specified place: *ʿinda sidrati l-muntahā / ʿindahā jannatu l-maʾwā*, "at the lote tree at the furthest end / there where the garden of the retreat is" (Q I 53:14–15). Here too it is a tree (or shrub) that is disturbingly altered. In place of the burning bush of thorns, or "the fire" of Moses (Ex 3:2–3 and Q II 20:10), is a "covered tree": *idh yaghshā l-sidrata mā yaghshā* "when the lote tree was covered by what covered [it]," Q 53:16.

Reading the two stories of encounter in context, it emerges that the middle Meccan story of Moses, together with its introduction, highlights just those details that are also relevant for the early Meccan vision report of the proclaimer; Moses's calling (Q II 20:1–5, 9–14):

> Ta ha. We have not revealed the *qurʾān* to you
> to make you unhappy
> but only as a reminder to him who fears
> a sending down from him
> who created the earth and the highest heavens
> The compassionate—he sits upright on the throne.
> . . . .
> Has the story of Moses reached you?
> When he saw a fire, he said to his people:
> "Wait, I have noticed a fire,
> perhaps I can bring you a torch from it
> or find guidance from it."
> Then when Moses approached it, there was a calling out to him:
> "Moses, I am your Lord, take off your shoes,

81. Cf. chap. 2, 68–71.

you are in the sanctified valley Ṭuwā
I have chosen you, so listen to what is being inspired.
I am God, there is no God but I!
So worship me and perform the prayer in my remembrance."

One can compare this to the vision of the proclaimer (Q 53:4–10, 13–18):

It is only an inspiration being given to him
taught to him by a mighty one
steadfast to look at. Enthroned
on the upper horizon.
Then he came closer and hung suspended,
only two bows' lengths or nearer.
And he inspired to his servant what he inspired. . . .
He saw him still another time
at the lote tree at the farthest end,
where the garden of retreat is
when the lote tree was covered by what it was covered by.
His sight did not fail nor did he err.
Of the signs of his Lord he saw the greatest.

Both Moses and the proclaimer are at first granted a visible sign: a mysterious fire for Moses and an appearance of God on the horizon for the proclaimer in a first vision a "covered" tree in a second. Moses then experiences an audition that seals his calling: God calls him directly, gives him his name, and instructs him to worship (Ex 3:4.15; Q II 20:9–14); he announces to him inspirations (Q II 20:13). The proclaimer also experiences an inspiration, though without being called by a voice; for him the encounter with God remains above all without a verbally unambiguous communication and instead lingers as a non-verbal "inspiration": *wa-awḥā ilā ʿabdihi mā awḥā*, "He inspired to his servant what he inspired" (Q I 53:10).

The second vision of the proclaimer remains limited wholly to vision: here, only the location in a specified place and the tree changed in its form recall the Moses scenario (Q I 53:14–15). Although the report about Moses's call in sura 20 is to be dated later than sura Q 53, the earlier text on the vision of the proclaimer clearly orients itself to the apparently familiar model of the call of Moses. But the differences between the two experiences are hard to ignore: the visions of the proclaimer are not an experience of calling. God does not reveal himself to him with his name, nor does he give him an unambiguous assignment, but rather grants to him a sign of his appearance (Q 53:10) or lets him witness a natural wonder (Q 53:18), without the inspiration thus received marking the beginning of his mission.[82] The double

82. For this reason, in looking for a text referring to a calling, the tradition has not made use of this vision report but rather made reference to other suras; on sura 96, see chap. 7, 247–250.

report in sura 53 is preceded by a still earlier vision report (Q I 81:15–29), which remains wholly without references to Moses. The relatedness to Moses seems to first become important at the end of the early Meccan period, as the discourse related to the followers of the people of God emerges, a discourse that dominates the middle Meccan texts.

Later presentations come to complete the image of the events of Moses's divine calling to prophethood through further details, but without whitewashing his ambivalent actions: while Moses remains in Egypt, he unintentionally kills a man (Q II 20:40, III 38:19–33) and must then go into hiding. On his way back from Midian, his place of exile, he then experiences his calling. But while the story of his childhood, the miraculous salvation from the Egyptian murder of children, and his stay in Midian all form parts of the narrative, the main focus in the Qur'an clearly lies in his debates with the unbelieving ruler, Pharaoh, whom he is not able to convince, and who instead triumphs over the messenger. There is no collective exodus that first has to be fought for, no founding of the feast of Passover—and thus no dramatic crisis of events to culminate in the Exodus. Instead, these events are mentioned later, and rather cursorily, without any connection to Moses's confrontation of Pharaoh. Taking the attempt of the conversion of Pharaoh as the central point of the Qur'anic story of Moses, which is linked to the biblical narrative only through the episode of Moses's magic tricks performed at Pharaoh's court, the story remains bound to the textual genre of the punishment legend, even if the messenger attempts to convert not his own people but rather his personal opponent, Pharaoh. As in other punishment legends, the unbelieving Pharaoh is indeed punished in the earthly world, but he awaits his more serious punishment in the next. The believers are saved, in this case not a small crowd but rather the people of the Israelites led by Moses in the Exodus, to whom is granted a miraculous crossing of the sea on dry feet.[83]

11.4.2 Moses's Exodus as a Model for the "Inner Exodus" of the Proclaimer

In the Jewish Moses tradition, there are two episodes that stand above all at the center: the deliverance of the people through the Exodus and the granting of the scripture, *matan tora*. Strikingly, these have no outstanding position in the Qur'an; Moses's confrontation with Pharaoh and his magicians clearly occupies the center of the story. However, the two biblically central events will figure as the model for the perception and presentation of key events in the life of the proclaimer himself. Indeed, the Exodus, reported three times in the Qur'an and which could seem to be a prefiguration of the *hijra*, is never linked explicitly to the *hijra* experience; rather, the experience of liberation conveyed by the Exodus

83. See Neuwirth, "Erzählen als kanonischer Prozess."

re-appears other Qur'an contexts. This is consistent with the paradigmatic character of the Exodus. Complete absence of this particular Mosaic experience in the Qur'an would have been surprising, since the "Exodus . . . is the central experience of the deliverance of Israel, treated in the scripture as a story of liberation in detailed or concise form in different places. Also in post-biblical time, the Exodus remains one of the key elements of Jewish history writing, of the reading of biblical tradition for the ascertainment of one's own identity and the lasting relation to YHWH, the deity of Israel; it becomes a central element of the cultural memory of Israel and is thus transferable to the respective present."[84] As such, it would seem also to be transferable to the experience of the Qur'anic community.

Yet, in what seems to be the clearest reference to Exodus in the Qur'an, the "nocturnal visionary journey," what is presented is, remarkably, not a collective liberation but a personal experience of liberation of the proclaimer. The event, which is resonant with the Qur'anic designation of Exodus, *isrāʾ/asrā*, "night journey," "to (make) travel at night," enables the proclaimer to gain—spatially conceived—spiritual freedom: the word *asrā*, in reference not to Moses but rather to the proclaimer, stands in Q II 17:1 for a new model of exodus, which is achieved not physically but rather in the imagination: the "visionary journey" from the place of social oppression, Mecca, which had become an unbearable place of sojourn for the believers, to a place of spiritual freedom, the sanctuary of Jerusalem.[85]

On the Mosaic Exodus, in Q II 26:52 it says: "We inspired to Moses: go out in the night with my servants [*asri bi-ʿibādī*], you will be followed." The story that is then narrated (verses 53–68, especially 61–66) dramatically reports the persecution of those in flight and their final salvation through a miracle: Moses parts the sea with his staff, so that the Israelites can pass drily between the towering waves, while Pharaoh drowns with his armies. While this punishment of Pharaoh is evoked numerous times (Q II 17:103, III 10:90, III 44:23–24, III 43:55, III 7:138, M 2:50, M 8:54), the Exodus as such occurs only two other times, and there in the same very condensed form (Q II 20:77 and III 44:23).

The striking verb *asrā bi-*, to "make (someone) journey at night," to "drive (one) out at night," occurs, apart from the Exodus context, in two mentions of the "nightly flight" of the people of Lot from Sodom (Q II 15:65 and III 11:81), and a single time in reference to the proclaimer. In Q II 17:1:

subḥāna lladhī asrā bi-ʿabdihi laylan
mina l-masjidi l-ḥarāmi ilā l-masjidi l-aqṣā
lladhī bāraknā ḥawlahu
li-nuriyahu mina āyātinā innahu huwa l-samīʿu l-baṣīr

84. Schiffner, *Lukas liest Exodus*, 20.

85. On the whole, see Neuwirth, "Erste Qibla—fernstes Masjid?" Cf. also Rubin, "Muhammad's Night Journey"; Cf. chap. 8, 282–290.

> Praised be He, who let his servant travel by night
> from the sacred place of worship to the far/further place of worship,
> whose precincts we have blessed, to show him our signs.
> He is the all-hearing, the all-seeing.

The verse is striking, since it does not introduce the proclaimer in second-person address, as is usual, but rather speaks about him in the third person. As Wansbrough has noted, the beginning sentence of the verse—whose internal rhyme eventually indicates that the passage was originally formulated as a short independent verse group—could be taken to refer to Moses if treated in isolation from the rest of the sura. But this interpretation is excluded by the two following sentences, which clearly mention a movement between the endpoints "sanctuary of Mecca" and the "site of the Jerusalem temple," and thus presuppose a scenario for which only the proclaimer sojourning in Mecca can be the actor. His mention in the third person is not unique in the Qur'an. An early sura even begins with a speech about, rather than to, the proclaimer: "He frowned and turned away" (Q I 80:1).

Verse Q II 17:1 can most probably be interpreted in the sense of an experience perceived as miraculous by the proclaimer, who was taken from his location, the Meccan sanctuary, *al-masjid al-ḥarām*,[86] to an apparently comparably sacred place, *al-masjid al-aqṣā*, the "far/further sanctuary." There, he received "signs," *āyāt*—a detail that recalls the earlier reported experiences of the vision of God in sura 53. The supernatural experience is, according to Islamic tradition, most probably to be imagined in the frame of prayer, where the "visionary transfer" of the proclaimer, here communicated through allusion, is most probably explainable. The idea of prayer also fits well with the interpretation of the majority of scholars of the destination site as Jerusalem,[87] whose temple Mount according to biblical and Jewish tradition is the crystallization point of prayer par excellence. With the assumption of the direction of prayer, *qibla*, toward Jerusalem, which—according to our hypothesis—belongs in the context of a set of middle Meccan cult reforms, the community had drawn symbolically closer to the local center of the biblical tradition. The salvation historical past that thus comes to the fore forms a text world in competition with reality, which one approaches in prayer through the physical gesture of bowing toward Jerusalem, as well as with cultic recitation. The experience of liberation innate in the Exodus thus becomes

86. The designation of the Meccan sanctuary as *al-masjid al-ḥarām* is striking; it first becomes frequent in Medina. In Mecca there is mostly reference to *al-bayt*, "the temple." The new expression may have been coined in analogy to the title *al-masjid al-aqṣā* for the Jerusalem temple, whose historical fate is discussed in the course of the sura.

87. But see Horovitz, *Koranische Untersuchungen*, 140, who views *aqṣā* as a reference to the seventh heaven; on this position, see Busse, "Jerusalem." Busse presents the same interpretation in "Jerusalem in the Story of Muhammad's Night Journey." This interpretation, which contradicts the explicit statement in verse 93 of the same sura, is problematic.

a model for the praying community's "inner exodus," their "emigration" into the memory world of the Israelites, which is actualized anew with every ritual prayer.

That the Exodus, as prototype of the taking of refuge of the believers from repressive, unbelieving wielders of power, is the decisive intertext for Q II 17:1 is suggested above all, however, by the structure of the sura itself, which, as has been shown, is underlain by a pattern of multiple parallels between Moses and the proclaimer,[88] to which the beginning verse of sura 17, with its recollection of an experience of Moses by the proclaimer, forms the prelude.

What is apparently less important in the Qur'anic understanding of the Exodus is the geographical location of the "Promised Land." This is located simply in a place where it is possible for the believers to practice their worship unmolested, be it because the unbelievers themselves are annihilated, as in the Moses story where the Israelites "inherit" the land left by their opponents (Q II 26:58–59), or be it because they simply no exposed after they have found their refuge elsewhere through a *hijra*, as for example in the story of Abraham (Q II 37:99). Finally, an Exodus, *isrāʾ*, can be achieved non-physically, that is, spiritually, as is shown in the example of the "night journey" of the proclaimer, his imagined displacement to the "far/further place of worship," the Jerusalem temple (Q 17:1).

11.4.3 Moses's Covenant on Sinai—A Qur'anic Shibboleth

Similarly to the Mosaic Exodus as a whole, the second great salvation historical event connected to Moses, the reception of the tablets, *matan tora*,[89] which together with the Exodus plays a central role in Jewish tradition, in the Qur'an remains an episode that is not unfolded narratively in a single instance but is rather summarized in two verses (Q 7:145–154) and evoked in one other verse (Q 20:80). This striking fact is comprehensible within the Qur'an: on the one hand, with the early developed concept of the transcendent "preserved tablet," *al-lawḥ al-maḥfūẓ* (Q I 85:22),[90] there is an intact replacement for the tablets that were shattered after first being handed over to Moses. In addition, according to a Qur'anic conception that was already developed early, the written divine word is kept in the transcendent realm, in a "hidden writing," *fī kitābin maknūn* (Q I 56:78), or on a "preserved tablet," from which it is communicated to the individual proclaimers. In that this mode of the reception of revelation, shared by all prophets, is conceived as oral, it is difficult to reconcile it with a handing over of scripture or parts of scripture in history to a privileged receiver.

But if the mode of biblical reception of revelation by Moses falls out of the Qur'anic schema, nevertheless the central element of the event on Sinai, the drawing of the covenant between the Israelites and God, is an event that is also

88. Neuwirth, "From the Sacred Mosque."

89. Fishbane, *Sacred Attunement*.

90. Cf. chap. 2, 282–290.

treated in the Qur'an. It is around this very event that a controversy rose up in Medina. The controversy culminates in the uncovering of what the community perceived to be a breach of trust, an act of hermeneutical deceit committed by the Medinan Jews. The presentation of the Sinai event by the Jewish interlocutors was understood, in any case, as a wanton deception, although it could also be explained simply as an unbiased recourse to a rabbinic tradition that reinterprets the biblical text in a self-critical way—a shibboleth that retrospectively can hardly be illuminated.[91] The evidence for the controversy over this story, which as such had already been proclaimed in late Meccan times, is scattered across several Medinan texts. What develops into a point of controversy is a recollection, at first quite uncontroversial, of the gathering at Sinai in Ex 19:18–19 (a description followed, in Ex 20:2–17, by the anticipatory revelation of the Ten Commandments):

> Moses led the people out to God from the camp. . . . The mountain was entirely covered with smoke, because the Lord had come down to him in the fire. The smoke rose like the smoke of a furnace. The whole mountain shook violently.

The scene is condensed in the late Meccan sura Q III 7:171 into a single verse:

> Then, when we shook the mountain over them
> as though it were a canopy,
> and they thought that it would fall on them:
> "Hold fast to what we have given you,
> and remember what it contains!
> Perhaps you will be God-fearing."

The answer of those addressed, which is not communicated in the cited text, is in the Pentateuch: *naʿse wa-nishmaʿ*, "We will do and hear" (Ex 24:7), or *shamaʿnu weʿasinu*, "We hear it and will do it" (Dtn 5:24). An analogous answer from the Israelites is at first lacking in the Qur'an, but is added in a later Medinan text, Q M 2:93, which reassumes the scenario of the drawing of covenant. It appears there however, disfigured:

> When we made the covenant with you
> and raised above you the mountain and said:
> "Take what we have given you and obey!"
> They said: "We hear and we disobey!" [*samiʿnā wa-ʿaṣaynā*].
> They were instilled with the love of the calf in their hearts.
> Say: "Evil is what your faith commands you, if you truly believe!"

91. The controversy is treated in detail in Hartwig, "Urvertrag."

This new answer of the Israelites, so contrary to the biblical one, cannot be linked to any verse of scripture, but is only explainable through oral tradition. It does not necessarily spring from an absolute error, but rather, as Julian Obermann has shown,[92] may go back to a play on words, specifically a calque.[93] In the biblical Hebrew wording *ʿasinu*, "we will do (it)," one can hear with only slight audible change the Arabic *ʿaṣaynā*, "we disobey," alternately—and this is the alleged stumbling block—this could have been deliberately produced through calculated manipulation. For, as a slightly later Qur'an text commenting on this verse attests, the irritating wording of the Israelite answer was understood as a wanton falsification of the biblical text. The Jewish interlocutors of the community are accused of having done this intentionally to their illiterate and ignorant compatriots in the new community.

Such an intention did not necessarily exist. Julian Obermann[94] has drawn attention to the fact that rabbinic tradition itself has preserved such a negative evaluation of the intention of the Israelites at Sinai. He cites *Shemot Rabba*, a Midrash to Exodus, where we read: "On the day when they stood at Sinai and said with their mouth: 'We will do it and hear it [*naʿase we-nishmaʿ*],' their hearts were already concerned with worship of idols [literally: astral bodies—*libbam haya mekhuwwan li-ʿavodat kokhavim*]." This interpretation is supported, according to Dirk Hartwig,[95] inter alia, by Psalm 78:36–37: "They deceived Jim with the mouth, and with their tongue they lied to Him. Their heart did not hold fast to Him, and they did not stay true to His covenant." This tradition already presupposes the insincerity of the Israelites addressed at Sinai to the God who demands to be worshipped alone, which they will then go on to prove through the worship of the calf. They would already have vowed their own disobedience, "we disobey," at Sinai. Whether the Jewish informants of the community had this interpretation in mind or not, the formulation of the answer of the Israelites in Q M 2:93 was in any case understood by the Qur'anic community as a wanton deception, which, according to the Qur'an, did not even stand alone. In the late Medinan verse Q M 4:46, it is brought together with comparable instances:

> Some of the Jews take words out of their context and say:
> "We hear and we disobey" [*samiʿnā wa-ʿaṣaynā*] . . .
> and thus they twist their tongues and abuse the religion. . . .

92. Obermann, "Koran and Agada."

93. On this language play, see Rippin, "The Poetics of Qurʾānic Punning," which however does not take account of the numerous cases of calques in the Qur'an.

94. Obermann, "Koran and Agada." This important article asserts for the first time—against the misleading interpretation in Wheeler, *Moses in the Qurʾān*, 1–3—the ambiguity of the judgment on the Israelites obtaining already in Judaism itself and which is attested in rabbinic tradition, as a possible vantage point of the Qur'anic community's perception of the other.

95. All of the texts discussed here, as well as important further evidence, have been treated by Hartwig, "Urvertrag."

It would have been better and more upright for them to say:
"We hear and we obey" [*samiʿnā wa-aṭaʿnā*],
but God has cursed them on account of their disbelief.
So they disbelieve except for a few.

Without being able to reconstruct this scenario of interreligious engagement with any final clarity, it can be asserted here that we are not dealing with a polemic of the new community against the biblically grounded Jewish foundational text, even if we find in Q M 2:93 a thrust diverging from the biblical text. Rather, this community feels misled in their effort toward the "right" reception of scripture by their Jewish interlocutors. Since the biblical and the post-biblical materials are difficult to distinguish in oral tradition, the community remained unaware of the fact that post-biblical exegesis had long interpreted the text in diverse ways. The key event of the divine drawing of a covenant with the Israelites thus fell outside of its politically neutral salvation historical context, so to speak; it became instead the site of remembrance of an incident of failed communication that was felt as humiliating. It may have been experiences and perceptions of this kind that finally led to the indictment of the manipulation of scripture, *taḥrīf al-kitāb* (Q M 2:75).[96]

11.4.4 *The New Covenant*

But it cannot be overlooked that the biblical establishment of covenant as such, which was understood as including the Israelites uniquely, did not fit well conceptually into the Qur'an, which had already in late Meccan time developed the conception of successive divine covenants with individual prophets,[97] and thus had advanced to a kind of prophet genealogy. It therefore should not be surprising that the Mosaic drawing of covenant is rethought in the Qur'an and given a universal form. A rabbinic tradition had already given a new thrust to the drawing of covenant at Sinai, questioning the exclusive privileging of the entitlement of the recipients. In the Midrash to the Song of Songs, *Shir ha-Shirim Rabba*, we read:

> As Israel stood before Mount Sinai to receive the Torah, God spoke to them: should I give to you the Torah undeservedly? Bring me warrantors for that, and I will give it to you! They said: Lord of the world, let our fathers be warrantors for us! Then God said: Your fathers need warrantors for themselves. They said: Let our prophets be warrantors for us! Then God said: I even object to them. They said: then let our children be our

96. See Lazarus-Yafeh, *Intertwined Worlds*, 18–35, and McAuliffe, "The Qur'ānic Context."

97. Cf. Samir, "The Theological Christian Influence," whose construction of dependency has, however, already been disputed by Marx, "Mariology in the Qur'an."

warrantors. Then God said: truly, those are good warrantors; for their sake I give you the Torah.

Dirk Hartwig has demonstrated that this text throws light on the Qur'anic discussion.[98] It has to be juxtaposed with Q M 7:172. That Qur'anic text, which marks the conclusion of the debate about the covenant in the Qur'an, formulating the Mosaic divine covenant anew, equally withdraws from the sacred historical past, orienting itself instead to the future. Here too, it is the "descendants" who should be the partners of the covenant. But the verse goes a step further than the rabbinic text, in that it removes the event entirely from history and transfers it—as had already occurred with the Mosaic tablets, which assumed a new form in the Qur'an as *al-lawḥ al-maḥfūẓ*, the "preserved tablet"—into the transcendent realm. The Medinan verse Q 7:172, which in the Qur'anic text follows immediately the verse on the Mosaic drawing of covenant, takes on for later Islamic theology the status of the decisive equivalent of the Mosaic covenant, it is the so-called *ʿahd al-last*, that is, the covenant sealed with the words *a-lastu bi-rabbikum*, "Am I not your Lord?":

When your Lord brought forth
from the loins of the children of Adam their posterity
and made them testify against themselves:
"Am I not your lord [*a-lastu bi-rabbikum*]?"
They said: "Yes, we testify to it" [*balā shahidnā*]—
Lest you should say on the day of resurrection:
"we were not aware of this."

This new covenant, which is a covenant in the transcendent realm,[99] could not be more universal—it is made outside of history, in preexistence, and is valid for all the descendants of Adam, whether or not they believe. They are all addressed by God, and are determined "naturally" for monotheism, so to speak, by their declaration of readiness delivered already before their birth.

With this episode, a central Moses event has made history again, in the communal engagement. It has however been detached from Moses, in that his role was obscured by the incident of a distorting wordplay, and "superseded" by the more universal covenant drawn in the transcendent realm. Certainly, the model of the drawing of covenants with distinguished prophets is maintained—these even yield a sequence that, opening with Adam or Noah, includes also Moses and the proclaimer. *Wa-idh akhadhnā mina l-nabīyīna mithāqahum wa-minka wa-min Nūḥin wa-Ibrāhīma wa-Mūsā wa-ʿĪsā bni Maryam* . . . , "Then, when we

98. Hartwig, "Urvertrag."

99. The covenant has been interpreted variously in the research; cf. Gramlich, "Der Urvertrag," and Kadi, "The Primordial Covenant."

made a covenant with the prophets, with you and with Noah, Abraham, Moses, and Jesus son of Mary . . ." (Q M 33:7). The decisive covenant with the people of Moses is replaced by a covenant, no longer privileging a prophet and his elect community of believers, that is drawn between God himself and men as a whole in preexistence.

11.4.5 Moses and Muhammad

We must not overlook, however, the fact that Moses, together with Abraham, is the model, indeed the "type," of the proclaimer. The performance of leadership and the lawgiving function that distinguish both the proclaimer and Moses come fully into view in Medinan texts, in which we also find reflections of the political activities of the proclaimer. Sura 2 links the instruction to fast on Ramadan (Q M 2:187–190) with the corresponding lawgiving of Moses, setting its narration into the frame of the Jewish Day of Atonement, Yom Kippur. Shlomo Dov Goitein remarks: "Moses's stay at Mount Sinai, the sin of the Golden Calf, God's forgiveness and his granting of scripture . . . are presented in sura 2 with particular emphasis."[100] But it is not the biblical text itself that provides the background here; instead it is obviously its oral reception in the liturgy. Goitein convincingly identified elements of the Yom Kippur liturgy in the text of sura 2—findings that fit together with reports from Islamic tradition attesting to a particular interest of the proclaimer and the community in this particular Jewish holiday. Goitein himself has shown that the Islamic fast grew out of the Jewish fasting practice, beginning, as is known, with the adoption of the one-day Yom Kippur fast. The successive formation of the Islamic Ramadan fast, which is reflected in the Qur'an, is apparently connected less to biblical textual than to liturgical traditions of the Jewish community in Medina.[101]

Yet another characteristic connects the work of Moses and Muhammad: both are granted a decisive, saving, victory over overwhelming enemies. The proclamation of sura 2 that contains the institution of the fast seems to have come soon after an important military victory, the Battle of Badr; both the saving victory *and the reception* of revelation are mentioned together in Q M 2:185, as the occasions for the establishment of the fast, so that the fasting month appears as "proofs of the right guidance and the saving decision,"[102] *bayinātin mina l-hudā wa-l-furqāni* (cf. Q M 44:1–4). The ambiguous word *furqān*—it can mean "decision" but also "salvation"—recalls the verse of commemoration of the Battle of Badr: "What we have sent down to our servants on the day of the saving decision [*yawma l-furqāni*], on the day, when the two armies went out against each

100. Goitein, "Zur Entstehung des Ramadans," 190.

101. Neuwirth, "Ramadan."

102. The word *furqān* as an inner-Arabic derivation denotes "decision"; as a Syriac loan word it denotes "saving."

other" (Q M 8:41). In this last context, *furqān* means a decisive, liberating victory over threatening enemies. *Furqān*, apparently in the sense of a saving victory, is a privilege of Moses: "Then, when we granted to Moses the scripture and the saving decision [*al-furqān*], so that he may be able to lead you" (Q M 2:53; cf. M 21:48).[103] It is these *two* experiences, the decisive victory and the communication of scripture, that the Qur'anic community shares with the people of Moses and that, as Kees Wagtendonk has concluded,[104] gave the occasion for the introduction of the Ramadan month of fasting.

This double etiology of the Islamic fast, as a thanksgiving for both the salvation *and* for the reception of scripture, fits in with the double role of Moses, who at once institutes a fast and at the same time is the recipient of scripture and the leader of his people. Even if Moses's double performance, both delivering scripture and effecting a national liberation, is not brought into connection in the Qur'an with his third role as giver of the law of fasting, it is these three services that Muhammad can lay claim to as a "second Moses": the transmission of a revelation, the leading out of his people/community from the situation of oppression that threatened their existence, the "liberation," and the implementation of orders of worship.

103. Marshall, *God, Muhammad and the Unbelievers*, 117–137, sees in the event at Badr the climax of a Prophetological development, which begins already with the early Meccan punishment legends: the enforcement of the inner-worldly punishment of the unbelieving opponents of the Prophet. They were annihilated in earlier history through the intervention of God. In Medina, the proclaimer and his dependents themselves become the instruments of the inner-worldly punishment of the unbelievers.

104. Wagtendonk, *Fasting in the Koran*.

12

The Qur'an and Poetry

12.1 Prophecy and Poetry

The close kinship between poets and prophets[1] is not a discovery of European Romanticism; it is manifest first in Antiquity. If we look at the books of the Bible that contain prophetic and poetic texts, we see that, as James Kugel shows,[2] there is a clear distinction between these two types apparent already in the procedure of the redactors who assigned the two categories to different text blocks. Kugel[3] sees this intention confirmed in the fact that the books of the "prophets," *nevi'im*, make up their own partial text corpus held distinct from other "writings," *ketuvim*. He also sees a similar distinction active in the later marking of reading pauses, *ṭeʿamim*, which distinguish the three books received as poetic—the Psalms, Proverbs, and Job, the so-called *Libri Metrici* of the Renaissance—by a unique system of reading techniques. Slightly later, in rabbinic Judaism, we even meet with an explicit and rigorous division between prophecy and poetry. Poetry is disdained to such a degree that the poetic activity of the biblical prophetess Deborah, for example, is presented as a demotion from her rank as a prophetess, even a punishment.[4] But such boundaries were blurred among Hellenized Jews. Among them, we even observe a close proximity between the literary forms of the Bible and those of the local cultural environment. Thus Josephus compares Moses and David to Greek poets, an approach that was continued and developed in the early church. Kugel cites the *Didascalia apostolorum*: "If you wish to read histories, take those of the Book of Kings; if you want poetry and wisdom, take the Prophets . . . if you desire songs, you have the Psalter."[5] He summarizes: "In the world of Western Christianity, Scripture in effect became a 'surrogate literature,' for a time rivaling classical texts in the curriculum; although the classics managed, more or less, to stay on in their educational role, learned churchmen from Jerome to the Renaissance did not tire of exalting the literary values of Scripture over classical (pagan) models."[6] Thus, the poetic side of prophecy over time came to be a subject of intense interest. On the other hand, the prophetic dimensions

1. See the illuminating remarks by Kermani, *Gott ist schön*, 342–456.
2. Kugel, "Introduction," 1–25, esp. 8–9.
3. Ibid., 9.
4. Ibid., 11.
5. Ibid., 13.
6. Ibid.

of certain poetic texts were pondered on, starting from Vergil's Fourth Eclogue to the books of the Sibyl. With the proliferation of the Greek concept of inspiration, a common mode of the mediation of prophecy and poetry became determined. Indeed, this concept opened the possibility for the understanding of all the books of the Hebrew Bible as inspired, and therefore prophetic—here, Kugel detects a decisive step toward canonization. It is to this debate that the field of tension between poetry and prophecy in the Qur'an is linked as well. In the Qur'an, however, instead of explicit debates we find implicit evidence, intertextual traces of an exchange. In what follows, five types of poetic-prophetic intertextuality in the Qur'an will be presented. The central reference text here is ancient Arabic poetry, which existed in the same language as the Qur'an.

12.1.1 *The Qur'anic Relationship to Poetry: A Terra Incognita*

While the relationship of the Qur'an to the neighboring monotheistic traditions across various language barriers has been a central critical interest since the beginnings of Qur'an research, the highly developed and extensively transmitted literature in the Qur'an's own language, ancient Arabic poetry, has rarely been contextualized with the Qur'an.[7] It is only in recent times that the request has been expressly raised for a connection of the two major early Arabic text corpora within a shared Late Antique research program.[8] Partially to blame for the neglect of poetry in Qur'an research is the verdict against the "authenticity" of early Arabic poetry that is connected to the figures of Taha Hussein[9] and Samuel Margoliouth.[10] For some researchers, even down to the present day, the dating of the initial systematic codification of the poetry in the eighth century, alongside that of the early Arabic heroic prose narratives, the *ayyām al-ʿArab*, raises questions about the authenticity of that poetry even as documentary evidence of intellectual history and is enough reason to ignore pre-Islamic literature altogether, even in the face of the widespread consensus among literary scholars about its authenticity. Thomas Bauer, in his programmatic essay of the relationship between poetry and Qur'an,[11] points also to a further prejudice, the claim that the *literary* texts of early Arabic poetry are irrelevant to the *religious* document of

7. Neither the introductory works Paret, *Mohammed und der Koran*; Bobzin, *Koran*, Cook, *Der Koran*; and Déroche, *Le Coran*, nor either of the two "companions," McAuliffe, *The Cambridge Companion*, and Rippin, *The Blackwell Companion*, discuss the significance of poetry in the Qur'an.

8. Montgomery, "The Empty Ḥijāz."

9. The Egyptian historian and cultural philosopher in 1926 raised the claim that ancient Arabic poetry was mostly the product of later philologists; see Hussein, *Fī l-Shiʿr al-Jāhilī*.

10. Margoliouth considered the poetry to be influenced by the Qur'an and to have first emerged in a later period; cf. his *Mohammed and the Rise of Islam*, 60; also Margoliouth, "Muhammad," 874, and especially Margoliouth, "The Origins of Arabic Poetry." His hypothesis raised a controversy into which significant researchers of his period entered, e.g., Lyall, "Some Aspects of Ancient Arabic Poetry," 374; Bräunlich, "Versuch einer literargeschichtlichen Betrachtungsweise," 826; Brockelmann, *GAL* I, 32–33; Levi Della Vida, "Pre-Islamic Arabia"; Blachere, *Histoire de la littérature arabe*, 83–117 (Gottfried Müller, personal communication).

11. Bauer, "The Relevance of Early Arabic Poetry," 702.

the Qur'an. Early Arabic poetry, it is true, contains little evidence relevant to the history of religion (apart from that of individual town dwellers such as Umayya ibn Abī Ṣalt);[12] but this overly strict limiting of source texts to clearly religious material is highly questionable. "Early Arabic literature," writes Bauer,

> will prove to be a far more productive source for the cultural background at the time of the Prophet if it is approached using current literary and cultural methods of inquiry appropriate to the sources at hand. An inquiry would need to turn—more systematically than has been done until now—to cultural patterns, attitudes and values, beliefs, and mores. One could attempt to explore concepts like virtue, honor, manliness and others as displayed in poetry, on the one hand, and in the Qur'an, on the other, and study basic issues such as ideas about death[13] and sexuality, expression of feelings such as fear, sorrow, and joy. Inquiries such as these would without doubt demonstrate the "originality of the Arab Prophet,"[14] which manifests itself not only vis-à-vis the earlier religious cultures but equally vis-à-vis his Arabian milieu, more effectively than any singular or one-sided approach limited to a history-of-religions approach.[15]

In several studies, James Montgomery has shown the productivity of such comparisons.[16] Until now, this avenue of research has remained largely unpursued, despite Toshihiko Izutsu's otherwise important studies on the ethical positions represented in the two text corpora.[17] Indeed, Izutsu's results are strongly limited by his neglect of a diachronic reading of the Qur'an; based on general judgments about the Qur'an as an undifferentiated whole, they are ill-suited to producing a reliable image.[18] There are only a few isolated investigations that throw light onto central concepts from both poetry and Qur'an, above all Werner Caskel's study on fate[19] and Tilman Seidensticker's study on the heart.[20] First steps toward a mental-historical comparison between poetry and Qur'an have been taken by Agnes Imhof, in her pathbreaking monograph on the image of man reflected in

12. On this poet, see Borg, "Umayya b. Abi al-Salt as a Poet"; Seidensticker, "The Authenticity of the Poems"; Montgomery, "Umayya b. Abi l-Salt"; Nöldeke, "Umaija." One should nonetheless assume a significant though still underestimated presence of Christian and Jewish Arabic poetry before and around the genesis of the Qur'an; cf. Nöldeke, "Samau'al"; Jacobi, "Mukhaḍram"; Dmitriev, "A Christian Arabic Account"; Hainthaler, "Adī ibn Zayd al-ʿIbādī."

13. For a short contrasting of death in battle in poetry and in the Qur'an, see Neuwirth, "From Sacrilege to Sacrifice"; on funeral poetry, see Borg, *Mit Poesie*.

14. This is the title of an essay by Fück that was programmatic for the Qur'anic scholarship of his time (1936), "Die Originalität des arabischen Propheten."

15. Bauer, "The Relevance of Early Arabic Poetry," 702–703.

16. Montgomery, *Vagaries of the Qasida*, 260–208.

17. Izutsu, *The Structure of the Ethical Terms*.

18. The same applies to Farrukh, *Das Bild des Frühislam*, which remains a valuable collection of work.

19. Caskel, *Das Schicksal*; see also more recently Dmitriev, *Das poetische Werk*, 105–128.

20. Seidensticker, *Altarabisch "Herz,"* and Seidensticker, *Das Verb sawwama*, which explore the meaning of Qur'anic expressions on the basis of early Arabic poetry; cf. also Seidensticker, "Herumirrende Dichter."

the work of several poets who were contemporary with Muhammad,[21] and by Ludwig Ammann, whose essay on the pre-Qur'anic Arabs coming to terms with contingency[22] reflected in poetry and the Qur'an will be resumed in what follows.

It is not just the "originality of the (Arab) Prophet" that would be brought into relief by the inclusion of poetry in Qur'an research but also the innovative, indeed revolutionary, dimension of the Qur'an itself, which only becomes clear against the background of early Arabic poetry. As Thomas Bauer emphasizes,[23] it should be assumed, contrary to the standard position of research, that poetry was an integral part of the formation of the Meccan and then Medinan countrymen of the Prophet. The heroic worldview that takes shape in poetry must have been a constant challenge and a central object of dispute for the Qur'anic community. In order to oppose a new social conception to the ideals constructed and enunciated in the poetry, that is, the anthropocentric ethos of Arab heroism, or *murū'a*, central concepts from the world of the poetry had to be confronted, and their compatibility with the new theocentric worldview had to be tested. In his contrasting of poetry and Qur'an, Bauer introduced the criterion of a "negative intertextuality," founded on the assertion that certain elements of the poetic canon are consciously bypassed or excluded in the process of the Qur'an's self-definition in relation to poetry. Beyond this assertion of an absence, it is also worthwhile to search for traces of the negotiation of such elements, in order to trace the process of their reformation or suppression. According to the hypotheses pursued here, the Qur'an is not merely a counter-model to poetry, but rather in its central points it is also a trans-formation or metamorphosis of poetry, which becomes the blueprint for a radical rethinking and which—as the spiritual achievement of an emerging community—would bring the revolutionary dimension of the new scripture into relief no less strikingly than the amalgamation of biblical and post-biblical traditions, which has so long functioned as the center of research.

12.1.2 *Inversion and Subversion of Poetic Discourse in the Qur'an*

Although on first view there may subsist an apparent discrepancy between the Qur'an, which calls for the self-submission of man to the will of God, and the poetic corpus, which calls for heroic self-assertion, nevertheless on closer study a more intricate relation come to the fore: The Qur'an highlights a number of central values that had been shaped in poetry, sometimes rigorously criticizing them but in other instances engaging them in negotiation and debate. Among these values reflected in the Qur'an are the cardinal virtues of the heroic ethos: "generosity," *jūd*; "bravery," *ḥamāsa*; "ancestral nobility," *nasab*; and the goal of self-immortalization, the striving after *khulūd*, with which the poet-hero seeks to

21. Imhof, *Religiöser Wandel*; Imhof, "The Qur'ān and the Prophet's Poet."
22. Ammann, *Die Geburt des Islam*.
23. Bauer, "The Relevance of Early Arabic Poetry."

combat the dominant perception of transitoriness, of time's destruction.[24] That these ideas are also major themes of the Qur'an is easily obscured by the fact that in the Qur'an they are not treated consistently but rather sporadically and, above all, because they are rigorously reinterpreted. *Jūd* is reconstrued in the Qur'an as a social behavior derived from man's createdness, and the *jūd*-motivated honor of the hero is thus replaced by the sovereignty of God. *Ḥamāsa*—tempered in its exuberance and extended in its application—is carried on in the form of the Qur'anic cardinal virtue of patient "persistence," *ṣabr*.[25] Finally, *nasab* is displaced in the Qur'an and transferred from the biological forefathers of the Bedouin elite to the spiritual forefathers of the community. Genealogy is re-embodied Qur'anically in the succession, *dhurriyya*, of Prophets, the new guarantors of authority of whom the proclaimer of the Qur'an is himself the final one, according to a late Qur'anic testimony (Q 33:40). These Qur'anic re-readings have not been the object of systematic investigation.

To examine, in the present state of research, the relationship between Qur'an and poetry, we must proceed from the Qur'an itself, investigating the explicit and implicit Qur'anic references to poetry. In several early suras, the proclaimer himself fends off insinuations from opponents who wish to discredit him as a *shāʿir*, "poet" or *kāhin*, "seer." This confrontation with what—in view of to the exclusive truth claim raised in the proclamation—had become a problematic counter-model of public speech is particularly relevant, in that it sheds light on the perception of poetry and mantic discourse in early Arab society. Even stronger evidence for the practical power of the poetical discourse is offered by the cases of poetic intertextuality in the Qur'an itself, where poetic topoi are negotiated in a new way, as can be shown by an initial sketch of the Qur'anic treatment of generosity, *jūd*.

Thomas Bauer's "negative intertextuality" not least refers to formal features that are avoided in the Qur'an.[26] In fact, Qur'anic discourse is not poetry in the conventional sense. But, with a broader perspective of poetry in mind, one could speak of a new form of religious poetry in a large range of texts of the Qur'an. The Qur'an with its short text units bundled by a distinctive rhyme, displays a viable alternative form to the metrically bound monorhyme poetry—which no less could justly claim to be "poetic." This praxis of the simultaneous employment of semantic, morphological, and phonetic references within the limited space of just a few verses—succeeds in generating an innovative form of utterance. It is operative above all in the early Meccan suras. To proceed from these rather minute commonalities and divergences to the more fundamental questions of the history of mentalities, one has to discuss, building on the work of Ludwig Ammann, the

24. See Ammann, *Die Geburt des Islam*.
25. Cf. Cragg, *The Event of the Qur'ān*, 157–160.
26. See Bauer, "The Relevance of Early Arabic Poetry."

Qur'anic claim to have inherited from poetry the age-old function of coping with contingency.

Early Arabic poetry deserves the intense interest of Qur'an research, not only because it is a literary corpus that formed part of the "formative canon" shared by the proclaimer and his hearers. Poetry, as an authoritative expression of mental, social, and political conditions, is also instrumental in the history of the proclamation itself. During the ministry of the proclaimer, individual poets appeared who, in competition with him, used the authority of their ancestral function as public speakers to engage the proclaimer in disputes though occasionally also to support him. Twice we find explicit mention of these figures in the Qur'an, in Q 26:224–226 and Q 26:227. Bauer's new interpretation of verses 224–226 represents an attempt to revise the earlier reading of the entire sura 26, "The Poets," and to make sense of its emphasis on the "untruthfulness" of poetry in contrast to the "truthfulness" of mantic discourse.

The relationship between Qur'an and poetry can also be investigated in a still broader aspect: it is a uniquely felicitous accident in the history of transmission that, in addition to the Qur'anic evidence, texts have been transmitted authored by poets who interacted with the proclaimer in Medina, which become relevant as Qur'anic paratexts, parallel evidence for the Qur'anic assessment of the social situation and general atmosphere in Medina. In several cases, these texts throw light on particular political events that are merely alluded to in the Qur'an. These texts have not been consistently taken into account in Qur'an research, although some of the events mentioned here, such as slanders of the Prophet and the arranged killings of poets, have long been integrated into the Prophet-biographical literature. A thorough analysis of the relevant poems has been offered in a recent study by Agnes Imhof,[27] which can here be merely referred to.

12.2 The Ambivalent Heritage of Poetdom and Seerdom

> The Prophetic type that Muhammad represents is not easy to grasp. There are mentions of visions in the Qur'an, but we do not know whether they occurred at the earliest phase. Ecstatic experiences are reported; Muhammad apparently covered himself in these instances, as is familiar from other visionaries. But the Qur'an gives only hints, and the later exegeses have often obscured them. . . . The only firm criterion that we possess is the diction: short, frequently elliptical, abbreviated sayings, reminding one of outbursts and introduced by puzzling oath forms, held together by urgent prose rhymes, gripping images brought into closely packed succession with each other—the style of a fortune teller, well-known to the

27. Imhof, *Religiöser Wandel*.

> Arabs. It is to them that Muhammad is probably related most strongly in his behavior; of prophecy in the sense of the Old Testament, he knew nothing. . . . For that reason, it is to fortune tellers or the possessed that his contemporaries most often compared him—or to poets, who were also thought to be possessed or inspired by a *jinn*. He himself indignantly rejected this accusation, most likely because he was well aware of his vitiating closeness to these false predecessors. Of course, he was correct to emphasize the difference: what he brought forward was no longer a telling of signs, and, above all, he sought no payment for his visions. He worked under holy compulsion.[28]

Van Ess's classic presentation presents the proclaimer, at least at the start of his activity, alongside models from the pagan Arab world: the two older speaker types of his environment, who shared the essential characteristic of excited, emphatic speech in *saj*ʿ, concise rhymed discourse: the "seer," *kāhin*, and the poet, *shāʿir*.

12.2.1 The Seer

The connection to the early Arabic "seer," *kāhin*, pl. *kuhhān*, who articulated his speech in an ecstatic state, is most problematic for the proclaimer of a strict monotheism: the early Arab *kāhin* belongs to the cultic personnel of the pagan shrines, whose cult was soon to be brought to an end by the victory of Islam. Seers who continued to perform until the onset of Islam are—if we follow the largely unexamined evidence of the traditional literature—persons who under supernatural compulsion articulated oracular pronouncements, often introduced by mysterious oaths and accompanied by magical practices, without rational control over their expressions, which were presented as messages received from inspiring forces in the form of direct "second-person" address. They performed these tasks at the order of groups or individuals that sought counsel or help, and sometimes also accepted payment for this. Although the Qur'an offers only polemic against the seers, it nonetheless attests a clearly perceived formal relationship to the mantic forms of discourse of the early Arab seers, whose oracular pronouncements were characterized by metrically undefined rhyming prose, which shared with the early Meccan suras the form of the introductory oath cluster, a form that is nowhere else in evidence. Qur'anic features that could formally be perceived as a break with early Arabic poetry becomes plausible in connection to the pronouncements of seers. Yet, a source-critical and hermeneutically grounded processing of the early Arabic mantic traditions still remains to be carried out. Reports regarding seers, from the fifth to sixth centuries recorded in later sources, were collected by Julius Wellhausen;[29] but the

28. Van Ess, "Islam," 38; Hirschfeld, *New Researches* (1906), is already more critical. See in general Neuwirth, "Der historische Muhammad im Spiegel des Koran."

29. Wellhausen, *Reste*, 130–140.

authenticity of these pronouncements must always be interrogated, since *kāhin* traditions are essentially dubious, representing evidence of rites that had long become obsolete and could thus easily be distorted or even fabricated. More recent researchers, such as Toufic Fahd, have placed the Arabic *kāhin* in a comparative ancient Near Eastern context, and have attempted to draw conclusions about various seer functions but do not go beyond defining the *kāhin* in the immediate pre-Islamic period as "a bearer of supernatural wisdom inspired by a demon or *ṭābiʿ*," or "a proclaimer and interpreter of oracular communications from an individual deity."[30]

12.2.2 *The Poet*

In comparison, the second association that the Meccan opponents draw for the speaker, that with the poets, at first seems innocuous. But who is meant by the poet? It is not entirely clear that the *shāʿir* references in the pagan accusations refer to the authors of socially prestigious qasidas, the complexly constructed long-form poems. Typological similarities would rather suggest the authors of spontaneously produced occasional poetry in the vernacular, following none of the complex meters of long-form poetry but rather the primitive iambic meter *rajaz*.[31] The *shāʿir* of this simpler type shares with the *kāhin* the verbal form of utterances composed out of a few closely linked parallel verses, which, although organized metrically through the simple iambic verse meter, still clearly reflect an emergence from strong psychic excitement. It is this type above all who, as Ignaz Goldziher showed,[32] is traditionally considered to be possessed, *majnūn* by a demon (*jinn, shayṭān, ṭābiʿ*) bound to him personally. But the Qur'anic denigration of the proclaimer as a poet is not unambiguous. At least once, he is also connected to the qasida poets. This form seems to be referred to in the polemical evocation of a poetic motif, which the Meccan mockers "quote" in order to illustrate their disdain of poets: in Q 52:30 they ridicule the proclaimer: *am yaqūlūna shāʿirun natarabbaṣu bihi rayba l-manūn*, "Or do they say: 'A poet! Let us wait and see what the powers of fate do to him!' "[33] The *rayb al-manūn* is a topos of the qasida, where the power of fate is a central object. With this reference, it seems that they attempt to fight the putative poet with his own weapons. The proclaimer is likewise instructed to play at the same game: *qul tarabbaṣū fa-innī maʿakum mina l-mutarabbiṣin*, "Say: just wait, I wait with you!" (verse 31). Despite these references to the qasida, the association with *rajaz* poets cannot be dismissed out of hand. Even if we were to assume that the belief in inspiration through *jinn* had

30. Fahd, "Kāhin" 421. But see the contrary position—presented somewhat selectively—in Stewart, "Soothsayer."

31. Ullmann, *Untersuchungen zur Rajazpoesie.*

32. Goldziher, *Abhandlungen.*

33. Bauer, "The Relevance of Early Arabic Poetry," 723–725.

faded at the time of the Qur'anic proclamation,[34] so that invoking the *jinn* had become a mere verbal convention, nevertheless the Meccan accusations seem to be related to reminiscences of these sources of inspiration, originally relevant to both *kāhin* and *shāʿir*.

Seen from the social perspective, the proclaimer's arguments should have been convincing. For in their social function or in the particular thrust of their articulation, the two old speaker types, *kāhin* and *shāʿir*, do not show much similarity to the proclaimer: the *kāhin* is responsible for the communication of practically useful supernatural knowledge, while the *shāʿir* is generally responsible for the (occasionally aggressive) public representation of his clan; the proclaimer, as against that, is primarily communicating a pious teaching. Where then should we look for the shared characteristics that might have triggered the insinuations of the Meccans? Might they lie in the ecstatic disposition of the proclaimer, as described in the opening quotation above? Or do they lie rather in the alleged sources of inspiration for the two speaker types? Let us look at the Qur'an itself on this matter, and then at some literary evidence from early Islam.

12.2.3 *The Proclaimer as Ecstatic Speaker? The Meccan Insinuations*

The characterization quoted at the start, which concludes in favor of an ecstatic disposition, is in no way a construct of Western criticism but is indeed supported in large part by the Qur'an and by a significant body of indigenous exegesis. In fifteen places within the Qur'an, we find energetic defenses mounted against the insinuations, brought forward forcefully and repeatedly by the Meccans, that the proclaimer is *majnūn*, possessed by *jinns*, demons, or inspiring spirits, or that he is a *kāhin* or *shāʿir*. In later suras, this defense takes on a stereotyped character; but its initial aspects convey the impression of a primarily real shock effect that shozld have triggered these insinuations. Of the total fifteen places in which we find language related to pagan types of inspiration, two early Meccan pieces of evidence will be presented more closely in what follows: Q 81:19–27 and 52:29–34.[35] For clarification of the particular steps of the argumentation, we offer a schematic classification:

I = (a) transmitter of the discourse to the proclaimer; (b) rejection of the "false" transmitter

II = producer of the message

III = receiver of the message; a/b/c/d/e/f each defense against an allegation of the receiver as (a) possessed, (b) suppressing secret knowledge, (c) accepting wages, (d) *kāhin*, (e) *shāʿir*, (f) devising something arbitrarily

34. The survival of the belief in *jinn* inspiration, which for the time of the Prophet had already been questioned by Goldziher, *Abhandlungen*, cannot be proven by the reports drawn from the *Kitāb al-Aghānī* presented by Shahid in "A Contribution to Koranic Exegesis," 563–580. On invective poetry, see van Gelder, *The Bad and the Ugly*.

35. The other two early Meccan statements of self-defense are Q 68:1–4, 46–52, and 69:40–48.

IV = reception situation
V = qualification of the discourse as liturgical text
VI = performance situation

Q 81:19–27

innahu la-qawlu rasūlin karīm
dhī qūwatin ʿinda dhī l-ʿarshi makīn
muṭāʿin thamma amīn
wa-mā ṣāḥibukum bi-majnūn
wa-la-qad raʾāhu bi-l-ufuqi l-mubīn
wa-mā huwa ʿalā l-ghaybi bi-ḍanīn
wa-mā huwa bi-qawli shayṭānin rajīm
fa-ayna tadhhabūn
in huwa illā dhikrun li-l-ʿālamīn

It is none but the speech of a noble messenger (Ia),
with power before the Lord of the throne (Ia, II),
to be obeyed and be trusted (Ia).
Your companion is not possessed (IIIa),
he saw him on the clear horizon (IV),
He is not greedy about what is hidden (II).
It is not the speech of a cursed Satan (Ib),
So where are you heading?
It is but a reminder to the worlds (V).

In suras 69 and 52 we find an additional accusation, that the proclaimer invents parts of his message independently: sura 52, belonging already to the end of the early Meccan period, contains a challenge; Q 52:29–34:

fa-dhakkir fa-mā anta bi-niʿmati rabbika bi-kāhinin wa-lā majnūn
am yaqūlūna shāʿirun natarabbaṣu bihi rayba l-manūn
qul tarabbaṣū fa-innī maʿakum mina l-mutarabbiṣīn
am taʾmuruhum aḥlāmuhum bi-hādhā am hum qawmun ṭāghūn
am yaqūlūna taqawwalahu bal lā yuʾminūn
fa-l-yaʾtū bi-ḥadīthin mithlihi in kānū ṣādiqīn

So recall! By the grace of your Lord,
you are not a seer or one possessed. (IIId, a)
They say: "A poet! Let us await the ill-doings of fate for him!" (IIIe)
Say: "Wait. I shall be one of those waiting with you."
Do their whims command them to do this? They are an insolent people!
Or do they say: "he has invented it?" No, they do not believe! (IIIf)
Let them bring a discourse like it, if they are truthful!

Again and again the proclaimer defends himself against the ranking of his experience of revelation alongside older models of inspiration: he defends himself against the *kāhin* accusation with the remark that he receives no payment (Q 68:46) and harbors no hidden wisdom; he defends himself against the charge of being a *shāʿir* and *majnūn* by claiming he has a more wholesome attitude (Q 68:4) and defends himself against the accusation of arbitrary fabrication of parts of his message by pointing to the mortal danger of such actions (Q 68:44–46). Clearly, he understands these accusations also as insinuations of the compromising *social/moral* behavior characteristic of seers and poets-for-pay. That his own personal chief argument, the steadfast reference to his own other sources of inspiration, does not catch on, should not be surprising in view of his opponents' expectations. His whole project of self-justification comes to nothing, since for the Meccans these were clearly not concrete, objectively founded accusations. The identification of Muhammad as *shāʿir* and *kāhin*, which are mutually exclusive if taken in a strict sense, already points to the Meccan dilemma described aptly by Albrecht Noth:[36] "The shared feature in these attempts by *Quraysh* to classify Muhammad among their common personal categories, can be seen in the fact that they identify him as a social outsider. . . . For [the *Quraysh*], it was . . . difficult to comprehend *functionally* the self-understanding of Muhammad . . . , [someone who] had the task of warning his fellow tribespeople, since for them, this was no such current character type [and] thus they were never able to properly classify the proclaimer from the *Hāšim* clan."

Corresponding to this, the proclaimer himself has no verbal designation for the role available to him; he resorts to functional terms such as "warner," *nadhīr* (Q 51:50–51) and *mundhir* (Q 79:45), and "recaller," *mudhakkir* (Q 88:21); the title of the receiver of the divine message, *rasūl*, envoy, apostle, which will later be used as his personal title of honor, is connected not to him in the early Meccan suras but instead to the divine messenger. The reference to the message itself with the ambiguous word *dhikr*, "reminder," or rather "recitation,"[37] seems also to have been unfamiliar, particularly in light of its constant qualification by the Aramaic loanword *li-l-ʿālamīn*, "for the worlds," which makes reference to a Jewish-Christian context that was not highly appreciated to the pagan Meccans.

12.2.4 *Sira versus Qur'an*

Should we interpret the Meccan accusations, clearly received as harmful, in terms of a psychological insecurity on the part of the proclaimer, in terms of an initially suspected nearness to the earlier speaker types? The inner-Qur'anic evidence does not make this clear; the confrontations culminate rather in the

36. Noth, "Früher Islam," 20.

37. On this understanding of *dhikr*, literally "reminiscence, remembrance, warning," in the sense of an abbreviation of *udhkuri sma rabbika*, "Praise the name of your Lord! Recite, praise!" see Rubin, "*Iqra bi-smi rabbika . . . !*"

statement that the speech being performed is a liturgical text, a *dhikr*, not an ephemeral communication in fulfillment of a seer's or poet's task. It is in this, in the misperception of the message, that we have to see what was truly harsh and shocking about the insinuations, not in the disclosure of embarrassing similarities suggested by tradition; if it were not so, the telltale diction would hardly have been maintained for so long after these accusations were lifted. We do find attestations of Muhammad's fears of being closely related to the *kāhin* type, but this occurs only in the Sira, which was codified some hundred years after the Qur'an and from which the linking of the proclaimer to the *kāhin*, and only to this type, was carried over into the Western discussions. In the Sira, we find for example the attribution to the Prophet of a confession to his wife Khadīja: "I see a light and hear a voice. I am afraid I may be a *kāhin*."[38]

The Sira should possess no documentary value, yet this particular piece of evidence, because it diverges notably from the elevated image of the Prophet that later became canonical, has frequently been accepted as historical. Rudi Paret speaks approvingly of the presentation in the Sira of "a kind of obsession on the part of Muhammad, creeping into his consciousness."[39] Were this taken for granted, the Prophet would have to have suffered from such a complex until around the end of the middle Meccan period—since corresponding polemic passages are found still in later suras. Even a superficial acquaintance with the Sira is sufficient to recognize a pattern in such passages that is characteristic of its type of exegesis, that is, imposing of a narrative-edifying interpretation on a Qur'an verse that was felt to be devoid of dramatic pathos.

12.2.5 Qur'anic Testimonies on the Reception of Revelation

But it is primarily the Qur'anic testimony about the reception process of revelation that makes an ecstatic disposition of the proclaimer extremely unlikely, above all suras 73 and 74, in which he is portrayed preparing himself for the reception of new revelations during nighttime. What we find here are outlines of divine worship largely on the model of the monastic night worship, the vigil, familiar in the region. A special emphasis is laid on the particular liturgical performance, on the *tartīl* required from the proclaimer, probably a reference to techniques of psalm-chanting.[40] The notion is conveyed that at this special time

38. The quotation attributed to the proclaimer in Ibn Sa'd, *Al-Ṭabaqāt al-Kubrā*, 195, referred to by Paret, *Mohammed und der Koran*, 51, and which could be supplemented with an abundance of parallels, can be easily explained through the "Midrashic technique" of the Sira, whereby individual elements of Qur'anic verses are expanded into independent narratives.

39. Paret, *Mohammed und der Koran*, 51.

40. On the vigils, see chap. 2, 71–73. For the requirement of cantilena as a ceremonial form of reciting the suras, we need not rely on evidence from the native lexicography, which understands *tartīl* in Q73:4 in the technical sense of the Qur'an recitation with cantilena that was developed later. The form of the Qur'anic verse itself suggests this designation; cf. Neuwirth, *Studien zur Komposition*. 117–174; cf. chap. 5, 189–190.

of day, and particularly in the situation of the conducting of the liturgy,[41] words become more effective. There is no reference to a state of trance, in which divine contact usually occurs according to the ancient Near Eastern concepts of seerdom and prophethood, *ḥazon* and *nevu'a*;[42] neither is there any clear reference to ritual self-covering in the face of present shock. The two supposed references to the proclaimer's self-covering in the beginning verses of suras 73 and 74 both appear on closer inspection to be no more than references to the specific gown worn by the proclaimer at night, who by this time of late vigil has put on a kind of cape, called either a *dithār* or *zimāl*.[43]

Nor does the argument linking the proclaimer with the *kāhin* on account of his visions carry much weight, as the visions, which are limited expressly to two in sura 53, the first of which perhaps corresponding to the earlier vision in sura 81, are mentioned in a subdued tone and are connected there to the legitimization of the Qur'anic message through claims of a truly divine origin.[44]

Thus, the only remaining proof from the catalogue presented by Josef van Ess for the hypothesis of an essentially ecstatic disposition of the proclaimer would be the diction of the Qur'an itself.

12.2.6 The Real "Offense": Proximity to Ancient Discourse Types in the Qur'an

It certainly cannot be denied that certain formal markers of the early suras were meant to raise associations with the discourse of an ecstatic speaker, the *kāhin* discourse or, in the case of one single complete sura, sura 111,[45] *rajaz* poetry and the *shāʿir* discourse. Here we should think above all of the oaths, and in particular the suras that are introduced with entire oath clusters. One of these suras will now be compared with an example of seer discourse, the sayings of the seer Saṭīḥ before the Yemeni king Rabīʿa ibn Naṣr.

The *Life of the Prophet* by Ibn Isḥāq in its section dedicated to pre-Islamic history transmits an episode, that can shed light on the function and structure of the discourse of the ancient Arab seer.[46] The Yemeni king Rabīʿa ibn Naṣr has a dream vision, which he wants to have interpreted by his seer, Saṭīḥ; in order to show his

41. Apart from the specific reference in Q 73:1–8 to the development of early Meccan suras from the context of vigils, individual introductions to the suras also refer to this same process; see Neuwirth, "Images and Metaphors"

42. On *ḥazon*, cf. Jepsen, "Hazon"; on *nevuʿa*, see H. P. Müller, "Nebhu'ah.

43. See Rubin, "The Shrouded Messenger."

44. See chap. 3, 68–71.

45. See Fischer, *Der Wert der vorhandenen Koran-Übersetzungen*; cf. chap. 5, 182–184; cf. van Gelder, *The Bad and the Ugly*, 20–24.

46. Ibn Isḥāq, *Sīra*, 15–17; Guillaume, *The Life of Mohammad*, 4–6.

competence, Satīḥ must first repeat back the dream itself.[47] His pronouncement has the following structure:

Enigma:
ra'ayta ḥumama
kharajat min ẓuluma
fa-waqa'at bi-arḍi tahama
fa-akalat minhā kulla dhāti jumjuma

Something hot and glowing you saw
come forth out of darkness.
It fell over the flat land
and consumed everything that had life.

Presented first is the enigmatic dream, the enigma: a threatening phenomenon emerging from the darkness, descending over the land, and finally obliterating all life. This dream vision, which is apparently politically intended, permits a concrete interpretation.

The interpretation of the enigma begins with an oath, which likewise refers to threatening phenomena, but ones known through social experience; this is then followed, in the form of the pronouncement of an oath, by the identification of the aggressors and the revealing of the catastrophe.
Analysis of the enigma:

aḥlifu bi-mā bayna l-ḥarratayni min ḥanash
la-tahbuṭanna arḍakumu l-ḥabash
fa-la-yamlukunna mā bayna Abyana ilā Jurash

By the snakes between the lava plains I swear:
The Ethiopians will fall upon your land,
They will rule from Abyan to Jurash.

This discourse model can also be observed in several early suras, particularly in sura 100, "The Runners," which was discussed in chapter 10. The short sura[48] consists also of these two parts, enigma and analysis of the enigma, divided by a brief paraenetic interlude: the riddle, corresponding to the obscure vision of the king, is formed into a series of oaths, in which coded elements of social experience (horses, riders) are conjured and conveyed with a sense of fast approach.

47. For the historical background, see Rothstein, *Lakhmiden*, 39.

48. For a discussion of this sura's structure and its typological counterparts in the Qur'an, see Neuwirth, "Images and Metaphors," 6–12. The sura is discussed in chap. 10, 359–365, for a second time, in relation to allegorical speech.

The oath series culminates in the disclosure of aggression in verse 5, though this aggression cannot be concretely identified.

Enigma (Q 100:1–5):[49]
wa-l-ʿādiyāti ḍabḥā
fa-l-mūriyāti qadḥā
fa-l-mughīrāti subḥā
fa-atharna bihi naqʿā
fa-wasaṭn bihi jamʿā

By the snorting runners
Striking sparks with their hooves
Venturing an attack in the morning
Raising dust with stomps
Penetrating the middle droves.

Just as the epithet "hot and glowing" (*ḥumama*) stands for fire or for some totally destructive power in the speech of the seer, so here "runners" (*ʿādiyāt*) stands for horse/rider, a cipher for threatening aggressors. This is followed immediately by a paraenetic reflection about mankind in the form of an oath pronouncement (Q 100:6–8). These explicit verses fall outside the frame of the encoded enigma discourse and, with their calming monotony, serve to decelerate the previously accumulated movement. This movement is then restored in its intensity, when after this delay we find the solution of the enigma (Q 100:9–12):

a-fa-lā yaʿlamu idhā buʿthira mā fī l-qubūr
wa-ḥuṣṣila mā fī l-ṣudūr
inna rabbahum yawmaʾidhin la-khabīr

Then does he not know: when what is in the graves is brought back
and what is in the heart is revealed,
that nothing remains hidden before his Lord?

No surprising and unexpected danger is presented as a solution to the riddle expressed by the fast movement of the riders; we find no fatal political phenomenon such as in the seer's speech, but rather something that is long familiar in the frame of the proclamation: the coming of the Final Day, when the dead, torn from their graves, undergo a testing of their hearts and are led before their judge—a scene that takes on an additional connotation of fatedness through the flash-forward in the oath series. Although the old elements of seer discourse can easily be recognized structurally in the sura, the function of the discourse has

49. The translation is influenced by Rückert, *Der Koran*, which conveys the dynamics of the tableau quite clearly.

changed: in the case of Saṭīḥ's pronouncement the enigma was an actual puzzle concerning an unknown and deadly political phenomenon pressing on the person or group seeking council, but in the case of the suras introduced by oath clusters, the enigma represents something that must have been known by the Meccan hearers previously. A survey of the suras introduced by these types of encoded oath objects shows that they all stand for the catastrophic phenomenon of the Final Day, not a fated event that is limited to the group seeking council but rather a universal catastrophe announced through the encoded communication.

We see here a repurposing of the previous discourse, which no longer relates to what is actually known; the old seer formula has been blunted by an implosion of its literary genre. Nowhere in the earlier seer speeches do we find an intervening paraenetic text that delays the moment between enigma and solution. Precisely for that reason, because the schema of the seer's speech is imploded by the insertion of a strikingly different formal religious language in the Qur'an, we can trace the successful "negation" of an old pagan discourse form and its integration in the frame of monotheistic forms of expression. That the solution passage is not purely ancient Arabic in its phrasing but rather is marked by biblical tradition should not be surprising: the *ghazwa* or "raid" that is evoked in the enigma is ultimately revealed to be an attack on the human heart, which is "attacked" on the Last Day, emptied out, and tested for the value of its contents—like the containers in the tents of enemies surprised by an attack. The "test of the heart" by the Lord of the Worlds who is "aware of all things" is a motif that, in terms of content and history, stands entirely outside of the horizon of the early Arabic seer. Their rhythm, diction, and structure faithfully preserve the earlier form, so that if the words referring to eschatological or psychological matters, "graves," *qubūr*, and "hearts," *ṣudūr*, were replaced by concrete elements of the nomadic environment, the passage could refer to a *ghazwa*. But we see here the abandonment of an old pattern and the emergence of a new form that can be used liturgically, in a prayer service to God.[50]

12.3 Poetical Topoi in the Qur'an

One of the central virtues of the Bedouin code of values, and a standard subject of the poetry, is the hero's generosity, *jūd* or *karam*.[51] It is often linked to ostentatious expenditure of possessions, denounced reproachfully by a critical observer as *ihlāk al-māl*, "the exhaustion of possessions." This Bedouin virtue achieves greater pathos because its ambivalence, the heroically undertaken self-harming of the generous man, is clearly recognized and referred to by name in

50. On the overall characteristics of early Meccan suras, cf. Neuwirth, "Einige Bemerkungen."

51. Further poetic motifs and topoi are discussed in Caskel, *Schicksal*; Ammann, *Die Geburt des Islam* (*khuld*, "immortality"); Bauer, "The Relevance of Ancient Arabic Poetry" (*rayb al-manūn*, "unpredictability of fate").

the poetry. A figure is introduced precisely to serve this critical function, that of the "rebuker," *al-ʿādhila*, who contests the poet with pragmatic arguments. The topos of the intervention of the rebuker (male or female) is widespread; it occurs, for example, in Taʾabbaṭa Sharran, where a rebuker reproaches the hero: *ahlakta mālan law ḍaninta bihi*, "You have wasted your goods, when you should have preserved them!"[52] In response to this, a poet proudly defends his own heroic principle. For what would be seen as a loss in practical terms is transmuted into a display of manly honor, *murūʾa*, in the Bedouin worldview. Excessive giving and sharing is also bound up with excessive consumption. The poet ʿAntara says proudly of himself: *fa-idhā sharibtu fa-innanī mustahlikun mālī*, "If ever I drink, then it is to the ruin of my wealth!"[53]

Toshihiko Izutsu, in the context of a comparison between the values of *murūʾa* in poetry and their reception in the Qur'an,[54] saw early Arabic generosity as an attitude related essentially to the Qur'anic concern for the poor, which would later be institutionalized as an alms tax. Surely, stinginess is frowned upon in the Qur'an, as in the early Meccan period, Q 104:1–2: *waylun li-kulli humazatin lumazah / alladhī jamaʿa mālan wa-ʿaddadah*, "Woe to every backbiter and whiner / who accumulates and counts wealth," or, in the Medinan period, Q 4:128: *wa-uḥḍirati l-anfusu l-shuḥḥa wa-in tuḥsinū wa-ttaqū fa-inna llāha kāna bi-mā taʿmalūna khabīra*, "The souls are set before greediness. If you do good and are pious before God—he is aware of what they do." The implication here is not a positive attitude toward *jūd/karam*, the excessive generosity of the Arabic hero, which arises from quite different motives. On the contrary, this attitude is parodied and antagonized in the Qur'an, from the very beginning, as a form of self-deception, or *istighnāʾ*, the "deeming oneself rich or independent," which is opposed in the Qur'an by the idea of *taqwā*, "dependence" or "piety." The later collective obligation for almsgiving develops out of a protracted negotiation, employing biblical arguments, in tension with the old ideal.

Already in an early sura, we find a reproach of the type of the generous man who exhausts his possessions. In Q 90:6, we even find a direct representation of the voice of one such type, who defends himself: *yaqūlu ahlaktu mālan lubad*, "He says, I have exhausted a great deal of possessions." This verse is a rare example of a paraphrase of poetry in the Qur'an. What would be invoked in the poetry as a rebuke of the poet-hero's *ihlāk al-māl*, his "exhaustion of possessions," is reformulated in the Qur'an into a proud boast of one's own deeds by the spender himself, making his flawed behavior seem all the more grave. It is useful here to look at the entirety of the short sura 90, *al-balad*, "The City," because, uniquely

52. Taʾabbaṭa Sharran, *Mufaḍḍaliyyāt*, 1:21, quoted in Hamori, *The Art of Medieval Arabic Literature*, 11; cf. also Izutsu, *The Structure of the Ethical Terms*, 67–75.

53. Antara, *Muʿallaqa*, 40, quoted in Hamori, *The Art of Medieval Arabic Literature*, 11.

54. Izutsu, *The Structure of the Ethical Terms*, 65–99.

in the Qur'an, it embeds the treatment of property into an elaborate theology of creation.

The three-part sura is introduced by an oath series upon the town of Mecca, thematized as a place of settled life where the proclaimer himself stays. It is also presented as a place of social coherence, ensured by blood ties and father-son genealogies (verse 3). Conveying ideas about procreation, here imagined as the essential foundation of all communal social life, the oath series preludes the middle section, which is filled out with signs of creation (verses 8–9). Through this initial double setting that unites creation and divine providence, which is evoked by the naming of the holy city of Mecca, an expectation is awoken. It is directed toward the eschatological resolution of creation and man's rendering on the Final Day of the pledge received in divine communication. But the fulfillment of this expectation is initially delayed, and is only redeemed in the final verses.

A reprimand of man follows in the form of an oath statement (verse 4), an early Meccan topos that asserts an instability and ambivalence instilled in man from creation, while he is charged concretely with the burden of toil and perhaps sluggishness.[55] This is offered as the explanation of his insistent wastefulness, an attitude inherited from the anthropocentric world of the Bedouin hero. Desire for expenditure is ultimately an expression of the contempt for death that was celebrated as a virtue in the pre-Qur'anic Arab Bedouin world,[56] an attitude that is, however, diametrically opposed to the fear of God and the restrained lifestyle that are propagated by the proclaimer. In that the unrepentant person's speech that originally carried positive connotations in the earlier poetic context is rigorously overturned, the sura reveals itself to advocate an alternative social model, opposed to the Bedouin lifestyle. This interpretation is also suggested in the text by the parallelism between the microcosm of the human body and the macrocosm of the city, Q 90:1–7:

lā uqsimu bi-hādha l-balad
wa-anta ḥillun bi-hadhā l-balad
wa-wālidin wa-mā walad
la-qad khalaqnā l-insāna fī kabad

I swear by this town
—you are a dweller in [or: you dwell legally in] this town—
by one who begets, and by what he begot,
we have created man in distress.

55. This connotation is suggested by the Semitic etymology; the translation with "travail" or "heaviness" seems to be preferable to the common "hardship," or "distress"; cf. Ambros, *A Concise Dictionary*.

56. Cf. Hamori, *The Art of Medieval Arabic Literature*, 3–19.

a-yaḥsabu an lan yaqdira ʿalayhi aḥad
yaqūlu ahlaktu mālan lubad
a-yaḥsabu an lam yarahu aḥad

Does he think that none has power over him?
He says: "I have exhausted much wealth."
Does he think that no one has seen him?

The Bedouin heroic ideal of a licentious lifestyle is confronted in the second part (verses 8–16) with arguments from biblical tradition, first by a recollection of God's special creation of man that takes up psalmic formulations. God "installed" sense organs in man, giving him eyes and lips and a tongue (verses 8–9), which represent the organs of understanding (quite in the sense of psalms such as Psalms 94:9, "He who planted the ear, shall he not hear, who formed the eye, shall he not see?" or Psalms 40:47, "Sacrifice and oblation is not pleasing to you, ears you have drilled into me, whole burnt offerings and sin offerings have you not required"). Q 90:8–10:

a-lam najʿal lahu ʿaynayn
wa-lisānan wa-shafatayn?
wa-hadaynāhu l-najdayn?

Have we not given him two eyes
And a tongue and two lips?
And guided him along the two high paths?

The sense organs enable and compel man toward insight into the divine order. This is followed by a recollection of the guidance that brings man to a fork in the road, evoking a New Testament image. What is brought out here is the ethical requirement of experience, illustrated by the choice that has to be taken between two differing and demanding ways—that is, one must walk the "steep way," *ʿaqaba*, and this requires selflessness.

This challenge at first remains enigmatic, until it is decoded by means of an interposed rhetorical question, in initiatory question ("Do you know what is X?"), which increases the tension. The solving of the *ʿaqaba* riddle translates ideas that were evoked in the oath cluster, such as the symbol of Mecca as original place of theophany and divine devotion to man and the emergence of man from the act of procreation as the basic fundament of social life, translating the universal idea of the pledge of divine devotion that must be rendered into an individual obligation: the steep way consists of the accomplishment of social acts such as freeing a slave and feeding poor relatives and the needy (verse 11–16):

fa-lā qtaḥama l-ʿaqabah
wa-mā adrāka mā l-ʿaqabah

fakku raqabah
aw iṭʿāmun fī yawmin dhī masghabah
yatīman dhā maqrabah
aw miskīnan dhā matrabah

But he has not climbed the steep way.
Do you know what the steep way is?
The loosening of a neck
or feeding on the day of hunger
an orphan of relation
or a poor person lying in dirt.

It is interesting to see that the Bedouin approach to the consumption of wealth (verse 6) is contrasted with an opposing model that is rooted in the known biblical tradition: the three acts of charity—the liberation of the oppressed, the feeding of the hungry, and the provisioning of the poor—already form an ensemble in Isaiah (Is 58:6–7): "Is the fast that I have chosen not rather the loosing of the chains of evil, the untying of the straps of the yoke, to free the downtrodden and break every yoke? Is it not the sharing of bread with the hungry and that you receive in your house the poor man, who is outcast? That you, when you see a naked man, cover him and not hide yourself before your own flesh?" The three acts of freeing, feeding, and providing for the poor are also featured in Mt 25:34ff. The Lord praises those on his right for having fulfilled the three benefactions. On the other hand, he lets those on his left, who have denied these three acts, go into the fire: Mt 25:41ff. The three acts of charity of the Isaiah tradition thus take on an additional eschatological dimension in their rereading in Matthew, which, just as in the Qur'an text, picks up the image of those on the right and left. More surprising is the new thrust of the Qur'anic text, which no longer thematizes the righteous man as a responsible individual, but rather treats him, quite in harmony with the ideal space of the town, as a part of a collective, where individuals encourage each other to deliver charitable services (third part, verses 17–20).

The text, however, stands in both the ancient Arab and the biblical traditions. In the sura's rhetoric and progression of thought, the proclaimer fulfills an aim suggested by the references to poetry: to outdo the poetry and the heroic worldview that it transmits. This is done structurally: in sura 90, the town as a macrocosm matches the microcosm of man. The physiology of man and the topography of the place correspond in their harmonic-symmetrical structure (verses 8–10), in that the natural symmetry of man's physiology adds persuasive power to the topographical symmetry of the two ways: "two ways," "two lips," "two ears." The imposing "steep way," *ʿaqaba*, corresponds to the psychological challenge of burdensome practices, the "climbing" *iqtiḥām*, which again is translated immediately from the physiological-psychological into the ethical. Just as the solution of the metaphor of the *ʿaqaba* (verses 13–16) makes recognizable the charitable activity, so too is the topographical-physiological cosmos of the town ethically coded. God's accomplishment of creation gives an ethical thrust to both elements—providing man with knowledge and capabilities of articulation (eyes, lips, tongue), and providing the town with symbolically readable signs (ways, the steep path). A tension is named through the reference to the inherent flaw in man's nature (verse 4, *kabad*, "toil," "difficulty'), and this tension is solved only through the redress of this flaw through insight (the eyes) and responsible conduct (the lips and tongue) (verse 13–16), reflecting also the divinely willed ideal of the political body, the polis.

This train of thought is expressed less through argumentation than through the insertion of imagery. Indeed, beyond its semantic content the "image matrix"[57] constituted in the oath series remains effective throughout the entire sura; proceeding from the topographical *balad*, "city," on the one hand and the physiological *walada*, "beget," on the other to evoke associations of both topographical and physiological-social links. Thus, *balad* finds its echo in such toponymic metaphors as *najdayn*, "two high roads" (standing for the choice given to man between good and evil), and above all *ʿaqaba*, "steep way" (for the compulsory difficult choice). Related to *walada*, on the other hand, in the physiological realm, there are such terms for organs as *ʿaynayn*, "two eyes," *lisān*, "tongue," *shafatayn*, "two lips" (as the means of knowledge and insightful conduct), and *raqaba*, "neck" (as an image for servitude), and, in the social realm, such classifications as "orphan," "relations," and "the poor."

Through a supplement to this idiosyncratically formulated catalogue of virtues (verse 13–16) in a later passage (verse 17–20), the actions compelled by the model of the city are "translated" into eschatological value categories and the tension built up with the double incipit of creation and instruction of man is released through the rendering account of both, physis and reason, at the last judgment on the Final Day (verse 17–20):

thumma kāna mina lladhīna āmanū
  wa-tawāṣaw bi-l-ṣabri wa-tawāṣaw bi-l-marḥamah
ulāʾika aṣḥābu l-maymanah
wa-lladhīna kafarū bi-ayātina
  hum aṣḥābu l-mashʾamah
ʿalayhim nārun muʾṣadah

Then is he one of those who believe
  and spur each other on to patience and spur each other on to mercy.
They are the companions of the right hand.

57. Neuwirth, "Der Horizont der Offenbarung."

And those who lie about our signs
they are the companions of the left hand.
Upon them a blazing fire!

Although this final verse group, with its clarity, stands out from the largely ambiguous earlier topics of the sura, it can nonetheless claim a basic formal unity with the rest of the text, through its proportional correspondence to the beginning section (each four verses) and through its continuation of the rhyme scheme, sometimes through spontaneously formed neologisms (*mash'ama*, "the left" for *shimāl*, "left," and *maymana*, "the right," for *yamīn*, "right").

Charitable behavior is thus not a new form of the Bedouin praxis of generosity, but rather its antithesis. The distinction does not just lie in the Qur'anic disavowal of the pre-Islamic boasting about generosity and its practice for the sake of glorification and the self-aggrandizement of the hero, as Izutsu claimed, but in fact it lies much deeper.

Even the verse Q 2:264, adduced by Izutsu as evidence,[58] goes beyond a mere critique of falsely motivated generosity:

O you who believe, do not render your alms void
by reproach or vexation,
like the one who spends his possessions
to make a show to the people
and does not believe in God and the Last Day.
He is like a rock on which is soil,
which is struck by heavy rain, leaving it bare.
They have no power over any of that which they have acquired. God does not guide the unbelievers.

Here the one who gives out of a selfish motive is accused of hypocrisy, which will be immediately debunked in a test. The seemingly empirical statement gains additional impact through its application of a New Testament simile (*mathal*),[59] which is given a different meaning than that developed in Christian theology, where it refers to a transcendent world beyond apparent reality. The Qur'anic simile likewise through its final clausula turns out to be an expression of divinely warranted truth. Sincerely practiced charity—in contrast to feigned—reflects not apparent but rather true stability of the cosmos.

As the poetically dense sura 90 shows, true charity is not warranted by mere avoidance of excesses and bragging. Rather, it is bound up in a creation theology that requires certain behaviors from man toward his creator, as a being endowed

58. Izutsu, *The Structure of the Ethical Terms*, 69.
59. See Ben-Shammai, "The Status of Parable and Simile"; cf. chap. 8, 305–313.

with physical capacity and the capacity for reason—accomplishments that form the basis for urban life and piety in the Qur'an.

12.4 Poetical Operations in the Qur'an

Not only do we find poetic topoi in the Qur'an—alongside the local Arabic topoi, anthropomorphic divine predicates familiar from biblical tradition such as the Light Verse, Q 2:155, would deserve mention—but we can also trace particular poetic techniques. A remarkable feature of the Qur'an is its neologisms: previously unattested word forms that can best be understood as spontaneous coinages, which were later considered so exclusively Qur'anic that they are never used outside of the Qur'an. For the most part, they designate empirically unknown issues, such as the eschatological site of hell (presented in places as *hāwiya*, "abyss," literally "collapsing," Q 101:9–10, or *al-ḥuṭama*, "the crusher," Q 104:4), or individual actors or circumstances involved in the resolution of the cosmos (*al-nāziʿāt*, "the tearers," Q 79:1; *al-qāriʿa*, "the knocker," Q 101:1–3). These neologisms, which are for the most part metonymic, that is, they stand as adjectival or participial qualifiers in place of the expected nominal signifier, are not to be considered something entirely new, for we find a frequent use of metonymical expressions in the poetry as well. They serve not simply as semantically unfamiliar designations but also function on the morphological and phonetic level as components of an argument. Introduced right at the beginning of their sections, they establish reference points for a network of individual thoughts, which only crystalize into an argument through their "amalgamating" effect.

In sura 104, "The Backbiter," the two unfamiliar forms *humaza/lumaza*, "backbiter/grumbler," at the start of the sura and the new coinage *al-ḥuṭama*, "the crusher," at the beginning of the second section, serve the function of reference points for an argument, verses 1–9:[60]

waylun li-kulli humazatin lumazah
alladhī jamaʿa mālan wa-ʿaddadah
yaḥsabu anna mālahu akhladah
kallā la-yunbadhanna fī l-ḥuṭamah
wa-mā adrāka mā l-ḥuṭamah
nāru llāhi l-mūqadah
allatī taṭṭaliʿu ʿalā l-afʾidah
innahā ʿalayhim muʾṣadah
fī ʿamadin mumaddadah

60. For a contrasting attempt at interpretation with stronger emphasis on formally surprising effects than logical structure, see Robinson, *Discovering the Qurʾān*, 164–166.

Woe to every backbiter and grumbler
who has gathered and counted riches
thinking his riches make him immortal.
No indeed! He will be thrown to the crusher.
Do you know what the crusher is?
The fire of God, kindled,
it ascends unto the hearts
its flames clash together over them
in high towering columns.

The sura stands in the tradition of invective poetry (*hijāʾ*) and consists mainly of exclamations marked through elements such as *waylun li-*, "woe to" (verse 1), *kallā*, "indeed no!" (verse 4), and the polemic *wa-mā adrāka mā . . .* , "do you know what is . . . ? (verse 5). Structurally, it consists of an exclamation of woe, declared against the backbiter and the grumbler, followed by a short catalogue of vices (verse 1–2), which is countered by the exposure of wrong behavior (verse 3) and the threatening of otherworldly punishment, which will take place in an enigmatic site (verses 4–9) designated by *ḥuṭama*. More than half of the text is dedicated to this place and the conditions there; its puzzling quality is further underscored by a rhetorical question ("do you know what is . . . ?"). But above all, the wordplay triggered by the neologism *ḥuṭama*, the playful repetition of references, is a clear sign that hearers are to be impressed: those reprimanded as *humaza/lumaza*, "backbiters and grumblers" here appear for the only time in the Qur'an in the rare morphological form *fuʿala*,[61] while the same type elsewhere appears in the more common form *hammāz*, as in Q 68:10–13:

And do not obey everyone who swears much and is lowly,
who rushes and spreads base slander [is a backbiter; *hammāz*]
who hinders the good,
a transgressor who sins,
a rude person and a bastard.

In both cases, the accusation against the *hammāz/humaza* is rooted in social misbehavior. In sura 104, the two-part, penultimate-stressed form *humaza/lumaza* binds together the accusation and its substantiation across the verse break and acts as a prelude to the unusual rhyme of the statement *ʿaddadah*, "he counts it." The unfamiliar *humaza/lumaza* echoes the rhyme of the absurd assumptions of the greedy one (verse 3), who claims that his possessions "will give him immortality" (*akhladahu*).

61. An intensive form with reference to human behavior, not listed in Brockelmann, *Semitische Grammatik*; but see Grande, *Kurs arabskoj*, 82 (personal communication from Kirill Dimitriev).

The naming of the *ḥuṭama* then makes new recourse to the beginning word pair *humaza/lumaza*, now through precise iteration of the morphological form *fuʿala*. The otherwise unknown name *al-ḥuṭama* in this context can only signify hell, which seems to be personified here, as is the case elsewhere. This alone would explain the morphological form, which is an analogue to *humaza/lumaza* expressing intensive or constant behavior. There is thus a close relationship between the offenders and their otherworldly destination: they follow their wild cravings on a path toward debasement, while the place itself pursues its cravings toward their dismemberment. In other words, for the behavior of the *humaza/lumaza*, a suffering in the hereafter is decreed that is "homeopathichally" equivalent in intensity.

Yet the answer given in verse 5 to the rhetorical question connected to *ḥuṭama* is not congruent with the image, since fire does not crush or grind, but rather consumes, and the associations of the familiar etymologically related Qur'anic *ḥuṭām*, "dry chaff" (Q 56:65, 39:21, 57:20), are difficult to bring together with fire. It is difficult also to associate it semantically to the familiar element of the Meccan shrine known as al-Ḥaṭīm, which served as a place for sacrifice and other activities.[62] But what stands out above all is the use of a form reserved for animated beings. Clearly, there are two images of hell superimposed here, that of a place of fire and that of a mythical being—distinguished by insatiability, and crushing its victims—as in Q 50:30: "On the day, when God speaks to hell: 'have you been sated?' And she replies: are there more supplies?"

After the conventional image of hell as a place of fire in verse 6, the perspective turns from physical punishment to psychic punishment, to the affecting of the hearts. *Fuʾād*, "heart," is not primarily a bodily organ in the Qur'an, but rather the site of feelings.[63] Elsewhere we find similar language for eschatological experiences that affect the "heart" or the "breast," as in: "When what is in the heart is brought forth" (Q 100:10). The punishment through enclosure in flames, which stands alongside the terrifying image of high blazing flames, resumes the antepenultimate-stressed rhyme of *muʾṣada, afida, ʿamada*, which now feeds back into the misconduct (*humaza, lumaza, ʿaddadahu*) and miscalculation (*akhladahu*) of the punished, while in the final *fī ʿamadin mumaddada*, "high towering columns," we find audible and morphological reference to the intensive counting of the greedy, *ʿaddadah*.

The coherence of this text is due above all to the operation of semantic-morphological-phonetic reference points introduced right from the beginning. The accusation of *hamz*, "jibing," and the closely related *lamz*, "grumbling," becomes a forceful beginning signal through the doubling of its morphological

62. See Rubin, "The Kaʿba."

63. Cf. Seidensticker, *Altarabisch "Herz,"* 42–62.

expression (*humaza/lumaza*). Further accusations are bound closely to these phonetically related rhymes. The deterrent site of hell then "works" continuously like the punished himself, taking shape as its counterpart through a shared morphological form *humaza/lumaza/ḥuṭama*. The newly introduced signifier of hell, *ḥuṭama*, is thus closely linked poetically to the specified group of people of the *humaza/lumaza*, or is even generated because of this group, whose verdict and punishment thus receive a convincing legitimation.

12.5 Coping with Contingency in Poetry and Qur'an

While a number of theologically and liturgically important concepts shared by the Qur'an and its predecessor traditions still indicate their historical origin through their expression in loan words, it is remarkable that the central designation for the message received by the proclaimer is indicated with a genuine Arabic word. It is a word that is first introduced almost casually, to indicate the modality of the divine communication (Q 53:4, 10–11) and that does not become a technical term in later Qur'anic texts either, but maintains a variety of meanings—namely, *waḥy*, "inspiration." For a long time in Qur'anic usage, *waḥy* remains a *nomen actionis* derived from *awḥā*, "to inspire, to indicate through signs, to suggest," a behavior displayed almost always by God.[64] It often denotes the act of inspiration, not in connection to revelation, but rather with quite pragmatic implications.[65] Because *waḥy* is also directed at nonhuman entities such as the heavens (Q 41:12), earth (Q 99:5), and bees (Q 16:68), it is to be understood in the Qur'an as including nonverbal communication. It is in this sense, that is, as a nonverbal communication converted into an understandable message only by the messenger, that *waḥy* should be understood when it is connected to revelation. This nonverbal understanding of *waḥy* can be found in ancient Arabic poetry as well, where it even plays a prominent role. It is therefore probable that the concept, which appears already in the early Meccan suras, of "inspiration," of "that which is inspired" (*in huwa illā waḥyun yūḥā*, Q 53:4), did not develop in complete isolation from a "topos of *waḥy*" that was already extant in ancient Arabic poetry.

64. Satan only interferes once: Q 6:121. On *waḥy*, see also chap. 2, 68–71.

65. Noah "is inspired" to build the ship (Q 11:37; 33:27); something "is inspired" to the mother of Moses (Q 20:31); Zachariah "inspires" his community to sing praises in the morning and evening through a language of signs (Q 19:11); the bees "are inspired" to build habitations on the mountains (Q 16:68); and finally the heavens and earth themselves figure as receivers of *waḥy* (Q 41:12, 99:5). In all other places however, *awḥā* is reserved for Prophets: Noah, Abraham, Ishmael, Isaac and Jacob, Moses, Jesus and his disciples, and the proclaimer. Although often admonitions for behavior can be the object of *waḥy* (Q 10:87 to Moses, Q 16:123 to the proclaimer), as a rule what is "inspired" is the divine word, which must be communicated further. From the middle Meccan period onward, "inspiration" often designates a concrete mass of texts that is already available, Q 18:27; 12:3; 17:86.

This topos is manifest in the initial sections, *nasīb*, of the qasida, the standard long poem, where the poet in his nostalgic contemplation of the weathered camp traces, the *aṭlāl*, the remains of a former dwelling of his tribe, expresses a complaint about transience. The poet "questions" the weathered traces or bare rocks, addressing them directly, and censures himself at the same time for this act, which he recognizes as a senseless turning toward mute and time-resistant natural phenomena. That this address relates to the question of the whereabouts of a once flowering but now extinct social life, the *ubi sunt qui ante nos fuere*,[66] "Where have they vanished to who came before us?" is suggested by the theme of transience that dominates ancient Arabic poetry. In this situation of aporia, the poet compares the traces of the settlement to the writing on a rock, which he attempts to identify, but which, although it is made up of signs, is not readable to him, and which thus carries for him a locked message.[67] In view of its non-accessibility as a signifier, it is—analogous to other nonverbal messages—indicated by *waḥy*.[68]

The traces of the encampment, that is, of one's own history that is no longer accessible, convey an incomprehensible message, whose interpretation the poet strives for in vain. Following the work of Gottfried Müller,[69] Ludwig Ammann has attempted to bring this particular mental situation of the poet, and of ancient Arabian society, to a point:

> The dramaturgy of the polythematic *qasida* . . . gives an implicit answer to the "question of sense." The first part describes the Bedouin experience of transience triggered by the remains of an earlier inhabited campsite, which evokes the memory of the poet's parting with the beloved. This part ends with a questioning of the remains, for which there are no words. Then, for example, we read: "I asked them, but how can we ask deaf and immutable things, whose speech is not clear," or "No clarifying word do they offer for him who asks, only riddles." This question (*suʾāl*) is the total question, the question about sense, and this remains unanswered, at least in the first part.[70]

Ammann then adds, following the accepted notion that the poet's aporia is overcome by his departure from the devastated place and the return to his tribe: "Yet the *qasida* moves on, toward the praising of self and tribe, . . . the poetic immortalization of heroic deeds; and this praise stands—as we read in a verse of *al-Hādira*—as immortality. The practical answer consists in no more than the heroic conduct of life, the turning away from all reflection and toward courageous

66. Cf. Becker, "Ubi sunt qui ante nos in mundo fuere."
67. For citations, see Montgomery, "Dichotomies."
68. There are also other terms, such as *zubūr*, cf. the citations in ibid.
69. Müller, *Ich bin Labīd*.
70. Ammann, *Die Geburt des Islam*, 32–33.

action."[71] But then Ammann concedes: "For that very reason, the question about sense remains theoretically virulent. The integration of both, the question about sense that is still not conceptualized and the fact of achieved awareness of meaning through heroic conduct, into a coherent whole, takes place only aesthetically, through verse measure and rhyme that binds it all together."[72] One could add: through the restitution of that which appeared as frustratingly inaccessible and incomprehensible, *waḥy*, which has now become comprehensible in language. But this restitution is not accomplished for good, but rather must be constantly reformulated from case to case in poems and is only realized through performance; in poetry, there is thus no stable restitution of sense warranted with poetry. Though Ammann in his reconstruction of a Qur'anic answer to the ancient Arabic situation of loss does not discuss the particular aporia captured by the *waḥy* reference, he nonetheless takes up the idea of a necessary perpetuation, which he sees as the Qur'an's trumping of the poetic question. He supports this through reference to Q 50:2–3, 9–11, 15:

> The unbelievers say: that is a wondrous thing. O how!
> When we are dead and turned to dust—
> a return to life is surely far-fetched!
> . . . From heaven we send down blessed water and let gardens grow and grain for the harvest
> and high palms with compact spathes,
> for the subsistence of the servants, and thereby revive the dead land. So is the coming forth.
> . . . Did the first creation make us weary?
> No! But they are in darkness about the new creation.[73]

Ammann interprets this as follows: "The argumentation connects to what is already believed, the first creation and the giving of vivifying rain, and concludes from the primordial dealing with contingency and its perpetuation in the world that there will be a final coping with contingency as well: the resurrection of the dead. The given sense is thus continued. This leads to the result of an entirely new answer to the question about sense: there is a life in the hereafter."[74]

This is certainly a convincing interpretation as far as the semantic development of the message is concerned. But with *waḥy*, perceived as problematic, the poet has opened up yet another question, which is hermeneutical in nature, namely, the question of the comprehensibility of history.[75] The aporia that

71. Ibid., 33.
72. Ibid.
73. The translation reflects the understanding of Ammann.
74. Ibid., 36–37.
75. Cf. chap. 3, 127–129.

crystalizes in the incomprehensible script so momentous in poetry is canceled from the outset in the Qur'an. Already, the earliest suras bind the idea of physical creation to that of the providing of *knowledge*, emphasizing the privilege of man, who is "addressed" from the beginning of creation by God.[76] The question about sense that is raised in poetry would not be fully answered in the Qur'an by the guarantee of the cancelation of physical transience alone, however; it is only answered through the solution of the hermeneutic puzzle of the *waḥy*, that is, the removal of the aporia in face of the verbally inaccessible message of history that is symbolized by the unreadable writing of *waḥy*. That the Qur'an offers this solution is signified most clearly in the newly acquired positive connotation of *waḥy*, which is not aporetic anymore, but is manifest in the divine message to the community. The proclaimer is instructed to transfer what he receives as preverbal inspiration into articulated discourse (*tilāwa*) and to communicate it on to his hearers. "Signs of God's reign, such as procreation and birth, are embedded in nature as proofs to reason of his omnipotence. They are embedded also in history, in which God intervenes to save and condemn, to reward and to punish—a noticeable extension of the conception of God as the driver of fate."[77] *Waḥy* is thus a conceptual "puzzle picture." Although its verbal form *awḥā*, "inspire," continues to denote a preverbal form of communication in the Qur'an, which requires a particular natural or cultural deciphering code, it has obtained a new valence in the Qur'anic nominal form *waḥy*: it stands for the communication of God, successfully decoded by the proclaimer, to men, whose "writing" no longer consists of unreadable signs, but rather of a system of proof signs amenable to reason, engendering a sensible ordering of the world.

12.6 Poets in the Qur'an

The "Poet Verses" in Q 26:224–226

In light of such intense disputes over the central problems of the worldview of the poets, it is surprising that in the Qur'an we only find two places where poets are directly mentioned, and even there the language is hardly unambiguous. Numerous studies have addressed the fact that the ending verses of the middle Meccan sura 26 allude to something known to contemporary hearers and that its points can only be deduced from knowledge of these intertexts. But it is only in a recent reinterpretation by Thomas Bauer that this problem has been brought closer to a solution.[78] This interpretation now permits us to fit these verses meaningfully into the context of the sura, and thus to form a new understanding of the

76. Cf. chap. 7, 264–277.
77. Ammann, *Die Geburt des Islam*, 39.
78. For earlier interpretations, see "The Relevance of Early Arabic Poetry."

sura as a whole. In the conventional translation of Q 26:224–226, the verses read as follows:[79]

wa-l-shuʿarāʾu yattabiʿuhumu l-ghāwūn
a-lam tara annahum fī kulli wādin yahīmūn
wa-annahum yaqūlūna mā lā yafʿalūn

The poets, they are followed by those who go astray.
Have you not seen that they wander in every valley
and say what they do not do?

Thomas Bauer has shown that this translation cannot be maintained and has demonstrated on the basis of poetical references that the verb *hāma, yahīmūn* instead denotes "suffering from thirst pangs." The verses seek to demonstrate the mendacity of the poets, and thus to discredit the worldview of "those who follow them," or those who are dedicated to the ancient Arabian ideals. He clarifies:

> The worldview of the aristocratic elite stemming from powerful Bedouin tribes is characterized by the concept of the *murūʾa*, which describes a heroic and manly ethos held by a social group. . . . The virtue of *murūʾa* includes bravery, generosity, courage, a sense of honor, and other similar qualities. All of these values are glorified in early Arabic poetry. Talks of fights, wine and feats, the *maysir* game, of the hunt, of conquests in love with pampered and elegant women, and other such subjects occur frequently. When the poets spoke of these subjects, to be sure, they might exaggerate and embroider them, but it cannot be claimed that they were outright lying. In Q 26:226, instead, the poets are accused of "say[ing] what they do not do." Consequently, we have to look for a common motif in pre- and early Islamic poetry, in which the poets boast of acts which in reality they did not perform. . . . One of the actions by which one proves one's *murūʾa* is suffering deprivation and facing dangers. As one of the most common of themes in poetry, proving oneself is often achieved by fighting bravely or in bearing the hardships of a long desert journey. The "desert journey" is not only mentioned alongside the other *murūʾa*-themes in the self-praise or *fakhr*-section of Qasidas, which serve for the presentation of one's own bravery, but also became a fixed constituent part of a particular type of Qasida, in which this motif binds together two parts of the Qasida. . . . There could hardly be any poet of any importance who did not treat this subject in one fashion or the other for whom this theme did not occur. . . . And therein lies the explanation for the Qur'anic verse 26:225. What the poets say but do not in fact do is found in the Qur'an

79. The translation reflects the understanding of Paret, *Der Koran*, 309.

> itself: *fī kulli wādin yahīmūn*, "to die from thirst in all those wadis". . . . In countless pieces of poetry poets claim to have crossed wastes where for days on end there was no water to drink, where they and their camels were dying of thirst. But this is exactly what the poets, as members of an aristocratic and wealthy upper class, did not do.[80]

Building on this, Bauer's new translation is as follows:

> And the poets: Those who go astray follow them.
> Don't you know that they "die from thirst in all kinds of valleys
> And that they (as you can see) do not do what they say?"

He comments on this:

> This passage makes two points: it begins as a straightforward and rather simple statement about the path of righteousness: whoever follows the poets is not following the right path, the path that leads to salvation. But it also contains a somewhat surprising point, which is that, in the end, this is exactly what the poets themselves say! The poets themselves are being quoted, as they themselves say that they constantly "die from thirst in all those wadis!" The same destiny thus awaits those who follow the poets. Or maybe not. For there is also a second surprising twist to this saying: in reality, poets do not die of thirst at all in the valleys, but are just boasting. That of course makes the accusation here even worse: those who follow the poets have lost their way because poets are liars, when they glorify the deceitful ideal of the virtue of the *murūʾa*.[81]

But what motivates this designation of the poets at the end of a sura, which, after a short address to the proclaimer (verses 1–9), refers in detail in its main part (verses 10–191) to no fewer than ten prophet stories? The sura, which, with this contrasting of proclamation and poetic performance, has been read as a "mantic manifesto,"[82] offers a narrative tour de force, presenting a larger number of prophet stories than any other Qur'an text. The stories are always concluded with a double-verse refrain: *inna fī dhālika la-āyatan wa-mā kāna aktharuhum muʾminīn*, "Truly, in that is a sign, which however most of them do not believe." In this multiplication of the model of ethical exhortation practiced by the proclaimer himself, which is achieved through its projection of diverse earlier prophets, we find a suggestive communication of the monotheistic worldview. What is at stake, then, is the persuasive character of prophetic discourse and the truth value of the message of the new worldview. The status that obtains for the

80. Bauer, "The Relevance of Early Arabic Poetry," 727.

81. Ibid., 729; but see the modification of this thesis by Seidensticker, "Herumirrende Dichter," according to which the poets are denigrated for their exalted, erotic lifestyle rather than for mendacity.

82. Following Zwettler, "A Mantic Manifesto."

poet polemic in this context becomes recognizable through the analysis of the entire ending part of the sura (verses 192–226).[83]

The concluding section begins with an affirmation of the truth of the proclamation:

> It [the Qur'an / the reading] is a sending down from the lord of the worlds,
> which the reliable spirit
> has sent down on your heart, so that you may be a warner,
> in clear Arabic speech. (Verses 193–195)

The Qur'an thus clearly stands in competition with other Arabic pronouncements. It is a proclamation that is also accepted by Jewish scholars (verse 197), and the Arabness of the proclamation is of central significance: "Had we sent it down on a non-Arab / and he had read it out to them, they would not have believed" (verse 198–199). After this follows a complaint against the unbelief of individual hearers (verses 200–209). The ensuing rejection of the idea of an inspiration of the Qur'an through Satan—the model that applies to the inspiration of the poets—indicates that an insinuation that the proclaimer is a poet had preceded. This accusation can only be countered by the worship of God alone and the performance of liturgies (verses 210–220).

The hymnic predication in verse 220 (*innahu huwa l-samīʿu l-ʿalīm*, "He is the hearing, the seeing") is followed by a polemic postscript that typologically could easily serve as conclusion to the sura. It is, however, directed to a plurality of hearers, unlike the preceding twenty-eight verses of the concluding part, which were directed toward the proclaimer (verses 221–223): "Should I announce to you all, onto whom the satans truly come down? They come down upon every sinful liar! / They attempt to eavesdrop [on the edge of the heavenly spheres, in order to overhear divine wisdom];[84] indeed, most of them are liars." This disavowal, not unique in the Qur'an, of inspiring spirits that are "for the most part insincere," in contrast to the "reliable spirit" (*al-rūḥu l-amīn*, verse 193) responsible for the inspiration of the proclaimer, is an index of the untruth of any discourse in competition with the proclamation that would lay claim to supernatural origin—an allusion to the poets and seers, who were known to be "inspired" by the *jinn* or satans. The allusion is made explicit in what follows by the mocking of the poets (verses 224–226), who, as representatives of the heroic worldview, were the most dangerous competitors of the proclaimer. Their truthfulness is mocked sarcastically—an important strategic step in the context of the double contest with the poets: about the "right worldview" and about the more verbally convincing presentation.

83. On the structure of the entire sura, see Neuwirth, *Studien zur Komposition*, 276–277.
84. See Hawting, "Eavesdropping."

12.6.1 *Postscript to the Poet Verses*

This polemical closing of the sura, in the late Meccan, or more likely early Medinan period, is finally appended by a modified statement about the poets, Q 26:227:

> *illā lladhīna āmanū wa-ʿamilū l-ṣāliḥāti*
> *wa-dhakarū llāha kathīran wa-ntaṣarū min baʿdi mā ẓulimū*
> *wa-sa-yaʿlamu lladhīna ẓalamū ayya munqalabin yanqlibūn*

> Except those who believe and do good works and praise God often, and defend themselves after they have suffered wrong. Those who do wrong will come to know what kind of turn they will take.[85]

Stylistically, it is hard to decide clearly when this addition was appended. Later clarifications or exceptions from general judgments are frequent in the Qur'an in the Meccan and Medinan periods.[86] But how can the mendacity of the poets and their lack of credibility, which is asserted in Q 26:224–226, be relativized through the exception of single individuals? Obviously, a special poet type is being given protection with these verses and brought forward as an exception: those who have become believers, thus having renounced the heroic worldview, and who—in addition to observing the elementary religious duties—also show personal zeal, which in the case of poets should not be military zeal but rather verbal engagement. As to Mecca, we know nothing of poets who exerted themselves through poems on behalf of the believers; for Medina, however, transmitted collections of poetry show evidence of poets who interfered into the political conflicts of the community. Within the ranks of the "zealous poets," we might therefore most plausibly count those famous figures known from tradition who defended the new political entity by means of their *hijāʾ* poems, putting themselves and their polemical poetic art into service for the community.

Some of these poets were active in Medina, or in the wider vicinity of the Prophet; these include Labīd, Ḥassān b. Thābit, Kaʿb b. Zuhayr, and Kaʿb b. Mālik, whose poems have been discussed by Agnes Imhof in her study *Religiöser Wandel und die Genese des Islam* (Religious change and the genesis of Islam).[87] The contextualizing of these and other poems with the Qur'anic depiction of contemporary events that feature in both the Qur'an and poetry, as for example the battle of Badr, which is treated by Ḥassān, still remains a desideratum. Imhof's study of

85. Paret, *Der Koran: Kommentar*, 372, remarks: "In 227 the little flattering statements about enthusiasm and boasting are retrospectively restricted."

86. Cf. chap. 5, 185–187.

87. Cf. Imhof, *Religiöser Wandel*. She discusses Labīd, Ḥassān b. Thābit, Kaʿb b. Mālik, and Kaʿb b. Zuhayr.

the image of man in the early Arabic panegyrists of the seventh century can be supplemented by Suzanne Stetkevych's discussion of the "mantle ode" (*qaṣīdat al-burda*) by Kaʿb ibn Zuhayr[88] and Werner Diem's *Studies on the Transmission and Intertextuality* on the same poem—all of these studies already present a promising entry into the comparative study of poetry and Qur'an as part of a history of mentalities.

88. S. Stetkevych, "Pre-Islamic Panegyric and the Poetics of Redemption."

13

The Rhetorical Qur'an

13.1 The Qur'an—Document of an "Age of Rhetoric"

13.1.1 Answer to the Expectations of Hearers

> To every prophet is given a sign that proves the truth of his message: God sent Moses at a time when Pharaoh believed in the omnipotence of magic, and so his sign was the transformation of his staff into a snake. He sent Jesus in an age at a time when the art of healing stood in the highest regard, therefore Jesus had to outdo the craft of the doctors—by raising the dead. In Muhammad's time, one could no longer impress with such sensory miracles, since he came before listeners for whom the art of speech possessed the highest rank, and so his sign needed to be a linguistic one: the rhetorical miracle of the Qur'an.

This is the report of the ninth-century encyclopedist al-Jāḥiẓ (160–255/777–869), who worked in Basra.[1]

This classification of the prophets can be easily recognized as an Islamic continuation of the Christian theological topos of successive divine covenants, each with its own prophet.[2] But Muhammad now forms the apex, whose rank clearly rises above that of the others, since his sign is not physical but rather spiritual in nature. Yet, however disparaging the evaluation of the earlier prophetic messages may be, which are presented as relying for their authentication on theologically insignificant miracles, the text nevertheless brings to a point a central trait of the Qur'an itself: the simultaneous claim of theological-semantic and aesthetic-hermeneutical value. This claim is historically grounded by al-Jāḥiẓ in the emergence of the Qur'an in an age of special sensibility vis-à-vis the word, and through the linking of its proclamation to a particularly literarily sophisticated hearership. Even if this idea in al-Jāḥiẓ is difficult to separate from his apologetic-linguistic position in confrontation with non-Arabs,[3] still he addresses an important aspect that connects the Qur'an to Late Antiquity. Because the Qur'an makes

1. This citation summarizes a longer explanation in al-Jāḥiẓ, *Ḥujaj al-Nubūwa*, 3:221–281, esp. 278–280. Pellat, *Arabische Geisteswelt*, also offers a paraphrasing translation, 80.

2. Samir, "Theological Christian Influences."

3. See Heath, "Adab and the Art of the Essay"; Agha, "Language as a Component."

use of the highly rhetorical ancient Arabic language employed by the poets of the sixth and seventh centuries, and even surpasses this register innovatively in many ways, it gains access to a hermeneutical potential for the display of its supernatural origin to an Arabic audience that is more effective than any sensory miracle could be. James Montgomery has recently pointed to the vast ideological radiation of ancient Arabic poetry, which thanks to the strategy of cladding its world view in a Bedouinizing guise[4] had become the central manifestation of Arab cultural and political autonomy. High linguistic standards were thus set, which the Qur'an had to meet in order to confront this worldview. At the same time a new discourse had been opened that was to steer the entire proclamation, which one could without much exaggeration term a "contest for the optimal art of persuasion." It is a contest that was staged with various opponents, whether they were personally present on the stage of the debate (like the pagan Meccan opponents), heirs of differing Late Antique religious traditions present among the hearers (as in Medina), or, finally, absentees, to be identified as "hermeneutical Jews"[5] (or Christians).

The strategy of raising the linguistic form to the rank of a proof of the authentication of the message is also suggested by another observation: the Qur'an, unlike the Hebrew Bible and Gospels, consists throughout—notwithstanding the great number of narrative passages—of direct speech and often even exchanges of speech. In Ludwig Ammann's words, "The Qur'an is the word of God without narrative frame. This word can be understood as continuous reflection, to convey to the notion of God's rulership . . . an ever increasing, comprehensive validity."[6] But this prophetic speech not only operates in the sphere of lived reality; it also operates, to no lesser degree, in a text world as well. This is not surprising historically. In biblical tradition, already centuries earlier the "wise man," that is, the man who is aware of tradition and capable of interpreting scripture, had replaced the spontaneously articulating prophet, since, as James Kugel claims, the "word of God was regarded as having already been laid down in scripture."[7] This perspective is shared also by the Qur'an, which continuously refers to and interprets the earlier "writings." Yet the Qur'an is also to a high degree spontaneous mantic speech, a practice that had remained alive in the Arabian Peninsula, perhaps because biblical tradition did not circulate there in written form, but rather in oral transmission. Thus, the role of Muhammad is not captured satisfactorily by that of a prophet in the biblical sense: Muhammad is at once a mantic speaker and the

4. Montgomery, "The Empty Ḥijāz."

5. The term "hermeneutic Jew" goes back to Jeremy Cohen. In his work the term refers not to an actual person but rather to the stereotypical image of a representative of Judaism whose understanding of the Bible is perceived to be unacceptable in Christian polemic; see Cohen, *Living Letters of the Law* (Dirk Hartwig, personal communication).

6. Ammann, *Die Geburt des Islam*, 44–45.

7. Kugel, *The Bible as It Was*, 17; cf. chap. 10.

interpreter of tradition. In light of its expressive pathos, the Qur'an as a whole can be seen as an Arabic prophet text closely related to biblical prophet texts, but at the same time, and with only slight exaggeration, one could assign it to the genre of "exegesis." In fact, semantically, it consists to a great extent of interpretations and reformulations of already known biblical and post-biblical traditions; as to its form, however, it is replete with apologetical-polemical argumentation.[8] These observations confirm the close relationship to rhetoric claimed by al-Jāḥiẓ: the Qur'an enters the stage in an epoch that is rightly distinguished by al-Jāḥiẓ from the earlier periods, an epoch that corresponds to our category of Late Antiquity.

Looked at from a more universal perspective, al-Jāḥiẓ's statement places the text into an epoch that is acclaimed in literary history for its rhetorical productivity, even if in established scholarly presentations Arabic is seldom discussed; what are discussed are rather works in Greek, the language of rhetoric par excellence. Thus, Albin Lesky's comprehensive history of Greek literature[9] includes for the fourth century a number of Near Eastern rhetoricians who, although themselves pagan and having Semitic-language backgrounds, became the teachers of Christian scholars who wrote in Greek. Thus the most significant among them, Libanios of Antioch (314–393),[10] was the teacher of the later church fathers Chrysostom, Basil the Great, and Gregory of Nazanius[11]—founding a rhetorical tradition that was to span centuries. Sophronios, patriarch of Jerusalem from 634–638, who gave the city over to the Muslims five years after the death of the Prophet, bore the honorary title "the Sophist" and enters into history as the poet of highly rhetorical Greek hymns.[12] Rhetorical praxis was clearly not reliant on professional discipline alone. Daniel Boyarin has recently reclaimed Hellenistic satirists such as Menippos to have provided the indirect models for individual structures of argumentation of the Talmudic Amoraim.[13] Exegesis, especially as it was practiced dialogically, was often produced by means of rhetoric. Indeed, the Qur'an emerged contemporaneously with parts of the Talmud and important patristic literature, to name only the most central corpora. Read together with the writings of the Late Antique rhetoricians, the church fathers, and the rabbis, all of whom are commonly claimed as part of the European legacy, the Qur'an actually becomes a text that is familiar to us—or it would, if our own intellectual preconceptions did not skew our perceptions.

8. McAuliffe, "Debate with Them in a Better Way." Sinai, *Studien zur frühen Koraninterpretation*, 1–22, also summarizes "intra-Qur'anic" and "extra-Qur'anic exegesis" as "scripture interpretations." A similar treatment of scripture is common in Syrian religious poetry; cf. Brock, "Syriac Dispute Poems."

9. Lesky, *Geschichte der griechischen Literatur*, 907.

10. On him, see Brown, *Macht und Rhetorik*.

11. Lesky, *Geschichte der griechischen Literatur*, 907, 972.

12. Donner, *Anakreontische Gedichte*.

13. Boyarin, "The Talmud as a Fat Rabbi."

13.1.2 *The Qur'an as the Site of Late Antique Knowledge Transfer*

The fact that the assignment of the Qur'an to this particular epoch has not yet been noted in Western research in its full dimension is due not least to another problematic chronological assignment: the usual dating of the first Hellenistic imprint on Arabic culture within the Abbasid period, when an official translation movement sought to make the decisive texts of Greek theoretical literature available in Arabic translations,[14] laying out explicit translation principles and transmitting texts in philologically integral versions under professional supervision.[15] But as momentous as this philological movement surely was, it represents only the tip of the iceberg, the institutionalization rather than the initial moment of the reception of Hellenistic learning in Arabic. One should however assume a living oral transmission of forms of thought and knowledge, above all from philosophy and the disciplines preparatory for it in the Hellenistic curriculum, already in the period before the official translation movement. Fahmi Jadaane[16] has spoken of a *voie diffuse*, an unofficial and hard to control trajectory of transmission by which Stoic doctrines reached the Arabic language area. If reflections of Aristotelian terms can already be seen in the Qur'an, as for example the antinomy *amphibolos* and *pithanos* in the forms *mutashābih* and *muḥkam* in Q 3:7,[17] then this too would be an example of the communication of elements of Hellenistic language-related sciences into the Arabic language area, reaching far back before the Abbasid period.

Historical study has long been devoted to a number of abstract terms in the Qur'an that can be recognized as loanwords of non-Arabic origin, mainly from Hebrew[18] and Syriac-Aramaic.[19] On the other hand, those abstract terms in genuine Arabic dress, which just as surely presuppose theoretical debates in Hellenistic circles, have not yet been studied in relation to their corresponding Hellenistic terms. The Qur'anic word *ta'wil* (Q 3:7), for example, which denotes an explanation of something through "reference back to a first (*awwal*)," seems related to the notion of deduction, but this remains a still unclarified issue in the history of tradition. We can assume a wide proliferation of theoretical knowledge in the Arabian-language area in Late Antiquity, whose full dimensions can only be assessed through the analysis of those *literary* text corpora that have for too long been neglected as evidence of Late Antique culture—namely, ancient Arabic poetry and the Qur'an. On the other hand, historical research has made important new discoveries in recent times:[20] G. W. Bowersock[21] has detected

14. See Strohmeier, *Hellas im Islam*.
15. See Rosenthal, *Das Fortleben der Antike im Islam*.
16. Jadaane, *Stoicisme dans l'Islam*.
17. See chap. 9, 327–330.
18. Horovitz, *Jewish Proper Names*.
19. Jeffery, *Foreign Vocabulary*.
20. Easily accessible in Hoyland, *Arabia and the Arabs*; see also the comprehensive bibliography there on 256–315.
21. Bowersock, *Roman Arabia*.

clear traces of Hellenistic culture in the southeast of the Arabian Peninsula, such as a universally distributed nomenclature and iconography of pagan deities represented in locally differing modes. According to Peter Brown,[22] the spread of a linguistic koine that united culturally different groups, which was characteristic of Hellenism,[23] offered the ideal precondition for the fast spread of Islam in its own new koine, Arabic. Based on ancient Arabic poetry, one could speak justifiably of Arabic-language culture as an Arabic analogue to the Greek-language culture and rhetorical education known as *paideia*,[24] which has been illuminated by Peter Brown as a unifying bond among the elites of the Late Antique world.[25] By activating this linguistic culture that united tribal societies, the message acquired a dimension of persuasive power, *persuasio*, which in the Qur'an successively becomes an integral part of its theological self-grounding. The Arabic language of the Qur'an, which was to trigger debates over dogma in later Islamic theology,[26] is already perceived in the course of the proclamation as an integral part of the Qur'anic message itself.[27]

But in historical research, the most important text of Arab Late Antiquity has hardly ever been considered: the Qur'an itself, which is as a rule excluded from the historical presentations of Late Antique Arabia.[28] It is true that the Qur'an through its very structure defies its own immediate historical evaluation; yet its significance as a theological-historical document of Late Antiquity cannot be overlooked. The obscuring of this perception is often grounded teleologically. Treated from a bird's eye view, and viewed from a perspective shaped by the shifts of power brought about by the victory of Islam, the Qur'an, which was the trigger of these developments, must appear to represent a break, as a radical "other" that breaches the frame of Late Antiquity as an epoch imprinted by Hellenism.

As against that, al-Jāḥiẓ had valorized the special rhetorical character of the Qur'an as a sign of its belonging to an "age of rhetoric." Although al-Jāḥiẓ should not be taken to be referring consciously to a pluricultural milieu imprinted by Hellenism for the Qur'an, his "age of rhetoric" strikingly coincides with the rhetoric-oriented Late Antiquity. Al-Jāḥiẓ's pointed formulation is only the beginning of a learned engagement with the form of the Qur'an that was to stretch over centuries, carried forward in the tenth century by ʿAlī ibn ʿĪsā al-Rummānī (d. 384/994), Muḥammad al-Khaṭṭābī (d. 386/996), and Abū Bakr al-Bāqillānī (d. 403/1013).[29] Navid

22. Brown, *The Making of Late Antiquity*.

23. See already von Grunebaum, "Arab Unity before Islam."

24. The later educational canon of the Islamic elite was in fact denoted by the term *adab*, equivalent to *paideia*.

25. Brown, *Macht und Rhetorik*; Brown, "Late Antiquity and Islam."

26. Caspar, "Parole de Dieu."

27. See chap. 2, 95–100.

28. Thus even Hoyland, one of the most energetic advocates of the conception of a Late Antique Arabia, in his *Arabia and the Arabs*, 139–166, refers only cursorily to the Qur'an, placing it in the context of wider Arabic literature references, without setting it into relief as a significant innovation of Late Antique theology.

29. Von Grunebaum, "Arab Unity before Islam."

Kermani[30] has seminally described this history of impact. He aptly refers for the bulk of his evidence to ʿAbd al-Qāhir al-Jurjānī (d. 471/1078), a literary scholar who authored what is, in Arabic tradition and Western research alike, celebrated as the subtlest theoretical reflection on the linguistic form of the Qur'an. But al-Jurjānī only marks the peak of a long development: within Islamic tradition, the Qur'an was perceived from an early point onward to be a poetic-rhetorical masterpiece, and from the Abbasid period onward it became the object of an extensive stylistic-theoretical learned literature. In this literature, the boundaries between theology and literary theory are fluid: forceful language, that is, applied rhetoric, is acknowledged as a decisive characteristic of the Qur'an, not only in poetological literature but also in standard prophetology. According to the Islamic view, rhetorically high standards not only support but *prove* the truth of the message, quite unlike what applies according to Islamic perception to the scriptures of the past, to which is conceded no comparably close relation between verbal form and pronouncement. Although the classical Arabic rhetorical literature treats Qur'an and poetry in close connection, this synoptic view is almost entirely lacking in critical research: there are no monographs available on this close aesthetic-rhetorical connection between ancient Arabic poetry and the Qur'an.[31] It appears that the rigorous distinction between "profane" and "sacred" literature, which arose in modernity, has been projected into the past.

In what follows, a an examination of the status of Qur'anic rhetoric, focused first from outside and then from within, is meant to shed light on the scene of the continuous rhetorical contest with other traditions that is reflected in the Qur'an. Once we presuppose religious variety—bridged by Hellenistic culture as a shared legacy—to have been the characteristic of the milieu of the Qur'an's genesis, the question appears promising to the degree to which rhetorical praxis and reflection were involved in this reception of Late Antiquity.

13.2 "Incapacitating" Rhetoric

13.2.1 *The Later Dogma of Iʿjāz al-Qurʾān*

If one takes seriously the notion attested in the Qur'an itself, that with the successively occurring inspiration and proclamation a text took shape that was newly formed, not wholly identical with its transcendent templates but rather adapted for the communication situation and its respective receivers,[32] then the inner-worldly side of the process, the process of the Qur'anic genesis from the

30. See Kermani, *Gott ist schön.*

31. A pioneering work is Bauer, "The Relevance of Early Arabic Poetry"; cf. chap. 12.

32. See Sinai, "Qurʾānic Self-referentiality"; Sinai, *Studien zur frühen Koraninterpretation*, 84–85; cf. chap. 2, 73–76.

reinterpretation of older traditions, becomes of central interest. Traditions are not simply "taken up" by the emerging Qur'anic community, but rather taken as challenges to be answered dialectically through new readings. With the adoption of this perspective, we can observe a *muʿāraḍa*, a "textual contest," or collision of concepts and ideas strong enough to set free an energy that results in the genesis not only of a new scripture but also of a new community, a religious movement.

This Qur'anic "eclipsing" of older traditions through new readings would be unthinkable without the particular linguistic factor to which the Qur'an makes numerous references, for example, with its self-designation as an "Arabic reading," *qurʾānun ʿarabīyun* (Q 12:2 and passim). This Qur'anic self-reference calls for a short comment: *ʿarabīyun* here stands not simply for a national language but for the high Arabic standard language that was in use alongside a number of dialects and that—according to one of its most diligent scholars, Anton Spitaler—"is the original Arabic language surviving from earliest times, which had long been withdrawn from everyday use and was *kābiran ʿan kābirin*, "from generation to generation,"[33] . . . transmitted together with particular texts."[34] Spitaler assumes a situation of diglossia: "To learn this language according to patterns heard again and again, to speak in it, was . . . a matter of natural talent, of an inborn sense of hearing, that distinguished poetic speech from the everyday language in a purely formal way, and this talent could be found just as well among the *ʿāmma*, the 'lowly people,' as among the *khāṣṣa*, 'the elite.' "[35] The high Arabic language, which had been given form in the highly developed poetry practiced already for centuries and which was particularly rich in evocations thanks to its unexampled lexical polysemy, granted the Qur'an a high degree of pathos from the very beginning, a gravity that is registered consciously by the proclaimer and community. It is due to this power of expression, based on various rhetorical figures and on a very free handling of syntax, that the Qur'an achieved that aura by which, according to tradition, it deterred its opponents already during the communication process.

This rhetorical "incapacitation," Arabic *iʿjāz*, becomes a keyword, which would have a major career as a central characteristic of the Qur'an in the ninth century, giving its name to the Islamic "dogma" of *iʿjāz al-qurʾān*, "the inimitability of the Qur'an."[36] The dogma of the Qur'an's "inimitability" (as *iʿjāz* is usually

33. In his review of Fück, Arabiya, 145, Spitaler adds: "The expression is of course to be taken *cum grano salis.* August Fischer (ZDMG 59 [1905] 662) . . . wanted to assume a particular dialect as the foundation of the classical language, and in principle that would hold true; but it seems to me quite difficult, almost impossible, to locate this dialect more precisely in place and time. It cannot be determined when and in which phase it was extracted from the everyday language, and at what point in time it became a high language recognized by all the speakers of dialects, whose use was required under certain conditions." On the other hand, Retsö, *The Arabs in Antiquity*, 49–53, has now put forward a new theory on the significance of *ʿarabīya* in the Qur'an; on this, see Wild's criticism in "An Arabic Recitation."

34. Spitaler, *Rezension zu Fück, Arabia*, 144–145.

35. Ibid., 145.

36. Martin, "Inimitability"; on the aesthetic implications, see Kermani, *Gott ist schön*, 233–314.

rendered, though it is better translated literally as "incapacitation, disablement") is not elaborated only through rhetoric. It also belongs to a theological context,[37] where the divine "deterrence" or "turning away," *al-ṣarfa* (of opponents from imitation), of the Qur'an is often foregrounded vis-à-vis the Qur'an's rhetorical perfection.[38] It is hard to understand the *iʿjāz* debate independently of the Christian-Muslim rivalry over the consummate manifestation of the word of God. The Qur'an, as the Muslim equivalent to the incarnate word of God in the Christian tradition, becomes, in the wider context of the *iʿjāz* debate and the confrontation between the rational theologians of the Muʿtazila and their opponents, the object of reflections that clearly relate to Christian theological patterns. The closeness of the Islamic and Christian debates goes so far as to produce "trans-confessional" reactions. Thus, in the eighth/ninth century, Theodor Abū Qurra, bishop of Harran, heard in the Muʾtazilites' thesis of *khalq al-qurʾān*, "the createdness of the Qur'an," a "denial of the logos," which motivated him toward a polemic against the advocates of the created Qur'an.[39] The unmistakable analogy between Christ and Qur'an as embodiments of the word of God[40] had already struck numerous early Islamic theologians as problematic. The judgment of the Qur'an to be *makhlūq*, "created," articulated by the Muʾtazila, can be recognized as a negative echo of the Nicene Creed on the nature of Christ: Greek *genēthenta ou poiēthenta*, Arabic *mawlūd ghayr makhlūq*, "born, not created."[41] But the Qur'an retained the quality of miraculous perfection shared with the incarnate word. The *iʿjāz* debate gave rise to theological tractates, and to a sequence of rhetorical-poetological works, among which is the work of al-Jurjānī, *Dalāʾil al-īʿjāz, The Proofs of Inimitability*, which is rightly celebrated as the high point of Arabic poetics.

The dogma of *iʿjāz al-qurʾān*, which in Western research was never taken seriously, has until now not been discussed in its Christological context. The frequent low evaluation of the literary character of the Qur'an itself would make the doctrine seem baseless, and the lack of a synopsis of Byzantine and Islamic theology further inhibited its systematic treatment in the theological context of confrontations around the createdness or eternity of the Qur'an. The previous dialogue between the traditions, which led to the formation of the dogma, still awaits investigation.

37. See van Ess, *Theologie und Gesellschaft*, 3:410–413, 4:609–612.

38. Even for al-Jāhiẓ, *iʿjāz* is not a permanent, static trait of the Qur'an "but rather a kind of shock, which is set loose by the challenge"; see van Ess, *Theologie und Gesellschaft*, 3:411.

39. Ibid., 3:137.

40. See chap. 2, 89–94.

41. In the Muʿtazilite declaration that the Qur'an is the created word of God, we should see not least the attempt to dispute any nearness to the Trinitarian conception of God; cf. Nader, *Le systeme philosophique*, 101; Maalouf, *La place du verbe*, 85–107. The contextualization of Islamic and Christian theological debates still remains to be done; it has long been a neglected avenue of research; see Martin, "Inimitability."

Research so far has treated the dogma above all from the cultural-historical perspective, as an index of an exaggerated Arabic cultural pride. Behind this perspective may have often loomed a contrary expectation suggested by the Christian tradition, the opinion that an especially glamorous verbal dressing of a scripture would be inappropriate. For just as Christ, according to Phil 2:5–8, "though he was in the form of God, did not count equality with God a thing to be grasped, but emptied himself, by taking the form of a servant, being born in the likeness of men,"[42] so must the word of God, the scripture, "make its way through history in the form of a servant." It thus consciously employs a "humble way of speech," the so called *genus humile*.

Gustav von Grunebaum, who dwells on this idea, comes to the conclusion that the early church laid emphasis on the theory of the *genus humile* because a comparison of the Gospels with classical Greek literature compelled them to take this stance. The Qur'an, however, for which no comparable previous writings existed, was not confronted by such standards.[43] But even in relation to Christianity, this claim only touches the surface. If one wanted, one could also recover from the Christian Bible sufficient poetical and rhetorical "pearls" to set against the classical authors. After all, Longinus, a pagan aesthetician of Late Antiquity, cited the beginning of Genesis in his treatise *On the Sublime* as an example of particular linguistic magnificence.[44] On the Arabic side, the claim is grotesque: the low literary evaluation of pre-Islamic poetry and the often unquestioned assumption of the isolation of the Qur'an from the culture that preceded it could hardly be expressed more clearly than in von Grunebaum's verdict. It is all the more astonishing in view of the fact than the theoreticians of *iʿjāz*, among whom is al-Bāqillānī (one of whose tractates was edited by von Grunebaum himself),[45] continuously contextualize their Qur'an-specific observations with observations on the poetry.

13.2.2 *Iʿjāz in the Qur'an*

Although these are later developments, they heuristically offer a promising approach. The Qur'an does not yet use the term *iʿjāz*, nor does its self-reference throughout the proclamation as a qualitatively unmatchable text refer to any tradition outside the text. Again and again, the Qur'an text pronounces the

42. This epistolary passage belongs to the particularly well-known texts of the Eastern Church; it figures as a reading on the Day of the Assumption of Mary. In that it makes an important statement about the Christian representation of the word of God, it belongs also in the context of the discourse within the *iʿjāz* dogma about the particular form of the word of God. This quotation follows the English Standard Version (ESV).

43. Von Grunebaum, *A Tenth-Century Document*, xv.

44. On the work attributed to the otherwise unknown Longinus, *Peri hypsous*, whose composition dates to the first half of the first century CE, see Fuhrmann, *Die Dichtungstheorie der Antike*. For further testimonials of the perception of aesthetic coequality between the Bible and classic literature, see Kugel, "Poetry and Prophecy"; cf. also chap. 12, 419–421.

45. Von Grunebaum, *A Tenth-Century Document.*

challenge to individual hearers to bring something comparable and of equal rank, reflecting the ideological and verbal contest between different stakeholders striving to convey the most persuasive message, the rivals of the proclaimer addressed in the Qur'an being apparently not monotheist but pagan critics of his message. No firm judgments about the chronology of the challenge verses can be made, since they already develop during the proclamation into a topos. Yet the Qur'an does not simply lay out a challenge; Qur'anic speech itself also responds to a challenge. Following Ludwig Ammann, one might see the emphasis on language as evidence of transcendent origin in relation to the conservative position of the Meccan hearers:

> The Meccans do not trust that Muhammad is the messenger of God. His extraordinary textual creation could also be explained otherwise in their view: with the help . . . of the *jinn*, the lower spiritual beings that inspire the soothsayers and poets. Thus, in view of the hints at the speech of soothsayers in the earliest suras, they concede Muhammad to be supernaturally inspired, not however by God, and rank him among the charismatic figures of weaker authority. . . . The speech of revelation must therefore strive to attest to its privileged mantic status. To this end, it lays out the challenge of a contest in verbal art, for which the following assumption is the basis: "Even if men and *jinn* united together, they would not bring forth something equal to the Qur'an!" (Q 17:89). . . . The Qur'anic speech is thus—based on the power of its inimitability—its own miracle of authentication. The claim of inimitability "tops" the observation that the Qur'anic speech art is exceedingly creative. It regards the continuously forceful otherness of this speech, in that the new pattern remains unachievable, as a performance of a wholly "other" speaker, as divine inspiration.[46]

In Ammann's view this is a triumphal claim of rupture with tradition: this "sura corpus, which would replace the qasida as the founding text of the Bedouin form of life, knows no predecessor as a literary genre; as an art work in language, the Qur'anic event of reflection stands unique in history."[47]

In the Qur'an itself, the confrontation with anonymous opponents is presented on several levels. Already in an early Meccan sura, the charge of arbitrary invention of speech is met with the challenge to bring "a speech such as this," *bi-ḥadīthin mithlihi*. In the middle Meccan sura 17, on the other hand, the superiority of the Qur'anic recitation over all conceivable rivals is already affirmed triumphally (verse 88):

46. Ammann, *Die Geburt des Islam*, 45–46.
47. Ibid., 46.

> Say: "Were humans and *jinn* to band together to produce a semblance of this Qur'an [*an ya'tū bi-mithli hādhā l-qur'ān*], they could not do so, even if they backed one another up."

In the late Meccan texts, an open confrontation is even staged, and the challenge of bringing ten text units for recitation, "suras" (*suwar*), is raised (Q 11:13):

> Or do they say: he fabricated it? Say: "Bring forth ten suras like it [*fa-'tū bi-'ashri suwarin mithlihi*], and call upon whomever you can, apart from God, if you speak the truth."

Finally, we find language of *one* sura (*fa-'tū bi-sūratin mithlihi*, "Bring yet a sura, which is equal to it," Q 10:38). The debate reaches its climax with the explicit reference to the unattainability of the sura performance, whose disdain brings with it the loss of life in the hereafter, in the Medinan text Q 2:23–24:

> If you doubt what we revealed to our servant, bring forth one sura like it [*fa-'tū bi-sūratin mithlihi*]. And summon your witnesses, any other than God, if you are truthful. But if you do not, and surely you will not, beware of the fire whose fuel is mankind and stones, made ready for the unbelievers.

It is irrelevant here whether the Arabic word *sūra* already designates the unit "sura" as it was later determined or if it is used here rather to indicate a text for recitation undefined in length. What is important is that we see here a contest around the verbal, and the exclusion of the possibility that the performed speech can be outdone by an opposing speech from outside. This occurs, as the quoted verses show, according to a fixed rhetorical scheme, in which a text performance is required as proof of the validity of the opposing truth claim.

The historicity of the staging of these particular challenges is not certain. Matthias Radscheit takes the so-called *taḥaddī* verses, the "challenge verses," as wholly fictive,[48] which however would say nothing about their effectiveness for Qur'anic argumentation. Even if they are merely rhetorical challenges, or "simulations," they nonetheless represent the expression of a new self-consciousness based not least on verbal competence. The verses give expression to the scenario, characteristic of the Qur'an, of an enduring rhetorical challenge reflected in the dialectical form of the suras,[49] which grows ever more dominant from the middle Meccan period onward.

48. Radscheit, *Herausforderung*, and Radscheit, "Ijāz al-Qur'ān im Koran?" argues on the basis of Wansbrough's scenario of a later anonymous compilation of the Qur'an, so that all Qur'anic dialogues would then have to be only retroactive simulations. His explanation is rejected by Ammann, *Die Geburt des Islam*, 45, and Gilliot, review of Radscheit, *Herausforderung*, 130.

49. See McAuliffe, "Debate with Them in a Better Way."

Within the context of the Qur'anic affirmation of its rhetorical dimension belongs also the insistence on the point that it is a proclamation in Arabic language, which crops up in the middle Meccan period (Q 20:113):

> Hence we sent it down, an Arabic Qur'an [*anzalnāhu qurʾānan ʿarabīyan*], and we detailed in it all kinds of threat; perhaps they will turn pious, or else it may inspire them to remembrance.

Such references to the Arabic language occur into the late Meccan period: Q 12:1–3, 26:192–201, 16:101–103, 39:27–28, 41:1–4, 42:7, 43:1–4, and 46:12. Stefan Wild[50] points out that the Arabness of the Qur'an attested here is occasionally contrasted with the foreign-language form of the earlier scriptures. This special self-referentiality does not yet seem to stand in a religious polemical context, however, but rather to be the triumphal expression of a purely empirical perception. The rabbinic confrontations around the particular rank of Hebrew as *leshon ha-qodesh*, "the sacred language" of the Bible, will be reflected further in the later Islamic discussion of the divine "setting," *tawqīf*, of the language in Arabic,[51] but these discussions remain unconcerned with the Qur'anic understanding of language as a part of the transcendent message.[52] It is striking that no other scripture besides the Qur'an thematizes its own particular language, let alone insists on it as a significant medium of the revelation.[53]

The conviction that stands behind the challenges, that the proclamation as such should be sufficient to render opponents and opposing claims silent, already stands firm and is articulated in a sequence of Meccan debates, in which the Qur'anic proclamation presents itself as its own proof of validity, as a "sign," *āya*, that should fulfill the opponents' demand of a "miracle," *āya*, such as in the late Meccan verse Q 29:50–51:

> They say: "If only some miracles had been sent down on him from his Lord!" Say: "Miracles are with God. I am only a manifest warner." Was it not enough for them that we sent down the scripture on you to be recited to them? In this is a mercy and a remembrance to a people who have faith.

Though we already find an even higher rank given to the recitation as a reproduction of the preexistent word of God (Q 55:1–4),[54] this rank was not made explicit in the challenge debates. But the challenge to bring forth something equal to the

50. Wild, "An Arabic Recitation."

51. Caspar, "Parole de Dieu."

52. Wansbrough, *Quranic Studies*, 93–106. On *leshon ha-qodesh*, see Veltri, *Gegenwart der Tradition*, 51ff. The expression, which does not occur before the Mishna, indicates particular pericopes, which are to be read out in the *leshon ha-qodesh*. Veltri connects the concept with a historical situation in which the Hebrew text of the Torah had become unintelligible (Dirk Hartwig, personal communication).

53. Wild, "An Arabic Recitation," 136, which makes reference to the merely occasional mentions of the respective languages in the biblical books.

54. See chap. 2, 89–94.

reading, which is made six times, and behind which lies the conviction of the ability to overwhelm all opponents through the Qur'anic speech, carries a triumphal tone that is not frequent elsewhere in the Qur'an.

Such a triumphal tone is in no way alien, however, to the reflections in the neighboring traditions about the persuasive power, *persuasio*, of their own believed truths. A hymn to Mary composed around one hundred years before the Qur'an, the Akathistos Hymn,[55] praises the power of persuasion, exceeding all opposing rhetorical professionalism, of a central theological message, the incarnation symbolized by Mary:

> We see articulate orators struck dumb as fish, in view of you, mother of God. . . . Hail to you, who have stripped philosophers of their philosophy, hail to you, who have made the teachers of rhetoric speechless. Hail to you, for the powerful in contest have become dumb because of you, hail, for through you the inventors of follies have become still. Hail, for you have torn the captious entanglements of the Athenians, hail, for you have filled the fishermen's nets.[56]

This degree of hyperbolic rhetoric is foreign to the Qur'an—but a triumphal tone of victory, of the verbally convincing guise of its own transcendent message, is nevertheless unmistakably present in the Qur'an from the middle Meccan period on.

13.2.3 Contest of Traditions

However clearly the "challenge verses" indicate a concrete interaction scenario in which contesters of the Qur'anic message are brought to silence, the definitive challenge should be assumed to have come less from individual opponents, who then had to be encountered with further challenging speeches, than from "hermeneutic opponents," effective older traditions that had to be dealt with as such. The perception that central traditions of the two older religions were dressed in verbally convincing form, and that they drew authority from this form, is reflected in the Qur'an in numerous places. It was above all ubiquitous texts clad in "convincing" formulations, such as creeds, prayers, and hymns, from which a challenge came forth, and this challenge had to be answered by the Qur'anic community through the replica of a new text that would be stylistically close enough to the precursor text to integrate it as an authority-founding reference. In this process, individual personal representatives of these traditions did not necessarily need to be present and involved. Rather, we should understand

55. On the Akathistos Hymn see Peltomaa, *Image of the Virgin*; cf. chap. 9, 324–332.

56. The Greek text is as follows: "rhētoras polyphtongous, hos ichtyas aphonous, oromen epi soi, Theotoke. Chaire, philosophous asophous deiknyousa . . . , chaire, technologous alogous elenchousa. Chaire, hoti emoranthēsan hoi deinoi syzētētai. Chaire, hoti emaranthēsan hoi ton mython poiētai. Chaire, ton Athēnaion tas plokas diasposa. Chaire ton alieon tas sagenas plērousa."

"textual contest" here in a wider sense, in that the response to older traditions was addressed less to the heirs of these traditions, so that the goal was not the triumph over an opposing religious group but rather a continuous reform within the community, in which the traditional material belonging to the formation of individual hearers was checked, sharpened, and modified according to the new consensus taking shape. This can be shown at the end of the early Meccan period in relation to Psalm 136, which is reformulated in an entire sura—without the Jewish or Christian "heirs" of this psalm appearing on the stage.[57] A similar state of affairs holds true for the Christian text models, which are newly formed in the Fātiḥa.[58] The rhetorical moment in this lies not in a polemical address to the hearer but rather in the verbally convincing reformulation of the traditions available in various text types into a new form of rhythmical rhymed prose characteristic of the early Meccan suras.

13.3 A Contest Before Polemic: From Biblical Hymn to Qur'anic Paraenesis

13.3.1 Psalm 104 and Sura 78

An actual contest with the older traditions was already underway in the early Meccan period. The powerfully effective and much cited traditions of the dominant belief communities demanded a response, irrespective of their individual origins. In the beginning, we still sense nothing of that polemical atmosphere that resonates in the challenge (*taḥaddī*) verses cited above. Yet in the early, still unpolemical handling of the challenge coming from the older traditions, we already find a central role played by the moment of *persuasio*, persuasive power, and thus the art of rhetoric. One could even claim that in the Qur'an, older traditions are effectively reformulated not only semantically but also rhetorically, in that they are recast from narrative or hymnic speech into paraenetic speech. One can only trace this reception of older traditions in the final result, for in view of the purely oral transmission of the predecessor texts that we must presuppose for the community, the concrete process of the amalgamation of these traditions cannot be reconstructed. It can be ascertained that a sequence of Qur'anic texts reformulate biblical traditions in accordance with the Qur'anic worldview, without thereby making the older authority-bearing text wholly unrecognizable. The older text remains preserved in important details in the new text, and thus forms the still-comprehensible premise for the Qur'anic antithesis.

57. Neuwirth, "Psalmen."
58. On this, see chap. 8, 282–290.

Several examples of such "antithetical" readings pertain to the new interpretation of psalms. The tension-rich relation between Psalm 104 and sura 78, "The Tidings," is an example that has not yet received due notice, although this very psalm does figure in Heinrich Speyer's list of Qur'anic references to the Psalms.[59] The numerous Qur'anic traces of this Psalm can be explained though its outstanding significance in Jewish and Christian liturgy.[60] The discussion should be premised with the Qur'anic text that is related to the psalm (Q 78:6–17):

a-lam naj'ali l-arḍa mihādā
wa-l-jibāla awtādā
wa-khalaqnākum azwājā
wa-ja'alnā nawmakum subātā
wa-ja'alnā l-layla libāsā
wa-ja'alnā l-nahāra ma'āshā
wa-banaynā fawqkum sab'an shidādā
wa-ja'alnā sirājan wahhājā
wa-anzalnā mina l-mu'ṣirāti mā'an thajjājā
li-nukhrija bihi ḥabban wa-nabātā
wa-jannātin alfāfā
inna yawma l-faṣli kāna mīqātā

Did We not make the earth a couch for you?
And the mountains pegs?
Did We not create you in pairs?
Did We not make your sleep a time of rest
and the night a garment,
and the day a source of livelihood?
Did We not build above you seven firmly established,
and fix a glowing lantern?
Did We not send down rich water on you from clouds, flooding,
to sprout seeds and vegetation, and gardens intertwined?
The day of decision shall be a date appointed.

The short introductory part of the sura (verses 1–5),[61] with its rhetorical question, sounds a theme that is apparently controversial to the hearers, but which itself remains unpronounced. The "great tidings" (verse 2) are—in view of the centrality of eschatology in the early suras—not difficult to identify as the Day of Judgment, especially since it is followed by a threat to the doubters (verses 4–5).

59. Speyer, *Die biblischen Erzählungen im Qoran*, 498, names thirteen Qur'anic references to Psalms 104.
60. See the evidence from the Jewish tradition in Neuwirth, "Psalmen."
61. Neuwirth, *Studien zur Komposition*, 217.

The second part that follows (verses 6–16, presented here) responds to the beginning dialectically: the catalogue of divine acts of creation (*āyāt* series) should disperse all doubt about the omnipotence of God, which for some still block the belief in the Final Judgment. The third part (verses 17–40), setting in with an evocation of the day of Judgment, merges into an eschatological scene, followed by a detailed double image.

Sura 78 offers one of the rare cases in which a non-narrative biblical subtext becomes clearly evident: the *āyāt* series in the middle part, verses 6–16, is unmistakably evocative of Psalms 104:1–23[62] (Ps 104:1–5, 13–14, 19–23):

Praise the Lord, my soul.
Lord my God, you are very great;
you are clothed with splendor and majesty.
The Lord wraps himself in light as with a garment;
he stretches out the heavens like a tent
and lays the beams of his upper chambers on their waters.
He makes the clouds his chariot
and rides on the wings of the wind.
He makes winds his messengers,
flames of fire his servants.
He set the earth on its foundations;
it can never be moved.[63]

He waters the mountains from his upper chambers;
the land is satisfied by the fruit of his work.
He makes grass grow for the cattle,
and plants for people to cultivate—
bringing forth food from the earth . . .

He made the moon to mark the seasons,
and the sun knows when to go down.
You bring darkness, it becomes night,
and all the beasts of the forest prowl.
The lions roar for their prey
and seek their food from God.
The sun rises, and they steal away;
they return and lie down in their dens.
Then people go out to their work,
to their labor until evening.

62. The translation is influenced by Gunkel, *Die Psalmen*; the name of God used in Gunkel's historical reading, YHWH, was supposedly replaced by Adonai/Kyrios already in the psalm reception of Late Antiquity.

63. Verses 6–12 depict the myth of the parting of the waters.

13.3.2 *Comparison of the Texts*

Despite the differing frameworks—in the psalm, the praises enumerated are an integral part of a great hymn, while in the sura they are framed as eschatological descriptions—the two texts nonetheless show significant commonalities. Most striking is the image that occurs nowhere else in the Qur'an of the earth as a tent[64] (Q 78:6–7), set on pillars (Ps 104:2; cf. Q 78:7), holding up the heavens as a roof (Ps 104:2), held in place by pegs (Q 78:7). In both texts, however, the image of the tent is not exclusive: in the sura text, the "seven firmly established," which presuppose the Ptolemaic cosmology with the sun as light source (Q 78:12–24), cannot be united without tension with the metaphor of the tent; in the psalm, the image of the tent runs counter to the conception of the cosmos as a multistoried house of God, from whose upper "chambers," *'aliyot* (Ps 104:3; 13), God provides for his creation.[65] Furthermore, in both texts, clouds (Ps 104:13, Q 78:14), mountains (Ps 104:13, Q 78:7), sun and moon (Ps 104:19; 22, Q 78:13), and night (Ps 104:20, Q 78:10), as well as the nourishment through the growth of plants (Ps 104:14, Q 78:15–16), are presented as divine supports. The time of mankind is the bright day for earning his living (Ps 104:13, Q 78:11), a thought that is not taken up elsewhere in the Qur'an. But the two texts diverge in the depiction of the nighttime, since, going beyond the psalm, the sura mentions the idea that humans have been created as gendered pairs, for whom the night is given as the time of their sexual fulfillment—a remarkable Qur'anic addition to the psalmic image of the human habitat, which does not thematize sexuality. This thought is expressed with a metaphor that is unique in the Qur'an:[66] the two sexes appear wrapped in a cosmic garment (Q 78:10: *wa-ja'alnā l-layla libāsā*, "Have we not given to you the night as a garment?"). Such a cosmic metaphor in the psalm is conceded only to God as a depiction of his majesty ("with glory and majesty you are doned [*lavashta*]. You wrap yourself in light as in a garment [*ka-samla*]," verse 1–2). In the Qur'an, this anthropomorphism is "corrected," so to speak, in that the perspective of God is directed away to humans. The cosmic metaphor thus does not need to be relinquished; it is transferred to the human couple. Not only through the strategy of "correcting anthropomorphisms" that was current in contemporary Bible exegesis as well but also through the reference to the contemporary state of knowledge, the cosmic structure based on seven planetary spheres, the Qur'an text shows itself as a document of Late Antiquity.

But what is unmistakable above all is a fundamental difference: the psalm draws a great mythical tableau in which a deity is presented in an anthropomorphic shape who—before the eyes of the psalmist, so to speak—rules in a lordly way, drives along in a heavenly chariot, and personally shapes the living

64. On the ancient Near Eastern context of this image, see Lumpe and Bietenhard, "Himmel."

65. The translation follows Gunkel, *Die Psalmen*; see his commentary, 448; cf. also Zenger, *Psalmen*, 2:27–43.

66. It is quoted again in Q 25:47 from Q 78:10.

conditions of his creation, taking care of their sustenance. Creation itself seems dynamically affected, set in motion by his presence; wild creatures come forward and retreat and request from him their nutrition (Ps 104:20–22). One could speak here of the topos of the *locus amoenus*,[67] the "pleasant place" that from Greek Antiquity down to the Renaissance was a dominant motif in descriptions of nature, including those of the afterlife, and which, according to Ernst Robert Curtius, involves the setting of a light grove, trees, and running water or springs forming an idealized scenery of human and especially animal interaction. It is true that in the psalm the description of nature is set in service of the praise of God, but without losing its aesthetic appeal: the world, particularly in view of the presence of God who rules in it, is distinguished as a "pleasant place" marked by natural riches and the lively interaction of men with their environment. This judgment cannot be readily applied to the nature description in the sura. As harmoniously as the human habitat is described there, it does not combine into a coherent scenario. The individual elements stand for themselves and, instead of being components of an image, are charged with meaning in themselves: as the paraenetic form of the rhetorical question that holds the whole tableau together demonstrates these individual components are meant to point to a theological message.

For here the work of creation is not envisioned as a *creatio perpetua*, as in the psalm, but rather it appears as having been long completed. God is no longer present as the agent of creation but rather as a speaker, who in first-person speech calls his deeds to memory as *instruction*. All the provisions for his creatures enacted by God appear as frozen into timeless divine *speech*. It is the field of eschatological tension created by the new Qur'anic context that has reconfigured the narrative report of creation anew, transforming it from an *image* to a part of a *discourse*: the text answers in rhetorically expressive speech, through the use of the figures of speech of anaphor (Q 78:9–13) and the (cosmic) metaphor (Q 78:10), and also the consistent use of personal address, to the doubt that still exists among the hearers about the omnipotence of God, which was expressed in the initiatory provocative rhetorical question. It is a discursive offer that is proposed to the hearers: to decide between the correct side, in view of the judgment presented in conclusion, and the "opposite place" of hell, a *locus terribilis*. The passage is not a hymn, as in the psalm, an expression of spontaneous emotion, but rather a warning reminder, an argument.

Just as the Qur'an with its unemotional gaze at creation distances itself from the psalm, which revels in its mythic dynamic and cosmic metaphoric, its positive reinterpretation of the great predecessor text is all the more significant and theologically enriching for the new perception of the world. The tent that the

67. Curtius, *Europäische Literatur*, 202–209.

Qur'anic verse group sketches is not part of the cosmic dwelling place of God but rather a "habitation" trimmed back to human dimensions. Man, who in the pre-Islamic worldview is abandoned to nature,[68] is presented in the Qur'an as housed. For him, unlike the pre-Islamic hero, neither maintenance nor sexual fulfillment are denied or made unavailable. The Qur'an reverses the ancient Arabic relation of man and nature.[69] It does this not through an argumentation derived from reality but rather by means of referentiality, with the help of the psalmic intertext, from which it excises, so to speak, the elements relevant for man. The psalmist praises the monumental glory of God with a view directed upward, while the Qur'anic speaker has God, looking down on man from above, explain to man his earthly habitation as a work of divine creation: a quasi-paradisiacal scenario of interaction, in which man stands in the center. Set against the psalm text, we find a Qur'anic counter-version, in which the change of speaker from man to God, and the reversal of perspective thus achieved, has led to a frigidly argumentative presentation of the world that appears—in comparison to the psalm—emotionally withdrawn. The hymnics of the psalm give way to Qur'anic rhetoric.

In all this, we should not overlook that the Qur'an, based on its textual, that is, psalmic, images of nature, describes a turn in relation to the pre-Islamic perception of nature.[70] In the pre-Islamic worldview, the natural milieu occurs as a challenge to mankind; it is not immediately accessible but rather a disputed space, which must first be conquered by the Bedouin hero. The image of nature sketched by the early poets in the opening sections of their odes expresses no aesthetic delight in nature, but presents rather the hero's struggle to restore the lost form of that space, which was earlier filled with felicitous social interaction but is now abandoned and obliterated by nature.[71] Even the descriptions of spring looming large in the presentation of the "camel journey," which do praise the bounties of nature, restrict the undamped enjoyment of these blessings to the realm of animals, while the phenomenon of nature's cyclical self-renewal exerts the opposite effect on man, only bringing to his mind his own temporality. In contrast to this heroic or melancholic position toward space in poetry, the early Qur'an texts present, in their psalm-imprinted *āyāt*-passages, the earthly space as trust-inspiring, as a habitation, at times even as an idyllic scenario. They present it as a place of happiness and leisure, of the enjoyment of divine benefactions and ethically directed human interaction. Later parables and even polemics equally reflect, as Patricia Crone has shown,[72] rural life. The Qur'anic orientation to biblical images that is detectable in the reworkings of Psalm 104 and Psalm

68. Müller, *Ich bin Labīd*.
69. Neuwirth, "Geography."
70. See Neuwirth, "Geography."
71. See Neuwirth, "Geography."
72. Crone, "How Did the Qur'ānic Pagans Make a Living?"

136[73] clearly suggest the assumption of a fundamentally text-referential rather than reality-referential pronouncement in the Qur'an, though this problem still requires more precise treatment.

13.4 Rhetorical Bonding of Earthly Events to the Transcendent Lord of the Worlds: Paraenetic Clausulas

13.4.1 From Sajʿ Rhymed Verse to Clausula Verse

Rhetorical innovation manifests itself in the Qur'an not only in the reformulation of existing traditions but even more in the production of a prose style unknown in Arabic up to that time, the clausula discourse.[74] With the new form of prose interspersed throughout with recollections of God, valuations, and admonishments for behavior, we see the creation of an effective stylistic medium of sacrally coded speech and a uniquely flexible theological strategy of connecting innerworldly relations to the transcendent God. This has not been closely observed as such in research up to now.[75] Thus, Friedrich Schwally[76] states rather pejoratively: "Muhammad's style becomes ever more slack, so that in the late Meccan and Medinan suras only two types of rhyme, easy to achieve through grammatical endings and frequent words, prevail. . . . The carelessness in the use of rhyme becomes more palpable, the less rhyme comes to suit the prosaic tone of the later pieces, and we have to regard it—particularly in legal instructions and the like—as a heavy fetter, which does not at all decorate the speech." But already Josef Horowitz[77] drew attention to the parallels with the law texts in the Pentateuch, where the individual prosaic provisions likewise end with warning or with strengthening of God's authority, such as Leviticus 19–20. Clausula speech thus can be regarded as thoroughly suitable for the communication of religiously established laws, particularly if these are meant as oral public proclamations. Yet later researchers have remained dependent on Nöldeke's and Schwally's mistaken evaluation of the long verses as prose units flawed by an unsuitable rhyme.[78]

73. Neuwirth, "Psalmen"; cf. also chap. 3, 119–131.

74. Neuwirth, *Studien zur Komposition*, 56–178; cf. chap. 5, 192–196.

75. Nöldeke's verdict, *GdQ*, 30, repeated in *GdQII* (second edition), 6, has persisted into later research: "But even with the strict care that he dedicated to rhyme or assonance, he shows a lack of appreciation for the form, and he shows this yet more in that he persists with rhymed verse even though his revelations have become closer to pure prose. On account of this admittedly imperfect rhyming, his language was subject to much compulsion, although the individual verses of the respective sections often varied greatly with respect to length. Muhammad certainly meditated greatly over the content of his revelation before he brought it to light, but very little over its form."

76. Schwally, *GdQ2*, 40.

77. Horovitz, *Koranische Untersuchungen.*

78. Bell, *Introduction to the Qur'an*, 69–70, taken over by Watt, *Bell's Introduction to the Qur'an*, 70–71; Blachère, *Histoire de la Littérature arabe* 2:216, 221, 225; Gibb, "ʿArabīya," 585; Gabrieli, *Storia della letteratura araba*, 89; Müller, *Untersuchungen zur Reimprosa*, 3–4; cf. also Wansbrough's review of Müller. All these positions are discussed by Neuwirth, *Studien zur Komposition*, 171–174.

Within the dominant approach, the clausulas—not being current in profane narrative technique and not required for the progress of the narrated event—are still today treated as disturbing or at best superfluous. What is overlooked here is that the introduction of the widely stereotypical cola of the long verses, in place of the rhyming endings of the short verses, signals not only a stylistically and mnemotechnically relevant change of form but also a change of the intended function of the Qur'an texts. The clausula endings of the verses are indeed not only end-markers of a complex semantic-syntactic speech unit and elements to support the memorizing of intended sense-units, but they are in most cases paraenetic comments on what is presented, metatextual "recollections" of the source of the speech, God himself, or at least of his admonishments and claims. Thus, every statement, even descriptive or reporting ones, becomes a direct or indirect "appeal,"[79] an instigation to resume communication. Even Qur'anic salvation history thus turns into cultic address.

The Qur'anic effectiveness of this device will be demonstrated in an example. The early Meccan sura 97, "The Determination," and the introduction to the middle Meccan sura 44, "The Smoke," (verses 2–8) are dedicated to the same object, the "night of the determination."[80] Both texts work with metatextual elements, sura 97 through rhetorical questions, and the later sura 44 through clausulas.

innā anzalnāhu fī laylati l-qadr
wa-mā adrāka mā laylatu l-qadr
laylatu l-qadri khayrun min alfi shahr
  tanazzalu l-malāʾikatu wa-l-rūḥu fīhā
  bi-idhni rabbihim min kulli amr
salāmun hiya ḥattā maṭlaʿi l-fajr

We sent it down in the night of determination.
Do you know what the night of determination is?
The night of determination is better than a thousand months.
  In it angels and the spirit descend
  by permission of their Lord in every matter.
It is a blessing until break of day! (Q 97:1–5)

ḥāʾ mīm
wa-l-kitābi l-mubīn
innā anzalnāhu fī laylatin mubārakatin
  innā kunnā mundhirīn

79. Cf. the three-part division of speech into declaration, description, and appellatory speech in Bühler, *Sprachtheorie*.

80. On the two suras, see Neuwirth, *Studien zur Komposition*, 157.

fīhā yufraqu kullu amrin ḥakīm
amran min ʿindinā
    innā kunnā mursilīn
raḥmatan min rabbika
    innahu huwa l-samīʿu l-ʿalīm
rabbi l-samawāti wa-l-arḍi wa-mā baynahumā
    in kuntum mūqinīn
lā ilāha illā huwa, yuḥyi wa-yumītu
    rabbukum wa-rabbu abāʾikumu l-awwalīn

Ha mim
By the clear writing!
We sent it down in a blessed night—
    It is We who are the warners -
In which all the wise decisions are taken
By instruction from us—
    It is We who send down,
Out of mercy from your Lord—
He is the all-hearing, the all-knowing,
From the Lord of the heavens and the earth and what is between them,
    If you would indeed recognize it!
No God but him! He brings to life and lets die,
    Your Lord and the Lord of your forefathers! (Q 44:1–8)

Three statements are shared between the two texts: (1) the sending down of the *qurʾān* figuring as a medium of divine-human communication, in a blessed night, (2) the glorification of the night, and (3) God's position on this. In the early Meccan sura 97,[81] these statements are distributed over four short verses: verse 1 = statement (1), verses 3 and 4a = statement (2), and verse 4b = statement (3). This distribution avoids the stylistic flaw of overly compressing the weighty message into verses following immediately on each other; therefore in verse 2 a rhetorical question[82] halts the progression of the discourse and thus lends additional weight to the statements. In sura 44, whose style is already more syntactically complex, multipartite, verses, that is, verses consisting of more than one sentence, the prevailing verse rhythm requires longer verse units. To compress more than one of the important statements into a single longer verse, which would be technically possible, would deprive them of their particular pathos. The three statements are therefore isolated from each other through clausulas: statement (1) is additionally accounted for in verse 3b through a self-praising of God as *mundhir*,

81. It is considered here in its final form. On verse 4, which was added later, see Sinai, *Studien zur frühen Koraninterpretation*, 157.
82. On the structural elements of the suras, cf. chap. 5, 166–187.

"warner"; statement (2) borders directly on statement (3), but the sequence is loosened stylistically through the enjambement *yufraqu . . . / amran*, "decisions are taken . . . / by instruction." A clausula is used for closure, which now praises God as the sender of messengers (verse 5b). Then statement (3) is taken up again in verse 6a, focusing now on the divine motif, after which comes another clausula—about God as the all-hearing, the all-knowing (verse 6b). Connected to both closing verses of the passage we find further hymnic praises, expressed in 7b by a paraenetic and verse 8c by a hymnic clausula. Both texts, sura 97 and Q 44:1–8, employ stylistic strategies to avoid an overly strong amassment and thus a devaluation of important statements. This is effected in sura 97 by a rhetorical question, while in sura 44 it is achieved by the employment of clausulas, which has become a regular strategy from the middle Meccan period on.

13.4.2 *What Exactly Are Clausulas?*

On the one hand, clausulas are markers of verse endings. In the early Meccan period, individual marked rhymes signaled the verse ends unambiguously; but this effect can no longer be brought about by the rhyme alone, after the adoption of rhymed prose composed of long verses with rhymes largely based on the morphologically easily achieved *-ūn/-īn* pattern. The element that is to be repeated, which now signals the close, is thus no longer purely phonetic, but rather takes on syntactical dimensions, since the masculine plural ending (*-ūn/-īn*), which is now necessary for the completion of the rhyme at the conclusion of the sentence, can only be achieved through particular syntactical constructions. But not all concluding cola[83] are clausulas; the term should only be applied for those cola that structurally resemble formulas and thus have a clear concluding character.[84] These stand out from their context semantically as well, containing for the most part transcendence referents that give the text a sacral encoding. The following types can be distinguished:[85]

1. Clausulas confirming the revelation (Q 44:3 and 5)
2. Hymnic clausulas, often predications of God (Q 44:6 and 8)
3. Evaluative clausulas, the chief function of which is to judge the actors of the narrated story or their behaviors positively or negatively from a religious or moral aspect, e.g., *wa-mā anā mina l-mushrikīn*, "I am not one of those who associate others with God" (Q 12:108c)

83. On the term, see chap. 5, 192–196.

84. The author has attempted to classify the specific formal characteristics on the basis of the constituents of sentences in *Studien zur Komposition*, with reference to the criteria developed for the formulaicity of early Arabic poetry by Monroe, "Oral Composition."

85. In what follows, the description of the clausulas provided in an earlier study is taken up again; cf. Neuwirth, "Yūsuf-Sure."

4. Clausulas focusing on conditions or behaviors. These determine actions or temporary conditions that are value neutral but significant for the progress of the plot, so, e.g., *wa-hum yamkurūn*, "while they were intriguing" (Q 12:102c).
5. Paraenetic clausulas in a stricter sense. These appeal directly to the insight or gratitude of the hearers. They can entail a direct exhortation or a warning against wrong behavior, e.g. *in kuntum mūqinīn*, "if you but would recognize clearly" (Q 44:7), or *la'allakum ta'qilūn*, "that perhaps you might comprehend" (Q 12:2b).

In sura 12, the evaluative clausulas and the predications of God alone amount to nearly half of all verse endings, fifty of a total 111, which is not surprising in a sura that is claimed in the Qur'an itself to be "the most beautiful narration" (verse 3), and which therefore is acknowledged as especially formidable and well-suited for meditation. In sura 12, which has been specially studied with regard to its clausulas, we find an extraordinary intensive employment of that hermeneutical element, which deserves to be termed the *basso continuo* of the later Qur'anic discourse, namely, the all-penetrating remembrance of God as the absolute ruler and consequently the awareness of the division of men into those who act according to the will of God and those who act against it. It is worth noting that the evaluative clausulas not only make statements about the respective persons in question but implicitly contain an appeal to the reciter and his hearers to join the positive group or at least endure with them and part ways with or remain separate from the negative group. We should also understand accordingly the analytic constructions with *min*, "one of," + plural. In sura 12, this construction appears nine times: in the verses 24, 26, 27, 29, 33, 36, 51, 78, and 108. Q 12:78 is an example:

qālū yā ayyuhā l-'azīzu inna lahu aban shaykhan kabīran
fa-khudh aḥadanā makānahu
innā narāka mina l-muḥsinīn

They said: O powerful Lord, he has a father who is very old,
So take one of us in his place;
we see that you are one of those who do good.

It is not merely the compulsion of rhyme that prompts the choice of the unwieldy means of expression; rather, in view of the frequent Qur'anic division of mankind into two camps without any intermediary levels, this kind of recouping of rhyme simply comes in handy. The fact that it also imported from poetry which is rich in analogous constructions, the flair of sophisticated speech, was certainly welcome.

In sura 12, which itself includes no hymn as such, elements of hymn are strewn throughout the entire narrative part in the form of verse-ending clausulas. For a contemplative hearer, these predications of God could even appear as the actual backbone of the narrative. Seen as such, the narrative is not intertwined and adorned with epithets of God, but rather the various praiseworthy characteristics of God are unfolded by means of a narrative. The short clausula, limited to the ending colon of individual verses, can be considered as a Qur'anic coinage of what in Christian-Jewish contexts takes the form of hymnic speech across entire verse groups.

This change of hermeneutical keys, by which the discourse occasionally transcends its actual themes, also made an impact on some unbiased intellectuals of markedly European training. Just one example is Hugo von Hofmannsthal, whose testimony is all the more valuable as it is based not directly on the Qur'an but rather on the strong aftereffect of this Qur'anic mode of discourse in later Islamic culture. In his classic introduction to *One Thousand and One Nights* (first printed in 1907) he writes:

> In the story of *ʾAlī Shār* and the faithful *Zumurrud*, to hit on just one of a thousand pages, there is a moment that I would not trade for any of the most sublime places in our most venerable books. And it is almost nothing. The lover wants to free his beloved, who has been stolen away by an evil old ghost. He has scouted out the house, and is under the window at midnight; a sign is agreed upon, and he merely needs to give it. But he must wait a short while. Then he is overtaken by a leaden sleep, as inconvenient as it is irresistible, as if fate from the darkness had breathed stultifyingly onto him. "Indeed then sleepiness overtook him," it says, "and he fell asleep—mighty is he, who never sleeps!"[86]

13.5 Rhetorical Triumph over the Jewish and Christian Credos

There is yet a further contest recognizable in sura 112, "The Pure Belief,"[87] see table, which is represented by the single voice of the Qur'an itself, although which other voices can still be heard in it; here we will lay out a discussion of this contest in its rhetorical aspects.[88]

It is difficult not to hear the beginning verse *qul huwa llāhu aḥad*, "Say: He is God is one," as a free translation of the Jewish credo, *Shmaʿ Yisraʾel, adonai*

86. Von Hofmannsthal, "Tausendundeine Nacht," 473, reprinted in Littmann, *Tausendundeine Nacht*, 1:12.

87. For the reference texts to sura 112, see the databank of "intertexts" in the project Corpus Coranicum, Berlin-Brandenburg Academy of Sciences. The first part of the sura was already connected with various biblical texts, including the Shemaʿ Yisraʾel, by Paçacı, "Sura 12." However, Paçacı does not understand the Qur'anic relation to these texts dialectically, but rather assumes a shared store of traditions that has been incorporated in the Qur'an. The contextualization of the second part is due to a conversation with Michael Marx. The studies by Newby, "Sūrat al-Iskhlāṣ"; Rubin, "al-Ṣamad"; and Ambros, "Sura 112," which do not contain discussion of the Jewish-Christian credo intertexts, do not recognize the dialectical character of the sura.

88. Cf. chap. 3, 116–119.

Nicene-Constantinopolitan Creed (381 CE)		Dtn 6:4		Q 112: "Sincerity" (*al-ikhlāṣ*)	
English	Greek	English	Hebrew	English	Arabic
We believe in one God,	Πιστεύομεν εἰς ἕνα Θεόν,	Hear, Israel, the Lord is our God, the Lord is One.	שְׁמַע, יִשְׂרָאֵל: יְהוָה אֱלֹהֵינוּ, יְהוָה אֶחָד.	Say: He is God, one,	وَلَمْ يَكُن لَّهُۥ كُفُوًا أَحَدٌ
The Father ***Almighty***, Maker of heavens and earth, and of all things visible and invisible.	Πατέρα, Παντοκράτορα, ποιητὴν οὐρανοῦ καὶ γῆς, ὁρατῶν τε πάντων καὶ ἀοράτων.			God, the absolute,	وَلَمْ يَكُن لَّهُۥ كُفُوًا أَحَدٌ
And in one Lord Jesus Christ, ***the only-begotten Son of God, begotten of the Father*** before all worlds (aeons), Light of Light, very God of very God, ***begotten, not made***,	Καὶ εἰς ἕνα Κύριον Ἰησοῦν Χριστόν, τὸν Υἱὸν τοῦ Θεοῦ τὸν μονογενῆ, τὸν ἐκ τοῦ Πατρὸς γεννηθέντα πρὸ πάντων τῶν αἰώνων· φῶς ἐκ φωτός, Θεὸν ἀληθινὸν ἐκ Θεοῦ ἀληθινοῦ, γεννηθέντα οὐ ποιηθέντα,			He did not beget, nor is he begotten,	وَلَمْ يَكُن لَّهُۥ كُفُوًا أَحَدٌ
being of one substance with the Father.	ὁμοούσιον τῷ Πατρί.			And there is none like him.	وَلَمْ يَكُن لَّهُۥ كُفُوًا أَحَدٌ

elohenu adonai eḥad, "Hear Israel: the Lord, our God, is one" (Dtn 6:4). The key-word "one" *eḥad*, resonates unmistakably in the Arabic text with *aḥad*, "one." This "multivocity" "polyphony," of two texts in one is achieved through an "ungrammaticality," a violation of Arabic grammar, which in place of the noun *aḥad* in rhyme position would require the adjective *wāḥid*. According to the theory of the researcher of poetics Michael Riffaterre, ungrammaticality denotes a verbal phenomenon that, by standing out from a certain text, makes reference to another text where this form is "normal." What initially appears as an irregularity shows itself, through knowledge of the "other text," to be a bridge between two texts that mutually illuminate each other: Riffaterre speaks here of a *dual sign*, a sign of double significance: "The sign of double significance works through a play on words. . . . It is initially perceived as mere ungrammaticality, until one discovers that there is another text in which the word is 'grammatical.' Once this text is identified, the sign of double significance becomes significant in its form, which makes reference to that other code."

As we have seen, the Jewish text remains hearable through the Qur'anic version. This audible "citation," hearable across linguistic borders, underlines the new Qur'an-specific turn, which transfers the old credo, a confession-specific text marked by address to Israel, into a universal text to be repeated by all men. To make the Jewish credo universally valid, and thus also acceptable to a non-Jewish hearership, the text is reformulated, but without losing the distinct form in which it already possesses authority.

Not quite so striking on first glance is the fact that the short sura makes reference to a further credo. The text that was central in Judaism had long been interpreted in Christian theology in terms of a Trinitarian credo. In the Nicene Creed, it takes this form: "We believe in one God, the Father, the all-powerful, who created everything, heaven and earth, all that is sensible and insensible. And in the one Lord Jesus Christ, the Son of God, who was born as the only child from the Father before all time, light out of light, true God out of true God, born, not created, of one essence with the father." The Qur'anic verse 112:3, *lam yalid wa-lam yūlad*, "he did not engender a child, nor was he born," resonates as an echo of the Nicene Creed "born, not created." But the verse unmistakably rejects the statement of the Nicene Creed, *genēthenta ou poiēthenta*, "born, not created." It is remarkable that it thereby employs a double expression that is no less emphatic than the original, *lam yalid wa-lam yūlad*, "he did not engender child and was not born," and thus remains close to the "translated" text in its rhetorically marked form. A negative theology is here established, achieved through a recognizable inversion of a key text that is prominent locally—though among Christians rather than Jews. This negative theology is condensed in verse 4: *wa-lam yakun lahu kufuwan aḥad*, "and no one is equal to him."[89]

89. Riffaterre, *Semiotics of Poetry*, 92.

This verse, which up to now has been read simply as a particularly forceful confession of monotheism, is striking. It introduces *kufuwan*, "equal," which occurs only once in the Qur'an, as a reproduction of the important theological concept *homoousios*, Greek for "equal in nature." It thus not only inverts the Nicene Creed's statement of the essential likeness of Christ with the Father, *homoousios to patri*, but also goes beyond it to epistemically exclude the mere thought that any created being could be equal to God—to say nothing of the essential likeness of a son. This is yet another ambitious rhetorical translation, but one that induces a rigorous reinterpretation of an older text.

Where do such probings of the Qur'anic wording lead? Not least to the traces of that "conversation" from which the Qur'anic text, as we have it, came forth. For the text that opposes the Nicene Creed is of course not simply a polemical address to the Christians but also forms a part of a new cross-confessional formulation of the two familiar credos as they may have been acceptable not just to the Qur'anic community but also to hearers from among the Jewish community of Medina: a reformulation of the Jewish confession of God's unity, expanded by a delimitation against Christological interpretations of the unity of God.

This kind of historical illumination of the structure of Qur'an texts stands at a far remove from inner-Islamic exegesis. Yet inner-Islamic exegesis attributes the highest significance to the structure of the discourse. The classical scholar of rhetoric al-Jurjānī based his defense of the uniqueness of the Qur'an predominately on "structure," that is, the "meaningful linking of word signs to the communication of an intention," *naẓm*. Navid Kermani has cited the programmatic passages in his work on Qur'anic rhetoric:

> We say that the qualitative excess (*mazāyā*) appeared to them (i.e., the contemporaries of Muhammad) in the *naẓm* of the Qur'an, that it was the peculiarities they found employed in the linking of verbal expressions (*alfāẓ*) that incapacitated them in the face of any response or challenge; we say that it was the figures of word and sense (*badā'i'*) comprised within the individual elements of the verses that filled them with shudders, and that every expression was in its place and in harmony with the others. . . . They found a well-structuredness that overwhelmed their spirits through its majesty and paralyzed all men on the basis of verbal order and harmony, by its inner perfection and the conclusiveness of its construction. No longer did any speaker feel the ambition to set something against it; he would rack his brains if he wanted, but nothing would come to him, so that no tongue was able any longer to say anything or make claims, and even the greatest of the opponents admitted defeat and withheld every word of resistance.[90]

90. Al-Jurjānī, *Dalā'il al-I'jāz fī l-Qur'ān*, 44; translation by Kermani, *Gott ist schön*, 256.

Although it is itself a paradigmatic example of hyperbole or "exaggeration," *mubāligha*, this encomium brings to a point a central characteristic of the Qur'anic language: its particular pathos due to conscious rhetorical molding. The social frame of this success is, in al-Jurjānī's view, that of a contest. In agreement with the literary genre of his tractate on "inimitability," he thinks in particular of the rhetorical triumph over verbally gifted rivals of the Prophet. What he describes as a trump card of the Qur'anic style, however, the impressive figures of word and sense in the individual verses, stands out all the more if one contrasts it with familiar older formulations from the Jewish/Christian predecessor texts. In the two examples already presented, suras 78 and 112, we see a tendency to eclipse the Christian or Jewish texts taken as challenges, through the heightening of expression: this was achieved in sura 112 through the universalization of particulars, *qul*, "speak!," instead of "Hear, Israel," or "he did not engender a child nor was he born," which is clearly more categorical in comparison to "born, not created." It was achieved in sura 78 through the redistribution of anthropomorphic or cosmic attributes from God to mankind. Ornamental rhetorical figures, *badāʾiʿ*, are also instrumental in this, such as anaphor *[qul huwa] Allāhu aḥad, Allāhu l-ṣamad*, "[say, he] God is one / God, the constant" in Q 112:1–2, or the anaphoric sequence *khalaqnākum . . . wa-jaʿalnā . . . wa-jaʿalnā . . .*, "We created you . . . / We made . . . / We made . . . ," in Q 78:8–11;13. It was not only that contemporary opponents, as the "challenge verses" might suggest, were to be overcome, but also, and above all, it was necessary to confront the powerful traditions of the predecessor religions on the same level.

Rhetoric in the Qur'an is thus not only a means for spontaneous persuasion; it also stands in the service of the creation of a new speech form. It is concerned with the communication of theological positions, which subliminally accompanying the semantic message, suggest the epistemic verifiability of the message. It is for the sake of this new speech form that the emotionally affecting image of Psalm 104 was "recast" in the Qur'an into an epistemically oriented structure that aims at rational insight, thus pursuing the goal of *persuasio*, persuasion, through consciously employed means. This new structure can be termed the specific "rhetorical structure" of the Qur'an.

What we have presented in this last section is not transmitted in the Islamic tradition. The biography of the Prophet shows little interest in the debates with the older communities, and even less does it allow for these to be the triggers of Qur'anic textual production. No one would read sura 112 or sura 78 against the background of their pre-Islamic, Christian and Jewish, intertexts. The reasons for this refusal to face the multifacetedness and polyphony of the Qur'an as ultimately a reflection of the pluriculturality of pre-Islamic Arabia are too complex historically and politically to be discussed in detail in this framework.

One important reason, however, can certainly be identified: it is concern for the integrity of the Qur'an. The problematics inherent in our new perspective on the history of the Qur'an's genesis should therefore not be downplayed: the reading we have suggested would make sensible a wide spectrum of "buried" theological and liturgical traditions that were once transmitted in the Arabic language. The great wealth of long ignored and forgotten traditions thus would become recognizable again. It would however also require—and this, seen from the conservative standpoint, would be an imminent negative result—breaking taboos: the exclusivity of the classical Arabic language, which reaches its climax in the Qur'an, is problematized. Looking at the Qur'an through a historical-critical lens, we can glimpse the diversity of the "inartificial" linguistic and cultural idiom that circulated in the Near East before Islam shining through the varnish of the aesthetically developed and unprecedentedly successful medium of Arabic, a diversity that was obscured from historical consciousness by canonization. Ultimately, the Qur'an's—historically unique—unifying achievement, once the text is reconnected to the diversity that it came to cover up, would be available for discussion again.

At the same time—and this seems to be the most important argument *for* our approach—it is only through historical reflection that the text becomes fully recognizable in its dimensions of innovation. Only when the epistemic revolution achieved by the Qur'an is set into relief against a historically illuminated background can the Qur'an be recognized as both an Islamic inheritance and a Late Antique legacy to Europe. And only then can we begin to perceive it, finally, on the same level as the two more ancient scriptures.

Bibliography

Abbott, Nabia. *The Rise of the North Arabic Script and Its Kur'anic Development, with a Full Description of the Kur'anic Manuscripts in the Oriental Institute*. Chicago, 1939.

Abbott, Nabia. *Studies in Arabic Literary Papyri*; vol. 2: *Qur'anic commentary and tradition*. Chicago, 1967.

ʿAbd al-Baqi, Fuʾad. *Al-Muʿjjam al-mufahras li-alfāz al-Qurʾān al-karīm*. Cairo, 1364/1944.

Abd al-Rahman, A'isha (Bint al-Shati'). *Al-Iʿjāz al-bayānī li-l-Qurʾān wa-Masāʾil Ibn al-Azraq*. Cairo, 1971.

Abdel Haleem, M. A. "The Qur'anic Employment of the Story of Noah," in: *JQS* 8.1 (2006), 38–57.

Abduh, Muḥammad, and Rashid Rida. *Tafsīr al-Manār*, 12 vols. Cairo, 1346–1353/1906–1934.

Abu Zaid, Nasr Hamid. *Mafhūm al-Naṣṣ: Dirāsa fī ʿulūm al-Qurʾān*. Cairo, 1990.

Abu Zaid, Nasr Hamid. *Islam und Politik: Kritik des religiçsen Diskurses*. Frankfurt am Main, 1996.

Adang, Camilla. "Tawrat," in: *EQ*, vol. 5. Leiden, 2005, 300–311.

Adjina, Muhammad. *Mausūʿat asāṭīr al-ʿarab* [Encyclopedia of Arab mythology]. Beirut, 2005.

Adler, William. "The Jews as Falsifiers: Charges of Tendentious Emendations in Anti-Jewish Christian Polemics," in: *Translations of Scripture: Proceedings of a Conference at the Annenberg Research Institute, May 15, 1989, JQR Supplement* 1990, 1–27.

Agha, Saleh. "Language as a Component of Arab Identity in al-Jahiz: The Case of Ismaʾil's Conversion to Arabhood," in: *Al-Jahiz: A Muslim Humanist for our Time*, ed. Arnim Heinemann, John L. Meloy, Tarif Khalidi, and Manfred Kropp, 67–90.

Ahlwardt, Wilhelm. *The Divans of the Six Ancient Arabic Poets: Ennabiga, 'Antara, Tharafa, Zuhair, 'Alqama and Imruulqais; Chiefly According to the Mss. of Paris, Gotha, and Leyden; and the Collection of Their Fragments with a List of the Various Readings of the Text*. London, 1870.

Ahrens. Karl Ahrens. "Christliches im Qoran," in: *ZDMG* 84 (1930), 15–68; 148–190.

Albayrak, Ismail. "Qur'anic Narrative and Isra'iliyyat in Western Scholarship and in Classical Exegesis." Dissertation, University of Leeds, 2000.

Ali, Jawad. *Al-mufassal fī tāʾrīkh al-ʿarab qabl al-islām* [A detailed history of the Arabs before Islam]. Beirut, 1970.

Alter, Robert. *The Art of Biblical Narrative*. New York, 1981.

Alter, Robert. *The Art of Biblical Poetry*. New York, 1985.

Alter, Robert. *Canon and Creativity: Modern writing and the authority of scripture*, New Haven. London, 2000.

Alter, Robert. "Von der Kunst, Sinn zu erzeugen," in: *Bibel als Literatur*, ed. Hans-Peter Schmidt and Daniel Weidner. Munich, 2008, 31–56.

Alter, Robert, and Frank Kermode, eds. *The Literary Guide to the Bible*, Cambridge, 1987.

Ambros, Arne A. "Die Analyse von Sure 112. Kritiken, Synthesen, neue Ansätze, in: *Der Islam* 63 (1986), 219–247.

Ambros, Arne. *A Concise Dictionary of Koranic Terms*. Wiesbaden, 2004.

Amir-Moezzi, Ali. *Dictionnaire du Coran*. Paris, 2007.

Amir-Moezzi, Mohammad Ali, and Etan Kohlberg. *Revelation and Falsification. The Kitāb al-qirāʾāt of Ahmad b. Muhammad al-Sayyārī*. Leiden, 2009.

Ammann, Ludwig. *Die Geburt des Islam: Historische Innovation durch Offenbarung*. Göttingen, 2001.

Andrae, Tor. *Mohammad, sein Leben und sein Glaube*. Göttingen, 1932.

Andrae, Tor. *Die Person Muhammads in Lehre und Glauben seiner Gemeinde*. Stockholm, 1918.

Andrae, Tor. *Der Ursprung des Islams und das Christentum*, Uppsala and Stockholm, 1926 (Hildesheim, [2]1977).

Arazi, Albert, and Salman Masalha. *Six Early Arab Poets: New Edition and Concordance*. Jerusalem, 1999.

Arberry, Arthur J. *The Koran Interpreted*. Oxford, 1964.

Arkoun, Mohammed. *Lectures du Coran*. Paris, 1982.

Arkoun, Mohammed. "The Notion of Revelation from Ahl Al-Kitab to Societies of the Book," in: *Die Welt des Islam* 28 (1988), 62–89.

Arkoun, Mohammed. *Rethinking Islam: Common Questions, Uncommon Answers*. Boulder, 1994.

al-Ansari, Zakariya. *Sharh matn al-Djazarīya fī maʿrifātt tadjīd al-āyāt al-Qurʾānīya*. Blida, 1950.

Assmann, Aleida, and Jan Assmann. "Kanon und Zensur als kultursoziologische Kategorien," in: *Kanon und Zensur: Archäologie der literarischen Kommunikation*, vol. 2, ed. Aleida und Jan Assmann. Munich, 1987, 7–27.

Assmann, Aleida, and Jan Assmann. "Nachwort," in: *Schrift und Gedächtnis: Beiträge zur Archäologie der literarischen Kommunikation*, ed. Aleida Assmann, Jan Assmann and Christof Hardmeier. Munich, 1983, 265–284.

Assmann, Jan, ed. *Das Fest und das Heilige*. Munich, 1991.

Assmann, Jan. *Das kulturelle Gedächtnis: Schrift, Erinnerung und politische Identität in frühen Hochkulturen*. Munich, 1992.

Assmann, Jan. *Politische Theologie zwischen Ägypten und Israel*. Munich, 1993.

Atwan, Husain. *Al-Qirāʾāt al-Qurʾānīya fī Bilād al-Shām*. Beirut, 1982.

Aurelius, Erik. "Durch den Glauben gehorsam—durch Werke gerecht," in: "*Abraham, unser Vater*": *Die gemeinsamen Wurzeln von Judentum, Christentum und Islam*, ed. Reinhard G. Kratz and Tilman Nagel. Göttingen, 2003, 98–111.

Ayoub, Mahmoud M. "Das Mystische im Koran: Muhammads mystische Vision," in: *Hermeneutik in Islam und Christentum: Beiträge zum interreligiösen Dialog: Rudolf-Otto-Symposium 1996*, ed. Hans-Martin Barth and Christoph Elsas. Hamburg, 1997, 127–140.

al-Azmeh, Aziz. "Chronophagous Discourse: A Study of the Clerico-Legal Appropriation of the World in Islamic Tradition," in: *Religion and Practical Reason*, ed. Reynolds and Tracy. Albany, 1994, 163–213.

al-Azmeh, Aziz. *Ibn Khaldun in Modern Scholarship: A Study in Orientalism*. London, 1981.

al-Azmeh, Aziz. "The Muslim Canon from Late Antiquity to the Era of Modernism," in: *Canonization and Decanonization*, ed. Arie van der Koij. Leiden, 1998, 191–228.

al-Azmeh, Aziz. "Rome, New Rome and Baghdad: Pathwings of Late Antiquity," in: *Europa im Nahen Osten—Der Nahe Osten in Europa*, ed. Angelika Neuwirth and Günter Stock. Berlin, 2010, 53–73.

Bacher, Wilhelm. *Die exegetische Terminologie der jüdischen Traditionsliteratur*. Leipzig, 1899, repr. Hildesheim, 1990.

Bandt, Cordula. *Der Traktat "Vom Mysterium der Buchstaben": Kritischer Text mit Einführung, Übersetzung und Kommentar*. Texte und Untersuchungen zur Geschichte der alt-christlichen Literatur 162. Berlin, 2007.

al-Bannā, Ahmad ad-Dimyātī. *Ithāf fudalā al-bashar fī qirā āt al-arba ata ashar*. Būlāq, 1868.

Barlas, Asma. "Women's Readings of the Qur'an," in: *The Cambridge Companion to the Qur'an*, ed. Jane McAuliffe. Cambridge, 2006, 255–271.

Barth, Hans-Martin, and Christoph Elsas, eds. *Beiträge zum interreligiösen Dialog: Rudolf-Otto-Symposium 1996*. Hamburg, 1997.

Barth, Jakob. *Studien zur Kritik und Exegese des Qorans*. Strasbourg, 1915.

Barton, John, ed. *The Cambridge Companion to Biblical Interpretation*. Cambridge, 1998.

Barton, John. "Historical-Critical Approaches," in: *The Cambridge Companion to Biblical Interpretation*, ed. John Barton. Cambridge, 1998, 9–20.

Barton, John. "Introduction," in: *The Cambridge Companion to Biblical Interpretation*, ed. John Barton. Cambridge, 1998, 1–6.

Bauer, Hans. "Über die Anordnung der Suren und über die geheimnisvollen Buchstaben im Qoran," in: *ZDMG* 75 (1921), 1–20.

Bauer, Thomas. *Altarabische Dichtkunst*. Harrassowitz, 1992.

Bauer, Thomas. "The Relevance of Early Arabic Poetry for Qur'anic Studies Including Observations on Kull and on Q 22:27, 26:225, and 52:21," in: *The Qur'ān in Context: Historical and Literary Investigations into the Qur'ānic Milieu*, ed. Angelika Neuwirth, Nicolai Sinai, and Michael Marx. Leiden, 2010, 699–732.

Bauschke, Martin. *Jesus im Koran*. Cologne, 2001.

Bauschke, Martin. *Der Spiegel des Propheten Abraham im Koran und im Islam*. Frankfurt am Main, 2008.

Baumstark, Anton. "Jüdischer und christlicher Gebetstypus im Koran," in: *Der Islam* 6 (1915), 113–148.

Beaumont, Daniel. "Simile," in: *EQ*, vol. 5. Leiden, 2005, 13–14.

Bechert, Heinz, Josef van Ess, Hans Küng, and Heinrich von Stietencron, eds. *Christentum und Weltreligionen: Hinführung zum Dialog mit Islam, Hinduismus und Buddhismus*. Munich and Zürich, 1984.

Beck, Edmund. *Des Heiligen Ephraem des Syrers Hymnen de Paradiso und Contra Julianum*. Corpus Scriptorum Christianorum Orientalium 174, Scriptores Syri 78. Louvain, 1957.

Beck, Edmund. "Die Ibn-Mas'ūd-Varianten bei al-Farrā'," I, II, III, in: *Orientalia* 25 (1956), 353–383; 28 (1959), 286–205, 230–256.

Beck, Edmund. "Die Mariologie der echten Schriften Ephräms," in: *Oriens Christianus* 40 (1956), 22–39.

Beck, Edmund. "Studien zur Geschichte der kufischen Koranlesung," I, II, III, IV, in: *Orientalia* 17 (1948), 326–355; 19 (1950) 328–250; 20 (1951) 316–328; 22 (1953) 59–78.

Beck, Edmund. "Der uthmanische Kodex in der Koranlesung des zweiten Jahrhunderts," in: *Orientalia* 14 (1945), 355–373.

Beck, Edmund. "Die Zuverlässigkeit der Überlieferung von außer uthmanischen Varianten bei al-Farrā'," in: *Orientalia* 23 (1954), 412–435.

Becker, Adam. *Fear of God and the Beginning of Wisdom: The School of Nisibis and Christian Scholastic Culture in Late Antique Mesopotamia*. Philadelphia, 2006.

Becker, Carl Heinrich. "Ubi sunt qui ante nos in mundo fuere," in: *Aufsätze zur Kultur- und Sprachgeschichte vornehmlich des Orients: Ernst Kuhn zum 70. Geburtstag am 7. Februar 1916 gewidmet von Freunden und Schülern*. Breslau, 1916, 87–105, repr. in: Carl Heinrich. *Islamstudien*, vol. 1. Leipzig, 1923, 509–519.

Becker, Carl Heinrich. "Zur Geschichte des islamischen Kultus," in: *Der Islam* 3 (1912), 374–399, repr. in: Carl Heinrich Becker, *Islamstudien*, vol 1. Leipzig, 1923, 472–500.

Bell, Richard. *A Commentary on the Qur'an*, edited by C. Edmund Bosworth and M. E. J. Richardson, 2 vols. Manchester, 1991.

Bell, Richard. *Introduction to the Qur'an*. Edinburgh, 1953.

Bell, Richard. *The Origin of Islam in Its Christian Environment*. London, 1926, repr. 1968.

Bell, Richard. *The Qur'ān: Translated, with a Critical Re-arrangement of the Suras*, 2 vols. Edinburgh, 1937–1939.

Bellamy, James A. "The Mysterious Letters of the Koran: Old Abbreviations of the Basmalah," in: *JAOS* 93 (1973), 267–285.

Bencheikh, Jamel Eddine. "Iram ou la clameur de Dieu: Le mythe et le verset," in: *Revue des mondes musulmans et de la Méditerranée* 58 (1990), 70–81.

Ben-Shammai, Haggai. "The Status of Parable and Simile in the Qur'an and Early Tafsir: Polemic, Exegetical and Theological Aspects," in: *JSAI* 30 (2005), 154–169.

Berg, Herbert. *The Development of Exegesis in Early Islam: The Authenticity of Muslim Literature from the Formative Period*. London, 2000.

Berg, Horst Klaus. *Ein Wort wie Feuer: Wege lebendiger Bibelauslegung*. Munich, 1991.

Berger, Klaus, and Christiane Nord, trans. and eds. *Das Neue Testament und Frühchristliche Schriften*. Frankfurt am Main, 2005.

Berger, Monroe, M. A. Rauf, and Bernhard Weiss. *The Recited Koran: A History of the First Recorded Version*. Princeton, 1973.

Bergsträsser, Gotthelf. "Die Koranlesung des Hasan von Basra," in: *Islamica* 2 (1926), 11–57.

Bergsträsser, Gotthelf. "Koranlesung in Kairo," in: *Der Islam* 20 (1932), 1–42; 21 (1933), 110–140.

Bergsträsser, Gotthelf. "Plan eines Apparatus Criticus zum Koran," in: *Sitzungsberichte der philosophisch-philologischen Klasse der Bayerischen Akademie der Wissenschaften*, vol. 7. Munich, 1930, 3–11.

Bergsträsser, Gotthelf, and Otto Pretzl. *Geschichte des Qoran*; vol. 3: *Die Geschichte des Korantexts*. Leipzig, 1938.

Bieberstein, Klaus. "'Zum Raum wird hier die Zeit': Drei Erinnerungslandschaften Jerusalems," in: *Jahrbuch für biblische Theologie* 22 (2007), 3–39.

Birkeland, Harris. *The Lord Guideth: Studies on Primitive Islam*. Oslo, 1956.

Blachère, Régis. *Histoire de la littérapture arabe*, 2 vols. Paris, 1964.

Blachère, Régis. *Introduction au Coran*. Paris, 1947.

Blachère, Régis. *Le Coran: Traduction selon un essai de réclassement des sourates*, 2 vols. Paris, 1949–1950.

Blair, Sheila. *Islamic Calligraphy*. Edinburgh, 2006.

Blair, Sheila. "What Is the Date of the Dome of the Rock," in: *Bayt al-Maqdis: Abd al-Malik's Jerusalem*, ed. J. Raby and J. Johns. Oxford, 1992, vol. 1, 66–87.

Bloch, Alfred. *Vers und Sprache im Altarabischen Metrische und syntaktische Untersuchungen*. Basel, 1946.

Bludau, August. *Die Schriftfälschungen der Häretiker. Ein Beitrag zur Textkritik der Bibel*. Neute-stamentliche Abhandlungen 11. Münster, 1925.

Bobzin, Hartmut. *Der Koran: Aus dem Arabischen neu übertragen von Hartmut Bobzin unter Mitarbeit von Katharina Bobzin*. Munich, 2010.

Bobzin, Hartmut. *Der Koran: Eine Einführung*. Munich, 1999.

Bobzin, Hartmut. *Der Koran im Zeitalter der Reformation*. Beirut, 1995.

Bobzin, Hartmut. *Muhammad*. Munich, 1999.

Bobzin, Hartmut. "Pre-1800 Preoccupations of Qur'anic Studies," in: *EQ*, vol. 4. Leiden, 2004, 235–253.

Bobzin, Hartmut. "The 'Seal of the Prophets': Towards an Understanding of Muhammad's Prophethood," in: *The Qur'ān in Context: Historical and Literary Investigations into the Qur'ānic Milieu*, ed. Angelika Neuwirth, Nicolai Sinai, and Michael Marx. Leiden, 2010, 565–585.

Bodman, Whitney. "Stalking Iblis: In Search of an Islamic Theodicy," in: *Myths, Historical Archetypes and Symbolic Figures in Arabic Literature: Proceedings of the International Symposium in Beirut, June 25th—June 30th, 1996*. Beiruter Texte und Studien 64, ed. Birgit Embalo et al. Beirut and Stuttgart, 1999, 247–269.

Boitani, Pietro. *The Bible and Its Rewritings*. Oxford, 1999.

Bonitz, Hermann. *Index Aristotelicus*. Berlin, 1870, repr. Graz, 1955.

Borg, Gert. *Mit Poesie vertreibe ich den Kummer meines Herzens: Eine Studie zur altarabischen Trauerklage der Frau*. Istanbul, 1997.

Borg, Gert. "Umayya b. Abi l-Salt as a Poet," in: *Pilosophy and Arts in the Islamic World*, ed. U. Vermeulen and D. de Smeet, Leuven, 1998, 3–13.

Bothmer, Hans Caspar Graf von. "Architekturbilder im Koran: Eine Prachthandschrift der Umayyadenzeit aus dem Yemen," in: *Pantheon* 45 (1987), 4–29.

Bothmer, Hans Caspar Graf von, Karl-Heinz Ohlig, and Gerd-Rüdiger Puin, eds. "Neue Wege der Koranforschung," in: *Magazin Forschung: Forschungs-magazin der Universität des Saarlandes* 1 (1999), 33–46.

Böwering, Gerhard. "Chronology," in: *EQ*, vol. 1. Leiden, 2001, 319–20.
Bowersock, Glen. *Hellenism in Late Antiquity*. Ann Arbor, 1993.
Bowersock, Glen. *Roman Arabia*. Cambridge, MA, 1983.
Boyarin, Daniel. *Borderlines: The Partition of Judaeo-Christianity*. Philadelphia, 2004.
Boyarin, Daniel. "The Eye in the Torah: Ocular Desire in Midrashic Hermeneutic," in: *Critical Inquiry* 16 (1990), 532–550.
Boyarin, Daniel. "The Genealogy of Indeterminacy," in: *The Talmud Yerushalmi and Graeco-Roman Culture*, vol. 3, ed. Peter Schäfer. Tübingen, 2003, 273–299.
Boyarin, Daniel. "'The Gospel of the Memra': Jewish Binitarianism and the Prologue to John," in: *ThR* 94 (2001), 242–284.
Boyarin, Daniel. *A Radical Jew: Paul and the Politics of Identity*. London, 1994.
Boyarin, Daniel. "The Talmud as a Fat Rabbi: A Novel Approach," in: *Text and Talk* 28 (2008), 603–619.
Boyarin, Daniel, and David Stern. "Exchange on the Mashal," in: *Prooftexts* 5 (1985), 269–280.
Boyd, James Oscar. "Sin and Grace in the Biblical Narratives Rehearsed in the Koran," in: *Biblical and Theological Studies by the Members of the Faculty of Princeton Theological Seminary*, ed. David B. Calhoun. New York, 1912, 423–445.
Bräunlich, Erich. *Bistām Ibn Qais, ein vorislamischer Beduinenfürst und Held*. Leipzig, 1923.
Bräunlich, Erich. "Versuch einer literargeschichtlichen Betrachtungsweise altarabischer Poesien," in: *Der Islam* 24 (1937), 825–833.
Bräunlich, Erich. "Zur Frage der Echtheit der altarabischen Poesie," in: *OLZ* 29 (1926), 825–833.
Bravmann, Meir M. *The Spiritual Background of Early Islam and the History of Its Principal Concepts*. Louvain, 1951.
Brettler, Marc Zvi. *God Is King: Understanding an Israelite Metaphor*. Sheffield, 1989.
Brinner, William M. "Noah," in: *EQ*, vol. 3. Leiden, 2003, 540–543.
Brock, Sebstian P. "Syriac Dispute Poems the Various Types," in: *Dispute Poems and Dialogues in the Ancient and Medieval Near East: Forms and Types of Literary Debates in Semitic and Related Literatures*, ed. Gerrit Jan Reinink and Herman L. J. Vanstiphout, Leuven, 1991, 109–119 (reper. *From Ephrem to Romanos*, Aldershot, 1999).
Brockelmann, Carl. *Geschichte der Arabischen Literatur*, 2 vols., Weimar 1898–1902, suppl. vols. 1–3. Leiden, 1937–1942.
Brockelmann, Carl. *Lexicon Syriacum*. Berlin, 1895.
Brockelmann, Carl. *Semitische Grammatik, mit Paradigmen, Literatur, Chrestomathie und Glossar*. Berlin and New York, 1912.
Brown, Norman O. "The Apocalypse of Islam," in: *Apocalypse and/or Metamorphosis*, ed. Norman O. Brown. Berkeley, 1991, 69–94.
Brown, Peter R. L. "Late Antiquity and Islam: Parallels and Contrast," in: *Moral Conduct and Authority: The Place of Adab in South Asian Islam*, ed. Barbara D. Metcalf. Berkeley, 1984, 23–37.
Brown, Peter R. L. *Macht und Rhetorik in der Spätantike. Der Weg zu einem 'christlichen Imperium.'* Munich, 1995.
Brown, Peter R. L. *The Making of Late Antiquity*. Cambridge, MA, 1978.
Brown, Peter R. L. *The World of Late Antiquity: AD 150–750*. London, 2002.

Brueggemann, Walter. *Theology of the Old Testament, Testimony, Dispute, Advocacy*. Minneapolis, 1997.

Brumlik, Micha. *Schrift, Wort und Ikone: Wege aus dem Bilderverbot*. Frankfurt am Main, 1994.

Brunner, Rainer. “Einige schiitische Stimmen zur Frage der Koranfälschung,” in: *Akten des 27. Deutschen Orientalistentages: Bonn, 28. September bis 2. Oktober 1998; Norm und Abweichung*, ed. Stefan Wild et al. Würzburg, 2001, 447–457.

Brunner, Rainer. *Die Schia und die Koranfälschung*. Abhandlungen für die Kunde des Morgenlandes 53. Würzburg, 2001.

Bruns, Gerald L. “Midrash and Allegory,” in: *The Literary Guide to the Bible*, ed. Robert Alter and Frank Kermode. Cambridge, 2002, 625–646.

Buhl, Frants. *Das Leben Muhammeds*. Translated by H. H. Schaeder. Leipzig, 1930, repr. Heidelberg, 1955.

Buhl, Frants. “Über Vergleichungen und Gleichnisse im Qoran,” in: *Acta Orientalia* 2 (1923/1924), 1–11.

Buhl, Frants. “Zur Koranexegese,” in: *Acta Orientalia* 3 (1924), 97–108.

Bühler, Karl. *Sprachtheorie: Die Darstellungsfunktion der Sprache*. Stuttgart, 1965.

Bukharin, Mikhail D. “Mecca on the Caravan Routes in pre-Islamic Antiquity,” in: *The Qurʾān in Context: Historical and Literary Investigations into the Qurʾānic Milieu*, ed. Angelika Neuwirth, Nicolai Sinai, and Michael Marx. Leiden, 2009, 115–135.

Bultmann, Rudolf. *Die Geschichte der synoptischen Tradition*. Göttingen, 1931.

Bultmann, Rudolf. *Glauben und Verstehen: Gesammelte Aufsätze*, 2 vols. Tübingen, 1958.

Burgmer, Christoph, ed. *Streit um den Koran: Die Luxenberg-Debatte; Standpunkte und Hintergründe*. Berlin, 2004.

Burton, John. *The Collection of the Qurʾān*. Cambridge, 1977.

Busse, Heribert. “Herrschertypen im Koran,” in: *Die Islamische Welt zwischen Mittelalter und Neuzeit: Festschrift für Hans Robert Roemer zum 65. Geburtstag*, ed. Ulrich Haarmann and Peter Bachmann. Beirut and Wiesbaden, 1979, 56–80.

Busse, Heribert. “Jerusalem,” in: *EQ*, vol. 3. Leiden, 2003, 2–7.

Busse, Heribert. “Jerusalem in the Story of Muhammad’s Night Journey and Ascension,” in: *JSAI* 14 (1991), 1–40.

Busse, Heribert. *Die theologischen Beziehungen des Islams zu Judentum und Christentum: Grundlagen des Dialogs im Koran und die gegenwärtige Situation*. Darmstadt, 1988.

Cachia, Pierre. *Taha Husayn: His Place in the Egyptian Literary Renaissance*. London, 1956.

Cantineau, Jean, and Leo Barbès. “La recitation coranique à Damas et à Alger,” in: *AIEO* 6 (1942–1947), 66–107.

Carroll, Robert P. “Poststructuralist Approaches: New Historicism and Postmodernism,” in: *The Cambridge Companion to Biblical Interpretation*, ed. John Barton. Cambridge, 1998, 50–66.

Caskel, Werner. “Ajjām al-Arab, Studien zur altarabischen Epik,” in: *Islamica* 3 (1930), 1–99.

Caskel, Werner. *Das Schicksal in der altarabischen Poesie*. Leipzig, 1926.

Caspar, Paulin, and Jacques Jomier. “L’exegèse scientifique du Coran d’après le Cheikh Amin al-Khouli,” in: *MIDEO* 4 (1957), 269–280.

Caspar, Robert. "Parole de Dieu et langage humain en Christianisme et en Islam," in: *Islamochristiana* 6 (1980), 33–60.

Chabbi, Jacqueline. *Le Coran décrypté: Figures bibliques en Arabie*. Paris, 2008.

Chabbi, Jacqueline. "Histoire et tradition sacrée: la biographie impossible de Mahomet," in: *Arabica* 1 (1996), 190–194.

Chabbi, Jacqueline. "Jinn," in: *EQ*, vol. 3. Leiden, 2003, 43–50.

Chabbi, Jacqueline. *Le seigneur des tribus: L'islam de Mahomet*. Paris, 1997.

Childs, Brevard. *Biblical Theology in Crisis*. Philadelphia, 1970.

Childs, Brevard. *Introduction to the Old Testament as Scripture*. Philadelphia, 1979.

Childs, Brevard. *The New Testament as Canon: An Introduction*. Philadelphia, 1985.

Childs, Brevard. *Die Theologie der einen Bibel*, vol. 1: *Grundstrukturen*, vol. 2: *Hauptthemen*. Freiburg, 1994–1996.

Cohen, Jeremy. *Living Letters of the Law: Ideas of the Jews in Medieval Christianity*. Berkeley and Los Angeles, 1999.

Colpe, Carsten. "Aus der Geschichte des Teufels im Abendland," in: *Das Böse: Eine historische Phänomenologie des Unerklärlichen*, ed. Carsten Colpe and Wilhelm Schmidt-Biggem. Frankfurt am Main, 1993.

Combs-Schilling, M. Elaine. *Sacred Performances: Islam, Sexuality and Sacrifice*. New York, 1989.

Cook, David. *Martyrdom in Islam*. Cambridge, 2007.

Cook, Michael. *Der Koran: Eine kurze Einführung*. Stuttgart, 2000.

Cragg, Kenneth. *The Event of the Qur'an: Islam in Its Scripture*. Oxford, 1971.

Crone, Patricia. "The First-Century Concept of Hijra," in: *Arabica* 41 (1994), 352–387.

Crone, Patricia. "How Did the Quranic Pagans Make a Living?," in: *BSOAS* 68 (2005), 387–399.

Crone, Patricia. *Meccan Trade and the Rise of Islam*. Oxford, 1987.

Crone, Patricia. "The Religion of the Qur'anic Pagans: God and the Lesser Deities" (unpublished manuscript).

Crone, Patricia. "Two legal Problems Bearing on the Early History of the Qur'an," in: *JSAI* 18 (1994), 1–37.

Crone, Patricia. "What Do We Actually Know about Mohammed?," in: *OpenDemocracy*, June 10, 2008, https://www.opendemocracy.net/faith-europe_islam/mohammed_3866.jsp.

Crone, Patricia, and Michael Cook. *Hagarism: The Making of the Islamic World*. Cambridge, 1977.

Curtius, Ernst Robert. *Europäische Literatur und Lateinisches Mittelalter*. Bern, 1954.

Cuypers, Michel. *The Banquet: A Reading of the Fifth Sura of the Qur'an*. Miami, 2008.

Dayeh, Islam. "Al-Hawamim:Intertextuality and Coherence in Meccan Surahs," in: *The Qurʾān in Context: Historical and Literary Investigations into the Qurʾānic Milieu*, ed. Angelika Neuwirth, Nicolai Sinai, and Michael Marx. Leiden, 2010, 461–498.

Dayeh, Islam. "Plain Sense and the Allegorical Lessons from the Egyptian School" (lecture, July 15, 2009, at the Wissenschaftskolleg zu Berlin).

de Blois, François. "Islam in Its Arabian Context," in: *The Qurʾān in Context: Historical and Literary Investigations into the Qurʾānic Milieu*, ed. Angelika Neuwirth, Nicolai Sinai, and Michael Marx. Leiden, 2010, 615–624.

Dehghani, Sasha. *Messianismus und Märtyrertum: Die Geschichte der Babis*, Wiesbaden, 2011.

Delaney, Carol L. *Abraham on Trial: The Social Legacy of Biblical Myth*. Princeton, 1998.

Denny, Frederick M. "Islamic Ritual: Perspectives and Theories," in: *Approaches to Islam in Religious Studies*, ed. Richard C. Martin, Arizona, 1985, 63–77.

Déroche, François. *Le Coran*. Paris, 2005.

Déroche, François. *Islamic Codicology: An Introduction to the Study of Manuscripts in Arabic Script*. London, 2005.

Déroche, François. "Manuscripts of the Qur'an," in: *EQ*, vol. 3. Leiden, 2003, 254–275.

Déroche, François. *Les Manuscrits du Coran*, vol. 1: *Aux origines de la calligraphie coranique*; vol. 2: *Du Maghreb à l'Insulinde*. Paris, 1983–1985.

Déroche, François. *La transmission écrite du Coran dans les débuts de l'Islam*. Leiden, 2009.

Dettinger, M. "Beiträge zu einer Theologie des Corans," in: *Tübinger Zeitschrift für Theologie*, 1831 vol., pt. 3, 1–74.

Dettinger, M. "Beiträge zu einer Theologie des Corans—Fortsetzung," in: *Tübinger Zeitschrift für Theologie*, 1834 vol., pt. 1, 3–86.

Deutung zu Tausendundeine Nacht, 1907 (repr. in: Hugo von Hofmannsthal, *Erzählungen und Aufsätze*, Frankfurt am Main, 1957, and in: Enno Littmann, *Tausendundeine Nacht: Übersetzt von Enno Littmann*, Wiesbaden, 1953).

Diem, Werner. *Studien zur Überlieferung und Intertextualität der altarabischen Dichtung: Das Mantelgedicht des Ba'b ibn Zuhayrs*. Wiesbaden, 2010.

Diem, Werner. "Untersuchungen zur frühen Geschichte der arabischen Orthographie," I: "Die Schreibung der Vokale," II: "Die Schreibung der Konsonanten," III: "Endungen und Endschreibungen," IV: "Die Schreibung der zusammenhängenden Rede," in: *Orientalia* 48 (1979), 207–257; 49 (1980), 67–106; 50 (1981), 332–383; 52 (1983), 357–404.

Dmitriev, Kirill. *Das poetische Werk des Abu Sakhr al-Hudhalī*. Harrasowitz, 2009.

Dmitriev, Kirill. "An Early Christian Arabic Account of the Creation of the World," in: *The Qur'ān in Context: Historical and Literary Investigations into the Qur'ānic Milieu*, ed. Angelika Neuwirth, Nicolai Sinai, and Michael Marx. Leiden, 2010, 349–388.

Dohmen, Christoph. *Die Bibel und ihre Auslegung*. Munich, 1998.

Dohmen, Christoph, and Manfred Oeming. *Biblischer Kanon—warum und wozu?* Freiburg, 1992.

Donner, Fred McGraw. *The Expansion of the Early Islamic State*. Aldershot, 2008.

Donner, Fred McGraw. "The Historical Context," in: *The Cambridge Companion to the Qur'an*, ed. Jane McAuliffe. Cambridge, 2006, 23–40.

Donner, Fred McGraw. *Narratives of Islamic Origins: The Beginnings of Islamic Historical Writing*. Princeton, 1998.

Donner, Fred McGraw. "The Qur'ān in Recent Scholarship: Challenges and Desiderata," in: *The Qur'an in Its Historical Context*, ed. Gabriel Said Reynolds. London and New York, 2008, 29–50.

Donner, Herbert. *Die anakreontischen Gedichte Nr. 19 und Nr. 20 des Patriarchen Sophronius von Jerusalem*. Heidelberg, 1981.

Dreibholz, Ursula. *Early Quran Fragments from the Great Mosque in Sanaa, DAI*. Sanaa, 2003.

Drory, Rina. "The Abbasid Construction of the Jāhiliyya: Cultural Authority in the Making," in: *Studia Islamica* (85) 1996, 33–49.

Duri, Abdalaziz. "Jerusalem in the Early Islamic Period: 7th–11th Centuries A. D.," in: *Jerusalem in History*, ed. Kamil J. Asali. Essex, 1989, 105–125.

Dutton, Yasin. "The Qur'ān as a Source of Law: The Case of Zakāt (Alms-Tax)," in: *Islamic Reflections, Arabic Musings: Studies in Honour of Professor Alan Jones*, ed. Robert G. Hoyland and Philipp F. Kennedy. Oxford, 2004, 201–216.

Dutton, Yasin. "Some notes on the British Library's 'Oldest Qur'ān Manuscript' (Or. 2165)," in: *JQS* 6 (2004), 43–71.

Dutton, Yasin. "An Umayyad Fragment of the Qur'an and it's dating," in: *JQS* 10 (2008), 157–187.

Encylopaedia of Islam, 2nd ed. 11 vols. and supplement vol. Leiden, 1960–2004.

Ehlich, Konrad. "Text und sprachliches Handeln: Die Entstehung von Texten aus dem Bedürfnis nach Überlieferung," in: *Schrift und Gedächtnis: Archäologie der literarischen Kommunikation*, vol. 1, ed. Aleida Assmann, Jan Assmann and Christoph Hardtmeier. Munich, 1983, 24–44.

Ehrman, Barth D. *Lost Christianities: The Battles for Scripture and the Faith We Never Knew*. New York, 2004.

Ehrman, Barth D. *Lost Scriptures: Books That Did Not Become the New Testament*. New York, 2003.

Eickelman, Dale F. "Musaylima," in: *Journal of the Economic and Social History of the Orient* 10 (1967), 17–52.

Eickelman, Dale F. "Muslim Politics: New Prospects for Democracy in North Africa and the Middle East," in: *Islam, Democracy and the State in North Africa*, ed. John P. Entelis. Bloomington, 1997, 17–41.

Elbogen, Ismar. *Der jüdische Gottesdienst in seiner geschichtlichen Entwicklung*. Berlin, 1913.

Elsas, Christoph. "Religionswissenschaftliche Vermittlung gemeinsamer Arbeit von Christen und Muslimen an Texten aus Bibel und Koran," in: *Hermeneutik in Islam und Christentum. 2. Rudolf-Otto-Symposion, 16.-19. Mai 1996. Beiträge zum interreligiösen Dialog*, ed. H.-M. Barth and Christoph Elsas. Hamburg, 1997, 180–196.

Endreß, Gerhard. "Handschriftenkunde," in: *Grundriß der arabischen Philologie*, vol. 1, ed. W. Fischer and Helmut Gätje. Wiesbaden, 1982, 271–314.

Endreß, Gerhard. "Herkunft und Entwicklung der arabischen Schrift," in: *Grundriß der Arabischen Philologie*, vol. 1, ed. W. Fischer and H. Gätje. Wiesbaden, 1982, 165–197.

Ettinghausen, Richard. "Antiheidnische Polemik im Koran." Dissertation, Frankfurt am Main, 1934.

Fahd, Toufic. "Kāhin," in: *EI*², vol. 4, 421.

Fahd, Toufic. *Le Panthéon de l'Arabie Centrale à la veille de l'Hégire*. Paris, 1968.

Farrukh, Omar A. *Das Bild des Frühislam in der arabischen Dichtung: von der Higra bis zum Tode 'Umars 1–23 D. H./ 622 n. Ch.* Leipzig, 1937.

Feldman, Louis H. "Josephus' Portrait of Noah and Its Parallels in Philo, Pseudo-Philo's Biblical Antiquities, and Rabbinic Midrashim," in: *Proceedings of the American Academy of Jewish Research* 55 (1988), 31–57.

Finster, Barbara. "Arabia in Late Antiquity: An Outline of the Cultural Situation," in: *The Qur'ān in Context: Historical and Literary Investigations into the Qur'ānic Milieu*, ed. Angelika Neuwirth, Nicolai Sinai, and Michael Marx. Leiden, 2009, 61–115.

Firestone, Reuven. "Abraham," in: *EQ*, vol. 1. Leiden, 2001, 1–11.

Firestone, Reuven. "Jihād," in: *The Blackwell Companion to the Qur'an*, ed. Andrew Rippin. Oxford, 2006, 308–320.

Firestone, Reuven. *Journeys in Holy Lands: The Evolution of the Abraham-Ishmael Legends in Islamic Exegesis*. Albany, 1990.

Fisch, Harold. "Prophet und Publikum. Ein gescheiterter Vertrag," in: *Bibel als Literatur*, ed. Hans-Peter Schmidt and Daniel Weidner. Munich, 2008, 175–186.

Fischer, August. *Der Wert der vorhandenen Koran-Übersetzungen und Sure 111*. Leipzig, 1937.

Fishbane, Michael. *Biblical Myth and Rabbinic Mythmaking*. Oxford, 2003.

Fishbane, Michael. "Inner-Biblical Exegesis: Types and Strategies of Interpretation in Ancien Israel," in: *Midrash and Literature*, ed. Geoffrey H. Hartmann and Sandford Budick. New Haven, 1986, 19–37.

Fishbane, Michael. *Sacred Attunement: A Jewish Theology*. Chicago, 2008.

Flügel, Gustav. *Concordantiae Corani arabicae*. Leipzig, 1842.

Flügel, Gustav. *Corani textus arabicus*. Leipzig, 1834.

Flusser, David. *Jesus*. Jerusalem, 1998.

Flusser, David. "The Magnificat, the Benedictus and the War Scroll," in: *Judaism and the Origins of Christianity*, ed. David Flusser. Jerusalem, 1988, 126–149.

Foskett, Mary F. *A Virgin Conceived: Mary and Classical Representations of Virginity*. Bloomington, 2002.

Fowden, Elizabeth, and Garth Fowden. *Studies on Hellenism, Chistianity and the Umayyads*. Athens, 2004.

Fowden, Garth. *Qusayr 'Amra: Art and the Umayyad Elite in Late Antique Syria*. Berkeley, 2004.

Frutaz, A. P. "Märtyrer," in: *Lexikon für Theologie und Kirche*, vol. 5, 128.

Frye, Northrup. *The Great Code: The Bible and Literature*. San Diego, 1983.

Fück, Johann. "Die Originalität des arabischen Propheten," in: *ZDMG* 90 (1936), 509–525, repr. in: Johann Fück, *Arabische Kultur und Islam im Mittelalter: Ausgewählte Schriften*, ed. Manfred Fleischhammer. Weimar, 1981, 142–152.

Fuhrmann, Manfred. *Die Dichtungstheorie der Antike: Aristoteles, Horaz, "Longin."* Düsseldorf and Zürich, 2003.

Gabrieli, Francesco. *Storia della letterature araba*. Milan, 1962.

Geiger, Abraham. *Was hat Mohammed aus dem Judenthume aufgenommen?* Berlin, 1833.

Gerock, Carl F. "Versuch einer Darstellung Die tahaddī-Verse im Rahmen der Polemikpassagen des Korans," in: *Arabica* 46 (1999), 130.

Geyer, Rudolf. "Rezension zu Karl Vollers Volkssprache und Schriftsprache im alten Arabien, Straßburg 1906," in: *Göttingische Gelehrte Anzeigen* 1909, 10–56.

al-Ghazālī, Muhammad. *Ihyā der Christologie des Koran*. Hamburg and Gotha, 1839.

Gibb, Hamilton A. R. "Arabiyya," in: *EI*[2], vol. 1, 561–565.

Gilliot, Claude. "Exegesis of the Qu-r'an, Classical and Medieval," in: EQ, vol. 2. Leiden, 2002, 99–124.

Gilliot, Claude. "Informants," in: *EQ*, vol. 2. Leiden, 2002, 512–518.

Gilliot, Claude. "Les 'informateurs' juifs et chrétiens de Muhammad: Reprise d'un problème traité par Aloys Sprenger et Theodor Nöldeke," in: *JSAI* 22 (1998), 84–126.

Gilliot, Claude. "Reconsidering the Authorship of the Qur'an: Is the Qur'an Partly the Fruit of a Progressive and a Collective Work?," in: *The Qur'an in Its Historical Context*, ed. Gabriel Reynolds. London and New York, 2008, 88–108.

Gilliot, Claude. "Zur Herkunft der Gewährsmänner des Propheten," in: *Die dunklen Anfänge: Neue Forschungen zur Entstehung und frühen Geschichte des Islam*, ed. Karl-Heinz Ohlig and Gerd Rüdiger Puin. Berlin, 2005, 148–169.

Goerke, Andreas, and Gregor Schoeler. *Die ältesten Berichte über das Leben Muhammads: Das Korpus Urwa b. az-Zubair*. Princeton, 2008.

Goitein, Fritz [Shlomo Dov]. "Beholding God on Friday," in: *Islamic Culture* 34 (1960), 163–168.

Goitein, Fritz [Shlomo Dov]. "Das Gebet im Koran." Dissertation, Frankfurt am Main, 1923.

Goitein, Fritz [Shlomo Dov]. "The Muslim Month of Fasting, Its Early Development and Religious Meaning," in: *Studies in Islamic History and Institutions*, ed. Fritz [Shlomo Dov] Goitein. Leiden, 1966, 90–110.

Goitein, Fritz [Shlomo Dov]. "The Origin and Nature of the Muslim Friday Worship," in: *Studies in Islamic History and Institutions*, ed. Fritz [Shlomo Dov] Goitein. Leiden, 1966, 111–125.

Goitein, Fritz [Shlomo Dov]. "Prayer in Islam," in: *Studies in Islamic History and Institutions*, ed. Shlomo Dov Goitein. Leiden, 1966, 73–84.

Goitein, Fritz [Shlomo Dov]. *Studies in Islamic History and Institutions*. Leiden, 1966.

Goitein, Fritz [Shlomo Dov]. "Who Were Mohammad's Chief Teachers?," in: *Tarbiz* 23 (1952), 146–59 (Hebr.).

Goitein, Fritz [Shlomo Dov]. "Zur Entstehung des Ramadans," in: *Der Islam* 18 (1929), 189–195.

Goldin, Judah, trans. *The Fathers According to Rabbi Nathan*. Yale Judaica Series 10. New Haven, 1955.

Goldziher, Ignaz. *Abhandlungen zur arabischen Philologie*. Leiden, 1896.

Goldziher, Ignaz. "Muruwwa und Din," in: Muhammedanische *Studien*, ed. Ignaz Goldzieher, vol. 1, Halle 1888, repr. Hildesheim, 1971, 1–39.

Goldziher, Ignaz. "Was ist unter al-Ǧāhilijja zu verstehen?," in: *Muhammedanische Studien*, ed. Ignaz Goldzieher, vol. 1, Halle, 1888, repr. Hildesheim, 1971, 219–228.

Goosens, Eduard. "Ursprung und Bedeutung der koranischen Siglen," in: *Der Islam* 13 (1923), 191–226.

Goßmann, Hans-Christoph. "Die Darstellung Noahs im Koran und ihr traditionsgeschichtlicher Kontext," in: *Begegnungen zwischen Christentum und Islam: Festschrift für Hans-Jürgen Brandt zum 65. Geburtstag*. Perspektiven der Weltmission: Wissenschaftliche Beiträge 20], ed. Hans-Christoph Goßmann. Ammersbek, 1994, 35–40.

Grabar, Oleg. *The Shape of the Holy: Early Islamic Jerusalem*. Princeton, 1996.

Grabar, Oleg. "The Umayyad Dome of the Rock of Jerusalem," in: *Ars Orientalis* 3 (1959), 33–62.

Graf, Friedrich Wilhelm. *Moses Vermächtnis: Über göttliche und menschliche Gesetze*. Munich, 2006.

Graham, William. *Beyond the Written Word: Oral Aspects of Scripture in the History of Religions*. Cambridge, 1987.

Graham, William. "Islam in the Mirror of Ritual," in: *Islam's Unterstanding of Itself*, ed. Richard G. Hovannisian and Speros Vryonis. Malibu, 1983, 53–72.

Graham, William. "Scripture and the Qur'ān," in: *EQ*, vol. 4. Leiden, 2004, 558–569.

Graham, William. "'The Winds to Herald His Mercy': Nature as Token of God's Sovereignty and Grace in the Qur'an," in: *Faithful Imagining*, ed. Sang Hyun Lee and Wayne Proufoot. Atlanta, 1995, 19–38.

Graham, William, and Navid Kermani. "Recitation and Aesthetic Reception," in: *The Cambridge Companion to the Qur'an*, ed. Jane Dammen McAuliffe. Cambridge, 2006, 115–141.

Gramlich, Richard. "Der Urvertrag in der Koranauslegung (zu Sure 7, 172–173)," in: *Der Islam* 60 (1983), 205–230.

Grande, Bencion M. *Kurs arabskoj grammatiki v sravnitelno-istoričeskom osveščenii* [Course on Arabic grammar in a comparative-historical light]. Moscow, [2]1998.

Griffith, H. "Gospel" in: *EQ*. Leiden, 2002, vol. 2, 342–343.

Griffith, Sidney. "Christian Lore and the Arabic Qur'an: The 'Companions of the Cave' in Surat al-Kahf and in Syriac Christian tradition," in: *The Qur'an in Its Historical Context*, ed. Gabriel Reynolds. London and New York, 2008, 109–137.

Griffith, Sidney. "Christians and Christianity," in: *EQ*, vol. 1. Leiden, 2001, 307–316.

Griffith, Sidney. "The Gospel in Arabic: An Inquiry into Its Appearance in the First Abbasid Century," in: Sidney Griffith, *Arabic Christianity in the Monasteries of Ninth-Century Palestine*. Aldershot, 1992, 126–167.

Grintz, Yehoshua M. "Jubilees, Book of," in: *EJ*[2], 473–474.

Grohmann, Adolf. *Arabische Paläographie*, 2 vols. Vienna, 1967.

Grohmann, Adolf. "Die Entstehung des Korans und die ältesten Koranhandschriften," in: *Bustan* 1 (1961), 33–38.

Grohmann, Adolf. "The Problem of Dating Early Qur'ans," in: *Der Islam* 33 (1958), 213–231.

Groß, Markus, and Karl-Heinz Ohlig, eds. *Schlaglichter: Die beiden ersten islamischen Jahrhunderte*. Berlin, 2008.

Grözinger, Karl-Erich. "Middat ha-din und middat ha-rahamim: die sogenannten Gottesattribute 'Gerechtigkeit' und 'Barmherzigkeit' in der frühen rabbinischen Literatur," in: *Frankfurter Judaistische Beiträge* 8 (1980), 95–114.

Gründler, Beatrice. *The Development of the Arabic Scripts: From the Nabatean Era to the First Islamic Century According to Dated Texts*. Atlanta, 1993.

Von Grunebaum, Gustav E. *Islam: Experience of the Holy and Concept of Man*. Los Angeles, 1965 (German: "Die Erfahrung des Heiligen und die Auffassung vom Menschen," in: *Studien zum Kulturbild und Selbstverständnis des Islams*, ed. Gustav E. von Grunebaum, Zürich, 1969, 29–47).

Von Grunebaum, Gustav E. "Islam: Its Inherent Power of Expansion and Adaptation," in: *Modern Islam: The Search for Cultural Identity*, ed. Gustav E. von Grunebaum. New York, 1964, 3–18 (German: "Ausbreitungs- und Anpassungsfähigkeit," in: Studi*en zum Kulturbild und Selbstverständnis des Islams*, Zürich, 1969, 11–22).

Von Grunebaum, Gustav E. "The Nature of Arab Unity before Islam," in: *Arabs and Arabia on the Eve of Islam*, ed. F. E. Peters. Aldershot, 1999, 2–19.

Von Grunebaum, Gustav E., ed. *Studien zum Kulturbild und Selbstverständnis des Islams: Gesammelte Schriften*. Zürich, 1969.

Von Grunebaum, Gustav E. *A Tenth Century Document of Arabic Literary Theory and Criticism: The Sections on poetry of al-Bāqillānī's Kitāb I jāz al-Qur'ān*. Chicago, 1950.

Guillaume, Alfred. *The Life of Mohammad: A Translation of Ishaq's Sirat Rasul Allah with Introduction and Notes*. Oxford, 1955, repr. Karachi, 1967.

Gunkel, Hermann. *Die Psalmen*. Göttingen, [6]1986.

Günther, Sebastian. "Muḥammad the Illiterate Prophet: An Islamic Creed in the Qur'ān and Islamic Exegesis," in: *JQS* 4 (2002), 1–16.

Günther, Sebastian. "O People of the Scripture! Come to a Word Common to You and Us: The Ten Commandments and the Qur'ān," in: *JQS* 9 (2007), 28–58.

Haase, Claus-Peter. "Gärten und Paradies im Islam," in: *Begegnungen zwischen Christentum und Islam: Festschrift für Hans-Jürgen Brandt zum 65. Geburtstag*. Perspektiven der Weltmission: Wissenschaftliche Beiträge 20, ed. Hans-Christoph Goßmann. Ammersbek, 1994, 11–33.

Haddad, Yvonne. *Contemporary Islam and the Challenge of History*. New York, 1982.

Hainthaler, Theresia. "Adī ibn Zayd al-Ibādī, the Pre-Islamic Christian Poet of al-Hira and His Poem Nr. 3 Written in Jail," in: *Parole de l'Orient* 30 (2005), 157–172.

Hamdan, Omar. "The Second Maṣāḥif Project: A Step Towards the Canonization of the Qur an," in: *The Qur'ān in Context: Historical and Literary Investigations into the Qur'ānic Milieu*, ed. Angelika Neuwirth, Nicolai Sinai, and Michael Marx. Leiden, 2010, 795–836.

Hamdan, Omar. *Studien zur Kanonisierung des Korantextes: Al-Hasan al-Basrīs Beiträge zur Geschichte des Korans*. Wiesbaden, 2006.

Hämeen-Anttila, Jaakko. "Arabian Prophecy," in: *Prophecy in Its Ancient Near Eastern Context: Mesopotamian, Biblical and Arabian Perspectives*, ed. Martti Nissinen. Atlanta, 2000, 115–146.

Hamori, Andras. *The Art of Medieval Arabic Literature*. Princeton, 1974.

Hartwig, Dirk. "Der 'Urvertrag' (Q 7:172): Ein rabbinischer Diskurs im Koran," in: *"Im vollen Licht der Geschichte": Die Wissenschaft des Judentums und die Anfänge der kritischen Koranforschung*, ed. Dirk Hartwig, Walter Homolka, Michael Marx, and Angelika Neuwirth. Würzburg, 2008, 191–202.

Hartwig, Dirk. "Die 'Wissenschaft des Judentums' und die Anfänge der kritischen Koranforschung: Perspektiven einer modernen Koranhermeneutik," in: *ZRGG* 61 (2009), 234–256.

Hartwig, Dirk, Walter Homolka, Michael Marx, and Angelika Neuwirth, eds. *"Im vollen Licht der Geschichte": Die Wissenschaft des Judentums und die Anfänge der Koranforschung*. Würzburg, 2008.

Hasselblatt, Gunnar. *Herkunft und Auswirkungen der Apologetik Mohammed Abduhs (1849–1905) untersucht an seiner Schrift: Islam und Christentum im Verhältnis zu Wissenschaft und Zivilisation, Dissertation*. Göttingen, 1968.

Hawting, Gerald R. "Calf of Gold," *in*: EQ, vol. 3. Leiden, 2003, 273–276.

Hawting, Gerald R., ed. *The Development of Islamic Ritual*. Aldershot, 2006.

Hawting, Gerald R. "Eavesdropping on the Heavenly Assembly and the Protection of the Revelation from Demonic Corruption," in: *Self-Referentiality in the Qur'an*, ed. Stefan Wild. Wiesbaden, 2006, 25–38.

Hawting, Gerald R. *The Idea of Idolatry and the Emergence of Islam: From Polemic to History*. Cambridge, 1999.

Hawting, Gerald R. "Introduction," in: *The Development of Islamic Ritual*, ed. Gerald R. Hawting. Aldershot, 2005, xiii–xxxiv.

Hawting, Gerald R. "The Tawwābūn, Atonement and 'Ashura,'" in: *The Development of Islamic Ritual*, ed. Gerald R. Hawting. Aldershot, 2006, 172–188.

Heath, Peter. "Al-Jahiz, Adab, and the Art of the Essay," in: *Al-Jahiz: A Muslim Humanist for our Time*, ed. Arnim Heinemann, John L. Meloy, Tarif Khalidi, and Manfred Kropp. Würzburg, 2009, 133–172.

Heath, Peter. "Creative Hermeneutics: Comparative Analysis of Three Islamic Approaches"; in: *Arabica* 36 (1989), 173–210.

Heemskerk, Margaretha T. "Speech," in: *EQ*, vol. 5. Leiden, 2005, 108–112.

Heidemann, Stefan. "The Evolving Representation of the Early Islamic Empire and Its Religion on Coin Imagery," in: *The Qur'ān in Context: Historical and Literary Investigations into the Qur'ānic Milieu*, ed. Angelike Neuwirth, Nicolai Sinai, and Michael Marx. Leiden, 2009, 149–196.

Heiler, Friedrich. *Erscheinungsformen und Wesen der Religion*. Stuttgart, 1979.

Hennecke, Edgar. *Neutestamentliche Apokryphen in deutscher Übersetzung*. 3rd ed., 2 vols. Tübingen, 1959, 1964.

Henninger, Joseph. "Spuren christlicher Glaubenswahrheiten im Koran," in: *Neue Zeitschrift für Missionswissenschaft* 1 (1945), 306–307.

Herrmann, Klaus. *Sefer Jezira: Das Buch der Schöpfung*. Frankfurt am Main, 2008.

Heschel, Abraham Joshua, *Heavely Torah: As Refracted through the Generations*. Edited and translated by Gordon Tucker. New York, 2005.

Hirschberg, Joachim W. *Jüdische und christliche Lehren im vor- und frühislamischen Arabien: Ein Beitrag zur Entstehungsgeschichte des Islams*. Krakow, 1939.

Hirschfeld, Hartwig. *New Researches into the Composition and Exegesis of the Qoran*. London, 1902.

Hock, Ronald F. *The Infancy Gospels of James and Thomas: Introduction, Greek Text, English Translation, and Notes*. Santa Rosa, 1995.

Hofmannsthal, Hugo von. *Einlei-al-islāmīya*. Beirut, 2010.

Hooke, H., ed. *Myth, Ritual and Kingship: Essays on the Theory and Practice of Kingship in the Ancient Near East and Israel*. Oxford, 1958.

Horovitz, Josef. "Bemerkungen zur Geschichte und Terminologie des islamischen Kultus," in: *Der Islam* 15–16 (1926–1927), 249–263.

Horovitz, Josef. *Jewish Proper Names and Derivatives in the Koran*. Hildesheim, 1964.

Horovitz, Josef. "Das koranische Paradies," in: *Scripta Universitatis atque Bibliothecae Hierosolymitana*. Jerusalem, 1923, 1–16, repr. in Rudi Paret, *Der Koran*, Darmstadt, 1975, 53–73.

Horovitz, Josef. *Koranische Untersuchungen*. Berlin and Leipzig, 1926.

Horsch, Silvia. "Tod im Kampf: Figurationen des Märtyrers in frühen islamischen Schriften." Dissertation, Freie Universität Berlin, 2009.

Hossfeld, Frank-Lothar, and Erich Zenger. *Die Neue Echter-Bibel: Kommentar zum Alten Testament mit der Einheitsübersetzung; Die Psalmen*. Würzburg, 1993.

Hoyland, Robert. *Arabia and the Arabs: From the Bronze Age to the Coming of Islam*. London and New York, 2001.

Hoyland, Robert. "New Documentary Texts and the Early Islamic State," in: *BSOAS* 69 (2006), 395–416.

Hoyland, Robert. *Seeing Islam as Others Saw It: A Survey and Evaluation of Christian, Jewish, and Zoroastrian Writings on Early Islam*. Princeton, 1997.

Hughes, Aaron. "The Stranger at the Sea: Mythopoesis in the Qur'an and Early Tafsir," in: *Studies in Religion* 32 (2003), 261–279.

Husain, Taha. *Fī l-Shi r al-Jāhilī*. Cairo, 1926.

Ibn al-Djazarī. *Kitāb al-Nashr fī l-qirā āt Abū Sahr al-Hudalī: Eine literaturanthropologische Studie*. Diskurse der Arabistik 15. Wiesbaden, 2008.

Ibn Isḥāq. *Sīra*, in: *al-Sīra al-nabawīya li-Ibn Hishām*, ed. Muhammad al-Saqqa et al., Cairo, 1955.

Ibn Mujāhid. *Kitāb al-Sabʿa*, ed. Shawqi Ḍayf. Cairo, 1972.

Ibn Qaiyim al-Jauzīya. *Al-tibyān fī aqsām al-qurʾān*, ed. Muḥammad Ḥāmid al-Fiqī. Beirut, 1982.

Ibn Sa'ad. *Al-Tabaqāt al-Kubrā*, vol. 1: *As-sīra al-sharīfa al-nabawīya*. Beirut, 1960.

Imhof, Agnes. "The Qur'an and the Prophet's Poet: Two Poems by Ka'b b. Mālik," in: *The Qurʾān in Context: Historical and Literary Investigations into the Qurʾānic Milieu*, ed. Angelika Neuwirth, Nicolai Sinai, and Michael Marx. Leiden, 2009, 389–403.

Imhof, Agnes. *Religiöser Wandel und die Genese des Islam: Das Menschenbild altarabischer Panegyriker im 7. Jahrhundert*. Würzburg, 2004.

Irsigler, Hubert. "Gott als König in Berufung und Verkündigung Jesajas," in: Ein Gott eine Offenbarung: Beiträge zur biblischen Exegese, Theologie und Spiritualität; Festschrift für Notker Füglister OSB zum 60. Geburtstag, ed. Friedrich V. Reiterer. Würzburg, 1991, 127–154.

Izutsu, Toshihiko. *Ethico-Religious Concepts in the Qur'an*. Montreal, 1966.

Izutsu, Toshihiko. *God and Man in the Quran: Semantics of the Koranic Weltanschauung*. Tokyo, 1964.

Izutsu, Toshihiko. *The Structure of the Ethical Terms in the Koran: A Study in Semantics*. Tokyo, 1959.

Jacobi, Renate. "Mukhaḍram," in: *Encyclopedia of Arabic Literature*, ed. Julie Scott Meisami and Paul Starkey, 2 vols. London, 1998, 548.

Jacobi, Renate. *Studien zur Poetik der altarabischen Qaside*. Wiesbaden, 1971.

Jadaane, Fahmi. *Stoicisme dans l'Islam*. Beirut, 1968.

al-Jāḥiẓ, *Ḥudjadj al-nubuwa*, in: *Rasā il al-Djāhiz*, ed. Abdassalam Muhammad Harun, 6 vols., Cairo, n.d.

James, David. *Qur'ans and Bindings from the Chester Beatty Library: A Facsimile Exhibition*. London, 1980.

Jeffery, Arthur. "Abu Ubayd on the Verses Missing from the Qur'an," in: *Muslim World* 28 (1938), 61–65.

Jeffery, Arthur. *Foreign Vocabulary in the Qur'an*. Baroda, 1937.

Jeffery, Arthur. *Materials for the History of the text of the Qur'an: The Old Codices*. Leiden, 1937.

Jeffery, Arthur. "The Mysterious Letters of the Koran," in: *Muslim World* 14 (1924), 247–260.

Jeffery, Arthur. "The Present Status of Qur'anic Studies," in: *The Middle East Institute: Report of Current Research* 1957, 1–16.

Jeffery, Arthur. "Progress in the Study in the Qur'an Text," in: *Muslim World* 25 (1935), 4–16.

Jeffery, Arthur. *The Qur'an as Scripture*. New York, 1952.

Jeffery, Arthur, and I. Mendelsohn. "The Orthography of the Samarqand Qur'an Codex," in: *JAOS* 62 (1942), 175–195.

Jepsen, Alfred. "Hazon," in: *ThWAT*, vol. 2, 822–835.

Jomier, Jacques. *The Bible and the Koran*. New York, 1964.

Jomier, Jacques. *Le commentaire coranique du Manar: Tendences modernes de l'exégèse coranique en Egypte*. Paris, 1954.

Jomier, Jacques. *The Great Themes of the Quran*. London, 1997.

Jomier, Jacques. "La place du Coran dans la vie quotidienne en Egypte," in: *Revue de l'Institut des Belles Lettres Arabes* 15 (1952), 131–165.

Jomier, Jacques. "Quelques positions actuelles de l'exégèse coranique en Egypte révélées par une polémique récente (1947–1951)," in: *MIDEO* 1 (1954), 39–72.

Jülicher, Adolf. *Die Gleichnisreden*, 2 vols., Freiburg i.B., 1888–1899, repr. Darmstadt, 1976.

al-Jurjānī, *Dalā il al-i jāz fī l-Qur ān*, ed. Muhammad Abduh and Rashīd Riḍā. Rev. ed. Beirut, 1994.

Kadi, Wadad (al-Qāḍī). "The Primordial Covenant and Human History in the Qur'an," in: *Proceedings of the American Philosophical Society* 147 (2003), 332–338.

Kadi, Wadad (al-Qāḍī), and Mustansir Mir. "Literature and the Qur'ān," in: *EQ*, vol. 3. Leiden, 2003, 205–227.

Kandil, Lamya. "Die Schwüre in den Mekkanischen Suren," in: *The Qur'an as Text*, ed. Stefan Wild. Leiden, 1996, 41–57.

Kandil, Lamya. "Die Surennamen in der offiziellen Kairiner Koranausgabe und ihre Varianten," in: *Der Islam* 69 (1992), 44–60.

Kassir, Samir. "Das arabische Unglück: Von historischer Größe, Selbstverlust und kultureller Wiedergeburt," in: *Lettre Internationale* 71 (2005), 62–69.

Kassir, Samir. *Das arabische Unglück*. Berlin, 2006.

Kellermann, Andreas. "Die Mündlichkeit des Koran: Ein forschungsgeschichtliches Problem der Arabistik," in: *Beiträge zur Geschichte der Sprachwissenschaft* 5 (1995), 1–33.

Kellermann, Andreas. "Koranlesung im Maghreb." Dissertation, Freie Universität Berlin, 1996.

Kermani, Navid. "Appelliert Gott an den Verstand? Eine Randbemerkung zum koranischen Begriff aql und seiner Paret'schen Übersetzung," in: *Encounters of Words and Texts: Intercultural Studies in Honor of Stefan Wild on the Occasion of His 60th Birthday, March 2, 1997, Presented by His Pupils in Bonn*, ed. Lutz Edzard and Christian Szyska, Hildesheim, 1997, 43–66.

Kermani, Navid. *Gott ist schön: Das ästhetische Erleben des Koran*. Munich, 1999.

Kermani, Navid. *Offenbarung als Kommunikation. Das Konzept wahy in Nasr Hāmid Abū-Zayds Maf-hūm an-Nass*. Frankfurt am Main, 1996.

Kermani, Navid. *Offenbarung Übersetzung und wissenschaftlicher Kommentar*, 12 vols. Gütersloh, 1990–2001.

Kessler, Christel. "Abd al-Malik's Inscription in the Dome of the Rock: A Reconsideration," in: *JRAS* 1 (1970), 2–64.

Khalafallah, Muhammad Ahmad. *Al-Fann al-Qasasī fi-l-Qur'ān al-Karīm*. Cairo, 1953.

Khalafallah, Muhammad Ahmad. *Al-Qur'ān wa-Mushkilat Hayatinā al-Mu āsira*. Repr. Cairo, 1982.

Khalidi, Tarif. *Arabic Historical Thought in the Classical Period*. New York, 1994.

Khalidi, Tarif. *Images of Muhammad: Narratives of the Prophet in Islam across the Centuries*. New York, 2009.

Khuli, Amin al-. *Manāhidj at-tadjdīd fi-n-nahw wa-l-balāgha wa-l-tafsīr wa-l-adab*. Cairo, 1961.

Kimbler, Richard. "The Quranic Law of Inheritance," in: *Islamic Law and Society* 5 (1998), 291-325.

Kinberg, Leah. "Ambiguous," in: *EQ*, vol. 1. Leiden, 2001, 70–77.

Kinberg, Leah. "Muhkamat and mutashabihat (Koran 3/7): Implications of a Koranic Pair of Terms in Medieval Exegesis," in: *Arabica* 35 (1988), 143–172.

Kindy, Salam al-. *Le voyageur sans Orient: Poésie et philosophie des Arabes de l'ère préislamique*. Arles, 1998.

Kister, M. J. "The Campaign of Ḥulubān: A New Light on the Expedition of Abraha," in: *Le Muséon* 78 (1965), 425–436.

Kister, M. J. "Labbayka, Allahumma, Labbayka . . . On a Monotheistic Aspect of a Jahiliyya Practice," in: *JSAI* 2 (1980), 33–57.

Klinghardt, Matthias. "'. . . auf daß du den Feiertag heiligest': Sabbat und Sonntag im antiken Judentum und frühen Christentum," in: *Das Fest und das Heilige*, ed. Jan Assmann. Munich, 1991, 206–233.

Knauf, Ernst Axel. "Arabo-Aramaic and Arabiyya: From Ancient Arabic to Early Standard Arabic, 200 CE–600 CE," in: *The Qur'ān in Context: Historical and Literary Investigations into the Qur'ānic Milieu*, ed. Angelika Neuwirth, Nicolai Sinai, and Michael Marx. Leiden, 2009, 197–254.

Knauf, Ernst Axel. "Audiatur et altera pars: Zur Logik der Pentateuch-Redaktion," in: *Bibel und Kirche* 53 (1998), 118–126.

Kohlberg, Etan. "Shahīd," in: *EI*, vol. 9, 203–207.

Kopf, Lothar. "Religious Influences on Medieval Arabic Philology," in: *Studia Islamica* 5 (1956), 33–59.

Körner, Felix. *Revisionist Koran Hermeneutics in Contemporary Turkish University Theology: Rethinking Islam*. Würzburg, 2005.

Körner, Felix, ed. *Alter Text—neuer Kontext: Koranhermeneutik in der Türkei heute; Ausgewählte Texte, übersetzt und kommentiert von F. K. SJ*. Freiburg, 2006.

Krone, Susanne. *Die arabische Gottheit al-Lāt*. Heidelberger orientalische Studien 23. Bern, 1992.

Küchler, Max. *Jerusalem: Ein Handbuch und Studienführer zur Heiligen Stadt*. Zürich, 2007.

Kugel, James. *Traditions of the Bible: A Guide to the Bible as It Was*. Cambridge and London, 1998.

Kugel, James. "Early Interpretation: The Common Background of Later Forms of Biblical Exegesis," in: *Early Biblical Interpretation*, ed. James Kugel and Rowan A. Greer. Philadelphia, 1986, 9–106.

Kugel, James. *Poetry and Prophecy: The Beginnings of a Literary Tradition*. Ithaca and New York, 1990.

Kugel, James. "Poets and Prophets: An Overview," in: *Poetry and Prophecy: The Beginnings of a Literary Tradition*, ed. James Kugel. Ithaca and London, 1990, 1–25.

Lacocque, André. "'Apocalyptic Symbolism': A Ricoeurian Hermeneutical Approach," in: *Biblical Research* 26 (1981), 6–15.

Lammens, Henri. *Fatima et les filles de Mahomet: Notes critiques pour l'étude de la sira*. Rome, 1912.

Lammens, Henri. *L'Arabie occidentale avant l'higire*. Beirut, 1928.

Lane, Andrew J. *A Traditional Mu tazilite Qur an Commentary: The Kashshāf of Jār Allāh al-Zamakhsharī*. Leiden, 2006.

Lassner, Jacob. "Abraham Geiger: A Nineteenth-century Jewish Reformer on the Origins of Islam," in: *The Jewish Discovery of Islam: Studies in Honor of Bernard Lewis*, ed. Martin Kramer. Tel Aviv, 1999, 103–136.

Lassner, Jacob. *Demonizing the Queen of Sheba: Boundaries of Gender and Culture in Postbiblical Judaism and Medieval Islam*. Chicago, 1993.

Lausberg, Heinrich. *Handbuch der literarischen Rhetorik: Eine Grundlegung der Literaturwissenschaft*. Munich, 1960.

Lawson, Todd. *The Crucifixion and the Qur'an: A Study in the History of Muslim Thought*. Oxford, 2009.

Lazarus-Yafeh, Hava. *Intertwined Worlds: Medieval Islam and Bible Criticism*. Princeton, 1992.

Lecker, Michael. "Muhammad at Medina: A Geographical Approach," in: *JSAI* 6 (1985), 29–62.

Lecker, Michael. *Muslims, Jews, and Pagans: Studies on Early Islamic Medina*. Leiden and New York, 1995.

Lecker, Michael. "On the Markets of Medina (Yathrib) in Pre-Islamic and Early Islamic Times," in: *JSAI* 8 (1986), 133–147.

Leemhuis, Fred. "Codices of the Qu-r'ān," in: *EQ*, vol. 1. Leiden, 2001, 337–346.

Leemhuis, Fred. "From Palmleaves to the Internet," in: *The Cambridge Companion to the Qur'an*, ed. Jane McAuliffe. Cambridge, 2006, 145–162.

Lehmann, Manfred R. "Biblical Oaths," in: *ZAW* 81 (1969), 74–92.

Leicht, Reimund. "The Qur'anic Commandment of Writing Down Loan Agreements (Q 2:282)—Perspectives of a Comparison with Rabbinical Law," in: *The Qur'ān in Context: Historical and Literary Investigations into the Qur'ānic Milieu*, ed. Angelika Neuwirth, Nicolai Sinai, and Michael Marx. Leiden, 2009, 593–615.

Lesky, Albin. *Geschichte der griechischen Literatur*. Munich, 1999.

Levi della Vida, Giorgio. *Frammenti coranici in carattere cufico*. Vatican City, 1947.

Levi della Vida, Giorgio. "Pre-Islamic Arabia," in: *The Arab Heritage*, ed. N. A. Faris. Princeton, 1944, 41–48.

Lichtenstädter, Ilse. "Das Nasib der altarabischen Qaside," in: *Islamica* 5 (1932), 17–94.

Lindqvist, Pekka. "Sin at Sinai: Three First Century Versions," in: *Ancient Israel, Judaism, and Christianity in Contemporary Perspective: Essays in Memory of Karl-Johan Illman*, ed. Jacob Neusner and Alan J. Avery-Peck. Lanham, 2006, 225–246.

Lings, Martin. *The Qur'anic Art of Calligraphy and Illumination*. London, 1976.

Littmann, Enno, trans. *Tausendundeine Nacht*. 6 vols. Wiesbaden, 1953.

Loades, Ann. "Feminist Interpretation," in: *The Cambridge Companion to Biblical Interpretation*, ed. John Barton. Cambridge, 1998, 81–94.

Lohmann, Theodor. "Die Gleichnisse im Koran," in: *MIO* 12 (1966), 75–118 and 241–287.

Lotman, Jurij M. *Die Struktur literarischer Texte*. Munich, 1972.

Lüling, Günter. *Über den Ur-Qur'an: Ansätze zur Rekonstruktion vorislamischer christlicher Strophenlieder im Qur'an. Erlangen*, 1974, rev. ed. 1990, 3rd ed. 2004.

Lumpe, Adolf, and Hans Bietenhard. "Himmel," in: *Reallexikon für Antike und Christentum*, vol. 15. Stuttgart, 1991, 173–212.

Luxenberg, Christoph. *Die syro-aramäische Lesart des Koran: Ein Beitrag zur Entschlüsselung der Koransprache*. Berlin, 2000, repr. Berlin, 2008.

Lyall, Charles. *Some Aspects of Ancient Arabic Poetry as Illustrated by a Little-Known Anthology*. Oxford, 1918.

Maalouf, Nayef. *La place du verbe dans la pensée arabe*. Beirut, 2006.

Madigan, Daniel. "Gottes Botschaft an die Welt: Christen und Muslime, Jesus und der Koran," in: *Internationale katholische Zeitschrift—Communio* 32 (2003), 100–112.

Madigan, Daniel. "Preserved Tablet," in: *EQ*, vol. 4. Leiden, 2004, 261–263.

Madigan, Daniel. *The Qur'an's Self-Image: Writing and Authority in Islam's Scripture*. Princeton, 2001.

Magermans, A. H., comp. *Index of Qur'anic Verses to the English Part of Materials for the History of the text of the Qur'an: The Old Codices*. By Arthur Jeffery. Leiden, 1951.

Maghen, Zeev. "First Blood Purity, Edibility, and the Independence of Islamic Jurisprudence," in: *Der Islam* 81 (2004), 49–95.

Makī ibn Abī Ṭālib al-Qaisī. *Al-Riwāya fī l-qirāʾa*, ed. Aḥmad Ḥasan Farḥān. Damascus, 1973.

Mariès, Louis, and Charles Mercier, trans. *Hymnes de Eprem conservées en version arménienne*, in: *Patrologia Orientalis* 30. Paris, 1961.

Margoliouth, Samuel. "Muhammad," in: *Encyclopaedia of Religion and Ethics*, vol. 8, 878.

Margoliouth, Samuel. *Mohammed and the Rise of Islam*. London, 1905.

Margoliouth, Samuel. "The Origins of Arabic Poetry": in: *JRAS* 1925, 417–449.

Marmorstein, Arthur. *The Doctrine of the Merits in Old Rabbinical Literature*, 2 vols. New York, 1968.

Marshall, David. *God, Muhammad and the Unbelievers*. Richmond, 1999.

Martin, Richard C. "Inimitability," in: *EQ*, vol. 2. Leiden, 2002, 526–536.

Martin, Richard C. *Islam: A Cultural Perspective*. Englewood, 1982.

Martin, Richard C. *Islam in Local Contexts*. Leiden, 1982.

Martin, Richard C. "Understanding the Qur'an in Text and Context," in: *History of Religions* 21 (1982), 361–384.

Marx, Michael. "Glimpses of a Mariology in the Qur'an: From Hagiography to Theology via Religious-Political Debate," in: *The Qurʾān in Context: Historical and Literary Investigations into the Qurʾānic Milieu*, ed. Angelika Neuwirth, Nicolai Sinai, and Michael Marx. Leiden, 2010, 533–564.

Marx, Michael. "The Koran according to Agfa: Gotthelf Bergsträssers Archiv der Koranhandschriften," in: *Trajekte: Zeitschrift des Zentrums für Literatur- und Kulturforschung Berlin* 19 (2009), 25–29.

Marx, Michael. "Ein Koranforschungsprojekt in der Tradition der Wissenschaft des Judentums: Zur Programmatik des Akademienvorhabens Corpus Coranicum," in: "*Im vollen Licht der Geschichte*"—*Die Wissenschaft des Judentums und die Anfänge der Koranforschung*, ed. Dirk Hartwig, Walter Homolka, Michael Marx, and Angelika Neuwirth. Würzburg, 2008, 41–54.

Marx, Michael. "Ein neuer Impuls für die Erforschung des Koran," in: *inamo* 33/34 (2003), 45–47.

Marx, Michael. "Was ist eigentlich der Koran?," in: *inamo* 37 (2004), 53–54.

Massey, Keith. "Mysterious Letters," in: *EQ*, vol. 3. Leiden, 2003, 471–476.

Massey, Keith. "Mysterious Letters of the Qur'an," in: *Arabica* 43 (1996), 497–501.

McAuliffe, Jane Dammen, ed. *The Cambridge Companion to the Qur'an*. Cambridge, 2006.

McAuliffe, Jane Dammen. "Chosen of all Women: Mary and Fatima in Qur'anic Exegesis," in: *Islamochristiana* 7 (1981), 19–28.

McAuliffe, Jane Dammen. "'Debate with Them in a Better Way': The Construction of a Qur'anic Commonplace," in: *Myths, Historical Archetypes and Symbolic Figures in Arabic Literature*, ed. Angelika Neuwirth et al. Beirut and Stuttgart, 1999, 163–188.

McAuliffe, Jane Dammen. *Qur'anic Christians: An Analysis of Classica and Modern Exegesis*. Cambridge, 1991.

McAuliffe, Jane Dammen. "The Qur'anic Context of Muslim Biblical Scholarship," in: *Islam and Christian-Muslim Relations* 7 (1995), 141–158.

McAuliffe, Jane Dammen. "Text and Textuality: Q 3:7 as a Point of Intersection," in: *Literary Structures of Religious Meaning in the Qur'an*, ed. Issa J. Boullata. Richmond, 2000, 56–76.

McDannell, Colleen, and Bernhard Lang. *Heaven: A History*. New Haven, and London, 1988.

Meier, Andreas. "Gotteswort in Knechtgestalt—ein islamischer Luther in Ægypten? N.H. Abu Zaids provokante Koranexegese als säkulare Reform des Islam," in: *Begegnungen zwischen Christentum und Islam. Festschrift für Hans-Jürgen Brandt zum 65. Geburtstag*. Perspektiven der Weltmission: Wissenschaftliche Beiträge 20, ed. Hans-Christoph Goßmann. Ammersbek, 1994, 57–73.

Meier, Fritz. "Almoraviden und marabute," in: Die Welt des Islam 21 (1983), 80–163. Repr. in: Fritz Meier, *Bausteine II: Ausgewählte Aufsätze zur Islamwissenschaft*, ed. Erika Glassen and Gudrun Schubert. Beirut and Stuttgart, 1992, 712–796.

Meyer, Eduard. *Der historische Gehalt der Ayyâm al-'Arab*. Wiesbaden, 1970.

Mingana, Alphonse. "Syriac Influences on the Style of the Kur'an," in: *Bulletin of John Rylands Library* 2 (1927), 77–98.

Mingana, Alphonse, and Agnes Smith Lewis. *Leaves From Three Ancient Qurâns, Possibly Pre-'Othmânic, With a List of Their Variants*. Cambridge, 1914.

Mir, Mustansir. *Coherence in the Qur'an: A Study of Islahi's Concept of nazm in Tadabbur-i Qur'an*. Indianapolis, 1986.

Mir, Mustansir. "The Qur'anic story of Joseph: Plot, themes and characters," in: *Muslim World* 76 (1986), 1–15.

Mir, Mustansir. "The Sura as an Unity: A Twentieth Century Development in Qur'an Exegesis," in: *Approaches to the Qur'an*, ed. Gerald R. Hawting and Abdel Kader Shareef. London, 1993, 211–224.

Mittwoch, Eugen. *Zur Entstehungsgeschichte des islamischen Gebets und Kultus*. Abhandlungen der Preußischen Akademie der Wissenschaften 2. Berlin, 1913.

Monroe, James T. "Oral Composition in Pre-Islamic Poetry," in: *JAL* 3 (1972), 1–53.

Montgomery, James E. "Dichotomy in Jāhilī Poetry," in: *JAL* 17 (1986), 1–20.

Montgomery, James E. "The Empty Ḥijāz," in: *Arabic Theology, Arabic Philosophy, From the Many to the One: Essays in Celebration of Richard M. Frank*, ed. James E. Montgomery, Leuven and Paris, Dudley, 2006, 37–97.

Montgomery, James E. *Vagaries of the Qasidah: The Tradition and Practice of Early Arabic Poetry*. London, 1997.

Montgomery, James E. "Umayya b. Abi 'l-Salt," in: *EI*², vol. 10, 905–906.

Motzki, Harald. "Alternative Accounts of the Qur'an's Formation," in: *The Cambridge Companion to the Qur'an*, ed. Jane Dammen McAuliffe. Cambridge, 2006, 59–78.

Motzki, Harald. *Die Anfänge der islamischen Jurisprudenz: Ihre Entwicklung in Mekka bis zur Mitte des 2./8. Jahrhunderts*. Stuttgart, 1991.

Motzki, Harald, ed. *The Biography of Muhammad: The Issue of the Sources*. Boston and Leiden, 2000.

Motzki, Harald. "The Collection of the Qur'an: A Reconsideration of Western Views in Light of Recent Methological Developments," in: *Der Islam* 78 (2001), 1–34.

Mourad, Suleiman A. "From Hellenism to Christianity and Islam: The Origin of the Palm tree Story con-cerning Mary and Jesus in the Gospel of Pseudo-Matthew and the Qur'ān," in: *OC* 86 (2002), 206–216.

Mourad, Suleiman A. "Mary in the Qur'an," in: *The Qur'an in Its Historical Context*, ed. Gabriel Reynolds. London and New York, 2008, 163–174.

Mourad, Suleiman A. "On the Qur'anic Stories about Mary and Jesus," in: *Bulletin of the Royal Institute for Inter-Faith Studies* 1 (1999), 13–24.

Müller, David Heinrich. *Die Propheten in ihrer ursprünglichen Form: Die Grundgesetze der ursemitischen Poesie, erschlossen und nachgewiesen in Bibel, Keilschriften und Koran, und in ihren Wirkungen erkannt in den Chören der griechischen Tragiker*, 2 vols. Vienna, 1896.

Müller, Friedrun R. *Untersuchungen zur Reimprosa im Koran*. Bonn, 1969.

Müller, Gottfried. "Die Barmherzigkeit Gottes: Zur Entstehungsgeschichte eines koranischen Symbols," in: *Die Welt des Islams* 28 (1988), 334–362.

Müller, Gottfried. *Ich bin Labid und das ist mein Ziel: Zum Problem der Selbstbehauptung in der altarabischen Qaside*. Berlin, 1981.

Müller, Hans-Peter. "Nebhu'ah," in: *Theologisches Wörterbuch zum Alten Testament*, vol. 5, 140–163.

Munajjed, Salahuddin. *Le manuscrit arabe jusqu'au Xe siècle de l'Hegire*, vol. 1. Cairo, 1960.

Murray, Robert. *Symbols of Church and Kingdom: A Study in Early Syriac Tradition*. Cambridge, 1975.

Nabhan, Laila. *Das Fest des Fastenbrechens (Id al-Fitr) in Ægypten: Untersuchungen zu theologischen Grundlagen und praktischer Gestaltung*. Berlin, 1991.

Nader, Albert. *Le système philosophique des Mou'tazilas*. Beirut, 1956.

Nagel, Tilman. "Vom 'Qur'an' zur Schrift—Bells Hypothese aus religionsgeschichtlicher Sicht," in: *Der Islam* 60 (1983), 143–165.

Nagel, Tilman. "'Der erste Muslim'—Abraham in Mekka," in: "Abraham, unser Vater": *Die gemeinsamen Wurzeln von Judentum, Christentum und Islam*, ed. Reinhard G. Kratz and Tilman Nagel. Göttingen, 2003, 133–149.

Nagel, Tilman. "Medinensische Einschübe in Mekkanischen Suren: Ein Arbeitsbericht," in: *The Qur'ān as Text*, ed. Stefan Wild. Leiden, 1996, 59–68.

Nagel, Tilman. *Medinensische Einschübe in mekkanischen Suren*. Göttingen, 1995.

Nagel, Tilman. *Muhammad: Leben und Legende*. Munich, 2008.

Najman, Hindy. "Interpretation as Primordial Writing: Jubilees and Its Authority Conferring Strategies," in: *Journal for the Study of Judaism* 30 (1999), 379–410.

Nasr, Seyyed Hossein. *Ideals and Realities of Islam*. London, 1966, repr. London, 1979, 43–44, cited in: Daniel A. Madigan, *God's Word to the World: Jesus and the Qur'an, Incarnation and Recitation*, Leuven, 2009.

Nebes, Norbert. "The Martyrs of Najrān and the End of Himyar: On the Political History of South Arabia in the Early Sixth Century," in: *The Qur'ān in Context: Historical and Literary Investigations into the Qur'ānic Milieu*, ed. Michael Marx, Angelika Neuwirth, and Nicolai Sinai. Leiden, 2009, 27–59.

Nelson, Kristina. *The Art of Reciting the Qur'an*. Cairo, 2001.

Neuwirth, Angelika. "Adab Standing Trial—Whose Norms Should Rule Society? The Case of al-Harīrī's al-Maqāmah al-Ramlīyah," in: *Myths, Historical Archetypes and Symbolic Figures in Arabic Literature: Proceedings of the International Symposium in Beirut, June 25th–June 30th, 1996*, ed. Angelika Neuwirth, Birgit Embaló, Sebastian Guenther, and Maher Jarrar. Beirut and Stuttgart, 1999, 205–224.

Neuwirth, Angelika. "De-mythifying Islam: A Novel Hermeneutic Approach to the Relation of the Three Religious Traditions of Europe," in: *Islam in Europe: Case Studies, Comparisons and Overviews*, ed. Reuven Amitai and Amikam Nachmani. Jerusalem, 2008, 119–132.

Neuwirth, Angelika. "Eine europäische Lektüre des Koran," in: Jahrbuch des Dubnow-Instituts 7 (2008), 261–283.

Neuwirth, Angelika. "Einige Bemerkungen zum besonderen sprachlichen und literarischen Charakter des Koran," in: *ZDMG* suppl. 3/1 (1977), 736–739.

Neuwirth, Angelika. "Erste Qibla—fernstes Masjid? Jerusalem im Horizont des historischen Muhammad," in: *Zion-Ort der Begegnung: Festschrift für Laurentius Kleinzur Vollendung des 65. Lebensjahres*, ed. Ferdinand Hahn, Frank-Lothar Hossfeld, Hans Jorissen, and Angelika Neuwirth. Bodenheim, 1993, 227–270.

Neuwirth, Angelika. "Erzählen als kanonischer Prozess: Die Mose-Erzählung im Wandel der koranischen Geschichte," in: *Islamstudien ohne Ende: Festschrift für Werner Ende zum 65. Geburtstag*, ed. Rainer Brunner et al. Würzburg, 2002, 323–344.

Neuwirth, Angelika. "Form and Structure of the Qur'an," in: *EQ*, vol. 2. Leiden, 2002, 245–266.

Neuwirth, Angelika. "From Sacrilege to Sacrifice: Observations on Violent Death in Classical and Modern Arabic Poetry," in: *Martyrdom in Literature: Visions of Death and Meaningful Suffering in Europe and the Middle East from Antiquity to Modernity*, ed. Friederike Pannewick. Wiesbaden, 2004, 259–82.

Neuwirth, Angelika. "From the Sacred Mosque to the Remote Temple": Sūrat al-Isrā' between Text and Commentary," in: *With Reverence for the Word: Studies in Jewish,*

Christian and Islamic Exegesis, ed. Jane D. McAuliffe, Barry Walfish, and Jo-seph W. Goering. Oxford, 2003, 376–407.

Neuwirth, Angelika. "Das Gedicht als besticktes Tuch; Mahmud Darwischs Gedicht 'Ein Liebender aus Palästina', in: *Pracht und Geheimnis: Kleidung und Schmuck aus Palästina und Jordanien*, ed. Gisela Voelger, Karin v. Welck and Katharina Hackstein. Cologne, 1987, 110–117.

Neuwirth, Angelika. "Geography and the Qur'an," in: *EQ*, vol. 2. Leiden, 2002, 293–313.

Neuwirth, Angelika. "Gewalttexte und Versöhnungsliturgien in Judentum, Chri-stentum und Islam," in: *Europäische und islamisch geprägte Länder im Dialog: Gewalt, Religion und interkulturelle Verständigung*, ed. Jacques Poulain, Fathi Triki and Christoph Wulf. Berlin, 2006, 48–61.

Neuwirth, Angelika. "Der historische Muhammad im Spiegel des Koran: Prophetentypus zwischen Seher und Dichter," in: *Biblische Welten: Festschrift für Martin Metzger zu seinem 65. Geburtstag*, ed. Wolfgang Zwickel. Freiburg and Göttingen, 1991, 83–108.

Neuwirth, Angelika. "Der Horizont der Offenbarung: Zur Relevanz der einleitenden Schwurserien für die Suren der frühmekkanischen Zeit," in: *Gottes ist der Orient; Gottes ist der Okzident: Festschrift für Abdoldjavad Falaturi zum 65. Geburtstag*, ed. Udo Tworuschka. Cologne and Vienna, 1991, 1–39.

Neuwirth, Angelika. "The House of Abraham and the House of Amran: Genealogy, Patriarchal Authority, and Exegetical Professionalism," in: *The Qurān in Context: Historical and Literary Investigations into the Qur'ānic Milieu*, ed. Angelika Neuwirth, Nicolai Sinai, and Michael Marx. Leiden, 2010, 499–532.

Neuwirth, Angelika. "Images and Metaphors in the Introductory Sections of the Makkan sūras," in: *Approaches to the Qur'ān*, ed. Gerald R. Hawting and Abdul-Kader A. Shareef. London and New York, 1993, 3–36.

Neuwirth, Angelika. "Imagining Mary—Disputing Jesus: Reading Surat Maryam and Related Meccan Texts within the Qur'anic Communication Process," in: *Fremde, Feinde und Kurioses. Innen- und Außenansichten unseres muslimischen Nachbarn*, ed. Benjamin Jokisch, Ulrich Rebstock, and Lawrence Conrad. Berlin, 2009, 383–415.

Neuwirth, Angelika. "Das islamische Dogma der Unnachahmlichkeit des Korans in literaturwissenschaftlicher Sicht," in: *Der Islam* 60 (1983), 166–183.

Neuwirth, Angelika. "Jerusalem—Ort auch islamischer Erinnerung," in: *Die Reise nach Jerusalem*, ed. Hendrik Budde and Andreas Nachama. Berlin, 1995, 24–31.

Neuwirth, Angelika. "Der Koran—Mittelpunkt des Lebens der islamischen Gemeinde," in: *Weltmacht Islam*, ed. Rudolf Hilf. Munich, 1988, 69–92.

Neuwirth, Angelika. "Der Koran," in: *Grundriss der arabischen Philologie*, ed. Helmut Gätje. Wiesbaden, 1987, vol. 2, 96–135.

Neuwirth, Angelika. "Die Korangenese zwischen Mythos und Geschichte," in: *Die Religionen der Welt: Ein Almanach zur Eröffnung des Verlags der Weltreligionen*, ed. Hans-Joachim Simm. Frankfurt am Main, 2007 ([2]2008), 325–335.

Neuwirth, Angelika. "Koranlesung zwischen islamischem Ost und West," in: *Proceedings of the XIth Conference of the Union Europeenne des Arabisants et Islamisants*, ed. Adel Sidarus. Evora-Faro, 1983, 305–316.

Neuwirth, Angelika. "Mary and Jesus—Counterbalancing the Biblical Patriarchs: A Re-reading of Surat Maryam in Surat Al Imran (Q 3:1–62)," in: *Parole de L'Orient* 30 (2005), 231–260.

Neuwirth, Angelika. "Meccan Texts—Medinan Additions? Politics and the Re-Reading of Liturgical Communications," in: *Words, Texts and Concepts Cruising the Mediterranean Sea: Studies on the Sources, Contents and Influences of Islamic Civilization and Arabic Philosophy and Science; Dedicated to Gerhard Endress on His Sixty-Fifth Birthday*, ed. Rüdiger Arnzen and Jörn Thielmann. Leuven, 2004, 71–93.

Neuwirth, Angelika. "Myths and Legends in the Qur'an," in: *EQ*, vol. 3. Leiden, 2003, 1–21.

Neuwirth, Angelika. "'Oral Scriptures' in Contact: The Qur'anic Story of the Golden Calf and Its Biblical Subtext between Narrative, Cult, and Inter-communal Debate," in: *Self-Referentiality in the Qur'an*, ed. Stefan Wild. Wiesbaden, 2006, 71–91.

Neuwirth, Angelika. "Die Psalmen—im Koran neu gelesen (Ps 104 und 136)," in: "*Im vollen Licht der Geschichte*": *Die Wissenschaft des Judentums und die Anfänge der kritischen Koranforschung*, ed. Dirk Hartwig, Walter Homolka, Michael Marx, and Angelika Neuwirth. Würzburg, 2008, 157–190.

Neuwirth, Angelika. "Qur'an and History—A Disputed Relationship: Some Reflections on Qur'anic History and History in the Qur'an," in: *JQS* 5 (2003), 1–19.

Neuwirth, Angelika. "Qur'an, Crisis and Memory: The Qur'ānic Path towards Canonization as Reflected in the Anthropogonic Accounts," in: *Crisis and Memory in Islamic Societies: Proceedings of the Third Summer Academy of the Working Group Modernity and Islam held at the Orient Institute of the German Oriental Society in Beirut*, ed. Angelika Neuwirth and Andreas Pflitsch. Beirut. Würzburg, 2001, 113–152.

Neuwirth, Angelika. "Ramadan," in: *EQ* vol. 4 (2004), 338–348.

Neuwirth, Angelika. "Referentiality und Textuality in Surat al-Hijr: Some Observations on the Qur'ānic 'Canonical Process' and the Emergence of a Community," in: *Literary Structures of Religious Meaning in the Qur'an*, ed. Issa J. Boullata. London, 2000, 143–172.

Neuwirth, Angelika. "Rezension zu Richard Burton, *The Collection of the Qur'ān*": *OLZ* 76 (1981), 372–380.

Neuwirth, Angelika. "Rezension zu John Wansbrough, *Qur'anic Studies*," in: *Welt des Islams* 23–24 (1983), 539–542.

Neuwirth, Angelika. *Scripture, Poetry and the Making of a Community: Reading the Qur'an as a Literary Text*. Oxford, 2014

Neuwirth, Angelika. "The Spiritual Meaning of Jerusalem in Islam," in: *City of the Great King: Jerusalem from David to the Present*, ed. Nitza Rosovsky. Cambridge, MA, 1996, 94–129 and 483–495.

Neuwirth, Angelika. "Structural, Linguistic and Literary Features," in: *The Cambridge Companion to the Qur'ān*, ed. Jane Dammen McAuliffe. Cambridge, 2006, 97–114.

Neuwirth, Angelika. "Structure and the Emergence of Community," in: *The Blackwell Companion to the Qur'ān*, ed. Andrew Rippin. Oxford, 2007, 140–159.

Neuwirth, Angelika. *Studien zur Komposition der mekkanischen Suren*. Berlin, 1981, 2nd ed. 2007.

Neuwirth, Angelika. "Sura(s)," in: *EQ*, vol. 5. Leiden, 2005, 166–177.

Neuwirth, Angelika. "Symmetrie und Paarbildung in der koranischen Eschatologie: Philologisch-stilistisches zu Surat ar-Rahman," in: *Mélanges de l'Université Saint-Joseph* 50 (1984), 445–480.

Neuwirth, Angelika. "Verse(s)," in: *EQ*, vol. 5. Leiden, 2005, 419–429.

Neuwirth, Angelika. "Vom Rezitationstext über die Liturgie zum Kanon: Zu Entstehung und Wiederauflösung der Surenkomposition im Verlauf der Entwicklung eines islamischen Kultus," in: *The Qur'an as Text*, ed. Stefan Wild. Leiden, 1996, 69–106.

Neuwirth, Angelika. "Zur Struktur der Yū-suf-Sure," in: *Studien aus Arabistik und Semitistik. Anton Spitaler zum siebzigsten Geburtstag von seinen Schülern überreicht*, ed. Werner Diem and Stefan Wild. Wiesbaden, 1980, 123–152.

Neuwirth, Angelika. "Zeit und Ewigkeit in den Psalmen und im Koran," in: *Time and Eternity as Places of Divine Action / Zeit und Ewigkeit als Raum göttlichen Handelns*, ed. Reinhard G. Kratz and Hermann Spieckermann. Berlin and New York, 2009, 319–342.

Neuwirth, Angelika, and Karl Neuwirth. "Sūrat al-Fātiḥa—'Eröffnung' des Text-Corpus Koran oder 'Introitus' der Gebetsliturgie?," in: *Text, Methode und Grammatik: Wolfgang Richter zum 65. Geburtstag*, ed. Walter Gross, Hubert Irsigler and Theodor Seidl. St. Ottilien, 1991, 331–337.

Newby, Gordon D. "Sūrat al-Ikhlāṣ—A Reconsideration," in: *Orient and Occident: Essays Presented to Cyrus H. Gordon on the Occasion of His Sixty Fifth Birthday*, ed. Harry A. Hoffner. Neukirchen-Vluyn, 1973, 127–130.

Newby, Gordon D., and Vernon K. Robbins. "A Prolegomenon to the Relation of the Qur'an and the Bible," in: *Bible and Qur'an: Essays in Scriptural Intertextuality*, ed. John C. Reeves. Leiden and Boston, 2003, 23–42.

Niehoff, Maren R. "What Is in a Name? Philo's Mystical Philosophy of Language," in: *Jewish Studies Quarterly* 2 (1995), 220–252.

Nöldeke, Theodor. *Geschichte des Qorans*, 1st ed. Göttingen, 1860 [= GdQ]; 2nd ed., ed. Friedrich Schwally, Leipzig, 1909 [= GdQ^2], repr. Hildesheim, and New York, 1961.

Nöldeke, Theodor. "Hatte Muhammad christliche Lehrer?," in: *ZDMG* 12 (1858), 699–708.

Nöldeke, Theodor. *Orientalische Skizzen*. Berlin, 1892.

Nöldeke, Theodor. "Rezension zu Karl Vollers, Volkssprache und Schriftsprache im alten Arabien = 'Zur Sprache des Korans'," in: Theodor Nöldeke, *Neue Beiträge zur Semitischen Sprachwissenschaft*, Straßburg, 1910, 1–30.

Nöldeke, Theodor. "Samaual," in: *Zeitschrift für Assyriologie und verwandte Gebiete* 27 (1912), 173–183.

Nöldeke, Theodor. *Sketches from Eastern History*. Translated by John Sutherland Black. Beirut, 1963 (based on Nöldeke, *Orientalische Skizzen*).

Nöldeke, Theodor. "Umaija b. AbisSalt," in: *Zeitschrift für Assyriologie und verwandte Gebiete* 27 (1912), 159–172.

Norden, Eduard. *Die Antike Kunstprosa*. Leipzig, 1898, repr. 1958.

Noseda, Sergio Noja. *Les manuscrits de style Higazi*, vol. 1: *Les manuscrits de style Higazi BNF 328 a*, and vol. 2: *Les manuscrits de style Higazi British Library Or 2165 (fol. 1–61)*. Paris, 1998.

Noth, Albrecht. "Früher Islam," in: *Geschichte der arabischen Welt*, ed. Ulrich Haarmann. Munich, 1987, 11–100.

Noth, Albrecht. "Die Hiğra," in: *Geschichte der arabischen Welt*, ed. Ulrich Haarmann. Munich, 1987, 11–57.

Obermann, Julian. "Koran and Agada: The Events at Mount Sinai," in: *American Journal of Semitic Languages and Literatures* 58 (1941), 23–48.

Ohlig, Karl-Heinz. "Einleitung," in: *Die dunklen Anfänge: Neue Forschungen zur Entstehung der frühen Geschichte des Islam*, ed. Karl-Heinz Ohlig and Gerd R. Puin. Berlin, 2005, 7–13.

Ohlig, Karl-Heinz, and Markus Groß, eds. *Schlaglichter: Die beiden ersten islamischen Jahrhunderte*. Berlin, 2008.

Ory, Solange. "Un nouveau type de muṣḥaf: Inventaire des corans en rouleaus de provenance Damascenes conservés à Istanbul," in: *Revue des Etudes Islamiques* 33, 87–149.

O'Shaughnessy, Thomas. *The Development of the Meaning of Spirit in the Koran*. Rome, 1953.

Paçacı, Mehmet. "Sag: Gott ist ein einziger—ahad: Ein exegetischer Versuch zu Sure 112 in der Perspektive der semitischen Religionstradition," in: *Alter Text—neuer Kontext: Koranhermeneutik in der Türkei heute; Ausgewählte Texte, übersetzt und kommentiert von F. K. SJ*, ed. Felix Körner. Freiburg, 2006, 166–203.

Pagels, Elaine. *Das Geheimnis des fünften Evangelium: Warum die Bibel nur die halbe Wahrheit sagt*. Munich, 2006.

Paret, Rudi. "Das Geschichtsbild Mohammeds," in: *Welt als Geschichte* 11 (1951), 214–224.

Paret, Rudi. "Der Koran als Geschichtsquelle," in: *Der Islam* 37 (1961), 24–42.

Paret, Rudi. *Der Koran: Kommentar und Konkordanz*. Stuttgart, 1971.

Paret, Rudi. *Der Koran: Übersetzung*. Stuttgart, 1966.

Paret, Rudi, ed. *Der Koran: Wege der Forschung*. Darmstadt, 1975.

Paret, Rudi. "Leitgedanken in Mohammeds frühesten Verkündigungen (Besprechung v. Harris Birkeland, The Lord Guideth)," in: *OLZ* 1957, 389–392.

Paret, Rudi. *Mohammed und der Koran: Geschichte und Verkündigung des arabischen Propheten*. Stuttgart, 1957.

Paret, Rudi. "Textkritisch verwertbare Koranlesarten," in: *Islamwissenschaftliche Abhandlungen: F. Meier zum 60. Geburtstag*, ed. Richard Gramlich. Wiesbaden, 1974, 198–204.

Parrinder, Geoffrey. *Jesus in the Qur'an*. London, 1965.

Pearson, James D. "Translations of the Kur'an," in: *EI*[2], vol. 5 (1981), 429–432.

Pellat, Charles. *Arabische Geisteswelt*. Zürich, 1967.

Peltomaa, Leena-Mari. *The Image of the Virgin in the Akathistos Hymnus*. Leiden, 2001.

Peters, Francis E. *Arabs and Arabia on the Eve of Islam*. Aldershot, 1999.

Peters, Francis E. "The Quest of the Historical Muhammad," in: *International Journal of Middle Eastern Studies* 23 (1991), 291–315.

Petersen, Daniel Carl. "Creation," in: *EQ*, vol. 1. Leiden, 2001, 472–480.

Pines, Shlomo. "'Jāhiliyya' and 'ilm,'" in: *JSAI* 13 (1990), 175–194.

Pink, Johanna. "Sunnitische Korankommentare in der arabischen Welt, Indonesien und der Türkei (1967-2004). Lokaler Kontext und gemeinsame Traditionen," Habilitationsschrift, Freie Universität Berlin, 2009.

Plessner, Martin. "Generalindex zu August Fischers Arbeitern," in: *Islamica* 2 (1926), 618–644.

Popp, Volker. "Die frühe Islamge-schichte nach inschriftlichen und numismatischen Zeugnissen," in: *Die dunklen Anfänge": Neue Forschungen zur Entstehung und frühen*

Geschichte des Islam, ed. Karl-Heinz Ohlig and Gerd-Rüdiger Puin. Berlin, 2005, 16–123.

Poulain, Jacques, Fathi Triki, and Christoph Wulf, eds. *Al-tarbīya al-dīmūqrātīya Aqtar urubbīya wa-muslima wa-arabīya tatahawar*. Tunis, 2009.

Pregill, Michael E. "'The Living Calf of Sinai': Orientalism, 'Influence' and the Foundations of the Islamic Exegetical Tradition." Dissertation, Columbia University, New York, 2008.

de Prémare, Alfred-Louis. "Abd al-Malik b. Marwān et le Processus de Constitution du Coran," in: *Die dunklen Anfänge: Neue Forschungen zur Entstehung und frühen Geschichte des Islam*, ed. Karl-Heinz Ohlig and Gerd-R. Puin. Berlin, 2005, 179–211.

de Prémare, Alfred-Louis. *Joseph et Muhammad: Le chapitre 12 du Coran*. Aix-en-Provence, 1998.

Pretzl, Otto. "Die Fortführung des Apparatus Criticus zum Koran," in: *Sitzungsberichte der Bayerischen Akademie der Wissenschaften* 1934, pt. 5.

Pretzl, Otto. "Die Wissenschaft der Koranlesung," in: Islamica 6 (1934), 1–47, 230–246, and 290–331.

Pritchard, James B. *Ancient Near Eastern Texts Relating the Old Testament*. Princeton, 1950, 2nd ed. 1955.

Puin, Elisabeth. "Ein frühes KoranpalimpsestausSana (DAM01-27.1),"in: *Schlaglichter: D iebeiden ersten islamischen Jahrhunderte*. Inara: Schriften zur frühen Islamgeschichte und zum Koran, ed. Markus Groß and Kalr-Heinz Ohlig. Berlin, 2008, 462–493.

Puin, Gerd Rüdiger. "Leuke Kome/Laykah, die Arser/ Ashab al-Rass und andere vorislamische Namen im Koran: Ein Weg aus dem 'Dickicht'?," in: *Die dunklen Anfänge: Neue Forschungen zur Entstehung und frühen Geschichte des Islam*, ed. Karl-Heinz Ohlig and Gerd Puin. Berlin, 2005, 317–339.

Puin, Gerd Rüdiger. "Observations on Early Qur'ān Manuscripts in Sanaa," in: *The Qur'an as Text*, ed. Stefan Wild. Leiden, 1995, 107–111.

Qadi, Muhammad al-. "La composante narrative des 'Journées des Arabes' (Ayyâm al-'arab)," in: *Arabica* 96 (1999), 358–371.

Qutb, Sayyid. *Fī Ẓilāl al-Qurʾān*, 20 vols. Beirut, 1971, partial English trans.: *In the Shade of the Qur'an*, trans. M. Adil Salahi and Ashur A. Khamis. London, 1979.

Radscheit, Matthias. "Aktuelle deutsche Koranübersetzungen im Überblick," in: *CIBEDO Beiträge zum Gespräch zwischen Christen und Muslimen* 13 (1999), 124–135.

Radscheit, Matthias. "I'jaz al-Qur'an im Koran?," in: *The Qur'an as Text*, ed. Stefan Wild. Leiden, 1996, 113–123.

Radscheit, Matthias. *Die Koranische Herausforderung: Die tahaddi-Verse im Rahmen der Polemikpassagen des Korans*. Berlin, 1996.

Radtke, Andreas. *Offenbarung zwischen Gesetz und Geschichte: Quellenstudien zu den Bedingungsfaktoren frühislamischen Rechtsdenkens*. Wiesbaden, 2003.

Rahman, Fazlur. *Major Themes in the Qur'an*. Minneapolis, 1980.

Raven, Wim. "Sira and the Qur'an," in: *EQ*, vol. 5. Leiden, 2005, 29–51.

Reeves, John C., ed. *Bible and Qur'an: Essays in Scriptural Intertextuality*. Leiden, 2003.

Reeves, John C. "Problematizing the Bible . . . Then and Now," in: *JQR* 100 (2010), 139–152.

Reichert, Klaus. *Vierfacher Schriftsinn: Gesammelte Essays zu Finnegans Wake*. Frankfurt am Main, 1998.

Reiser, Marius. *Bibelkritik und Auslegung der heiligen Schrift: Beiträge zur Geschichte der biblischen Exegese und Hermeneutik*. Tübingen, 2007.

Retsö, Jan. "Arabs and Arabic in the Age of the Prophet," in: *The Qurʾān in Context: Historical and Literary Investigations into the Qurʾānic Milieu*, ed. Angelika Neuwirth, Nicolai Sinai, and Michael Marx. Leiden, 2009, 281–292.

Retsö, Jan. *The Arabs in Antiquity: Their History from the Assyrians to the Umaiyads*. London and New York, 2003.

Reynolds, Frank E., and David Tracy, eds. *Religion and Practical Reason: New Essays in the Comparative Philosophy of Religions*. Albany, 1994.

Reynolds, Gabriel. "Reading the Qur'an as Homily: The Case of Sara's Laughter," in: *The Qurʾān in Context: Historical and Literary Investigations into the Qurʾānic Milieu*, ed. Angelika Neuwirth, Nicolai Sinai, and Michael Marx. Leiden, 2009, 585–592.

Rezvan, Efim A. *The Qur'an of 'Uthmân*. St. Petersburg, 2004.

Richter, Gustav. *Der Sprachstil des Koran: Aus dem Nachlass herausgegeben von Otto Spies*. Leipzig, 1940.

Richter, Wolfgang. *Exegese als Literaturwissenschaft. Entwurf einer alttestamentlichen Literaturtheorie und Methodologie*. Göttingen, 1971.

Ricœur, Paul. *Essays on Biblical Interpretation*. Philadelphia, 1980.

Ricœur, Paul. *Hermeneutik und Psychoanalyse*. Munich, 1974.

Riffaterre, Michael. *Semiotics of Poetry*. Bloomington and London, 1978.

Rippin, Andrew. *Approaches to the History of the Interpretation of the Qur'ān*. Oxford, 1988.

Rippin, Andrew, ed. *The Blackwell Companion to the Qur'an*. Malden, 2006.

Rippin, Andrew. "'Desiring the Face of God': The Qur'anic Symbolism of Personal Responsibility," in: *Literary Structures of Religious Meaning in the Qur'an*, ed. Issa J. Boullata. Richmond, 2000, 117–124.

Rippin, Andrew. "The Exegetical Genre 'asbāb al-nuzūl': A Bibliographical and Terminological Survey," in: *BSOAS* 48 (1985), 1–15.

Rippin, Andrew. "The Function of 'Asbāb al-nuzūl' in Qur'anic Exegesis," in: *BSOAS* 51 (1988), 1–20.

Rippin, Andrew. "God," in: *The Blackwell Companion to the Qur'an*, ed. Andrew Rippin. Malden, 2006, 223–233.

Rippin, Andrew. "Muhammad in the Qur'ān: Reading Scripture in the 21st Century," in: *The Biography of Muhammad: The Issue of the Sources*, ed. Harald Motzki. Leiden, 2000, 298–309.

Rippin, Andrew. "The Poetics of Qur'anic Punning," in: *BSOAS* 57 (1994), 193–207.

Rippin, Andrew. "The Qur'an as Literature: Perils, Pitfalls and Prospects," in: *British Society for Middle Eastern Bulletin* 10 (1983), 38–47.

Rippin, Andrew. "Quranic Studies, Part IV: Some Methodological Notes," in: *Methods and Theory in the Study of Religion* 9 (1997), 39–46.

Rippin, Andrew, ed. *The Qur'an: Style and Content*. Aldershot, 2001.

Rippin, Andrew. "Reading the Qur'an with Richard Bell," in: *JAOS* 112 (1992), 639–647.

Rippin, Andrew. "Western Scholarship and the Qur'an," in: *Cambridge Companion to the Qur'an*, ed. Jane Dammen McAuliffe. Cambridge, 2006, 235–251.

Robbins, Vernon K., and Gordon D. Newby. "A Prolegomenon to the Relation of the Qur'an and the Bible," in: *Bible and Qur'an: Essays in Scriptural Intertextuality*, ed. John C. Reeves. Leiden, 2004, 23–42.

Robin, Christian-Julien. "Ḥimyar et Israël," in: *Comptes-rendus des séances de l'Académie des Inscriptions et Belles-Lettres* 148 (2004), 831–908.

Robin, Christian-Julien. "Les Filles de Dieu de Saba' à La Mecque: reflexions sur l'agencement des panthéons dans l'Arabie ancienne," in: *Semitica* 50 (2001), 113–192.

Robinson, Neal. *Christ in Islam and Christianity: The Representation of Jesus in the Qur'an and the Classical Muslim Commentaries*. London, 1991.

Robinson, Neal. *Discovering the Qur'an: A Contemporary Approach to a Veiled Text*. London, [1]1996 (Washington, [2]2003).

Robinson, Neal. "Jesus," in: *EQ*, vol. 3. Leiden, 2003, 7–21.

Roff, William R. "Pilgrimage and the History of Religions: Theoretical approaches to the Hajj," in: *Approaches to Islam in Religious Studies*, ed. Richard C. Martin, Arizona, 1985, 7886.

Rosenthal, Franz. *Das Fortleben der Antike im Islam*. Zürich, 1965.

Rosenthal, Franz. "The History of Heinrich Speyer's *Die biblischen Erzählungen im Qoran*," in: *"Im vollen Licht der Geschichte": Die Wissenschaft des Judentums und die Anfänge der kritischen Koranforschung*, ed. Dirk Hartwig, Walter Homolka, Michael J. Marx, and Angelika Neuwirth. Würzburg, 2008, 113–116.

Rosenthal, Franz. *Knowledge Triumphant: The Concept of Knowledge in Medieval Islam*. Leiden, 1970.

Rosenzweig, Franz. *Der Stern der Erlösung*. Frankfurt am Main, 1988 (first published 1921).

Rothstein, Gustave. *Die Dynastie der Lakhmiden in al-Hira*. Berlin, 1899.

Rotter, Gernot. *Das Leben des Propheten*. Tübingen, [2]1979, repr. 2004.

Rubin, Uri. "Al-Samad and the High God—An Interpretation of Sura XCXII," in: *Der Islam* 61 (1984), 197–217.

Rubin, Uri. *Between Bible and Qur'an: The Children of Israel and the Qur'anic Self-Image*. Princeton, 1999.

Rubin, Uri., ed. *The Biography of Muhammad*. Aldershot, 2007.

Rubin, Uri. "Hanifiyya and Ka'ba: An Inquiry into the Arabian Pre-Islamic Background of Din Ibrahim," in: *Arabs and Arabia on the Eve of Islam*, ed. Francis E. Peters. Aldershot, 1999, 268–293.

Rubin, Uri. "The Īlāf of Quraysh: A Study of Sura CVI," in: *Arabica* 31 (1984), 165–188.

Rubin, Uri. "Iqra' bi-smi rabbika! Some Interpretations of Sūrat al-'alaq (Vs.1–5)," in: *Israel Oriental Studies* 13 (1993), ed. Joel L. Kraemer. Leiden, 1993, 213–231.

Rubin, Uri. "Jews and Judaism," in: *EQ*, vol. 3. Leiden, 2003, 21–34.

Rubin, Uri. "The Ka'ba: Aspects of Its Ritual Functions and Position in Pre-Islamic and Early Islamic Times," in: *Arabs and Arabia on the Eve of Islam*, ed. Francis E. Peters. Aldershot, 1999, 313–347.

Rubin, Uri. "Meccan Trade and Qur'anic Exegesis (Qur'an 2:198)," in: *BSOAS* 3 (1990), 421–428.

Rubin, Uri. "Morning and Evening Prayers in Early Islam," in: *JSAI* 10 (1987), 40–67, repr. in: Gerald R. Hawing, ed. *The Development of Islamic Ritual*, Aldershot, 2006, 105–129.

Rubin, Uri. "Muhammad's Night Journey (isra') to al-Masjid al-Aqsa: Aspects of the Earliest Origins of the Islamic Sanctity of Jerusalem," in: *Al-Qantara* 29 (2008), 147–165.

Rubin, Uri. "Prophets and Prophethood," in: *The Blackwell Companion to the Qur'an*, ed. Andrew Rippin. Malden, 2006, 234–247.

Rubin, Uri. "Rezension zu Madigan, *The Qur'an's Self-Image*," in: *JSAI* 28 (2003), 381–386.

Rubin, Uri. "The Shrouded Messenger: On the Interpretation of al-Muzzammil and al-Muddaththir," in: *JSAI* 16 (1993), 96–107.

Rückert, Friedrich. *Amrilkais, der Dichter und König: Sein Leben dargestellt in seinen Liedern*. Stuttgart and Tübingen, 1843.

Rückert, Friedrich. *Der Koran*, ed. A. Müller, Frankfurt am Main, 1888, repr. Hildesheim, 1980.

Rudolph, Wilhelm. *Die Abhängigkeit des Qorans von Judentum und Christentum*. Stuttgart, 1922.

Saeed, Abdullah. "Fazlur Rahman: A Framework for Interpreting the Ethico-legal Content of the Qur'an," in: *Modern Muslim Intellectuals and the Qur'an*, ed. Suha Taji-Farouki. Oxford, 2004, 37–66.

Saʿfi, Wahid al-. *al-Qurbān fi l-djāhilīya wa-l-islām*. Beirut, 2007.

Saʿid, Labibal-. *Al-Djam al-Sawti al-awwal li-l-Qur'an aw al-Mushaf al-Murattal*. Krof, 1978. Partially translated as: *The Recited Koran: A History of the First Recorded Version*, ed. Morroe Berger, M. A. Rauf, and Bernhard Weiss. Princeton, 1973.

Sale, Georges. *The Koran: Commonly called the Alkoran of Mohammed*. London, 1734.

Saleh, Walid. "The Etymological Fallacy and Qur'anic Studies: Muhammad, Paradise and Late Antiquity," in: *The Qur'ān in Context: Historical and Literary Investigations into the Qur'ānic Milieu*, ed. Michael Marx, Angelika Neuwirth, and Nicolai Sinai. Leiden, 2009, 649–698.

Saleh, Walid. *The Formation of the Classical Tafsir Tradition: The Qur'an Commentary of al-Ta'labi*. Leiden, 2004.

Saleh, Walid. "'What if you refuse, when ordered to fight?': King Saul (Talut) in the Qur'an and Post-Qur'anic Literature," in: *Saul in Story and Tradition*, ed. Carl Ehrlich. Tübingen, 2006, 261–283.

Saleh, Walid. "The Woman as a Locus of Apocalyptic Anxiety," in: *Myths, Historical Archetypes and Symbolic Figures in Arabic Literature: Towards a New Hermeneutic Approach*, ed. Angelika Neuwirth et al. Beirut, 1999, 123–145.

Saleh, Walid A. *In Defense of the Bible. A Critical Edition and an Introduction to al-Biqāʿī's Bible Treatise* (Islamic History and Civilization, vol. 73). Leiden and Boston, Brill, 2008, viii, 223.

Samir, Samir Khalil. "The Theological Christian Influences on the Qur'an: A Reflection," in: *The Qur'an in Its Historical Context*, ed. Gabriel Reynolds. London and New York, 2008, 163–174.

Sanders, James A. *Canon and Community: A Guide to Canonical Criticism*. Eugene, 2000.

Sayyed, Redwan. *Die Revolte des Ibn al-Ash'ath und die Koranleser: Ein Beitrag zur Religions- und Sozialgeschichte der frühen Umayyadenzeit*. Freiburg, 1977.

Schäfer, Peter. *Rivalität zwischen Engeln und Menschen: Untersuchungen zur rabbinischen Engelvorstellung*. Berlin, 1975.

Schäfer, Peter. *Weibliche Gottesbilder im Judentum*. Frankfurt am Main, 2008.

Schechter, Salomon. *Aspects of Rabbinic Theology*. New York, 1909.

Scheliha, Arnulf von. "Religionen im Pluralismus—am Beispiel der christlichen Deutung des Islam," in: Begegnungen zwischen Christentum und Islam: Festschrift für Hans-Jürgen Brandt zum 65. Geburtstag. Perspektiven der Weltmission: Wissenschaftliche Beiträge 20, ed. Hans-Christoph Goßmann. Ammersbek, 1994, 105–114.

Schedl, Claus. *Muhammad und Jesus*. Vienna, 1976.

Schiffner, Kerstin. *Lukas liest Exodus: Eine Untersuchung zur Aufnahme ersttestamentlicher Befreiungsgeschichte im lukanischen Werk als Schrift-Lektüre*. Stuttgart, 2008.

Schimmel, Annemarie. *Die Zeichen Gottes: Die religiöse Welt des Islam*. Munich, 1995.

Schippers, Arie. "Psalms," in: *EQ*, vol. 3. Leiden, 2003, 314–318.

Schmid, Nora Katharina. "Quantitative Text Analysis and Its Application to the Qur'an: Some Preliminary Considerations," in: *The Qurʾān in Context: Historical and Literary Investigations into the Qurʾānic Milieu*, ed. Michael Marx, Angelika Neuwirth, and Nicolai Sinai. Leiden, 2009, 441–460.

Schmidt, Hans-Peter. "Von der Kunst, Sinn zu erzeugen," in: *Bibel als Literatur*, ed. Hans-Peter Schmidt and Stefan Weidner. Munich, 2008, 31–56.

Schmidt, Hans-Peter, and Daniel Weidner, eds. *Bibel als Literatur*. Munich, 2008.

Schmidt, W. H. *Königtum Gottes in Ugar it und Israel: Zur Herkunft der Königsprädikation Jahwes*. Berlin, 1966.

Schmidt-Biggemann, Wilhelm. "Vorwort," in: *Das Böse: Eine historische Phänomenologie des Unerklärlichen*, ed. Carsten Colpe and Wilhelm Schmidt-Biggemann. Frankfurt am Main, 1993.

Schmitz, Bertram. *Der Koran: Sure 2 "Die Kuh": Ein religionshistorischer Kommentar*. Stuttgart, 2009.

Schöck, Cornelia. "Adam and Eve," in: EQ, vol. 1. Leiden, 2001, 22–26.

Schöck, Cornelia. *Adam im Koran*. Berlin, 1993.

Schöck, Cornelia. "Moses," in: *EQ*, vol. 3. Leiden, 2003, 419–426.

Schoeler, Gregor. *Charakter und Authentie der muslimischen Überlieferung über das Leben Mohammeds*. Berlin and New York, 1996.

Schoeler, Gregor. "The Codification of the Qur'an: A Comment on the Hypotheses of Burton and Wansbrough," in: *The Qurʾān in Context: Historical and Literary Investigations into the Qurʾānic Milieu*, ed. Angelika Neuwirth, Nicolai Sinai, and Michael Marx. Leiden, 2009, 779–794.

Schoeler, Gregor. "Schreiben und Veröffentlichen: Zu Verwendung und Funktion der Schrift in den ersten islamischen Jahrhunderten," in: *Der Islam* 69 (1992), 1–43.

Scholem, Gershom. "Der Name Gottes und die Sprachtheorie der Kabbala," in: Gershom Scholem, *Judaica 3: Studien zur jüdischen Mystik*. Frankfurt am Main, 1987, 2–70.

Schöller, Marco. *Exegetisches Denken und Prophetenbiographie: Eine quellenkritische Analyse der Sira-Überlieferung zu Muhammads Konflikt mit den Juden*. Wiesbaden, 1998.

Schöller, Marco. *Mohammed*. Frankfurt am Main, 2008.

Schöller, Marco. "Post-Enlightenment Academic Study in the Qur'an," in: *EQ*, vol. 4. Leiden, 2004, 187–208.

Seale, Morris, ed. *Qur'an and Bible: Studies in Interpretation and Dialogue*. London, 1978.

Segal, Alan F. *Two Powers in Heaven: Early Rabbinic Reports about Christianity and Gnosticism*. Boston, 2002.

Seidensticker, Tilman. *Altarabisch "Herz" und sein Wortfeld*. Wiesbaden, 1992.

Seidensticker, Tilman. "The Authenticity of the Poems ascribed to Umayya Ibn Abi al-Salt," in: *Pilosopy and Arts in the Islamic World*, ed. U. Vermeulen and D. de Smeet. Leuven, 1998, 87–101.

Seidensticker, Tilman. *Das Verbum sawwama: Ein Beitrag zum Problem der Homonymenscheidung im Arabischen*. Munich, 1986.

Seidensticker, Tilman. "Quellen zur vorislamischen Religionsgeschichte," in: *Asiatische Studien* 57 (2003), 881–912.

Seidensticker, Tilman. "Sources for the History of Pre-Islamic Religion," in: *The Qur'ān in Context: Historical and Literary Investigations into the Qur'ānic Milieu*, ed. Angelika Neuwirth, Nicolai Sinai, and Michael Marx. Leiden, 2009, 293–323.

Seidensticker, Tilman. "Umherirrende, durstige oder verliebte Dichter? Noch einmal zu Sure 26 Vers 225," in: *Der Islam* 85 (2010), 156–163.

Sellheim, Rudolf. "Prophet, Chalif und Geschichte," in: *Oriens* 18 (1965–66), 33–91.

Sells, Michael. *Approaching the Qur'an: The New Revelations; Selections, Translations, and Commentaries*. London, 1999.

Sells, Michael. "A Literary Approach to the Hymnic Surahs in the Qur'an: Spirit, Gender and Aural Intertextuality," in: *Literary Structures of Religious Meaning in the Qur'an*, ed. Issa Boullata. Richmond, 2000, 3–25.

Sells, Michael. "Sound and Meaning in 'Surat al-Qari'a,'" in: *Arabica* 40 (1993), 403–430.

Sells, Michael. "Sound, Spirit and Gender in Surat al-Qadr," in: *JAOS* 11 (1991), 239–259.

Sezgin, Fuat. *Geschichte des arabischen Schrifttums*, vols. 1–9 Leiden, 1967–1984 (index to vols. 1–9, Frankfurt am Main, 1995), and vols. 10–12. Frankfurt am Main, 2000.

Shahid, Irfan. "A Contribution to Koranic Exegesis," in: *Arabic and Islamic Studies in Honor of Hamilton* A. R. Gibb, ed. George Makdisi. Leiden, 1965, 563–580.

Shahid, Irfan. "Najran" in: *EQ*, vol. 3. Leiden, 2003, 300–301.

Shahid, Irfan. "People of the Elephant," in: *EQ*, vol. 4. Leiden, 2004, 44–46.

Shāṭibi, Abū l-Qāsim al-. *Ḥirz al-amānī wa-wadj al-tahānī*, Cairo, n.d.

Shatibi, Ibrahim al-. *Al-muwāfaqāt fi usūl al-sharī'a*, vols. 1–4, Cairo, 1340/1922.

Shawqi, Aḥmad. *Al-Amal al-shi rīya al-kāmila*. Beirut, 1988.

Sinai, Nicolai. "Auf der Suche nach der verlorenen Vorzeit: Günter Lülings apokalyptische Koranphilologie," in: *Neue Zürcher Zeitung*, February 2, 2004.

Sinai, Nicolai. "Orientalism, Authorship, and the Onset of Revelation: Abraham Geiger and Theodor Noeldeke on Muhammad and the Qur'an," in: *"Im vollen Licht der Geschichte"—Die Wissenschaft des Judentums und die Anfänge der Koranforschung*, ed. Dirk Hartwig, Walter Homolka, Michael Marx, and Angelika Neuwirth. Würzburg, 2008, 145–154.

Sinai, Nicolai. "The Qur'an as Process," in: *The Qur'ān in Context: Historical and Literary Investigations into the Qur'ānic Milieu*, ed. Angelika Neuwirth, Nicolai Sinai, and Michael Marx. Leiden, 2010, 407–439.

Sinai, Nicolai. "Qur'anic Self-Referentiality as a Strategy of Self-Authorization," in: *Self-Referentiality in the Qur'an*, ed. Stefan Wild. Wiesbaden, 2006, 103–134.

Sinai, Nicolai. "Rezension zu Ohlig, Dunkle Anfänge," in: *Bibliotheca Orientalis* 3–4 (2007), 481–485.

Sinai, Nicolai. *Fortschreibung und Auslegung: Studien zur frühen Koraninterpretation*. Wiesbaden, 2009.

Sinai, Nicolai, and Angelika Neuwirth. "Introduction," in: *The Qurʾān in Context: Historical and Literary Investigations into the Qurʾānic Milieu*, ed. Angelika Neuwirth, Nicolai Sinai, and Michael Marx. Leiden, 2010, 1–24.

Sister, M. "Metaphern und Vergleiche im Koran," in: *Mitteilungen des Seminars für Orientalische Sprachen* 34 (1931), 194–254.

Smith, David E. "The Structure of surat al-Baqarah," in: *The Muslim World* 91 (2001), 121–136.

Sperl, Stefan. "The Literary Form of Prayer: Qur'an sura One, the Lord's Prayer and a Babylonian Prayer to the Moon God," in: *BSOAS* 57 (1994), 213–227.

Speyer, Heinrich. *Die biblischen Erzählungen im Qoran*. Gräfenhainichen, 1931 [1935], repr. Hildesheim and New York, 1971.

Spitaler, Anton. "Arabisch," in: *Linguistica semitica presente e futuro*, ed. G. Levi Della Vida. Rome, 1961, 115–138.

Spitaler, Anton. "Die Schreibung des Typus ṣalāh im Koran: Ein Beitrag zur Erklärung der koranischen Orthographie," in: *Wiener Zeitschrift für die Kunde des Morgenlandes* 56 (1960), 212–226.

Spitaler, Anton, ed. "Ein Kapitel aus den Faḍā il al-Qurʾān von Abū Ubaid al-Qāsim ibn Sallām," in: *Documenta islamica inedita*, ed. Johannes W. Fück. Berlin, 1952.

Spitaler, Anton. "Rezension zu Alfred Bloch, Vers und Sprache im Altarabischen, metrische und syntaktische Untersuchungen," in: *Oriens* 2 (1949), 317–322.

Spitaler, Anton. "Rezension zu Johann Fück, Arabiya: Untersuchungen zur arabischen Sprachund Stilgeschichte." in: *BO* 10 (1953), 144–150.

Spitaler, Anton. *Die Verszählung des Koran*. Munich, 1935.

Spuler-Stegemann, Ursula. "Die hermeneutische Diskussion im türkischen Islam und ihre gesellschaftliche Relevanz," in: *Hermeneutik in Islam und Christentum: Beiträge zum interreligiösen Dialog; Rudolf-Otto-Symposium 1996*, ed. Hans-Martin Barth and Christoph Elsas. Hamburg, 1997, 84–95.

Stegemann, Hartmut. "Gedanken zum Johannesprolog (Joh 1, 1–18)," in: *Hermeneutik in Islam und Christentum: Beiträge zum interreligiösen Dialog; Rudolf-Otto-Symposium 1996*, ed. Hans-Martin Barth and Christoph Elsas. Hamburg, 1997, 127–140.

Stein, Peter. "Literacy in Pre-Islamic Arabia: An Analysis of the Epigraphic Evidence," in: *The Qurʾān in Context: Historical and Literary Investigations into the Qurʾānic Milieu*, ed. Michael Marx, Angelika Neuwirth, and Nicolai Sinai. Leiden, 2009, 255–280.

Stern, David. "Midrash and Indeterminacy," in: *Critical Inquiry* 15 (1988), 132–161.

Stern, David. *Parables in Midrash: Narrative and Exegesis in Rabbinic Literature*. Cambridge, 1991.

Stern, David. "Rhetoric and Midrash: The Case of the Mashal," in: *Prooftexts* 1 (1981), 261–291.

Sternberg, Meir. *The Poetics of Biblical Narrative: Ideological Literature and the Drama of Reading*. Bloomington, 1985.

Stetkevych, Jaroslav. *Muhammad and the Golden Bough: Reconstructing Arabian Myth*. Bloomington, 1996.

Stetkevych, Jaroslav. *The Zephyrs of the Najd: The Poetics of Nostalgia in the Classical Arabic Nasib*. Chicago, 1993.

Stetkevych, Suzanne Pinckney. *The Mute Immortals Speak: Pre-Islamic Poetry and the Poetics of Rituals*. Ithaca, 1993.

Stetkevych, Suzanne Pinckney. "Pre-Islamic Panegyric and the Poetics of Redemption: Mufaddaliyah 119 of Alqamah and Banat Su ad of Ka b Ibn Zuhayr," in: *Reorientations: Arabic and Persian Poetry*, ed. Suzanne Pinckney Stetkevych. Bloomington, 1994, 1–57.

Stewart, Devin J. "Soothsayer," in: *EQ*, vol. 5. Leiden, 2005, 76–80.

Stowasser, Barbara F. "Mary," in: *EQ*, vol. 3, 288–296.

Strohmaier, Gotthart. *Hellas im Islam: Interdisziplinäre Studien zur Ikonographie, Wissenschaft und Religionsgeschichte*. Wiesbaden, 2003.

Suermann, Harald. "Early Islam in the Light of Christian and Jewish Sources," in: *The Qur'ān in Context: Historical and Literary Investigations into the Qur'ānic Milieu*, ed. Angelika Neuwirth, Nicolai Sinai, and Michael Marx. Leiden, 2010, 135–148.

al-Ṭabarī. *Djāmi al-bayān fī tafsīr al-Qur'ān*, 30 vols. Bulaq, n.d.

Tahry, Nevin Reda. "Textual Integrity and Coherence in the Qur'an: Repetition and narrative Structure in Surt al-Baqara." Dissertation, University of Toronto, 2010.

Talbi, Muhammad. "La qira'a bi-l-alhan," in: *Arabica* 5 (1958), 183–190.

Tamer, Georges. *Zeit und Gott: Hellenistische Zeitvorstellungen in der altarabischen Dichtung und im Koran*. Berlin, New York, 2008.

Teodorova, Maria. "Historische Vermächtnisse zwischen Europa und dem Nahen Osten (Erste Carl Heinrich Becker Lecture der Fritz Thyssen Stiftung 2007)," in: *Europa im Nahen Osten—der Nahe Osten in Europa*, ed. Angelika Neuwirth and Günther Stock. Berlin, 2010, 85–106.

Thomas, David, ed. *Early Muslim Polemic against Christianity: Abū Īsā al-Warrāq's "Against the Incarnation."* Cambridge, 2002.

Toelle, Heidi. *Le Coran revisité: Le feu, l'eau, l'air et la terre*. Damascus, 1999.

Toral-Niehoff, Isabel. *Die Ayyām al-Arab als "Tribal History" der arabischen Spätantike: Ein Beitrag zur literarischen und historischen Kontextualisierung der Koran- und Islamgenese* (in preparation).

Toral-Niehoff, Isabel. "The Ibad in al-Hira: An Arab Christian Community in Late Antique Iraq," in: *The Qur'ān in Context: Historical and Literary Investigations into the Qur'ānic Milieu*, ed. Angelika Neuwirth, Nicolai Sinai, and Michael Marx. Leiden, 2009, 323–347.

Toral-Niehoff, Isabel. *Stammesfürsten und Dichterkönige: Die arabischen Christen und das Reich der Lahmiden*, Berlin, 2008.

Torrey, Charles C. "Three Difficult Passages in the Qur'an, 3: His Mother Is Hawiya, 101–108," in: A *Volume of Oriental Studies Presented to Edward G. Browne*, ed. T. W. Arnold and Reynold A. Nicholson. Cambridge, 1922, 464–471.

Tottoli, Roberto. "Imran," in: *EQ*, vol. 2. Leiden, 2002, 509.

Tottoli, Roberto. *I profeti biblici nella tradizione islamica*. Brescia, 1999 (English translation: *Biblical Prophets in the Qur'an and Muslim Literature*, Richmond, 2002).

Tottoli, Roberto. "Origin and Use of the Term Isra'iliyyat in Muslim Literature," in: *Arabica* 46 (1999), 193–210.

Ullmann, Manfred. *Untersuchungen zur Ragazpoesie*. Wiesbaden, 1966.

Urbach, Efraim E. *The Sages: Their Concepts and Beliefs*, 2 vols. Cambridge, 1987.

Vajda, Georges. *Album de paléographie arabe*. Paris, 1958.

van der Koiij, Arie, ed. *Canonization and Decanonization*. Studies in the History of Religion 82. Leiden, 1998.

van der Toorn, Karel. *Scribal Culture and the Making of the Hebrew Bible*. Cambridge, MA, 2009.

van Ess, Josef. "Abd al-Malik and the Dome of the Rock: An Analysis of Some Texts," in: *Bayt al-Maqdis, Abd al-Malik's Jerusalem*, ed. Julian Raby and Jeremy Johns. Oxford, 1992, 89–103.

van Ess, Josef. "Islam," in: Christentum und Weltreligionen: Hinführung zum Dialog mit Islam, Hinduismus und *Buddhismus*, ed. Heinz Bechert, Josef van Ess, Hans Küng, and Heinrich von Stietencron. Munich and Zürich, 1984.

van Ess, Josef. *Theologie und Gesellschaft im 2. und 3. Jahrhundert Hidschra: Eine Geschichte des religiösen Denkens im frühen Islam*, 6. vols. Berlin, 1991–1995.

van Ess, Josef. "Vision and Ascension: Sūrat al-Najm and Its Relationship with Muḥammad's mi rāj," in: *JQS* 1 (1999), 47–62.

van Gelder, Geert Jan. *The Bad and the Ugly: Attitudes Towards Invective Poetry (Hijā) in Classical Arabic Literature*. Leiden and New York, 1988.

van Gelder, Geert Jan. *God's Banquet: Food in Classical Arabic Literature*. New York, 2000.

Veltri, Giuseppe. *Gegenwart der Tradition: Studien zur jüdischen Literatur und Kulturgeschichte*. Leiden, 2002.

Vermes, Geza. *The Changing Faces of Jesus*. London, 2001.

Vollers, Karl. *Volkssprache und Schriftsprache im alten Arabien*. Strasbourg, 1906.

Wagner, Ewald. *Grundzüge der klassischen arabischen Dichtung*, vol. 1: *Die altarabische Dichtung*. Darmstadt, 1987.

Wagtendonk, Kees. *Fasting in the Koran*. Leiden, 1968.

Waldman, Marilyn. "New Approaches to 'Biblical' Materials in the Qur'an," in: *Papers Presented at the Institute of Islamic-Judaic Studies: Center for Judaic Studies*, ed. William M. Brinner and Stephen David Ricks. Atlanta, 1986, 47–63.

Wansbrough, John. *Quranic Studies: Sources and Methods of Scriptural Interpretation*. Oxford, 1977.

Wansbrough, John. "Rezension zu Friedrun R. Müller, *Reimprosa im Koran*," in: *BSOAS* 33 (1970), 389–391.

Wansbrough, John. *The Sectarian Milieu: Content and Composition of Islamic Salvation History*. Oxford, 1978.

Watt, William Montgomery. *Bell's Introduction to the Qur'an*. Edinburgh, 1970.

Watt, William Montgomery. *Muhammad at Mecca*. Oxford, 1953.

Watt, William Montgomery. *Muhammad at Medina*. Oxford, 1956.

Watt, William Montgomery. *Muhammad: Prophet and Statesman*. London, 1961.

Weidner, Daniel. "Literatur und Antiliteratur," in: *Bibel als Literatur*, ed. Hans Peter Schmidt and Daniel Weidner. Munich, 2008, 173f.

Weil, Gustav. *Historisch-kritische Einleitung in den Koran*. Bielefeld, 1844.

Weiss, Bernard, trans. *Al-Djam al-sautī al-auwal li-l-Qur'ān*. Princeton, 1975.

Weiss, Bernard, and Labib Al-Sa'id. *The Recited Koran: A History of the First Recorded Version*. Princeton, 1975.

Welch, Alford. "Ḳur'ān," in: *EI*, vol. 5, 400–432.

Wellhausen, Julius. *Reste altarabischen Heidentums*. Berlin, 1887.

Wensinck, Arent J. *Concordance et indices de la tradition musulmane*, 8 vols. Leiden, 1937–1968 (2nd ed., 4 vols. Leiden, 1992).

Wensinck, Arent J. *The Ideas of the Western Semites Concerning the Navel of the Earth*. Amsterdam, 1916.

Wensinck, Arent J. *Muhammad and the Jews of Medina*. Freiburg im Breisgau, 1975 (orig. Leiden, 1928).

Westermann, Claus. *Vergleiche und Gleichnisse im Alten und Neuen Testament*. Stuttgart, 1984.

Wheeler, Brannon M. *Moses in the Quran and Islamic Exegesis*. London and New York, 2002.

Whelan, Estelle. "Evidence for the Early Codification of the Qur'an," in: *JAOS* 118 (1998), 1–14.

Whelan, Estelle. "Writing the Word of God," in: *Ars Orientalis* 20 (1990), 130–147.

Wiedenhöfer, Siegfried. "Offenbarung," in: *Neues Handbuch theologischer Grundbegriffe*, vol. 4, ed. Peter Eicher. Munich, 1991, 98–115.

Wielandt, Rotraud. "Exegesis of the Qur'ān: Early Modern and Contemporary," in: *EQ*, vol. 4. Leiden, 2004, 124–142.

Wielandt, Rotraud. *Offenbarung und Geschichte im Denken moderner Muslime*. Wiesbaden, 1971.

Wild, Stefan. "An Arabic Recitation: The Metalinguistics of Qur'anic Revelation," in: *Self-Referentiality in the Qur'an*, ed. Stefan Wild. Wiesbaden, 2006, 135–158.

Wild, Stefan. "Die andere Seite des Textes: Naṣr Ḥāmid Abū Zaid und der Koran," in: *Die Welt des Islam* 33 (1993), 256–261.

Wild, Stefan. "Lost in Philology? The Virgins of Paradise and the Luxenberg Hypothesis," in: *The Qur'ān in Context: Historical and Literary Investigations into the Qur'ānic Milieu*, ed. Michael Marx, Angelika Neuwirth, and Nicolai Sinai. Leiden, 2009, 625–647.

Wild, Stefan. *Mensch, Prophet und Gott im Koran: Muslimische Exegeten des 20. Jahrhunderts und das Menschenbild der Moderne*. Münster, 2001.

Wild, Stefan. "Die 'schauerliche Öde des heiligen Buches': Westliche Wertungen des koranischen Stils," in: *Gott ist schön: Er liebt die Schönheit; Festschrift für Annemarie Schimmel zum 7. April 1992, dargebracht von Schülern, Freunden und Kollegen*, ed. Christoph Bürgel and Alma Giese. Bern, 1994, 429–447.

Wild, Stefan. "The Self-Referentiality of the Qur'an: Sura 3:7 as an Exegetical Challenge," in: *With Reverence for the Word: Medieval Scriptural Exegesis in Judaism, Christianity, and Islam*, ed. Joseph W. Goering, Jane Dammen McAuliffe, and Barry D. Walfish. Oxford, 2003, 422–436.

Wild, Stefan, ed. *Self-Referentiality in the Qur'an*. Wiesbaden, 2006.

Wild, Stefan. "'We have sent down to thee the book with the truth . . .': Spatial and Temporal Implications of the Qur'anic Concepts of *nuzul, tanzil*, and *inzal*," in: *The Qur'an as Text*, ed. Stefan Wild. Leiden, 1996, 137–156.

Wild, Stefan. "Why Self-Referentiality?," in: *Self-Referentiality in the Qur'an*, ed. Stefan Wild. Wiesbaden, 2006, 1–14.

Wilken, Robert Louis. "In Defense of Allegory," in: *Modern Theology* 14 (1998), 197–212.

Winkler, Helmut. "Fatiha und Vaterunser," in: *ZS* 6 (1928), 238–246.

Witztum, Joseph. "The Foundations of the House (Q 2:127)," in: *BSOAS* 72, no. 1 (2009), 25–40.

Wolfson, Elliot R. "The Body in the Text: A Kabbalistic Theory of Embodiment," in: *JQR* 95 (2005), 479–500.

Wolfson, Harry A. *The Philosophy of the Kalam*. Cambridge, 1976.

Zahniser, A. H. Mathias. "Guidance and Exhortation: The Composition of Suratu n-nisa'," in: *Humanism, Culture, and Language in the Near East: Studies in Honour of Georg Krotkoff*, ed. Asma Afsaruddin and A. H. Mathias Zahniser. Winona Lake, 1997, 71–85.

Zahniser, A. H. Matthias. "Parable," in: *EQ*, vol. 4. Leiden, 2004, 9–12.

Zahniser, A. H. Mathias. "The Word of God and the Apostleship of Isa: A Narrative Analysis of Al Imran (3:33–62)," in: *JSS* 36 (1991), 77–112.

Zirker, Hans. *Christentum und Islam: Theologische Verwandtschaft und Konkurrenz*. Düsseldorf, 1989.

Zirker, Hans. *Der Koran: Übersetzt und eingeleitet von Hans Zirker*. Darmstadt, 2003.

Zirker, Hans. *Der Koran: Zugänge und Lesarten*. Darmstadt, 1999.

Zobel, Moritz. *Das Jahr des Juden in Brauch und Liturgie*. Berlin, 1936.

Zwettler, Michael. "A Mantic Manifesto: the Sura of 'the Poets' and the Qur'anic Foundations of Prophetic Authority," in: *Poetry and Prophecy: The Beginnings of a Literary Tradition*, ed. James Kugel. Ithaca, 1990, 75–119.

Zwettler, Michael. *The Oral Tradition of Classical Arabic Poetry: Its Character and Implications*. Columbus, 1978.

Index of Persons

General Index

Citations of Scripture

New Testament

Rabbinic Literature

Talmud

Midrash